Personality
Theories

SAGE was founded in 1965 by Sara Miller McCune to support the dissemination of usable knowledge by publishing innovative and high-quality research and teaching content. Today, we publish over 900 journals, including those of more than 400 learned societies, more than 800 new books per year, and a growing range of library products including archives, data, case studies, reports, and video. SAGE remains majority-owned by our founder, and after Sara's lifetime will become owned by a charitable trust that secures our continued independence.

Los Angeles | London | New Delhi | Singapore | Washington DC | Melbourne

Personality
Theories

A GLOBAL VIEW

ERIC SHIRAEV
George Mason University

Los Angeles | London | New Delhi
Singapore | Washington DC | Melbourne

Chapter 10. The Developmental Domain 298

Chapter 11. The Gender Domain   **334**

• Preface •

Welcome to the study of personality in the 21st century—welcome to a field that is enlightening, intriguing, and promising. It is enlightening because of the superb quality of the research in which this field is rooted. It is intriguing because of the fascinating assumptions that this research into personality offers. And it is promising because of its significant practical applications in so many areas of our lives.

This book will be your guide and companion in the journey to study personality. Why do we need this book? Indeed, today we have unprecedented access to global information: statistics, video clips, tweets, Facebook postings, eyewitness reports, theoretical articles, research summaries, and sensational stories—all are just a click away. Fifteen years ago, it would have taken many hours to locate an article that today's reader can "Google" in seconds. And then you can find another article. And a new clip on YouTube . . . and another one . . . and more . . . How many of them should we read? Which of these sources are valid? Which one is more accurate and trustworthy compared with others? This book aims to bring a significant measure of scientific certainty to your understanding of personality. This confidence is based on critical fact-analysis—the method that the author has already applied in his *A History of Psychology* (Sage).

Main Features

First, the science about personality presented in this book is *interdisciplinary*. The book's core is about personality psychology, which is inseparable from science and social science and which welcomes contributions from the fields of the humanities, history, and other disciplines.

Second, this book emphasizes *diversity*. It has a significant cross-cultural and cross-national focus to emphasize the global nature of our knowledge about personality. The author has significant background and expertise in cross-cultural studies.

Third, the book introduces and applies *critical thinking* as a main method of analysis of facts and theories. One of the book's goals is to help students learn to deduce facts from opinions and to be informed skeptics.

Finally, the book pays attention to the practical *relevance* of our knowledge of personality to students' diverse experiences today. It introduces applications from the fields of medicine, therapy, education, training, criminal justice, and entertainment, to name a few.

Structure

The book contains 14 chapters. The first discusses main definitions and assumptions, the second turns to scientific foundations of personality studies, and the third one focuses on methodology to study personality. The next six chapters examine personality from the standpoint of several major psychological traditions. Then, the following four chapters discuss personality within the developmental, gender, clinical, and adjustment domains. Finally, the concluding chapter asks students to use their critical and creative thinking while discussing contemporary research into personality.

You should notice the book's well-defined structure, which is consistent from chapter to chapter. After the first three introductory chapters, each subsequent chapter is organized around three general themes related to our research journey into personality. These themes can be presented in the form of three questions:

What are the basic ideas and facts that we focus on?

How do we study these ideas and facts?

How do we apply them?

The coverage of classical and contemporary research in this text remains both comprehensive and chronological. Most ideas and theories are presented as "products" of their own time, which are shaped by the unique social circumstances. These ideas and theories, in turn, influenced the society and the individual. Many of these theories made an instant and often lasting impact on other theories, the development of which is traced throughout the book's 14 chapters.

Academic Traditions

The scientific knowledge about personality over the past 120 years developed within major academic traditions generally associated with psychology as an academic discipline. Such traditions bring together scholars—who often lived and worked thousands of miles apart, yet who shared similar views on a particular scientific approach, subject, or method. There are real associations involving interacting individuals, and there are traditions as convenient symbols to indicate a similarity in views across borders and times. To illustrate, consider these points:

- In studying personality, psychoanalysis of the early 20th century and later turned to the *conflicting and feeling individual*. Psychoanalysts focused on various unconscious motivational forces and believed in the significant impact of early childhood on personality.

- Other scientists rejected psychoanalysis's assumptions and focused instead on the individual's reflexes, observable behavior, and learning mechanisms. To these scientists, the individual—who they studied—was seen mostly as *acting and learning*. The behaviorist tradition dominated academic and applied psychology for decades.
- While many researchers argued about the key sources of personality's features, others turned to measuring personality traits—the personality's most stable features. It was the tradition that emphasized the growing interest in the *structured individual*, which appeared as complex, interdependent, and measurable.
- The cognitive revolution in science in the middle of the past century meant a renewed interest in those inner mechanisms that define human experience. Again, the *thinking, information-processing individual* was back on the researchers' agenda. Cognitive science connected many disciplines together, including psychology, philosophy, neuroscience, and computer science.
- At the same time, many psychologists urged others to focus more on a different individual: the one that was loving, caring, and growing. They emphasized the uniquely human core of personality and the individual's relentless search for happiness.

Although this book examines these traditions in a linear sequence, they have never been isolated from one another. They, like beams of light, were coming from different projectors and illuminating one object: personality. Each beam brightened only one side of the object, but together, they show a much clearer and detailed picture. Each tradition brought something new, something promising, as well as something controversial and exciting to our knowledge of personality. Using this analogy, we could see various traditions as relentless attempts to deepen and broaden our knowledge. It is about enlightenment, after all.

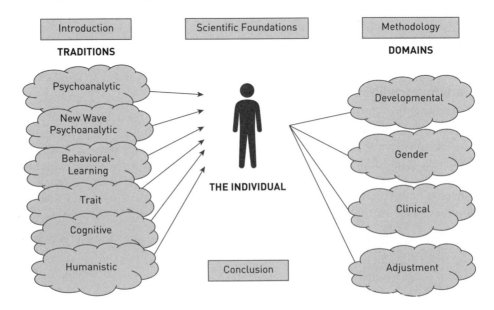

Domains

Our scientific journey in the fields of personality will be incomplete without a critical examination of knowledge in several specific "real-life" contexts or circumstances, which we will call for convenience *the domains*. We examine personality within the four of such domains: developmental, gender, clinical, and adjustment. This is how the next group of chapters is structured:

- Personality is never static. It is evolving, developing. We, as humans, are constantly growing, maturing, and changing. The *developmental domain* allows us to approach personality from the life-span, dynamic perspective.
- Personality is gendered. For centuries, societal traditions, values, beliefs, and laws have been rooted in the male–female dichotomy, yet the concept of gender is evolving. The gender domain in the study of personality is an area of many discoveries and new, fascinating questions.
- Personality can be described within the continuum of "normal" and "abnormal" features. The clinical domain approaches personality from the position of psychopathology and individual malfunction. True, there is always a way out of suffering. There must be. The chapter discusses it as well.
- Personality is about facing life's challenges and adjusting to them. We constantly cope with threats and sudden transformations, as well as long-awaited, life-changing events. Within the adjustment domain, we will focus together on the coping individual, who learns and adjusts—as the human being should.

Pedagogy

- Each chapter begins with learning objectives. For example, here are the objectives for Chapter 6 on the behavioral learning tradition:

Learning Objectives

After reading this chapter, you should be able to do the following:

- Identify the main features of the behavioral learning tradition as they apply to the study of personality
- Describe the opportunities and limitations of behaviorism and social learning theory
- Apply the key principles of the behavioral learning tradition to individual behavior

- Each chapter begins with a *vignette* or opening *case*, which serves as an informal introduction. Each vignette typically contains questions relevant to the chapter's contents. The following is how Chapter 11 introduces the discussion of gender, identity, and personality:

Kelsy has finally answered the question that most of us do not even have to ask: *Who am I . . . a boy or a girl?* Kelsy already knew that some people are born in female bodies but feel male inside, and some other people have male bodies but feel female. She also knew the meaning of the words *gay*, *unisex*, and *transgender*. They have become very common in the English language (although, frankly, some people still have only a superficial view of the meaning of these words). Today, more people speak freely about their true identity and overcome the fear of being condemned and discriminated against for their feelings. Yet Kelsey had a more complicated challenge—a feeling that neither *male* nor *female* categories were appropriate for her self-identity: She felt she was neither a girl nor a boy. . . .

- Several *Check and Apply Your Knowledge* boxes are placed strategically within chapters to help with immediate review of key points and facts. This is just one example of this feature from Chapter 13, which discusses adjustment and coping:

CHECK AND APPLY YOUR KNOWLEDGE

1. Define and explain *flexibility*.
2. Explain proactive approaching.
3. Ferrari (2010), in *Still Procrastinating? The No Regrets Guide to Getting It Done*, would like to see a general cultural shift from punishing procrastination to rewarding the "early bird." The author proposed, among other things, that the federal government and other agencies give financial incentives to those who do things (such as paying taxes) early, long before the deadlines. Discuss whether this strategy could reduce procrastination or would just reward the people who are too anxious and do everything very early.
4. In one of the most famous plays by Shakespeare, the main character Hamlet posed probably the most frequently quoted question: "To be or not to be?" In the monologue that followed, he complained about life's pains and unfairness yet was also afraid that the alternative, which is suicide, might be worse. What kind of coping was Hamlet choosing from?
5. Define *adjustment disorder*.
6. Explain burnout.
7. Have you ever experienced burnout? How did you cope with it?

- Each chapter has a *Self-Reflection* box, which typically presents a case in point, a life episode, or a research summary, and then asks students to apply the knowledge to themselves. This is just one example of this feature from Chapter 12, which discusses personality disorders.

SELF-REFLECTION

The Drama of the Gifted Child by Alice Miller (1994) put forward a controversial hypothesis: Many professional psychotherapists are likely to be narcissistic. They do not become narcissistic after they become professionals—quite the contrary, she writes. Many individuals seek degrees in psychology because of childhood experiences that make them narcissistic.

Imagine, she argues, a mother who is emotionally insecure, weak, or desperate, yet who always tries to appear confident, independent, and strong. This mother has a child who is sensitive and smart and who is capable of understanding her or his mother's struggles. The child wants to help and thus develops sensitivity to the needs of the mother and other people. The child earns a good reputation for helping others. Unlike business, such amateur "psychological practices" generate no money; however, they bring approval from others. The child, a teenager now, becomes a home-grown "therapist" and feels important. He or she now seeks people's praise. That is why many of these children later choose psychology as a profession. To them, Alice Miller argues, psychological practice is about much more than money. Helping other people with their emotional issues feeds the psychologists' childhood narcissism—the desire to maintain a good image of self and feel special.

Questions

As a high school student, were you ever asked to help other people with their emotional problems? Did you enjoy helping or guiding others? What is the difference between (1) enjoying every opportunity to help another person and (2) having narcissistic features?

- Each chapter has a *Visual Summary* at the end of it. This will help students to better prepare for exams and may serve as a reference as well.
- Additional support for the text can be found on the book website at **edge.sagepub.com/shiraev personality**, where you can find practice and discussion questions, research updates, facts, and links. Boxes in each chapter point the student to relevant online material, as shown in the example to the right from Chapter 4.

@

Freud was a man of many paradoxes and contradictions, as many of us are. Read about these paradoxes on the companion website. Then think about the most important decisions you've made to address your life's paradoxes and contradictions.

To the Student

Know thyself, says the ancient aphorism. *Learn about yourself,* encourages today's popular maxim. The journey to understand the individual's personality is as old as humankind. This book will help you navigate through a wide range of theories and empirical studies about personality. You will examine theoretical assumptions, research summaries, and critical-thinking exercises. Your professor will assign projects and administer tests based on this text. True, it is very important to be informed, knowledgeable, and confident with this knowledge. Yet today's professional is not a passive observer or a wise guru judging the word from a secluded place. Your knowledge will require action. When you turn a page or when you finish a chapter in the book, ask yourself these questions. Start looking for answers today.

"How did this study or this theory help me understand myself?"

Reliable knowledge takes more than observing things unfolding in front of you at this hour. Experts who study personality do more than register this event or that fact. They analyze the inner logic of these events and the ways these facts are interconnected. Therefore, we will need serious analysis, or the breaking up of something complex into smaller parts, to comprehend their important features and interactions. Apply this knowledge to yourself. Ask others to share their views and help you. It too takes skill to ask for help. Again, after turning another page, ask yourself this:

"How can I use this knowledge to help others?"

To answer this question, you will have to gain a broader, critical knowledge about other people. To make conclusions, you have to study, analyze, and generalize not only the headlines popping up on the screen of your mobile device but also the rich database of facts, opinions, and theories accumulated over the years. You will need to familiarize yourself with some general "rules" and patterns of human behavior as exceptions to these rules. You know that we, as individuals, are unique.

"How can I use this knowledge to make a bigger difference in life?"

Do not be surprised if you realize that with each chapter, the more you learn about personality, the more you will realize that there are many things you . . . don't know. This awareness of the limitations of your knowledge will be a sign that you are growing as a professional. Always patiently test your conclusions against the stubborn realities of this ever-changing, complex world. Whatever question, idea, or doubt you have, ask your professor or e-mail me, the author of this text. We will listen and, hopefully, answer. We also will learn from you.

Welcome to the journey, which we will undertake together.

Instructor Teaching Site

A password-protected site, available at **https://edge.sagepub.com/shiraev personality**, features resources that have been designed to help instructors plan and teach their course. These resources include an extensive test bank, chapter-specific PowerPoint presentations, lecture notes, sample syllabi for semester and quarter courses, discussion questions to facilitate class discussion, links to SAGE journal articles with accompanying article review questions, and links to video and web resources.

Student Study Site

A web-based study site is available at **https://edge.sagepub.com/shiraev personality**. This site provides access to several study tools including eFlashcards, web quizzes, links to full-text SAGE journal articles with accompanying article review questions, and links to video and web resources.

• Acknowledgments •

I am very grateful for the insightful feedback and help of my colleagues and reviewers, the constant efforts of several research assistants, and the patience and understanding of my family members. Valuable contributions, help, and encouragement for this book came from many individuals. In particular, I acknowledge Reid Hester for suggesting and supporting this project from the start. I appreciate the support of David Sears and Barry Collins from the University of California, Los Angeles, and of James Sidanius from Harvard University—they gave me a jump-start. I thank David Levy from Pepperdine University, Sergei Tsytsarev from Hofstra University, Denis Sukhodolsky from Yale University, Cheryl Koopman from Stanford University, Phil Tetlock from the University of Pennsylvania, Denis Snook from Oregon State University, Anton Galitsky from St. Petersburg State University, and Olga Makhovskaya from the Russian Academy of Sciences. A word of appreciation to John and Judy Ehle, Vladislav Zubok, Dmitry Shiraev, Dennis Shiraev, Nicole Shiraev, Alex Shiraev, and Oh Em Tee. I can never thank them enough.

This book received constant attention and support from the dynamic, highly professional team at SAGE: Reid Hester (again, he initiated this project), Nathan Davidson, Jane Haenel, Sarita Ramirez, Judith Newlin, Kassi Radomski, and Amy Harris. I thank them all.

A special word of appreciation is due to the administration, faculty, staff, and students at my academic institutions, where I have been consistently provided with an abundance of support, assistance, and validation.

Everything is to be continued . . .

Thanks to the following reviewers provided by SAGE:

Joan W. Bailey, *New Jersey City University*

Jeffrey S. Bedwell, *University of Central Florida*

Benjamin Bennett-Carpenter, *Oakland University*

John H. Bickford Jr., *University of Massachusetts Amherst*

Elizabeth Boger, *Rose State College*

Nicole M. Capezza, *Stonehill College*

Kyle De Young, *University of North Dakota*

Joanna Gentsch, *University of Texas at Dallas*

Carrie E. Hall, *Miami University*
Stella G. Lopez, *University of Texas at San Antonio*
Toby K. Marx, *Union County College*
Daniel Philip, *University of North Florida*
Daren Protolipac, *St. Cloud State University*
Kimberly Renk, *University of Central Florida*
Robert W. Seals, *University of Houston*
William T. Sharp, *Northeastern University*
James Sullivan, *Florida State University*
Melody Whiddon, *Florida International University, College of Education*

• About the Author •

Eric Shiraev is a professor, researcher, and author working and living in Virginia, near Washington, DC. He received his academic degrees at St. Petersburg University in Russia and completed a postdoctoral program in the United States at the University of California, Los Angeles. He has served in various teaching and research positions at St. Petersburg University, Northern Virginia Community College, Oregon State University, George Washington University, and at George Mason University. He has authored and edited 15 books, including several textbooks in multiple editions, such as *A History of Psychology* (SAGE). He has published numerous papers, essays, and reviews in the fields of global studies, cross-cultural psychology, political psychology, and the individual personalities of political leaders. In his publications, he develops a distinct multidisciplinary approach to human behavior and experience. His recent research involves the study—conducted together with a dynamic international scholarly team—of character attacks across times and cultures on the individual's reputation. He continues writing songs for pop singers in Europe, some of whom are famous. For updates and discussions of ongoing and new academic projects, visit his Facebook page.

And then you clearly understand that perhaps what matters most to you is all about the ability to continue the endless search for the things that matter. Let this book be a helper in this journey. It may also help with your next application.

Identifying Personality

Defining *personality* is one of the most challenging tasks in psychology. Psychologists often view personality according to their main theoretical positions held within the discipline. So if this is the case, what should we do? No matter how diverse the views of personality are, we need to have an initial point of reference. A working definition of **personality** is a stable set of behavioral and experiential characteristics of an individual (American Psychological Association [APA], 2014). We should also understand that this definition isn't carved in stone: During our learning journey, we will have more than ample opportunity to reexamine and clarify this initial definition. But it should help in starting the discussion of personality theories and their applications.

Personality
A personality is a stable set of behavioral and experiential characteristics of an individual.

Explaining the Definition and Asking Questions

Details are important. To make sure that we are on the same page, consider the following questions and answers about the personality definition and its interpretations.

Q. Which characteristics of an individual do psychologists associate with personality?

A. The American Psychological Association refers to patterns of *thinking, feeling,* and *behaving* (APA, 2014). Similarly, our working definition suggests *behavior* and *experience* (experience in psychology traditionally refers to thinking and feeling).

Q. Do we need to study every behavioral act and every moment of experience?

A. Of course not. We are looking only at relatively *stable* patterns and *enduring* features of behavior and experience. These features manifest in various life situations. Psychologists try to describe, measure, compare, and explain such patterns. Later we will turn to the study of personality traits as distinct and stable patterns of behavior and experience (Chapter 7 specifically focuses on traits).

Q. Does every individual have a personality?

A. It is logical to assume that personality has to be associated with, or remains inseparable from, a certain material or physical carrier, such as a human body. However, in many parts of the book and particularly in Chapter 8 (on the cognitive tradition) we will discuss whether personality can be viewed and understood independently from such a carrier.

knowledge in three areas: (1) health care, (2) education, and (3) social services. Therefore, you can apply your knowledge in global contexts in the following ways:

- Think about yourself and others from a greater perspective. What do you want to achieve globally? What is your role, your mission as an individual in this life, in this world?
- As a person, what are you bringing to the world? What do you want to be recognized for?
- Specifically, after reading a chapter or any part of it, ask this question: How can I use this knowledge to make a real difference in life? Ask others to answer this question. And then think, discuss, and do something useful.

Most of us probably will not be involved in national policy making or global decisions. Yet we all can make a difference by promoting scientific knowledge and critically discussing and applying it. During class discussions and seminars, in articles and public lectures, in the media and online social networks, or during face-to-face contacts, we can review both new and classical research findings, promote our original ideas, influence each other's opinions, change common stereotypes, and, most importantly, help other people. The first step is to gain knowledge. Let's get back to work.

Visual Review

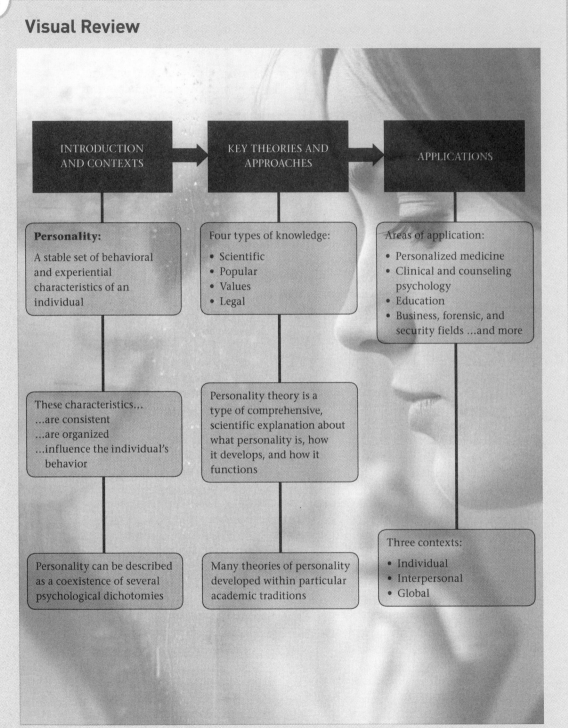

INTRODUCTION AND CONTEXTS → **KEY THEORIES AND APPROACHES** → **APPLICATIONS**

Personality:

A stable set of behavioral and experiential characteristics of an individual

Four types of knowledge:
- Scientific
- Popular
- Values
- Legal

Areas of application:
- Personalized medicine
- Clinical and counseling psychology
- Education
- Business, forensic, and security fields ...and more

These characteristics...
...are consistent
...are organized
...influence the individual's behavior

Personality theory is a type of comprehensive, scientific explanation about what personality is, how it develops, and how it functions

Personality can be described as a coexistence of several psychological dichotomies

Many theories of personality developed within particular academic traditions

Three contexts:
- Individual
- Interpersonal
- Global

© iStockphoto.com/fotostorm

Summary

- Personality is not easy to define, and there are several views on what personality is. We understand personality as a stable set of behavioral and experiential characteristics of an individual.

- Personality refers to both unique and typical, distinguishable patterns of behavior and experience; together, they will be called personality traits. Taken together, in a combination, an individual's traits form a certain type. Type refers to a kind or category of elements or features sharing similar characteristics or features.

- Some features can be called central because they tend to be broad and general. Peripheral personality features are associated with central ones, yet they tend to be more specific, more relevant to particular individuals and specific circumstances. Central features are not necessarily more important or valuable than peripheral.

- Personality can be stable and evolving at the same time. Stability and change are based on many interconnected influences. Research has established that during the life-span we as individuals keep many of our personality characteristics relatively stable. Most personality-related changes take place during childhood. Our personalities become more or less stable in the middle age, and are least changeable after people reach approximately age 50. Exceptions to these expectations are plenty.

- Personality can be viewed as normal and abnormal. Tolerance threshold is a measure of tolerance or intolerance toward specific personality traits in a society or a cultural group. Tolerance thresholds are tested in specific social situations. Personality disorders are enduring patterns of behavior and inner experience that deviate markedly from the expectations of the individual's culture.

- Our behavioral patterns and experiences that become a core of our personality are likely to be explained by a combination of biological and social factors. The debates about complex interactions of natural (biological) factors and social (cultural) influences have always been the focus of attention in social sciences and psychology.

- Understanding the mechanisms of the mind–body interactions has been one of the most challenging topics of research and intellectual debates in the history of science and one of the most intriguing problems in psychology.

- Personality is active and reactive. Determinism encourages psychologists to study how personality was formed (in the past) and how personality features affect behavior and experience now and in the future. Psychologists generally avoid fatalism, which states that we, as humans, are not in control of our actions and thoughts because something or somebody else (like God, fate, or chance) predetermines them.

- At least four types of knowledge related to personality are relevant to our discussion: scientific knowledge, popular beliefs, values, and legal knowledge. These types constantly interact.

- Knowledge requires analysis, which is the breaking of something complex into smaller parts to understand their essential features and relations. Applied to personality, theory is a type of comprehensive, scientific explanation about what personality is and how it develops and functions.

- Many theories of personality developed within particular academic traditions. These traditions bring together scholars that share similar views on a particular scientific approach, subject, or method.

- Personality theories find applications in many walks of life. Philosophers and natural scientists, doctors and educators, curious explorers and experimentalists, and then professional psychologists try to apply their knowledge of personality to a wide variety of human activities.

Key Terms

academic traditions 25	nature–nurture debate 14	scientific knowledge 19
analysis 24	peripheral 9	self-determination 16
censorship 26	personality 4	self-enhancement 10
central 9	personality disorders 13	theory 24
cynicism 10	personality psychology 25	tolerance threshold 13
determinism 16	pessimism 9	type 9
fatalism 16	pop psychology 21	values 21
knowledge 18	popular (or folk) beliefs 20	
legal knowledge 22	scarcity mindset 16	

Evaluating What You Know

Define *personality*.

Explain the three principles referring to personality.

Explain personality's dichotomies and give examples.

Describe the four types of knowledge related to personality; provide examples.

Explain how the four types of knowledge interact.

Describe the areas of application of knowledge about personality.

Describe the steps in applying knowledge.

A Bridge to the Next Chapter

Studying personality should be interesting yet challenging. We are not the first to start this journey. Early philosophers, doctors, and scientists have laid the foundations for personality theory. Year after year, decade after decade, psychologists, like prospectors, tried to gather different theories, concepts, methods, and approaches to find valuable "nuggets" of knowledge about personality. Offering their findings for critical peer review or other forms of evaluation, psychologists began to "filter" and accumulate the best, most successful, and effective methods of investigation and psychological intervention. Travel and publications made this knowledge available to more psychologists globally. More scientists began to combine methods received from different schools to critically examine personality and then apply this knowledge. Psychologists gain their knowledge from other disciplines, including biology, medicine, social sciences, computer sciences, sociology, behavioral economics, and philosophy. This list can easily be continued.

We are at the beginning of our journey. Our next step, in the following chapter, will be to examine how science, social sciences, and the humanities throughout their long histories have contributed to our knowledge of personality today.

WANT A BETTER GRADE?

Get the tools you need to sharpen your study skills. Access practice quizzes, eFlashcards, web exercises, and multimedia at edge.sagepub.com/shiraevpersonality

⑤SAGE edge™

perhaps sets only the general course for our individual features—not the final destiny. Research shows, for example, that economic and educational problems significantly affect IG: People who face poverty and economic uncertainty and people who are less educated tend to be more impulsive than the educated and those who grow up facing certainty (Chiraag & Griskevicius, 2014; Mischel, 2014; Perez-Arce, 2011).

We may be born with certain predispositions for stronger willpower and impulse control, but our lives and experiences contribute as well. We learn from our own victories and mistakes. We absorb from good and bad experiences of others. Our lives are often a lasting discovery of the worth of waiting.

Science and the Scientific Method

Scientific method
The scientific method uses careful research procedures designed to provide reliable and verifiable evidence.

Natural science
Natural science is concerned with the description, prediction, and understanding of natural phenomena.

Personality psychology draws on various types of knowledge (see Chapter 1). Scientific knowledge is the focus of our attention throughout the book. This knowledge is accumulated through research, systematic empirical observation, and evaluation of facts. Personality psychology is a scientific discipline rooted in the **scientific method,** which uses careful research procedures designed to provide reliable and verifiable evidence (Gergen, 2001). This method is about critically checking, rather than simply believing or uncritically accepting, knowledge (Shermer, 2015).

In the process of their research, scientists created various methods to gather facts and theories to explain personality. What is the difference between a scientific theory and just an assumption about personality? A theory should be considered scientific if and only if it is falsifiable—it is testable to prove if it is correct or wrong (Popper, 1992). In personality psychology, many theories are falsifiable (that is, testable), as we shall see throughout the book, and some are not. We will study some of them, though, because they may become testable in the future. If personality psychology is based on the scientific method, in which scientific fields does it obtain its facts? We now turn to a brief description of the three major sources of knowledge: basic science, social science, and humanities.

In very general terms, **natural science** is concerned with the description, prediction, and understanding of natural phenomena. Natural science has two key branches: physical science and biological science (often called life science), which focuses on living organisms, including human beings. Biological science includes many branches of biology involving anatomy, physiology, evolutionary sciences, genetics, and neuroscience. Personality psychology constantly receives new empirical data from life sciences. Which studies are most valuable for psychologists? Let's mention several of them.

For example, genetics is the field of biology involving multidisciplinary studies of heredity through genetic transmission and genetic variations. The term *genetics* has its roots in the ancient Greek word "origin." Indeed, genetics seeks out the origins of the bodily structures, physiological processes, and behavioral and cognitive

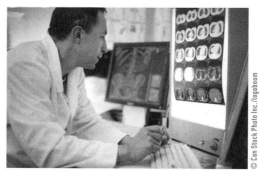

Photo 2.1
A researcher examines a CT scan. Do you mostly rely on scientific knowledge to make decisions? Think of situations wherein you relied on popular beliefs instead. Can you describe these situations?

functions of living organisms, including human beings. The impact of genetics on contemporary personality psychology is significant. We will discuss the research into genetics on many pages in this book.

Another field of life sciences that contributes to personality psychology is **neuroscience**, which is a scientific study of the nervous system. This is a vast field examining the molecular, structural, functional, medical, evolutionary, and many other aspects of the nervous system's work. **Cognitive neuroscience** has a special importance for personality psychology. It examines the brain mechanisms that support the individual's mental functions and subsequent behaviors. This field also includes neurochemistry, which examines how various neurochemicals, such as neurotransmitters, influence the network of neural operations. As a general rule, cognitive neuroscience treats psychological processes—such as thinking and emotions as well as human behavior—as the "products" of the brain's physiology.

Personality psychology also receives significant feedback from **evolutionary science**, which explains how large populations of organisms—plants, animals, and human beings—evolve over time. Evolutionary science, by definition, is interested in evolutionary changes. In very broad terms, evolution is transformation of the heritable traits of species and humans over successive generations. Evolutionary science contributes to personality psychology by providing assumptions about the roots of particular personality traits, especially those that are common in large populations and social groups, such as men and women or the young and the middle-aged.

From the opening vignette, you should remember that impulse gratification has something to do with poverty: The lack of resources and insecurity make individuals more impatient in their decisions. Studies show that poor children as a group are prone to opt for immediate rewards compared with other kids (Mischel, 2014). Being in school makes young people value their futures more and develop patience (Perez-Arce, 2011). Asian immigrants in North America tend to emphasize impulse control more than other families do—the fact that may partly explain the educational and professional success of Asian Americans as an immigrant group compared with others (Baumeister & Tierney, 2012). These were examples from studies conducted by social scientists. **Social science** is concerned with society and the relationships among individuals within it. This discipline includes anthropology, economics,

Neuroscience The scientific study of the nervous system is called neuroscience.

Cognitive neuroscience The study of cognitive neuroscience examines the brain mechanisms that support the individual's mental functions and subsequent behaviors.

Evolutionary science The study of evolutionary science explains how large populations of organisms—plants, animals, and human beings—evolve over time.

Social science The study of social science is concerned with society and the relationships among individuals within it.

@

Read more about religion in the context of personality psychology (including Buddhism, Hinduism, Judaism, Christianity, and Islam) on the companion website.

Question
Read and identify a few common features that these religions share in their reference to the individual's personality.

Behavioral economics The study of the effects of individual factors on personal economic decisions is behavioral economics.

Sociology Sociology is the study of society and the social action of humans.

Humanities In general terms, the field of humanities studies human culture.

Culture A large group of people share a culture, or a set of beliefs, behaviors, and symbols that is usually communicated from one generation to the next.

Philosophy Philosophy is the study of the most general and basic problems of nature, human existence, mind, and society.

political science, and sociology, among others. The goal of anthropology, for instance, is to provide scientific knowledge about human beings. Anthropologists as a group can be interested in such dissimilar topics as the biological roots of the human race, the common grammars of languages, or gender biases in religious rituals (Nanda & Warms, 2010). Yet as a vast field, anthropology provides an uninterrupted stream of knowledge to personality psychology about the universal and culture-specific roots of human beliefs, customs, rituals, and practices.

Economics analyzes and describes the production, distribution, and consumption of resources. Personality psychologists are especially interested in **behavioral economics,** which studies the effects of individual factors on individual economic decisions. These factors include reasoning, mistakes of judgment, habit, group pressure, and so on. These are our daily choices, for example, when we are buying an app for our phone, declining a wedding invitation, or choosing a roommate. Economists and personality psychologists share common interests: They study how people make typical decisions and their individual differences in patterns of behavior. The cooperation between psychology and economics has been very productive. For instance, the 2002 Nobel Prize in economics went to psychologist Daniel Kahneman for his research on biases of individual decision-making. We will turn to his research later in this chapter.

Sociology is the study of society and the social action of humans. This field is generally concerned with associations, groups, organizations, communities, and institutions, both large and small. Sociologists study social development, organization, and change. Personality psychologists obtain news facts and new applications from sociology. For example, psychologists learn from urban sociology about the impact of big-city communities on the adolescent lifestyle; from sociology of gender about the patterns of career choices of boys and girls; or from environmental sociology about how religious beliefs affect individual conservation efforts. These are just a few examples.

Personality psychology also relies on the humanities. In very broad terms, the **humanities** study human culture. **Culture** is a set of beliefs, behaviors, and symbols shared by a large group of people and usually communicated from one generation to the next. Sociology and anthropology are also interested in culture, but the humanities tend to use methods that are primarily critical and have a significant historical and creative element. The humanities study ancient and modern languages, literature, philosophy, religion, and visual and performing arts such as literature, music, and theater. We will discuss the impact of the humanities to the study of personality.

In Greek, **philosophy** means "love of wisdom." Philosophy is the study of the most general and basic problems of nature, human existence, mind, and society. Philosophy is based on rational argument in contrast to faith, belief, or trust, which doesn't have to be rational. Philosophers come from many areas and subdisciplines. Beliefs, practices, and prescriptions relevant to the supernatural and the relationships between the individual and the supernatural are commonly called **religion** (Smith, 1982). Religion is different from philosophy. When philosophy relies mostly on science and logic, religion turns to faith. When philosophy embraces critical reason, religion turns to prescriptions and trusts in tradition. As you should remember from Chapter 1, religious knowledge commonly appears in the form of human values usually supported by custom. Religion does not necessarily reject science—it actually embraces it. However, it requires putting faith before science when there is a contradiction between the two. We should keep in mind that for centuries religion's influence on science, social sciences, and the humanities was significant.

Religion The beliefs, practices, and prescriptions relevant to the supernatural and the relationships between the individual and the supernatural make up religion.

The expression of human imagination through creativity is called **art.** It typically includes, among many other forms, visual arts such as painting and sculpture and performing arts such as music, theater, film, and dance. Artists can be scientists, yet most of them aren't. They do not intend to convey scientific knowledge through their artistic designs. Artists create something that is supposed to be beautiful or carry emotional power and requires an act of judgment from the listener or viewer (Kandel, 2012).

Art Art is the expression of human imagination through creativity.

Personality psychology is rooted in the **humanist tradition** (or humanism) in science, which emphasizes the subjective side of the individual—the sense of freedom, beauty, creativity, and moral responsibility. Humanism encourages self-understanding and improvement, openness, and sharing of skills and experience (Dilthey, 1910/2002). A typical humanist is a person of virtues, knowledge, and passion. Humanism is also based on science and tends to be secular.

Humanist tradition Also called humanism, the humanist tradition in science emphasizes the subjective side of the individual—the sense of freedom, beauty, creativity, and moral responsibility.

Art gives personality psychologists a treasure trove of materials to enrich their scientific outlook of human beings, their behavior, and their inner world. *Ramayana,*

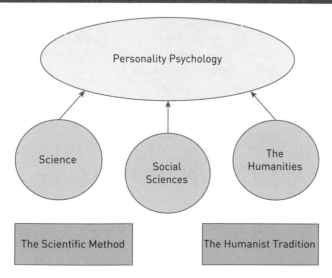

FIGURE 2.1 ● The Scientific Traditions in the Study of Personality

the ancient Indian epic, and *Dream of the Red Chamber*, an 18th-century Chinese classic, provide great accounts of the complexities of human behavior and individual choices. Writers such as Shakespeare in England and Tolstoy in Russia have created a long line of literary characters that millions of people continue examining today. Scores of artistic sources that originated in the Middle East, Iran, and central Asia also deal with the individual's personality. Creations of Firdawsi, Umar Hayyam, and Nizami teach us about passion and romantic love, anger, jealousy, pride, and generosity of people living centuries ago.

Science, social sciences, and the humanities interact when we study personality. Without science, personality psychology would certainly lose the power of the scientific method. Without social sciences, personality psychology would overlook the importance of social factors in shaping who we are as people. The humanities provide personality psychology with moral strength and encourage care about the individual (see **Figure 2.1**).

We are now turning to major contributions to personality psychology from life sciences, social sciences, and the humanities. These disciplines' intellectual legacy is diverse and vast. What did they bring to our understanding of personality? How can we apply this knowledge?

CHECK AND APPLY YOUR KNOWLEDGE

1. What is cognitive neuroscience? How does it contribute to the study of personality?

2. Explain behavioral economics and why it is important for the study of personality.

3. Compare the scientific tradition and the humanistic method to study personality. Consider two assertions:

   A. Social sciences, for example, provide evidence about the impact of education on reducing violence and crime.

   B. The French novelist Victor Hugo (1802–1885) wrote, "He who opens a school door, closes a prison." Do scientists and poets often convey similar ideas? What are the differences in their approaches to facts?

4. When scientists appeal to reason, artists inspire imagination. Think about and suggest the cases in which science appeals to imagination and art refers to reason.

Genetics Genetics is the study of heredity through genetic transmission and genetic variations.

Inheritance Inheritance refers to how certain traits in living organisms were handed down from parents to offspring.

Influences on the Study of Personality

Genetics

Genetics is the study of heredity through genetic transmission and genetic variations. For centuries, scientists tried to understand **inheritance**, or how certain traits in living organisms were handed down from parents to offspring. Many researchers looked for the most elementary bodily "units" responsible for inheritance of such traits. Charles Darwin (1809–1882), for example, believed that acquired characteristics are inherited. He attributed this to gemmules, some identifiable particles in the body. To test his hypothesis, he transfused blood from different breeds of rabbits to examine the resulting characteristics of the offspring. In the 20th century, science turned to molecular biology to

Photo 2.2 Have you met any identical twins? If yes, how different or similar did their behavior appear to you?

explain hereditary transition processes and patterns. These days, the union of genetics with molecular biology has created a powerful new science that provides personality psychology with a constant stream of new facts. What do we learn specifically from genetics research about heredity and its role in the individual's personality?

Some Personality Features Are Inherited

When we discuss heredity, we usually talk genetic transmissions and genes. What is a gene? In a simple way, a **gene** is a segment or portion of the DNA (a complex molecule) that contains codes or "instructions" as biological information about how to build new protein structures. Genetics offers several important facts and assumptions to personality psychology, thus helping better explain the development and behavioral manifestations of certain personality features—including traits, skills, emotional patterns, and so on.

The following summative arguments can help us better understand the impact of hereditary factors on personality.

- An individual's personality features, including traits, subsequent behaviors, and psychological experiences, are often influenced by genetic factors. Genetic information activates particular physiological "mechanisms" in the individual's body, thus affecting his or her physical development, as well as a wide range of behavioral, cognitive, and emotional features. The consistency of our behaviors and inner experiences has something to do with our genetic makeup.

- Genetic factors can explain many variations in personality traits and behaviors, including the similarities and differences among individuals. At the same time, we should accept that some personality features have a stronger genetic component compared to others.

- The individual's personality features, however, develop in a complex and constant interaction between genetic and environmental factors. Genes do not directly create or "build" individual traits or features. Genes are responsible only for "building materials," which, in the process of active interaction with the environment, influence the development of certain behaviors, thought patterns, and other personality features.

Gene A gene is a segment or portion of the DNA (a complex molecule) that contains codes or "instructions" as biological information about how to build new protein structures.

Research spreading over several decades in various countries shows the significant role of hereditary factors in the individual's life, behavior, and specific traits. Consider a few examples for starters. Our genes significantly affect our life expectancy. If your grandparents are alive and they are in their 80s, your parents and you are very likely to live as long and possibly even longer. Genetic factors have something to do with our susceptibility to many illnesses, such as certain cancers, heart diseases, or diabetes (Dubal et al., 2014). Genetic factors also affect our predisposition to serious psychological disorders, such as schizophrenia, bipolar disorder, and depression (Paul, 2014). A child's early measures of activity, emotionality, and sociability (these are major components of temperament and foundations of our personality) have a significant hereditary component (Buss & Plomin, 1984; Silva & Stanton, 1996). Genes influence a person's cognitive abilities as well as play a very important role in triggering intellectual disabilities (American Psychiatric Association, 2013). Our musical skills are rooted in genetic factors, too. Recent research (Mosing et al., 2014) shows that practicing music without the right genes to back up that practice could be unproductive. While it is true that Mozart and Lady Gaga spent long hours in training (in Salzburg and in New York, respectively) before they became famous, they also most likely had the right "musical genes."

Genetic factors also contribute to physiological variations among large groups. For example, ethnic groups living in Tibet developed a genetic variant that allows them to live at high altitudes, where most other people suffer because of the lack of oxygen (Wade, 2015). In North America, Europe, Japan, and other countries that have no significant shortages of food, people's height is determined mostly by their heredity (Bilger, 2004). Genetic factors also affect the stability of individual traits during the process of development (Hopwood et al., 2011). In other words, some of us are predisposed to have stable personality traits; others should expect their traits to change during their life-spans (the stability and change of personality traits is the focus of Chapter 10). However, our genetic "building blocks," or predispositions for developing stable psychological features of our personalities, should always be considered in the context of environmental conditions within which we develop and live.

Genes and the Environment Interact

Thirty years ago, personality studies borrowing from genetics focused on specific genes that correlate to specific personality traits (Davies, 2014). Today's understanding of the genetic transmission is more complex. Genes provide numerous options for varying cells to be expressed, but the environment determines which of these are activated. A fine illustration comes from the studies of twins: Despite sharing similar genetic backgrounds, their actual physical features (such as fingerprints) are extremely diverse. Identical twins—even those raised in the same environment—are not perfect replicas of each other; their experiences make them very distinctive from each other.

Studies of animals also provide ideas about the behavior of humans. Genetically identical mice, for example, are different in terms of the amount of activity in which they engage—some are explorers and some are not. In a study using microchips, scientists measured the amount of active and exploratory behavior in mice. Over the course of 3 months, the brains of the most explorative mice were building more new neurons in the hippocampus (a process called *neurogenesis*), which is the center for learning and memory, than the animals that were more passive. So even though these mice were genetically identical, their brains became different due to the differences in their experiences (Bergmann & Frisén, 2013).

Research shows that some genetic factors under certain environmental conditions result in particularly advantageous traits that help individuals in their lives. Genetic factors are also responsible for aggressiveness, inhibition, or propensity for anxiety. In certain conditions and in some individuals, these features develop into persistent psychological problems and disorders (Krueger & Markon, 2006). To reiterate, people's genetic predispositions for developing psychological features should always be considered in the framework of environmental conditions (Davies, 2014; Wade, 2015). For example, some people are genetically predisposed to be more socially sensitive, caring, and compassionate than others, but their environment contributes to the degree of sensitivity. Sensitivity is positively correlated with religiosity: People who tend to be sensitive also tend to be religious. Religiosity is also connected in surveys with the sense of happiness. However, people feel happier when they find opportunities for social connectedness and affiliation with others (Sasaki, Kim, & Xu, 2011). It is not enough to have certain inherited conditions for being happy. There must be a social environment that influences the individual's ability to be happy or unhappy.

Neuroscience

Recall that neuroscience is the scientific study of the nervous system. At least three disciplines within neuroscience contribute to personality psychology: electrophysiology, clinical pathology, and brain imaging studies. In university- and hospital-based laboratories, researchers use increasingly sophisticated methods and experimental devices to learn more about the mechanisms of neurophysiological processes and the brain's chemistry. The brain has about 86 billion neurons, 16 billion of which are in the cerebral cortex, the seat of many functions affecting an individual's personality (Jabr, 2015).

Clinical studies of brain pathology provide valuable knowledge about the brain's normal functioning as well as its dysfunctions. One of the many efficient methods involves studies of lesions in people who suffered brain damage that examine if or how their personality traits were affected by the trauma. For years, scientists using the **clinical–pathological method** compared clinical observations of a patient's abnormal symptoms with the reliable data about brain pathology, most likely obtained during an autopsy on the deceased patient's brain (Taves, 1999). Ideally, this method helps to establish cause-and-effect relationships between pathology of certain areas of the brain and various psychological functions and dysfunctions (Seitelberger, 1997). In reality, such cause-and-effect relationships are extremely complicated.

The rapidly developing methods of brain imaging added to the clinical–pathological method and provided cognitive neuroscientists with remarkable new facts. For example, by examining the location of neural activation generated by a behavioral or cognitive task, researchers learn more about the role of brain processes in thinking,

Clinical–pathological method Using the clinical–pathological method, clinical observations of a patient's abnormal symptoms are compared with reliable data of brain pathology, most likely obtained during an autopsy.

emoting, and decision-making. Electroencephalography (EEG) was introduced around the 1930s (Berger, 1994) and has been used ever since. This method allows scientists to study the dynamic aspects of brain activity under changing functional conditions. Computerized tomography used since the 1970s helps to identify the precise location of a brain lesion while the patient is alive, and for the past 20 years, magnetic resonance imaging (MRI) and functional neuroimaging have allowed us to see direct changing psychological conditions. The recent advances in EEG help study the neural dynamics associated with mental events at the millisecond level (Solms & Turnbull, 2011). Although almost 90% of neuroimaging studies were performed in Western countries (Chiao & Cheon, 2010), this situation is changing recently to include more culturally diverse subjects.

These are several summative and key assumptions of neuroscience relevant to personality psychology:

- Identifiable brain structures are contributing to particular behavioral, cognitive, emotional functions of the individual and his or her personality traits. Specific neurophysiological mechanisms in the brain are associated with particular behavioral, cognitive, emotional functions of the individual. These physiological mechanisms can explain differences in personality features.
- The relations between neurophysiological functions and behavioral responses are not that simplistic. Specific personality features can have something to do with different brain mechanisms; similarly, different features could be associated with similar physiological mechanisms. Brain centers do not operate independently, and their functions are continually influenced by the activities in other parts of the brain.
- To better understand the individual's personality using research in neurophysiology, we should always understand human physiology in its constant interaction with the environment (both social and physical).

Brain Activities Are Associated With Specific Behaviors

Consider a few examples. The functioning of a brain's frontal lobes has been associated with the individual's style of planning, the style of responses to reward and punishment, tendencies to procrastinate, and a wide range of executive functions related to decision-making (Carver & Harmon-Jones, 2009). Studies involving brain tomography showed a significant reduction in the development of the frontal lobes, compared with the control group, in individuals convicted of serious violent crimes such as murder (Raine, 2014). The frontal lobes contribute to individual self-control, including the ability to control anger and other emotions that contribute to violence. Studies show that some cultural differences (among other factors) in individual behavior also may have something to do with the functioning of frontal lobes (Chiao & Cheon, 2010).

Amygdala The amygdala is the almond-shaped part of the brain crucial for processing emotions.

The size and functioning of the **amygdala**, the almond-shaped part of the brain crucial for processing emotions, is also apparently correlated with the individual's violent traits (Raine, 2014). The hypothalamus function has something to do with our style of attachment and bonding as well as our predisposition to lying

(Shalvi & De Dreu, 2014). **Neurotransmitters**, or endogenous chemicals that enable neurotransmission between two cells, are associated with a variety of behavioral and psychological functions, including propensity to depression, anxiety, and even social delinquency (Raine, 2014; Rang, 2003).

Cognitive neuroscientists proposed various models of the brain process, largely comparing it to the way computers process data. In a nutshell, the brain receives information from the senses, encodes it, stores it, and then exercises decision-making and response selection. But how and where does all this information travel within the brain? Cognitive neuroscience comes to help and uses the model of neural networks to explain these dynamics. What are these neural network models? The brain neurons can be presented as "nodes." A node is like a communication device of some sort that is connected to other nodes and attached to a larger network. Such a node is able to send, receive, block, and forward information through various communication channels. In terms of the brain's operations, cognitive neuroscientists examine mental functions from the standpoint of the nodes functioning in networks (Glynn, 2009).

The Nervous System Interacts With the Environment

Psychologists have to be careful, however, and critically review the data they obtain from neuroscientists. An experimental fact that, for instance, one portion of the brain is more active than several adjacent areas during a certain mental operation could be interpreted in many ways. Leading physiologists of the past conveyed to future generations of scientists that the higher-level mental processes, such as making an important decision, or psychological traits such as openness to experience cannot be reduced to physiological processes, even the most complicated ones (Sperry, 1961). A mental function is more than a combination of billions of neurons firing. To understand psychology, one has to understand the complexity of multilevel interactions of physiological processes and mechanisms by which they interact. Most importantly, these physiological processes and mechanisms take place within specific environments, both physical and social. This interaction has created human beings.

Certain animals have very large brains. Billions of neurons in such brains support very sophisticated functions. But just the size of the brain does not make a living organism competitive with a human being in terms of intellectual and personality features. Of course, humans have the most cortical neurons of any species on Earth. Although it makes up only 2% of body weight, the human brain consumes about 20% of the body's total energy at rest. In contrast, the chimpanzee brain needs only half that (Jabr, 2015). In addition to the brain functions, human bodies also have certain advantages that are likely to distinguish human beings from other species. Dolphins have demonstrated elements of self-awareness. They can cooperate, plan ahead, and use simple elements of a language. However, dolphins don't have hands or can't build tools, like humans. Apes can mimic human behavior, perform complex operations, and understand words from human language. Yet their vocal tracts lack the ability to produce speech, which humans can do. Continuing the same logic, some parrots and crows have the vocal anatomy to imitate human speech, but their brains are not large enough or wired in the right way to master complex language and reasoning (Jabr, 2015).

Neurotransmitters
Neurotransmitters are endogenous chemicals that enable neurotransmission between two cells. They are associated with a variety of behavioral and psychological functions, including propensity to depression, anxiety, and even social delinquency.

What makes human beings who they are is a sophisticated combination of biological, physical, and environmental conditions in the context of human evolution. About 1.8 million years ago, human brains became larger. Humans started walking upright. They had transformed themselves from tree-climbing apes who needed to spend a lot of time searching for food to upright, meat-consuming hunters who could roam large distances. Learning to cook with fire, searching out new water sources, making tools, and using vocal cords to make sounds and develop language were several among many accomplishments made by our ancesters (Finlayson, 2014).

Evolutionary Science

Evolutionary psychology The study of evolutionary psychology combines the knowledge of evolutionary science and psychology and explores the ways in which complex evolutionary factors affect human behavior, experience, and personality features.

Personality psychology receives significant feedback from evolutionary science. Evolution, in very general terms, is transformation in the heritable traits of species over successive generations. Evolutionary science generally explains how large populations of organisms—plants, animals, and human beings—evolve over time. **Evolutionary psychology** combines the knowledge of evolutionary science and psychology and explores the ways in which complex evolutionary factors affect human behavior, experience, and personality features (Confer et al., 2010). Particular adaptive mechanisms of thinking and acting allowed humans to survive and adjust to challenging environmental conditions. These mechanisms have been transmitted—most likely genetically—from one generation to the next. It was a long process: Human beings were evolving during hundreds of thousands of years as a result of competition and natural selection.

Several summative assumptions of evolutionary psychology are most suitable for the study of personality:

- The individual's personality features can be explained as useful, adaptive functions of the individual interacting with the physical and social environment.
- Natural selection principles can explain similarities and differences in personality traits between different groups of people. Principles of natural selection are not necessarily useful in explaining individual differences between two individuals.
- To better understand how evolutionary factors influence the individual's personality, it is crucial to consider them in close interaction with other factors, including individual genetic variations, physiological mechanisms' underlying behavior, and specific social conditions within which an individual lives.

Evolutionary Factors

Today's evolutionary psychologists explain a diverse array of individual features, including curiosity and shyness, openness to new experiences, friendship and aggression, propensities to lie or suspiciousness of strangers, and many other behaviors—all by evolutionary mechanisms. Human beings struggle for resources and safety. They are supposed to approach with caution new, untested things in their lives. They are supposed to support and protect the members of their families and friends. The main assumption of evolutionary psychology is that most elements of human behavior should have a biological, evolutionary meaning. People survive because the things they do make sense. Infants, for instance, show a very early tendency to be wary of certain animals and plants. It should make good evolutionary sense to be afraid of plants when we are young and ignorant about which are useful and which are harmful (Wertz & Wynn, 2014). Other behaviors and habits, such as drug use or overeating, are harmful to evolution. Individuals who practice such behaviors are likely to die prematurely, reducing their chances of having offspring.

The "logic" of the evolutionary theory can be further illustrated with several examples. Let's discuss, for instance, the similarities and differences between men and women. Throughout history, especially during the early stages of human civilization, the **alpha males**, which are the strongest and most aggressive, were able to reproduce better than other, weaker males. Therefore, to survive, men in the past had to develop habits of aggressive and dominant behaviors to compete against one another. Thus, strong, dominant men created a particular culture to benefit the most competitive and the most aggressive. In history, this culture certainly benefited strong men. Today, men continue to dominate the upper echelons of business and politics. Yet men also suffer because of this evolutionary male-dominant culture: Far more men than women die in on-the-job accidents, are detained for crime, and are killed on the battlefield. For these and other reasons, men's life expectancy is lower than women's: It is between five and seven years, depending on several factors (Baumeister, 2010).

Furthermore, as evolutionary scientists suggest, men's desire for a variety of partners and women's desire for one committed partner also play a significant role in the evolution of human behavior. Evolutionary "strategies" for men and women are different in some ways. Men seek variety and try to multiply the number of their

Alpha males Alpha males are the strongest and most aggressive males and are able to reproduce better than other, weaker males.

SELF-REFLECTION

Studies show that people tend to attribute positive personality characteristics, such as kindness or high intelligence, to physically attractive individuals. Mothers tend to unintentionally treat attractive children more favorably than unattractive ones. As evolutionary psychologists maintain, a friendly face is seen as attractive and beautiful because friendliness is an important evolutionary feature (Elia, 2013).

Questions

Just for the sake of this exercise, contemplate for a minute whether other people find you (a) very attractive, (b) somewhat attractive, or (c) not very attractive—based only on your "external" physical characteristics. How did these perceptions of your physical characteristics affect your view of self or your individual features? (We will revisit this issue in Chapter 8.) Discuss whether other people, in your experience, tend to associate a person's physical characteristics, such as attractiveness, with his or her kindness.

Yet understanding the mechanisms of the mind–body and nature–nurture interactions has been and remains one of the most significant scientific challenges (Gergen, 2001).

Studying the individual in social contexts, social scientists acknowledge that the individual is an integral part of society. People create their social environment and depend on it. Personality psychologists put forward three key summative assumptions:

- The quantity and quality of resources available to the individual and the quality of surrounding physical and social conditions all affect the individual's personality.
- Specific interactions of the individual with the environment (both physical and social) affect the individual's specific traits, which develop as a result of these interactions.
- Individual differences and group differences can be explained, to a significant degree, by the variations in their social environments.

Abundance or scarcity of resources profoundly affects human behavior and an individual's personality features. Research shows that poverty, for instance, is distinctly linked to a shorter life span and poorer health (Wairaven, 2013). The poor tend to live in more harmful environments and are more likely to be exposed to diseases and other risks than those who are not poor. Malnutrition in childhood, particularly during the first year of life, childhood infections, and exposure to accidents and injuries all make chronic and sometimes disabling diseases more likely in adult life, causing substantial changes in individual activities. Poverty affects the way people make decisions, form habits, and see themselves and others (Banerjee & Duflo, 2011). This research will be addressed throughout the text.

Climate and environmental tendencies both have a tremendous impact on the individual. Harsher climates involve a wide variety of risks and challenges, including food shortages, strict diets, and health problems. People living in harsh climates persistently face greater risks compared with people living in mild climates and thus develop traits to tackle their regular problems (Van de Vliert, 2006). Consistent levels of pathogens (infectious agents such as microbes) could partly explain the individual's propensity to interconnectedness and collectivism. How? Groups facing high prevalence of local pathogens (to which they develop resistance) tend to protect themselves from strangers (who possibly carry new germs). Therefore, such groups develop behavioral norms to be more inward-oriented, protective, and collectivist (Cashdan & Steele, 2013). Moreover, in areas with pathogen prevalence, both men and women place greater value on a potential mate's physical attractiveness (Gangestad, Haselton, & Buss, 2006). Parasites tend to degrade physical appearance. Therefore, a person's looks may quickly suggest this person's health status.

Social scientists suggest that particular personality features develop in certain historic conditions. The American sociologist Fredrick Turner (1920) argued that while facing the challenges of the frontier, Americans developed their frontier spirit and individualistic features because they were mainly conquerors and builders. Similar speculative assumptions were common in social sciences in the past. More recent research, however, produces some intriguing conclusions. Japanese scholars (Kitayama, Ishii,

Imada, Takemura, & Ramaswamy, 2006) found that people in Hokkaido, the northern island of Japan with a history of frontier spirit, showed a greater degree of individualism than did mainland Japanese who don't have such a history. Another study turned to agricultural practices, such as rice and wheat growing. Both required significant cooperation among farmers; however, farmers who grew rice (before mechanization of agriculture) had to expend twice as many hours doing so as those who grew wheat. Therefore, rice-growing societies such as India, Malaysia, and Japan had to develop very "cooperative" labor practices and collectivist traits compared with Europeans, who mostly grew wheat (Talhelm et al., 2014). Wheat-growing societies also required cooperation and mutual help, yet to a smaller degree. These societies have developed less collectivist behavior and outlook in their members.

The Economics Dimension

Economists make their contribution to personality psychology because they study and explain the connections between economic factors and the individual's personality and behavior. Consider several illustrations.

Do you think wealthy individuals are different from poor ones in terms of their personality features? Would you say the thinking patterns and everyday habits of the super-rich are different from those in the middle class? Economist Karl Marx (1818–1883) and later his followers suggested that there are "higher" and "lower" classes based on their access to resources, and ultimately, power. How does a person's social class affect her or his behavioral and psychological features, according to Marx? Social classes pursue their fundamental class interests: The *haves* (the wealthy) want to keep the resources and power in their hands, and the *have-nots* (the poor) want to redistribute power and resources equally. Thus, social classes create their own values, customs, and even individual habits that serve their class interests. One of the most important ideas for personality psychology to examine is that individuals tend to develop **class consciousness**, a set of core beliefs and perceptions about their life and the world around them based on their social (class) position in the society. In practical terms, people born to luxury and privilege or those who are surrounded by poverty and injustice are expected to develop key personality features relevant to their socioeconomic status.

What specific personality features are developed, and how can researchers prove that individuals have different personalities because they belong to different classes? Sociologists and psychologists have tried to answer these questions for many years. Studies in the former Soviet Union showed that people in egalitarian societies such as the Soviet Union (where private property was outlawed so that people were economically and socially equal) tend to be more collectivist, honest, altruistic, generous, and optimistic than people living in more capitalist countries, where they tend to be more greedy, individualistic, and pessimistic. However, the results of such studies are questionable because they haven't been properly peer reviewed by independent scholars. Also many researchers who conducted such studies received incentives, and they were required by the government to demonstrate in their research the superior features of people living in communist countries (Shiraev, 2013). These criticisms

Class consciousness Members of social classes possess a set of core beliefs and perceptions about their life and the world around them based on their position in society.

should not diminish the importance of the economic dimension of academic research into personality. Access to resources (money, housing, education, and employment) affects many aspects of individual behavior and beliefs. Studies show that social and economic inequality, as well as discrimination of one group against others, can affect a host of psychological features (Fowers & Richardson, 1996; Jenkins, 1995).

Social Science and Typology

Social status
A social status is a position within the society and can be a measure of an individual's access to resources and power.

Stereotyping
Stereotyping is a generalization of others' behaviors and traits based on their social status or membership in a particular gender, age, ethnic, or professional group.

Social scientists also study individual types based on their **social status**, or position within the society. Social status can be a measure of an individual's access to resources and power. Sociologists most often put people in categories according to their income, education, gender, age, and occupation and then try to see similarities and differences in their behavior, opinions, and personality features. Studies show that an individual's perceived social status affects other people's perception of this individual. People tend to perceive and respond differently to a low-status person compared to a high-status person (Fiske, 2010). Social scientists also study **stereotyping**, a generalization of others' behaviors and traits based on their social status or membership in a particular gender, age, ethnic, or professional group. This book provides many examples of stereotyping and provides suggestions for ways to reduce it.

CHECK AND APPLY YOUR KNOWLEDGE

1. Name the two key summative assumptions (related to the study of personality) of social sciences.
2. Explain the phenomenon known as the "frontier spirit" in America and Japan.
3. What is class consciousness? How does it relate to the study of personality?

The Humanities

Philosophy

Philosophy, with history that spreads across centuries and millennia, is rooted in a global intellectual tradition. Across regions and times, philosophers emphasized the importance of education, honesty, friendship, cooperation, hard work, and the ability to persevere in difficult circumstances. "How should we live?" asked Aristotle (384–322 BCE), who lived in ancient Greece. He, like many other philosophers, believed that the individual should develop the capacity for virtue—a stable set of character traits to think, feel, and act in the right way (Pickard, 2011; Warburton, 2012). Moderation in desires and actions was valued by many European, Indian, and Chinese philosophers hundreds of years ago and thousands of miles apart from one another. Many philosophers search for the essence of moral behavior, which is often referred to as the "golden rule": Act according to your rational will but assume that your action, to be considered moral, should become a universal law for others to follow. In other words, treat others as you would like others to treat you (Gensler, 2013; Kant, 1785/1956).

Philosophers endorsed **enlightenment**, which is the view of validating knowledge and education based on science and reason rather than on religious dogmas. Philosophy celebrates the educated individual. The propensity to learn and reason is the essence of humans. Ancient Indian philosophers compared education with personal liberation from fear and despair. Chinese thinkers, such as Confucius (c. 551–479 BCE), emphasized the importance of education for an individual to become an efficient member of society. Philosophers expressed different ideas about how the individual should learn. Yet they emphasized the necessity for the learned to apply their knowledge in the right, ethical way. The ability to think critically was also desired (Collins, 1990).

Philosophers initiated the discussion about the interaction between the natural tendencies, or inborn factors, and the quality of the learning process. Philosophers commonly associated the lack of education with the inability to live a productive, fulfilled, and happy life. Many philosophers agreed with social scientists that a deliberate, planned intervention in many areas of society should be beneficial to human growth and improvement (Nugent, 2009).

Many philosophers wrote about various personality types and produced some interesting and detailed descriptions of such types. At least two clusters of their assumptions are important in the context of personality psychology. In vertical hierarchical typologies, philosophers placed the types in a particular ranked order to indicate the strength, purity, skills, or other features of the individual, such as social status (like in social sciences). For example, the Greek philosopher Plato (427–347 BCE) believed in different quality of the souls. Using his classification, philosophers and public officials are likely to possess the highest-quality rational souls. Warriors have strong affective souls. Slaves should have dominant desirous souls. In horizontal typologies, the types appear as somewhat loose clusters assembled by the philosopher's creative imagination. For example, English philosopher David Hume (1711–1776) described four personality types: The Epicurean type displays elegance and seeks pleasure; the Stoic is a person of action and virtue; the Platonist type regards philosophical devotion; and the Skeptic is the critical thinker (Hume, 1777/1987).

Enlightenment
Enlightenment is the view of validating knowledge and education based on science and reason rather than on religious dogmas.

Personality Psychology Learns From Studying Religion

For a psychologist, religious values are a rich source of knowledge about the individual's inner world, behavior, and personality. Religious knowledge is both descriptive and perspective. It describes various individual features and explains the individual's inner world and behavior. It also prescribes the rules and directions of thinking and action.

First, religious beliefs reflect the **transcendental** (spiritual, nonphysical) side of human experience. Religious beliefs contain the idea that something larger and more important than human beings should exist and govern our behavior (Park, 2005). Good and bad things can happen to us beyond our control. Research shows many individuals share the view that several aspects of our lives are out of our control or that our control is insignificant. We return to these studies and the phenomenon called locus of control in Chapter 6.

Transcendental
Transcendental refers to the spiritual, nonphysical side of human experience.

Second, religious beliefs offer individuals a distinct possibility of extending life beyond the time of their physical existence. This can happen because, according to religious teachings, we have a soul. Across religions, the soul is perceived as immortal, indivisible, active, and existing independently of the body (Collins, 1990; Fernandez, Castano, & Singh, 2010).

Third, religious teachings often embrace mysticism—a belief in the existence of realities beyond rational reflection or scientific scrutiny, but accessible by feelings. Mysticism is reflected in many teachings, including the Sufi tradition in Islam, the Kabbalah tradition in Judaism, and in the Christian tradition in general (Shiraev & Levy, 2013).

Fourth, religions teach that happiness is possible. Individuals can achieve this stage through their own efforts. For example, Buddhism and Hinduism teach about nirvana, or a state of profound peace of mind and perfect enlightenment (Collins, 1990). We shall return to these views when we discuss the humanistic views in personality psychology.

Finally, religious teachings tend to prescribe particular behaviors and urge the development of certain desirable personality traits, such as kindness, humility, and self-control. Behaviors such as learning, sharing, and helping others are also strongly encouraged. Religion postulates behavioral taboos—actions and behaviors individuals should eliminate or repress, which often cannot be negotiated or traded (Saroglou, 2011). For example, anger, impulsivity, and jealousy are rejected across cultures. People should not consider wealth and power as the main goals of their lives. Religious knowledge contains detailed descriptions of desirable and undesirable individual types. Some religious teachings provided a clear dichotomy: They separated divine beings (such as saints) from profane beings (such as demons). In other religions, such as Hinduism, the divisions appear more complex because good and evil are usually viewed as intertwined.

In prescribing particular behaviors, religious teachings introduce two interconnected types of action. One requires our individual effort and engagement of others. The other path is inaction and even disengagement based on self-limitations. These paths (for example, in Christianity or Buddhism) are not mutually exclusive. They both can lead toward moral behavior and happiness (see **Table 2.1**).

TABLE 2.1 ● Religious Prescriptions of Engagement and Disengagement		
Prescriptions	**Action and Engagement**	**Inaction and Disengagement**
Positive prescriptions and values	• Become an activist; volunteer. • Engage others. • Make a difference.	• Do not impose your views. • Grow inside through self-discipline, knowledge, and mediation.
Negative prescriptions and taboos	• Abstain from substances. • Abstain from sex before marriage. • Confront evil temptations.	• Reject wealth, greed, and material success. • Pursue a simple life; embrace asceticism.

Sources: Ellens, 2011; Graham and Haidt, 2010.

What does personality psychology gain from the study of religion? Just for starters, psychologists are interested in how religious values affect individual traits and other features, such as self-esteem. Psychologists working in drug rehabilitation programs can also learn how religious beliefs affect temperance and other forms of impulse control. Most important, religious teachings encourage self-improvement that certainly interests psychology theorists and practitioners (Dahlsgaard, Peterson, & Seligman, 2005). In summary, religious beliefs and prescriptions suggested valuable information about inner features such as self-cognition, self-growth, the nature of good and evil behavior, and overt features such as moral behavior.

The Arts

How does what is artistically created help our study of personality psychology?

Ancient philosophers and writers discussed the propensity of some people to postpone the gratification of their immediate needs for the sake of future returns. The Greek author Homer, about 3,000 years ago in approximately 800 BCE, immortalized Odysseus, the famed traveler, who overcame the temptation of the lure of the beautiful yet deadly Sirens. In today's terms, Odysseus had strong IG control. Poets and novelists masterfully described patience and endurance. Chinese authors 2,000 years ago and European playwrights of the 17th and 18th centuries praised restraint and moderation as most appropriate personality features and denounced impulsivity and immediate gratification of desires. Being a good person was almost always meant to be self-controlling.

Describing

In the 1951 book *Catcher in the Rye* by J. D. Salinger, we learn about the identity struggles, alienation, depression, and personal growth of the novel's main character, Holden Caulfield, through him. A stream of his experiences creates in our memory an image of a unique individual personality. Art, at its simplest, is a form of communication. Artists express their visions of human beings--their looks, postures, and actions—and then convey them to their audiences. Artists also attempt to portray, reflect, and even creatively explain the inner worlds of others—their thoughts, desires, insecurities, and emotions. Artists depict specific and recognizable individuals as well as create images of certain individual types. Some artists try to be as close to reality as possible, while others turn to imagination.

Artists (such as actors, directors, and writers) also convey to us their thoughts, beliefs, emotions, mood, and intentions. An artist's creation is often a window into his or her mind and personality. By studying their creative works, we learn about artists' personality traits as well. For example, in the classic film *Forrest Gump* (1994), we learn from the character played by Tom Hanks about the extraordinary power of kindness and forgiveness. In another example, the contemporary Norwegian author Karl Ove Knausgård, who began his six-book series *My Struggle* in 2009, masterfully reflects on the most complex and profound inner battles of the individual living in the 21st century.

Encouraging New Reflections

Artists also give the reader or viewer an emotional impulse to look around, ask questions about their lives, revisit the dilemmas they face, and think about the moral choices they make. Their work can encourage us to think critically and analyze other people's behavior, scrutinize their choices, and even speculate about their future actions. A stroke of a brush or a poetic verse makes us think about others and search for some yet unknown features of human experience and behavior. Art can also serve as a source of entertainment and relaxation by stimulating a particular emotion or mood.

Images and words can also bring about individual action by encouraging us to look inside our own minds and think about the meaning of our own lives, the decisions we make, the differences and similarities among humans, or the nature of good and evil within us. Art provides a means to express the imagination and bring about inner changes. People do not necessarily copy the behavior and thought of literary characters. The changes may be subtle but produce new perspectives on self and the world (Fairhall, 2012). And as we change our views, habits, and personality features, those individual changes may bring social action, which brings about social change (see **Figure 2.2**).

Affecting an Individual's Personality

How can we understand the impact of art on an individual's personality? Several influences should be considered. The first one is socialization, which can be direct and indirect (as is noted earlier in the chapter). Studies show that reading books and stories, sharing these stories, and thinking about them are all important elements of socialization and growth (Thorne & Nam, 2009). When parents read stories to children, the latter learn about the characters and their personality features. This knowledge may affect individual behavior and personality traits: After watching a film or reading a book, we often self-reflect and understand more about ourselves. Then a behavioral change is possible. A person may start thinking and acting differently; as his or her habits change, so do several personality features.

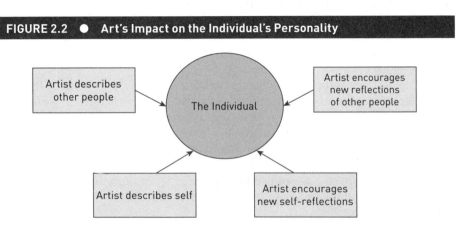

FIGURE 2.2 ● Art's Impact on the Individual's Personality

There is also evidence that suggests literary works had an impact on scientists who have contributed to personality psychology. To illustrate, literary creations of ancient Greeks and Romans influenced scores of social scientists and psychologists of modern times. Tragedies by Sophocles gave inspiration to Freud in conceptualizing his Oedipus complex. Epicurus's ideas about friendship were highly regarded by the philosopher Nietzsche (Dumont, 2010). Nietzsche also credited the influence of Dostoyevsky, whose impact on today's views of personality is significant. Petrarch influenced Renaissance humanist philosophers for at least a couple of centuries. Psychologist Lev Vygotsky was deeply inspired by Shakespeare's *Hamlet*. Other examples will follow in later chapters.

CHECK AND APPLY YOUR KNOWLEDGE

1. Explain the transcendental side of human experience.

2. How would you explain nirvana?

3. Does religion affect your behavior directly? Discuss a few examples illustrating the impact of your religious beliefs on your daily habits and behavior.

4. How does art impact an individual's personality?

5. Which literary or film character has had at least some impact on your ideas or behavior? The impact does not have to be direct and overwhelming. It can be limited and subtle.

How Do We Apply Knowledge?

Sciences, social sciences, and the humanities celebrate knowledge over ignorance, care over indifference, and moral values over indecency. The process of learning, as the Greek philosopher Aristotle believed, should essentially give us the capacity for virtue, a stable set of character traits to think, feel, and act in the right way (Pickard, 2011). Scientific knowledge provides personality psychologists with a vast arsenal of theories and facts to search for virtues in us and other people and apply them to various areas of life.

Applying Knowledge to Self

Know Yourself

Do you know yourself? No, this question is not about your complex inner world. We will examine the inner world of the self later in the book. For now, just describe your basic physical and social features. How well do you know them? Use **Table 2.2** to answer a few simple questions. To answer them with a measure of accuracy, we probably have to turn to measurements (to check weight, for example), pause for a

TABLE 2.2 ● Knowing Your Own Individual Features	
Individual Features	**Assessments**
Physical features: Describe your height, weight, body shape, and so on.	**Are you satisfied with your physical features?** Mostly satisfied Not sure Mostly dissatisfied
Health: Describe if you have health issues or concerns today.	**Are you satisfied with your health?** Mostly satisfied Not sure Mostly dissatisfied
Social status: Describe your income, living conditions, and education today.	**Are you satisfied with your social status?** Mostly satisfied Not sure Mostly dissatisfied
Personal relationships: Describe your friends, relatives, and people with whom you are close today.	**Are you satisfied with your personal relationships?** Mostly satisfied Not sure Mostly dissatisfied
Daily habits: Describe the things you do regularly—your daily routines.	**Are you satisfied with your daily habits?** Mostly satisfied Not sure Mostly dissatisfied

second and think (Do I really have health concerns?), and even contemplate for some time when the question asks about your personal satisfaction with your individual features.

These simple questions about some of the most obvious individual characteristics are not as superficial as they may seem. They can encourage us to pay more attention to our health, habits, or lifestyle. For instance, have you seen a doctor lately to judge with confidence about your health? Did you discuss lately your educational or work plans with someone? Whom did you discuss them with? Who are your friends now? Are most of your habits healthy and helpful? The study of personality psychology ought to start with simple self-evaluation of the facts about you.

Improve Yourself

Behavioral economists suggest that to be successful as an individual, you have to make most reasonable decisions by (a) maximizing your gains and (b) minimizing your losses (Levitt & Dubner, 2005). Psychologists propose effective techniques to improve the effectiveness of our decisions. However, these improvements require knowledge, critical thinking, and hard work. And, of course, you have to make a decision first: Do you want to improve yourself? Do you want to be a better person? Start with a simple step: Keep a daily journal to list all of the things for which

Photo 2.3 Do you exercise regularly? If you do, how does being active affect your individual traits? If you do not exercise, does this inactivity reflect your personality?

you are grateful. Research shows people who keep such a journal report significantly increased feelings of happiness and increased healthy behavior, which are interconnected (Emmons & McCullough, 2003). Contemplating and sketching a plan should be helpful (see **Table 2.3**).

We can change our minds and bodies and make more effective decisions if we commit to an effort to achieve this. Take **yoga**, for example, a system of beliefs and practices to facilitate the transformation of body and consciousness (Flood, 2012). It is rooted in various religious traditions, especially in Hinduism and Buddhism. Yoga is used these days in the West as well as globally as a comprehensive exercise program, focusing simultaneously on body and mind (Sutherland, 2014). Research shows that learning and practicing yoga helps individuals in addressing their emotional problems, such as depressed mood and excessive anxiety (Streeter et al., 2010). Yoga is a source of positive changes in behavior and thinking, staying focused, avoiding excessive stress, and learning about your own body and mind (Deshpande, Nagendra, & Nagarathna 2009). Yoga also teaches us to be ethical, honest, and nonviolent (Broad, 2012). It is important to practice concentration and self-discipline. An important role in self-improvement, attributed to meditation, is a broad range of principles and techniques of self-reflection, concentration, and contemplation. We will return to this subject in Chapter 9 and Chapter 13.

Yoga Yoga is a system of beliefs and practices to facilitate the transformation of body and consciousness.

Strive for Happiness

Some scientists and philosophers (we will learn more about them in Chapter 10) predicted a major crisis in the middle of every person's life—a crisis at which we all

psychologists historically embraced progressive values (Shiraev, 2013). For psychology professionals, progressivism means an opportunity to apply scientific knowledge to social issues. Progressivism also emphasizes the importance of applied psychological knowledge in three areas: (1) health care, (2) education, and (3) social services. There is nothing wrong with seeing yourself as a social reformer who is interested in pursuing the expansion of your professional role in social life and the increased role of psychology as an applied field. Yet to become reformers, we need to gain knowledge first.

CHECK AND APPLY YOUR KNOWLEDGE

1. What is yoga, and what can it do for self-improvement?
2. Explain positive psychotherapy.
3. What is social categorization? Give examples.
4. Read about the similarities and differences concerning religion while considering how different and how similar religions and their followers are.

   Similarities. Religiosity describes the degree or depth of one's cognitive, emotional, and behavioral dedication to a religion. There are levels or dimensions of religiosity, which involves believing, emotionally bonding with religious knowledge, behaving, and belonging (Saroglu, 2011). Religious teachings may have a relatively similar impact on individuals regardless of their specific religions. Religious rituals and the experience of related emotions seem rather universal across cultures (Saroglou, 2014). Religious teachings may have a different impact on individuals simply because these individuals are already different when they turn to their religions.

   Differences. The very specific forms, predictors, and outcomes of religion and personal religiosity should vary as a function of many factors referring to specific geographic region, climate zone, ethnicity, history, politics, and so on. Consider a simple example: Religious groups endorse a great variety of beliefs and rituals regarding food. Jews and Muslims don't eat pork, and Hindus don't eat beef. Catholics don't eat meat on Fridays during Lent. Consider (and research if necessary) other important differences—such as food, clothing, and rituals—among different religions.

Questions
Studies show that different religious teachings tend to inspire similar individual features in us, including honesty, goodwill, modesty, and kindness. In other words, if two people belong to different religions yet they are equally bright, kind, and generous, then what is the difference between their religious beliefs, in your view? Does their actual everyday behavior make it relatively unimportant what they eat and how they pray? Or does their diet or their style of praying matter in our understanding of them?

Visual Review

INTRODUCTION AND CONTEXTS → KEY THEORIES AND APPROACHES → APPLICATIONS

The **scientific method** uses careful research procedures designed to provide reliable and verifiable evidence

Personality psychology learns from:
- Genetics
- Neuroscience
- Evolutionary science
- Social sciences
- The humanities

Personality psychologists apply knowledge to:
- Self
- Others
- The world

Sources of knowledge about personality:
- Natural sciences
- Social sciences
- The humanities

Sciences, social sciences, and the humanities celebrate knowledge over ignorance, care over indifference, and moral values over indecency

© Can Stock Photo Inc./Lopolo

Summary

- Personality psychology is a scientific discipline rooted in the scientific method, which uses carefully designed research procedures to provide reliable and verifiable evidence. Personality psychology is rooted in science, social sciences, and the humanities.

- Personality psychology learns from genetics. An individual's personality features, including traits, subsequent behaviors, and psychological experiences, should be influenced by genetic factors. Genetic information activates particular physiological "mechanisms" in the individual's body that affect his or her physical development as well as a wide range of behavioral, cognitive, and emotional features. Genetic and environmental factors interact.

- Neuroscience is another important source of knowledge for personality psychology. Identifiable brain structures contribute to particular behavioral, cognitive, and emotional functions of the individual and her or his personality traits. Specific neurophysiological mechanisms in the brain are associated with particular behavioral, cognitive, and emotional functions of the individual. These physiological mechanisms can explain differences in personality features. Physiological and environmental factors interact.

- Personality psychology learns from evolutionary science. The individual's personality features can be explained as useful, adaptive functions of the individual interacting with the physical and social environment. Natural selection principles can explain similarities and differences in personality traits between different groups of people.

- Social sciences contribute to personality psychology. The quantity and quality of resources available to the individual and the quality of surrounding physical and social conditions all affect the individual's personality. Specific interactions of the individual with the environment (both physical and social) affect the individual's specific traits, which develop as a result of these interactions.

- Social science—including anthropology, economics, political science, and sociology—studies concerns with society and the relationships among individuals within it. The humanities, including philosophy, religion, and art, examine human culture.

- Human beings cannot be understood apart from social bonds and interpersonal relationships, yet they are part of nature as well. Individuals are not just passive "recipients" but rather active participants in the process of interaction with their natural environments. Scarcity, availability, and quality of resources, specific natural factors, and the types of interactions between humans and their environment all affect an individual's behavior, experience, and traits.

- Economists make their contribution to personality psychology by explaining several ways to link economic factors and the individual's personality and behavior. Economic features and individual behavior are interconnected.

- Philosophy is the study of the most general and basic problems of nature, human existence, mind, and society. Philosophy is based on rational argument in contrast to faith. Across regions and times, philosophers emphasized ethical imperatives, the importance of education, honesty, friendship, cooperation, hard work, and the ability to persevere in difficult circumstances. Philosophers endorse enlightenment by validating knowledge and education based on science and reason rather than on dogmas.

- Religion relates to beliefs, practices, and prescriptions relevant to the supernatural and the relationships between the individual and the supernatural. Religious beliefs reflect the transcendental side of human experience, its spiritual or nonphysical realm, and they offer believers the distinct possibility of extending their lives beyond the time of their physical existence. Religious knowledge contains detailed descriptions of desirable and undesirable individual types.

- The expression of human imagination through creativity is art. The acts of artistic creation and reflection are important processes in understanding personality. Artists describe themselves and other people, and encourage us to reflect on others as well as make new self-reflections. Art affects individuals via socialization processes, and psychologists' knowledge can be transformed and inspired by art.

- In the application fields, social sciences and the humanities—for the most part—celebrate knowledge over ignorance, care over indifference, and moral values over indecency. We are encouraged to know more about ourselves, understand our actions, and improve from within. Personal enlightenment should lead us toward a better understanding of others and the world around us. This will lead to an educated action.

Key Terms

alpha males 49

amygdala 46

art 41

behavioral economics 40

categorization 63

class consciousness 53

clinical–pathological method 45

cognitive neuroscience 39

culture 40

enlightenment 55

evolutionary psychology 48

evolutionary science 39

gene 43

genetics 42

humanist tradition 41

humanities 40

inheritance 42

marshmallow experiments 37

natural science 38

neuroscience 39

neurotransmitters 47

philosophy 40

positive psychotherapy 62

progressivism 63

religion 41

scientific method 38

social science 39

social status 54

sociology 40

stereotyping 54

transcendental 55

yoga 61

Evaluating What You Know

Define *scientific method*.

Explain the role of sciences in personality psychology.

Explain the role of social sciences in personality psychology.

Explain the role of the humanities in personality psychology.

Give examples of the three areas of application related to self, others, and the world.

A Bridge to the Next Chapter

Year after year, decade after decade, psychologists, like prospectors or gold seekers, tried different theories, concepts, methods, and approaches to advance their knowledge of personality. Offering their findings for critical peer review or other forms of professional evaluation, psychologists "filter" and accumulate the best, most successful, and effective methods of investigation of personality. First travel, then paper publications, and now online articles make this knowledge available to more people globally. Besides psychology, other disciplines now provide reliable and relevant facts. Yet how do psychology and other disciplines supply these facts? How do they obtain them? The next chapter turns to studying the methodology of personality psychology.

3

Research Methods

"Everything must be taken into account. If the fact
will not fit the theory—let the theory go."

—Agatha Christie (1890–1976), English novelist

Learning Objectives

After reading this chapter, you should be able to:

- Describe the primary research methods used in personality psychology
- List the steps involved in preparing and conducting research
- Identify ways to apply critical thinking skills in conducting research about personality

They will first check your identification documents to verify your birth date, birthplace, and your current address. Then they will measure your weight and height. Then they will verify your education and employment history. Your parents will be visited to learn about their parenting style. Then they will ask you to tie a necktie. Can you cook a meal? Please do. They will taste it. After reviewing your meal, they will ask you about your dating history. (You wonder if this is a bit private. They will say "no" and later verify your answers). They will ask you about how you manage your money. More questions will address the breadth of your general knowledge and your formal intellectual skills. A few questions will evaluate your life experience, attitudes about marriage and family, and plans for the future. Next, they will ask you how much money you would give to a beggar on the street. Finally, they will look at your self-introduction video.

Who are *they*? Maybe a government institution or a casting agency for a reality show? No, they are neither. In fact, they are a matchmaking agency in the Hunan province, China. The agency does an exhaustive background check and personality assessments of its applicants. This is not an average dating service. The company selects potential brides for very rich, single Chinese entrepreneurs. These entrepreneurs pay tens of thousands of dollars to prepare their "wish lists" of personality characteristics in an ideal bride. Although the majority of the potential grooms are looking for a "good woman, good wife, and good mother" (as they put in their applications), the specific requirements, as you can imagine, vary greatly.

If this service were available to you now, would you apply as a candidate to be matched with a successful entrepreneur or a professional man or woman?

Critics view the methods of this "matchmaking" service as vague and superficial. Yes, a person's height, weight, memory, and intellectual skills can be quantified, but how can an individual's compassion, empathy, or piety be measured? Supporters argue that the methods are good enough and in line with what we do daily. We all are engaged in spontaneous matchmaking: We seek and find new friends, business partners, intimate friends, and spouses. The difference between our daily "searches" and matchmaking services is that the latter does it seemingly professionally, with the use of psychological science.

What do you think? Is it possible to design a research method to predict whether two people will fall in love? Do your weight, height, moderate openness to experience, and good creative skills make you a better candidate to marry Person A but not B? Or, looking from the other point of view, if the assessment methods were to measure personality features and predict future behavior with some precision, would you be curious to see if someone is the best match for you?

As one of the candidates in China said, "What's wrong with wanting to love a rich guy? I am young, pretty, and smart, and I deserve someone who can match me."

Source: Coonan, 2012.

Personality Research Methods

This chapter deals with research assessment in personality psychology. Some of these methods and critical procedures should be familiar to you from introductory psychology classes. This chapter will give you more. It will provide an overview of several research strategies and offer critical suggestions about gathering, analyzing, and interpreting facts. Further discussions of specific methods for studying personality will follow in every chapter. Here, as an introduction, we will review several most important methods and outline some of their critical assessments. There is no the "one-size-fits all" standard research procedure that every psychologist must follow. In fact, almost every research procedure is unique. Psychologists who study personality pursue different goals, have different resources available to them, and work in different circumstances. Researchers' strategies often relate to the specific methods they use and the interpretations of the results they collect. In many ways, they can determine what the final product will be and what conclusions it will bring.

What do psychologists try to achieve in studying personality? They pursue at least two general strategies: nomothetic and idiographic. These strategies were proposed by the American psychologist Gordon Allport

(1897–1967). The **nomothetic** strategy, or approach, uses the same method to compare many people or subjects to a certain average, standard, or norm. This approach focuses on comparisons and generalizations. It pays attention to characteristics in which individuals may be similar to one another or vary. The **idiographic** approach is person-centered and focuses on many characteristics integrated in a unique person. It refers to specific features within an individual and uses various assessments and measurements. In the past, several prominent psychologists, such as American Henry Murray or Boris Ananiev from Russia believed that the ideographic approach should be the central in personality studies: Psychologists would coordinate research of many other specialists, such as doctors, anthropologists, sociologists, and physiologists, to study an individual. Today, most psychologists acknowledge the importance of both approaches.

What would you, as a researcher, want to know about an individual's personality? What type of data would you like to collect? The American psychologist Raymond Cattell (1905–1998), a pioneer in the scientific study of personality, proposed at least three types of methods, which should produce three kinds of data. The first one is L-data, which includes subjective assessment of biographical (life record) data, including age, sex, nationality, education, occupation, work and volunteer experience, and so forth. The second kind of data is produced in self-reports or questionnaires (often called Q-data). In such self-reports, individuals express their views of various real or hypothetical situations and give assessments of their own individual features in specific situations or in general. And finally, T-data, which include descriptions of people's behavior in standardized experimental situations, can be gathered through experimental methods. We will return to these methods again in Chapter 7.

If you look back at the opening case, you will notice the researchers used all three types of Cattell's methods as well as nomothetic and ideographic strategies to obtain comprehensive data about an individual or a group of people.

What specific research methods do psychologists use?

Observation

Scientific **observation** involves acquisition of information about identifiable variables from a primary source. Observation is not just spontaneous witnessing of something or somebody (it could be, of course, in some cases). As a research method, though, observation requires serious preparation. Observation can be of two types: naturalistic and laboratory-based.

In the laboratory observation, the participants or subjects are brought in, and you—as a researcher—prepare tasks or assignments for them to perform. Researchers in both natural and laboratory cases typically focus on certain manifestations of an individual's behavior. If you are observing from a distance how children share toys in the sandbox, this procedure is likely to be called naturalistic observation. A group of British psychologists, for example, conducted naturalistic observation and focused on the incidents of individual aggression on the streets. The researchers used street cameras, which are now commonplace in the United Kingdom. Using the camera footage, the scientists spent many hours observing various, although rare, street confrontations. They found that an individual's quick and decisive intervention into a potentially violent street confrontation deescalates this conflict. In other words,

Nomothetic A nomothetic strategy, or approach, uses the same method to compare many people or subjects to a certain average, standard, or norm. This approach focuses on comparisons and generalizations.

Idiographic The idiographic approach is person-centered and focuses on many characteristics integrated in a unique person. It refers to specific features within an individual and uses various assessments and measurements.

Observation Observation is the acquisition of information about identifiable variables from a primary source.

the study showed that our decisive peacemaking actions should make a difference (Levine, Taylor, & Best, 2011).

Direct observations such as this are often difficult or sometimes impossible. How can one examine the facts that took place some time ago? In this case, the researcher turns to eyewitness accounts. Sigmund Freud and William Bullitt (1966) published a study of the personality of the U.S. president Woodrow Wilson. This work was based on other people's observations of the president and many biographical facts. Of course, research data about an individual can be collected over various periods ranging from a few seconds to a life-span.

Observations can be both unstructured and structured. In an unstructured observation, the researcher plays the role of an observer to identify and describe various behavior manifestations involving an individual under observation. The method may be used, for instance, for preliminary investigation into a subject. To illustrate, before conducting a detailed assessment of an elementary school student's behavioral problems, a school psychologist may spend some time observing the student's conduct during recess. Nonstructured procedures are often necessary, especially if the psychologist has no other means to obtain information about behavior or individual traits.

A combination of observation and self-reporting was described in a study in the Philippines (IIo, 1998). The procedure is called *pagtatanung-tanong*, and it can be used in relatively small and culturally homogeneous communities. Researchers avoid making the people feel that they are "subjects" in a survey. Although researchers ask many questions, they are discussed in a very informal context. Researchers ask prepared and memorized questions in sequence, but the answers they get may lead to the formulation of new questions and further clarifications if needed. Conducting this type of research does not alert or frustrate people, and it allows some personal or other sensitive issues to be discussed. Answers to questions are gathered as research data.

Observer ratings Observer ratings are structured observations of behaviors or features that require assessment of these actions and features.

Structured observations are based on a plan (you identify the behaviors or features you want to observe) and often require **observer ratings**, or assessment of these actions and features. Studies show that observer ratings of other people, by and large, produce quite reliable assessments. One study examined data obtained from more than 40,000 people; it showed that personality ratings (evaluations) by friends, family members, or unrelated observers can more or less accurately predict behavior of the rated individuals based on their observed personality features (Connelly & Ones, 2010).

Observer ratings can be used in various situations and settings. For example, the members of a sorority could assess one another's leadership qualities and rank them. Each sorority member ranks every other member. Then two people with the highest scores become candidates for an office election. This method has been already used in the past in well-known studies when subjects knew each other relatively well, such as family members (Costa & McCrae, 1988). It is also effective in clinical settings when relatives and friends assess psychological features of individuals undergoing treatment—for example, patients with different forms of dementia, including Alzheimer's disease.

Of course, observation can produce inaccurate and biased data. One of the remedies is to use multiple observers who are likely to produce a more balanced record of observations of some enduring characteristics of individuals (Kenrick & Funder, 1988).

Whenever it is possible or appropriate, the researcher should verify the facts and check for sources of the received information—for example, when analyzing single recollections about an individual or detailed biographies and autobiographies.

Self-Reports

Written opinions, posted comments, e-mails, and private diaries may become sources of information about people even though they do not necessarily expect or plan that others will study these materials. Today, many employers study their job applicants' or employees' posted messages and public profiles on social networks such as Facebook to gather information and form impressions about applicants. Although these "impressions" tend to be biased (remember the discussion of popular knowledge from Chapter 1), they are increasingly common ways of personality assessments.

Other types of self-assessments, such as diaries and memoirs, are often the only sources that allow professionals to make judgments about personality features of particular individuals, including leaders and other historic figures. Psychology's history contains many such examples. For instance, Cardano (1501–1576), known also as Jérôme Cardan, was an Italian physician, mathematician, and astrologer. Cardano wrote a detailed autobiography filled with meticulous details about his daily activities, habits, and psychological experiences. From his unique self-report, we learn that he was an optimistic, hardworking, and conscientious person, yet he was bothered by excessive and occasional obsessive ideas (it looks somewhat like a contemporary profile!). In clinical settings these days, clients often provide detailed self-descriptions to help their therapists diagnose and treat their psychological problems. In cases involving legal judgments, psychologists often use personal statements to better describe individual features of defendants or plaintiffs.

Among self-assessment methods, self-report questionnaires have become dominant in studies of personality (Boyle & Helmes, 2009). For decades, the written questionnaire and the pencil were most common methods of assessment. Today, these methods are increasingly computerized. Questionnaires typically consist of several statements for a person to evaluate or a list of questions to answer. Respondents, for example, assess whether or not each statement applies to them, or they express the degree to which they agree or disagree with certain assertions related to their daily habits, mood, and views of self or other people.

Among the most typical forms of questions used in self-assessment are dichotomous, open-ended, and multiple-choice ones. Dichotomous questions give the subject only two choices: to respond with "Yes" or "No" or "True" or "False." Open-ended questions typically begin with "What do you think . . ." or "Describe . . ." and give subjects an opportunity to express themselves, explaining

Photo 3.1 More than 500 years ago, Gerolamo Cardano, a respected Italian mathematician, wrote a very detailed autobiography. How does such a biography differ from any individual's Facebook profile today? What kind of information could you gather studying someone's Facebook page?

some nuances of their thoughts and feelings. However, the answers to open-ended questions are difficult to analyze. Multiple-choice (or close-ended) questions are easier to analyze than open-ended ones. Nevertheless, these questions limit the choices from which the respondent can select.

Psychologists use some questionnaires to examine as many people as possible to establish common trends in the answers. (Remember the nomothetic approach?) Other questionnaires examine several features or traits of one person. (Remember the idiographic approach?) Any set of questions within a personality questionnaire that is designed to measure a particular personality trait is called a personality scale. Most personality questionnaires contain several different scales, which means they attempt to measure several personality traits (Johnson, 2001).

Studies conducted over the years suggest that many questionnaires used by professional psychologists can generally predict behavior of an individual based on the questionnaire assessment of his or her traits. However, self-reports are not bias free. Be aware, for example, of **social desirability bias**, which is the tendency of respondents to give answers that are supposed to be received favorably by others. As an illustration, many people might be tempted to give a positive answer to the question "Do you acknowledge your own mistakes?" To appear humble and self-critical is commonly viewed as a virtue (Levy, 1997). You should also be aware of a **self-serving bias**—people's tendency to assess their own features as better or more advanced than those of the "average" person. On the other hand, some people tend to diminish their accomplishments or potentials; respondents from Chinese, Korean, and Japanese samples commonly evaluate themselves among the least hardworking in the world. In self-reports, people from Western cultures (e.g., Australians, Americans, Canadians, or Germans) were far more likely to describe their individual traits in terms of internal psychological characteristics and were less likely to describe themselves in terms of roles and relationships than are people from non-Western populations (Heine, 2008; Schmitt, Allik, McCrae, & BenetMartínez, 2007). Respondents also have a tendency to present themselves in a socially appropriate way. For example, parents tend to be reluctant to admit certain practices, such as spanking and grounding their children (Iusitini et al., 2011). Studies also reveal that people's concerns about privacy affect the answers (Mills & Singh, 2007), especially when the survey examines sexual behavior (Alexander & Fisher, 2003). And then there are selective memories; for example, in testimonies and stories people tend to remember better the facts that support their points of view and tend to forget others (Browder, 2000). In the following chapters, we will study some of the prominent self-assessment methods, such as the Sixteen Personality Factor Questionnaire (16PF), Minnesota Multiphasic Personality Inventory (MMPI), Clinical Analysis Questionnaire (CAQ), and others.

Social desirability bias   The tendency of respondents to give answers that are supposed to be received favorably by others is the social desirability bias.

Self-serving bias   The tendency to assess our own features as better or more advanced than those of the "average" person is known as self-serving bias.

Experiments

Experimental methods allow psychologists to determine how an individual's behavior and experience vary across different situations. Experiments should give the researcher transparent and verifiable procedures; not only do they ask individuals about, for example, how fast they make decisions, but they can test the speed of such decisions in various experimental conditions (Johnson, 2001). By varying these conditions, psychologists try to detect specific changes in the subjects' behavior, judgments, opinions, and so on. In an experiment, the condition(s) that are controlled—that is, can be changed by you, an experimenter—are called the **independent variable(s)**. The aspect of human activity that is studied and expected to change under influence of the independent variable is called the **dependent variable(s)**. As an experimenter, you control the independent variable: You may change the conditions of the experiment.

Researchers using the experimental method should try to avoid the biases often found in observations and self-reports. In other cases, experimental procedures allow researchers to design conditions that are difficult or impossible to "assemble" in reality. A group of British scholars, for example, wanted to study why and when individuals intervene in a violent confrontation. Previous research paid the most attention to several outside factors, such as the size of the group. Yet under what individual conditions will a bystander attempt to stop a violent attack of one person against another (Slater et al., 2013)? Psychologists can use street cameras and examine hundreds of hours of video footage (as they did in the study described earlier in this chapter). Obviously, psychologists may not, just out of curiosity, stage real fistfights and brawls. What they may do in addition to observation is design an experimental procedure: a virtual-reality experiment in which the participants are asked to watch several versions of an animated confrontation between an attacker and a victim. The researchers found that at least two factors played a role in the behavior that stops a violent confrontation: the victim's direct pleas for help and whether or not the victim and the witness shared some common identity features, such as being followers of the same sports club. In the following chapters, we will illustrate and critically discuss many other experiments to study personality (see **Figure 3.1**).

Independent variable In an experiment, an independent variable is a condition that is controlled—that is, it can be changed by the experimenter.

Dependent Variable The aspect of human activity that is studied and expected to change under the influence of the independent variable is the dependent variable.

FIGURE 3.1   ●   A Visual Review of Dependent and Independent Variables in Experimental Research

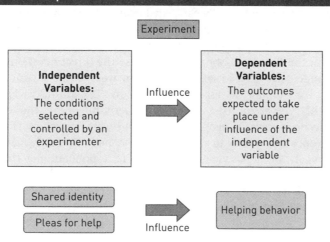

Content Analysis

Content analysis is a research method that systematically organizes and summarizes both the manifest (what was actually said or written) and latent (the meaning of what was said and written) content of communication. The researcher usually examines transcripts of conversations or interviews, television or radio programs, letters, newspaper articles, and other forms of communication. The main investigative procedure in content analysis consists of two steps. Initially, the researcher identifies coding categories; these can be particular nouns, concepts, names, or topics. First-level coding involves identifying properties of data that are clearly evident in the text. Second-level coding involves categorization and interpreting what the first-level categories mean.

To illustrate, Elker Weber from The Ohio State University compared thousands of American and Chinese proverbs and popular expressions to study wisdoms related to an individual's risky behavior as well as risk aversion. She assumed initially that in Chinese culture the number of proverbs related to the individual's cautious behavior would be significantly greater than in the West (in the English language). In fact, she found that in Chinese language, sayings related to risk-taking behavior (such as "Seize an opportunity and make good use of it") are more prevalent than similar expressions in English (Weber, 1998).

Projective Methods

If you were a tree, what kind of a tree would you be? Which character in *Sex and the City* are you likely to be? If you are skeptical of such questions because they seemingly provide little information about the respondent's personality, you are not alone. Some psychologists would argue, however, that this type of questions, if properly designed, could in fact generate valuable information about many individual features, such as a person's interests, concerns, imagination, and even some personality traits. **Projective methods** in personality psychology require the respondent to ask questions or perform particular tasks—the results of which are expected to reveal certain meanings that are typically concealed from a direct observation (Konnikova, 2014). These tasks may include interpreting pictures, drawing sketches, completing stories or sentences, and so forth. It is assumed that projective methods have an advantage over traditional questionnaires because the direct questions may encourage the respondents to give socially desirable answers (as we mentioned earlier in this chapter). For example, by asking the question "Do you have violent thoughts and how often?" you are unlikely to register exactly how often the respondent has those thoughts because many people do not want to appear violent. However, asking a person to propose an ending to a short story may not necessarily make the respondent think that she or he has violent tendencies (a respondent may think, "It is just a story after all"). Psychologists study the responses to projective tests and look for their meanings that may reflect certain consistent emotions or motivations that the respondent is unwilling or unable to reveal when preparing a self-report or answering a questionnaire.

Projective methods In personality psychology, projective methods require the respondent to ask questions or perform particular tasks—the results of which are expected to reveal certain meanings that are typically concealed from a direct observation.

The Swiss psychiatrist Hermann Rorschach (1884–1922) authored one of the best-known projective techniques known as the **inkblot test** (see **Photo 3.2**). An inkblot is a spot or stain of ink that has no particular geometrical pattern or meaning. In the procedure, an individual is shown several pictures (there were 10 in the original version) with symmetrical inkblots on each. The person is asked to generate associations or tell what he or she sees in these pictures. The researcher then analyzes the answers, the commentaries the person makes, the time of response, and other variables. Among the features to analyze can be the person's originality of thought, thinking patterns, aggressive or suicidal tendencies, and a range of clinical features (Weiner, 2003). Over decades, psychologists and psychiatrists in several countries offered and developed several assessment systems, allowing them to quantify the answers and create statistical norms. The inkblot test remains particularly popular in clinical assessments.

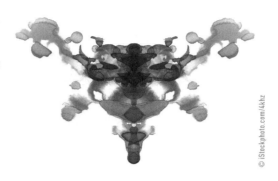

Photo 3.2 This is an example from an inkblot test. An inkblot is a stain of ink that has no particular geometrical pattern or meaning. The person is asked to generate associations or tell what he or she sees in these pictures.

© iStockphoto.com/4khz

Inkblot test An inkblock personality test involves the evaluation of a subject's response to ambiguous inkblots.

Mixed and Holistic Methods

In psychological research and practice, most researchers are likely to use several methods of assessment of an individual: self-reports, observations, experiments, and biographical data. To illustrate, in Chapter 9, Chapter 13, and others, we discuss individual features associated with happiness. This is not just about feeling good. Happiness is typically described as a complex feature that contains several interconnected states, such as stable subjective experiences and also decisions and actions involving other people. Therefore, to study happiness, researchers commonly use self-reports (to examine individual experiences), observers' ratings (to study a person's impact on other people), and also the subjects' accomplishments in life, such as their impact on other people—which is studied by biographical methods (Csikszentmihalyi, 1997; Csikszentmihalyi, 1990).

Increasingly often, personality psychologists implement holistic methods of research. In this context, **holistic** refers to the study of systems with multiple interconnected elements. Applied to personality psychology, holistic methods are based on the principle that scientific knowledge of personality cannot be obtained only from studying various features of an individual taken separately from one another—such as experiences, traits, actions, motivation, emotions, and so on. They must be studied together, as a "whole."

Holistic Holistic refers to the study of systems with multiple interconnected elements.

Holistic methods are not necessarily an "alternative" (or nonscientific) type of research in personality psychology. Some individuals use the term *holistic* to refer to intuition, folk knowledge, or rituals in studying an individual. However in science, holistic methods attempt to combine different scientific methods and thus produce a comprehensive set of data that can be analyzed on different levels. For a brief summary of research methods, see **Figure 3.2**.

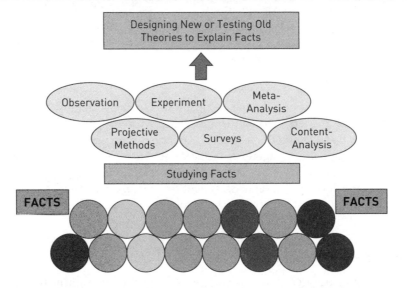

FIGURE 3.2 ● **Research Methods in Studying Personality**

CHECK AND APPLY YOUR KNOWLEDGE

1. Describe the differences between nomothetic and idiographic approaches (strategies).

2. What are observer ratings?

3. Give an example of self-serving bias.

4. What is the difference between dependent and independent variables in an experiment?

5. What are projective methods in psychology?

6. You have only 1 minute to draw an image of yourself—the one that would represent your personality in the best way (use a piece of paper or a tablet's screen). Imagine, this image will be preserved for the future generations to remind them about you. Use no words. What would you draw or assemble on paper (or on a screen)? When the image is ready, write down specific personality features you wanted to reflect in it. Ask other people to tell their interpretations of the image. What are most obvious weaknesses of this projective technique?

How Do We Prepare and Conduct Research?

We've reviewed several methods of assessment for studying an individual's personality, so the next step is to find the right method for the study. How do we choose the "right" methods of assessment and the correct number of them? Before starting your research, you will need to formulate and describe a problem you have to investigate. Why does this problem interest you? For example, you can study something that nobody has studied before. You can continue somebody's incomplete research. Or you can seek a solution to a certain practical problem. In the beginning, you should always ask, "What do I want to achieve by studying this problem?"

Reviewing Your Sources

Now you have identified the problem, and you are about to begin your research; first, you need to determine if anyone done this or similar research before. Often, a simple web search will reveal that someone else has already approached your problem. This finding should not discourage you. You may conduct your own study with different methods, and you may obtain different results. Ask these questions: What methods did the researchers use? What were the other studies' findings? Do you find them convincing?

It is also important, whenever possible, to examine the sources in other languages. Although English is probably the most commonly used language in personality psychology and the most prominent psychological publications appear in English, we need to avoid this bias and turn to sources in non-English publications, too.

Photo 3.3 How often do you use Wikipedia to get facts? What is an essential weakness of Wikipedia as a source of scientific knowledge?

© iStockphoto.com/cruphoto

of qualitative studies is biographical research, or an in-depth analysis of individuals. For example, how can we learn about people's emotions in ancient Rome? The British scholar Mary Beard examined ancient manuscripts on the art of rhetoric, transcripts of speeches, and jokes (Beard, 2014). She concluded that there were no exact words in Latin for *smile*. Of course, the Romans smiled out of joy; however, Beard suggests, they did not smile to indicate greeting or one's willingness to help.

As it has been mentioned, qualitative and quantitative methods are not mutually exclusive, and psychologists often choose both to use in one study. For example, it is common to use a qualitative method to better understand the studying sample and then design applied quantitative procedures to measure individual psychological features (Roer-Strier & Kurman, 2009).

Quantitative research is about systematic investigation of behavioral or psychological phenomena by means of statistical or mathematical data and various computational techniques. This research is based on measurement and involves recording, measurement, classification, assessment, and interpretation of data. As an illustration, using quantitative methods, the researcher can measure the emotional stability of an individual, compare the strength of organizational skills in a group of applicants for a job, or compare and contrast collectivist habits of two age or cultural groups. The researcher may also seek to establish correlations, or the relationships between two or among several variables.

> **Quantitative research**
> Quantitative research uses systematic investigation of behavioral or psychological phenomena by means of statistical or mathematical data and various computational techniques.

Being Aware of Biases

One important issue in evaluating personality assessment instruments involves the actual items and how they are phrased. Psychologists carefully approach subjects such as religion, sex, and politics. Questions are supposed to be gender-neutral unless the method is designed specifically for women or men. Psychologists often use focus groups and independent judges to check the words used in their methods.

So psychologists do try to avoid bias, but how do they know that the answers reflect what the respondents really think? Why would people lie or provide inaccurate answers? Some questions or items on the test can be very difficult to understand, or they can be ambiguous. Another reason is social desirability, which we have mentioned earlier in this chapter. There is widespread recognition of the nature of social desirability as an important personality variable (Boyle & Helmes, 2009). There are certain procedures that help avoid the negative impact of deliberately inaccurate, deceptive, or wrong answers to questionnaires. The question "Have you ever driven your car above the speed limit?" may be one of such questions. The answer "No" will likely indicate that a person may have a tendency to lie. Another reason for providing inaccurate answers is deception—the individual wants to obtain something, such as medical treatment, or avoid a punishment. A suspect who has been charged with a sexual crime, during a mandatory psychological assessment, may deny having had any sexual fantasies over the last 20 years. Therefore, many personality questionnaires have so-called correction scales. They measure inconsistency or deception in the individual's answers and provide the psychologists who administer tests with valuable information about the subjects.

Checking Reliability and Validity

Reliability is the extent to which a particular method gives consistent results. Each new method typically undergoes a reliability inspection. Several types of such inspection exist. Test–retest reliability is a measure obtained by administering the same test twice over a certain period (a day or a week) to the same person or group. Parallel-forms reliability is checked by giving two or several versions of the test to the same person or the same group. The scores from the two versions are then compared to evaluate the consistency of their results. Sometimes it is possible to check the method's split-half reliability. After "splitting" or dividing in half all items of a test, the researchers then administer these two halves and compare the results. Interrater reliability assesses the degree to which different observers or raters agree in their assessments of someone's behavior or other variables. Observers do not necessarily interpret facts the same way; however, the closer their assessments are, the higher the method's reliability is.

Validity of an assessment is the degree to which it measures what it is supposed to measure and not some other variables (Kelley, 1927). For example, if you want to assess leadership skills of children working on a group task, you have to make sure that you measure these leadership skills and not only children's knowledge or their propensity to speak loud. In most cases, a method you are using is supposed to measure a relatively stable personality trait and not some responses caused by the situation or other passing influences.

Different types of validity exist. Construct validity is used to ensure that the method assesses what it is intended to measure according to a theory. For example, you measure SDO (or social dominance orientation) in a group of trainees. The questionnaire you are using should measure SDO according to how psychologists understand this phenomenon. Using a panel of "experts" familiar with the construct is a way in which this type of validity can be assessed. Convergent validity is the extent to which a method yields the results obtained by other methods when they measure the same phenomenon. To make sure that the results of the study reflect a particular trend and are not due to chance alone, the researcher should repeat the same study to accept the data with confidence or find out about other similar studies. External validity of a method refers to the degree to which the results obtained by this method can be generalized to other individuals, groups, or conditions. Predictive validity is the degree to which a method accurately predicts something that will occur in the future with the phenomenon it studies. Recall the famous marshmallow experiments (Chapter 2) to measure willpower in children. The test might have demonstrated some predictive validity because it could predict general behavioral tendencies in the future.

Analyzing Your Data

Measuring a certain individual personality trait or someone's assessment of other people often requires several attempts. Therefore, among the most commonly used data are measures of central tendency. They indicate the location of a score distribution

Reliability The extent to which a particular method gives consistent results is its reliability.

Validity The degree to which an assessment measures what it is supposed to measure and not other variables is its validity.

on a variable; that is, it describes where most of the distribution is located. The most convenient and frequently used measure of central tendency in personality psychology is the mean. The mean indicates the mathematical central point of a distribution of scores.

Scales

When you measure distance, weight, volume, motion, or temperature, the results represent quantity, magnitude, or degree. Individual features can be measured along these dimensions, too. Choosing a correct measurement scale becomes a crucial factor for the overall success of any psychological research. There are four types of measurement scales: nominal, ordinal, interval, and ratio (Stevens, 1946). A *nominal* scale is primarily used for identification purposes. Each score on it does not indicate an amount. This scale does not measure any rank or order and is used mostly for identification purposes. In an *ordinal* scale, the scores designate rank order. A rank order may indicate the subject's preference, accomplishment, or opinion. In an *interval* scale, each score indicates some amount. There is presumably an equal unit of measurement separating each score. With a *ratio* scale, the scores reflect the true amount of the present variable, and zero truly means that zero amount of the variable is present (see **Table 3.1**).

Correlation

In studying personality, we often need to establish correlations, or the relationships between two or among several variables. If in one set of data, when Variable X

TABLE 3.1 ● Types of Measurement Scales		
Type of Scale	**Descriptions**	**Examples**
Nominal	The differences between items are based only on their names.	What is your major? Psychology— Business— Government— Communications— Other
Ordinal	Each item on the scale allows for a certain rank order.	What do you value the most in other people? Rank these five features: honesty, physical strength, intellect, sense of humor, kindness.
Interval	Items on the scale allow for relatively equal intervals between them.	Which year of your college life was the happiest? First Second Third Fourth
Ratio	This scale possesses an identifiable "zero" value.	How many hours did you sleep last night? 0 1 2 3 4 5 6 7 8 9 10 11 12 13 14

is low, Variable Y is also low, and when Variable X is high, Variable Y is also high, we have a positive correlation between the variables. If, according to another data set, when Variable A is low, Variable B is high, and when Variable A is high, Variable B is low, we have a negative correlation. A measure of correlation—correlation coefficient—contains two components. The first is the sign that indicates either positive or negative linear relationship. The second is the value. The larger the absolute value, the stronger the relationship. For example, the intelligence scores of identical twins raised either together or apart are highly correlated: +0.88. The intelligence scores of non-relatives raised together are relatively low: +0.20 (Bouchard, Lykken, McGue, Segal, & Tellegen, 1990). Does correlation establish a cause-and-effect relationship between the variables? A psychologist who, for example, finds a positive cross-cultural correlation between (1) violent crime and (2) level of poverty in a particular country, in most cases, would not be able to make a conclusion about which, if either, factor was the cause and which, if either, was the effect or result. In other words, poverty may cause crime, crime can contribute to poverty, or a third variable—unknown to the psychologist—may contribute to both.

Factor Analysis

Factor analysis is a statistical method for identifying clusters of items that tend to be answered the same way. This method, like the empirical method, begins with a large set of items that are administered to a group of respondents. If respondents who agree with Item A also tend to agree with Items B, C, D, and so forth, these items are deemed to measure the same psychological trait. We will return to this method in Chapter 7.

A special statistical method allows psychologists to do quantitative analysis of a large collection of scientific results and integrate the findings. This is **meta-analysis**, or the analysis of analyses (usually called combined tests) of a large collection of individual results in an attempt to make sense of a diverse selection of data. One of the attractive features of this method is the reliance on statistical formulas and an imperative to include a large selection of studies, not just those that appear to be "good" and "interesting." This method often shows results that are difficult to see in individual studies. For instance, meta-analysis of rewarding behavior such as praise, encouragement, and so on across cultures (25 studies altogether) has shown that results yielded by student samples differed from those collected from samples of employees (Fischer & Smith, 2003).

We need to be persistent and patient in the way we apply our knowledge. Yet we cannot simply take one study, read one report, examine one or even several theories, and start applying them immediately. First, we have to learn how to think about the facts we are learning—to *think critically*. We have heard this term before. But actually, what is critical thinking and why is it important to learn its skills?

Factor analysis
Factor analysis is a method to deal with large numbers of observed variables that are thought to reflect a smaller number of underlying variables.

Meta-analysis
Meta-analysis is the analysis of analyses (usually called combined tests) of a large collection of individual results in an attempt to make sense of a diverse selection of data.

CHECK AND APPLY YOUR KNOWLEDGE

1. Name the four goals of research.

2. Explain construct validity.

3. Explain one or two "reliability inspection" procedures.

4. Name and explain the four measurement scales.

5. Give examples of a positive and a negative correlation.

6. Research has shown, time and again, that estimates derived from large samples are more reliable than those derived from small samples. Nevertheless, when forming judgments, we typically do not take this principle into account. As a consequence, despite the fact that data collected from small samples cannot be counted on as trustworthy predictors of a population's characteristics, we often are prone to commit the error of overgeneralizing from too small a sample. Let us illustrate. What do you think: Does "7 out of 10" look like better odds than "60 out of 100"?

Answer: Yes, it looks as if the first one is better. However, the more reliable indicator is "60 out of 100" because it is drawn from a larger—that is, more reliable—sample.

Applying Critical Thinking to Research Methods

Critical thinking The process of critical thinking is an active and systematic strategy for understanding knowledge on the basis of sound reasoning and evidence.

Critical thinking is not all about passing skeptical judgments on everything. **Critical thinking** is an active and systematic strategy for understanding knowledge on the basis of sound reasoning and evidence (Levy, 2009). It is rather a set of constructive skills that you can improve and master. Critical thinking is about curiosity, doubt, and intellectual honesty. Curiosity guides in searching for and finding new facts. Doubt helps in producing new ideas and offering new solutions. Intellectual honesty helps in distinguishing facts from opinions and recognizing our own biases.

Imagine a test suggests that A has a higher score on a curiosity scale compared with B. What does this difference in scores mean? Does it say that A is a more curious person than B? So what? Assessments like this should not lead to quick generalizations and judgments about individuals or groups. Tests scores can be important indicators of how an individual thinks, decides, and acts. However, tests do not necessarily allow psychologists to hire or fire an individual. Just 80 years ago in the United States, some psychologists believed that in educational placement, employment and promotion should rely exclusively on psychological tests. However, a certain test performance might not necessarily and accurately predict this person's professional or social potential in the future (Vernon, 1969). Moreover, factors such as a test-taker's language proficiency and motivation, test content, and various contextual factors significantly contribute to people's test performance (Sternberg, 1997). Psychology's history teaches us that the tests created in one social and cultural environment (upper-middle class) tend to be biased against other groups (middle and lower class). Cross-cultural studies reveal that children tend to have many advanced practical skills that are not recognized on academic tests (Shiraev & Levy, 2013).

Psychologists seldom, if ever, take test responses and scores at face value. Extra procedures are necessary. For example, there is no shortage of online tests that ask you to answer a few questions and then quickly evaluate your mind skills and personality traits. Are these conclusions convincing? Such tests are likely to be based on nonrepresentative samples and produce invalid assessments.

Photo 3.4 Imagine a person says to you that she has the personality of a mermaid. Would you find this intriguing? Maybe. Yet this statement (hypothesis) is unscientific because it is not falsifiable. Explain why.

Although many online tests are entertaining, they do not provide reliable scientific knowledge about personality (Konnikova, 2014).

Distinguish Facts From Opinions

Scientific knowledge (discussed in Chapter 1) is rooted in procedures designed to provide reliable and verifiable evidence based on facts. We need to separate facts from opinions. On the surface, it appears easy: Facts are supposed to be verifiable. Something either happened or did not. On the other hand, opinions are speculations or intuitions about how and why such developments may have taken place. In reality, distinguishing facts from opinions can be complicated. Some facts are hidden: How do we know what a person is thinking about at the moment? Other facts can be distorted: People routinely misrepresent their intentions ("Oh, I didn't mean to say that") or feelings ("Oh, I am fine"). Sometimes such distortions are deliberate; sometimes they are not. Yet other facts can be in dispute. One research study suggests that children growing up with one parent develop more psychological and behavioral problems than those with two parents; another set of studies disputes these findings.

Many people tend to embrace the facts they like and events they approve of but ignore information that appears to challenge their views. A passionate supporter of one theory would select scientific facts to support the idea that dissociative identity disorder (often called multiple personalities) is linked to an early emotional trauma of childhood. However, the same person may easily ignore other facts challenging this assumption.

The opinions and beliefs that we hold toward other people can—with or without our intent—actually "produce" or encourage the very behaviors that we expect to find. In other words, a perceiver's assumptions about another person may lead that person to adopt those expected attributes. This phenomenon is known as the **self-fulfilling prophecy**.

Self-fulfilling prophecy A perceiver's assumptions about another person that may lead that person to adopt those expected attributes is known as self-fulfilling prophecy.

In what is probably the most famous—and still controversial—study of the self-fulfilling prophecy, Rosenthal and Jacobson (1968) informed teachers at a San Francisco elementary school that on the basis of a reliable psychological test, some of the pupils in their classroom would show dramatic spurts in academic performance during the upcoming school year. In reality, there was no such test, and the children designated as "intellectual bloomers" were chosen at random. Nevertheless, when the children's performance was assessed several months later, those students who had been earmarked as bloomers did indeed show an improvement in their schoolwork; even more remarkably, their IQ scores had increased. The teachers thus unwittingly created the very behaviors that they expected.

Separating facts from opinions should help you navigate the sea of information related to personality. It can start with looking for new and more reliable sources of facts. Some facts may appear more plausible on their surface than others. Whenever possible, try to establish as many facts as possible related to the issue you are studying. Check the credibility of your sources. If there is a disagreement about the facts, try to find out why the differences exist. What are the interests and motivations behind these disagreements? The more facts you obtain, the more accurate your analysis will be. If a person who indicates that he suffers from anxiety scores as high as other people known to have anxiety problems, that person can also be viewed as suffering from anxiety. If a person indicates in a questionnaire that she is "very generous" yet disagrees with statements such as "I regularly donate to other people," this person is unlikely to be considered generous (Wolfe, 1993).

We need to avoid quick generalizations, which often appear tempting. Although personal testimonies and vivid cases may be very persuasive, they are not inherently trustworthy indicators of fact. Also, when we generalize about research findings, we will remember that the best basis for drawing valid generalizations is from a representative sample of relevant cases. We can generalize, but we should do it carefully.

Describe, Not Prescribe

Language serves many functions. Certainly, one of its most common and most important purposes is to help us describe or evaluate an event, a situation, or a person. We constantly ask, "What is it? Is it good or bad? Is it useful or harmful?" Typically, we consider descriptions to be objective, while we consider evaluations to be subjective.

However, the distinction between objective description and subjective evaluation is not always clear. Words both describe and evaluate. Whenever we attempt to describe something or someone, the words we use are almost invariably value laden in that they reflect our own personal likes and dislikes. Thus, our use of any particular term serves not only to describe but also to prescribe what is desirable or undesirable to us (Shiraev & Levy, 2013).

This problem is not so prevalent in describing objects as compared with people. Take, as an illustration, the terms *cold* and *hot*. For material substances, both terms refer literally to temperature: That coffee is very cold, or that tea is very hot. When we use these same terms to describe an individual, however, they take on a distinctly evaluative connotation: J. J. is very cold, or E. E. is very hot.

SELF-REFLECTION

Are you a happy person? On a scale from 1 to 10, how happy are you most of the day? Studies show that, according to surveys, the happiest people live in Scandinavia and Singapore. They score the highest on the scale, around 8. Knowing this, if you met a person from Denmark or Singapore, would you expect him or her to be happy?

Although some people might be tempted to make such a generalization, we should think critically about this. Just because surveys indicate that people from Denmark and Singapore are the happiest people in the world, that doesn't mean all people from these countries are happy. This is true in other instances as well.

Questions

Try to generalize how many people around you are generally happy. A small proportion? About one half? A majority? What will be their average number be on a scale from 1 to 10? Ask people in class to define how happy they are using the same scale. Compare their actual scores with your prediction. How accurate were you?

Our best attempts to remain neutral are constrained by the limits of language. When it comes to describing people (e.g., in conducting research or clinical interviews), it is nearly impossible to find words that are devoid of evaluative connotation. Incredible as it may seem, we simply do not have entirely neutral adjectives to describe personality characteristics, whether of an individual or group. And even if such words did exist, we still would be very likely to use the ones that reflect our own personal preferences. You may be described as *idealistic* by your close friends, while other people may label you *naïve*. You can call someone *obsessed*, but this person will refer to himself or herself as *committed*. Do you see the differences in these evaluations?

Not only are we seldom aware of the extent to which our expectations can influence the behavior of others, but we probably are even less aware of how the expectations of others are capable of influencing our behavior. It is thus important to remember that our actions are shaped not only by our own attitudes but also by the expectations of those with whom we interact. Put another way, we are continually cultivating the constructions of each other's social realities.

Remember that descriptions, especially concerning personality characteristics, can never be entirely objective, impartial, or neutral. Become aware of your own personal values and biases and how these influence the language that you use. Avoid presenting your value judgments as objective reflections of truth. Recognize how other people's use of language reveals their own values and biases (see **Figure 3.3**).

Do Not Always See Correlation as Causation

As was mentioned earlier in this chapter, correlation does not establish a cause-and-effect relationship between two variables. A **correlation** is a statement about the

Correlation
A correlation is a statement about the relationship or association between two (or more) variables.

FIGURE 3.3 ● The Evaluative Bias of Language: To Describe Is to Prescribe

The Same Phenomenon as Described From Two Different Perspectives

From Jenny's Value System	From Lee's Value System
Irresponsible	Spontaneous
Troublemaker	Feisty
Cheap	Frugal
Spineless	Cooperative
Näive	Idealistic
Old	Mature
Weird	Interesting
Obsessed	Committed
Dependent	Loyal
Paranoid	Vigilant
Manic	Enthusiastic
Psychotic	Creative
Bum	Vocationally disadvantaged
Sociopath	Morally challenged
Dead	Ontologically impaired

Source: Shiraev & Levy, 2013.

relationship or association between two (or more) variables. Correlations thus enable us to make predictions from one variable or event to another. That is, if two events are correlated (or "coappear"), then the presence of one event provides us with information about the other event. However, a correlation does not necessarily establish a causal relationship between the variables. In other words, causation cannot be proven simply by virtue of a correlation or coappearance.

As an example, let us consider the correlation between creativity and psychological disorders (see, e.g., Andreason & Canter, 1974; Andreason & Powers, 1975; Jamison, 1993). Great painter Vincent van Gogh, Russian novelist Fyodor Dostoyevsky, and American writer Ernest Hemingway all suffered from psychological disorders that seriously disrupted their lives. The late U.S. comedians John Belushi and Chris Farley developed serious (and ultimately fatal) drug addictions. Based on these observations, what may we conclude? That psychological disorders cause creativity? Perhaps. But maybe creativity causes psychological disorders? Then again, isn't it possible that creativity and psychological disorders reciprocally affect each other? To complicate matters further, what about the possibility that some other variable, such as a genetic predisposition, causes both creativity and psychological disorders? Put another way, given a correlation between A and B, does A cause B? Does B cause A? Do A and B cause each other? Does C cause A and B? Could there be some combination of these causal relationships? Unfortunately, a correlation alone does not (in fact, cannot) provide us with the definitive answers to these questions.

The following are some examples of correlated variables about which some people may erroneously infer causality. You can do an exercise to interpret the following correlations found in research in the past.

One particular type of faulty, uncritical reasoning, the **post hoc error**, refers to the mistaken logic that because Event B follows Event A, then B must have been caused by A. This error, also known as parataxic reasoning (Sullivan, 1953), may be seen as a kind of "magical thinking" because events that occur close together in time are construed as causally linked. As it turns out, most superstitions are based on parataxic reasoning. For example, if a football coach does not shave before a game and his team then wins, he might assume that not shaving somehow caused the success. As a result, he may adopt this superstitious behavior for future games.

Post hoc error
With post hoc error, there is mistaken logic that because Event B follows Event A, then B must have been caused by A. This error is also known as parataxic reasoning.

CHECK AND APPLY YOUR KNOWLEDGE

1. Research has established a strong and positive correlation between aggression and meteorological conditions. For example, rates of homicide and rape are generally higher in warmer than in colder climates (Anderson, 1987). Do these findings suggest that only the climate (and not other factors) affect violence? Suggest factors that could affect incidents of violence.

2. Another study found that smoking cannabis, such as marijuana, is correlated with schizophrenia: People who smoke pot are found to be more likely to have symptoms of this illness (Power et al., 2014). Does this study suggest that smoking cannabis is a contributing cause of schizophrenia? Is it also possible that the drug can set off short-term psychotic episodes—such as hallucinations and delusions—in those already suffering from the condition? Or is it possible that people who have already been diagnosed with schizophrenia are more likely to smoke pot, compared to the nonsmoking?

3. A study conducted in four countries—France, Germany, Poland, and the United States—examined more than 1,000 adolescents. The study showed that a person's religiosity is correlated with this person's family orientation, which is also correlated with life satisfaction. The correlations were stronger in cultures with a high overall religiosity (Poland and the United States) as compared to one of the two cultures that places the least importance on religion (Germany; Sabatier et al., 2011). How would you interpret these results? Which factors should affect which, in your view?

Look for Multiple Causes

Let's return to research on happiness. Which factors affect happiness in individuals? Why do some people report that they tend to be happy most of the time when others do not feel the same? There are many reasons why. First, people who say they are happy may have good things happen to them more often than to others. Second, it is also possible that people feel they are happy because they have material resources and good health. In fact, these reasons can be true, as several studies show. For example, researchers Lyubomisrsky (2007) and Veenhoven (2008) have shown that people judge their happiness based on economic factors, such as money or good jobs. However, there are also many individuals who were probably born with a predisposition to be happy. Further, many of us learn how to feel happy and how to maintain a positive outlook on life despite difficulties. In other words, we learn how to be happy. Cross-cultural studies also show that people tend to assess their happiness based on cultural patterns. In predominantly individualistic cultures people tend to rely on their emotions when they assess their own happiness. In predominantly collectivist cultures, people tend to seek social cues or other people's responses to make a judgment (Suh et al., 2008).

Virtually anything in an individual behavior and experience has at least several underlying reasons or causes. As critical thinkers studying personality, we need to consider a wide range of possible influences and factors, all of which could be involved to varying degrees in the shaping of certain traits. Although we typically tend to think of causal relationships as being unidirectional (Event A causes Event B), frequently they are bidirectional (Event A causes Event B, and Event B causes Event A). In other words, variables can, and frequently do, affect each other. Consider also the bidirectional relationship between psychological disturbance and one's social environment. Specifically, it is probable that cold, rejecting, and hostile parents can cause emotional and behavioral problems in their children. At the same time, do not ignore the possibility (even the likelihood) that children with emotional and behavioral problems also might cause their parents to become colder, more rejecting, and even hostile. Virtually every significant behavior has many determinants, and any single explanation is inevitably an oversimplification. Thus, in this case, we would need to consider a wide range of possible factors (e.g., genetic, dietary, stress, family norms, and cultural traditions), all of which could, to varying degrees, be involved.

In sum, when facing an issue or problem that is presented in terms of *either/or*, try replacing either/or with *both/and*. For example, the statement "Prejudice is caused by either ignorance or hatred" becomes "Prejudice is caused by both ignorance and hatred" (and probably many other factors as well).

Critically Compare

Without comparisons, there is no study of personality. When comparing any two phenomena, initially they may "match" with respect to their mutual similarities. But no matter how many features they share in common, there is no escaping the inevitable fact that at some point there will be a "conceptual fork" in the road, where the phenomena will differ. Two people that seem to be completely different may share many similar features, just as two individuals who appear to be similar may be different in many ways.

We make judgments based on comparisons. Consider human height. Who is a tall person? A 5-foot, 10-inch man is likely to be seen as tall in some contexts (e.g., compared to most 7-year-old children) and short in others (e.g., compared to professional basketball players). Individual characteristics of one person are compared to the similar characteristics of others. Yet our comparisons tend to be incomplete, narrow. For example, Chinese people tend to evaluate themselves in comparison with other people in China, while people in the United States most likely evaluate themselves with reference to Americans (Heine, Lehman, Peng, & Greenholtz, 2002). Do you consider people in Japan and South Korea as generally hardworking? If you asked around, many people might say yes. However in surveys, Japanese and Koreans tend to evaluate themselves critically, considering themselves as less hardworking compared to other countries. To understand why people in these countries give themselves such low evaluations, we should realize that hard work and conscientiousness are usually estimated with respect to larger social cultural norms. Speaking hypothetically, if everyone is expected to be hardworking, punctual, and reliable, many people may see themselves as not meeting the standards of "ideal" set by cultural norms. As a result, most people report in surveys that they are less organized and less determined than they ought to be. These are examples of cultural response bias (Schmitt et al., 2007).

Whenever we learn facts about a person or a group of people, it is important to compare these facts, if possible, with other facts. When comparing and contrasting any two phenomena, we should ask ourselves, "In what ways are they similar?" and "In what ways are they different?"

Recognize Continuous and Dichotomous Variables

Some phenomena may be divided into two mutually exclusive or contradictory categories. These types of phenomena are **dichotomous variables**. For example, when you flip a coin, it must turn up either heads or tails—there is no middle ground. Similarly, a text message that you have typed is either sent or not. An individual next to you was either born in the United States or she wasn't. Other phenomena, by contrast, consist of a theoretically infinite number of points lying between two polar opposites. These types of phenomena are **continuous variables**. For example, consider such variables as an individual's weight and height. Many features that we will use to describe personality are likely to be continuous phenomena, such as masculinity, femininity, abnormality, consistency, conscientiousness, collectivism, individualism, and so forth. In Chapter 7, we will study the trait called openness to experience, which refers to, among other characteristics, a person's preference for variety and intellectual curiosity. Is openness to experience a dichotomous or continuous variable? Can you be totally "open" to experience and another person totally "closed" to it?

People around us (hopefully, not us) often confuse these two types of variables. Specifically, people have a natural tendency to dichotomize variables that, more accurately, should be conceptualized as continuous. In particular, most person-related phenomena are frequently presumed to fit into one of two discrete types (either Category A or Category B), rather than as lying on a continuum (somewhere between End Point A and End Point B). In the vast majority of cases, however, continuous variables are more accurate and therefore more meaningful representations of the phenomena we are attempting to describe and explain.

When comparing large samples, do not forget that these groups are far from homogeneous. Among them are individuals who are educated and those who are not, who are wealthy and poor, and who live in cities and small towns. It is always useful to

Dichotomous variables Dichotomous variables are phenomena that may be divided into two mutually exclusive or contradictory categories.

Continuous variables Continuous variables consist of a theoretically infinite number of points lying between two polar opposites.

FIGURE 3.4 ● Dichotomous and Continuous Variables

Which of these variables would you consider dichotomous?
Which appear to you as continuous? Explain your choices.

Feminine–Masculine: ____   Perfect–Imperfect: ____

Married–Single: ____   Young–Old: ____

Conscious–Unconscious: ____   Present–Absent: ____

Prejudiced–Unprejudiced: ____   Rich–Poor: ____

Liberal–Conservative: ____   Homosexual–Heterosexual: ____

Enemy–Ally: ____   Licensed–Unlicensed: ____

Racist–Nonracist: ____   Dead–Alive: ____

Guilty verdict–Not guilty verdict: ____   Power on–Power off: ____

Tolerance–Intolerance: ____   Subjective–Objective: ____

Politically correct–Politically incorrect: ____

Source: Shiraev & Levy, 2013.

request additional information about the groups that you study. For example, the diversity or homogeneity of the population and people's experience of such diversity may affect observation procedures. According to Matsumoto (1992), individuals from homogeneous societies (Japan, for example) may detect and identify other people's emotions less accurately than people from heterogeneous societies do (the United States, for example).

Learn to differentiate between variables that are dichotomous and those that are continuous. Remember that most person-related phenomena—such as traits, attitudes, and beliefs—lie along a continuum. To practice, see **Figure 3.4**.

Be Aware of Possible Ethnocentrism

Ethnocentrism
Ethnocentrism is the view that supports judgment about other ethnic, national, and cultural groups and events from the observer's own ethnic, national, or cultural group's outlook.

The view that supports judgment about other ethnic, national, and cultural groups and events from the observer's own ethnic, national, or cultural group's outlook is called **ethnocentrism**. Ethnocentrism is the tendency (often unintentional) to produce knowledge about personality from a specific national or cultural point of view. Let's illustrate. Imagine you develop a new method to assess "online shyness"—a tendency to feel awkward, worried, and tense while interacting on social networks. You studied this type of shyness in a large sample of college students in the United States. Can you be sure that your method could measure shyness in individuals living in China, Mexico, or South Africa? We know that social and cultural factors may impact the way people act, think, and feel. Sometimes this impact is great, and sometimes it is not. Before testing a method on samples from different social and cultural environments, the researchers may not conclude that their study describes some psychological phenomenon or personality feature. If a study is conducted on just one ethnic or national sample, the results of this study should not be extrapolated onto the entire global population.

To avoid ethnocentrism, personality psychology should rely on **cross-cultural psychology**, which is the critical and comparative study of cultural effects on human psychology (Shiraev & Levy, 2013). Cross-cultural psychology examines psychological diversity and the underlying reasons for such diversity. In particular, cross-cultural psychology examines—again, from a comparative perspective—the links between cultural norms and behavior and the ways in which particular human activities are influenced by different, sometimes dissimilar social and cultural forces (Segall, Dasen, Berry, & Poortinga, 1990). Cross-cultural psychology attempts not only to distinguish differences between groups but also to establish psychological universals and phenomena common to all people and groups. For example, cross-cultural psychology seeks to identify commonalties with regard to personality traits, the relatively enduring patterns of thinking, feeling, and acting (McCrae & Costa, 1997; Schmitt et al., 2007).

Cross-cultural psychology
The critical and comparative study of cultural effects on human psychology is cross-cultural psychology.

CHECK AND APPLY YOUR KNOWLEDGE

1. Describe continuous and dichotomous variables.

2. Explain ethnocentrism.

3. Until very recent times, more than 90% of research samples in psychology came from a small sample of countries representing only 12% of the world's population (Henrich et al., 2010). The vast majority of people who participate in psychological surveys, experiments, and other studies come from the United States, Canada, the United Kingdom, Germany, France, and Australia. Because psychology has been focusing so far on only a narrow sample of the population coming from only a few countries, what should be done, in your view, to correct this trend and, most importantly, how?

Visual Review

| INTRODUCTION AND CONTEXTS | → | KEY THEORIES AND APPROACHES | → | APPLICATIONS |

There are nomothetic and idiographic approaches to studying personality

Psychologists use:

- Observation
- Self-reports
- Experiments
- Content analysis
- Projective methods
- Mixed and holistic methods

In preparing and conducting research:

- Review your source
- Describe your goals
- Suggest a hypothesis
- Choose a sample
- Choose a method
- Be aware of biases
- Check for reliability and validity
- Analyze your data using interpretive procedures

In applying critical thinking to research methods:

- Be cautious about quick conclusions
- Distinguish facts from opinions
- Describe, not prescribe
- Do not always see correlation as causation
- Look for multiple causes
- Critically compare
- Recognize continuous and dichotomous variables
- Be aware of ethnocentrism

Summary

- Studies of personality are based on nomothetic and idiographic approaches, quantitative and qualitative studies rooted in a variety of research methods, including observation, surveys, experiments, content analysis, and many others.

- Personality psychology uses observation, self-reports, experiments, content analysis, projective methods, and holistic methods (among others). In many studies, researchers use mixed methods.

- Before starting their research, scientists need to formulate and describe a problem to investigate, review the available sources, and describe the goals of their study.

- Hypotheses are expectations or proposed explanations for something that you study. They should be testable and falsifiable.

- A sample is a part of a larger group, and by studying this sample, the researcher generalizes the results to that larger group. The sample should be representative.

- By and large, research methodology to study personality can be divided into two categories: quantitative and qualitative. This division is imprecise because these categories of assessment usually overlap.

- Reliability is the extent to which a particular method gives consistent results. Validity of an assessment is the degree to which it measures what it is supposed to measure and not some other variables.

- Measuring a certain individual personality trait or someone's assessment of other people often requires several attempts. Therefore, among the most commonly used data are measures of central tendency. They indicate the location of a score distribution on a variable; that is, it describes where most of the distribution is located.

- Studying personality, researchers often need to establish correlations, or the relationships between two or among several variables.

- Factor analysis is a statistical method for identifying clusters of items that tend to be answered the same way.

- Meta-analysis allows psychologists to do quantitative analysis of a large collection of scientific results and integrate the findings.

- Critical thinking is an active and systematic strategy for understanding knowledge on the basis of sound reasoning and evidence. As a critical thinker, you will be encouraged to distinguish facts from opinions, critically generalize about facts and compare them, look for multiple causes of facts, avoid prescriptions, and see both continuous and dichotomous variables in many things you learn about.

Key Terms

continuous variables 95	idiographic 73	quantitative research 84
correlation 91	independent variable(s) 77	reliability 85
critical thinking 88	inkblot test 79	representative sample 83
cross-cultural psychology 97	meta-analysis 87	sample 83
dependent variable(s) 77	nomothetic 73	sampling error 83
dichotomous variables 95	observation 73	self-fulfilling prophecy 89
ethnocentrism 96	observer ratings 74	self-serving bias 76
factor analysis 87	post hoc error 93	social desirability bias 76
holistic 79	projective methods 78	validity 85
hypotheses 82	qualitative research 83	

Evaluating What You Know

What are the key research methods in personality psychology?

What are advantages and disadvantages of self-evaluation?

Explain holistic methods.

Name and describe the steps in preparing research.

What are potential types of biases in research?

Explain reliability and validity.

Name and describe at least three rules of critical thinking to interpret research data.

A Bridge to the Next Chapter

As you should remember from Chapter 1, many theories of personality and their applications developed within academic traditions. These traditions bring together scholars who share similar views on a particular scientific approach, subject, or method. Some traditions remain relevant for a short period. Others remain influential for decades. In the next chapter, we begin examining psychoanalysis—a dominant field that provided major theoretical views of personality until approximately the 1960s. It has generally lost its influence, yet its impact on psychology and personality psychology is constantly reevaluated.

4

The Psychoanalytic Tradition

"Your vision will become clear only when you can look into your own heart. Who looks outside, dreams; who looks inside, awakes."

—Carl Jung (1875–1961)

Learning Objectives

After reading this chapter, you should be able to:

- Identify the founders and historical contexts of the psychoanalytic tradition
- Summarize the key theories of Freud, Adler, and Jung
- Identify ways to apply the key principles of the psychoanalytic tradition to individual experience and behavior

Some years ago, journalist Stephen Glass wrote false stories for more than 40 articles for the *New Republic*, *Rolling Stone,* and other popular magazines in the United States. He didn't just add a few creative details to those stories: He simply fabricated them. He made up his interviewees and created fake business cards, websites, and fictitious letters—all to make his articles appear legitimate. When his superiors uncovered his lies, he confessed. Then he was immediately fired.

A lie is an intentional false statement. Studies show that most of us tell small lies or twist facts daily. But why do we lie? To get ahold of a thing. To avoid or delay something. Psychological studies also reveal that people lie especially when they try to impress others. There are certain external incentives to lie, but can it be that the incentives to lie come not from the outside world but from within an individual? What if these incentives to lie reflect unresolved issues from the past?

Some psychologists who studied the case of Stephen Glass (and some of them argued on his behalf in court when he tried to restore his damaged reputation) explained that his lying was a result of his traumatic childhood experiences. Allegedly, his parents put immense psychological pressure on him, which was intense and often subtle. His parents cultivated in him a strong need for approval. As a result, he developed a powerful drive: To feel happy, he did not necessarily need to achieve; what he needed was to please his parents. How? It didn't matter. Even when he grew up and was working for a prestigious magazine, his parents were dismissive of his successes as a journalist. And that's when he began making things up in order to impress. As Stephen describes it, "I was anxious and scared and depressed. Outwardly I was communicating fun, but inside all I felt was anxiety." His work was a desperate attempt to impress his parents.

Many psychologists maintain that we all have a propensity to act in a certain way to address unresolved psychological conflicts from the past. Such conflicts may have deep roots in early family experiences. At any rate, something happened in the past, and we try to address those issues and conflicts through some of our present actions. Some of us fight for social causes; others write poetry; and others turn to lying. The question of who is "good" or who is "bad" in these cases is a matter of value judgment.

Sources: Dolan, 2014; Feldman, Forrrest, and Happ, 2002; Glass, 2003; Rosin, 2014.

The Essence of the Psychoanalytic Tradition

The psychoanalytic tradition, or *psychoanalysis*, as we call it for convenience, is probably the most scrutinized and controversial of all traditions in personality psychology. Supporters praise psychoanalysis for its significant contribution to the scientific knowledge of the individual. Critics see psychoanalysis as an immense yet misleading speculation, brilliantly disguised in a fake academic uniform. Yet both critics and supporters acknowledge that the influence of psychoanalysis on psychology in general and personality psychology in particular was vast and lasting (Karlsson, 2010).

Social and Cultural Contexts

The emergence of psychoanalysis can be traced to the end of the 19th century. It was the time of an early globalization—the massive exchange and cross-influence of various products and ideas. Trade barriers were easing, and commerce grew rapidly. Most Europeans could travel around the continent without visas. Telephones, telegraphs, daily newspapers, popular magazines, indoor plumbing, and orders by mail—all were bringing a relative and increasing comfort to daily life. Women everywhere were fighting for and gaining their basic political rights. Higher education was available to a greater number of people. Studies and research abroad were common, and psychologists traveled freely across borders. Publishers earned money from social science books, and psychological literature was increasingly popular. Old customs and fashions were changing. The traditional, authoritarian way of life was under pressure from almost every direction. But these developments were only one side of the ongoing changes. Paradoxically, the first 15 years of the new century were also a period of boiling nationalism and blind militarism. World War I (1914–1918) took more than 19 million lives and left another 21 million wounded worldwide.

In science, alternative views of nature rapidly developed. The emerging quantum physics challenged the traditional Newtonian understanding of the world as a mechanical unity. The seemingly undivided atom now contained numerous particles. Albert Einstein formulated the theory of relativity (Einstein,

1905/2000). Time and space, according to this theory, are not absolute but relative to the observer. Matter appeared as a form of energy. Social scientists portrayed life as complex and multidimensional. The theme of the irrational core of human existence reemerged; it gained support among many young and educated readers. It was the time when the German philosopher Friedrich Nietzsche (1844–1900) introduced the idea that irrational forces dominate human motivation. The rationality of a capitalist society and its reliance on orderliness was a sign of weakness and future defeat. Only the strong and the power driven should rule the world, Nietzsche believed. This was the time of impressionism, cubism, symbolism, abstract painting, and conceptual poetry, as well as an era of bold experimentations with form, sound, and color (Kandel, 2012). Artistic imagination and the scope of creative genres appeared limitless.

In summary, psychoanalysis was developed in a mixed social atmosphere of optimism and doubt, enthusiasm and pessimism, and irrationality and reason.

Founders and Influences

The founders of the psychoanalytic tradition—mostly psychiatrists—wanted to remain on a solid scientific foundation. They innovatively borrowed from physics and biology, history and medicine, anthropology and sociology, and literature and psychiatry. Based on these sources, psychoanalysts created their own ideas about the individual's personality. These ideas have been evolving for more than 100 years.

The Founder

Psychoanalysis has many contributors yet one indisputable founder: Sigmund Freud (1856–1939). Sigmund Freud was born in Freiberg (today the city is in the Czech Republic) in the Austrian Empire. His parents were Jewish, and his native language was German. An excellent student during his school years, he studied neurology in college and chose medicine as a profession. His work and ideas brought him global exposure and recognition in the 20th century and beyond. It is hard to find a psychology textbook today that does not mention his name or does not discuss his views. Very few psychological theories have had such a significant impact on such a wide range of disciplines and applied fields, including psychiatry, anthropology, history, sociology, literature, and the visual arts. These views are as influential as they are controversial. Freud called his views and his method **psychoanalysis**.

Psychoanalysis Psychoanalysis is a broad term that encompasses the psychological views and the psychotherapeutic methods attributed to Sigmund Freud and his followers.

Key Assumptions

What is psychoanalysis? Which ideas make it different from other traditions? Which of its main ideas are most relevant for personality psychology? Let's highlight the four most important points relevant to the study of personality.

© Can Stock Photo Inc./Jsoltseva

Photo 4.1 Sigmund Freud remains one of the most controversial thinkers of all time. Which of Freud's ideas do you find most applicable to your personal experiences and why?

their desire to gratify their immediate wishes. Controlled by the reality principle, they continue to live in the state of constant delay of their desires (see **Figure 4.1**).

Instinctual Drives Are Repressed

Freud gained his experience as a researcher in his clinical work with patients who were seeking treatment for their psychological problems. Analyzing the records of his therapeutic sessions, Freud became convinced that the words conveyed to the therapist are not actual feelings and memories but rather specially coded messages. Why did patients code them? Did they feel embarrassed to share stories about themselves? Possibly. Freud assumed there is an internal "censor" that distorts these messages and alters the memory contents so that they become less anxiety-provoking to the patient. To explore his assumptions, Freud studied his own childhood memories as well as the memories of his patients.

Freud hypothesized that an individual's early disturbing or traumatic experiences, primarily of a sexual nature, might cause some forms of abnormal psychological symptoms during life. These disturbing events may cause an accumulation of unreleased energy, which later manifests in a variety of symptoms, such as elevated anxiety, phobias, obsessive behavior, or depressive symptoms. Not only psychological problems but also all aspects of human behavior and experience could be a manifestation of unconscious conflicts within the individual. Whatever is revealed in seemingly insignificant behaviors such as a mispronounced word, a misspelled name, a lost

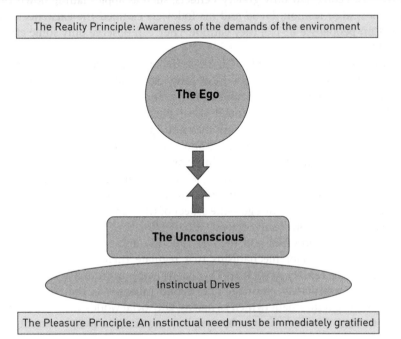

FIGURE 4.1 ● The Interactions Between the Unconscious and the Ego

The Reality Principle: Awareness of the demands of the environment

The Ego

The Unconscious

Instinctual Drives

The Pleasure Principle: An instinctual need must be immediately gratified key, a forgotten appointment, an angry reaction, or procrastination—all these could be reflections of an individual's unconscious inner struggles (Freud, 1901/2009). The problem is that we typically deny the existence of these conflicts.

What is the nature of this instinctual force that causes these inner conflicts? Freud suggested that it was a type of "sexual energy," or **libido**, which is the energy of the sexual drive or an erotic desire common in women and men (English & English, 1958). People who are passionately in love or individuals who care, cure, design clothes, write songs, strive for perfection, or seek new friends—they all are influenced by their libido.

Freud later connected libido with the universal *life drive*, often called **Eros**. Eros defines all the tendencies that strive toward the integration of a living substance. As with libido, Eros is about birth, creation, building, preserving, and loving. It manifests in love, friendship, courtship, altruistic help, kindness, and the creative work of carpenters and artists, among other things. Eros is responsible for love, bond, and the survival of the individual.

Freud was developing his views of personality during the first quarter of the 20th century. World War I (1914–1919) had a deep impact on him, his family members, and his colleagues. Millions of people perished in trenches, and many more died of disease and starvation. Unemployment, inflation, crime, and food shortages—they all appeared as a collective suicide by human civilization. His worldview became increasingly pessimistic. The years after 1914 provided Freud with ample evidence to contemplate the reasons behind human self-destructive behavior. He adopted the concept of the **death wish** (often labeled as *death instinct* or *death drive*)—the repressed instinctual tendencies that lead toward destruction. In simple terms, this is a repressed desire to destroy and kill self and others. **Thanatos** ("death" in ancient Greek), according to Freud, means striving for destruction, humiliation, pain, and death. It manifests not only in direct violence against people, including self, or objects but also in offensive jokes, jealous outbursts, criticisms, envious comments, racial slurs, character attacks, or contemptible responses—in anything that involves competition against another person or advancement at the expense of others. In Freud's view, this is a biological instinct based on natural, self-preservation to destroy or be pushed away and exterminated. Why do we slam the door when we are angry? Why do we spew profanities when we are irritated? Why do we people enjoy watching horror movies? These all could be indirect indications that the death wish affects our behavior. After describing the competing instinctual drives, Freud began to understand human experience as a constant conflict between these two primal drives—the creative and the destructive forces.

Freud argued that people tend to avoid pain and seek pleasure. Pain and pleasure are the first feelings to remain in the memory of an infant. We try to secure pleasurable moments in the memory and want to reexperience them. However, this is difficult for two reasons. First, society restricts many pleasure-related activities—such as sexual excitement, especially in children—by imposing moral taboos and regulations. Second, some pleasurable activities related to these memories are deemed shameful: A child who destroys a sand castle being built by another child is supposed to experience

Libido
In psychoanalysis, libido is the energy of the sexual drive or an erotic desire common in women and men.

Eros
In psychoanalysis, Eros refers to all the tendencies that strive toward the integration of a living substance.

Death wish
Often called a death instinct or death drive, a death wish is the repressed instinctual tendency that leads toward destruction.

Thanatos
According to Freud, thanatos ("death" in ancient Greek) means striving for destruction, humiliation, pain, and death.

guilt, not pleasure. Therefore, children are told to repress their violent and sexual fantasies, including anger, excitement, or jealousy. These feelings usually surface later—for the most part unconsciously—in various experiences and activities, including dreams, jokes, fantasies, hobbies, attachments, and, often, abnormal psychological symptoms such as excessive anxiety, depression, or obsessive thoughts (Freud, 1901/2009).

Repressed Desires in Action

Before "surfacing" at some point in the individual's life, where are these repressed features "stored"? Here, Freud evoked the idea of unconscious processes. Some experiences can be forgotten but can be later remembered, such as recalling someone's name at a party. However, they are not part of unconscious experiences, which are unlikely to be recalled simply by trying. The unconscious process is a reservoir of repressed guilty wishes and indecent feelings. The desire to reexperience some of them is matched by a powerful force that keeps them inside. What keeps the desires inside is conscience, or a moral guardian, which is a process that develops under the pressure of social norms. The repressed memory says to us, "You had this thought." The conscience replies, "No, I did not." To illustrate, think of someone explaining his or her inappropriate act (such as loudly saying an expletive in front of a group of small children) by saying, "I don't know how it happened; I felt like it wasn't *me* saying it," as if the person is trying to suggest that the "real" he or she could not have said it. Freud argued that the dynamics of the unconscious mind are similar to the act of denial. The content of the unconscious reservoir is filled early in life, and the power of the conscious mind keeps these memories repressed.

The Id, the Ego, and the Superego

Id In psychoanalysis, the id is the component of the psyche that contains inborn biological drives (the death wish and the life instinct); the id seeks immediate gratification of its impulses.

An individual's psyche (we can label it the *inner world* or *personality*) is made up of three levels (parts). The most primitive part of the personality is the **id**. This term was borrowed (and modified) from the German philosopher Friedrich Nietzsche. The id is the component of the psyche that contains inborn biological drives (the death wish and the life instinct); the id seeks immediate gratification of its impulses. The id, like unmanaged will, operates exclusively according to the pleasure principle. It represents a constant struggle between love and destruction (Freud, 1930/1990).

Neither Nietzsche nor Freud should get credit for discovering the good and the evil sides of an individual. Religious knowledge of the past contained these assumptions for many centuries. For example, Manichaeism, one of the oldest religions formed about 2,000 years ago on the territory of today's Iran, teaches that the individual is a "battleground" of good and evil forces. Christian theologian Augustine (354–430 CE) formulated the principle of two wills within the individual: the virtuous *caritas* and the sinful *cupiditas*. They are in continual battle against each other. They divide the self into struggling entities: lust versus chastity, greed versus self-control, and cravings versus moderation (Hooker, 1982). What makes Freudian ideas different from the religious assumptions is that in religion, the potential for a moral action is based on God's will. In Freud's system, the potentials for moral and immoral thoughts and acts are imbedded in the individual.

Making compromises between the id and the environment is the ego, which is guided by the reality principle. During an individual's development, the ego starts within the id but gradually changes to accept reason. Not every feature of the ego is conscious. Children learn moral rules as inner regulators restricting their behavior, emotional expressions, and thinking. The especially harsh and unexplainable restrictions are applied to the child's sexual interests (children are unaware yet of what decency means and are guided by the pleasure principle early in their lives). As infants, children see their parents as objects of love and aggression. Almost immediately, the children find that many of their emotional attachments are inappropriate, and they transfer the feelings into themselves. The children learn how to act like their parents. This moment launches the development of the **superego**, the moral guide passing on imperatives regarding appropriate or inappropriate actions and thoughts.

Among the first lessons children learn is what clothes they have to wear at home and in public. They also learn about specific circumstances when they should cover certain body parts (for example, the child learns to cover his or her mouth during sneezing). Being naked in front of a stranger automatically launches shame—a powerful and protective emotion. Then the child learns about appropriate and inappropriate words. Some words related to their body parts—such as *nose* or *knee*—are appropriate and may be spoken freely. Others—like *butt*—are not appropriate. Later, the child learns about social topics that are divided into proper, such as discussing a new toy or a book, and not proper, such as talking about poop and toilet activities. Overall, the superego, transmitted to the child by parents, older siblings, and teachers, represents the values and the customs of society.

Superego
In psychoanalysis, the superego is the moral guide that passes on imperatives regarding appropriate or inappropriate actions and thoughts.

Developmental Stages

Libido is associated with many pleasurable sensations, including those that come from the body. Children and adults enjoy a wide range of tactile experiences, such as touching, fondling, scratching, tasting, and kissing. Children go through several developmental stages in which the libido focuses ("fixates" in the psychoanalytic language) on different body areas. Such early fixations often manifest later in various patterns of repeating behaviors and thoughts. Because all children experience such fixations differently, when they grow up they display different behavioral and thinking patterns. One child enjoys his or her experiences and thus desires to repeat them in the future. Another child experiences sensory deprivation or frustration and thus does not crave such experiences in the future. These experiences develop in stages.

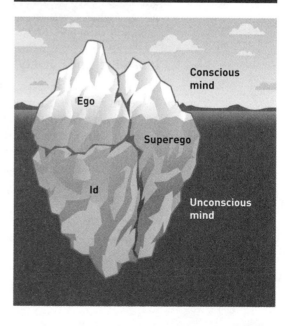

FIGURE 4.2 ● Interactions Among the Id, the Ego, and the Superego

Conscious mind

Ego

Superego

Id

Unconscious mind

The first developmental stage, called the *oral stage*, begins in infancy and is linked to an infant's nursing and eating. The infant who fixates on these activities, many years later as an adult, will often be prone to overeating, drinking, smoking, and excessive talking. The infant deprived of joy coming through the mouth should show angry and envious tendencies as a grownup.

The next stage, which lasts until the age of 4, is called the *anal stage*. During the period of toilet training, the child should use the bathroom regularly, follow the rules, and develop self-discipline. The child who develops a fixation during this stage (referred to in popular literature as an anal fixation) later shows obsessive tendencies, preoccupation with rules, orderliness, and delayed gratification (we discussed delayed gratification in Chapter 2). The child who felt miserable during toilet training later rebels by challenging the norms.

At the *phallic stage*, which lasts up to six or seven years, the focus of pleasure is the genitalia. According to Freud, at this point some boys may develop the castration complex, or an irrational fear of losing their penis (boys see people with missing limbs or teeth and assume that the penis can be "lost" too). Later in life, these boys become indecisive and lack initiative. Some girls may develop *penis envy,* an unconscious desire to have a penis. Such girls later on become submissive and dependent on men. Other girls will develop opposite tendencies rooted in unconscious hostility to boys and men. During the *latency stage*, which lasts until puberty, the child combines individual responses that he or she developed during the previous stages. The fifth stage is the *genital stage*, which lasts through adulthood. During this stage, the ego is formed. Many adults are now capable of gratifying the instinctual drives through society-approved activities, such as friendship, creativity, education, travel, and so forth.

Freud believed his works would help others better understand society and culture, and he pursued two major goals. The first one was to search for the societal sources of psychological conflicts within individuals. The second was a daring attempt to apply the main principles of psychoanalysis to history and the social sciences.

Individual and Society

Freud saw psychoanalysis as both a scientific method and a reliable theory. As such, it should apply to many areas of life and should help in resolving social problems. In *Civilization and Its Discontents* (1930), Freud wrote that the cause of most social problems is buried deep in people's anxiety: Humans don't know how to be happy because they are facing too many choices (Freud, 1930/1990). Freud frequently commented on social and moral issues. Religious behavior was one of his favorite topics.

Religion as an Analysand

Analysand An analysand, also known as a psychoanalyst's patient or client, is a person undergoing psychoanalysis.

In psychoanalytic vocabulary, an **analysand** is a person undergoing psychoanalysis, a psychoanalyst's patient or client. A committed atheist (he acknowledged his religious identity but did not practice Judaism), Freud used psychoanalysis to examine religion as if it were one of his patients. In general terms, Freud described an individual's religious behavior as an obsessive neurosis, compatible in contemporary terms to some symptoms of obsessive-compulsive disorder. He thought of parallels between religious rituals—such as regular praying, attachment to symbols, obsession with small details in religious rituals, and fears—to similar actions in his neurotic patients. Freud believed that an individual's behavior in both religious and neurotic contexts addresses similar internal anxieties. A person's adherence to religious rituals is like acting to address anxiety: It often serves a protective function. However, it may also deepen the underlying anxiety.

Freud wrote that people's embrace of religion comes from the individual's unconscious sense of helplessness. Religion also lets people accept the order and restrictions passed on to them by their parents. To criticize your religion, for example, is as problematic and morally offensive as insulting your parents. In the 1960s, years after Freud's passing, the famous German American theorist Herbert Marcuse (1898–1979) creatively used the ideas of psychoanalysis to inspire the young to revolt against capitalism and religion. In his view, every social revolution is also a personal event; in actuality, it is the young's revolt against their parents.

For a child, religion becomes a continuation of fantasy. Adults also maintain religion as an extension of their unconscious infantile fantasies and fears. Freud also viewed religion as a restraining force on human choices. The individual is trapped in a maze of fears and superstitions. The fear of eternal damnation, for instance, prevents people from questioning the existing social order. Infantile fears perpetuated by religious beliefs generate human passivity or, on the other hand, irresponsible and destructive acts (Freud, 1927/1990).

Views of Women

Freud's views of women were controversial and reflected the prevailing norms and perceptions of the time. Although most of Freud's patients were women, most of his original postulates related to males and were only later modified to describe women as well. Freud tended to see women as "failed" men because they do not have the same anatomical organs that men have. According to Freud, girls tend to develop an envious reaction toward men, which later manifests in some women in various forms of submissive behavior. Other women attempt to overcome envy by expressing constant hostility toward men.

Freud considered women as sexually more passive than men. Freud thought that such passivity was the result of social inequalities and cultural restrictions imposed on women. Nevertheless, he disliked the feminist movement in Europe. He did not accept the feminists' radical idea of eliminating the traditional order of the family and society. Yet he encouraged women to have access to sex education, learn about contraceptives, and seek choices in marriage. He also believed that women should have the right to divorce. He encouraged women who decided to become psychoanalysts to pursue education and training. One of the best illustrations of his position was his enthusiastic support of the professional advancement of his daughter, Anna, who became a world-renowned psychologist (Chapter 5).

CHECK AND APPLY YOUR KNOWLEDGE

1. Compare and contrast the pleasure principle and the reality principle.

2. What is the opposite drive to the death wish?

3. Using Freud's psychoanalysis, how would you explain the motivation of the person who sacrifices her safety and well-being on behalf of another person? In your view, is this a manifestation of the death wish or the love instinct?

4. The id is the component of the psyche that contains what?

5. What is the superego? Is it conscious or not?

6. Choose one developmental stage and describe it.

7. If you were a psychoanalyst, how would you apply these developmental stages to explain the lying behavior in the opening case?

8. From your personal standpoint now, suggest at least two strengths and two weaknesses of this Freudian classification.

Studying Alfred Adler's Views

One of Freud's most outstanding followers was Alfred Adler (1870–1937). He was born near Vienna. His father was a middle-class Jewish grain merchant. Young Alfred's health was poor, and he had to overcome numerous physical difficulties as he grew up. He went to medical school, became a doctor, and established a practice in Vienna. In 1902, Adler began to attend weekly meetings in Freud's home and became a dedicated follower of Freud's ideas. However, they never became close friends, and a few disagreements between Adler and Freud surfaced early. Adler, for example, particularly emphasized the importance of the relationships among siblings, not between the parents and the child, as Freud did. Adler also questioned sexuality as the most dominant force in human life and one of the central points of Freud's psychoanalysis. Their disagreements deepened. Until the end of his days, Freud criticized Adler's work. Their critical exchanges became personal sometimes. Freud claimed that Adler had paranoid ideas. Adler accused Freud of being power hungry and authoritarian. Researchers sometimes get passionate about their ideas.

Photo 4.2 Alfred Adler believed that adversities in our lives could spark the development of our previously hidden talents. Are you able to apply this theory to your life? Were any significant difficulties helpful in developing some of your personality traits?

© Sueddeutsche Zeitung Photo/Alamy

Organ Inferiority

Like Freud, Adler thought of the body as the source of pleasure and desires (Adler, 1930). The

SELF-REFLECTION

Adler first (1930) and then others (Sulloway, 1996) studied birth order and argued that it makes a difference on an individual and his or her behavior and personality features. Adler believed that firstborn children, because of their upbringing, should be more serious, conscientious, aggressive, conservative, organized, responsible, independent, fearful, high achieving, and competitive than their siblings. The youngest should be more outgoing, spontaneous, selfish, irresponsible, dependent, less competitive, and less achievement-oriented than other siblings. Children who are born in the middle are "mediators"; they need to take care of the conflicts between other siblings, take middle ground, and find compromises. The only child can assume features of both categories and is likely to be selfish.

According to Sulloway's (1996) research, firstborn children tend to be more supportive of status quo and the existing social and political establishment than their younger siblings (*later-borns*). For example, during the French Revolution, royalists (supporters of the king) were largely firstborns. But so were the most irreconcilable opponents of the monarchy. Moderates tended to be middle children.

Questions

Identify from their biographies the birth order of the past 10 U.S. presidents. Were they older or younger brothers in their families? What was their party affiliation? According to theory, older siblings are supposed to be more conservative, and younger ones are supposed to be more liberal. Discuss in class if the assumptions of Adler and Sulloway about birth order are applicable to you and your siblings (if you have them).

body is also a source of pain and frustration. Out of this assumption came one of Adler's central concepts called **organ inferiority**. The term stands for a wide range of physical problems that become psychological impediments. Organ inferiority refers not only to organs as such (for instance, the eye, the hand, the heart, etc.) but also to the nervous system. These problems can be physical or psychological. They appear at birth or may develop later in life. Organ inferiority manifests in many ways. For example, a very short boy does not play rough games at school, so children tease him for being short and reject him. Thus, his height is the source of his organ inferiority. Similarly, a girl with a mild learning disability, which is an obvious weakness in the classroom, feels embarrassed for scoring lowest on the test. In this case, the girl's learning disability is the source of her organ inferiority. According to Adler, a physically defective organ or a malfunctioning system sends signals to the brain suggesting that something is wrong or insufficient. However, the person cannot suffer continually. The body then needs to compensate for an emerging insufficiency, find energy resources to address the problem, and reduce the unpleasant feelings.

Based on lengthy observations of children, Adler concluded that organ inferiority is particularly common in the physically weak and in those with poor learning or

Organ inferiority
In Adler's view, organ inferiority refers to a wide range of physical problems that become psychological impediments.

Compensation In Adler's vocabulary, compensation refers to attempts to overcome the discomfort and negative experiences caused by a person's feelings of inferiority.

adaptation skills. These children thus attempt to overcome the discomfort caused by their inferiority. These attempts are called **compensation**. This is not necessarily a steady change resulting in the individual's improvement and growth. Compensation can bring different outcomes.

Degeneration, Neurosis, Genius

Genius In Adler's vocabulary, a genius is the type of individual who overcomes the old inferiority problems and achieves success and happiness.

There are three general outcomes of an individual's compensatory efforts. The **genius** overcomes the old inferiority problems and achieves success and happiness. Compensation in this case brings success and delivers a new life free from pain of inferiority. In the case of degeneration, the attempted compensation is unsuccessful. The person falls out of the normal course of life and is unable to adjust to social rules. The third outcome is neurosis. This happens when an individual is sliding from comfortable to difficult times. Imagine a 12-year-old girl who suddenly believes she is unattractive when someone jokingly tells her she has a big nose and pointy ears. Now the girl looks in the mirror and feels ugly for the first time in her life. As a result, this girl who was once an outgoing and happy person becomes anxious and withdrawn. She loses interest in many activities she previously enjoyed. She turns to fantasies. In her dreams, she becomes a supermodel, creates her own fashion line, and returns to her school years later to confront her peers who all turned out to be stupid and ugly losers. The fantasy is a temporary substitute for real action. Adler explains why the famous Cinderella fairy tale remained popular across generations: It was an example of a powerful childish expectation of a better outcome, a form of personal liberation from humiliation and pain caused by Cinderella's stepmother.

People tend to develop their own ideal world of fantasy because there, in that world, not necessarily in real life, they achieve redemption. In some cases, fantasies may cause action because the person realizes the difference between the dream and the reality. Such actions may, in some cases, lead to a change in habits, a different view of self and others, self-improvement, growth, and eventual success. However, in other cases, the individual may become increasingly withdrawn. The old bad habits remain, and the old psychological problems persist. The person sees the world as cold and hostile. Even family members and friends appear to be enemies. This is the beginning of neurosis, according to Adler. It may continue for years. Imagine for a moment a woman with heart problems; she needs attention and care. Later, however, to prolong care and to continue to enjoy the compassion of other people, she may perpetuate the existing heart problem or refuse to admit that her heart condition has improved. This is not a case of deliberate lying or malingering simulation of one's symptoms to get benefits. This is done without conscious efforts. Physical deficiency brought on the feeling of psychological deficiency: She feels that she now suffers more than anyone else, that she doesn't deserve to suffer alone, that no one understands her and her feelings, and that the world around her is mean and uncaring. These feelings, accurate or false, according to Adler, are key features of a neurosis. Any neurosis is a person's failed attempt to compensate for an infantile imperfection.

In cases of degeneration, some people withdraw deeply into the world of dreaming, thus becoming incapable of social functioning. Others may turn to violence to address their hostile fantasies against their abusers. Adler, in fact, described children who compensate by engaging in violent acts. Adler described this example as *protesting behavior*, which can manifest in many ways and in people of all ages.

Individual Psychology

Adler was particularly impressed with the work of Hans Vaihinger, who published *The Philosophy of "As If"* (1911). In this fascinating book, the author maintains that people live primarily by a fiction that does not correspond with reality (Vaihinger, 1952). Some of us, for example, believe that the world is disorderly. Yet we reject this belief and behave as if the world were well-ordered. Similarly, people create God, ignoring the idea that God could be a fiction. Why do people create and live by such falsifications? One of the reasons is that to achieve an ambitious goal, we have to believe in it. We also have to know how to achieve it. While Freud was interested in the past of his patients, Adler assumed that people are motivated primarily by future expectations. By forming them, people pursue their fictional final goal, called *self-ideal*. This is the unifying principle of an individual's personality. Self-ideal can be achieved if an individual engages in **striving toward superiority**. It is not about domination or other types of physical or social superiority. Adler meant that individuals strive for security, improvement, and control in all activities they undertake. Whether they win or make mistakes—it doesn't matter. What matters is the great upward drive, as Adler put it. The human feeling of imperfection is never ending, which should be accepted. But people should constantly seek for a solution to this problem by using the imperatives, "Achieve! Arise! Conquer!" (Adler, 1930).

> **Striving toward superiority**
> In Adler's view, striving toward superiority is an individual's vigorous exertion or effort to achieve security, improvement, control, and conquest.

[handwritten: Get up Dress up run]

Social Interest   *[handwritten: occupations, society, love]*

Recall that Adler viewed the power drive within individuals as a response to feelings of inferiority. He later modified his view, adding another important motivational feature to his views of personality: **social interest**, or the desire to be connected with other people and to adapt positively to the perceived social environment. Adler realized that while a person strives for self-advancement, he or she has to take into consideration other people's interests (because these people are striving for power, too). There are three major and interconnected social ties appearing in social interest.

The first social tie is *occupation.* People are engaged in different activities that provide food, water, safety, and comfort. People then create a division of labor. *Society* is the second tie. People join different groups based on their occupations or other interests. The third tie is *love.* People are attracted to one another. The division of labor and social requirements influence love.

> **Social interest**
> In Adler's view, social interest is the desire to be connected with other people and to adapt positively to the perceived social environment.

People create their own **style of life**. This concept is helpful in summarizing Adler's views. Every person's style of life develops in stages. First, a child has inferiority issues. Second, this developing individual is set to overcome this inferiority, which involves compensation. Compensation may manifest in behavior, imagination, or both. Pursuing compensation, an individual strives toward superiority and self-enhancement. There could be good and bad decisions on this path. This quest for

> **Style of life**
> In Adler's view, the style of life is a technique for dealing with one's inadequacies and inferiorities and for gaining social status.

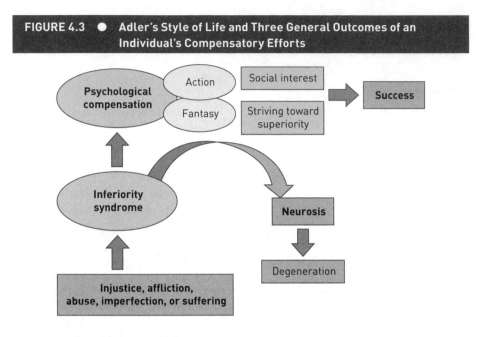

FIGURE 4.3 ● **Adler's Style of Life and Three General Outcomes of an Individual's Compensatory Efforts**

superiority involves an individual's engagement in social life and the establishment of social ties. All together, these elements form a unique style of life for each individual (see **Figure 4.3**).

Adler (1930) used the life of Johan A. Strindberg (1849–1912), one of the most prominent Swedish cultural icons of the modern era, to portray a typical neurotic personality. As a child, Johan suffered from interiority feelings. To compensate, he tried many professional paths and activities in life. He was a writer, a painter, a playwright, and a journalist. In search of his own artistic style, he tried naturalism and then switched to symbolism. He was married three times but was romantically involved with many more women as if he were trying to establish a firm control over them. He kept failing in marriage and kept looking for new romances as a way to exercise his power over women. He was a socialist and atheist, yet later in life, he returned to Christianity. He kept repeating his old mistakes, continuously returning to the place from which he started. Using this case, Adler emphasized that neurotic behavior and thinking are altered when an individual does not understand the difference between goals attached to reality and goals from the world of fantasy.

Although Adler (1930) acknowledged factual inequality between men and women, he also believed that mistakes of the history of civilization must be corrected and the social gap between men and women should be narrowed. However, as a man of his time, Adler accepted the long-established construction of gender roles. He used his theory to explain social and political aspects of gender inequality. He believed, for example, that women's protests against sexism and discrimination were wrong because, in reality, as he insisted, it was a protest against women's natural roles as mothers and caregivers.

CHECK AND APPLY YOUR KNOWLEDGE

1. What is organ inferiority?

2. What is compensation, according to Adler? Give examples.

3. What is the self-ideal, according to Adler?

4. What is your personal self-ideal? What difficulties do you have to overcome to achieve this self-ideal?

Alfred Adler always made relentless attempts to reach a broader audience, popularize psychology, and explain it in nonacademic, lay terms. He specifically mentioned that individuals and society together form a dynamic structure. When conditions change, social ties tend to change as well. So do our individual perceptions of them.

Early Transitions of Psychoanalysis: Carl Jung

Carl Jung (1875–1961) was frequently called the "crown prince" of psychoanalysis. For several years early in his career, like Adler, Jung was a firm and loyal supporter of Freud, his theory, and his method. In letters, Freud used to address Jung cordially as "dear friend and colleague" (Eisold, 2002). Their friendship lasted for several years. Their academic and personal breakup has become one of the most discussed stories in psychology's history.

The son of a Protestant preacher, Jung suffered from anxiety and obsessive symptoms early in life. Carl grew imaginative and creative, showing early interest in self-analysis. After getting a medical degree in 1900 from the University of Basel, he worked as a psychiatrist in a mental asylum. Freud was impressed with Jung's erudition and commitment to study unconscious phenomena. He suggested Jung for the leadership position in the newly formed international psychoanalytic movement. However, their friendship and cooperation did not last. Jung was hesitant to embrace the Freudian concept of sexuality and libido. He considered *mental energy* as a better term. Jung was also critical of Freud's views of human sexuality. Scientific disagreements gradually turned into mutual intolerance (Jung, 1961). The uncrowned prince of psychoanalysis would never be king. Yet Jung's own original theory and his view of personality would attract a growing posse of dedicated followers across the world.

Forming the Ideas

In one of his earlier works, Jung explored the idea that human dreams contained experiences beyond conscious awareness (Jung & Hinkle, 1912). He thought of dreams as a multistory house in which the basement represents the most fundamental and ancient features. Contradicting Freud, Jung thought that dreams do not necessarily reflect a child's unrealized wishes but are rather mythological stories and images from the experiences of our ancestors. Fantasy, too, like dreams, serves as a connector between our ancestors' experiences thousands of years ago and our experience at this moment.

Jung was fascinated with mysticism and spirituality. The roots of his theory are in the ideas of the Christian Middle Ages, Greek philosophy, and alchemy. Later, he gradually incorporated into his theory the ideas of Eastern philosophy, theology, and mythology. This was an eclectic combination of many designs. Yet they were shaped around a central message, or an assumption: The individual's unconscious contains mental relics from earlier generations (Drob, 1999). How do these mental relics appear? To explain, Jung turned to symbols, which are the unconscious aspects of the individual's perception of reality (Jung, 1964). When we are awake, we do not remember everything that happened to us a few hours ago. We tend to lose our conscious awareness of our memories. However, memory exists below the threshold of consciousness and manifests on the symbolic level. In dreaming, for example, the symbols appear spontaneously.

Analytical Psychology

Jung used the term **analytical psychology** to distinguish his views from Freud's psychoanalysis. He turned to two major sources of information to support his ideas. The first one was the folklore: fairy tales, myths, legends, drawings, and rituals. Jung suggested an impersonal layer in human psyche, which he called the **collective unconscious**. It is different from the individual unconscious. It is inherited and even shared with other members of the species. Jung agreed with Freud that the individual unconscious consists primarily of repressed ideas, yet the content of the collective unconscious consists of **archetypes**, or images of the primordial (elemental, ancient) character. These are people's ancestral experiences, which appear in three universal ways: dreams, fantasies, and delusions. Jung believed that certain delusions of his patients (e.g., a belief that the sun has wings or a fear of being swallowed by a giant animal) resemble mythological beliefs and images of the past. While our ancestors did not separate these beliefs from their everyday experience, we, in modern times, view them as unusual manifestations or even abnormal symptoms. How many archetypes are there? Jung and his followers did not attempt to give the exact number because the archetypes tend to combine with one another. There is considerable confusion in literature about specific issues related to archetypes, and Jung's position on archetypes evolved throughout his career. Therefore, the following are examples of a few categories of archetypes.

An archetype called the shadow contains the unconscious aspects of the self. In a way, the shadow in Jung's theory resembles the id in Freud's psychoanalysis. The shadow obeys instinctual forces. It manifests in a person's romantic attachments, aggressive acts, fears, persistent interests, avoidant behavior, and so forth. Another archetype called persona appears as a symbolic mask to trick other people into the belief that the carrier of the mask is playing a particular social role. The persona represents an individual's public image (the word *persona* comes from the Latin word for

Analytical psychology Jung called his views analytical psychology to distinguish them from Freud's.

Collective unconscious In Jung's theory, the collective unconscious is an impersonal layer in the human psyche that is different from the individual unconscious, as well as inherited and shared with other members of the species.

Archetypes According to Jung, archetypes are the content of the collective unconscious that consist of images of the primordial (elemental, ancient) character. These archetypes manifest in three universal ways: dreams, fantasies, and delusions.

"mask"). Jung used the label *personal man*—referring to both men and women—to refer to individuals who identify themselves with real or imaginary social roles. Such identification can be successful and adaptive; it also can be pathological when the person suffers from a split between the "real" personality features and his or her actual social roles. Imagine a woman, for example, who tries presenting herself to others as rich, independent, and superior (unconsciously playing the role of a fashion supermodel or a pop star). Playing this role could be hurtful because this woman invests so much psychologically into appearing as someone she is not.

Men have an inherited collective image of the feminine human essence called *anima*. In contrast, every woman has an inherited image of masculine essence, called *animus*. These two archetypes stand for unconscious masculine and feminine psychological qualities. Anima, for example, represents the man's unconscious expectation of women but also is a symbol of a man's feminine potentials. Animus is the analogous image of the masculine that occurs in women (Odajnyk, 2012). Every individual has the fundamental unconscious feminine and masculine features. Anima and animus, as archetypes, according to Jung, serve as an unconscious guide to an individual's love life. People often fall in love with little rational reason because the archetypes take over and direct the individual's feelings and subsequent behavior.

Jung believed that many symbols in our lives represent concepts that we cannot fully comprehend. For example, what symbolic meaning do numbers have? Jung referred to even numbers such as *2*, *4*, *8*, and so on, as "feminine" because they are round and associated with harmony. In contrast, Jung believed odd numbers are "masculine" because they are pointy and associated with power. Jung wrote that Christianity for the most part produced masculine symbols, such as the Trinity (the Father, the Son, and the Holy Spirit).

Symbolic actions fill our days. Have you ever drawn circular patterns on a piece of paper during a lecture or when you are sitting and waiting for an appointment? Jung called such spontaneous circular drawings *mandala*. From his view, these drawings are our attempt to calm down, to restore inner peace. Mandala is also a word from the classical Indian language of Sanskrit. Loosely translated, it means "a circle." It also represents a geometric pattern, a symbol of the divine, or the meaning of the universe from the human perspective. In Jungian terminology, mandala also refers to the archetype of wholeness. Jung believed that the circular patterns that people draw represent an archetype symbolizing the wisdom of life. The center of the mandala represents individuation, the process of psychological growth.

Jung hoped that his theory could help people become aware of the existence of their archetypes. This, Jung also believed, could be accomplished through an interpretation of cultural symbols, dreams, and fantasies (Jung, 1967). These patterns of cultural symbols appeared to Jung consistently across similar cultures and times. If people in the past created images and artifacts that are comparable to the images and artifacts created today, then the mental patterns of people today are similar to the mental patterns of people in the past. It was an optimistic outlook.

CHECK AND APPLY YOUR KNOWLEDGE

1. What is the collective unconscious?

2. What are Jung's archetypes? Name any two and explain them.

3. Why is it important to us to be aware of our archetypes?

4. How did Jung explain the mandala?

5. How would you personally interpret your own circular patterns on a piece of paper?

6. What are primordial fears? Are you aware of having primordial fears? What are they? How difficult will it be to discuss these fears with somebody else? How about in class? (If this is too difficult, you don't have to do this).

7. Have you ever wondered how it would feel if a giant animal swallowed you? Think about it. Does this idea scare you or fascinate you?

Jung believed that fear of being swallowed is one of the universal human fantasies related to death and rebirth through the act of eating. Jung compared the dreams and fantasies of his patients with different fairy tales. He turned to several such tales. One was the famous Red Riding Hood story, in which the wolf eats the grandmother, who is later rescued by the huntsman. Jung also considered ancient myths in which the sun is swallowed by a sea monster. The sun rises again in the morning. The story of Jonah in the Christian tradition and of Yunus in the Islamic tradition both contain the plot element in which a man is swallowed by a giant fish but then rescued. We can find many similar examples. In the *Adventures of Pinocchio* by the 19th-century Italian author Carlo Collodi, a giant fish swallows the little wooden puppet, who later escapes. In a famous Russian fairy tale by Kornei Chukovsky, a giant crocodile swallows the sun. In the ensuing darkness, the distressed people force the crocodile to spit out the sun. In the film trilogy of *Pirates of the Caribbean*, Captain Jack Sparrow is swallowed by a giant sea beast in the second film, only to reappear in the third.

Using these examples, Jung's followers maintain that the similarities in these stories are based on the common human archetypes attached to fears and fascinations. Critics maintain that children (and adults as well) hear such stories about beasts swallowing a character first and then develop fantasies and fears related to these stories, not the other way around.

Questions

Could you suggest other tales or films involving the act of swallowing and rebirth or reappearance? How do these stories end? Discuss a possibility to test Jung's ideas about primordial fears experimentally or by other methods.

Psychological Types

Jung did not conduct laboratory experiments. He was a theorist who relied on his encyclopedic knowledge and clinical observations. The idea of psychological types came to Jung earlier in his career when he compared the experiences of patients with schizophrenia with those of patients with hysteria (Jung, 1924). In Jung's view, the patient with hysteric symptoms attaches his or her energy to other people. Jung termed this behavior **extroversion**. Conversely, most patients with schizophrenic symptoms turn energy back to themselves. Jung called this **introversion**. In fact, in Jung's view, all people can be described along these directional lines. Extroversion and introversion, he argued, are about an individual's sense of direction (Odajnyk, 2012).

Extroverts, or individuals prone to extroversion, spontaneously embrace the world. Extroverts stream their libido outward, toward external objects. They commonly turn to other people and their ideas. Extroverts, however, can be shallow and their interests lie in the outside world. They are often inconsistent. Their many projects often do not materialize. Extroverts may start a new project because they see potential rewards and seldom anticipate failure. Yet they frequently miscalculate their options because they are too optimistic and don't clearly see potential problems arising.

On the other hand, introverts tend to shy away from the world and turn their attention and interest to themselves. The introvert's libido streams inward, toward a subjective realm of thoughts and fantasies. Introverts tend to seek internal resources to act. Introverts make mistakes too because they often see things from a gloomy, pessimistic perspective. Introverts tend to be reluctant to start new projects because they anticipate few rewards in the end and forecast difficulties ahead. In the end, both types, introverts and extroverts, can fail or win, but for different psychological reasons.

Jung believed, however, that the introverts have a harder time in contemporary society than extroverts. To an introvert, the world appears too challenging, pushy, annoying, and demanding. These critical perceptions are uncommon in the mind of an extrovert. Extroverts agree that the world is demanding, but as they argue, who says it shouldn't be? Introversion is not necessarily about the soul's depth. Some of their inner worlds are not that sophisticated and complex; they can be dull and banal (see **Table 4.1**).

Jung also believed that people have four ways to deal with reality: thinking, feeling, intuition, and sensation. These features help the individual organize and evaluate experiences. Sensation and intuition provide knowledge. Thinking organizes this knowledge and sorts out in terms of its significance, but thinking is not equal to high intelligence. Feeling brings evaluation, including moral judgments, likes and dislikes, and attachments to people and things. Extroversion and introversion are different orientations, in the same way that thinking and feeling as well as sensation and intuition are opposite in function. Sensation focuses on details, while intuition embraces the whole; thinking is about connecting ideas and structuring them, while feeling is about value judgments. Overall, Jung introduces eight psychological types. In these dyads, both functions have to be compatible, not contradictory. For example, a thinking type cannot simultaneously be a feeling type (see **Table 4.2**).

Extroversion
(E) In Eysenck's system, extroversion (E) is characterized by talkativeness, positive emotions, and the need to seek external sources of stimulation.

Introversion
In Jung's view, introversion happens when a person attaches his or her psychological energy back to self.

Jung believed that such categories should help psychologists in their theoretical and practical work. However, he warned against overusing the psychological types. Human beings are different from one another not only because of their types but also because of their distinctive individual qualities, strengths, and weaknesses (Odajnyk, 2012).

TABLE 4.1 ● Features Associated With Extroversion and Introversion

Features Associated With Extroversion	Features Associated With Introversion
Generally directed to others.	Generally directed to self.
Tries to participate in events; joins many groups and feels comfortable when there are many people around.	Stays away from participating in events; doesn't join many groups and feels uncomfortable when there are many people around.
Most tasks and problems appear easy, manageable, positive, and rewarding.	Most tasks and problems appear too demanding, overpowering, negative, and menacing.
Tends to trust people, tends not to be envious, and tends to feel competent.	Tends to be distrustful, envious, and often prone to inferiority feelings.
Has a generally positive attitude about other people and the world in general; tends to see the world in rosy colors. Self-criticism is infrequent and insignificant.	Tends to be critical about other people and the world in general; always finds "a hair in every soup." Self-criticism is frequent and significant.
Relations with other people do not require a guaranteed safety. In relationships, trust prevails.	Relations with other people tend to be warm only if safety is guaranteed. In other cases, defensive distrust is common.
Views of others and group pressure frequently affect judgments and actions.	Views of others and group pressure only infrequently affect judgments and actions.

Source: Jung, 1924.

TABLE 4.2 ● Jung's Function Types

The Extrovert			
Thinking Type	**Feeling Type**	**Sensation Type**	**Intuition Type**
Rejects most things based on feelings or intuitive or irrational ideas, including religious beliefs and experiences. Common among men. Jung considers Freud to be in this category.	Feelings are based on the impact of external circumstances and less on subjective experiences. This type tries to do right things. Pleasure seeking is typical. Common among women.	Lacks an intellectual potential and tries to find pleasure under any circumstances.	This type cares about relationships among several things and tries to exploit social situations. Common among entrepreneurs, politicians, and women.

The Introvert			
Thinking Type	**Feeling Type**	**Sensation Type**	**Intuition Type**
Less concerned with new facts and more preoccupied with new ideas. Follows own way of thinking and tends to ignore criticism. Frequently is impractical.	Cares about personal experience and often appears negative or indifferent. Common among women and creative artists.	Behavior is guided less by the object than by the intensity of own, subjective experiences.	Focuses on the background process of consciousness. This type is common among musicians, dreamers, or artists. Jung considers himself in this category.

Principles of Therapy

In the world of rationality, individuals fail to recognize their archetypes. These unrecognized archetypes, however, often appear in the form of neurotic symptoms (Jung, 1967). The intent of therapy is to provide an individual with a way to ease the impact of such symptoms. The first goal of therapy is to teach patients how to learn about their neurosis. Patients do not necessarily cure their own neurosis; exactly the opposite is true. Neurosis provides a cure to patients who acquire the skills to understand it. One of the differences between Freud and Jung is that Freud attempted to eliminate neuroses in his patients; conversely, Jung attempted to help his patients come to terms with their neuroses.

The second goal of Jungian therapy was balance restoration. Applying the concept of energy conservation, Jung believed that the mental energy in us is limited, and if we pursue one activity, other activities receive less energy. The third goal was **individuation**. This is the process of fulfilling an individual's potential by integrating opposites into a harmonious whole, by getting away from the aimlessness of life (the condition most of his patients were suffering from, according to Jung). Psychopathology is disorganization. Sanity is harmony. Jung was in a constant search for harmony within the individual.

Criticisms of Ethnocentrism

Jung was among the first psychologists to critically review the ethnocentric worldview of Western psychology. He confronted a widespread opinion of the time that the European type of thinking (pragmatic, analytical, and science-oriented) was far superior to other cultural types (holistic and spiritual). Consider an example. In present-day terms, a college-educated person from New York or Tokyo who catches a seasonal infection and thus becomes sick may explain this small health problem as a result of "bad luck" during the flu epidemic. A person who lacks formal education may explain the fever and coughing as a result of a malevolent act committed by an evil force. Both these people believe that the infection is only the means for delivering

Individuation
In Jung's view, individuation is the process of fulfilling an individual's potential by integrating opposites into a harmonious whole and by getting away from the aimlessness of life (a condition most of his patients were suffering from).

Psychoanalysis earned a reputation as a theory and method valid primarily within the Western culture. At the center of attention was a white person from the upper social class who was trapped in an internal conflict related to childhood and relationships. Although Freud understood the necessity of examining psychoanalysis in non-Western cultural conditions, he did not do much in this direction (DaConceição & De Lyra Chebabi, 1987).

Over the years, some psychoanalytic ideas were critically examined in different countries (Devereux, 1953; Kakar, 1995). Jung focused on non-Western cultural traditions. There were psychoanalytic studies of African witchcraft, social customs of Australian aboriginal natives, the impact of mainstream culture on African Americans, or ego defenses in people from Buddhist communities (Tori & Bilmes, 2002). Some studies suggested that the Western psychoanalytic tradition has difficulty interpreting, for example, the complexity of gender relations in Muslim communities, the importance of male bonding common in South Asia, or the role of religious identity (Kurtz, 1992). Criticism was also directed at the cultural applicability of psychoanalysis as a therapeutic method. For many years, the principles of interaction between the therapist and the client in the West have been generally based on the assumption that patient and analyst were essentially equal, although the analyst was more knowledgeable. It is not always the case in other cultural environments. Recent research shows that many immigrants from traditional cultures, for instance, expected a great deal of advice and direct guidance from the therapist, much as they expected guidance from the authority figure or family elders (Roland, 2006). Unlike behaviorism, in the 20th century, psychoanalysis remained, for the most part, a psychological theory rooted in the Western cultural tradition.

Today, one of the most important applications of psychoanalysis is its ability to constantly generate fascination about us, as human beings—about how we develop, feel, and act.

CHECK AND APPLY YOUR KNOWLEDGE

1. Compare the characteristics of extroverts and introverts. Are there any similarities between them?

2. Compare the feeling and the thinking types (according to Jung).

3. Which type do you feel resembles your personality features the most and why?

4. What is individuation? Give an example.

5. Why did Jung call the Western psychology's worldview *ethnocentric*?

6. What did Jung call religion a product of?

7. Why was psychoanalysis often labeled as a *self-fulfilling prophecy*?

Applying the Psychoanalytic Tradition

Understanding Self

Psychoanalysis would have probably remained an obscure and even an elitist theory known to a few educated enthusiasts had it not found its way to the hearts and minds of millions of people. It offered them a choice and an educated opportunity to look into the depths of consciousness, to examine a world of experiences hidden from direct or superficial observation.

Freud taught psychologists to be careful and critical observers. They should apply their theoretical knowledge to interpret their own experiences as well as experiences of others. From the early days of psychoanalysis, many of its educated followers believed that they were skilled practitioners capable of understanding the deep-seated individual problems hidden in the murky waters of unconsciousness, covered with a thick layer of resistance. Only trained psychoanalysts could finally reveal the "truth" about other people's personalities as well as causes of their problems. The professional language of psychoanalysis was straightforward: "It is not your bad luck that made you lose; it is your repressed fear of your mother!" or "You are not just late for the test. Your tardiness is a reflection of hidden hostility toward the professor!" Despite such apparent simplification in explaining human behavior, psychoanalysis encouraged the observer's curiosity, constant attention to details, and a relentless search for answers. Would you agree that these are fine qualities of a true psychology professional today?

Freud legitimized the distinction between "higher," prosocial structures of the individual personality and "lower," primitive, and largely antisocial formations. The problem in the patient was not in the prevalence or deficiency of certain personality traits (as Greek and many later thinkers would refer to deficiency or surplus of bodily fluids) but in the individual's inability to adequately resolve an inner conflict. Attempts to resolve a conflict led to the formation of behavioral traits that were deemed inappropriate, inept, and harmful within a social context. A person who consistently exhibits outrageous childish behavior—such as someone who *regresses*, in Freudian terminology—attempts to gain attention and love from others, which, unfortunately, does not happen because others not only refrain from expressing love but also reject or even condemn this childishness. This conceptual understanding of dysfunctions of personality as unresolved conflicts had a significant impact on contemporary views on personality disorders, which we will study in Chapter 12.

Jung and Adler encouraged psychologists to understand and appreciate similarities and cultural differences in human experiences. The Western world, according to Jung, was based on rationality and needed to be in touch with a deeper view of self and other, non-Western cultures. Contemporary psychology has generally accepted Jung's encouragements to develop an inclusive, cross-cultural approach to psychological knowledge (Shiraev & Levy, 2013). Jung also inspired scores of psychology researchers to enlighten themselves, broaden their cultural and intellectual horizons, and turn to a wide range of new educational sources created in India, Central Asia, Latin America, and other world regions.

Although psychoanalysis was often incorrect about the mechanisms of the individual's unconscious actions, it has brought significant attention to what we label today *spontaneous reactions*. For example, experimental studies show that individuals too often make quick, spontaneous, yet seemingly illogical decisions about complex and sophisticated products, such as buying kitchen furniture or a car (Dijksterhuis, 2004). There are certain "mechanisms" within the individual's mind that may explain why such decisions take place. What are the lessons of such studies? We have to be aware of this and sometimes wait longer, check again, or ask a friend or a family member to help us with certain decisions, especially if they are personally important or costly (Dijksterhuis, Bos, Nordgren, & van Baaren, 2006). The ability to wait, take time, and reflect on certain events or circumstances is another practical lesson that we learn from psychoanalysis. Very often our reactions are spontaneous or, as we sometimes call them, "natural." Experimental studies show, for example, that aggressive humor (when a person in a cartoon, for example, punches someone in the face) usually distracts people so that they are not fully aware of the content they are laughing at. When people are asked to first explain an aggressive joke or a cartoon, they consider them not as funny as other people do when they are not asked to pay attention to the violent content of a joke (Gollob & Levine, 1967).

Helping Others: Therapy

Perhaps one of the most significant applications of psychoanalytic theories is the method (or rather a range of methods) of treatment of psychological problems. Psychoanalytic ideas and practical work helped in making psychotherapy a legitimate occupation early in the 20th century. People began to understand mental illness

Photo 4.3 Do you have individual skills and traits that would make you a fine therapist? What are they?

© iStockphoto.com/Christopher Futcher

better, thus challenging the stigma of mental illness (Shiraev, 2015). Jung's therapy also won global recognition. Many people from different countries sought his treatment. They paid significant sums of money and settled in hotels near Jung's lakeshore residence in Switzerland, devoting weeks and months of their lives to therapy. In addition to individual sessions, Jung offered lectures and seminars attended by groups of his patients, who could receive an abbreviated course in his analytical psychology. Adler was also a sought-after therapist who believed that mental health was inseparable from the problem of social inequality.

In the past century, most practicing psychiatrists in the United States were not psychoanalysts. Yet many studied psychoanalysis in medical schools and freely applied its principles in diagnosis and therapy of mental illness. The first edition of *The Diagnostic and Statistical Manual of Mental Disorders* (*DSM*), published in 1952, was filled with psychoanalytic terminology and arguments. By the third edition of the *DSM*, published in 1980, psychoanalysis and psychoanalytic theory were excluded from its pages (Menand, 2014). Psychoanalysts, however, did not give up and continued improving the scientific foundation of their theory. They modified their research and practical work to pursue three principles or imperatives: (1) use clinical data to generate testable hypotheses, (2) test these hypotheses by scientific methods, and (3) look outside the discipline to exchange data with other fields in psychology (Bornstein, 2001; Mills, 2001). Many analysts began to implement these principles in their studies. Jonathan Metzl (2005), for example, in the book *Prozac on the Couch*, provides evidence of the effective use of psychoanalysis in combination with prescribed medication. Other researchers began to analyze the effectiveness of psychoanalysis as a therapeutic method using controlled methods and statistical analysis (Karon & Widener, 2001). Studies of the American Psychological Association (Gerber et al., 2011) and other clinical studies (Hilsenroth, 2007; Leichsenring, Biskup, Kreische, & Staats, 2005) show that psychoanalysis as a therapeutic method can be as effective as other popular forms of therapy.

Some researchers turned to psychoanalysis to apply some of its ideas of unconscious processes to the scientific study of the spiritual side of human existence. **Transpersonal psychology**, for example, is a theoretical and applied field that focuses on spiritual and transcendent states of consciousness (Vich, 1988), and it continues to attract attention today. Overall, the contemporary view of spirituality is that spiritual factors such as strong religious beliefs, prayer, meditation, and combinations thereof affect at least four interacting physiological systems: (1) the brain, (2) the endocrine system, (3) the peripheral nervous system, and (4) the immune system. These data are published in top peer-reviewed psychology journals (Powell, Shahabi, & Thoresen, 2003; Ray, 2004).

Transpersonal psychology
Transpersonal psychology is a theoretical and applied field that focuses on spiritual and transcendent states of consciousness.

Applying to History and Politics

Freud applied psychoanalysis to study personalities of historic figures; one of the most famous cases he studied was Leonardo da Vinci (1452–1519), the creator of the *Mona Lisa*. Freud explained Leonardo's scientific and artistic creativity as the result of his repressed inner conflicts. The *Mona Lisa*'s smile, according to Freud,

Summary

- Psychoanalysis is one of the most prominent traditions used to understand personality. Supporters praise psychoanalysis for its significant contribution to the scientific knowledge of the individual. Critics see psychoanalysis as an immense yet misleading speculation, brilliantly disguised in a fake academic uniform.

- First, psychoanalysis emphasized the dominant role of unconscious processes in human experience and behavior. Next, psychoanalysts stressed the importance of human sexuality in an individual's life. Then psychoanalysis emphasized the significance of early childhood experiences in the individual's life. And last, which is not least important for us, psychoanalysis was a type of treatment, or a sophisticated method of interaction between a professional therapist and a client.

- Freud accepted the prevailing scientific outlook of the 19th century that multiple forces, external and internal, cause humans to think and act. Some of these forces are instinctual drives. The individual, of course, seeks their gratification. Freud formulated and described two major mechanisms that regulate their activities: the pleasure principle and the reality principle.

- Freud advocated that boys and girls mature in similar ways but also differently. They both develop emotional attachment to their parents. The boys, however, are attached to their mothers, and girls are attached to their fathers. These conflicting attachments create a foundation for future psychological problems and influence every element of the child's and family's functioning.

- An individual's psyche (we can label it the *inner world* or *personality*) is made up of three levels (parts). The most primitive part of the personality is the id. The superego is the moral guide passing on imperatives of appropriate or inappropriate actions and thoughts. Making compromises between the id and the environment is the ego, which is guided by the reality principle.

- Adler was Freud's follower, yet he emphasized the importance of the relationships among siblings, not between the parents and the child as Freud did. Adler also questioned sexuality as the most dominant force in human life and one of the central points of Freud's psychoanalysis.

- Adler emphasized the importance of concepts such as organ inferiority and compensation. There are three general outcomes of an individual's compensatory efforts. The genius overcomes the old inferiority problems and achieves success and happiness. Compensation in this case brings success and delivers a new life free from pain of inferiority. In the case of degeneration, the attempted compensation is unsuccessful. The person falls out of the normal course of life and is unable to adjust to social rules. The third outcome is neurosis.

- Adler assumed that people are motivated primarily by future expectations. By forming them, people pursue their fictional final goal, called a self-ideal. This is the unifying principle of an individual's personality. Self-ideal can be achieved if an individual engages in striving toward superiority. People have social interest, or the desire to be connected with other people and to adapt positively to the perceived social environment.

- Jung used the term *analytical psychology* to distinguish his views from Freud's psychoanalysis. Jung suggested an impersonal layer in human psyche, which he called the collective unconscious. The content of the collective unconscious consists of archetypes, or images of the primordial (elemental, ancient) character. These are people's ancestral experiences, which appear in three universal ways: dreams, fantasies, and delusions.

- Jung theorized about extroversion and introversion. Extroverts, or individuals prone to extroversion, spontaneously embrace the world. Extroverts stream their libido outward, toward external objects. They commonly turn to other people and their ideas. Introverts tend to shy away from the world and turn their attention and interest to themselves. The introvert's libido streams inward, toward a subjective realm, thought, and fantasies. Introverts tend to seek internal resources to act.

- Jung was among the first psychologists to critically review the ethnocentric worldview of Western psychology.

- Over years, mainstream personality psychology based on experimental research developed unsettled relations with psychoanalysis. Some of its assumptions have been accepted. Many others have been criticized and rejected. Nevertheless, psychoanalysis offered them a choice and an educated opportunity to look into the depths of consciousness, to examine a world of experiences hidden from direct or superficial observation.

Key Terms

analysand 112

analytical psychology 120

archetypes 120

collective unconscious 120

compensation 116

death wish 109

ego 107

Eros 109

extroversion 123

genius 116

id 110

individuation 125

introversion 123

libido 109

organ inferiority 115

pleasure principle 107

psychoanalysis 105

psychobiography 132

reality principle 107

social interest 117

striving toward superiority 117

style of life 117

superego 111

thanatos 109

transpersonal psychology 131

unconscious 107

Evaluating What You Know

Describe the essence and the sources of the psychoanalytic tradition.

What were its major assumptions related to an individual?

In three or four sentences, describe the major views of Freud, Adler, and Jung as they are related to personality.

What are the most noticeable similarities and differences among these three scholars?

Explain the id, the ego, and the superego.

Explain the inferiority complex.

Explain and give an example of an archetype.

What did psychoanalysis give to scientific psychology?

How did psychoanalysts contribute to therapy?

A Bridge to the Next Chapter

Over the years, mainstream psychology based on experimental research developed unsettled relations with psychoanalysis. Two opinions related to personality psychology coexist:

- *Positive.* The works of Freud, Adler, and Jung had a notable impact on personality psychology. Psychoanalysis paid serious attention to the unconscious side of the individual's experience. Psychoanalysis also focused on early childhood and its role in the development of the individual's personality and elevated human sexuality as a legitimate research topic. Psychoanalysis had a big impact on modern psychotherapy as a key method of treatment of psychological problems.

- *Critical.* Psychoanalysis grossly exaggerated the role of unconscious processes in the individual's life. The impact of sexuality on individual development and interpersonal relationships was also overestimated. Psychoanalysts' focus on early childhood was valid, but their assumptions were wrong: It is clear now that infantile unconscious experiences do not play the central role in an individual's life.

Attempting to overcome the deficiency of "classical" (or the "first wave") psychoanalysis and hoping to address its key weaknesses, many doctors, social scientists, and psychology practitioners moved away from several initial postulates of psychoanalysis and created their own theories, which produced noticeable applications. However, they remained loyal to other key ideas of psychoanalytic theory. We will turn to their studies and applications (which we will call "the new wave") in the next chapter.

Maybe you think Adler's logic is applicable here as a way to explain that Gelhorn's journalism was a chance for her to overcome her "inferiority" and ineptness in social relationships, but that doesn't fit either, as Gellhorn had a very busy social life. She befriended many powerful politicians, renowned writers, and famous musical conductors. Her house was full of guests. She was married several times, and one of her spouses was the famous writer Ernest Hemingway. She had several love affairs, including ones with a legendary World War II general and a billionaire. She was acquainted with Eleanor Roosevelt. She wanted to create more, and she was never satisfied with what she had achieved. She often mistrusted top generals and politicians and preferred to interview the rank and file.

Perhaps Gelhorn was motivated by her anger. She was once asked if she was ever afraid, and she replied, "I feel angry, every minute, about everything." She maintained a consistent, lifelong anger toward the liars and frauds. She believed that the main problem with the world was that the crooks were running it. She also complained about a fear of boredom. Paraphrasing a Russian poet, she said, "If there is nothing else to do, scream." Gellhorn was longing to scream (Moorehead, 2003).

According to her own admission, there is "too much space in the world. I am bewildered by it, and mad with it. And this urge to run away from what I love is a sort of sadism I no longer pretend to understand" (Amidon, 2006, para. 3). She also revealed that she had never known complete love—except from Miss Edna, her mother. Gellhorn often compared herself to her mother, specifically to her integrity and honesty—ideals Gellhorn always wanted to achieve.

Maybe the true source of her motivation was her own self-challenge. She believed it was a constant desire to discover something within, to make a difference. Maybe her motivation was coming out of the search for a bigger, more meaningful self.

Are we all searching for a better self? Some of us quit in the middle of the search. Others never stop.

Sources: Amidon, 2006; Kozaryn, 1998; Moorhead, 2003.

Psychoanalysis and Society

Psychoanalysis influenced the studies of personality in several directions. The first influential wave already discussed in Chapter 4 included the development of the original psychoanalytic concepts of Freud, Jung, and Adler. We will call it classical psychoanalysis, for convenience. Its popularity grew in various aspects of society in the United States and in other parts of the world in the first half of the 20th century. The second wave included the new psychoanalytic theories that significantly advanced and changed classical psychoanalysis later in that century. The wave path involved the expansion and practical advancement of psychoanalysis in the fields of history, the humanities, and social sciences. We will discuss the new wave in this chapter.

Professional Applications

Few people in the early 1900s could foresee the degree of public fascination with psychoanalysis that would appear two decades later. In Europe, North America, and South America, classical psychoanalysis was gaining recognition as a legitimate theory and a form of therapy. Psychoanalytic clinics appeared. Clinicians used these facilities for at least two purposes: (1) to provide psychological help and (2) to train professionals interested in psychoanalysis. One of the earliest clinics was opened in London in 1920 and became an important center for training mental health specialists (Fraher, 2004).

Many followers of psychoanalysis wanted to study all areas of human behavior, not only those limited to mental illness. Psychiatrists, anthropologists, literary critics, journalists, and other professionals gradually discovered that their use of psychoanalysis generated money and could even bring a stable income. Where did the money come from? It came from several sources. One key source was paying clients with psychological problems. These people had money and needed help from professional therapists. Others were people who paid for books, journals, and magazines. Many also attended psychoanalytic lectures for a fee. They already had medical degrees and paid tuition to study psychoanalysis and learn therapeutic skills with the goal to become practitioners in the fields of psychoanalysis. Psychoanalysis, in a way, became a "product" for sale and purchase. Psychoanalysts could advertise their ideas, generate the demand for them, and create jobs. University students saw in psychoanalysis an interesting and rewarding career.

Popular Appeal

Learn about *self*! A new trend emerged among the educated circles mostly in the United States and Europe as early as in the 1920s. Newspaper articles, magazine stories, and pop-psychology books contributed to this frenzy. Upper-middle-class professionals, students, professors, and artists wanted to be psychoanalyzed or "psyched" (as people called it then). People were analyzing one another at home parties and other informal gatherings. Words such as *ego* and *libido* from the Freudian dictionary entered the vocabulary of the educated. In the spirit of American entrepreneurship, some people in the United States registered new educational companies and offered crash courses in psychoanalysis. For a fee, they promised a top-rated training in psychoanalysis. Criminologists turned to psychoanalysis to understand the personalities of violent criminals, thieves, habitual sex offenders, and swindlers. Educators learned about the superego to understand the inner world of the student. To explain an individual's behavioral problems as having something to do with his or her parents (as Freud taught), inferiority problems (as Adler suggested), or archetypes (based on Jung's theory) appeared scientific and modern. Serious discussions of human sexuality and its psychological attributes produced significant magazine sales.

The books by fiction writers such as Fyodor Dostoevsky (1821–1881), Franz Kafka (1883–1924), James Joyce (1882–1941), and Stefan Zweig (1881–1942), among others, generated special attention of the educated. These writers emerged to the reading public and critics as skilled "analysts" in their own way because they exposed the intimate, conflict-ridden, and seemingly bizarre worlds of some of their literary characters. Their obsessions, insecurities, suicidal thoughts, fantasies, psychological metamorphoses, and their constant soul searching appeared somewhat understandable, less mysterious, and in a way, human. The individual's inner world, thanks to psychoanalysis, was emerging as an interplay of identifiable forces. Psychoanalysts studied real, not imaginary, people with real problems (Karon & Widener, 2001). This focus on helping others and applying psychoanalytic theories contributed to a rise in the academic reputation and legitimacy of psychoanalysis.

Psychoanalysis and Ideology

Each country's conditions influenced the fate of psychoanalysis as a theory, as well as the application of its ideas in clinical, educational, and other spheres. Psychoanalysis gained attention in many countries. Freud's works appeared in several translations, including French, English, Spanish, Italian, and Russian. In the Soviet Union in the 1920s, some government officials initially supported psychoanalysis. Although they followed the official communist doctrine of "banning" or limiting the spread of scientific knowledge from capitalist countries, they saw psychoanalysis differently. They believed that psychoanalysis could help them reveal all the psychological weaknesses and flaws of the individual living in a capitalist society (Mursalieva, 2003). Several Soviet scholars received government funding to start psychoanalytic centers. For example, the Soviet psychoanalyst Sabrina Spielrein (1885–1942), Jung's former patient and confidante, returned to the Soviet Union in hopes of using psychoanalysis in her work with children (her life was popularized in the 2011 Hollywood movie *A Dangerous Method*, in which Keira Knightley played the role of Sabrina Spielrein).

However, official support of psychoanalysis in the Soviet Union ended by the 1930s. The theory of the power of unconscious processes in the life of the individual did not fit into communist ideology, which emphasized the importance of logic and reason. According to the communist ideology, all inner conflicts within the individual should disappear as soon as this person is placed in the conditions of social equality under the rules of communism (Etkind, 1993). From the 1930s to the 1980s, psychologists in the Soviet Union were permitted to write or teach about Freud and his views of personality only from a critical perspective.

In Germany after the Nazi party came to power in 1933, people who studied and taught psychoanalysis found themselves under attack. Nazism as an official ideology of the German state was rooted in deep-seated attitudes of racism, nationalism, and homophobia. Psychoanalysis was attacked for its alleged "decadent" and "perverted" views of the individual because it undermined the values of the German nation. In a short

CHECK AND APPLY YOUR KNOWLEDGE

1. What was the purpose of psychoanalytic clinics?
2. Why did many professionals turn to psychoanalysis in the first half of the 20th century?
3. Which movie or literary character (classic or modern) would you consider most interesting for psychoanalysis and why?

period, psychoanalysis was declared a "Jewish" science (because many early psychoanalysts were Jewish), which allowed the government to launch an open attack on professors and clinicians. Freud's books were confiscated from libraries and bookstores and burned; professors were openly insulted and physically attacked. Only a few lucky ones were able to emigrate from Germany to the United States or other countries. Many others perished in concentration camps. Psychoanalysis soon was officially banned in Germany as a theory and treatment method (Frosh, 2009).

Psychology and Psychoanalysis

Over the years, Western (and later non-Western) psychologists maintained an ambivalent position about the psychoanalytic view of the individual. From the early days of psychoanalysis, some psychologists saw it as just a fashionable trend. The American psychologist James Cattell, for example, called psychoanalysis an educated obsession. Many critics evaluated psychoanalysis as something that should be forgotten (Scott, 1908). Others saw psychoanalysis as a sophisticated conversational technique that could be useful in psychological therapy. Others saw the works of Freud, Adler, and Jung as an innovative contribution to psychology and an in-depth step into the study of the individual's personality. Still others reserved their judgment of psychoanalysis and wanted to see more studies before expressing their opinions about psychoanalysis and its theoretical and applied value (Dunlap, 1920).

Despite criticisms, psychoanalysis generated a growing public interest worldwide, especially in the West, and motivated many people, especially the young, to read psychology books and take psychology classes. A new crop of psychoanalysts, who were coming mostly from the clinical field, emerged. Not all of them liked to be called "psychoanalysts," yet the impact of the original psychoanalysis on their work was obvious. At the same time, they significantly changed the classical psychoanalysis and introduced a more dynamic, sophisticated view of personality.

Theoretical Expansions: Ego Psychology

Very few theories have had such a long-lasting impact on psychology as psychoanalysis. The followers of this theory were supporting some elements of it, refining others, and outright rejecting yet others. Overall, they were contributing to personality psychology by paying serious attention to a wide range of social factors contributing to an individual's development and experience.

Most of Freud's followers accepted the general idea that infantile conflicts should affect the individual's adult experiences and thus his or her personality features later in life. They also acknowledged that the individual is generally unaware of such conflicts. The awareness may be achieved in psychoanalytic therapy. After this point, with years passing, the interpretations grew increasingly diverse. Several trends in the new wave of psychoanalysis emerged (Fairbairn, 1963). Some psychoanalysts focused on a further examination of the ego and its functioning. As you remember, in Freudian theory the ego mostly represents the conscious aspects of the individual's personality. At this point, instead of looking at unconscious motives and their impact on the ego, researchers approached the individual as functioning in real-life circumstances. A new field of research called **ego psychology** began to focus on how the ego interacts with this social environment.

Ego psychology
Ego psychology focuses on how the ego interacts with its social environment.

It was a promising approach. The emerging ego psychology was in some ways a compromise between classical psychoanalysis and experimental psychology taught at universities: Psychoanalysts could now claim more legitimacy among professional psychologists who still had a difficult time accepting major postulates of psychoanalysis. Ego psychology also reintroduced consciousness as a legitimate area of study (Hartmann, 1958). Because of the emphasis of ego psychology on rationality, its basic research and findings were seemingly applicable not only to therapy but also to learning, education, and psychological testing (Sandler, 1985).

Ego psychology has never been a cohesive theory with an undisputed list of key terms and an advanced methodology. Ego psychology was frequently used to describe a wide range of studies generally focusing on the mechanisms of ego functioning. To describe the most important findings of ego psychology, as well as its contributions to personality psychology, we will examine the work of two prominent psychologists: Anna Freud and Erik Erikson.

Works of Anna Freud

Anna Freud (1895–1982) was the youngest of Sigmund Freud's six offspring. Born and raised in Vienna, she expressed her interest in psychoanalysis very early in her life. She started reading her father's articles and books at the age of 15 (some commentators considered this inappropriate because of the strong sexual context of these works). She chose a career as a schoolteacher, for which she received professional training in Germany. Anna escaped persecution by the Nazis and emigrated with her parents from Austria to London in 1938. There she founded a child therapy clinic, which is still in existence and is now called the Anna Freud Centre. She continued to work in the United Kingdom for many years, earning many awards and honorary degrees, including the Decoration of Honor for Services to the Republic of Austria, which was her birth land.

Anna could not escape the fact that she was the daughter of an internationally famous researcher and therapist. Nevertheless, it wasn't her father's reputation alone that brought Anna worldwide recognition and a place in psychology textbooks. She was above all a talented scholar, a dedicated teacher, and a successful therapist. Her training as a teacher and work with children informed her later work as a therapist.

Photo 5.1 Anna Freud helped to break the "glass ceiling" for women in psychology. Today, more women than men in the United States and Canada major in psychology. Why do you think this trend occurred?

Everett Collection Historical/Alamy

She emphasized that children could not explain their psychological problems as efficiently as most adults could. Medical and educational professionals working with children, she argued, should develop special skills to understand children's symptoms and interpret them (Bruehl, 1990).

Her most influential book was *The Ego and the Mechanisms of Defense* (1966), in which she focused on the inner struggles of the individual. It was above all the struggle of the ego with the overwhelming demands of the id, on the one hand, and powerful restrictions imposed by reality, on the other. Ego defenses or **defense mechanisms** are specific unconscious structures that enable an individual to avoid awareness of unpleasant, anxiety-arousing issues. The function of the ego is to defend itself from these issues. Such a defense is set to protect a person's ego against anxiety, shame, guilt, or other emotional challenges. The defense is launched automatically and remains mostly unconscious. This means that a person's defenses occur without this individual's awareness of them.

To an outside observer, there is quite often a puzzling connection between specific circumstances and the person's responses to them. For example, why does a young man suddenly start acting immaturely and irresponsibly after announcing an engagement to his girlfriend? One would expect quite the opposite type of behavior from a man who is about to get married, right? The problem is that we sometimes cannot find rational explanations for someone's behavior because defenses are launched to

Defense mechanisms The specific unconscious structures that enable individuals to avoid awareness of unpleasant, anxiety-arousing issues are called defense mechanisms.

schools that included Yale, the University of California at Berkeley, and Harvard. Erikson made a significant contribution to the psychoanalytic tradition by turning to sociocultural influences on an individual's development.

On the basis of his observations of hundreds of patients, Erikson proposed that the ego is supposed to develop in stages. The individual is likely to pass through eight of such **developmental stages** (see **Table 5.2**). At each of them, the ego faces age-related developmental challenges resulting in a conflict. Different challenges may lead to different types of thinking and acting. A person's ego may be weakened or strengthened by gaining a greater adaptation capacity (Erikson, 1950). Only then, through a healthy adaptation, is a positive, healthy outcome of a conflict possible. But if the crisis has not been resolved, the ego loses strength, which results in poor adaptation. For instance, a 4-year-old girl helps her parents clean the table after dinner (the girl initiates this action), but unfortunately while doing so, she breaks an expensive plate. However, the parents do not punish the girl for this accident and even praise her for her willingness to help. In this case, her initiative has been rewarded. This reward contributes to the development of a sense of direction or purpose. If the parents had focused on the broken plate instead and angrily told their daughter not to help anymore, this could have generated a negative outcome—the girl would have begun forming a sense of unworthiness. We will return to another discussion of these stages in Chapter 11.

Erikson coined the term **identity crisis**—an inner state of tension due to a person's inability to see and accept self with confidence and certainty (see **Figure 5.1**). Erikson maintained that every individual has to possess the sense of personal sameness and continuity. This sense should not be significantly different from the image we form of the outside world, which also has these features of sameness and continuity. Identity crisis is a result of tension or conflict between the developing ego and the changing world.

Developmental stages (Erikson's) In Erikson's view, developmental stages are the periods of a life-span in which the ego faces age-related developmental challenges, usually resulting in a conflict.

Identity crisis An identity crisis is an inner state of tension due to a person's inability to see and accept self with confidence and certainty.

TABLE 5.2 ● Developmental Stages According to Erikson (1950)

Stage	Ego Crisis	Age	Positive Outcome
1	Basic trust versus mistrust	0–2	Hope
2	Autonomy versus shame and doubt	2–3	Will
3	Initiative versus guilt	3–5	Purpose
4	Industry versus inferiority	5–12	Competence
5	Ego identity versus role confusion	Adolescence	Fidelity
6	Intimacy versus isolation	Young adult	Love
7	Generativity (nurturing things that outlast the individual) versus stagnation	Adulthood	Care
8	Ego integrity versus despair	Maturity	Wisdom

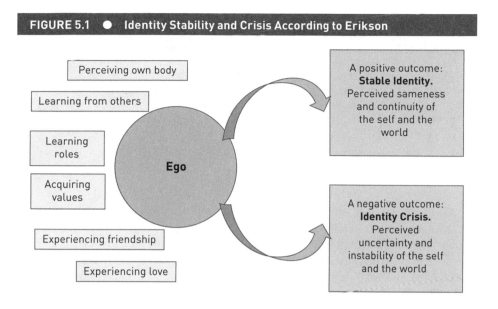

FIGURE 5.1 ● Identity Stability and Crisis According to Erikson

Perceiving own body

Learning from others

Learning roles

Acquiring values

Experiencing friendship

Experiencing love

Ego

A positive outcome: **Stable Identity.** Perceived sameness and continuity of the self and the world

A negative outcome: **Identity Crisis.** Perceived uncertainty and instability of the self and the world

Because the world is continuously transforming, new challenges continuously arise. This is where Erikson broke with a main postulate of psychoanalysis, according to which the personality is shaped primarily during infancy and early childhood. He insisted on the importance of continuing experiences and adjustments in an individual's life.

Identity crisis is not necessarily a problem or a malady. It can simply be the source of a person's new mode of thinking and actions. To illustrate, Erikson turned to historic figures and speculated about their lives. For example, he interpreted the life of Martin Luther (1483–1546), one of the most significant, historic figures of the Protestant Reformation (Erikson, 1962). Erikson claimed that Luther's challenge against the Catholic Church was, in fact, an attempt to address his personal identity crisis. He speculates that Luther carried an unconscious goal to do something significant in life, and when he did not achieve this goal, he experienced an inner crisis, which was exacerbated by his conflict with his father. So the inner conflict of one man apparently resulted in the historic transformation of the entire Western culture!

In another book (1969) written about the great Indian revolutionary Mohandas Gandhi (1869–1948), Erikson further developed the idea of different forces shaping the individual's personality. The early death of Gandhi's father and an unsuccessful marriage brought Gandhi significant challenges. Along with these challenges came the powerful unconscious desire to overcome his personal imperfections. Yet his early experiences with political protest in India helped Gandhi reach a conclusion about the dangers and uselessness of violence. In his view, nonviolence, called *Satyagraha*, should be the solution to most social injustices. *Satyagraha* should come not from our weakness but rather from our strength. This strength is found not in muscles but rather in our sense of dignity. Erikson sincerely believed that nonviolence was a perfect condition to develop a healthy ego. Longitudinal studies showed that engagement

Eight virtues

in multiple roles during early adulthood was positively correlated with generativity in Erikson's theory (Vandewater, Ostrove, & Stewart, 1997). Erikson defined an individual with a healthy or mature personality as one whose ego possesses the eight virtues—hope, will, purpose, competence, fidelity, love, care, and wisdom. These virtues emerge in progression, from a positive resolution at each stage of development. Erikson believed the goal of psychotherapy was to encourage the growth of whatever virtues a person was missing so that person could achieve happiness (Erikson, 1968). His ideas generated interest and found support with many psychologists in the West.

Erikson and Global Applications

Erikson's views allow us to approach the issue of whether psychological ideas established in one culture are applicable to another. Some studies show that on the one hand, Erikson's theory of the developmental stages could be applicable to various cultures (Gardiner, Mutter, & Kosmitzki, 1998). For example, Erikson's views correspond in many ways with Indian philosophical traditions aimed at self-transformation through insight into the nature of self (Paranjpe, 1998). However, Erikson's developmental stages indicate a general sequence that is not necessarily parallel to the stages of other ethnic groups. Unlike most adults in economically developed societies, people in many underdeveloped parts of the world face a very insecure reality. Hunger, violence, instability, chronic ecological problems, and political cataclysms are often the permanent focus of these people's daily concerns. Various erratic disturbances present a wide range of unpredictable problems, and the sequence of these problems is different from what appears in Erikson's classification. Therefore, more immediate strategies of survival "here and now" are likely to dominate these people's lives, not necessarily long-term inner conflicts related to the past. Furthermore, the issue of an individual's identity is likely not concluded by adolescence, as Erikson suggested. Studies of immigrants to the United States show that identity continues to evolve in many people during adulthood, long after the period Erikson had proposed in his classification (Shiraev & Levy, 2013). With increasing global migration, people's identity is likely to undergo changes as they experience social transition in their lives. Erikson assumed that people should have choices in terms of their identity or beliefs. However, in many parts of the world, people's identities and lifestyles are prescribed at birth. They have to accept a particular religion, social status, profession, and place

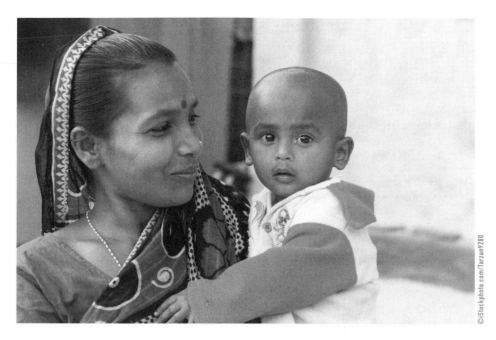

Photo 5.2 Erikson said that people should have choices when selecting identities, such as religious, social, and political views. In your opinion, are most people really free to choose their identities?

to live. People have fewer choices, and therefore, their transition from one stage to another may be "smoother" than for people who have more choices.

It is also important to realize that in some cultures, social maturation is not associated with increased independence, as happens in the West, but rather with increased interdependence. In India, for example, the Hindu concept of self historically has not been focused on one's autonomy but rather on being an integral part of a larger whole or group (Kurtz, 1992). Studies show that the sequence and timing of the developmental stages may be at times similar and yet different in varying ethnic groups—for example, in black and white samples in South Africa: White women were expected to solve the identity crisis earlier than men, and black men tended to resolve the identity crisis only after age 40 (Ochse & Plug, 1986).

Like Erik Erikson and Anna Freud, other prominent scientists preserved some of the initial ideas of psychoanalysis, but moved further away from it.

CHECK AND APPLY YOUR KNOWLEDGE

1. What is an identity crisis?

2. Why did Erikson study Martin Luther and Mohandas Gandhi?

3. Is Erikson's theory applicable across cultures? What are these theory cross-cultural limitations?

Theoretical Expansions: Away From the Libido Concept

This section focuses on the works of Karen Horney, Henry Murray, Harry Stack Sullivan, and Jacques Lacan, who made significant contributions to personality psychology. One of the major areas of their revision of classical psychoanalysis was the libido concept.

The Individual's Basic Anxiety

A significant revision of the Freudian concept of libido came from Karen Horney (1885–1952). Born and raised in Germany, she received a medical degree from the University of Berlin. In 1920, Horney took up a position within the Institute for Psychoanalysis in Berlin, where she lectured for several years. She immigrated to the United States in 1930, where she continued her medical work and research. She recognized the power of unconscious conflicts and their roots in infancy and childhood. Yet she criticized Freud's approach to sexuality and the concept of libido. She moved beyond these classical postulates as she began focusing more on the psychology of women.

Horney rejected the Freudian view that the main source of female unconscious conflicts is the woman's sense of inferiority. Men also have reason to feel inferior to women and to be envious of women, she argued. One of the several reasons for envy is men's inability to bear children. She also critiqued the concept of the Oedipus complex, suggesting that children's ambivalent relationships with their parents are most likely caused by specific circumstances of their lives and not necessarily by sexual factors alone (Horney, 1950).

Karen Horney broadened the traditional understanding of *neurosis*, a catchall label popular in the 20th century to describe a range of the individual's persistent anxiety- and mood-related symptoms. She considered neurosis a more common, widespread phenomenon among individuals than most psychologists believed. In Horney's view, neurosis was a general maladjustment between an individual and a traumatic event or development. She argued that we pursue our basic needs, including but not limited to affection, power, companionship, perfection, and achievement; we try to satisfy these needs, yet we cannot satisfy them all. So we develop coping strategies: In some cases, we move forward to satisfy our needs, and in others, we shift away from our needs or defy them. For example, a person feeling lonely after a breakup will be open to new experiences and seek new acquaintances. This could be a healthy solution. Under different circumstances, however, loneliness can lead to a deepening frustration, further social isolation, depression, irritation, or even aggressive behavior.

Horney referred to **basic anxiety** to describe an individual's feelings of loneliness and hopelessness. Basic anxiety often causes *counterhostility*, which is an individual's emotional response to intimidating situations. Such negative feelings originate mostly during childhood and are based on the child's relationships with parents. Horney emphasized that the nature of these early traumatic events does not have to be sexual. The child's fear of becoming helpless or lonely creates anxiety, which may produce abnormal responses that constitute the foundation for a neurosis. Looking for sources

Basic anxiety In Karen Horney's system, basic anxiety is exhibited in feelings of loneliness, hopelessness, and counter-hostility (emotional responses to hostile situations).

of basic anxiety, Horney focused on broad social and cultural factors affecting the child's development (Paris, 1994).

She paid particular attention to the psychological development of women and the problems they faced in society. She pointed out that many psychological problems relating to women's self-esteem, confidence, and psychological stability are due to old sexist customs and traditional societal expectations about women's role in society. In her view, society encourages women to depend on men and worship their strength and wealth, but she sees therapy, including self-therapy, as the solution to social inequalities between men and women.

Interpersonal Psychoanalysis

Harry Stack Sullivan (1892–1949) made an important contribution to the study of personality. He focused on interpersonal relationships. Born in the United States, he enriched and expanded psychoanalysis based on his theoretical research and clinical work with patients. Sullivan laid the groundwork for understanding the individual based on the network of relationships in which he or she is involved. He believed that cultural forces are largely responsible for the individual's psychological problems (Rioch, 1985). He was among the first to introduce the term **significant other** to refer to the most intimate and important person in the individual's life: a partner, a fiancée, or a spouse (Sullivan, 1953). Sullivan also wrote about self-esteem as a special arrangement of traits developed in childhood. These traits often receive positive appraisal and support from adults, which helps the child avoid excessive anxiety.

Sullivan preserved several core concepts of the Freudian system by emphasizing the importance of unconscious mechanisms and dedicating significant attention to a person's early childhood experiences. Like Karen Horney, he studied loneliness and its early impact on psychological development of the child. Like Anna Freud, he believed that defenses reduce an individual's anxiety, yet they often lead to inaccurate interpretations of reality. During early development, children develop certain self-perceptions and thus construct the world based on such perceptions. For example, early in life, the child develops the concept of the **bad-me**: an early awareness of self as disapproved by the adults. This awareness is a center for the development of later anxiety. However, children can see themselves from a different angle. The **good-me** is the child's awareness of an aspect of self that brings rewards, such as approval or kindness from the parents or other adults. This awareness serves as a foundation for understanding the whole self as good. The **not-me** refers to awareness of certain individual features that the child does not want to consider as part of his or her life and experience. The not-me is kept out of awareness by pushing it deep into the unconscious. An individual's personality is formed through a complex set of relationships and interactions. Sullivan maintained that people develop their psychological traits during adolescence and even later during adulthood.

A Complex Identity

The French psychiatrist and social scientist Jacques Lacan (1901–1981) made a contribution to personality psychology in his studies of the individual's identity and its

Significant other The most intimate and important person in a person's life—a partner, a fiancé(e), or a spouse—is known as a significant other.

Bad-me In Sullivan's system, the bad-me is an early awareness of self as disapproved by the adults.

Good-me In Sullivan's system, the good-me is an early awareness of an aspect of self that brings rewards from the parents or other adults.

Not-me In Sullivan's system, not-me refers to the early awareness of certain individual features that the child does not want to consider as part of his or her experience.

CHECK AND APPLY YOUR KNOWLEDGE

1. What is a significant other? Who are your significant others? Why are they so significant to you?
2. Explain the good-me, the bad-me, and the not-me concepts.
3. Which role do "they" (in Lacan's theory) play in a person's development?

development. Lacan was a practicing therapist whose educational seminars in the 1950s attracted significant attention in France and beyond. His theory was rooted in a diverse set of ideas from psychiatry, history, philosophy, and anthropology. One of his assumptions referred to the significance of others in an individual's formation of identity. By the middle of the second year, children are capable of recognizing their own images in the mirror. This experience brings the child pleasure because he or she perceives this image as something unified, holistic, and separate. Children perceive their own bodies as a collection of poorly coordinated pieces. The child initially feels tension because of the contradiction between the image of the self and the image of the body. To reduce this tension, the child soon identifies with the image, which forms the ego (Evans, 2005). This is a moment of joy because the child is capable of feeling his or her mastery over the body. However, soon the child realizes this mastery is insufficient because of the parent's power over the child. This may cause the formation of anxiety (Lacan, 2007).

Lacan retained one of the main postulates of the classical psychoanalysis: The individual is born into the world with essential needs that require constant gratification. However, other people begin to play a crucial role in the development of these needs. Early in life, individuals learn to desire things not because they need them, but because other people *tell* them that they need them (Lacan, 1988). In early years, as Lacan suggested, the child primarily tries to grasp what the mother or father desire. Then come symbols, such as the spoken and written language. What is important in our lives is largely decided by others. Certain words begin playing an important regulatory role in our lives. For example, using the name of the father ("Your father will be very angry") emphasizes a prohibitive function of the father (Johnston, 2014; Sharpe, 2008).

Psychoanalysis and Social Behavior

Psychology of Women

Many ideas of psychoanalysis that applied psychoanalysis to the individual's social behavior were positively received among social scientists. Helene Deutsch (1884–1982), was Freud's favorite student and a follower as a researcher and professional. After working in Vienna as a therapist, she moved to the United States in 1935 to escape her imminent arrest and death due to the unfolding political terror in her country. There she published a number of scholarly articles, but she became well-known for her two-volume book *The Psychology of Women* (Deutsch, 1944, 1945).

This book was a major early contribution to the field of psychology of women (Chapter 11), and it received attention from many professionals. Like Karen Horney, she received significant support and at the same time faced criticisms for her vision of the woman's role in contemporary society. She described women's ego as affected by the unconscious desire to overcome psychological deficiencies associated with their realization as young girls that their destiny is as a wife and mother. Deutsch believed that women have to challenge and overcome many complexes associated with their biological and social roles. Among such problems were their unconscious tendency to masochism (self-inflicted pain and suffering) and self-enslavement. While most social scientists at that time were looking into social and political causes of gender inequality, Deutsch emphasized psychological ones. Critics dismissed these ideas and believed Deutsch focused on the wrong causes, claiming problems that women faced were not about their psychological complexes but rather about social injustice and gender inequality.

Personality and Politics

A creative view of personality emerged from the works of Erich Fromm (1900–1980). His *Escape From Freedom* (published first in Britain as *Fear of Freedom*) is one of the most significant early significant contributions to psychology and social sciences (Fromm, 1941/1994). True freedom, Fromm wrote, is the individual's ability to have power and resources to realize their own potentials. Unfortunately, many people cannot embrace their freedom because they cannot make their own choices. They have too many of them. As a result, people follow three destructive paths: conformity, authoritarianism, and destruction. When people conform, they avoid anxiety by uncritically accepting someone else's ideas and actions. They also accept authoritarianism as an uncritical, judgmental form of intolerance against other people and ideas. Ultimately, some individuals turn to destruction because the authoritarian social order causes anxiety and insecurity (Fromm, 1947).

Fromm criticized dictatorship, Nazism, fascism, and communism as abusive forms of government and destroyers of individual freedom. He was also critical of capitalism. In his view, capitalism forces people to embrace consumerism and makes them long for material success. Fromm believed that the individual could be improved only if capitalism undergoes a transformation after the government chooses collectivist policies of equality.

Fromm researched **authoritarian personality**—a complex pattern of behavior and thought based on the individual's faithful acceptance of the power of authority, order, and subordination (see **Figure 5.2**). Discussions about authoritarian personality drew significant attention and sparked new research on this subject for many years (Adorno, Frenkel-Brunswik, Levinson, & Sanford, 1950). The interest in these studies continues today. One of the main assumptions of this research, which used

Authoritarian personality An authoritarian personality is exhibited in a complex pattern of behavior and thought based on the individual's faithful acceptance of the power of authority, order, and subordination.

FIGURE 5.2 ● Model of the Authoritarian Personality

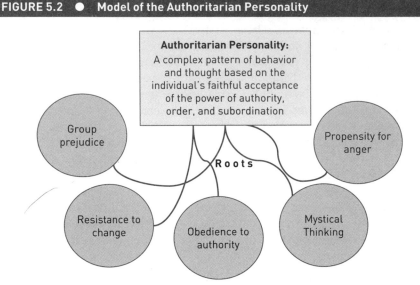

methods including psychobiography, surveys, and laboratory experiments, was that some individuals develop a stable pattern of authoritarian traits due to their childhood experiences. Such individuals are prone to mystical thinking and prejudice against particular individuals and social groups, especially ethnic minorities and gays. They are obedient to authority figures, such as parents, teachers, and political leaders, and resistant to social innovation while rejecting new societal trends. These individuals are also prone to anger and violence. The most remarkable finding of early and later studies was that the authoritarian personality type is very common in ordinary people. These individuals tend to endorse authoritarian methods of government and enthusiastically support dictators. They also tend to welcome injustice, oppression, and discrimination because they feel comfortable discriminating and oppressing. High scorers on authoritarianism have been associated with a punitive parenting style that had adverse consequences for parent–child relationships (Peterson, Smirles, & Wentworth, 1997). We will return to this subject again in Chapter 7.

Psychoanalysis and Judaism

Stereotypical claims that psychoanalysis was a cultural "creation" of a few Jewish researchers and doctors are as old as psychoanalysis itself. Sigmund Freud was aware of this critical view and constantly denied that psychoanalysis had something to do with Judaism (Freud, as you remember, did not practice his religion). Yet among the founders of psychoanalysis, there were many from the Jewish faith. At least two points of view exist on this matter.

Some historians believe that psychoanalysis as a theory and movement was indeed rooted in Jewish cultural and group identity. For the Jews, psychoanalysis of the early 20th century appeared as a cultural affair—a source of confidence and collective self-verification. It was a suitable way out of the collective mentality of an oppressed people (Cuddihy, 1974). Until the 20th century, most European countries had legal restrictions limiting the participation of Jews in public education, politics, and social life. Russia simply restricted most Jews early in the century from living in big cities. The rapid development of psychoanalysis coincided with both political and social liberation of the European Jews. Many young Jewish college graduates and doctors turned to psychoanalysis because it offered them inspiration, a chance to have an occupation, and a stable income.

On the other hand, a critical thinker should express caution about a strong connection of psychoanalysis to the Jewish culture. Fechner, Wundt, James, Watson, Bekhterev, and Skinner were Christians, but there is little reason to define experimental psychology as a Christian cultural phenomenon. Furthermore, in countries such as Great Britain, Russia, and Switzerland before the 1920s, there were few Jews among psychoanalysts (Leibin, 1994; Shorter, 1997). An influx of Jewish psychoanalysts to North America in the 1930s was part of a massive emigration of European Jews from Germany and Austria due to genocidal policies. However, a sizable portion of these psychoanalysts as well as other scientists and professionals were secular, and some of them were distinct atheists.

Contributions of the New Wave's Psychoanalysts

Most psychoanalysts of the "new wave," despite disagreements, shared several basic views of the individual's experience and behavior:

1. They focused on unconscious processes regulating an individual's experience, action, and personality. They also emphasized the crucial role of unconscious factors in psychological abnormalities.

2. They all stressed the crucial role of childhood and its impact on an individual's personality and its development.

3. They offered a therapeutic method to address a patient's psychological problems and treat them.

4. Many psychoanalysts maintained that not only an individual's life but also society and culture could be explained with the help of psychoanalytic ideas.

The main reformation of "classical" psychoanalysis in the mid-20th century was taking place in several areas. Anna Freud and Karen Horney turned to a more rational or conscious aspect of an individual's experience and began to examine the functioning of the ego. This focus allowed them to turn to empirical data accessible through direct observation, which improved the reputation of psychoanalysis among psychologists. Next, most psychoanalysts moved away from the Freudian assumptions about the sexual nature of the unconscious conflicts. Furthermore, social scientists such as Helene Deutsch and Erich Fromm began to apply psychoanalytic ideas to other fields of social sciences and the humanities.

CHECK AND APPLY YOUR KNOWLEDGE

1. Who wrote *The Psychology of Women*? What was the book about? *Hellen Deuch*
2. Who wrote *Escape From Freedom*? What was the book about? *From Erich*
3. Explain the authoritarian personality. Describe its main features. What is a modern example of this type?

Psychoanalysis was based on scientific determinism, a fundamental position according to which mental processes are determined by past events (Bjerre, 1916). The belief that human behavior and experience could be explained in terms of their predetermining causes—the idea defended in behaviorism and psychoanalysis—is a mainstream view of today's academic psychology.

Psychoanalysts also shared a view that an individual should adjust to the demands of inner drives and societal restrictions. Psychological problems reflect a person's inability to adjust. The major goal of psychoanalysis as a therapeutic method is to restore lost balance or reduce the suffering caused by inner conflicts. Psychoanalysts believed in guided therapies, deeper self-understanding, and gradual self-improvements. Furthermore, many analysts expanded the earlier suggestions of Freud about the necessity to improve humanity via societal changes. This was not about a social revolution. The main idea was that people could improve as human beings if they encountered fewer restrictions and social taboos related to gender roles, unlearned their ethnic and religious prejudices, and found socially accepted ways of displaying their aggressive tendencies.

On the companion website, see a discussion of the Murray report on Hitler. Get access to the original report.

Questions
What were Hitler's most significant psychological problems reflected in the report? What evidence did the report provide to support these conclusions?

Applying the Psychoanalysis of the New Wave

Psychoanalysts believed that the path to understanding the minds of other people begins with an examination of our own mind. Personal letters, diaries, and self-portraits become rich sources of information about the individual's personality. Nobel Prize winner Eric Kandel, for example, examined self-portraits of several famous artists living about 100 years ago. Knowing facts of their biographies, he compared these facts with their self-portraits. His goal was to find the connections between the portraits and emotions that the artists should have experienced in their lives (Kandel, 2012). If self-portraits are a way of knowing about the personalities of their artists, then we should be able to apply the same method to analyzing people's online posts.

Early Political Psychology

Another noticeable application of the psychoanalytic view belongs to Henry Murray (1893–1988). Murray built foundations for **political psychology**—the field examining psychological factors in politics as well as an individual's political behavior. Murray and his colleagues wrote a psychological profile of German dictator Adolf Hitler (Murray, 1943). Their report was a detailed psychological examination of the facts known about Hitler combined with psychoanalytic discussions about the causes of his cruelty and erratic behavior. Murray gave specific recommendations for anti-Hitler propaganda that could have been launched via mass media and leaflets. This analysis of a political leader was one of the earliest attempts at "long-distance" psychological profiling—a method that is used today by practitioners as a source of supplementary information about certain individuals, such as political leaders of foreign countries. Today, political psychology is an influential field of studies and applications.

Political psychology Political psychology is the field of study that examines psychological factors in politics as well as an individual's political behavior.

Testing

Main ideas of psychoanalysis influenced testing methods used in clinical practice. One of Henry Murray's major contributions to psychology was the Thematic Apperception Test (TAT) developed with Christina Morgan (Murray, 1938). It was a projective test, which in its original form contained 19 pictures. A person undergoing testing was asked to tell a story about each of these pictures, which were sufficiently vague to leave enough to the imagination of the person taking the test. Murray's main idea was that the test taker in the process of picture interpretation would reveal specific psychological needs that are difficult to identify by other methods. Murray used the term **themas** to describe stories or interpretations projecting fantasy imagery onto an objective stimulus, such as a picture. When a person experiences a press (an external influence) on his or her needs, a thema is activated to bring this person satisfaction and the sense of power, affiliation, and achievement. By studying these themas, a trained psychologist could reveal the true nature of this person's hopes, wishes, or specific psychological problems (Murray, 1938). TAT received global recognition and was translated into many languages.

Themas In Murray's system, themas are stories or interpretations that project fantasy imagery onto an objective stimulus.

Contributing to Neurophysiology

Many psychoanalysts believed that the structure and functions of the human mind were intimately related to the structure and functions of the brain. For example, an individual obsessive or avoidant behavior or defense mechanisms that make one individual different from another were supposed to be explained by the brain's functioning. Yet for decades in the past century, brain researchers did not have the

© Photo Researchers, Inc./Alamy

Photo 5.3 Murray believed that by studying a person's descriptions of pictures, a trained psychologist could better understand this individual's inner world. What are the weaknesses of this method?

Visual Review

INTRODUCTION AND CONTEXTS	→	KEY THEORIES AND APPROACHES	→	APPLICATIONS

The **new wave** included several psychoanalytic theories that significantly advanced and changed classical psychoanalysis later in the 20th century

Anna Freud studied the ego and key defense mechanisms

Early political psychology

Erikson proposed the main stages of individual development

Psychological testing

The wave path involved the expansion and practical advancement of psycho-analysis in the fields of:

- Psychology
- History
- The humanities
- Social sciences

Horney focused on the individual's basic anxiety

Neurophysiology

The new wave contributed to the study of society and social behavior

Therapeutic methods

Summary

- Psychoanalysis influenced the studies of personality from several directions. New intriguing theories and their applications appeared. Despite criticisms, psychoanalysis generated a growing public interest worldwide and motivated many people, especially the young, to read psychology books and take psychology classes.

- Each country's conditions influenced the fate of psychoanalysis as a theory as well as the application of its ideas in clinical, educational, and other spheres.

- Most Freud followers accepted the general idea that infantile conflicts should affect the individual's adult experiences and thus his or her personality features later in life. They also acknowledged that the individual is generally unaware of such conflicts. The awareness may be achieved in psychoanalytic therapy.

- A new field of research called ego psychology began to focus on how the ego interacts with social environment.

- Anna Freud's *The Ego and the Mechanisms of Defense* focused on the inner struggles of the individual. She wrote about the struggle of the ego with the overwhelming demands of the id, on the one hand, and powerful restrictions imposed by reality, on the other.

- Ego defenses can be described as defense mechanisms, or specific unconscious structures that enable an individual to avoid awareness of unpleasant, anxiety-arousing issues.

- On the basis of his observations of hundreds of patients, Erik Erikson proposed that the ego is supposed to develop in stages. The individual is likely to pass through eight of such developmental stages. At each of them, the ego faces an age-related developmental challenge

that results in a conflict. Different challenges may lead to different types of thinking and acting.

- Erikson coined the term *identity crisis*—an inner state of tension due to a person's inability to see and accept self with confidence and certainty.

- Karen Horney rejected the Freudian view that the main source of female unconscious conflicts is the woman's sense of inferiority. Men also have reason to feel inferior to women and to be envious of women, she argued.

- Horney broadened the traditional understanding of *neurosis*, a catchall label popular in the 20th century to describe a range of the individual's persistent anxiety- and mood-related symptoms. She considered neurosis a more common, widespread phenomenon among individuals than most psychologists believed. Neurosis, in her view, was a general maladjustment between an individual and a traumatic event or development. Horney referred to basic anxiety to describe an individual's feelings of loneliness and hopelessness.

- Harry Stack Sullivan focused on interpersonal relationships. He was among the first to introduce the term *significant other*, which refers to the most intimate and important person in an individual's life: a partner, a fiancé(e), or a spouse.

- The French psychiatrist and social scientist Jacques Lacan made a contribution to personality psychology in his studies of the individual's identity and its development. Lacan retained one of the main postulates of the classical psychoanalysis: The individual is born into the world with essential needs that require constant gratification. However, other people begin to play a crucial role in the development of these needs. Early in life, the individuals learn how to desire things not because they need them but rather because other people *tell* them that they need them.

- Erich Fromm researched authoritarian personality—a complex pattern of behavior and thought based on the individual's faithful acceptance of the power of authority, order, and subordination. Discussions about authoritarian personality drew significant attention and sparked new research on this subject for many years.

- Henry Murray and other psychoanalysts built foundations for political psychology—the field examining psychological factors in politics as well as an individual's political behavior.

- Besides political psychology, psychoanalysts of the "second wave" contributed to psychological testing, social psychology, psychological therapy, and views of sexuality, among other things.

Key Terms

authoritarian personality 155

bad-me 153

basic anxiety 152

defense mechanisms 145

developmental stages
    (Erikson's) 148

ego psychology 144

good-me 153

identity crisis 148

neuropsychoanalysis 160

not-me 153

political psychology 159

psychodrama 161

significant other 153

themas 159

Evaluating What You Know

What are the main features of psychoanalysis's new wave in the study of personality?

What are the most important differences between Freud's views and the views of the new-wave psychologists?

What are the major ideas of Anan Freud and Erik Erikson?

Explain a defense mechanism and give two to three examples.

How do individuals move from stage to stage, according to Erikson?

What are the areas of application of the new wave of psychoanalysis?

What is neuropsychoanalysis?

A Bridge to the Next Chapter

Because of their belief in the possibility of improving humanity through social changes, psychoanalysis shared progressive ideas. Supporters of progressivism, as you should remember from Chapter 2, believed in the opportunity to apply scientific knowledge to improve many spheres of social life. Progressivism in psychology also emphasized the importance of applied knowledge in three areas: health care, education, and social services. Psychoanalysts believed in their science as a new force, capable of changing society and providing people with a new vision of a peaceful and healthy life. It is probably true that psychology today is rooted in the same genuinely progressive view.

Yet psychoanalysis was most likely missing, as its critics insisted, a few important features. It did not embrace measurement. It did not accept the audacity of carefully crafted experimental research. It was somewhat indifferent to the person's acting, moving, and making decisions. Other psychologists saw the individual's personality from other angles.

At this point, we are ready to study another remarkable and highly influential tradition in psychology that focused exclusively on the individual's overt behavior.

WANT A BETTER GRADE?

Get the tools you need to sharpen your study skills. Access practice quizzes, eFlash-cards, web exercises, and multimedia at edge.sagepub.com/shiraevpersonality

⑤SAGE edge™

Anna Bryukhanova/E+/Getty Images

The Behavioral Learning Tradition

"What is love except another name for the use of positive reinforcement?"

—B. F. Skinner (1904–1990), American psychologist

Learning Objectives

After reading this chapter, you should be able to:

- Identify the main principles and historical contexts of the behavioral learning tradition
- Explain why early comparative psychologists linked animal and human behavior
- Discuss the principles of reflexology and conditioned reflexes
- Identify Watson's three founding principles of behaviorism
- Discuss Holt's and Tolman's findings on molar responses and purposive or operational behaviorism
- Discuss Skinner's principles of operant conditioning
- Discuss Rotter's and Bandura's social learning theories
- Identify ways to apply the principles of the behavioral learning tradition to individual experience and behavior

A few hours on the plane, a short bus trip through the mountains—and finally I had a chance to see this amazing place for the first time. It was a small town, conveniently located at the foot of the hill near a lake.

"How many people are living here?" I asked my guide.

"About 700," she replied. "There are more moving in this year."

What attracts people to this place?

People here live simple lives and own property collectively. Their economy is small. Residents work for only 4 hours daily. All people here have been trained to recycle, consume only what is necessary, and not to overproduce. They educate children together. Although marriages are monogamous, each family must take turns spending time with other children. To facilitate that, children spend each month with a new family. Parents treat every child with care and affection.

Everyone goes to school, and education is separate for boys and girls. Children begin their vocational training at age 16. Boys learn engineering, science, medicine, and manufacturing, while girls learn cooking, home management, child rearing, and sex education. Adults and children alike learn daily—useful habits are preserved, and mistakes are remembered.

There are no police in town because people train themselves to respect and enforce the rules. Occasional behavioral problems are corrected by mandatory training in the reeducation camp nearby. There are no elected officials or office bureaucrats. The power in the community belongs to a few people called behaviorists. They observe, judge, describe, and prescribe because they know how to develop an "ideal" personality. Most individuals are happy, virtuous, and they all look forward to a new day . . .

You have probably figured out that this is not a true story. This is actually a short summary of the futuristic projects by two influential American psychologists of the past century, John Watson (in 1929) and B. F. Skinner (in 1948). Watson and Skinner, as well as a handful of scientists of their time, believed that science, if used in the right way, could help in creating an ideal person: happy, educated, nonviolent, creative, and moral. Skinner held that most human problems were because people put too much trust into incompetent, sinister, and selfish politicians. As soon as trained psychologists replace such incompetent rulers, and scientists name the right conditions for growth and improvement, a new society and a new personality type will emerge.

Psychology as a discipline encourages the individual's growth and social improvement through scientific knowledge and education. What would be the advantages and disadvantages of giving professional psychologists the opportunity to train the best individual features in specially organized communities? If such communities existed today, would you like to work in one of them, maybe just for a year, as a psychologist? Explain your choices. If you have children, would you agree to educate your own children there? Why or why not?

Behaviorism
The rich and diverse interdisciplinary tradition that focuses on observable behavior is called behaviorism.

The Behavioral Learning Tradition

This tradition in personality psychology is closely connected to **behaviorism**, which is the incredibly rich and diverse interdisciplinary tradition that focuses on observable behavior. Its contribution to various personality theories is vast. Behaviorism gained strength at the beginning of the 1900s within a favorable social and educational climate. The rapidly developing industrial societies needed more technocrats— educated and skilled individuals. Social progress was increasingly seen as rooted in experimental science and modern technology. Behaviorists were technocrats of psychology; they turned to science to explain people's problems and then improve everyone's lives. Don't we need such technocrats today?

For more than 100 years, behaviorists continued to offer a somewhat unpretentious, yet clear and intelligent view of personality: An individual's development,

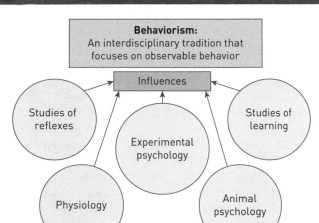

FIGURE 6.1   ●   The Behavioral Learning Tradition: An Illustrative Model

actions, complex behavior, and traits are all based on the underlying learning processes, which should be similar in most, if not in all, people. Because people are not completely identical at birth, because they are exposed to different physical conditions, and because they live in different social and cultural environments, their learning experiences result in different habits. Such habits then evolve and become traits. This is how different personalities appear (Banks & Rose, 2010). In the mind of the behaviorist, personality is something that "occurs" between behavior and the environment (see **Figure 6.1**; Mischel, 1993). Gaining knowledge about the universal learning principles and the different conditions in which this learning takes place is a key contribution of behaviorism to the study of personality. Behaviorism as a tradition grew and evolved within psychology, biology, and physiology. More scientists saw human life and mental activities as measurable. Unlike thoughts, perceptions, and will, which psychologists struggled to study experimentally, behavior and learning appeared observable and quantifiable. The teachings of Descartes and La Mettrie, both from France, portrayed human and animal behavior as reflexes and in mechanical terms. Mechanics meant measurement. Simple reactions and movements of individuals, as well as complex actions of the crowd, were now suitable to be explained by mathematical formulas. Behaviorists' logic was strikingly simple: We may have difficulty explaining the subjective side of, for example, embarrassment, but we can measure a person's behavioral responses in an embarrassing situation.

When psychologists apply behavioral principles to study personality, they tend to emphasize the importance of situational, environmental, and developmental factors in an individual's learning. They also study habits, traits, and the ways people change and develop in particular conditions. Some traits are learned early and remain stable during an individual's life-span. Studies show, for instance, that personality traits detected in childhood are strong predictors of adult behavior (Nave, Sherman, Funder, Hampson, & Goldberg, 2010).

Several developments contributed to behaviorism's rapid development. The first was the success of animal psychology. Researchers studying animals believed in the principle of continuity: Both humans and animals represent one natural world and must be subject to similar laws. The second development was the accomplishments of physiology. The success of general physiology in the early 20th century encouraged psychologists to turn to physiology of the brain and the nervous system. Researchers looked for measurable facts that are subject to verification and further experimentation. As with physics and the study of the atom, psychologists hoped to find physiological "atoms" of human behavior. Finally, there was the development of new research methods. Psychology as an experimental science was turning to a new generation of experiments, which many behaviorists called "objective methods" to distinguish them from introspection and other forms of self-observation.

A significant contribution of behaviorism to personality psychology was in its emphasis on education and learning. To optimize them, three conditions should exist (Skinner, 1938). First, behaviorism as a scientific discipline should provide knowledge in explaining how and under what circumstances habits and other personality features form and change. Second, successful learning takes place under specific conditions that must be created. Remember the idea about special communities at the beginning of the chapter? And finally, there should also be a group of highly educated and properly trained behavioral specialists, or *behaviorist physicians*. They should plan, manage, and protect human society in the same way that physicians conduct preventive care and treatment. These tasks are difficult; therefore, behaviorist physicians must be licensed. They will carry special observational devices to carefully examine every person's daily behavior. Behaviorists will correct deviant behavior and heal mental illness. Behavioral errors should be fixed; excellent behavior will receive recognition and rewards. Behaviorists encouraged psychologists to exclusively use behavioral terms in describing the individual's psychological features.

CHECK AND APPLY YOUR KNOWLEDGE

1. Describe yourself from a "behavioral" standpoint. Compose five short statements containing five verbs that reflect what you do as a person (it is a challenging task, but it should help in grasping the essence of behaviorism). Emphasize things you do and not how you feel or what you like and dislike. Compare your profile with one composed by another person. How different or similar are the profiles? What is the main limitation of such descriptions?

2. Who were behaviorist physicians? Imagine this profession existed today and you got a job as a behaviorist physician. What would you ideally want to do? Be creative and discuss in class.

Understanding Personality by Studying Animal Behavior

Comparative psychologists pioneered behavioral research into personality. Although the term *comparative psychology* became broadly accepted only in the 20th century (Johnston, 2002), studies in this field go deep into history. Comparative psychologists embraced the evolutionary ideas of Darwin and Spencer (Chapter 2), believed in the adaptive nature of animal behavior, and argued that animals and humans should be subject to essentially similar laws. To understand complex phenomena, a scientist should seek the simplest explanations. This principle, known as **parsimony**, became a working rule in comparative research. Studying animal behavior and comparing it to human conduct, scientists often assumed that many basic mechanisms of learning should be similar. Studying animals, we ultimately study humans. Humans, like animals, seek food, safety, and comfort and avoid danger and pain.

Parsimony
Parsimony is the scientific principle that refers to the necessity to seek the simplest explanations available to explain complex phenomena.

Anthropomorphism

More than 60% of Americans own at least one pet, according to the American Veterinary Medical Association (AVMA, 2016). You probably hear (or maybe even tell) stories about the surprisingly "human" behavior of those animals. In these stories, dogs may display "stubborn" personalities, cats have introverted tendencies, or parrots project a superb sense of humor. Portraying animal behavior in human terms is **anthropomorphism**. Among the most vivid examples of anthropomorphism are fairly tales, cartoons, and, of course, children's animations. Early comparative psychologists were anthropomorphists to some degree. They often elevated popular beliefs to the level of scientific knowledge. A pioneer ethnographer of Native American culture, Lewis Henry Morgan (1818–1881), argued that animals, like individuals, possess reason, creativity, and moral judgment. He maintained that the differences between humans and animals are based on the sophistication of their habits and the difficulty of their projects: In fact, both humans and beavers build dams! Animals too could develop their mental abilities if only they had access to special training (Johnston, 2002).

Anthropomorphism
Anthropomorphism is portraying animal behavior in human terms.

The British physiologist George J. Romanes (1848–1894) published *Animal Intelligence* in which he argued that sophisticated emotional dilemmas regulate animal behavior, and animals can display fortitude and patience (Romanes, 1882). Contemporary research shows how animals, such as dogs, display their emotions through muscular movements (Nagasawa, Kawai, Mogi, & Kikusui, 2013). However, this and similar studies do not support the assumption that animals experience deep moral conflicts and struggle with complex ethical predicaments.

Theories of Social Instincts

Supporters of anthropomorphism also found a convenient concept to explain behavior and individual traits: the **instinct**, which is an inherent pattern or a complex behavior. Humans belong to social groups in which they acquire social instincts

Instinct A person's instinct is an inherent pattern or a complex behavior.

Photo 6.1 There is a monument to the unknown dog in St. Petersburg (Russia), near the Institute of Experimental Medicine, where Ivan Pavlov headed the physiology laboratory for many years; it was commissioned and partially designed by Pavlov himself to honor the animals that died for the sake of scientific progress. Is it possible for animals to be used in research of personality psychology? Dogs, for example, play a big therapeutic role in helping people with psychological problems. Are there other areas in which animals can be studied and used?

Deindividuation
After joining a group, an individual may go through deindividuation, or the weakening of the awareness of self.

Habit formation
The process by which new behaviors become automatic is habit formation.

as automatic responses. The French psychologist Gustave Le Bon (1841–1931) believed, for instance, that aggressiveness as an individual trait initially emerges in a large crowd. A nonviolent person can act aggressively in a crowd (Le Bon, 1896). Gabriel Tarde (1843–1904), another Frenchman, focused on the mechanism of imitation. The entire learning process is imitation. We build our individual psychological qualities when we copy others (Tarde, 1903). The English scholar William McDougall (1871–1938) argued that human behavior could be traced to initial animal instincts, such as parenting (people, like animals, tend to take care of the young), self-display (individuals and animals tend to show off), or hoarding (people, like animals, tend to congregate in groups; McDougall, 1908).

Only some of these assumptions later found support in research. Take **deindividuation,** which is a process of weakening of an individual's awareness of self when he or she joins a group, as an example. Research shows that people who perform an exciting group activity tend to become less careful, less assertive, and less attentive than they normally are. In addition, group members tend to become less critical of one another (Lea & Spears, 1991). However, these and other studies did not produce evidence about human instincts.

Learning Laws

Comparative psychologists believed that animals learn according to some uniform principles that are applicable to all humans. Researchers turned to the study of **habit formation**, the process by which new behaviors become automatic. They offered a simple yet intriguing hypothesis that favorable conditions stimulate one type of behavior, and unfavorable conditions suppress this behavior. For example, a dog may learn to bark and then receive a treat after the dog's trainer says, "Speak!" Or a person learns to be honest because honesty is a habit, which develops in the situations when honesty is required. Similarly, another person learns how to lie because lying in some earlier situations helped this person avoid punishment.

Among many researchers who turned to experimental studies of habit formation, the American scholar Edward Thorndike (1874–1949) stood out. He introduced a new method, according to which research animals, such as chickens or cats, were placed inside a "puzzle box," which was a specially designed small cage or enclosure. An animal could escape by tripping a latch mechanism that opened a door or lifted a small barrier. Using this method, Thorndike observed the behavior of his experimental animals. But he did not just sit and draw sketches of them. First, he counted the number of trials attempted before each animal escaped from the box. Second, he measured the time it took the animal to escape. Third, he repeated the procedure several times and measured habit formation (Thorndike, 1911).

Thorndike showed the improvement of learning with experience. He called it the **learning curve**. He showed that with each new trial, the animal was spending less time in the puzzle box and making fewer trials before escaping from it. Most animals that attempted to get out of the puzzle box first initiated a kind of trial-and-error behavior. Even after they formed a required and useful habit, their behavior still involved many useless movements. Thorndike's experiments also disproved an assumption common at the time: that animals possess the unique ability to imitate behavior (Thorndike, 1911). The experience of an animal, its familiarity with the experimental situation, the quality of the reward, and the presence of distracting signals, such as noises, all may affect learning. Humans, according to Thorndike, are supposed to learn and unlearn in the same way.

Thorndike suggested several **laws of learning**, which are the most essential principles on which learning is based. For example, the *law of exercise* stated that the more one repeats a movement, the better it is retained. Describing the *law of effect*, Thorndike maintained that of several responses made to the same situation, those accompanied or closely followed by satisfaction are likely to be learned. When the same situation occurs again, the response associated with satisfaction will likely follow. Thorndike believed that the law of effect also explains how some people acquire harmful habits. For example, eating food in large quantities or drinking alcohol may bring immediate satisfaction to these individuals, yet they don't realize that the long-term consequences of these habits can be devastating. They overeat and become intoxicated again and again to satisfy themselves (see **Figure 6.2**; Thorndike, 1911).

Learning curve
In Thorndike's theory, the learning curve is a concept that describes the dynamic of learning a habit; it also indicates the connection between learning and the time it takes to learn.

Laws of learning
In Thorndike's system, the laws of learning are the most essential principles on which learning is based.

FIGURE 6.2 ● The Impact of Edward Thorndike

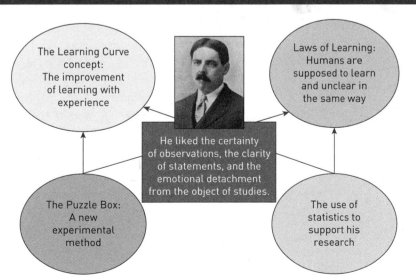

Source: Photo in the public domain.

CHECK AND APPLY YOUR KNOWLEDGE

1. What is parsimony? Recall a relatively important decision you have made recently. Explain this decision in a few sentences, using the parsimony principle. The causes of your behavior should appear as simple as possible.

2. Watch television and pay attention to all the commercials over a 30-minute period. Count and describe in a short sentence every display of anthropomorphism in these commercials (such as talking dogs, dancing cats, etc.). What exactly did the animals do or say? In which social activities is anthropomorphism also common?

3. Give an example of the learning curve using a recent episode from your life.

4. Which life situations involving humans should resemble, in your view, Thorndike's "puzzle box"? Have you ever been in such situations, and what did you do?

5. Assume you have a video of seven people stuck in the elevator for 15 minutes and later freed. As a behaviorist who could examine the video, what can you learn about these seven individuals?

Studies of animal behavior made an important contribution to the study of personality. This research encouraged some psychologists to consider humans and animals similar in principle yet different in complexity. The differences between them were substantial but not profound. Humans appeared more sophisticated than primates; monkeys appeared more advanced than cats and dogs, which in turn seemed more sophisticated than turtles and fish, and so forth. These specialists believed that animal research could help in the understanding of human individual traits and complex behavior.

Studying Reflexes

Psychology's interest in reflexes stemmed from the teachings of René Descartes and the physiologists of the 19th century (Chapter 2). In the 20th century, psychologists turned to reflexes to better understand human action and experience. At least two theories deserve our attention.

Reflexology and Personality

Reflexology In Bekhterev's system, reflexology is a unifying science to study reflexes.

Vladimir Bekhterev (1857–1927) was a Russian physiologist and doctor. He was among the first to use the term *personality* in his research (Strickland, 1997). He was among the most active promoters of the idea that science must study the individual from a multidisciplinary perspective, at the center of which he saw **reflexology**, which is a unifying science to study reflexes. He hoped that one day reflexology would become a universally accepted discipline, like biology or physics. He also believed that reflexology could explain practically all aspects of human behavior and personality as transformations of energy in the brain and nervous system (Bekhterev, 1904).

Bekhterev called the nervous energy that accumulates in the cerebral cortex of the brain *emotions*. When the energy affects action after a delay, this is called *thinking*. When energy is stored in some modified fashion by past experience and a stimulus affecting the organism puts it into action, Bekhterev called this type of stored energy *consciousness* (Frost, 1912). Bekhterev also wrote about special social reflexes. Like many of our individual reflexes such as blinking and yawning, which are influenced by external signals, social reflexes such as feistiness or stubbornness emerge under certain social conditions, such as when people face injustice or abuse (Bekhterev, 1921/2001; Strickland, 2001).

What is personality, according to Bekhterev? At least two points are important. Personality is, first of all, a "foundation," or an inner core that integrates and manages an individual's thoughts, actions, and complex behavior. Personality is an integrative

SELF-REFLECTION

Bekhterev used the concept of energy to explain immortality. Trying to cope with the mystery of death, he argued, many people turn to religion as a great source of hope. Many believe in the immortal soul or the resurrection of the dead. However, in his view, science could provide the most profound justification of immortality.

According to the principle of energy conservation (he borrowed it from physics), energy cannot disappear without a trace, and it cannot appear without being caused by another source of energy (Bekhterev, 1916/2001). Human internal energy transforms into the energy of muscles, thoughts, and actions. When a person dies, the decay of the body leads to decomposition of the organism into simple elements. Yet life is not over; according to Bekhterev, our personality continues into new forms of energy, including the thoughts and actions of other people. Our lives still influence the lives of other people! This is, in fact, the life cycle of immortality (Dobreva-Martinova & Strickland, 2001).

Questions
Animals don't seem to care how their offspring will remember them. Why do people care about how they will be remembered? Do you personally care? Why or why not? If our immortality is predetermined by our actions, as some behaviorists have proposed, would you agree that some people become more "immortal" than others because they have accomplished more and impacted more people during their lives? As a behaviorist, discuss and suggest an "index of immortality," which is a composite measure of a person's impact. What criteria would you suggest for this index (for example, the number of Google "hits" related to this person)?

Pavlov understood personality from the standpoint of reflexes, behavior, and learning. He clearly understood that the complexity of human life couldn't be reduced to simple reflexes. But he had to begin somewhere; he had to study those original "elements" or reflexes.

FIGURE 6.3   ●   Pavlov: Types of the Nervous System and Their Behavioral Profiles

Strong	**Balanced**	**Agile**	Strong, balanced, and agile type. Inhibition and excitement are balanced. The person adjusts quickly to changing conditions and can stand up to difficulties. Makes quick decisions and changes strategies when necessary.
		Inertial	Calm and slow type. Able to resist significant pressure. The person can handle difficult situations by ignoring them or by making carefully planned decisions. Changes in habits and behavioral strategies are difficult to make.
	Imbalanced		Strong and imbalanced type. Excitement dominates over inhibition. Explosive and temperamental, feisty and energetic. The person can stand up to difficulties but often cannot control emotions. Frequently and in various situations may lose self-control.
Weak			Weak type. Experiences difficulties under the pressure of challenges, including lack of time. Highly avoidant and sensitive to external signals such as other people's opinions. The person often has a hard time making quick decisions or selecting among choices.

CHECK AND APPLY YOUR KNOWLEDGE

1. Let's assume Bekhterev was right about energy transformation. Now recall the activities that consumed your "energy" today. Consider two variables such as (1) the time spent on these activities and (2) the effort (small—significant—very significant) you have used in these activities. Which activity has drained most of your energy and why? How could you—or not—save more energy next time around?

2. Choose a character from a book or a movie. Design a brief behavioral profile of this character using Pavlov's three functions of the nervous system: strength, balance, and agility. How strong or weak, balanced or imbalanced, and agile or inertial is this character?

3. Write a brief behavioral profile of yourself (your behavioral characteristics) using Pavlov's three functions of the nervous system. What type are you likely to be? Strong, balanced, and agile? Or imbalanced and inertial? Or will it be weak? Maybe you will discover another combination.

Watson: Studying and Applying Behaviorism

The American psychologist John Watson (1878–1958) took the discipline of psychology by storm. Ambitious and sharp, he was at the helm of the American Psychological Association at the age of 38. After that, his academic career did not last long: He was forced to resign his professorship when he was 42 due to an extramarital affair. Despite this personal turmoil, Watson's influence on psychology was significant. Essentially, Watson's (1919) views can be stated as follows:

1. Behavior is a set of responses to specific signals.

2. Behavioral responses become useful and thus retained.

3. Some simple reactions develop into complex acts.

Simple and complex reactions, under particular conditions, form habits. Different habits then integrate into functions of an individual's organism. Functions are organized, integrated habit systems, such as writing or swimming. Functions may be explicit and observable, like speech, or implicit, like thinking. They too are activated under specific conditions. Psychologists (Watson often called them "behaviorist physicians") study various stimuli and conditions under which particular habits are formed. Then they help people improve, strengthen, or change certain habits. Psychology's goal was to develop principles that would explain, predict, and control behavior (Watson, 1919). Remember the opening case to this chapter? Watson believed a knowledgeable and skilled behaviorist physician should have the right to "shape up" an individual's personality and change human lives for the better.

Personality, in Watson's view, is a totality of organized behavioral acts, such as habits, instincts, emotions, and their combinations (see **Figure 6.4**). Personalities are different because different people have different **plasticity**—a capacity for new habit formation or change of old habits. People are also different because some keep their habits ready to be used in a new situation, while others lose them. He called this **retention**.

Plasticity Plasticity is the capacity for new habit formation or change of old habits.

Retention In behaviorism, retention is the ability of individuals to keep their habits ready to be used in a new situation.

Habit Formation

How do habits—the foundation of personality—develop? John Watson considered emotions as conditioned responses or habits learned during childhood. Emotion formation thus is a process of habit formation. To examine it, Watson studied the development of conditioned reflexes on a 9-month-old baby. The experimenters wanted to show that emotions created in a laboratory were retained later in life (Watson & Rayner, 1920). Watson paired unconditioned stimuli that should cause initial alarm and fear in the child (e.g., a very loud noise) with live animals and toys that initially did not cause any emotional reaction, so in his experiments, Watson attempted to experimentally develop fears in children. Today, this procedure is questionable from the ethical standpoint: A psychologist has no right to scare a child for the sake of the psychologist's academic curiosity.

Like Bekhterev and Pavlov, Watson rejected the "subjective" side of an individual's personality. Watson was skeptical about so-called mental tests, which were common during the time. He wrote that by judging someone's answers on a piece of paper, he

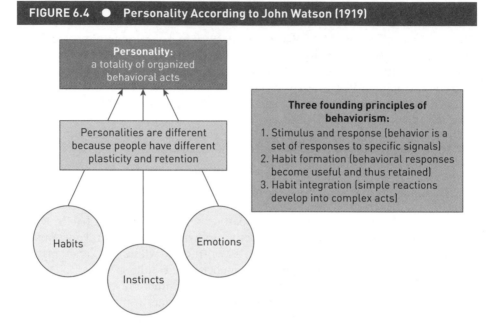

FIGURE 6.4 ● Personality According to John Watson (1919)

Personality: a totality of organized behavioral acts

Personalities are different because people have different plasticity and retention

Three founding principles of behaviorism:
1. Stimulus and response (behavior is a set of responses to specific signals)
2. Habit formation (behavioral responses become useful and thus retained)
3. Habit integration (simple reactions develop into complex acts)

Habits

Instincts

Emotions

would not be able to detect whether or not this person is a liar or if this individual is capable of working with other people (Watson, 1927). Only individuals' observable behavior, such as their responses, decisions, and habits, could provide reliable facts (see **Table 6.1**).

Habit Disturbances: Abnormal Behavior and Deviance

Watson argued that a healthy personality consisted of well-functioning habit systems in most situations. Abnormal features were characterized by an individual's inability to get rid of old habits and old emotions in new situations in which those old habits were no longer efficient. Mental illness was a kind of **habit disturbance**. Watson interpreted abnormal symptoms differently than most clinical psychologists of the time did. Symptoms of hysteria or neurosis, defensive reactions, guilt, irrational fears—all these and scores of other symptoms were maladaptive reflexes. How did they develop? There must have been a situation or condition in the past, an emotional trauma, physical or sexual abuse, masturbation, or something else—as Watson believed—that triggered the development of a dysfunctional habit. This habit, in a chain reaction, then triggers the development of other progressively maladaptive habits. Watson also suggested treatment for abnormal habits and functions. He believed that behavioral training and retraining of individuals to help them acquire new habits should be a foundation of a new kind of therapy (Wozniak, 1993).

Watson also believed that the individual's criminal behavior is rooted in this person's maladaptive habits (Watson, 1919). Psychologists, in Watson's opinion, were capable of providing treatment for such people through special behavioral programs funded by the government. Subsequently, after spending some time in such a program, a troubled individual would form new behavioral habits. This would result in crime reduction.

Habit disturbance
In Watson's system, the habit disturbance is the cause of mental illness.

TABLE 6.1 ● Psychology's Objectives and Their Applications to the Study of Personality	
Psychology's Objectives	**What It Means in the Study of Personality**
All speculations about the mechanisms of "the mind" and "consciousness" should be abandoned.	An individual is better understood when psychologists focus on what he or she does.
All experiments should be verified and controlled. Specifically, introspection should be ruled out as a method of scientific investigation.	New experimental procedures should be developed and implemented. Psychologists should not ask "How do you feel?" but measure an individual's actions.
Psychology should become an experimental branch of natural science. Psychology should resemble biology.	It is desirable to compare an individual's behavior to the behavior of an animal, especially in experimental situations.
The ultimate goal of psychology should be to describe, predict, and control human behavior. To achieve these goals, psychology must embrace behavior as the subject of studies.	Studying personality is also about applying the received data in various fields, including work, education, communications, advertisement, health care, and so on. Psychologists should play a bigger role in society.

Watson's ideas were simple, understandable, and attractive to many specialists in education, business, and psychology. He gave psychologists inspiration and built their confidence as researchers and practitioners. He influenced a large and enthusiastic audience, professionals and ordinary people alike, who were ready to learn, accept, support, and apply his ideas.

Studying Behavior From Different Angles

While supporting behaviorism in general, psychologists wanted to alter its focus. Edwin Holt (1873–1946), who served as a professor at Harvard and later at Princeton, argued that in real-life situations, behavior is more complex and must be understood as a complex unity of many behavioral acts. Holt introduced the concept of **molar responses**. The responses require interpretation. The concept of "interpretation" signaled a departure from a traditional behaviorism that generally ignored the concepts of goal or purpose. Individuals are different because they pursue different goals. One of Holt's supporters and students was Edward Tolman (1886–1959).

Working as professor of psychology at the University of California at Berkeley, Tolman was often called a purposive behaviorist, and his views were labeled **purposive or operational behaviorism**. Tolman suggested an expansion of the traditional $S \rightarrow R$ (stimulus–response) model of behaviorism and added $S \rightarrow O \rightarrow R$, in which O stood for measurable processes or variables within an organism. These variables are heredity (some animals or individuals have certain inborn abilities), age (e.g., strength of responses may decline with age), quality of previous training (some of us develop specific habits), features of stimuli (responses depend on various signals),

Molar responses
In Holt's system, a molar response is the reaction that has something to do with the meaning of the situation—that is, the way an animal or human interprets the situation.

Purposive or operational behaviorism
In Tolman's system, purposive or operational behaviorism involves the idea of purpose or a goal.

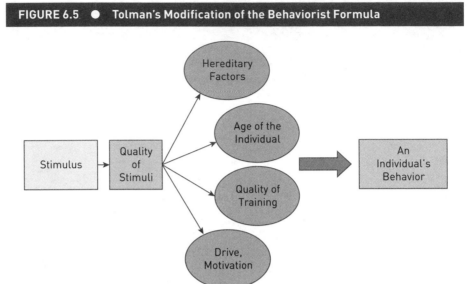

FIGURE 6.5 ● Tolman's Modification of the Behaviorist Formula

Cognitive map
In Tolman's system, a cognitive map results from the internal processing by which individuals code, store, recall, and decode information about particular elements of their experience.

and an organism's drive (Tolman, 1932). Drive is caused by frustration; although we cannot see it, we can perfectly describe frustration in operational terms as a degree of tension caused by an inability to reach a goal. The more time you spend or the more unsuccessful attempts you make to achieve your goal, the stronger your frustration is felt. It will direct your behavior for some time. Studying rats, Tolman believed that animals could learn the connections between stimuli and did not need any biologically significant event to make their learning occur (see **Figure 6.5**).

Tolman introduced the concept called a **cognitive map**, which refers to internal processing by which individuals code, store, recall, and decode information about

CHECK AND APPLY YOUR KNOWLEDGE

1. Could you improve your own plasticity? Recall what Watson meant by it. Think of one habit (a) you do not particularly like in yourself (like procrastination) or (b) you think needs development (like being more punctual, for example). Think of the circumstances in which this habit appears. Without delay, prepare a plan to change this habit. Start today. Monitor the changes.

2. Imagine a dilemma. You can get a B+ as a final grade in this class now, and then you do not have to attend this class any longer. If you reject this offer, you stay in this class, but no particular grade is guaranteed. What will you do? Explain your decision by using Tolman's cognitive map concept. What factors did you include in your decision?

particular elements of their experience (Tolman, 1948). It is not just a memory of vivid events. Cognitive maps represent a complex pattern that guides a person's behavior based on some learned behaviors. New learning experiences, either successful or not, build new cognitive maps. Tolman and his followers believed that the concept of cognitive maps could explain how an individual's personality develops and functions. Individuals constantly learn and develop new cognitive maps, which should result in new behaviors (Tolman, 1948).

Optimistic Behaviorism of B. F. Skinner

One of the most dynamic devotees of behaviorism in the mid-20th century was Burrhus Frederick Skinner, who is commonly known as B. F. Skinner (1904–1990). His theory and applications have generated enthusiastic support, heated debates, and outright rejections. Today, his name and his ideas (often simplified and sometimes misinterpreted) still appear in popular literature and scholarly journals around the world. Although he continued the line of research by John Watson, Skinner moved farther ahead of his prominent predecessor.

He embraced the idea that psychologists in their experiments need not rely so much on physiology (as Pavlov did) but could focus on overt behavior instead. He was not really interested in what was going "inside" the brain. Accurate measurement of behavior was a key challenge, which he recognized. To study behavior, Skinner designed many devices, but one, often referred to as the "Skinner box," was particularly successful. A mouse placed inside a specially made box was free to move around in it. As soon as the animal pressed a lever (at first accidentally), a small food pellet was automatically released on a tray so the mouse could eat it. In behaviorist terms, the mouse's lever-pressing act was reinforced by the food being delivered immediately afterward. Skinner next realized that he could measure many elements (or variables) of the process: the time elapsing before the mouse pressed the lever, the number of repetitions before the animal learned a habit, and so forth.

Skinner turned to study *behavioral reinforcements*, the term borrowed from Pavlov. Skinner believed that people always learn about the consequences of their behavior because they receive rewards and punishments. This type of learning is called **operant conditioning**. The word *operant* meant activities producing effects. Like the rat in the box presses the button (an activity) and then receives food (an effect), the individual engages in the same type of learning and habit development based on operant conditioning (Skinner, 1938).

Skinner came up with the idea of **schedules of reinforcement**, or conditions involving different rates and times of reinforcement. By changing the schedules of reinforcement, Skinner was able to measure behavioral responses. For example, at the beginning of an experiment, the rat received food every time it pushed the button. Next, Skinner gave reinforcement precisely in 1-minute intervals, regardless of how many times the rat pushed the button. Or he released food exactly after the rat pushed the button three consecutive times. Now he believed he could measure the behavior of his experimental animals with precision and sophistication.

Operant conditioning
In Skinner's system, operant conditioning is based on using activities to produce effects.

Schedules of reinforcement
In Skinner's system, schedules of reinforcement are conditions involving different rates and times of reinforcement.

From Animals to Humans

Skinner always believed it would be just a matter of time before everyone could see the practical value of his behavioral research (Skinner, 1960). His goal was to apply his studies to humans. For example, if scientists experimentally established the stimuli that produce useful reactions and behaviors, why don't they design and put together such stimuli? If we know, for example, that certain conditions influence the formation of certain habits, why can't we design such conditions? In 1944, Skinner built the **Aircrib**—a thermostatically controlled crib with a safety-glass front and a stretched-canvas floor—for his second daughter, Deborah. The boxlike crib contained soundproof walls and a window. If the baby cried, the insulation would reduce the noise, yet the parent could hear the baby very well. It had warming and moistening devices as well as air filters to control the quality of the air inside. Skinner believed that his invention would provide both safety and freedom of movement for a baby, a secure, controlled environment for the child, and better opportunities for parents to develop useful habits in their children. Yet both manufacturers and consumers remained skeptical about the safety of his invention. Many people who saw the promotional materials about Aircrib immediately called it as a small "jail" for babies. Critics rejected the idea of "building" habits in their children as if they were some kind of robots responding to external signals and commands. Skinner was upset by such critical reviews. More than 60 years have passed. Today, numerous patented devices and gadgets to simplify infant care for parents surround the child from birth—disposable diapers (they did not exist in 1944), video monitoring devices, portable cribs, developmental gadgets, and multifunctional strollers—they may all serve as reminders that Skinner's idea was not necessarily far off target. However, the idea of a strict, behavioral training device or program to raise a good child has been generally rejected. Or maybe Skinner was simply ahead of his time?

Aircrib   Designed by Skinner to form good habits in children, an Aircrib is a thermostatically controlled crib with a safety-glass front and a stretched-canvas floor.

@

On the companion website, read a summary of a study showing that children's behavioral styles at age 3 are linked to their adult personality traits at age 26.

Questions

Which methods were used in this study? What does this study suggest about the formation of early behavioral styles of children? Does this study also suggest that environmental factors do not play a significant role in influencing an individual's traits in late childhood and adolescence? Why or why not?

Social Engineering

From the behaviorist's view, animals and humans learn a habit not because they "understand" the purpose of learning. They retain useful habits because they are likely to secure food, shelter, pleasure, or safety. People and animals alike adapt to changing conditions by constantly modifying their reflexes. If this is true, as behaviorists believed, then it would be possible to design educational and social programs to develop people's healthy habits and effective decision-making strategies. Skinner believed his research, if it was properly applied, could change the individual and society. Two of his books, *Walden Two* (1948/2005) and *Beyond Freedom and Dignity* (1971), brought him worldwide fame and sparked heated discussions. In *Walden Two*, Skinner returned to the question posed by the philosopher and writer Henry D. Thoreau (1817–1862). In the first *Walden*, published in 1854, Thoreau argued for the psychological and moral benefits of a simple lifestyle. Skinner went even further. He claimed that humans could build an entire society that embraces a simple lifestyle by applying positive reinforcement. Who would manage such an enterprise? Skinner, as you remember from the introduction, emphasized that one of the problems with human civilization is that across centuries, the power of conditioning belonged to the wrong leaders. They were, for the most part, incompetent and selfish. In Skinner's version of the new world, educated behaviorists would take over, and they would help people build many useful, socially approved personality features. People would be honest, modest, and hardworking, and they would live in harmony with one another.

Skinner's ideas, as you can imagine, received a storm of criticism. Critics accused him of being a misguided scientist who believed in conditioned slavery (Jessup, 1948). Critics also pointed out that this utopian theory was no more than a disguised attempt to justify the transfer of political power to unelected scientists. Who would guarantee that they would not use behavioral methods to advance their own selfish interests? To others, *Walden Two* was a harmless reflection of a naïve belief of a Harvard professor.

Skinner's biggest publishing "hit" was *Beyond Freedom and Dignity* in which he applied behaviorism to explain the modern individual. People, he wrote, are misguided in their overconfident belief in individual freedom. In fact, what is called "freedom" had been defined by the ruling elites, such as government and powerful corporations, who treat us, ordinary citizens, as experimental animals in the box. The elites use behavioral reinforcement to make us buy certain products, order particular services, watch prime-time shows, join specific associations, and vote for certain parties. We, as individuals, blindly follow these pressures, mistakenly calling them freedom. To avoid this trap, we have to choose a different path in our lives instead and accept different sources of behavioral conditioning (*not* products or money). The key is in exercising self-control and moderation. To learn them, we should turn to behavioral scientists (see **Figure 6.6**).

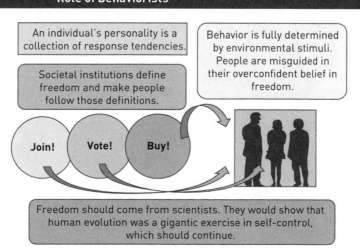

FIGURE 6.6 ● Skinner's Views of Personality, Freedom, and the Societal Role of Behaviorists

An individual's personality is a collection of response tendencies.

Behavior is fully determined by environmental stimuli. People are misguided in their overconfident belief in freedom.

Societal institutions define freedom and make people follow those definitions.

Join!   Vote!   Buy!

Freedom should come from scientists. They would show that human evolution was a gigantic exercise in self-control, which should continue.

Criticism of his book came from scholars and philosophers, including a champion of liberal ideas, Noam Chomsky, and a top conservative intellectual, Ayn Rand. They both criticized Skinner for his alleged disbelief in the individual's freedom. Skinner, of course, fought back. He claimed that the alleged freedom that Americans thought they possessed was merely a set of their conditioned reactions called consumerism, which he believed to be destructive. According to Skinner, true freedom can occur only when people use behavioral science to identify the morally "right" kinds of conditioning based on restraint, rational choice, and common good. Skinner wanted to free the individual from the abusive forces of selfishness.

Social Learning Theory

Social learning theory Generally, social learning theory states, among other things, that learning does not necessarily need reinforcement and conditioning.

While some behaviorists were studying reinforcements and conditioning, other researchers turned to social factors in learning as the process of acquisition of new knowledge and habits. **Social learning theory** is a general term to outline, among other things, that learning does not necessarily need reinforcement and conditioning. An individual learns and makes decisions within a particular social environment. Learning can take place through observation of other people's behavior, personal curiosity, through direct and deliberate instruction from one person to another, or through exposure of an individual to certain events.

Psychologist Julian Rotter (1916–2014) focused on an "inner" factor regulating human behavior: the expected outcome. A person's anticipation of a particular result, such as success or failure, produces specific motivation to act or not to act. People tend to avoid defeats or penalties and seek victories or rewards (of course, there are exceptions). We tend to engage in behaviors in which we anticipate a successful outcome. If we experience success or victory, we are likely to repeat this behavior. Of course, success is based on many factors and conditions, which may or may not be under an

CHECK AND APPLY YOUR KNOWLEDGE

1. Based on what you know about Rotter's research, do you think you are more external, internal, or somewhere in between?

2. After you've made your best guess, go to the companion website to find the original Rotter scale to measure your locus of control. Does your score reflect your expectation about your locus of control? As in previous examples and self-evaluations, use the knowledge about yourself critically and wisely.

individual's control. Think of the weather, for instance: Can we change it by working harder on a psychology research paper? There are also events that appear beyond our control because of the complexity of the world around us. We don't know what's causing those events, but even if we don't know what's causing a specific event, just explaining connections between events will lead to more predictability, which will give the appearance of more control (Kelley, 1967).

Rotter (1966) further developed this idea about control in experiments that showed consistent differences among individuals in the degree to which they attribute or explain personal control. Rotter categorized them into two groups. One group tends to explain events as influenced by somewhat controllable, internal, relatively permanent characteristics such as skill, preparedness, will, and the like. This group is labeled *internals* because they display an **internal locus of control**. Those with an **external locus of control** (*externals*) tend to explain events as influenced by uncontrollable external factors, such as powerful others, luck, the great complexity of the "outside" forces, and so on. Rotter's research sparked significant interest and follow-up studies. For example, people with an external locus of control are more likely to engage in persistent gambling (Hock, 2013). People with an internal locus of control tend to be "difficult" patients because they are less likely than externals to follow the doctor's recommendations. Strangers do not easily persuade internals, who tend to have stronger achievement motivation than externals (Rotter, 1990). We will discuss this research on achievement motivation in Chapter 10 and Chapter 13.

The Canadian-born psychologist Albert Bandura (b. 1925) worked at Stanford University and published the influential book *Social Learning and Personality Development* in 1963. In the early 1960s, Bandura and associates conducted a series of experiments that gained global recognition as the *Bobo doll experiment* (Bobo was a 5-foot, inflatable toy made out of vinyl; when pushed or hit, it would fall and then return to an upright position). In this experiment, boys and girls between the ages of 3 and 6 were told they could play with various toys, including the Bobo doll, that were presented to them. In some experimental scenarios, the children were in the room with an adult (a member of the team). The adult then would kick, punch, and verbally assault the doll. In other cases, the children would watch a film in which

Internal locus of control A person's internal locus of control is the individual tendency to explain events as influenced by somewhat controllable, internal, relatively permanent characteristics such as skill, preparedness, will, and the like.

External locus of control An external locus of control is an individual tendency to explain events as influenced by uncontrollable external factors, such as powerful others, luck, the great complexity of the "outside" forces, and so on.

©iStockphoto.com/Don Bayley

©iStockphoto.com/Stock Shop Photography LLC

Photo 6.2 The Bobo doll experiments sparked a discussion about the role of imitation in behavior. Do you find that people tend to imitate "bad" behavior easier than they imitate "good" behavior? Why?

an adult would assault the doll. As a result, the children exposed to direct and indirect violence were significantly more likely to express aggression toward the Bobo doll than those boys and girls who did not see violent acts during the experiment (Bandura, Ross, & Ross, 1961, 1963). The experiment was replicated many times and produced similar results: Children learned violence through imitation, just by observing the behavior of an adult. This study sparked a discussion among both professionals and the public about violence in the media and its impact on actual behavior of children and adults.

The Bobo doll experiment, replicated in many countries, showed that the children exposed to direct and indirect violence were significantly more likely to express aggression toward the Bobo doll than those boys and girls who did not see violent acts during the experiment.

This experiment was only one in the series of studies in which Bandura showed that learning occurred by observing a person's behavior and its consequences (Bandura, 1977). Learning takes place through demonstration (when we witness an event or behavior of other people), verbal instrumentation (like the safety instructions aboard a plane), and symbolic demonstration (such as watching a movie). The learner, however, is not a passive observer. People are active thinkers, paying and not paying attention to the information, retaining it in memory, forgetting it, or being able to recall it or not. According to **reciprocal determinism**, individuals influence their environment and vice versa. Bandura referred to his research as *social cognitive theory* to emphasize the importance of cognitive processes in social learning. In 1986, he published research showing that individuals were not passive agents of social influences but rather active, stubborn, developing, and self-regulating (Bandura, 1986).

Based on his research, Bandura formulated the principle of **self-efficacy,** which is people's belief in their ability to manage their lives and to exercise control over events that affect their lives (Bandura, 1997, 2001). People who have developed self-efficacy tend to believe they have enough power to produce desired outcomes in most cases. Therefore, they tend to persevere when facing difficulties or disagreements. They also tend to resist stress, stand up to misfortunes, and overcome bad moods. People with low self-efficacy tend to lose motivation and interest in fighting for their happiness. Instead, they succumb to despair when facing serious challenges.

Reciprocal determinism Reciprocal determinism offers the suggestion that individuals influence their environment and vice versa.

Self-efficacy Self-efficacy is our belief in our own ability to manage our lives and to exercise control over events that affect our lives.

What Behaviorism Accomplished and What It Missed

Behaviorists provided a solid foundation for future research into personality. Their followers agreed on the major principles of behaviorism but differed in the ways they interpreted it. They were often called neobehaviorists, although very few of them wanted to accept this one-dimensional label. Besides the differences among them, at least two issues unified neobehaviorists: their unrestrained belief in the possibility and necessity of objective measurement of behavior and their support for the reductionist belief that psychology should be a science of behavior and conditioning. Several researchers distinguished themselves because of valuable theoretical and practical innovations they added to the mainstream assumptions of behaviorism and learning.

Instead of describing self-observed feelings, behaviorists turned their attention to learned reactions, reflexes, reaction times, and emotional responses. Many of their findings were presented with amazing clarity. There were clear suggestions about where and under which circumstances behavioral research should be applied to education, therapy, work, and other areas. Many conclusions about human behavior and personality were almost commonsensical, as well as clear and often encouraging. They converted the language of common sense into the language of experimental research and vice versa. To many people, behaviorism appeared as a straightforward and simple theory in a confusing world. It was an unambiguous statement of clarity in a world of ambiguity. It was also an honest promise of confidence in a world of skepticism. Behaviorists emphasized that psychology could have done more to contribute to education, health care, professional training, and many other areas of life.

What did behaviorism miss? Psychologists working within the behavioral learning tradition did not produce a simple "magic" formula to describe an individual's personality in behavioral terms. Critics predictably describe behaviorism as reductionist and simplistic. Critics considered early behaviorist assumptions—that consciousness is a bodily reaction, emotion is a chaotic instinctive reaction, and thinking is internal

CHECK AND APPLY YOUR KNOWLEDGE

1. Self-efficacy is not a dichotomous (one either has it or not) but rather a continuous variable (see Chapter 3 on methodology). Self-efficacy can be high and low and anywhere in between. It can be stable, or it can change. Pick a difficult life situation you have encountered either recently or some time ago. How would you evaluate your self-efficacy in that situation? Describe your self-observations in a paragraph.

2. Who among your friends or family members has high self-efficacy? Describe briefly this person's behavior indicative of his or her self-efficacy.

speech—as ridiculous. The behavioral learning tradition viewed reflex as an important physiological model; however, this model had only limited applicability to an individual's personality. Behaviorism rejected subjectivity, yet only a few psychologists agreed that psychology must abandon "subjectivity" altogether and switch to behavioral or physiological models.

Applying the Behavioral Learning Tradition

Behaviorism carried an optimistic message about the possibility to form, shape, and change skills, habits, and personality features through exercising, training, and organized learning. Therefore, there was no shortage of attempted applications of behaviorism to practical fields, including education, business, law enforcement, and health care. Animal psychologists showed that proper training could "override" instinctual drives. For example, Zing-Yang Kuo (1898–1970), who worked in the United States and in China, raised kittens and rats together to demonstrate that the cats did not chase and kill the rats as they normally would in natural conditions. Doctors applied the key principles of learning to help people get rid of bad habits such smoking and drinking (Bekhterev, 1918/1933). Criminologists insisted that criminal behavior is not inborn but rather learned and thus could be corrected through special training with proper reinforcement (Burgess & Akers, 1966). Some applications were effective, yet others were not.

For example, *Taylorism* was a short-lived behavioral training program named after Frederick Taylor (1911), an engineer by education and occupation. According to the program, every worker's movement must be regulated—every simple operation should be effective, every movement should be useful. No long lunch breaks. No meaningless conversations or jokes at the workplace should be allowed. Initially, this program was met with enthusiasm. Soon, however, the euphoria about the Taylor method evaporated. Managers and workers alike hated the "sweatshop" atmosphere imposed by Taylorism. This system ignored the role of individual motivation, pride, and interpersonal relationships at the workplace and focused exclusively on production. As psychologists gradually realized, an individual's sense of comfort at the workplace and good relationships with coworkers and management were far more important for efficiency.

Other applications of the behavioral learning tradition were more successful.

Behavioral Economics

Behavioral principles find significant and promising applications in behavioral economics. As was noted in Chapter 2 personality psychology uses research from behavioral economics that focuses on how various individual factors affect people's choices. Behavioral economics is an experimental field and, like behaviorism, studies observable outcomes of human actions. It studies the effects of individual factors, such as reasoning, emotional stability, or habit, and group factors, such as traditions, group pressure, or competition, on individual economic decisions. These are our daily choices—for example, buying an app for your phone, declining

Photo 6.3 Behavioral economists bring an individual dimension to the study of economic decisions. Think about yourself. Do you have the particular personality features of a good entrepreneur or not? Explain why.

a wedding invitation, or choosing a roommate. Economists and personality psychologists find common interest in studying typical, consistent decisions that people make in their daily routines. In fact, the cooperation between psychology and economics has been extremely productive. For instance, the 2002 Nobel Prize in economics went to psychologist Daniel Kahneman for his research on biases of individual decision-making.

Consider chronic poverty. So far in this century, 1 billion to 2 billion people have remained chronically poor. Abhijit Banerjee and Ester Duflo (2011) looked into poverty from the position of an individual and his or her consistent patterns of action. The researchers have demonstrated that (besides social and political factors) many people remain poor because they do not have (or did not learn) the necessary habits and skills to climb out of poverty. For example, across countries, the poor consistently make similar mistakes in starting and operating small businesses. They tend to make bad decisions about their own health. Also, the poor tend to give up easily when they believe they cannot succeed. What is one common denominator of these constant errors? It is their lack of patience. It is poverty that makes people more impatient because they have not been conditioned in the past to receive rewards for being patient. So what is the remedy? The remedy is learning and acquiring new and useful skills that emphasize patience and perseverance. However, this learning requires qualified teachers.

Now consider deviant behavior. Why do some people engage in risky behavior while others do not? Tolman's ideas about the individual's "inner variable" find applications in safety policies. Studies show, for example, that people tend to avoid unnecessary risk. However, people also tend to adjust their behavior facing a risk in response to the perceived level of risk. In simple terms, we tend to act more carelessly when we feel more protected, and we act cautiously when we don't feel safe. We know that riding a bike without a helmet is dangerous, so why don't we initiate a policy to make helmets mandatory and thus reduce the number of injuries? In reality, the outcome of this policy is less than certain. People tend to immediately reevaluate their risks. They think because they are wearing a helmet, they are better protected, and they can ride faster and make more dangerous moves on the road. This is an example of risk compensation as a behavioral adaptation that may diminish the impact of safety rules.

Economist Sam Peltzman showed how risk compensation works (Peltzman, 2011). People in general show a consistent tendency: They tend to act more dangerously today if they feel that they are safer than yesterday. For example, one of the most significant medical breakthroughs in human history for fighting infections was the development of antibiotics—people know they no longer face inevitable death because of scarlet fever or tuberculosis. Yet this knowledge lets some people take more risks, such as not washing their hands before meals, eating unwashed products, and so on. The discovery of new treatments for heart disease and the development of the anti-AIDS medication have saved many lives, yet they could have triggered even riskier behavior in many individuals. Why so? An individual falsely assumes that his or her behaviors—unhealthy eating, overeating, smoking, or unprotected sex—are no longer harmful because there are great medical products and procedures that could easily provide a cure for any health malady. As mandatory car safety belts have saved many lives, their positive impacts would be greater if there were no risk-takers. They falsely believe they can drive faster and more recklessly because they are safer with a seatbelt. This also means that a safety ruling or policy by itself may not produce a fully desirable effect. It must be explained to people time and time again that it's necessary to follow safety rules and reduce risky behavior. What behavioral methods would you personally suggest to improve safety?

Coping With Traumatic Events

Traumatic experiences are part of life. Serious accidents, terrorist attacks, sexual assaults, natural disasters, military combat, and other traumatic events cause significant impact on millions of people. Many people continue having painful psychological symptoms long after the traumatic events took place. Such symptoms include elevated anxiety, sleep disturbances, nightmares, irritability, emotional detachment, and profound behavioral disengagement. Behaviorists such as Bandura and colleagues have found that building up self-efficacy is instrumental in overcoming the most painful post-traumatic symptoms (Bandura, 1997). Psychologists these days put together therapeutic procedures to help the sufferers build confidence and inner strength in dealing with their painful symptoms. People who suffer post-traumatic symptoms learn that taking charge of their own lives is a beginning of the healing process (Benight & Bandura, 2004). These methods help tens of thousands of natural disaster survivors, refugees, accident victims, and returning veterans (Bemak & Chung, 2004). We will return to several coping methods in Chapter 13 related to adjustment.

Behavior Therapy

Classical behavioral studies showed that **extinction**—which can involve abandoning a bad habit or a decrease in a fearful reaction—is not only a disappearance of something previously learned but is also a form of learning in its own right (Myers & Davis, 2002). Behavioral principles have found important applications in today's behavioral methods of treatment for a wide range of psychological disorders. Behavioral theories generally suggest that certain circumstances, such as stress, may lead to constant anxiety or depressive symptoms because they reduce the number of positive stimuli in a person's environment. Certain conditions in our lives may either increase or decrease the probability of abnormal or dysfunctional emotional symptoms. Overall, behavior therapies based on principles of operant conditioning have often been effective (Lewinsohn, Rohde, Seeley, Klein, & Gotlib, 2003; Nolen-Hoeksema, 1991).

Self-control therapy is used in dealing with emotional problems. It contains three phases. During the first phase—*self-monitoring*—the person receives a homework assignment, which consists of monitoring positive activities with immediate and delayed reinforcement value (Craighead, Miklowitz, & Craighead, 2013. In the second phase—*self-evaluation*—clients are taught to use self-monitoring data to define realistic and reachable goals in behavioral terms. For example, the person describes the specific steps that he or she should take to solve specific life situations. In the third phase—*self-reinforcement*—people are helped to create self-administered reinforcement programs. Behavioral distraction techniques, such as blocking negative thoughts, are sometimes used as well to help individuals avoid ruminations (or constant focusing on one's negative emotions). In particular, patients learn that their behavior is controlled by rewards and punishments, and that is the way to control their own actions, too. They also learn that people tend to self-punish too much and self-reward too little. At the end of therapy, patients construct individual self-reinforcement programs aimed at maintaining and increasing the level of positive activities in which they should engage. It results in an inventory of activities that contains various kinds of reinforcement.

Education

Many teaching strategies use principles of social learning. These strategies aim at enhancing students' knowledge acquisition and retention. For example, rather than just explaining things to their students, teachers could try using the technique of guided participation. For example, the teacher says a short statement and then asks the students in class to repeat it. While repeating aloud, the students imitate their teacher and develop and retain the information. Then the class and the teacher exchange opinions about the statement. The teacher delivers positive reinforcement to those students who participate. The students are encouraged to make evaluations themselves, and they begin playing a more active role in the process. By encouraging the students to adopt the position of active observers, the teacher improves the students' retention and their learning outcomes (Kumpulainen & Wray, 2002).

Extinction The process of extinction is the act of abandoning a bad habit or decreasing a fearful reaction.

Self-control therapy A behavioral method in dealing with emotional problems, self-control therapy contains three phases: self-monitoring, self-evaluation, and self-reinforcement.

CHECK AND APPLY YOUR KNOWLEDGE

1. Taylorism is psychology's convenient target to criticize, yet you can find some of its ideas applicable to our daily lives. For example, how much time do you waste every day on something that's under your control? Reflect on your day today. Identify the moments that you consider a waste of time (it could be anything, like chatting with someone, spending time on social networks, browsing the web aimlessly, just hanging out, etc.). Now make an authoritative decision: Tomorrow, try to regain at least some of the time that you think you wasted today. Shorten, cut, or avoid just one of the activities you listed. Do the same the next day. Make saving time a habit. After 2 or 3 days of such habit formation, describe your impressions. Discuss them in class. Was Taylor right or wrong for "pushing" us to change our habits? Will you continue practicing your time saving? Why or why not?

2. Behavioral economics teaches about rational and irrational choices. Return to the example on subjective safety and risky behavior. These days, car accidents are down, and cars are getting safer. However, one of the biggest risks now is the use of electronic devices when driving. Just 2 seconds of taking your eyes off the road may lead to a tragedy.

   a. In the following practicum, for 1 week, conduct a self-monitoring exercise: Join with two or three people and pledge not to use a smartphone while driving— the driver shall not text or browse the web while sitting behind the wheel.

   b. During this week, recall the episodes when you were really tempted to use the device. What were the occasions? Did you use the phone or not? Did you stop your car first before using it?

   c. Discuss your observations with others. Has your pledge helped you not to use the phone and to what degree?

   d. How would personal examples help persuade others not to text or browse while driving?

Visual Review

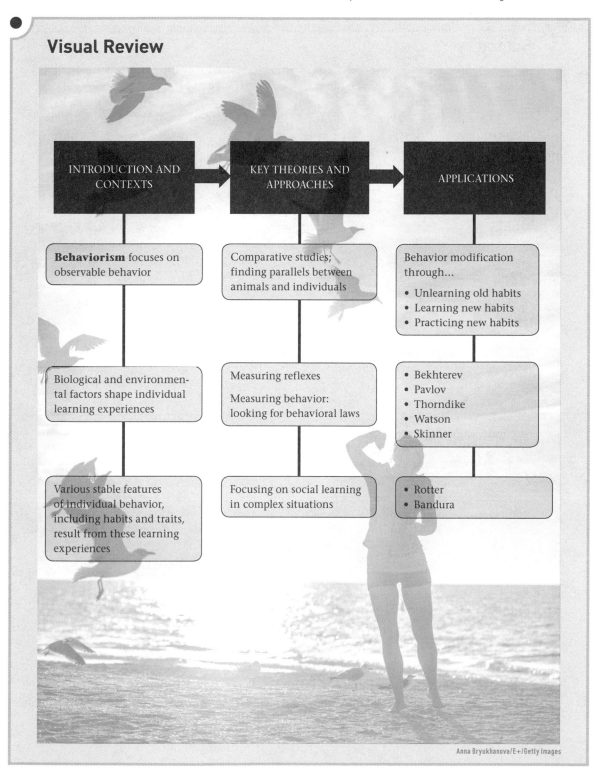

INTRODUCTION AND CONTEXTS → **KEY THEORIES AND APPROACHES** → **APPLICATIONS**

Behaviorism focuses on observable behavior

Comparative studies; finding parallels between animals and individuals

Behavior modification through...
- Unlearning old habits
- Learning new habits
- Practicing new habits

Biological and environmental factors shape individual learning experiences

Measuring reflexes

Measuring behavior: looking for behavioral laws

- Bekhterev
- Pavlov
- Thorndike
- Watson
- Skinner

Various stable features of individual behavior, including habits and traits, result from these learning experiences

Focusing on social learning in complex situations

- Rotter
- Bandura

Anna Bryukhanova/E+/Getty Images

Summary

- Behaviorism is the psychological and interdisciplinary tradition that focuses on observable behavior. Behaviorists offer a clear view of personality: an individual's development, actions, complex behavior, and traits are all based on the underlying learning processes. Behaviorism as a tradition primarily grew within psychology. It also evolved together with other disciplines, including biology and physiology.

- A behavioral learning approach emphasizes the importance of situational, environmental, and developmental factors in an individual's learning, choices, habits, traits, and the ways they change and develop.

- Comparative psychologists accepted the evolutionary ideas of Darwin and Spencer and believed in the adaptive nature of animal behavior. To understand difficult, complex phenomena, a scientist should seek the simplest explanations. This principle, known in science as parsimony, became a working rule for comparative researchers. Portraying animal behavior in human terms is called anthropomorphism. Early comparative psychologists tended to support anthropomorphism to some degree and sought scientific data to connect animal and human behavior. Supporters of anthropomorphism also found a seemingly convenient concept linking animal and human behavior: the instinct, or the inherent pattern of a complex behavior.

- The learning process of animals was called habit formation and means the process by which new behaviors or responses become automatic. Thorndike, using new experimental methods, described the learning curve: the improvement of learning with experience.

Thorndike's experiments provided him empirical data to suggest several laws of learning, which are the essential principles on which learning is based.

- Researchers' interest in studying reflexes has been consistent and stemmed from the teachings of René Descartes and the physiologists of the 19th century. Bekhterev suggested reflexology, a unifying new science to study reflexes. Reflexology used the principle of energy transformation. Personality, in his view, was an integrative core of reflexes.

- Pavlov turned to an objective study of the highest nervous activity (i.e., behavior) referring to physiological activities of the brain's cortex. He recognized two categories of reflexes: unconditioned and conditioned. He introduced the concept of physiological associations to explain an individual's complex behavior. Pavlov introduced behavioral types from the standpoint of three functions of the nervous system: strength, balance, and agility. According to Pavlov, there are four types of personalities based on four types of nervous systems: (1) strong, balanced, and mobile; (2) strong, balanced, and slow; (3) strong, unbalanced, and spontaneous; and (4) weak. Within this structure, psychopathological syndromes could be defined as exaggerations of the normal traits.

- Watson considered behavior as actual movements of the body: legs and arms, glands, and specific muscles. Watson saw any complex behavior as containing numerous smaller behavioral elements. Watson suggested three founding principles of behaviorism: stimulus and response, habit formation, and habit integration. Watson saw personality as a totality of organized behavioral acts, such as habits, instincts, emotions, and their combinations. Personalities are different because individuals have different capacity in new habit formation or change of old habits. Watson argued that a healthy personality consists of well-developed and efficient habit systems. Abnormal features are characterized by an individual's inability to get rid of old habits and old emotions in new situations in which those old habits are no longer efficient. Mental illness was a kind of habit disturbance.

- Holt followed Watson but argued that in real-life situations, behavior is different, more complex, and must be understood as a multifaceted unity of many behavioral acts. He introduced the concept of molar responses. Tolman offered key ideas of purposive or operational behaviorism. He also suggested an expansion of the traditional $S \rightarrow R$ (stimulus–response) model and added $S \rightarrow O \rightarrow R$, in which O stood for measurable processes or variables within an organism. Tolman moved further away from traditional behaviorism by introducing the concept called a cognitive map.

- Skinner believed psychologists should focus on overt behavior instead. He was not really interested in what was going "inside" the brain. He turned to descriptive behaviorism and the study of behavioral reinforcements. Learning

through reward and punishment received the name operant conditioning. Skinner came up with the idea of schedules of reinforcement, or conditions involving different rates and times of reinforcement. By changing the conditions of schedules of reinforcement, the researchers were able to measure behavioral responses. Skinner, a social designer, applied his research to address human problems and explain the modern individual. People, according to his works, are misguided in their overconfident belief in individual freedom.

- *Social learning theory* is a general term that means, among other things, that learning does not necessarily need reinforcement and conditioning. Instead, an individual's experiences and social environment play a powerful role in learning.

- Julian Rotter showed consistent differences among individuals in the degree to which they attribute or explain personal control. Albert Bandura showed that learning occurred by observing a person's behavior and its consequences.

- Behavioral learning principles can be used in many fields of applications, including behavioral economics, organizational development, education, and coping with traumatic stress.

Key Terms

agility of the nervous system 177	behaviorism 168	extinction 193
Aircrib 184	cognitive map 182	habit disturbance 180
anthropomorphism 171	conditioned reflexes 176	habit formation 172
balance of the nervous system 177	deindividuation 172	instinct 171
	external locus of control 187	internal locus of control 187

Evaluating What You Know

What are the main principles of the behavioral learning tradition?

What is anthropomorphism?

Explain the learning curve.

What was Watson's view of introspection?

Explain Tolman's cognitive map.

Define *operant conditioning*.

Give an example of schedule reinforcement.

What were major ideas of *Walden Two* and *Beyond Freedom and Dignity*?

Explain Taylorism.

What are practical applications of behavioral economics?

A Bridge to the Next Chapter

Skinner was probably the most recognizable representative of the behaviorist-learning tradition and should have taught us several valuable lessons. First, in our continuing quest to understand personality, we certainly need to learn more about behavior and its reinforcement. However, we must not ignore the complexity and the beauty of an individual's experiences. Our personalities are not necessarily combinations of reactions and reflexes—no matter how sophisticated these reactions can be. Your traits are not simply a selection of habits. The supporters of psychoanalytic tradition have already presented their case in favor of the "subjective" side in the previous chapters. Their arguments are intriguing but vague. At this point, we are ready to study the subjective side of personality using contemporary science.

Jonathan Knowles/Stone/Getty Images

7

The Trait Tradition

"I was always an unusual girl. My mother told me I had a chameleon soul, no moral compass pointing due north, no fixed personality; just an inner indecisiveness that was as wide and as wavering as the ocean."

—Lana Del Rey (b. 1985), American singer and songwriter

Learning Objectives

After reading this chapter, you should be able to:

- Identify the main principles and historical contexts of the trait tradition
- Discuss Allport's four columns, Cattell's 16PF, and Eysenck's E and N
- Explain the Big Five approach to personality
- Discuss personality from religious and cross-cultural perspectives
- Identify ways to apply the key principles of the trait tradition to individual experience and behavior

D r. Henry Jekyll and his alternative personality, Mr. Edward Hyde, are fictional characters in Robert L. Stevenson's famous book *Strange Case of Dr. Jekyll and Mr. Hyde* (1886). After drinking a special potion, Dr. Jekyll changes from a nice, friendly man to his alter-personality, Mr. Hyde, who is nasty, violent, and bad. Two personalities lived in one person, changing control of the body's behavior and the mind's functioning. This story and its characters have become widely recognized symbols symbolizing "good" and "bad" individual types—one oriented toward respect and peace, the other toward lust and violence. Some psychoanalysts would say that both these types demonstrate the existence of aggressive and impious impulses in all human beings. Dr. Jekyll represents the superego, while Mr. Hyde embodies the id. Some behaviorists would probably emphasize the environmental conditions surrounding the two types and the ways both types were conditioned to become who they were.

Yet what else can we learn about these characters? It looks that they appear to be more complex and controversial that they seem. For example, Dr. Jekyll, who has a "good" personality, was very unhappy and felt guilty for having an evil side within him. On the other hand, Mr. Hyde, who was a "bad" person, was thrilled to be engaged in violent and illegal acts. Dr. Jekyll was able, for the most part, to control his impulses. Mr. Hyde did not. Besides labeling these two types (or other types of individuals) as *good* and *evil*, we certainly need to know more about their specific individual features. Speaking of these two characters, what do we know about their emotional stability, their openness to new learning experiences, their dependability, or their ability to be patient or forecast their life? Is it very important for psychologists to pay more attention to specific individual features and characteristics and to measure or assess these characteristics.

Public domain

Photo 7.1 In Stevenson's book, Dr. Jekyll had good traits, while Mr. Hyde had evil ones. Yet in reality, can a "bad" person still have several good traits?

The Trait Approach

Traits
Traits are distinguishable and stable patterns of behavior and experience.

The trait tradition in personality psychology focuses on identifying and measuring **traits,** which are distinguishable and stable patterns of behavior and experience. Recall from Chapter 4 and Chapter 5 that the psychoanalytic tradition focuses on unconscious mechanisms directing the inner world of the individual. The behavioral learning tradition discussed in Chapter 6 brings our attention to the individual's observable behavior. Psychoanalysis emphasizes the subjective side of the individual's life, while behaviorism diminishes it. The trait tradition focuses on both behavior and experience and pays some attention to their causes. Yet it is mostly interested in identification and measurement of individual traits. These traits, as you remember from Chapter 1, include stable patterns of physical actions, decisions, emotions, and thoughts. The combination and interaction of various traits form a personality that is unique to each individual. The trait tradition to personality also focuses on differences between individuals and describes such differences as quantifiable, or measurable.

Like behaviorists and psychoanalysts, psychologists working within the trait tradition generally accept several common principles or general expectations related to their research and applications. First, traits are not just single behavioral manifestations or isolated emotional reactions. Your patient may appear nervous and timid during his first therapy session.

Or a new acquaintance of yours appears outspoken and funny in the afternoon during lunch and then quiet and reserved in the evening. Which situation was more telling about these individuals' traits? Probably neither because we haven't examined their behavior over a longer period of time. Traits are supposed to be stable, or relatively unchanging over a significant period. Traits are different from what we call "states." In our daily English vocabulary, we sometimes describe ourselves or other people as being in a particular emotional or motivational state. We say, "I don't want you to be in such as sad state," or "She is going through a state in which she is only focused on her work." Or a person may go through a period of dysphoria, such as exaggerated sadness, lack of motivation, fatigue, and the like. In the opening vignette, Dr. Jekyll was likely going through two different states: One was his natural state, and the other was induced by a chemical concoction. However, states are likely to evolve with or without an individual's deliberate effort or an outside intervention. Psychologists usually understand states, compared to traits, as more transitory or dynamic (Steyer, Mayer, Geiser, & Cole, 2015).

Second, traits should also impact the individual's actions, emotions, and overall experiences. In other words, if we recognize and measure a particular trait in a person, we should anticipate that he or she should react, think, or feel in a certain way in many other situations. For example, if somebody displays a trait such as openness to experience (we will look later at it as a trait), then we should anticipate that this individual is likely in most situations to have a tendency to learn, explore, study new materials, read, meet new people, take chances, and seek novel things in life.

Third, traits are expected to be dichotomous, or in many cases, measured as a point on a continuum. It is not very common that a person either "has" or "does not have" a particular trait, such as impulsivity; there are times when nearly all of us will do some things impulsively, without giving much thought to the actions. It is likely that we each have certain levels of individual traits somewhere along this spectrum.

Yet how many traits are there? In the past 100 years or so, psychologists proposed, studied, and measured a significant number of individual personality traits. A few include aggressiveness, assertiveness, propensity for anxiety, extroversion, conscientiousness, and so on. Some psychologists suggested dozens of traits to describe an individual, while others offered just a few (Corr & Matthews, 2009). Some psychologists, as we will see in this chapter, also offered their own original scales to measure the traits. They have proposed these and their **taxonomies**, which are descriptive models or classifications based on similarity, functioning, structure, size, origin, and the like. Taxonomies are supposed to be scientifically based, of course, and provide opportunities for further examination and careful review. These models should also be understood in a relatively simple way. Furthermore, to examine the similarities and differences among individuals, psychologists have to examine a relatively small (or at least manageable) number of individual traits rather than go through hundreds and maybe thousands of characteristics that may describe individual features that make us, humans, different. A "good" taxonomy should also allow psychologists to efficiently compare their findings with other psychologists' research, use a common language to describe these traits, and improve research communication among other researchers (John & Srivastava, 2001).

Taxonomies
Taxonomies are descriptive models or classifications based on similarity, function, structure, size, origin, and the like.

The trait tradition is not a lone theory but a way researchers think about and conduct research related to personality traits. It is a distinct type of research that recognizes and measures the strength or salience of personality traits. The degree or similar measure referring to these traits should indicate an "identification card" of each individual's personality.

Ancient Philosophies

The ideas about personality as a distinct combination of traits appeared in many ancient philosophical teachings. Buddhist thinkers referred to an individual uniqueness as a combination of various traits. Five constituents of personality (*khandha*) exist: body, perception, feeling, mental formations, and consciousness (Collins, 1990). The ancient Greek philosophers believed that individual traits should refer to the work of different parts of the body, such as the heart, the liver, or the brain; the heart and the liver had something to do with courage, lustfulness, stamina, and awareness, and the brain had something to do with judgment, patience, and intellectual skills. Many early classifications described the individual's bodily humors as foundations of stable traits. A misbalance in bodily humors—either due to inborn factors or other natural forces—likely caused this person to be either persistently and unreasonably elated or constantly withdrawn and grumpy or stubbornly belligerent and unpredictable or persistently sad or easily disturbed.

In the teachings of Hinduism, people had obligations in regard to their positions in society and to their stages of individual development. They had to act and think according to the prescribed models. The Brahmins (the highest class) taught religion; the nobles practiced defense; the commoners plowed, tended cattle, and lent money; and the lowest class served the upper ones. The caste system has had a profound impact on India's society, as well as on the individual behavior and thinking of many generations of Indians. It is outlawed in contemporary India, but its prescriptions are likely to be embedded in customs and subsequent thought and behavior of many individuals (Collins, 1990). Hinduism suggests various combinations of traits based on an individual's stages. For example, one can be labeled *the moral student* for combining good learning habits of religion with obedience. Another can be labeled *the dreamer* for combining faith and affection, but pursuing only little knowledge and obedience (Robbie, 2014).

In the Islamic tradition, there are several "levels" or qualities of personality traits distinguished according to the quality of *nafs* (self or soul): The lowest is characterized by the tendency toward evil; the middle level is associated with conscience and concern with moral rectitude; the highest level is associated with gradual movement toward perfection in thought and action (Kasule, 2000).

Astrological explanations of personality traits appeared in ancient times and remained very common for centuries (they remain very popular today as part of popular beliefs). According to these explanations, specific personality traits largely depend on celestial bodies. For example, the planet Jupiter was associated with an individual's predominant happiness and optimism. The impact from the planet Saturn could make certain people constantly bitter or sardonic. Mars as a planet affected traits such as bravery and conscientiousness. Did you know that the meaning of the term *lunatic* (in Latin, it is *lunaticus*) comes from the belief that the moon could negatively influence a person's behavior, which becomes unpredictable and irrational under the moon's influence?

Early Research in the Humanities and Psychology

It is hard to find a philosopher from the past who didn't write about personality traits. The prominent English thinker David Hume (1711–1776) described at least four most significant traits: pleasure seeking (which is a commitment to fun, variety, and entertainment), virtue seeking (a commitment to good deeds and action), philosophical devotion (a commitment to thinking), and critical thinking (a commitment to skepticism and evaluation). Another English philosopher, David Hartley (1705–1757), distinguished two groups of traits. The first group includes imagination, ambition, and self-interest. The second group includes sympathy, theopathy, and the moral sense. *Imagination* refers to objects as sources of pleasure or displeasure. *Ambition* is the realization of one's own status in the eyes of other people. *Self-interest* manages the demands of imagination and ambition. *Sympathy* refers to the feelings of other people. *Theopathy* refers to the individual's moral sense and connection with spiritual issues, such as religion. Although Hartley's theory of personality is based on theoretical assumptions, his approach shared common ground with various trait theories of personality developed during the 20th century by Gordon Allport, Raymond Cattell, and others. As in Hartley's writings, these theories state that individuals tend to possess relatively stable and unique characteristics.

Early experimental psychologists were looking for empirical descriptions and explanations of individual traits. The German psychologist Wilhelm Wundt (1832–1920), one of the founders of experimental psychology, believed that language had a big role in forming individual traits. When an individual speaks a particular language, this person then follows a particular custom and thus acquires a specific order of thinking. Wundt described Greek and Latin languages as relatively loose in terms of the positioning

SELF-REFLECTION

Meyer Friedman and his coworkers (Friedman & Ulmer, 1984) defined what they called Type A and Type B patterns. Type A traits include impatience and assertive competitiveness; people with them tend to challenge other people. They are intense and hard driving and do not mind engaging in conflicts. Type B people, on the other hand, tend to be patient and less competitive, possessing traits that help them be kind to others. They are not intense and prefer to avoid conflicts. There was also a Type AB, which is a mixed profile of traits that are between the Types A and Type B. Type AB people are likely to be intense and hard driving in some situations and less intense in others.

Questions

Which type of traits are you likely to have: A, B, or AB? How do you know that? Would you like to change these traits in yourself? Why or why not?

Photo 7.2 The German psychologist Wilhelm Wundt (1832–1920), one of the founders of experimental psychology, believed that language had a big role in forming individual traits.

Public domain

of words in comparison to the German language, which, according to Wundt, requires discipline, precision, and order. Thus, people who spoke German beginning in childhood were more likely to become most organized, orderly, and responsible compared to others who do not speak German (Wundt, 1916).

Recall from Chapter 4 that Carl Jung studied personality traits such as introversion and extroversion, and he provided detailed descriptions about them (these are described in Chapter 4 on pages 122–125). Jung used a pure observational method in describing personality traits, but other researchers were turning to more empirical methods. German-born psychologist William Stern (1871–1938), who is also known for his early studies of intelligence, studied personality as a unique, active, and self-contained entity. According to his research, individual traits are formed in the process of constant interaction among the environment, the individual's characteristics, and the individual's motivation, intellectual skills, and personal goals. He also gave a classification of individual types.

The American psychologist James McKeen Cattell (1860–1944) coined the term *mental test* in 1890 to indicate the procedures used to measure "mental energy" of the participants in psychological experiments. Attention was paid to the difference between (a) an individual's performance and (b) the performance of large populations on the same test. The goal of such measurements was mostly educational: Cattell believed that university counselors would use mental testing to make speedy assessments of students' potentials and give reasonable advice about their futures. He first began to administer tests in 1894 to students at Columbia University, where he worked as a professor. In the early 1900s, many universities and private businesses asked psychologists to help them with assessments of individual traits of students, potential employees, and workers (von Mayrhauser, 2002).

CHECK AND APPLY YOUR KNOWLEDGE

1. Define *traits*.

2. What are taxonomies?

3. Who were lunatics, and why were they called this?

4. Find any astrological horoscope online. What does the horoscope tell you about your personality traits? How accurate or inaccurate is the description of your traits? Is the description equally accurate in describing other people, such as your friends?

Most of the teachings in philosophy and the humanities about individual traits were speculative and based on a particular doctrine, or ideological knowledge. However, early psychologists were determined to bring science to their study of traits. They often disagreed about the sources of their knowledge and about the theory and methods of their investigation.

Trait Theorists and Perspectives

Several prominent psychologists have contributed to the trait tradition. Unlike psychoanalysts or behaviorists, they did not call themselves *trait psychologists*. The label arrived later, mostly out of convenience, when other psychologists began their evaluations of this rich legacy of studies of individual traits.

Gordon Allport

The American psychologist Gordon Allport (1897–1967) was a pioneer psychologist who created a new field of study dedicated to the measurement of personality. He was born in Indiana and from the beginning of his life witnessed and appreciated the hard work, perseverance, and religious dedication of his parents. As a Harvard social ethics student, Allport was genuinely committed to science. A formative experience for Allport was his postdoctoral fellowship in Germany in the fall of 1922. He was influenced by the works of the German psychologist William Stern, especially by Stern's attempts to measure and categorize an individual's traits (Allport, 1937; Nicholson, 2000).

Allport argued that "character" and "personality" were distinct and different entities. Borrowing this idea from the behaviorist John Watson, Allport maintained that character was a moral category associated with societal prescriptions and the manner with which people follow these directions. Personality, on the other hand, referred to the objective self, or the fundamental adjustment patterns that an individual forms over the course of his or her life and in various situations. Allport described both internal and external forces that influence an individual's personality traits. Two of them included genotypes and phenotypes. **Genotypes** are our individual forces that relate to how we keep information and use it to interact with the social and physical world around us. **Phenotypes** reflect the way individuals accept their environments and how others influence their behavior.

Throughout his career, Allport repeatedly emphasized the "unique" quality of individuals. The study of personality, he believed, should focus on the way in which traits join together (Allport, 1924). He maintained that there was a stable core of traits in every person (Allport, 1937). Allport also believed that only experimental procedures and measurements (as was done with intelligence testing) could bring psychology a new understanding of personality, free from theoretical speculation.

Allport and his colleagues wanted to find one or more unifying principles that could help them create a reliable, science-based taxonomy of personality traits. Yet to study such principles and create a classification, they had to have a comprehensive list of personality traits. Where could such a description be obtained? One of Allport's assumptions was that the daily language we speak and write should contain

Genotypes
In Allport's theory, genotypes are individual forces that relate to how we keep information and use it to interact with the social and physical world around us.

Phenotypes
In Allport's theory, phenotypes are internal and external forces that reflect the way individuals accept their environments and how others influence their behavior.

a very exhaustive database of labels, tags, and markers that people historically and commonly attached to other people's behavior, feelings, and a great variety of other manifestations. A few psychologists before them had already studied dictionaries in search of the words that would describe mental states and had identified thousands of such words related to traits in German and English (Klages, 1929). Yet what should be done with these words to study personality? Allport and Odbert (1936) identified 17,953 unique terms used to describe the individual's personality, behavior, feelings, and so on. Next, they separated these into four categories (or columns) based on their own criteria for classification (see **Table 7.1**).

This placement of traits into columns appears both logical and arbitrary. The researchers were aware of the subjectivity of such a classification and used several research assistants for independent reviewing to increase the consistency of their evaluations. Yet the degree of consistency among different assistants was relatively low. Allport also realized that many individual traits are too complex to be limited to single words. Moreover, he was also aware that the words related to personality meant different things in different languages and cultural groups.

Allport presented personality traits as cardinal, central, and secondary. Cardinal traits dominate an individual's personality and should explain most of his or her important decisions or actions. These traits stand out. For example, referring to the opening vignette, propensity for cruelty would likely be Mr. Hyde's cardinal trait. Propensity for nonviolence would probably be Mohandas Gandhi's cardinal trait (he was the preeminent leader of the Indian independence movement). We easily recognize some people among our friends and relatives because of their cardinal traits.

Next, individuals have several central traits, which are viewed as basic building blocks of an individual's personality. In the case of Mr. Hyde, it could be his thrill-seeking activities, such as indecent acts and impulsivity. As a rule, cardinal traits influence central traits, and their influence is mutual.

Finally, there are more than a few secondary traits. They tend to appear as patterns in particular circumstances. They are less dominant in their ability to influence behavior compared with the cardinal and central traits.

Allport's research into personality was inspired by a deep belief in social progressivism: He believed in the transformational power of the educated action. Like

TABLE 7.1 ● Gordon Allport's Classification of Personality Traits			
Column I	**Column II**	**Column III**	**Column IV**
Descriptions of seemingly stable personality traits such as polite, extroverted, assertive, aggressive, kind, and so on	Descriptions of passing emotional states, and attitudes such as frantic, calm, and so on	Reflections of other people regarding an individual's character, such as valuable, respectable, and the like	Important personality descriptive terms that did not fit into the other three columns, such as physical abilities or skills

many of his colleagues at the time, he also believed that the solutions to problems such as poverty, crime, and violence should be found in the works of scientists—psychologists in particular. He understood, however, that psychology as a discipline could not change social institutions at will. Psychology provides knowledge, yet this knowledge, if applied correctly, should change many people's traits, and subsequently, their behavior for the better.

Raymond Cattell

Raymond Cattell (1905–1998) was a British American psychologist who joined the ranks of many colleagues and contemporaries in his belief that only science and the scientific method could explain human behavior and experience. He received his undergraduate and advanced college degrees in the United Kingdom. After moving to the United States, he was invited by Gordon Allport to join Harvard University in 1941. As did most American psychologists during World War II, he contributed to the war effort as a consultant to the U.S. government, working on various tests for selecting officers in the armed forces. After the war, he joined the University of Illinois, where he worked for almost 30 years. He is considered among the most quoted psychologists of the 20th century and beyond (Tucker, 2009).

Like Allport, Cattell felt that psychology should distance itself from speculation and embrace measurement (Cattell, 1965, 1983). Such measurements should be available for verification, or retesting by other scientists (peer review), and the results should be explained in an open discussion. Earlier in his career, Cattell was working with Charles Spearman, who studied human abilities and with whom he learned about factor analysis (see Chapter 3)—a method to deal with large numbers of observed variables that are thought to reflect a smaller number of underlying variables (Cattell, 1978). Factor analysis performs complex calculations on the correlation coefficients among the variables within a particular domain (personality features) to determine the basic, primary factors for the particular domain. This method gave him confidence that a long list of human traits (different psychologists provided various lineups of traits) could be shortened and not necessarily by subjective reasoning and prejudgments. He believed that factor analysis could identify basic "building blocks," such as honesty or aggressive tendencies (like molecules in chemistry) of human personality (Cattell, 1946).

To apply factor analysis to personality, Cattell used three kinds of data: life, experimental, and questionnaire-based. He taught that to obtain life data (or L-data) the researcher should gather facts from the individual's behavior patterns in the real world. This could include jobs she or he has held, number of friends, frequency of visits to a doctor, and even eating and sleeping habits. Experimental data (or T-data) are about responses to standardized experimental situations created in a psychology laboratory where a subject's behavior is investigated and measured. And finally, questionnaire data (or Q-data) are about self-assessments or answers to a series of questions about specific behaviors or experiences.

He reexamined the largest compilation of words representing personality traits available to him (Allport & Odbert, 1936) and collected adjectives related to human personality. He then organized the list of adjectives into fewer than 200 items by eliminating redundancies, and then he asked subjects to evaluate people they knew with each of the adjectives on the list. Using data from three of the measurement domains (L-data, Q-data, T-data) and then applying factor analysis, Cattell identified a number of trait factors within the personality (Cattell, 1978). He used a technological device that was new at that time—the computer—to conduct a programmatic series of factor analyses on the data derived from each of the measurements (Cattell, 1983). In the end, Cattell was able to reduce the list of hundreds of psychological traits into 16 basic groups or dimensions that he believed were the core of the individual's personality (Kaplan & Saccuzzo, 2013). It appeared to observers that because of Cattell's background in the physical sciences he saw personality traits as fundamental underlying elements of daily human behavior and experience. To reiterate, Cattell believed that as chemical elements in the periodic system, psychological and behavioral features of individuals should be identifiable and measurable (see **Table 7.2**; Cattell, 1965).

16PF The Sixteen Personality Factor Questionnaire was developed by Raymond Cattell.

Cattell developed a test known as the Sixteen Personality Factor Questionnaire (**16PF**) to measure these personality features. This self-report method was revised at least four times, translated in several languages, and adopted for use in many

TABLE 7.2 ● Sixteen-Factor Structure of Personality by Raymond Cattell (1965)		
Factor	**High-Degree Manifestations**	**Low-Degree Manifestations**
Warmth	Outgoing	Reserved
Reasoning	Abstract	Concrete
Emotional stability	Stable	Volatile
Dominance	Forceful	Submissive
Liveliness	Spontaneous	Restrained
Rule-Consciousness	Conforming	Nonconforming
Social boldness	Uninhibited	Shy
Sensitivity	Sensitive	Tough-Minded
Vigilance	Suspicious	Trusting
Abstractedness	Imaginative	Practical
Privateness	Discrete	Open
Apprehension	Anxious	Confident
Openness to change	Flexible	Inflexible
Self-Reliance	Self-Sufficient	Dependent
Perfectionism	Controlled	Undisciplined
Tension	Impatient	Relaxed

countries. This has been one of the most popular psychological methods used globally for clinical, educational, and other purposes (Cattell & Mead, 2008; Shiraev & Levy, 2013). Just browse a few introductory psychology books, and you will see that Cattell remains one of the most talked-about psychologists (Tucker, 2009).

Hans Eysenck

Hans Eysenck (1916–1997) was a German-born psychologist who lived and worked in the United Kingdom. He is known for his work on a wide range of topics within psychology, including intelligence. One of his most significant contributions to psychology was in personality psychology. Like Cattell, he used empirical data and factor-analytic research to design and develop his theory. He emphasized two major personality dimensions: extroversion and neuroticism (Eysenk, 1948). Psychologists frequently refer to these dimensions as **Eysenck's E and N.**

Extroversion (E) is characterized by talkativeness, positive emotions, and the need to seek external sources of stimulation. Eysenk believed that traits should have a strong biological background, and he maintained that extroversion, for example, is based on brain activities that determine a person's level of arousal. People who are prone to extroversion tend to be underaroused (bored) so that they need to seek new experiences to achieve the optimal level of arousal. Introversion, on the other hand, is characterized by quietness, doubt, and the need to stick to inner experiences. People who are prone to introversion tend to be overaroused (jittery) and thus need calm and peace to achieve their optimal level of arousal.

Neuroticism (N) refers to an individual's level of emotionality. People who measure high in neuroticism have the tendency to see danger in many people, events, and developments around them. Their brains are activated quickly when they face a new situation or encounter a new problem. They tend to experience negative reactions associated with fear or anger. They tend to be easily upset and are also prone to depression and anxiety. People who measure low in neuroticism tend to be emotionally stable. Their brains are not activated quickly in new circumstances. They tend to control their negative emotions and are likely to be calm and collected under pressure. Depression and anxiety are not typical among them (see **Table 7.3**).

Eysenck's E and N Hans Eysenck studied two personality dimensions, extroversion (E) and neuroticism (N).

Extroversion (E) In Eysenck's system, extroversion (E) is characterized by talkativeness, positive emotions, and the need to seek external sources of stimulation.

Neuroticism (N) In Eysenck's system, neuroticism (N) refers to an individual's level of emotionality. People who measure high in neuroticism have the tendency to see danger in many people, events, and developments around them

TABLE 7.3 ● Extroversion–Introversion and Emotional Stability–Instability, According to Eysenck (1948)

Extroversion	High Neuroticism	Low Neuroticism
High	Tend to be quick-tempered, restless, edgy, changeable, impulsive, irresponsible	Tend to be outgoing, talkative, responsible, friendly, carefree, and display leadership
Low	Tend to be quiet, reserved, pessimistic, solemn, rigid, anxious, and often moody	Tend to be calm, even-tempered, consistent, controlled, peaceful, thoughtful, careful, and passive

Eysenck emphasized that these two dimensions were somewhat similar to the four personality types (commonly called temperaments) first proposed by the Greek physician Hippocrates: the Choleric (high N and E), the Melancholic (high N and low E), the Sanguine (Low N and high E), and the Phlegmatic (both N and E are low). The famous Greek speculated about the individual; Eysenck provided empirical research.

Later on in his career, Eysenck added another dimension to his model of the individual's personality. He called it **psychoticism,** which is a personality pattern that manifests as persistent aggressiveness and hostility toward others (Eysenck & Eysenck, 1976). Specifically, people with a predisposition to psychoticism tend to be tough-minded and nonconforming, as well as prone to recklessness, unfriendliness, anger, and impulsiveness. They tend not to experience remorse. Dr. Jekyll, from the introduction, would have scored low on psychoticism. Mr. Hyde's score, on the other hand, would have been very high.

Psychoticism also stands for impulsive tendencies in behavior (such as speaking before thinking or making a decision before assessing the decision's consequences) and **sensation seeking**, which is the constant tendency to search for new experiences and feelings. People who measure high on psychoticism tend to be sensation seekers. They need adventure. They tend to like wild parties and unusual activities. They tend to look for new psychological experiences using unconventional choices, including alcohol and other types of substances. They also feel bored in the company of "ordinary" people (Zuckerman, 2007). Eysenck believed that psychoticism has a significant biological component. This trait also positively correlates with artistic creativity (Eysenck, 1993).

Psychoticism
Psychoticism is a personality pattern that manifests as persistent aggressiveness and hostility toward others.

Sensation seeking
Sensation seeking is the constant tendency to search for new experiences and feelings.

CHECK AND APPLY YOUR KNOWLEDGE

1. Explain Gordon Allport's four columns.

2. Where did Gordon Allport obtain significant empirical data for his research into personality?

3. What are cardinal, central, and secondary traits? What would be your cardinal trait or traits? What traits would you like other people recognize in you?

4. What is factor analysis?

5. What is 16PF?

6. Describe briefly Eysenck's E and N.

7. Define *sensation seeking*. Suggest two situations in which sensation seeking has (a) a negative impact on the individual life and education and (b) a positive impact.

The Big Five

For many years in the 20th century, research of personality traits was associated with the original theories by Gordon Allport, Raymond Cattell, Hans Eysenck, and a few others. A new generation of psychologists offered their own versions of these theories, as well as their own new theories. One approach developed by several psychologists caught some attention, and once additional research was conducted, this approach eventually received global recognition (Goldberg, 1993). In fact, it is a data-driven analysis of verbal descriptors of human behavioral patterns that tend to cluster together. This theory is often called the **Big Five**, or as some call it OCEAN, a convenient acronym to outline and better remember these traits.

This five-factor structure of personality traits appears in most studies in different countries. The traits can be labeled *openness*, *conscientiousness*, *extroversion*, *agreeableness*, and *neuroticism*. According to the theory, other individual traits are likely to fall within these five. All five factors are rather continuous because they measure a certain degree for the manifestation of each trait. The opposite characteristics are often labeled as *dogmatism*, *irresponsibility*, *introversion*, *unfriendliness*, and *emotional stability* (see **Figure 7.1**).

Big Five The Big Five personality theory states that individual traits are likely to fall into these five categories: openness to experience, conscientiousness, extroversion, agreeableness, and neuroticism.

Openness to Experience

People who score higher on this measure tend to be curious, inventive, and exploratory. A person with high scores here is open to new experiences and tends to be intellectually and emotionally curious, likes travel to new places, is sensitive to beauty, and is willing to experience new things. Be careful, though. These features are not supposed to be judged as unconditionally "good" or most desirable. We should consider them in specific circumstances. Sometimes people who are open to various

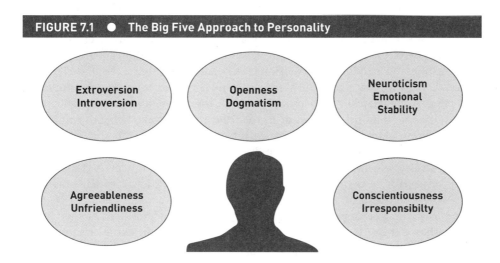

FIGURE 7.1 ● The Big Five Approach to Personality

Extroversion
Introversion

Openness
Dogmatism

Neuroticism
Emotional
Stability

Agreeableness
Unfriendliness

Conscientiousness
Irresponsibilty

experiences are viewed as lacking focus. On the other hand, those who score lower on openness tend to be cautious and more consistent in their interests and goals. Such people also tend to have more conventional, traditional interests in life. They prefer to plan things in advance and avoid ambiguity, rather than go with the flow. They prefer things that are familiar to them, while new things take some time to accept, if ever. They tend to be more resistant to change compared with those who are open to experience (McCrae & Costa, 1987).

Conscientiousness

People who score high on this measure tend to be organized, industrious, and efficient compared with those who display lower scores and tend to be less efficient and more carefree and blithe. Highly conscientious people strive for achievement and base their behavior on a plan. They tend to be less spontaneous and prefer an articulated strategy rather than improvisation. Nevertheless, high scores on conscientiousness may also indicate a person's stubbornness, making them be unreasonable and prone to mistakes. On the other hand, low scores on conscientiousness may indicate an individual's lack of a reliable behavior pattern. Low scores on conscientiousness may also indicate a person's ability to change and his or her spontaneity. A high level of conscientiousness is often related to the propensity to control, regulate, and direct desires and tame exciting ideas. These traits may change with age and changing social circumstances. Studies show that the average level of conscientiousness rises among young adults and then declines among older adults (Costa & McCrae, 1992).

Extroversion

A person who scores high on this variable tends to seek new contacts and attention, as well as be outgoing, full of energy, talkative, and dominant. People low on extroversion tend to be more reserved, not seek much attention, and not look for new contacts. They are more reflective and less talkative compared with others. Extroversion is usually about the scope and number of activities in which you are engaged. The opposite side of the spectrum is about depth and often attention to the quality of relationships and activities. Extroversion is associated with high levels of social interaction, along with being constantly energetic and action-oriented. People who are in this category are relatively visible simply because their presence is usually detectable: They talk more than listen, often sit in the front row, or make frequent comments. People low on extroversion (often called introverts—but remember, labels usually attempt to describe the entire person, and such simplistic descriptions are often inaccurate) display less intense social engagement and lower energy levels compared to others, especially to "extroverts." They tend to seem quiet, low-key, deliberate, and less involved in the social world. Their lack of social involvement should not be interpreted as shyness or depression; instead, they are more independent of their social worlds than extroverts. Introverts need less stimulation than extroverts and more time alone. This is not to suggest that they are unfriendly or antisocial; rather, they are reserved in social situations (Laney, 2002). Studies show that children with high scores on extroversion tend to be energetic, talkative, and more dominant in their play with children and interaction with adults. Children who score low on extroversion tend to be quieter, calmer, and appear more reserved than other children (Shiner & Caspi, 2003).

Agreeableness

People who rank high on this measure tend to appear friendly, cooperative, and compassionate to other individuals and to other people's concerns and problems. Lower scores on this measure are associated with an individual's detachment from other people's issues, a tendency to be unfriendly and even antagonistic. Agreeableness is also about a tendency to trust people, make new friends, listen to others, and cooperate with them. It is about an individual's desire to get along with neighbors, coworkers, and even strangers. It is about a tendency to seek approval from others and compromise by considering other people's plans and interests. Agreeableness may also appear as a negative, socially undesirable trend in an individual because it may be seen as a tendency of being weak, spineless, and "soft." On the other hand, low levels of agreeableness embody competition, challenge, skepticism, and a general tendency not to trust others. Trusting or not trusting others is not about being a good person or a bad one—it is highly contextual. Based on specific conditions, low and high levels of agreeableness may be useful or harmful to the individual's activities.

Neuroticism

A person who scores high on this variable tends to be more sensitive, concerned, and anxious compared to others. High scores indicate that the individual passionately cares about others and life in general. Low scores are associated with being calm, confident, and tough. Neuroticism typically refers to an individual's degree of emotional stability and the ability to handle incoming information and address real and imaginary threats. Neuroticism is also associated with a tendency to frequently experience negative emotions, such as anger and fear, and a tendency to experience anxiety or depression. High measures of neuroticism are associated with emotional instability—that is, the propensity to move back and forth from being in a good mood to being in a bad one (Jeronimus, Riese, Sanderman, & Ormel, 2014). Individuals who score high in neuroticism are likely to be vulnerable to stress. They are also more likely to interpret many everyday situations as threatening, difficult, and simply bad. Neuroticism is usually connected to a somewhat cynical (bitterly contemptuous and pessimistic) approach to work and social life (Fiske, Gilbert, & Lindzey, 2009). For people who score high on neuroticism, life usually appears as filled with negative events and new daily threats. At the other end of the scale, individuals who score low in neuroticism tend to be emotionally stable.

Why are there five and only five factors and not four or 10? Supporters of this approach say they are not using theoretical assumptions. Rather, they are deploying a data-driven method of analysis, which reduces the element of subjectivity. The five factors (no more or less) appeared because they are an empirical fact (Costa & McCrae, 1992). The mathematical method, supporters say, gives them confidence that they are learning the basic dimensions of personality (Block, 2001).

The five-factor theory has received significant empirical support. Studies have been conducted on various groups and in more than 50 countries. Twin studies suggest that both heritability and environmental factors influence all five factors to the approximately same degree (Bouchard & McGue, 2003; Jang, Livesley, & Vemon, 1996). Studies of longitudinal data, which correlate people's test scores over time, and cross-sectional data, which compare personality levels across different age groups, show a high degree of stability in personality traits during adulthood (McCrae & Costa, 1990). Cross-cultural studies also strongly suggested that personality trait structure is likely to be universal (Costa & McCrae, 1992; McCrae & Costa, 1997). The data obtained from comprehensive studies conducted in 28 languages and administered to almost 18,000 individuals from 56 nations show that the five-dimensional structure was present across major regions of the world. Moreover, people showed some differences as groups on certain measures. For example, people from the geographic regions of South America and East Asia were significantly different in openness from those inhabiting other world regions (Schmitt, Allik, McCrae, & BenetMartínez, 2007).

A study of gender differences in more than 50 countries found that women tended to be somewhat higher than men in neuroticism, extroversion, agreeableness, and conscientiousness. Gender differences in personality traits tended to be larger in prosperous, healthy, and more gender-equal–based cultures. Perhaps women's behaviors and traits in free and egalitarian countries are more likely to be attributed to their personalities, rather than to certain ascribed gender roles within more collectivist or traditional communities (Costa, Terracciano, & McCrae, 2001).

Certainly, the Big Five model has some weaknesses. One common criticism is that the theory explains an individual only superficially without looking at deeper structures and inner experiences. In addition, people tend to describe their own behavior differently than they describe other people's behavior (Piekkola, 2011). Psychologists also criticize the Big Five model for failing to include many other important features of human beings, such as honesty, masculinity and femininity, sense of humor, cynicism, selfishness, and so forth (we will return to these features in later chapters). The personalities of Dr. Jekyll and Mr. Hyde could not perfectly be described by the Big Five model; however, this model could have provided one of the best models available to psychologists these days.

Photo 7.3 Which specific personality traits would you like to develop in yourself to be more competitive in the job market?

© iStockphoto.com/PeopleImages

CHECK AND APPLY YOUR KNOWLEDGE

1. Why is the theory of personality called the Big Five?
2. Pick any trait from the list of the Big Five and describe yourself from the view of this trait.
3. Briefly explain why the Big Five model does not adequately explain the personalities of Dr. Jekyll and Mr. Hyde.

The Humanities and Personality Traits

Studies in the humanities reveal that religious knowledge contains detailed descriptions of desirable and undesirable individual types. These are not just individual acts or states; they are somewhat stable behavioral traits. Some religious teachings provide a clear dichotomy: They separate divine beings (such as saints) and profane beings (such as demons). In other religions, such as Hinduism, the divisions appear more complex because good and evil can be intertwined.

The Perfect. The sacred figures of saints, angels, and prophets provide a collective portrait of ideal, desirable individual qualities. Many religions distinguish an individual who carried the holiest, most divine, and important message from the supernatural entity. Muslims were taught to use the life of the prophet Mohammed as the touchstone for proper thought, decision, and action. Christians admire the life, the thought, and the deeds of Jesus Christ, which represented ultimate kindness, justice, wisdom, and compassion. Similarly, Siddhartha Gautama, or Buddha, has the complete set of personality traits admired by Buddhists.

Angels in most religious teachings usually appear as innocent and helpful transcendental beings who are universal helpers and rescuers. People attribute great, yet unexpected events to the work of angels. The saints are generally people who are believed to have holiness, which is a very high measure of perfection, purity, and righteousness. Saints commonly (1) sacrifice themselves for the sake of many, (2) refuse material possessions and bodily pleasures, and (3) inspire many followers to think, act, and feel in a different, positive, uplifting way (Hawley, 1987).

The Cursed. The devil is the ultimate evil; in fact, the most repulsive traits and individual features are often attributed to the devil. Evil characters appear in many shapes and forms, and they are labeled differently across cultures and religions. *Demons* and *ghosts* in Christianity; *jinn* in Islam; *vetala*, *bhoot* (and others) in Hinduism; *dybbuks* in Judaism; and *mara* in Buddhism all possess evil features such as greed, trickery, ire, jealousy, and pride. The cursed, such as demons and ghosts, often (1) interfere in and obstruct human affairs, (2) evoke fear and other negative emotions such as jealousy, and (3) seduce and provoke people to commit evil deeds. They lie, seduce, destroy, and spoil.

In the Western religious tradition, the most undesirable traits appear in descriptions of witches and demons. Belief in witches was widespread in Europe in early medieval society and continued through the scientific revolution. We learn about witches through the description of **witchcraft**, which is the alleged practice or art of witches, including their use of supernatural power, sorcery, enchantments, and sexual contact with evil entities.

Witchcraft
Witchcraft is the alleged practice or art of witches.

A Cross-Cultural Approach to Personality

The idea behind the existence of culture-bound or specific "national" or "ethnic" personality traits was explored by many intellectuals of the past and present. From the times of the Greek philosopher Aristotle (fifth century BCE), who claimed that the Greeks had a particular inclination to philosophy while people of other nations developed skills, there were numerous written statements or scientific theories about personality traits developed on entire peoples and cultural groups (Cooper, 2003). Little empirical evidence, of course, was produced to back up the theories espousing the existence of a distinct Greek, Babylonian, or any other collective personality. Even in more recent times at the dawn of scientific psychology, there has been no shortage of such stereotypical theories about the prevalence of specific personality traits in national or cultural groups.

Most popular assumptions were established about the differences between European and Asian cultures. Karl Jung, for instance, believed in substantial differences between Eastern and Western types of individuals based on their traits. The Western type is rooted in reason but has little connection to intuition and emotion, which is more common in the Eastern type. The Western type is mostly an extrovert, while the Eastern type is mostly an introvert (Kleinman & Kleinman, 1991). While evaluating Chinese and European personality types, other authors focused their attention on the peasant roots of the Chinese civilization associated with pragmatism and down-to-earth considerations, as well as mercantilism of Europeans with their love of numbers and abstract theories (Fung, 1948). Some scholars made sweeping assumptions about fundamental cultural differences that shaped different types of behavior in individuals who are brought up in different countries (Li, 2003; Mahbubani, 1999). Most of these assumptions—although intriguing—were not accompanied by strong empirical evidence or support. It is very difficult to validate assumptions about the existence of "national" personality types and personality disorders for a host of reasons. The most substantial is that there is a tremendous diversity of personality traits within an ethnic or national group. Furthermore, studies show with consistency that the variation of characteristics within national samples is typically greater than the differences between any two national samples (Barrett & Eysenck, 1984; Zuckerman, 1990).

CHECK AND APPLY YOUR KNOWLEDGE

1. Describe the most common personality traits of saints.

2. What are the Eastern and Western types of traits, according to Jung?

Applying the Trait Tradition

Individual traits are measured for a reason. Major goals for measuring individual differences are (a) making decisions about people in terms of their selection and promotion and (b) helping people make decisions (Johnson, 2001). In decision-making, personality assessments are used to predict how an individual will think, feel, behave, or be perceived by others in various life situations.

Marriage and Traits

Marriage is supposed to be an interaction, as both spouses have their own unique traits. At least two hypotheses based on common sense can be suggested here. First, in a successful marriage both spouses should have similar personality traits, and the more they match, the more stable the marriage. For example, it is better for a relationship if both individuals are open to experience, conscientious, and friendly. The second assumption is rooted in the theory that opposites attract—in other words, the most stable marriage is the one in which individual traits of both spouses are different so that they compensate each other. In this case, both spouses find attractive in their partner the traits that they lack. Which of these two hypotheses is more scientifically accurate?

Numerous dating sites boast the ability to help people find others with compatible personality traits; one such site is *eHarmony.* Customers fill out a lengthy questionnaire; then responses are evaluated, traits are identified, and finally, a match is (hopefully) found. *Match.com* also asks personal questions, yet it suggests finding people from a broader spectrum, as if suggesting "opposites attract." So what do personality psychologists say about the effectiveness of these two models?

At least two problems exist. The first is methodological. Although many dating sites claim they have a scientific model or an algorithm for partner matching, their methods do not allow for an independent verification or peer review, as is common in academic research. Only by offering their findings for critical peer review or other forms of evaluation can psychologists test their methods and select the most successful and effective methods of investigation and psychological advice (Finkel, Eastwick, Karney, Reis, & Specher, 2012).

The second problem is factual. Research-based psychology so far is skeptical about the claims that certain personality traits reliably predict compatibility and lead to more satisfying relationships in marriage. Specifically, research suggests that in a relationship, two people need not be similar in personality traits in order to have a successful, long-lasting union. Other factors, especially related to people's mutual attraction and their ability to communicate, are far more important (Orbuch, 2015).

So why do millions of people look for personality profile matches online? According to studies, about 15% of Americans use online dating sites, including mobile dating apps for several reasons (Pew, 2016). Communicating online can nurture intimacy, bring excitement, and build affection between two people who may not have met otherwise. There are many people who find happy, stable relationships from an online dating service—if there weren't, these services wouldn't exist. However, as studies show, hoping that an online company can help find an ideal mate with identical or best-fitting characteristics can lead to unrealistic expectations and disappointment when potential partners meet in real life. Unrealistic expectations rapidly turn to frustration; frustration becomes impatience; and impatience cultivates negative emotions that grow and ruin relationships and marriages. There is no single magic key to a successful relationship or marriage; contexts, circumstances, financial issues, intrusive in-laws, and many other small details—all can matter (Finkel et al., 2012; Orbuch, 2015). One of the most important things in any relationship is the *mutual* willingness and ability of two people to communicate and create a healthy, exciting, and long-lasting relationship (Orbuch, 2015). Still, the ability to communicate can be an individual trait that we can develop in ourselves and look for in others.

Which Personality Traits Are Most Important to Employers?

If you don't already have one, someday you will be looking for a job. During our professional careers, statistics show, we are likely we to apply for new jobs several times. Certainly, exceptions exist, yet most of us will have to compete for a job opening, hoping that our qualifications and skills are better than the qualifications and skills of other candidates. Is it possible to figure out which of our individual traits are considered the most desirable to give us the advantage over others? Which individual traits do employers look for most of the time?

Today, companies increasingly use personality measures to decide whether a candidate is a good fit. According to a survey from the Society for Human Resource Management, almost 20% of employers report that they use some personality test or a similar assessment procedure as part of the hiring process. Some experts estimate that almost 60% of potential employers are now asked to take some form of workplace assessments. The assessment industry is a growing $500-million-per-year business (Meinert, 2015).

In study published in *Perspectives in Psychological Science*, psychologists reviewed a database on hiring and job performance information to discover which personality characteristics companies value most (Sacket & Walmsley, 2014). The researchers chose to use the Big Five model to examine personality traits, and they investigated the materials of structured job interviews in which employers ask questions and evaluate candidates' responses to find out more about particular personality traits. The researchers' goal was to identify those traits that were chosen consistently and were considered "better" than others for particular job openings.

Most companies looked for conscientiousness as the most desirable trait. Agreeableness was the second-most sought-after trait. The researchers also examined how significant a factor conscientiousness was in determining an employee's success in the workplace. The researchers looked at the relationship between personality traits and three work performance criteria: whether an employee was able to satisfactorily complete work, how often an employee went above and beyond at work, and how often an employee engaged in negative behaviors. In this case, too, conscientiousness and agreeableness were the top two traits. These two traits are also listed in the Department of Labor Database (2016)—along with emotional stability—as the top three traits most important for professional success in the American workforce, regardless of experience and training. However, keep in mind that some professions and job descriptions require different traits.

Politics

Are there any distinct personality traits that determine political orientations and party preferences? Political scientists assume that our personalities motivate us to develop certain political attitudes later in life, and we will vote according to our personality traits (Gerber, Huber, Doherty, Dowling, & Ha, 2010; Mondak, Hibbing, Canache, Seligson, & Anderson, 2010). This assumption is founded on the simple correlation between the two constructs and the observation that personality traits are genetically influenced and developed in infancy, whereas political preferences develop later in life. **Table 7.4** provides a brief summary of some studies and their validation in further research.

TABLE 7.4 ● Studies of Traits Related to Political Behavior		
Research	**Interpretation**	**Validation**
Radicalism (R-factor) and tender-mindedness (T-factor)	People are likely to be divided into political categories based on their acceptance of toughness and force, on the one hand, and tolerance and consensus, on the other.	Partial support has been found.
Psychoticism, social desirability, and neuroticism	Psychoticism is substantially correlated with conservative military and social attitudes; social desirability (a tendency to respond in a manner consistent with perceived social norms) is related to liberal social attitudes; and neuroticism is related to liberal economic attitudes.	Limited evidence has been found.
Authoritarian personality	Some people develop a set of corresponding traits such as intolerance, obedience to authority, mystical view of life, rejection of new experiences, superstition, and propensity for violence.	Limited evidence has been found. New research continues to study terrorism.
Openness to experience, emotional stability, extroversion, and conscientiousness	Openness to experience may be related to liberal political views; emotional stability is correlated with conservative views in some studies but not in others; conscientiousness is negatively correlated with liberalism; and extroversion is not correlated with conservatism or liberalism.	Further supporting evidence has been found in cross-national studies.
Political preferences	Political preferences develop in childhood and are influenced by genetic factors, which means an individual has certain predispositions to be either liberal or conservative.	Limited evidence has been found.

Sources: Eysenck, 1956; Gerber et al., 2010; Mondak et al., 2010; Verhulst, Hatemi, and Martin, 2010.

The relationship between personality traits and political preferences in voting is more complex than it seems. Some personality traits do not necessarily cause people to develop specific political attitudes (Verhulst, Eaves, & Hatemi, 2012). Personality traits may direct a child to develop certain activities within which she or he learns about particular political ideas and values, and some traits are associated with political ideologies. For example, being conscientious increases your chances of being conservative (this is only a probability). Being highly open to experience is likely put you in the "liberal column." At the same time, these ideas and the experiences associated with them develop an individual's traits further in many unpredictable directions. An outgoing person is equally likely to be conservative, liberal, or neither. However, people who tend to display radical or violent behaviors may share similar traits regardless of their political orientation (such as liberal or conservative). In fact, studies suggest that the most active and vocal supporters *and* opponents of the death penalty or abortion rights may share similar personality traits. Studies also show that people form their political beliefs early in life, strengthen them during socialization, and further enhance them during their lives (Sears & Funk, 1999). In other words, we evolve individually and politically, yet this change is mutual.

Do "Stupid" People Have Distinctive Traits?

Is there a list of traits that applies to a person we label *stupid*? Psychologists from the University of Budapest (Aczel, Palfi, & Kekecs, 2015) gathered a sample of stories from the web and other publicly available literature in which an action of a main character was described as stupid. The stories were then presented to judges who were asked to fill out a questionnaire. According to their responses, the psychologists suggested a short list of traits that are associated with stupidity.

Confident arrogance The behavior and thinking to support people's belief that their ability to do something outweighs their actual ability to do it is called confident arrogance.

The worst type of stupidity is **confident arrogance**. This is behavior and thinking to support people's belief that their ability to do something outweighs their actual ability to do it. Think of drunk drivers, who erroneously believe they can manage driving and then crash their cars. Or think of a burglar who steals a cell phone, then calls several friends with it, and then posts selfies on Facebook bragging about a new phone.

Lack of control The intention of doing something important but getting engaged in some other unimportant activity instead.

Lack of control is the second "stupid" trait. In this case, someone is supposed to be doing something important but becomes engaged in some other unimportant activity instead. For example, a person misses a flight at the airport because he cannot resist an urge to eat at his favorite fast food restaurant just before it is time to board and the plane is due to take off. Lack of control often refers to particular forms of obsessive, compulsive, or addictive behavior (Aczel et al., 2015).

Absentmindedness In behavioral terms, absentmindedness can be called a lack of practical skills, common sense, or attention.

The third type is labeled **absentmindedness,** which in behavioral terms can be called lack of practical skills, common sense, or simply attention. People fail because they do not pay attention to something they should have, or they are unaware of their surroundings. How many people have fallen or bumped into a tree while texting? When this low awareness becomes constant, it becomes a trait.

There are individual traits and social conditions that contribute to the "stupid" traits. Having many supporting friends who constantly "like" your social media postings may contribute to confident arrogance. A habit of multitasking can contribute to absentmindedness. Intense feelings, both positive and negative (such as love or jealousy) can contribute to lack of control (Aczel et al., 2015).

Are There Criminal Traits?

For many years, social scientists and psychologists attempted to find out why people commit crimes or engage in antisocial behavior. Psychologists frequently turned to individual characteristics and traits. The Italian criminologist Cesare Lombroso (1835–1909) attempted to describe and explain the individual factors that affect criminal behavior. In 1876, he published a pamphlet in Italian, setting forth his theory of the origin of criminal traits. Lombroso believed that the most violent criminals have a biological predisposition, which is an **atavism,** or a reversion of behavior to some earlier developmental stages when theft, rape, and pillage contributed directly to male reproductive potential. Lombroso also argued that heredity interacts with environment to produce individuals with various potentials for criminality. These views brought his book popularity and respect (Gibson, 2002). Another book, *The Female Offender*, translated and published in English (Lombroso & Ferrero, 1895/1959), was based on Lombroso's observations of female criminals and women of deviant behavior, such as prostitutes. One of Lombroso's contributions to psychology was his typology of criminal behavior. He believed that some individuals have serious predispositions to break the law and be violent; others are less predisposed—willing to break the law but without resorting to violence (a certain prototype of what we now refer to as white-collar crime).

In the 20th century and today, psychologists worked and continue to work on theories to provide some evidence for particular traits associated with criminality. Can modern personality psychology identify some traits associated with criminal behavior? **Table 7.5** provides a summary of research referring to individual traits.

Consider just a few interesting research findings. Criminal behavior is linked to high novelty seeking, low harm avoidance, and low reward dependence (Reid, 2011).

Atavism Atavism is the reversion of behavior to some earlier developmental stages.

TABLE 7.5 ● Traits in Relation to Criminal Behavior	
Personality Traits	**Links to Criminal Behavior**
Agreeableness	Low scores associated with criminality
Conscientiousness	Low scores associated with criminality
Self-control and impulsivity	Lack of self-control associated with criminality
Novelty-seeking	High scores associated with criminality
Empathy and propensity to be remorseful	Research evidence inconclusive
Reward dependence	Research evidence inconclusive

Sources: Gottfredson, 2007; Kenny, 2015; Miller and Lynam, 2001; Reid, 2011.

Brain imaging studies showed the connection between frontal lobe executive functioning and impulsivity (Eme, 2008; Moffitt, 1990). Hyperactivity and a poor ability to perceive potential consequences of actions may result in antisocial behavior (Farrington, 2002). A tendency toward intense excitement in response to novel stimuli and the temptation for short-term pleasures in the face of escalating long-term risks are also among those traits (Kenny, 2015).

There is no a single cause or group of causes that shape the traits associated with criminality. Some causes are genetic; others are social. As we have learned in previous chapters, we are typically looking for a combination of biological, social, and situational factors to explain most psychological phenomena:

- Genetic factors alone do not "create" traits associated with criminality and do not "produce" criminal behavior.
- In addition to personality traits, a wide range of social conditions contributes to violent behavior—among them poverty, unemployment, discrimination, social instability, lack of education, and many others.
- There are also many factors (associated with social psychology), such as the impact of others, group pressure, obedience to authority, and others, that affect deviant and criminal acts.
- There are important contextual factors associated with crime, including the situation, circumstances, opportunity, low risk, and the like.

Visual Review

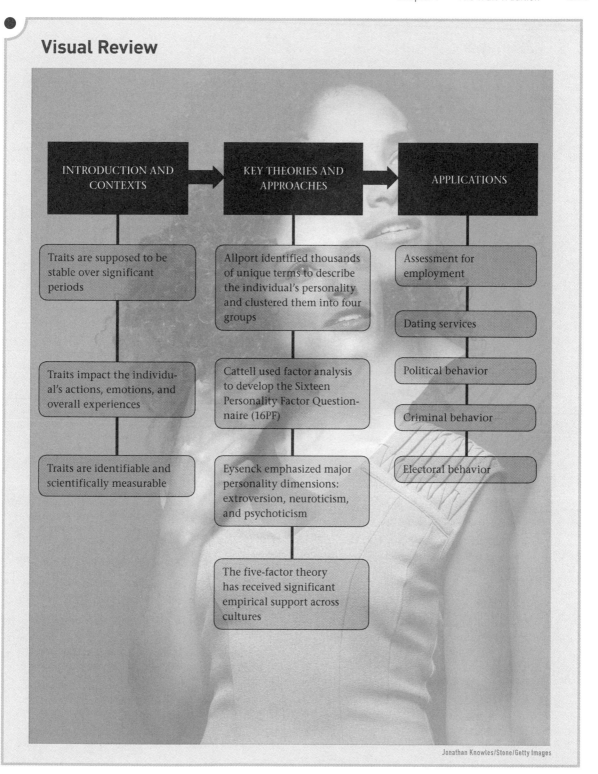

INTRODUCTION AND CONTEXTS → KEY THEORIES AND APPROACHES → APPLICATIONS

INTRODUCTION AND CONTEXTS

- Traits are supposed to be stable over significant periods
- Traits impact the individual's actions, emotions, and overall experiences
- Traits are identifiable and scientifically measurable

KEY THEORIES AND APPROACHES

- Allport identified thousands of unique terms to describe the individual's personality and clustered them into four groups
- Cattell used factor analysis to develop the Sixteen Personality Factor Questionnaire (16PF)
- Eysenck emphasized major personality dimensions: extroversion, neuroticism, and psychoticism
- The five-factor theory has received significant empirical support across cultures

APPLICATIONS

- Assessment for employment
- Dating services
- Political behavior
- Criminal behavior
- Electoral behavior

Jonathan Knowles/Stone/Getty Images

Summary

- The trait tradition in personality psychology focuses on identifying and measuring traits, which are distinguishable and stable patterns of behavior and experience.

- Like behaviorists and psychoanalysts, psychologists working within the trait tradition generally accept several common principles or general expectations. First, traits are not just single behavioral manifestations or isolated emotional reactions. Traits are different from what we call "states." Second, traits should also impact the individual's actions, emotions, and overall experiences. Third, traits are expected to be dichotomous or, in many cases, be measured as a point on a continuum.

- Psychologists also offered their own original scales to measure the traits that they have proposed and their taxonomies. Taxonomies are descriptive models or classifications based on similarity, functioning, structure, size, origin, and so on.

- Studies of personality traits have a long history in philosophy, the humanities, and early psychological studies.

- Allport argued that "character" and "personality" were distinct and different entities. He identified 17,953 unique terms used to describe the individual's personality, behavior, feelings, and so on. Next, he separated these into four categories (or columns), based on their own criteria for classification. Allport also presented personality traits as cardinal, central, and secondary.

- Cattell used factor analysis—a method to deal with large numbers of observed variables that are thought to reflect a smaller number of underlying variables. To apply factor analysis to personality, Cattell used three kinds of data: life, experimental, and questionnaire-based.

- Cattell developed a test known as the Sixteen Personality Factor Questionnaire (16PF) to measure these personality features. This self-report method was revised at least four times, translated into several languages, and adopted for use in many countries.

- Eysenck used empirical data and factor-analytic research to design and develop his theory. He emphasized two major personality dimensions: extroversion and neuroticism. Psychologists frequently refer to these dimensions as Eysenck's E and N. Later on in his career, Eysenck added another dimension to his model of the individual's personality. He called it psychoticism.

- The Big Five is a five-factor structure of personality traits that appears in most studies in different countries. The traits can be labeled *openness*, *conscientiousness*, *extroversion*, *agreeableness*, and *neuroticism*. As far as this theory goes, other individual traits are likely to fall within these five. All five factors are rather continuous.

- The five-factor theory has received significant empirical support. Studies have been conducted on various groups and in more than 50 countries. Twin studies suggest that heritability and environmental factors both influence all five factors to approximately the same degree.

- Studies in the fields of the humanities reveal that religious knowledge contains detailed descriptions of desirable and undesirable individual types. These are not just individual acts—these are somewhat stable behavioral traits.

- Trait theories find applications in many practical fields, including assessment for employment, dating services, political behavior and elections, and criminal behavior.

Key Terms

16PF 210

absentmindedness 222

atavism 223

Big Five 213

confident arrogance 222

extroversion (E) 211

Eysenk's E and N 211

genotypes 207

lack of control 222

neuroticism (N) 211

phenotypes 207

psychoticism 212

sensation seeking 212

taxonomies 203

traits 202

witchcraft 218

Evaluating What You Know

What is the trait tradition about?

What are common principles or general expectations that psychologists working within this tradition share?

Describe the major ideas of the studies into personality by Gordon Allport, Raymond Cattell, and Hans Eysenck.

Describe the main idea of the Big Five approach.

How do the humanities approach the individual's traits?

Explain the main idea of the cross-cultural approach to the individual's traits.

Explain several areas of applications of the trait domain, including marriage, employment, politics, criminal behavior, and others.

A Bridge to the Next Chapter

Perhaps the biggest strength of trait theory is that it's fairly understandable and straightforward. It appears unambiguous and finds support among practitioners. Trait theories usually rely on significant and comprehensive data, as well as statistical analysis. In contrast, psychoanalysts rely mostly on personal interpretation of subjective factors. The subjective experiences of the theorists affect the theory.

Trait researchers know that many unanswered questions still remain. For example, people do not always act according to their traits. Next, trait theories do not say enough about how our traits develop and change. It is still a challenge to understand how traits change and how people adjust their traits to face and address big and small challenges in their lives. We need to know more about this to help people strengthen their "positive" traits and correct the "negative" ones. Is this possible?

Finally, there is the big issue of self-reporting. If the trait theories we have studied on these pages claim they are "objective," why did they rely on self-reporting? Are we as individuals to remain the best interpreters of our own behaviors and traits? And if we are not, who can judge the process of our experience and self-reflection?

The next chapter will discuss this "subjective" factor in personality psychology and the importance of the cognitive factors in studying personality.

Martin Puddy/Photonica/Getty Images

8

The Cognitive Tradition

"Love is a striking example of how little reality means to us."

—Marcel Proust (1871–1922), French novelist

Learning Objectives

After reading this chapter, you should be able to:

- Identify the main principles and historical contexts of the cognitive tradition
- Describe the three fields of cognitive science and their impact on personality psychology
- Explain how attitude is studied in order to assess personality
- Discuss the personal-constructs approach to personality
- Identify cultural aspects associated with the self
- Explain how literature and the inner world are relevant to personality psychology

Abby and Brittany Hensel are conjoined twins: They have two arms and two legs total, but they have two separate heads, their own hearts, two stomachs, and two spinal cords. They learned from a young age to move and coordinate their body together, with Abby controlling the right hand side and Brittany the left. They can drive by controlling the steering wheel jointly, but they carry separate driver's licenses. When they fly, they buy one plane ticket since they use only one seat. However, Abby and Brittany have two passports for traveling overseas because they are considered two people. They both finished high school and graduated from college at the same time. They are both in good health and have a busy social life. They don't like to be photographed by visitors or strangers on the street.

They differ in some ways, too. They style their hair in different ways. They both like drinking coffee, but it affects them in different ways—Brittany gets jittery if she drinks more than one cup, and Abby thinks drinking several cups a day keeps her alert. They have their own food preferences, but they do not necessarily get hungry at the same time. They prefer different styles of clothing. Brittany is better at writing; Abby is good at mathematics. Brittany prefers to go out; Abby often likes to stay home. Brittany has a fear of heights; Abby does not. They can nap separately. They respond to their e-mails together but only when they agree on the answer. If their opinions differ, they give separate answers. They are two unique selves in the same body. They have two personalities.

Some psychologists say our bodies are hardware, and our self is software. The body is like a book, a device, while the mind is like a story, a program. You can touch and weigh the device, you can toss it in the air, and you can even crush it or take it apart.

Yet can you measure the mind? If so, how? How do we understand the essence of the self, or the unique reflection of our own existence? Furthermore, how does science help us understand our subjective existence?

Source: Wallis, 2013.

The Roots of the Cognitive Tradition: Early Psychology

The word *cognitive* refers to cognition, which relates to senses, experience, and thought. In the middle of the 20th century, psychology as a discipline was under the significant influence of psychoanalysis and behaviorism. Then it underwent a substantial change in its course called the **cognitive revolution**. This was a gradual yet significant shift of focus within university psychology from being primarily behavioral (regarding action) to being increasingly cognitive—that is, increasingly studying the work of the mind. Of course, the term *revolution* is used as a convenient label to describe several long decades of studies. Personality psychology also began paying more attention to the work of the human mind.

In cognitive theory, behavior is explained as guided by cognitions (e.g., understanding and expectations) about the world, other people, and the self. Cognitive theories are theories of personality that emphasize cognitive processes, such as thinking, imagining, and judging. It is about the functioning of an individual experience. The Hensel sisters described in the opening vignette undergo two unique individual experiences. They refer to themselves and their experiences as "my experiences."

The cognitive revolution, of course, had its roots and causes. Psychology's great scholars—from its early days as a research discipline in the 19th century—tried to find a way to measure the ever-elusive "internal" mechanisms of the mental life of an individual's personality. Psychologists wanted to measure mental life like physicists and chemists are able to measure molecules and electromagnetic fields; quantifying or explaining in precise terms the inner experience of a person seemed an intriguing and rewarding task.

An Era of Introspection

The founders of experimental psychology used the methods of **experimental introspection** by asking subjects to focus on their personal reflections and then relate them to outside signals. A subject (in the 19th century, it was most likely male) was usually asked to rate his experiences on a 1- to 10-point scale while looking at a light or listening to a sound within a dark research lab. The subject rated his experiences based on their quality, intensity, or duration.

It seemed to researchers that introspection had given them a sense of experimental validity to their studies. Psychologists believed that by studying mental elements such as sensations and feelings they would

Cognitive revolution The cognitive revolution refers to the gradual yet significant shift of focus within university psychology from being primarily behavioral (studying actions) to being increasingly cognitive (studying the work of the mind).

Experimental introspection Experimental introspection is the method according to which the researcher has to carefully observe his or her own experience as a response to a physical stimulus delivered in laboratory surroundings.

collect enough data to examine many sophisticated mental acts, such as thinking, decision-making, and even some lasting emotional states. It also appeared that using experimental introspection to examine immediate experiences by breaking them up into mental elements, such as feelings and sensations, would help in studying complex psychological processes and long-term states such as pride and envy or even some personality traits.

Photo 8.1 Supporters of experimental introspection believed in a scientific measurement of inner experiences, such as sensations. Yet can we measure a subjective side of our personalities?

Although the hope was that self-reported assessment numbers and mathematical formulas to interpret them would be suitable to describe the mind's action, they failed to provide sufficient and reliable information about the mind's work. It was imprecise and subjective.

Studying the Self

Psychologists who understood the limitations of introspection started to examine the subjective side of the individual—or the self—from a different angle. One such psychologist was Mary Calkins (1863–1930), the first female president of the American Psychological Association. She maintained that psychology was supposed to become the science of "selves" (Calkins, 1906), closely related to its environment, both physical and social. Calkins's self-psychology had three founding concepts: (1) the self, (2) the object, and (3) the self's relation or attitude toward that object.

She described the self on two levels: the first is contents of consciousness, and the second is the environment in which the content unfolds. As an illustration, an individual's direct experiences appear as a conscious process of sharing the experience of a number of other selves that are attached to memories, imagination, and the like. This approach is different from the one practiced in Indian philosophical traditions in which the act of reflection (as opposed to observation) is about the removal of all sensory content to access consciousness (Rao, Paranjpe, & Dalal, 2008). Calkins's view of the self reflected a Western cultural tradition that usually connects the self with the environment. Reflection and observation come together.

The Gestalt Tradition

Behaviorism (see Chapter 6) has been a mainstream orientation in Western psychology for many decades since the beginning of the 20th century. Nevertheless, studies of the "subjective" element of the individual's life have never stopped. The Gestalt tradition in psychology developed by the European psychologists Max Wertheimer, Wolfgang Köhler, Kurt Koffka, and others continued the experimental study of individual experience (Mandler, 2007). The main thesis taught in German universities in the first quarter of the 20th century as that an individual's experience consists of unrelated inert elements. The mind, from the traditional view, was a builder that collects multiple elements of experience and puts them together in an organized fashion under the laws of association (Köhler, 1959). Gestalt psychologists challenged this view and showed in their experimental research that it is not the elements but the integrated and constant patterns, or "wholes," that are likely to be the fundamental features of our psychological experience. A psychologist trained in the 19th century was likely to report this: "I perceive a pattern of sensations that usually occurs when I am engaged in the perception of a child's face." Now, a Gestalt psychologist would likely put it very simply: "I see a child."

Gestalt ideas were a significant departure from the ideas of the traditional psychology of perception. Subsequently, supporters of Gestalt psychology, after formulating the main principles of the organization of perception, applied these principles to thinking, learning, and behavior in general. This was an important step for personality psychology—it meant that our subjective "self" is not necessarily a bunch of elements bundled together. Instead, our inner world is a whole, or a coherent system with its own inner logic that interconnects all these elements. The challenge was to understand this logic.

Gestalt therapy
The Gestalt therapy uses ideas about the holistic nature of human experience, the disruption of its structure, and the emphasis on the actuality of the moment.

Gestalt theory had an initial impact on clinical psychology and a theoretical and practical field commonly referred to in clinical psychology as **Gestalt therapy**. Gestalt therapy uses the ideas about the holistic nature of human experience, the disruption of its structure, and the emphasis on the actuality of the moment (Perls, Hefferline, & Goodman, 1951). One of the founders of this method was Fritz Perls (1883–1970), a German American doctor who left Germany in 1933. His theoretical principles are founded on several assumptions of the classic Gestalt theory. The structure of an individual's experience is a dynamic summary that reflects needs, hopes, strengths, and weaknesses. Both satisfied and unsatisfied needs interact as figures and grounds of perceptual experience. Psychological problems arise when the form and structure of this interaction process are distorted. Another point connecting Gestalt theory to Gestalt therapy is that the latter focuses more on the process of our experience than on its content—that is, the emphasis is on what is being felt at the moment rather than on past memories. To summarize, Gestalt therapy focuses on a here-and-now method, embracing immediate experiences rather than past recollections (Perls, 1968).

Field Theory

Field theory
Lewin's approach to combining the main principles of Gestalt psychology and topology is called field theory. According to this approach, the acting and thinking individual is part of a dynamic field of interdependent forces.

Kurt Lewin (1890–1947) was one of the most prominent German American psychologists whose research legacy is constantly reevaluated. His **field theory** has been a significant contribution to personality psychology (Lewin, 1943). According to field theory, the acting and thinking individual lives in a dynamic field of interdependent forces. Life appears as a giant diagram with opposing forces, energy fields, obstacles, goals, conflicting interests, supportive aids, and obstructive opponents. To understand or predict someone's behavior (Lewin labeled it B), the researcher must understand the psychological, cognitive state of a person (labeled P) and of the psychological environment (E). In this system, P and E are interdependent variables. Behavior becomes a function (labeled f) of an individual's personality characteristics and of specific environmental or situational conditions.

$$B = f(P, E)$$

Field theory holds that an individual's choices depend on the characteristics of the present field at a particular moment. An individual's goals and past experiences all fit into the field characteristics of the moment. To describe the field, Lewin introduced terms such as *life space, field, existence, locomotion, force, valence, goal, conflict, interdependence,* and many others (Lewin, 1944).

In field theory, the individual becomes a calculating, conscious organism that constantly evaluates the options available at the moment and reevaluates new options available next. Field theory assumed that if the psychologist understands all the variables surrounding the individual and calculates this individual's rational calculations, then we can have a fairly understandable model explaining human existence. The problem, of course, is that in reality, we don't understand how many variables affect us every second. In addition, each individual's style of responses depends on a greater variety of other inner variables, rational and not, such as thoughts, expectations, beliefs, fears, prejudice, love, and so on.

Lewin was also an author of studies about **level of aspiration**, or the degree of difficulty of the goal toward which a person is striving. Whether or not a person will become successful is deeply influenced by that person's wish to be so. In most cases, a person's history of successes and failures determines a particular level of aspiration. In turn, they influence the expectation for the outcome of the future action and increase or decrease the level of aspiration accordingly (Lewin, 1942). For example, good students, in general, tend to keep their levels of aspiration slightly above their past achievements, while less successful students tend to show excessively high or low levels of aspiration—that is, ineffective students have not learned to be realistic in evaluating their past achievements and failures and today's opportunities.

Level of aspiration
The degree of difficulty of the goal toward which a person is striving is the level of aspiration.

In Europe, psychologists Jean Piaget and Lev Vygotsky (we will learn about their contribution to personality psychology in Chapter 10) examined the works of a child's thinking, paying special attention to the dynamic, developing mind. Psychoanalysts, along with examining a range of clinical symptoms, paid attention to various manifestations of the mind's work. So what was specifically innovative in the new wave of empirical studies of the human mind in the mid-20th century? What was its impact on personality psychology?

Here, we will examine a few principles of the cognitive tradition. We also will consider cognitive psychology in the context of a larger field of cognitive science. After that, we will turn to the cognitive tradition in personality psychology.

Cognitive Science

Several great scholarly minds working in various fields of science contributed to the development of the cognitive tradition in psychology. The American professor George Miller (1920–2012) was one of them. In 1960, Miller and his colleagues founded the Center for Cognitive Studies at Harvard University. This was also the year when Miller, Eugene Galanter, and Karl Pribram published their groundbreaking work *Plans and the Structure of Behavior* (1960). In this book, the authors explained several important principles of their approach to psychology. At least four of these principles are important for personality psychology.

First, anything we refer to as "mental" (which is traditionally viewed as subjective, even immeasurable) should be studied from the standpoint of information, which is measurable (Miller et al., 1960). While many psychologists emphasized the importance of traditional variables—such as behavioral habits, traits, learning principles, unconscious motivation, or complex bio-chemical mechanisms—to explain the individual, Miller and colleagues turned to information processing, which is the exchange of information in any way detectable by an observer. Consider the trait *openness to experience*, for example. According to the cognitive approach, this should be understood as a quantifiable, or measurable, amount of information that an individual receives, stores, and processes.

Second, Miller and colleagues (1960) believed that individuals should be viewed as extremely complex computing devices. If the nature of all mental aspects of our lives is information processing, then human beings should become natural processors of such information. If we know how machines process information, then by analogy, according to Miller, we could use this knowledge to understand the work of the individual's mind.

According to the third principle, understanding personality is like understanding computers: Computers conduct operations based on a set of instructions or programs, so if there is no program, there is no corresponding operation. The program compels the device's every operation in solving a particular problem or performing a task. When programming instructions change, the operations change accordingly. In general terms, every operation of the device refers to an underlying program, or a set of commands. Therefore, applying this analogy to personality, we can propose that every element of behavior—any emotion or any trait—can be explained as information processing based on a set of specific instructions or programs.

Fourth, such instructions underlying the work of the mind are very sophisticated and part of a multilevel plan, or long chain of operations. Each operation can be described as either *action* or *inaction*. Every psychological phenomenon—such as thinking or an aggressive act, for example—is a complex process, giving individuals special tools to control the schedule according to which chain of operations takes place.

CHECK AND APPLY YOUR KNOWLEDGE

1. What was the cognitive revolution?

2. Explain experimental introspection.

3. How does Gestalt therapy refer to the individual's cognition?

4. Explain field theory.

5. What is your level of aspiration: high, moderate, or low? Would you like to change your level of aspiration and why?

Psychology and Cognitive Science

Cognitive psychology belongs to the line of research that is commonly regarded today as part of an interdisciplinary field of **cognitive science**. This field includes studies in several areas, particularly cognitive neuroscience, computer science, philosophy, and linguistics, among others. To better understand cognitive psychology, let's briefly examine some key studies involved in the early development of cognitive science.

Cognitive science
The field of cognitive science includes cognitive neuroscience, computer science, philosophy, and linguistics, among others.

Cognitive Neuroscience

As an academic field, cognitive neuroscience examines the brain mechanisms that support mental functions (we also reviewed this field in Chapter 2). At least three areas of study exist. The first is experimental research in neurophysiology conducted in university- and hospital-based laboratories. Next, is research into the brain's pathology. Finally, rapidly developing methods of brain imaging provide cognitive neuroscientists with remarkable new facts. By examining the location of neural activation generated by a cognitive task, researchers can learn more about the brain's functioning and the role of psychological processes in thinking, emotions, and decision-making. Take free will, for example—historically, whether or not we have free will was a question philosophers examined. However, contemporary studies see free will as the result of electrical activity in the brain—that is, background noise, or patterns of brain activities that can be detected before a person makes a "free-will" decision. In other words, a person's brain seems to commit to certain decisions before the person becomes aware of having made them (Bengson, Kelley, Zhang, Wang, & Mangun, 2014). For instance, at this very moment you may believe you can think about anything you want, yet it appears that a new thought or one you want to bring back at this moment has already been determined by a set of random activities in the brain. It may be that our conscious "self" comes in at a later stage of our decision-making, not at the beginning of the decision-making process (Roskies, 2010; Smith, 2011).

Computer Science

After the advent of computers in the 1950s, for psychologists the most important assumption of the rapidly developing new discipline called computer science was that computers and human beings process information similarly. In a way, computer science represents a computational approach to psychology. One of the most prominent pioneers of the computational approach was the British scientist Alan Turing (1912–1954). Science historians agree that Turing's work is the theoretical and practical basis of the developing computer science (Hodges, 1983).

Turing's theoretical quests and remarkable practical accomplishments convinced him that human judgment, or the sophisticated work of the mind, could be explained with absolute certainty from the standpoint

Antoine Taveneaux/CC BY-SA 3.0

Photo 8.2 Alan Turing believed it would be possible in the future to mathematically describe and simulate virtually all operations taking place in a person's brain.

of mathematics and logic. Although he was not a psychologist, several of Turing's ideas were essential to the young field of cognitive psychology (Turing, 1950; Weizenbaum, 1976). What were these fundamental ideas?

First, Turing put forth that the brain has to use information from a variety of sources inside and outside the body to operate. The brain then has to store this information. A crucial point here is that this information is not as infinite or incalculable as it may appear; it is limited and measurable (Turing, 1950).

Second, the brain uses this information to solve problems. Therefore, mental functions can be viewed as problem-solving operations, programs, or procedures. If the information is finite and measurable, Turing proposed, then every problem the brain solves using this information is essentially mathematical.

Next, according to Turing, each problem-solving method is based on a particular rule or algorithm. Each algorithm can be viewed as a computable operation. All mental operations are computable, and computable operations should be sufficient to explain all mental functions the brain performs (Turing, 1950).

Turing believed that, if these assumptions were correct, then computer science could provide new insights into the mechanisms of the central nervous system. Sometime in the future, he thought, it would be possible to mathematically describe and simulate virtually all operations taking place in a person's brain. It also occurred to him that if problem solving was a computable operation, such operations should be available for a machine only if it was given a sufficient algorithm—ultimately, he was proposing a machine capable of thinking. Today, researchers and philosophers ponder whether we can create an artificial personality as well.

Philosophy, Consciousness, and the Self

Philosophy provided new inspiration to personality psychology. One of the most difficult questions coming from the philosophers was "How exactly do neurobiological processes in the brain result in consciousness and the self?" Supported by neuroscience and computer science, philosophers again turned to a holistic perspective on the functioning of the mind. The philosopher John Searle (b. 1932) believes that consciousness is a biological phenomenon; however, it has some important and unique features that cannot be understood by biology alone. The most important of these features is "subjectivity." If you were asked what it feels like to ask a student next to you in class for a spare pen, you could answer that question based on your previous experience. But if somebody asked you what it feels like to be a stone, you couldn't answer that question because stones are not conscious, so we can't know what it's like to be a stone (Searle, 1998).

Searle insisted that physiology causes consciousness. In other words, processes at the level of individual neurons and changes on the macrolevel of the whole brain create consciousness. Searle's views can be summarized briefly as follows: At least two crucial relationships between consciousness and the brain can be established. First, lower-level neuronal processes in the brain cause consciousness. Second, consciousness is simply a higher-level feature of the system that is made up of lower-level neuronal elements (Searle, 1992).

Studies of Attitudes

An individual's personality can be viewed and assessed from the standpoint of **attitudes**, which are the cognitive representations and evaluations of various features of the social and physical world. The study of attitudes gained significant popularity and research support in psychology and social psychology, especially in the second half of the past century. Attitudes are the psychological links, or associations between various cognitive images and their evaluations (Fazio, Williams, & Powell, 2000). Attitudes are based on personal experience. An individual's memory retains a particular image along with its appraisal.

The problem is that attitudes are not directly observable. Therefore, any description of attitude is an act of creative imagination. The question is "How do we bring measurable variables to the study of attitudes?" Consider physics. We cannot visibly see gravity as a form of energy, but we can observe and measure its effects: Apples fall down from trees, not up. The same is true with attitudes: Although we do not visibly see attitudes, we can judge them from people's verbal or written responses, as well as infer them from people's behavior. An individual's personality can be described based on what this person says and does. Unlike in the trait tradition, psychologists who study attitudes are interested in describing psychological "types" based on complex features and traits. They turn to the mechanisms that "connect" and "separate" attitudes and the ways by which attitudes regulate individual judgment and behavior.

It is assumed, based on the earlier tradition in psychology established by Wundt, that there are two general components to attitude: cognitive and affective.

1. *The cognitive component*: This is characterized by an individual's knowledge about a certain object, person (for instance, a fiancé, a presidential candidate), or issue (such as raising speed limits on the interstate), including learned facts, experiences, and assumptions about various aspects of reality.

2. *The affective component*: Often known as the emotional component, this is an evaluation of an object or issue linked to one or several basic human emotions, such as joy, fear, disgust, sadness, anger, and surprise. In general, the emotional component may not be only a dichotomous "positive-or-negative" evaluation of a particular object. Ambivalence, or presence of both positive and negative valuations, may coexist in many attitudes (Lavine, Bordiga, & Sullivan, 2000). Both emotional and cognitive components are likely to affect the individual's behavioral readiness to act in a certain way with respect to an object or issue he or she evaluates (Allport, 1935).

An attitude can be measured on a scale as being "weak" or "strong." Strong attitudes are enforced by the emotional-cognitive links that are based on a substantial amount of knowledge and reinforced by a sound emotional commitment to an object or issue the individual evaluates (Kallgren & Wood, 1986) and are likely to influence individuals' behavior. For example, industrious behavior and traits are linked to the strong attitude and knowledge about how to be an effective professional and a desire to be

Attitudes
The cognitive representations and evaluations of various features of the social and physical world are present in attitudes.

or become one. Weak attitudes tend to change because the emotional-cognitive connection is weak, and they are not based on knowledge or an emotional commitment.

Cognitive processes such as perception, memory, recognition, and decision-making play a critical role in attitude formation and expression. People's attitudes depend on the presence of other attitudes and specific cognitive mechanisms by which individuals receive, understand, and interpret the incoming facts. The studies in attitude accessibility, balance, and dissonance should help us understand this tradition better.

Attitude Accessibility

Some attitudes are easily accessible while others take an effort to retrieve. Think about your life: Certain facts and their evaluations are easily retrievable from your memory. Other facts and their assessments are not as easy to access, if you can access them at all. Why? Several reasons have been studied. The first is the frequency of the attitude's expression (Fazio, 1989). Research shows that if someone has a chance to explain or defend an attitude, it should be more easily accessible from memory in the future (Boninger et. al., 1995). Attitudes that are more accessible are more likely to be expressed and more likely to affect behavior than attitudes that are less accessible (Roese & Olson, 1994; Snyder & Swann, 1978). In addition, people are less likely to hold on to attitudes that are accessible to them if these attitudes are in conflict with the individual's other attitudes.

An attitude becomes more accessible if it contains a strong emotional evaluation of an issue—either positive or negative—but not both. Attitudes with a single composition of the affective component are called **single-evaluation attitudes**. Attitudes that contain an ambivalent emotional component are called **dual-evaluation attitudes**. If you develop a dual-evaluation attitude, the process of responding to a question should require the integration of positive and negative evaluations. Thus, the process of retrieving ambivalent components should be more time-consuming and require a greater cognitive effort than a single-evaluation attitude. Therefore, ambivalent attitudes are usually less accessible than single evaluation attitudes (Lavine et al., 2000). Overall, attitude accessibility is determined by the strength of the individual's cognitive connections between various images and their evaluations.

Single-evaluation attitudes
Single-evaluation attitudes have a single composition of the affective component, such as either liking or disliking.

Dual-evaluation attitudes
Dual-evaluation attitudes contain an ambivalent emotional component.

Attitude Balance

The ideas of Gestalt psychology described earlier made a distinct impact on the research of an individual's attitudes. One of these ideas was that people need a balanced, noncontradictory view of the world around them. Fritz Heider (1896–1988), an Austrian-born American psychologist, argued that people seek consistency among their judgments. They do not necessarily do this deliberately; rather, it is the nature of human experience to be "balanced" (Heider, 1944, 1958). To maintain their perception in "good form," people tend to seek explanations for their judgments, thus creating perceptual distortions. For example, if Person A has a good friend (Person B) and they both have a good opinion of a third individual (Person C), this situation is balanced because there is no tension or contradiction between Person A's attitudes. However, if Person A and Person B like each other but they have different views of Person

C, this creates tension, or a lack of balance, in Person A's attitudes. Person A must now bring the attitudes to a balanced state: Two people who like each other are supposed to see things in similar ways or, if they do not, they should like each other less. In general, a balanced cognitive system is one in which individuals agree with people they like or differ with people they dislike. This theory also proposes that we attach a greater value to things we like and lesser value to anything we dislike (Davidson & Thompson, 1980; Pratkanis, 1988). Experimental research also shows that the principles of cognitive balance had a cross-cultural validity (Triandis, 1994).

Attitude Dissonance

The idea that an individual is supposed to maintain a cohesive, noncontradictory view of the self and of the world was further developed in the studies of the American psychologist Leon Festinger (1919–1989), the author of the theory of **cognitive dissonance**. It has become one of the most recognizable theories in psychology. The term refers to an unpleasant psychological state experienced by an individual who performs an action that is contradictory to his beliefs and ideas or is confronted by new information that conflicts with his beliefs or ideas. Festinger maintained that people tend to experience tension, an unpleasant emotional state, caused by the perceived mismatch (dissonance) between the following:

- Their judgments (or two elements of knowledge, two facts)—for example, "I like this person but I have been told that she has lied to me on several occasions."
- Their judgment and behavior—for example, "I know I have promised to study for the test today, but I have also promised my parents to spend some time with them."

Whenever an individual must decide between two or more alternatives, the final choice is likely to be inconsistent and contradict some of this person's attitudes or previous decisions (Should I forgive and ignore my friend's lying? Should I conveniently "forget" about a promise I made?). This inconsistency generates dissonance (Festinger, 1957). Because this is an unpleasant state, to avoid it and to reduce or eliminate the tension, people have several choices. They can change their judgments to bring them back to harmony; they can modify their behavior somehow so that there is no longer an unpleasant dilemma; or they can avoid the unpleasant information or address their dissonance (Festinger, Riecken, & Schachter, 1956). This theory generated significant research and found many applications, especially in therapy and marketing.

Why do most people strive to balance their attitudes and avoid dissonance? The main motive is to avoid unpleasant emotions caused by cognitive tensions. A simple, harmonious, consistent, and meaningful view on issues is normally free of tensions. To achieve a harmonious view, people tend to use the **least-effort principle**: They minimize the number of cognitive operations to reach a goal. In other words, "bad" people are supposed to do bad things, while "good" people are most likely to do good things. If you have developed a set of beliefs about the world that is mean and unfair, you are likely to interpret most of the events around you from a

Cognitive dissonance Individuals experience the unpleasant psychological state known as cognitive dissonance when they perform an action that is contradictory to their beliefs and ideas or when they are confronted by new information that conflicts with their beliefs or ideas.

Least-effort principle The least-effort principle is the tendency to minimize the number of cognitive operations to reach a goal.

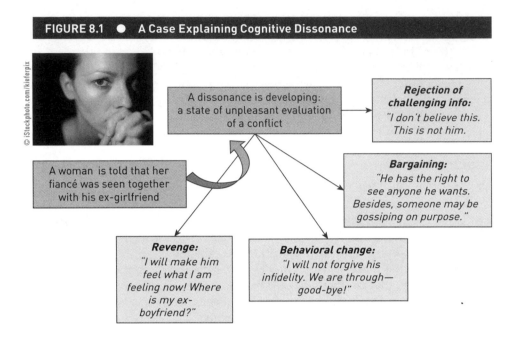

FIGURE 8.1 ● A Case Explaining Cognitive Dissonance

© iStockphoto.com/kieferpix

A woman is told that her fiancé was seen together with his ex-girlfriend

A dissonance is developing: a state of unpleasant evaluation of a conflict

Rejection of challenging info:
"I don't believe this. This is not him.

Bargaining:
"He has the right to see anyone he wants. Besides, someone may be gossiping on purpose."

Revenge:
"I will make him feel what I am feeling now! Where is my ex-boyfriend?"

Behavioral change:
"I will not forgive his infidelity. We are through—good-bye!"

pessimistic standpoint. The facts that contradict our attitudes are ignored, critically dismissed, or outright rejected (see **Figure 8.1**).

Attributions

Attribution
An attribution is the explanation individuals use to explain the causes of behavior and events.

Every second, something happens around us, and every second, people around us make decisions, express judgments, and take action. We tend to interpret other people's behavior in a particular, consistent way. This assumption is common in the cognitive tradition. Consistency is also an important adaptive function: We have to make sense of this world and explain most things that are relevant to us. We do this through **attribution**, or the process by which individuals explain the causes of behavior and events. Attribution involves an act of judgment, so the attribution approach shows from a particular angle how we explain the world and other people's actions. The UCLA psychologist Harold Kelley (1921–2003) showed in his research that people use attribution in a rational, logical fashion, and they assign the cause of an action to the factor that is connected (or appears connected) most closely with that action.

Kelley's (1967) research showed that people judge other people's behavior from at least three standpoints. The first one is consistency. Imagine that your professor expresses anger and disappointment when students come late to his class. How do we explain this reaction? We ask the question, "How frequent is this professor's behavior observed with a similar stimulus (such as when someone is late) but in different situations?" The second is distinctiveness, for which we ask, "How does the individual respond to different stimuli?" For example, you observe this professor in different

CHECK AND APPLY YOUR KNOWLEDGE

1. Describe the three fields of cognitive science. What are their impacts on personality psychology?

2. What are dual-evaluation attitudes?

3. Consider the following example: A man walks into a bar and sees a beautiful woman smiling at him. How does the man attribute her behavior? Does it mean she likes him? Or is it all in his mind? Research into this scenario has shown that, in general, men have a tendency to misjudge a woman's romantic intent, particularly after a few drinks. Studies also show that a man's attachment style influences his attribution of a woman's interest. There are secure, anxious, and avoidant styles of attachment. Those higher in attachment anxiety have a need for love and reassurance and a fear of rejection. People higher in attachment avoidance typically are reluctant to trust and rely on others, and they fear intimacy. Men on the higher end of the attachment anxiety spectrum are most likely to imagine a woman being sexually interested in them. Conversely, men higher in attachment avoidance felt the opposite (Hart, Nailling, Bizer, & Collins, 2015). Explain the result of this study from the standpoint of cognitive balance or cognitive dissonance.

situations during the day, at the cafeteria, or in the parking lot, and in those situations, you find this professor outgoing, cordial, and pleasant. And the third is consensus for which we ask, "Do most professors express anger and disappointment when students come late to their class?"

Of course, we as individuals are prone to mistakes. Nevertheless, in our daily interactions, we make generally accurate attributions about other people, which helps us function in this extremely complex world (Kelley, 1979).

The Personal Constructs Approach

Our inner world, the world of cognition, is an interconnected structure in which every element or function is attached to another element or function with a somewhat predictable connection. This means that certain ideas we have are likely to predict the existence of other ideas so that our inner world of experience is, in fact, a somewhat foreseeable or expectable system. To illustrate, the psychologists David Palermo and James Jenkins began amassing a huge database of word associations, which are the first thoughts that come to mind when people are asked to comment on a specific word. The researchers discovered that the vast majority of these associations were extremely predictable. If we say one word, most people who speak the same language are likely to respond with a certain word. For instance, when people are asked to free-associate about the word *blue*, the most likely first answer is *green*, followed by *sky* and *ocean*. When asked to free-associate about *green*, nearly everyone says *grass* (Lehrer, 2012). The same principle refers to more complex cognitive structures.

The American psychologist George Kelly (1905–1967) is one of the most recognized psychologists who combined the principles of cognitive psychology and applied psychotherapy to approach the individual personality. He believed that people, for the most part, are capable of making reasonable and rational judgments. People make cognitive constructs about themselves and the world around them. Constructs should provide a certain order, clarity, and prediction to a person's world. People then approach daily events and take steps as reasonable decision-makers. In fact, people can be seen as scientists of sorts. Although most of them do not apply the scientific method all the time to make their decisions, they still try to rely on evidence available to them and facts that they learn from other individuals. In fact, people are likely to be **naïve scientists**—individuals seeking rational and reasonable answers yet lacking scientific knowledge and critical judgment. This is how Kelly generalized about human beings (Kelly, 1963).

To make quick and hopefully correct judgments about the world, other people's behavior, and ourselves, we create a system of expectations. This system is based on our own experiences and beliefs. In science, each hypothesis put together by the scientist is supposed to be carefully verified and scrutinized by independent peer reviewers. Yet because most of us are in actuality "naïve scientists," we tend to rely on our own reviews or on the reviews that are easily available to us. Very often we use the views and ideas that we simply like or with which we are comfortable.

As a clinical psychologist, Kelly (1955) maintained that we constantly engage in coping with the psychological stresses of our lives, using our judgments from previous experiences that we think should help us now. However, our past experiences often have very little to do with our current challenges and problems.

Kelly (1963) wanted to know how individuals make sense of the world based on their constructs. Most of us pay significant attention to the words we use, and we tend to attach different meaning to these words based on the different experiences we have while learning these meanings. Recall from Chapter 3's discussion of studying the rules of critical thinking, one description of someone's behavior often means different things to different people. For example, consider the adjective *assertive* when referring to a person's individual traits. In some cases and for some individuals, this adjective should represent a person who is strong, decisive, and effective in her or his decisions. However, to another person, being assertive means using pushy, forceful, and even rude behavior.

It is probably expected that we all have different views of the world and attach different meanings to words. What is especially important about human beings is that we establish stable patterns of such assessments, and we use these patterns to judge small events, such as taking an exam, as well as significant developments, such as marriage or college graduation. In a certain way, we develop our own complex cognitive systems to filter the information about the world and make stable

Naïve scientists
Naïve scientists are individuals who seek rational and reasonable answers yet lack scientific knowledge and critical judgment.

judgments. Such systems or **constructs** are stable assumptions that the individual develops about other people, the self, and the world in general. Such assumptions tend to focus on two, opposing sides of the spectrum. For example, if a person believes that the world has to be stable and predictable, he or she will want the world to be well-organized and "nice": Busses should arrive on time, people should not lie or do bad things, and politicians should always deliver their promises. However, in actuality, every day that person encounters a different world—one that is unstable, unpredictable, and unfair. Busses are late, people lie and cheat, and the world of politics is apparently getting nastier. As a result, this individual develops a dichotomous view of the world: One is the view about how the world should be, and the other is about the world that is. This construct is filled with frustration and anger; the person wants to live in a "nice" world yet realizes this is impossible to do. As a result of this construct's impact on the individual's life, this person develops a contradictory view related to all areas of life, including work, education, family, and so on.

These constructs may or may not be adaptive. If a particular construct can be successfully applied to a situation and it is useful at predicting events, it is adaptive. Adaptive people are continually revising and updating their own constructs to match new information they encounter. All constructs are not used in every situation because they have a limited range of predicting power. To summarize briefly, our world is cognitively constructed by the ways in which we anticipate events (Kelly's constructs are summarized in **Table 8.1**).

There are 11 common and interconnected types of significant, basic assumptions, or corollaries, that people use in their daily lives. The first assumption (construction) means that each one of us anticipates events in the future by perceiving a similarity with a past event. In reality, events do not necessarily repeat themselves, yet we still construct something cognitively that allows us to perceive many events as similar: "I have seen people like this before! I can easily explain their behavior." Another option is the commonality corollary—we often make judgments simply because most people around us see them as "normal," "expected," and even "required." These choices affect our choice of lifestyle, friends, occupation, and faith, among others.

Most constructs are useful, and they help us adjust to the changing conditions of our world, yet there are "disordered constructs" in which the system of construction is not useful in predicting social events and fails to change to accommodate new information. If a person has many disordered constructs, then psychological and behavioral problems may be considered a mental illness. Kelly's **fixed-role therapy** was designed to change the individual's perception of self during a relatively short period. In a simple way, the person describes the self and emphasizes various problems that he or she has at present. Then the psychologist rewrites this self-description but instead of focusing on negative characteristics and mistakes, emphasizes helpful behaviors and positive self-evaluations. The individual is then asked to perform a new role with new behaviors and perceptions (Maltby, Day, & Macaskill, 2013).

Constructs
In Kelly's system, constructs are stable assumptions that the individual develops about other people, the self, and the world in general.

Fixed-role therapy
In Kelly's system, fixed-role therapy is a method to change the individual's perception of self during a relatively short period.

TABLE 8.1 ● George Kelly's (1963) Personal Constructs Approach to Personality	
Corollaries or Interconnected Assumptions	Description of the Assumptions
Construction	We assume, anticipate, and "construct" events that are supposed to happen based on our experience with past events.
Individuality	Each person constructs an internal model of external events, and those models differ from one person to another.
Organization	Each person develops a model or roadmap of external reality built upon their theories about external reality.
Dichotomy	The constructs that make up our personal maps of reality are paths between two polar opposites.
Choice	People "invest" in these constructs and are dependent on them; they will make choices that promise to develop the usefulness of these constructs.
Range	People establish a convenient zone within which the construct can be applicable.
Experience	People's construction systems change and develop as they successively construe the replication of events.
Modulation	Constructs are different in their ability to change people's circumstances.
Fragmentation	Constructs compete with one another. Each person may successively employ a variety of constructions that appear incompatible with one another.
Commonality	Most constructs are gathered through common learning in common situations. Individuals tend to share many common experiences.
Sociality	Interpersonal relationships matter. Together, people can change others' constructs.

Culture and the Self

Self   The self is the representation of one's identity or the subject of experience.

The term **self** refers to the representation of one's identity or the subject of experience. The cognitive tradition is based on the assumption that people make distinctions between the world within them and the world outside. Both these internal and external worlds shape our self-perception in a variety of ways that can reflect the most prominent, individual characteristics of ourselves and the culture in which we live. We have been turning to various aspects of the self throughout the book. We will turn to this again in the later chapters, but now we will look at certain cultural aspects associated with the self.

Recognizing the Self

Self-awareness   Self-awareness is a reflection of a state of awareness of our own existence; it allows us to perceive our existence with a sense of consistency.

Our ability to recognize self or "I" as something separate from the environment and other individuals is called **self-awareness**. Self-awareness is similar yet different from consciousness, which is a state of awareness of your existence. Self-awareness is, in fact, a reflection of this awareness; it allows us to perceive our existence with a sense of consistency—you are likely to remain the same "you" when you wake up tomorrow, right? We also see ourselves with a sense of distinction—we are different from other people!

Awareness can be viewed from two interconnected sides: private and social (public). Cross-cultural research on self-perception also shows distinctions between the "private" and "public" self (Benedict, 1946; Shiraev & Fillipov, 1990; Triandis, 1994). The private self indicates feelings and thoughts about oneself for oneself. The public self is the concept of self in relation to others for others. Research shows that many characteristics of self-perception are consistent across countries and cultures. In self-reports and online postings, men tend to exaggerate their height—they prefer to appear taller. Women, on the other hand, tend to lower their weight. On online dating sites, people routinely portray themselves as taller, younger, more athletic, and healthier than they actually are (Levitt & Dubner, 2009). It's common, for instance, for men to overestimate their own intelligence level and give themselves an average score of three points higher than females do (Furnham & Baguma, 1999; Furnham, Rakow, Sarmany-Schuller, & Fruyt, 1999).

People from collectivistic cultures produce more group-centric and fewer self-centric descriptions of self than people from individualistic cultures. In collectivistic—and therefore interdependent—cultures (e.g., China, Japan, and Korea), people tend to identify their self not as an independent entity but rather as part of particular social groups (Triandis, 1994, 1989). On the other hand, when U.S. subjects describe themselves, they tend to identify a great number of abstract traits—relatively unrelated to particular social groups. Asian subjects identify fewer of the same abstract traits (Bond & Tak-Sing, 1983). Surveys show that most Japanese subjects, for example, experience differences between their public and private selves. Those who cannot accept the dissonance between these two selves experience social alienation and insecurity (Naito & Gielen, 1992). U.S. respondents, on the contrary, try to eliminate the inconsistency between public and private self (Iwato & Triandis, 1993).

The individual's identity is not formed at once. It is a long process that goes through childhood and continues in adulthood (we will discuss some aspects of this process in Chapter 10 and Chapter 13). We change in the way we see our self due to the natural aging process, the social roles we acquire, and the transitions we go through.

Culture and Identity

Our **social identity** refers to our perceived membership in one or several social groups. It is a fluid category: We change our professions and earn different incomes; we migrate. We are getting more accustomed to the idea that people can permanently change their physical characteristics and even their sex. Further, your answer to the question "Who am I?" may be different based on who asks it and when. We are aware of the contexts in which we speak and act. We also learn from the social sciences and the humanities that the (1) ability and (2) willingness to change your socially prescribed self—the way you identify yourself—is probably a relatively recent cultural development.

Social identity
People's perceived membership in one or several social groups is their social identity.

Just several hundred years ago, people faced significantly fewer choices for their social identity. Most of their roles were prescribed to them by society through strict custom and law. The Indian religious caste system, the feudal Japanese system, the European structure of the so-called estates of the realm, or sectarian and tribal divisions in Islam typically prescribed people by their social category at birth. In the past, most individuals were typically born into their social class. These "spots" were inherited and changes in social position, if possible at all, occurred slowly (Huizinga, 1924/2013). For centuries, the predominant form of social organization in India was the caste system, which reinforced inequality and hierarchy among India's citizens. The caste system is formally outlawed yet it continues to exist in customs and beliefs. Accordingly, Indians tended to view themselves and their interpersonal relationships as more hierarchically structured than U.S. citizens (Sinha & Verma, 1983). A study conducted by Biswas and Pandey (1996) compared the self-perceptions of male members of three social groups in India. The respondents were asked to evaluate their quality of life, followed by which each respondent's answer was matched with his socioeconomic status. The researchers found that socioeconomic upward mobility—measured as an increase in income and occupational status—did not substantially affect the respondents' self-image or perception of their social status. In other words, a respondent may earn more money than he or she did several years ago, have a better job, and have a higher academic degree but still perceive her- or himself as a person of lower status. What can be concluded from these findings is that socioeconomic change alone does not necessarily bring about changes in the way people perceive themselves. Because many societies are still deeply divided along historical class, gender, ethnic, and caste lines, "older" identities may be more salient than "newer" ones, despite significant changes that have taken place in people's lives.

As an educated person living in the 21st century, you have a significantly wider scope of options for social self-identification. You can even invent and accept your own identity free from the most common social categories. Yet most people adapt to changes in response to economic and cultural globalization, though many people develop new self-perceptions based on old and "local" customs, ideas, and symbols, as well as new, cross-cultural ones (including new fashions, foods, leisure activities, and educational principles). However, for some people the process of change is more difficult than it is for others. The new values, norms, and behaviors may seem frightening and challenging when compared to old and "convenient" cultural images and norms. Some people may feel excluded from both their local culture and the global culture, truly belonging to neither (Arnett, 2002).

Self-Esteem

Self-esteem
Self-esteem is a person's general subjective evaluation, both emotional and rational, of his or her own worth.

A person's general subjective evaluation, both emotional and rational, of his or her own worth is called **self-esteem**. There are findings pointing to a correlation between individualism and collectivism in relation to self-esteem. Tafarodi and

Swann (1996) examined the self-esteem of more than 600 U.S. (predominantly individualistic) and Chinese (generally collectivistic) college students. The study revealed that Chinese participants were lower in perceived self-competence but higher in self-liking than U.S. students. The authors argued that in collectivistic cultures—which require sensitivity to the needs of others and subordination of personal goals to collective needs—it is expected that individuals develop self-liking. However, because of a relative loss of individual control often found in collectivistic societies, these cultures promote restraints on feelings of self-competence. On the contrary, in individualist cultures, independence and the self are prioritized. It might be that competence is related to material status, and in the United States, people feel more secure in terms of achievement than people in China. However, it is unclear why positive feelings of self-competence in U.S. students appear to have caused a decrease in positive feelings of self-liking. It appears as if reverse causation is at play: A relatively

Ethnic disidentification
Detaching an individual's self from the ethnic group with which he or she has been previously associated or is currently associated.

SELF-REFLECTION

Americans of Filipino descent, currently the second-largest Asian group in the country, have a long history within the United States: There are more than 3.5 million of them. How do those who live in the Philippines as well as Filipino Americans feel about their ethnic identity? How does their historical and contemporary relationship with America shape their identity? Do they keep it? Do they change it? Some researchers have written about this, including Dr. E. J. R. David (2013), who focused on an interesting phenomenon referred to as **ethnic disidentification**—detaching an individual's self from the ethnic group with which or she has been previously associated or is currently associated. Some common manifestations of this phenomenon are described as follows.

Filipinos in the Philippines often use skin-whitening products—endorsed by actors and other celebrities—to make their skin lighter; skin-whitening clinics and businesses are very popular as well. Children are told to stay away from the sun so they do not get "too dark." Filipinos tend to consider anything that is imported as "better" and more special than anything that is made in the Philippines.

Many Filipino Americans try to weaken their "Filipino-ness" by suggesting to other people that they are mixed with some other races or ethnic groups. Some Filipino Americans regard Filipinos who live in the Philippines as lower class (David, 2013).

Questions

How common is ethnic disidentification in your view? Ask around and search the Internet to find some examples. Discuss in class whether other ethnic or national groups have similar experiences. Why do you think ethnic disidentification takes place? What conditions (social and psychological) can trigger disidentification? Have you experienced it at some point in your life? If yes, describe your behavior and experiences.

low level of self-liking generates compensatory thoughts and behaviors that push individuals to achieve, produce, and accomplish. Cross-cultural research has also established that critical elements of self-perception are more typical in Japanese individuals than in U.S. citizens (Heine, Lehman, Markus, & Kitayama, 1999). In fact, many studies conducted over the years have established lower self-esteem scores in East Asian countries compared to North America and Europe (Boucher, Peng, Shi, & Wang, 2009; Brown & Cai, 2010). The findings do not suggest that Chinese, Japanese, or Korean individuals perceive themselves more negatively than their U.S. or Netherland counterparts. Rather, these lower scores are a form of expressed self-criticism, derived from a pervasive and complex cultural tradition of self-restraint. For example, the linguistic and behavioral emphasis in Japan on *kenson* (modesty) and *enryo* (reserve or restraint) lack analogous terms in Western culture. This emphasis constrains those who are Japanese from speaking or writing that which might be perceived as arrogant, presumptuous, or impudent. In contrast, in the West, people are conditioned to avoid statements portraying them as weak and insecure (Tafarodi et al., 2011).

Literature and the Inner World

Artists create characters, or fictional images of human beings. Most writers are not scientists. However, just as artists do, they use words to describe either extraordinary (unusual or improbable) or ordinary (common, everyday) characters in extraordinary and ordinary circumstances (see **Table 8.2**).

Extraordinary events and extraordinary characters are the most recognizable sources of knowledge about personality. Heroes and villains defying social order have always been popular literary characters. The Russian writer Dostoyevsky in *Crime and Punishment* (1866) created an remarkable character of a young man (Raskolnikov) who thinks of himself as a "superman" and whose actions must not be judged by moral rules. One of William Shakespeare's (1564–1616) most recognized characters, Hamlet, is an intellectual rebel, challenging cultural constrains and searching for his own new rules (Bayanova, 2013). The Spanish playwright Miguel de Cervantes (1547–1616) created Don Quixote, an ultimate idealist, a social misfit, and a hopeful dreamer driven by optimism, honesty, and honor.

Words and images spark the reader's imagination, especially when extraordinary characters perform in extraordinary situations. Writers present their characters in symbolic, allegoric ways in which unreal appears real. It takes the reader's cognitive ability to imagine (Djikic, Oatley, & Carland, 2012). In art, romanticism is a comprehensive viewpoint of society and human behavior based on the idealistic enchantment with individuality, spontaneity, and passion. In literature, romanticism as a genre glorified emotion and imagination, intuition and inspiration, and beauty and brilliance. Fairy tales—a fine example of the works in this genre—have been imbedded in many people's vocabulary, memories, and associations. German writers Jacob (1785–1863) and Wilhelm Grimm (1786–1859), known to most of

TABLE 8.2 ● Characters in Different Circumstances: What They Convey About Personality Features		
Characters and Circumstances	Extraordinary Situations	Ordinary Situations
Extraordinary characters	Outstanding characters with amazing abilities who are searching, fighting, and rescuing in unusual situations	Outstanding characters in everyday situations facing the circumstances and challenges that the average person usually faces
Ordinary characters	Ordinary individuals placed in extraordinary situations and showing outstanding personality qualities	Average, "next door" individuals acting and thinking in a typical, average way in everyday situations

us as "the Brothers Grimm," first published a volume of fairy tales in 1812 that included *Snow White* and their version of *Cinderella*, both stories of passion and commitment. The Danish writer Hans Christian Andersen (1805–1875) published *The Little Mermaid* and *The Steadfast Tin Soldier*. What associations do you have with these tales? More recently, today's popular mystery novels and horror stories stimulate the interest of the educated circles toward some veiled, hidden features of the human psyche. Fiction stories involving dreams, hypnosis, altered states of consciousness, uncontrolled impulses, and instincts consistently are in high demand.

Ordinary characters also appear in extraordinary circumstances in which men and women reveal their individual features. Read, for example, works by the Spanish playwright Lope de Vega (1562–1635). In his plays and essays, he reveals the complexity of human emotions and behaviors, mistakes in the pursuit of individual choices, and the power of human greed. Leo Tolstoy in *War and Peace* (1869) provides an extraordinary account of love, commitment, and loyalty—all tested in the time of war. American Mark Twain puts two of his main characters—just ordinary boys, Tom Sawyer and Huckleberry Finn—in adventurous contexts. Which adventures and personality features of these boys do you remember?

What about everyday people in ordinary situations? Russian writer Anton Chekhov and American Tom Salinger—very much different in their literary styles—elegantly carved individual traits of seemingly ordinary people. Some of their characters are appealing because they are full of humility, modesty, and perseverance, but others appear unattractive and even repulsive (Birmingham, 2014). Some literary characters are serious; others are comical. Jean-Baptiste Poquelin, better known as Molière (1622–1673), was an outstanding French playwright, director, and actor. A grand master of comic satire and exaggeration, he composed spectacular psychological profiles of his memorable characters in *Tartuffe* (1664), *Don Juan* (1665), *The Misanthrope* (1666), and *The Learned Ladies* (1672), among others.

CHECK AND APPLY YOUR KNOWLEDGE

1. Why did George Kelly call people "naïve scientists"?

2. What are Kelly's constructs, and how do they function? Think about and identify two or three constructs within your personality. Describe them.

3. Explain self-awareness and self-esteem. How would you describe your self-esteem? How does your self-esteem help you in dealing with your daily issues? Would you rather change your self-esteem or keep it as is? Why?

4. Extraordinary events and extraordinary characters are probably the most recognizable sources of knowledge about personality. Suggest a few of such characters that you think most other people should name as well. Discuss in class.

5. Name a book or a story that has had a significant impact on you and your understanding of yourself and other people.

Applying the Cognitive Tradition

How does our knowledge within the cognitive tradition help in practical matters related to personality? We will consider an example from psychotherapy, look at specific examples of the maladaptive style of behavior, and consider some ethical issues associated with artificial intelligence and digitalized personalities.

Cognitive Therapy

Cognitive therapy is not a single method of treatment; rather, it is an approach to psychotherapy rooted in the assumption that certain psychological disorders and many difficult psychological problems come from an individual's particular view of the world and the self. This is not about either accurate or inaccurate perceptions of the world (Whose perceptions are actually accurate?). The problem is that some individuals maintain perceptions that are linked to their emotional and behavioral problems and thus contribute to their disorders. In short, some individuals develop wrong information-processing styles and habits, so the goal of cognitive therapists is to help individuals change those styles (Beck, 1964; Beck, 1991). People who need help have to evaluate and change certain beliefs about self and others. Three essential concepts in cognitive therapy that help them to do this are collaborative empiricism, Socratic dialogue, and guided discovery (Beck & Weishaar, 2013).

Collaborative empiricism refers to a therapeutic alliance between a therapist and a client in which they become coinvestigators as they examine the evidence to accept, support, reevaluate, or reject the client's thoughts, assumptions, intentions, and beliefs. This process is conducted as a dynamic partnership between the patient and the therapist—they both learn from each other.

Collaborative empiricism
When a therapist and a client engage in collaborative empiricism, they form a therapeutic alliance in which they become coinvestigators and together examine the evidence to accept, support, reevaluate, or reject the client's thoughts, assumptions, intentions, and beliefs.

Socratic dialogue is named after the Greek philosopher Socrates. This method aims at helping the individual arrive at new, more logical conclusions by encouraging discussion—every argument is questioned and supposedly weakened by additional questions, and contradictions are emphasized. The Socratic method does not necessarily aim to demonstrate a person's ignorance or mistakes; instead, it encourages him or her to seek new solutions to the problems that appear unsolvable.

Photo 8.3
Psychologists are increasingly turning to spirituality as a positive factor in therapy. How do spiritual beliefs help individuals with their emotional problems?

© iStockphoto.com/AkaratPhasura

Through guided discovery, the individual modifies maladaptive beliefs and assumptions. The therapist serves as a critical but helpful "guide" who elucidates the person's errors in logic by designing new experiences (by means of behavioral experiments) that lead to the acquisition of new skills and perspectives (Beck & Weishaar, 2013). This aspect of therapy is based on the notion that the old reality could be reinvestigated and some new answers found.

Cognitive therapy is commonly combined with other therapeutic interventions. This combination should make sense: In order to change our thinking, it is necessary to perceive life differently and develop new habits. For example, ACT (acceptance and commitment therapy) is supposed to help individuals increase their psychological flexibility by changing their mode of judging as well as behavioral habits. It contains six principles: Individuals learn not to dwell on their negative emotions, to allow bad thoughts to come and go, to be more open to new experiences, to better understand and accept self, and to set new goals and carry them out with new plans. Empirical studies show the effectiveness of this form of therapy (Davis, Morina, Powers, Smits, & Emmelkamp, 2015).

"Applied" Spirituality

Psychologists are often increasingly turning to spirituality as a possible mediating factor in therapy and as a tool in helping individuals to recover from deep emotional traumas and many other personal problems. The key strategy is to apply particular principles of thinking (they can be religious, philosophical, or just associated with belief in a "higher power," which we typically call spirituality) to the process of individual growth and healing.

Religious scholars in the past provided interesting suggestions about self-healing and growth. In Christianity, Ignatius of Loyola (1491–1556), the founder of the Society of Jesus (known as the Jesuits), published a book under the title *The Spiritual Exercises* (1914). The book described 370 exercises by which people could advance their individual willpower. For example, the book teaches how to use meditation to focus on specific experiences of the past, as well as imagination about the future. During meditation, people focus on the memories of their own sinful behavior or imagine painful experiences they could encounter in hell. Is this too scary an exercise? Apparently not, because by focusing on the negative, the individual was supposed to find the way to his or her own individual growth. In the history of psychology, clinicians used religious principles and incorporated them into their therapeutic techniques. In the United States, the Emmanuel Church Healing Movement gained popularity between 1906 and 1910. This practice made an impact on the subsequent rapid development of psychotherapy in the United States and focused the attention of millions of people on psychology and its applications. People learned how to gain access to their psychological problems through the power of scientific knowledge and their own religious faith, and as a result, they gained moral control, self-knowledge, and willpower (Caplan, 1998).

Key principles of Buddhist philosophy continue to find their impact on modern therapy (Mathers, Miller, & Ando, 2009). The teachings of the **Four Noble Truths** are most central to the Buddhist tradition. First, Buddhism maintains that suffering (*dukkha*) is an inseparable part of life. Several types of suffering exist. One is everyday physical and psychological suffering that is inevitable and associated with physical pain, discomfort brought by illness, loneliness, aging, and dying. Another type of suffering is rooted in anxiety or stress caused by people's desire to hold on to things that are constantly changing (people often try to possess something that will not be there for them tomorrow). The third type of suffering is rooted in the lack of satisfaction about things not measuring up to our expectations or desired standards. Does this all mean that humans are destined to suffer? No. Moreover, acknowledging the existence of suffering is not about giving up. In fact, there is a way to avoid suffering (Gethin, 1998).

To find this way, one has to understand the true origins of suffering, and this is the Second Truth. People mistakenly believe that they need pleasurable experiences to get what they want: status, power, money, admiration, fame, and physical comfort. Their attachment to such pleasurable experiences is the key source of suffering, but realizing that there is an escape from cravings and ignorance is learning the Third Truth of Buddhism.

The Fourth Truth is about acting to reduce and eliminate suffering. This is essentially about becoming a moral person by looking at things carefully and critically, speaking truthfully, trying not to harm by deeds or words, making constant attempts at self-improvement, understanding self, avoiding being influenced by cravings, and practicing concentration and meditation. Contrary to a common misperception, Buddhism does not encourage people to turn to poverty and social disengagement. There is a path between two extremes of human existence: People should not succumb to greed and self-indulgence, but at the same time, they should not practice self-punishment and total asceticism (a lifestyle of restraint or abstinence from various worldly pleasures). Instead, people should adopt the Middle Way, a concept that has also become a distinct feature of Buddhism. It means that people should avoid the excesses of self-indulgence and self-punishment. Moderation and

Four Noble Truths
The four basic statements reflecting the key positions of Buddhism are known as the Four Noble Truths.

nonviolence should be practiced (Mathers et al., 2009). But everything starts in the individual mind first.

Gambling Fallacies

Gambling involves risking (wagering) something valuable, usually money (the stakes), on an episode, which involves an uncertain outcome: a card game or a sports game, for example. The key goal of gambling is to win additional value, such as money, if the gambler's prediction or choice is correct. Many gamblers often rely on luck to win, but other gamblers believe they can design a strategy that should allow them to beat the odds, or probabilities, to win. Those who place a bet on a single event once each year, such as a college basketball tournament, often have personal attachments to a certain team. Some regular gamblers place their bets differently: They observe several repetitive events and place their bets on several such events consecutively.

Most gamblers also know that over the long term, odds cannot be beaten. However, there are "hot hands" or long winning streaks—you win once, twice, and you continue to bet. Conversely, many also believe bad luck is not forever either—you lose once, twice, and you may win soon. In the end, losing gamblers feel certain they will recoup their losses. This is known as the *gamblers' fallacy*, or the false belief that if something happens more frequently than usual during a period, it will happen less frequently in the future. Conversely, if something happens less frequently than typical during a period, it surely will happen more frequently in the future (Xu & Harvey, 2014).

A study of more than 565,000 sports bets made by 770 online gamblers showed that people who won were more likely to win again, but apparently this was not happening because they believed in their hot hands and luck—it was because they chose safer, less risky odds than before. Yet those who lost were more likely to lose again because they tended to choose riskier odds than before. Being cautious after winning and riskier after losing indicates that online sports gamblers suffer from the gamblers' fallacy—both winners and losers expected their luck to reverse. But winners' winning streaks increased in length because they started choosing safer and safer odds, which led them to win more often (though less money). In contrast, those who had experienced a losing streak chose ever-riskier bets, making it more likely the streak would continue (Xu & Harvey, 2014).

In fact, cognitive psychologists suggest that the propensity for gambling can be rooted in the person's mind. Perhaps what are called hot hands and "losing streaks" in gambling are real, yet they are created by the cognitive fallacies of the gambler. Imagine that such fallacies are persistent in the person's mind, and as a result, this individual is back to betting on a regular basis, weekly or even daily. In fact, gambling disorder is an addictive disorder included in the *DSM–5* as a diagnosable condition (Section 312.31; American Psychiatric Association, 2013). This is a persistent and recurrent problematic gambling behavior leading to clinically significant impairment or distress. It could be that one of the ways to address this issue is to make sure that the person with this problem understands the cognitive fallacies involved in gambling behavior.

Is an Artificial Personality Ethical?

Artificial intelligence (AI)
Artificial intelligence, or AI, is the study and design of intelligent machines.

Early in this chapter, you read about the work of Turing. His work gave a significant boost to the field of studies of **artificial intelligence (AI)**, which is the study and design of intelligent machines. In the context of cognitive neuroscience, artificial intelligence is the study and creation of systems that perceive their environment and make decisions to maximize success. In the 1950s after Turing proposed his ideas, AI became a reasonable possibility, and even skeptics had to lower their critical voices.

Chess was one of several areas in which computers began to gain both strength and public attention. Digital computers provided both mathematical and sophisticated technical solutions for the game. Soon enough, chess computers began to compete with humans. Today, some computers can compete on the highest level of the game, winning against world chess champions (Hsu, 2002). Creative writing was another field that AI tried to infiltrate. Some assumed that poetry would become a routine procedure for machines as soon as mathematicians wrote clever programs for metaphors and rhyming. It didn't happen, however. Computer-produced poetry was sophisticated grammatically but awful as an art (Funkhouser, 2012).

Others suggest that creativity also can be programmed. Technology guru and futurist Ray Kurzweil suggested that by 2045 humans would have achieved digital immortality by uploading their minds to computers, allowing humans to overcome the need for a biological body for survival. According to Kurzweil (2005), advances in neural engineering and modeling of brain function will make it possible to reproduce human minds in a digital medium in the future. Kurzweil claims that even if a biological part dissolves and dies, it won't make any difference—people will be able to create virtual bodies and virtual reality that will be as realistic as the actual reality. There

Mindclones
Mindclones are digital versions of human individuals that live forever.

is also the concept of **mindclones**—digital versions of human individuals that live forever. A "mindclone" can be created from a "mindfile"—an online repository of an individual's personality that many believe is already taking shape in the form of social media, such as Facebook (Rothblatt, 2009). A mindclone is a software version of your mind: It is all of your thoughts, recollections, feelings, beliefs, attitudes, and values, and it allows a person to experience reality from the standpoint of whatever machine their mindware is running on (Rothblatt, 2011b). We tend to think of our personal identity as being "installed" into our body; the new idea is that it can be reinstalled and uploaded to a different hardware!

Even if mindcloning is scientifically and technologically possible, many puzzling philosophical and psychological questions arise. In popular culture, scores of authors long entertained the literary idea that "thinking" machines would eventually compete with humans in all intellectual and practical fields. Yet what if these clever computers and machines went out of control and rebelled against humans? One such example is in the movie *The Terminator* (1984). If we allow machines to think and give them the ability to develop their practical thinking, what will happen to us? What if mindclones inherit software glitches and catch viruses and bugs? Moreover, can we teach moral values to machines? And will mindclones have to pay taxes?

Visual Review

INTRODUCTION AND CONTEXTS	→	KEY THEORIES AND APPROACHES	→	APPLICATIONS

Cognitive refers to the individual's senses, experience, and thought

The cognitive tradition gains knowledge from:

- Introspection
- Studying the self
- The Gestalt tradition
- Cognitive science

The contemporary cognitive tradition includes the cooperation of:

- cognitive neuroscience
- computer science
- philosophy of the self

Studies of

- attitude
- accessibility
- attitude balance
- attitude dissonance
- attributions

have enriched our knowledge about personality

Studies of personal constructs and the self within cultural contexts have added a new dimension to our understanding of personality

Cognitive therapy

Applying knowledge about cognitive errors

Applied spirituality

Applied artificial intelligence

Martin Puddy/Photonica/Getty Images

Summary

- The term *cognitive revolution* refers to the shift of focus within university psychology that went from being primarily behavioral (regarding action) to being increasingly cognitive (regarding the mind). In cognitive theory, behavior is explained as guided by cognitions (e.g., understandings and expectations) about the world, other people, and the self.

- The cognitive revolution, of course, had its roots and causes. From its early days as a research discipline in the 19th century, psychology's great scholars tried to find a way to measure the ever-elusive "internal" mechanisms of mental life of an individual's personality. They used experimental introspection, studied the self, and applied the principles of Gestalt psychology and field theory to bring cognition to the study of personality. Gestalt therapy uses the ideas about the holistic nature of human experience, the disruption of its structure, and the emphasis on the actuality of the moment.

- Cognitive psychology belongs to the line of research that is commonly regarded today as part of an interdisciplinary field of cognitive science. This field includes studies in several fields, particularly cognitive neuroscience, computer science, philosophy, and linguistics.

- Philosophy and its studies of consciousness and the self brought new inspiration to personality psychology.

- An individual's personality can be viewed and assessed from the standpoint of attitudes, which are the cognitive representations and evaluations of various features of the social and physical world. The study of attitudes gained significant popularity and research support in psychology and social psychology, especially in the second half of the past century.

- Attitudes are not directly observable; yet they can be measured with various methods of assessment and self-assessment. We can judge them from people's verbal or written responses or infer them from people's behavior. The individual holds attitudes in a particular fashion, and the connections between attitudes and behavior can be studied and measured.

- There are relatively strong and weak attitudes. An individual has some attitudes easily accessible, while others take an effort to retrieve. This is a measure of availability and easiness of expression of the individual's attitude.

- Attitudes with a "unipolar" composition of the affective component are called single-evaluation attitudes. Attitudes that contain an ambivalent emotional component are called dual-evaluation attitudes.

- Balance theory maintains that people seek consistency among their judgments. They do not necessarily do this deliberately. It is the nature of human experience to be "balanced." To maintain their perception in "good form," people tend to seek explanations for their judgments, thus creating perceptual distortions.

- Leon Festinger, the author of the theory of cognitive dissonance, maintained that people tend to experience tension—an unpleasant emotional state caused by the perceived mismatch dissonance between their attitudes and behavior. The dissonance causes people to change either behavior or attitudes. To achieve a harmonious view, people tend to use the least-effort principle—they minimize the number of cognitive operations to reach a goal.

- The attribution approach shows from a particular angle how the individual explains the world and other people's actions. Attribution involves an act of judgment and is the process by which individuals explain the causes of behavior and events. Harold Kelly proposed that people judge other people's behavior from the standpoints of consistency, distinctiveness, and consensus.

- The American psychologist George Kelly combined the principles of cognitive psychology and applied psychotherapy to approach the individual personality. He believed that people for the most part are "naïve scientists" capable of making reasonable and rational judgments. Such construct systems or constructs are stable assumptions that the individual develops about other people, the self, and the world in general. Such assumptions tend to be "bipolar," or focus on two opposing sides of the spectrum. Constructs should provide a certain order, clarity, and prediction to a person's world. We as individuals develop our "construct systems" to filter the information about the world and make stable judgments.

- A disordered construct system does not accurately predict events and does not help the person adjust to new circumstances. Kelly's fixed-role therapy was designed to change the individual's perception of self. In a simple way, the person would describe self and emphasize various problems that he or she has at present. Then the psychologist would rewrite this self-description and, instead of focusing on negative characteristics and mistakes, would emphasize helpful behaviors and positive self-evaluations.

- The term *self* refers to the representation of one's identity or the subject of experience. The cognitive tradition is based on the assumption that people make distinctions between the world within them and the world outside.

- Consciousness is a state of awareness of our own existence. Self-awareness is, in fact, a reflection of this awareness that allows us to perceive our existence with a sense of consistency. Identity can be private and social. Social identity refers to the individual's perceived membership in one or several social groups.

- A person's general subjective evaluation, both emotional and rational, of his or her own worth is called self-esteem.

- Writers are not scientists, but as artists, they use words to describe either extraordinary (unusual or improbable) or ordinary (common, everyday) characters in extraordinary and ordinary circumstances. Extraordinary events and extraordinary characters are the most recognizable sources of knowledge about personality. Ordinary characters also appear in extraordinary circumstances where men and women reveal their individual features. Reflections about everyday people in ordinary situations bring valuable knowledge to the study of personality as well.

- Cognitive therapy is an approach to psychotherapy rooted in the assumption that certain psychological disorders and many difficult psychological problems are established in the individual's particular view of the world and the self. Three essential concepts in cognitive therapy are collaborative empiricism, Socratic dialogue, and guided discovery.

- Psychologists use spirituality as a mediating factor in therapy and as a cognitive tool in helping individuals to recover from deep emotional traumas and personal problems. The key strategy is to apply particular principles of thinking (they can be religious, philosophical, or just associated with the belief in a "higher power") to the process of individual growth and healing.

- Cognitive psychology studies cognitive errors related to gambling. Psychologists suggest that "hot hands" and "losing streaks" in gambling are real, yet they are created by the cognitive fallacies of the gambler.

- Cognitive psychology encourages the discussion about scientific and moral aspects of a digital personality and mindclones—digital versions of human individuals that live forever.

Key Terms

artificial intelligence(AI) 256	dual-evaluation attitudes 240	level of aspiration 235
attitudes 239	ethnic disidentification 249	mindclones 256
attribution 242	experimental introspection 232	naïve scientists 244
cognitive dissonance 241	field theory 234	self 246
cognitive revolution 232	fixed-role therapy 245	self-awareness 246
cognitive science 237	Four Noble Truths 254	self-esteem 248
collaborative empiricism 252	Gestalt therapy 234	single-evaluation attitudes 240
constructs 245	least-effort principle 241	social identity 247

Evaluating What You Know

What is the main idea of the cognitive tradition in personality psychology?

Summarize the contribution of early studies in psychology to the cognitive tradition.

What did cognitive science give to this tradition?

Describe the role of cognitive science in the study of personality.

What do studies of consciousness bring to personality psychology?

Explain attitude accessibility, attitude balance, and attitude dissonance. Give examples.

How do attributions and personal constructs affect behavior?

Explain the self, self-esteem, and social identity.

Identify several areas of applications of the cognitive tradition including therapy, spirituality, gambling problems, and others.

A Bridge to the Next Chapter

Critics of the cognitive tradition in personality psychology often claim that it overemphasizes cognition, rational choice, and formal operations, as well as pays significantly less attention to emotion and motivation, especially to the issues involving ultimate "human" attributes of people's existence and experience: ideals, moral choices, and values. In the next chapter, we turn to a tradition in psychology that holds a hopeful, constructive view of human beings and of their substantial capacity to be self-determining. It is guided by a conviction that ethical values are strong determinants of human behavior. This belief leads to an effort to emphasize human qualities such as choice, imagination, and the capacity to be free and happy.

WANT A BETTER GRADE?

Get the tools you need to sharpen your study skills. Access practice quizzes, eFlash-cards, web exercises, and multimedia at edge.sagepub.com/shiraevpersonality

⑤SAGE edge™

© iStockphoto.com/Susan Chiang

9

The Humanistic Tradition

"Thank goodness for the first snow, it was a reminder—no matter
how old you became and how much you'd seen, things could still
be new if you were willing to believe they still mattered."

—Candace Bushnell (b. 1958), American novelist, author of *Sex and the City*

Learning Objectives

After reading this chapter, you should be able to:

- Identify the main principles and historical contexts of humanistic psychology
- Discuss the four assumptions of existentialism and May's findings about fear
- Discuss Maslow's hierarchy of needs
- Explain what it means to be autotelic
- Discuss Rogers's person-centered approach and the principles of positive psychology
- Identify the accomplishments and shortcomings of the humanistic tradition
- Identify ways to apply the key principles of the humanistic tradition to individual experience and behavior

The purpose of life is a life of purpose.

The difference between ordinary and extraordinary is that little extra.

These are the words of a young girl named Athena Orchard who died at age 13 after a brief, stoic battle with cancer. Following her death, Athena's parents uncovered an unusual diary written on the back of her bedroom mirror. With whom did Athena want to share the 3,000 words written in marker? Maybe with her parents, siblings, and friends. Or maybe with all of us.

Happiness is a direction not a destination.

Thank you for existing.

Be happy, be free, believe, forever young.

Athena was first diagnosed with cancer when she was 12. She underwent a long emergency operation, which was followed by months of chemotherapy. The chances of survival were slim, but she fought. She gave everything to this battle, in which the illness prevailed. Despite all the treatments attempted, the doctors could no longer do anything for her.

Love is not about who you can see spending your future with; it's about who you can't see spending your life without.

Athena—before her illness—was very athletic and strong. She loved to write. The illness took away her physical abilities. She lost her hair. But she never lost her positive outlook. She always believed in the best outcome. She believed in life. She left behind her six sisters and three brothers.

> *People gonna hate you, rate you, break you, but how strong you stand, that's what makes you . . . you!*

Don't we all sometimes feel sorry about how life treats us? There are those days when we feel gloomy and desperate. Life seems unfair. There are nights when we dread the upcoming morning. We wish our tasks were easier, people nicer, workdays shorter, and vacations longer. Maybe today is that day. However, the next time you feel sad, think of Athena. She never gave up. She inspired others. She reminded us about dignity and hope. We can *feel* down sometimes, yet we should not let ourselves *be* down. We can be happy. It is up to us.

> *Happiness depends upon ourselves.*

> *Maybe it's not about the happy ending—maybe it's about the story.*

Maybe happiness is a state of mind. Maybe it is ephemeral. Yet happiness can also be a trait. There are happy people around us, and you may be or become one of them. You can also make other people happy. The humanistic tradition in personality psychology focuses on happiness—not only does it tells us about happy individuals, but it teaches us how to be and remain happy.

Sources: Perry, 2014; Spillett, 2014.

The Humanistic Tradition: Social Contexts

The humanistic tradition in personality psychology took shape during one of the most turbulent and uncertain periods in history. At least two major global developments contributed to this worldwide uneasiness. The first was World War II (1939–1945) and the massive international devastation that resulted. The second was the Cold War—a period of dangerous ideological and political struggle between capitalism and communism that lasted until the end of the 20th century. Scientists, politicians, and ordinary people alike were increasingly aware of the dangers of nuclear war.

In the second half of the past century, the United States became a powerful center of education and science. Colleges and universities in the United States were in much better shape compared with educational institutions in other parts of the world. A significant influx of immigrants from all over the world brought to America a fresh new wave of educated specialists.

Let us examine how all of these events relate to the humanistic tradition that we study in this chapter.

Debates Within Psychology

New and intriguing debates about the role of psychology in contemporary society emerged in the 1950s. Many professionals of that era believed that psychology had to use primarily experimental methods of investigation. In their view, psychologists should use science, including mathematics, biology, and neurophysiology.

But a good number of other psychologists thought differently. When behaviorists studied a person's useful habits and psychoanalysts scrutinized early childhood conflicts, more psychologists began asking a powerful question: Why do we study physical movements and painful memories? They further argued that psychology must change its focus and embrace something more human, such as happiness, self-improvement, and compassion instead of just studying "reactions" and "defenses." In the early 1960s, many psychologists began to reevaluate and emphasize the importance of humanitarian and moral issues in psychology. Group seminars on healthy relationships and educational sessions on self-esteem became popular. Psychologists reasoned that the mathematical precision of most behavioral studies was running a risk of losing the purpose and focus of psychological research. The attention should turn toward the individual: the comprehending, compassionate, and ever-evolving person who is not necessarily "responding" to stimuli but rather "growing" (Aanstoos, Serlin, & Greening, 2000).

Furthermore, early humanistic psychologists believed that psychology as a discipline should pay significant attention to human suffering and injustice. Psychology should be progressive and pursue an ambitious goal to make the society better. These arguments drew significant attention in the changing political culture of the 1960s. Dissatisfied with war, injustice, and unequal opportunity, many people, especially the young adults of the "baby-boomer" generation in the West, challenged the rules and attitudes of the traditional establishment. The focus of their attention was shifting toward civil rights and social obstacles, including discrimination, prejudice, racism, sexism, and bigotry. Many professors and students shared a popular opinion that psychology as a discipline should bring scientific wisdom and compassion to addressing lingering societal problems, especially in the fields of education, mental health, and individual development.

Photo 9.1 Humanistic psychologists believe that psychology should pursue an ambitious goal to make the society better. Suggest two or three social areas in which you think psychologists can help the most.

© iStockphoto.com/Cylonphoto

The Essence of Humanistic Tradition

The term *humanistic* is somewhat imprecise. It has several interpretations, which multiply in foreign translations. Applied to psychology, the humanistic tradition calls for renewed efforts to study the phenomena that distinguish human beings—love, happiness, and self-growth. It also focuses on "being and becoming somebody" rather than "having and accumulating something." Those who called themselves **humanistic psychologists** wanted to focus less on experimental procedures and statistics and more on the individual's care and self-growth. They wanted to celebrate the uniqueness of individual experiences and share them with others.

Humanistic principles are extraordinarily diverse and have deep roots in several academic disciplines. Almost every contributor to personality psychology in the past had somehow addressed humanistic ideas. Looking at their contributions, we will focus primarily on a few that have influenced personality psychology.

Humanistic psychologists
Humanistic psychologists encourage efforts to study the phenomena that distinguish human beings—love, happiness, and self-growth.

The Critical Aspect

The humanistic tradition is rooted in critical examinations of other traditions, especially behaviorism and psychoanalysis. Humanistic psychologists claimed that psychology was losing its main subject: the individual.

Behaviorism was the first target of criticism. Behaviorists, representing the "first force" in psychology, insisted that learning was the key influence in shaping the individual's actions. In essence, an individual's personality is a complex "ensemble" of various responses and habits predetermined by a specific genetic makeup of an individual and molded by environmental conditions. Psychologists within the humanistic tradition grew increasingly dissatisfied with behaviorism for this seemingly simplistic approach. Moreover, behaviorism practically ignored consciousness and the "inner" world of the feeling and striving individual. Critics argued that behavioral experiments, measurements, and correlation quotients could provide some knowledge about an individual. However, this knowledge would be grossly incomplete because it would convey very little about the individual's subjective experience.

Psychoanalysis was another target of criticisms. Many humanistic psychologists studied and practiced psychoanalysis early in their careers. They agreed that psychoanalysis encouraged individuals to address their problems through a dialogue with a therapist, self-discovery, and a sustained mental effort. However, they also criticized psychoanalysis for focusing primarily on psychological anomalies. Psychoanalysis, as they claimed, had overemphasized the importance of unconscious processes and had devalued the meaning of conscious, purposeful acts. The individual in many psychoanalytic theories appeared overwhelmed with the heavy weight of traumatic unconscious experiences stemming from childhood. The individual appeared helpless dealing with the "demons" of the past (Schneider, Pierson, & Bugental, 2014).

The Positive Aspect

Humanistic psychologists also claimed that the intriguing, provocative, controversial, and inspirational core of human existence was seemingly disappearing in the "forest"

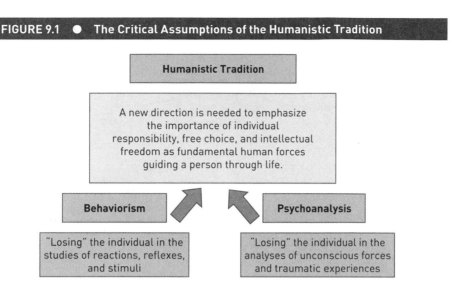

FIGURE 9.1 ● The Critical Assumptions of the Humanistic Tradition

Humanistic Tradition

A new direction is needed to emphasize the importance of individual responsibility, free choice, and intellectual freedom as fundamental human forces guiding a person through life.

Behaviorism

"Losing" the individual in the studies of reactions, reflexes, and stimuli

Psychoanalysis

"Losing" the individual in the analyses of unconscious forces and traumatic experiences

of technical terms to describe learned reactions and defense mechanisms. They challenged behaviorism and psychoanalysis by emphasizing the importance of individual responsibility, free choice, and intellectual freedom as fundamental human forces guiding a person through life. It was a very optimistic orientation, assuring people of the strength of their own unrealized power (see **Figure 9.1**).

Principles of Humanistic Psychology

The term **humanistic psychology** emerged in publications and academic presentations in the 1950s. Several psychologists, psychiatrists, and educators expressed their concerns about the growing and problematic trend in mainstream academic psychology. In a nutshell, humanistic psychology treats individuals as uniquely human. Humanistic psychologists themselves define this tradition as a value orientation that holds a hopeful and constructive view of people and of their substantial capacity to be self-determining (Association for Humanistic Psychology, 2014). The humanistic tradition is based on five theoretical principles (see **Figure 9.2**).

Five Theoretical Principles

The first principle of the humanistic tradition states that people should be viewed from a holistic perspective. Each individual is more than the sum of his or her habits, reflexes, mental operations, or decision-making strategies. This point may seem trivial because it would probably be difficult to find any psychologist in the 1960s who would state that a human being is "just a sum of several parts." Nevertheless, the focus on holism within the humanistic tradition was another way to express criticism of behaviorism. The message was as follows: In our humanistic study, we will focus on all aspects of an individual's existence and not necessarily on isolated behavioral acts, no matter how complex they are (Bugental, 1964).

Humanistic psychology
Humanistic psychology refers to a tradition or a value orientation in psychology that holds a hopeful and constructive view of people and of their substantial capacity to be self-determining.

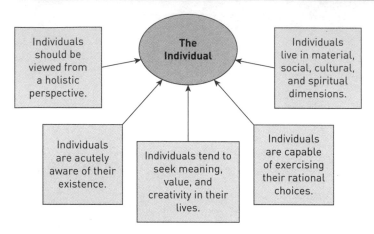

FIGURE 9.2 ● The Principles of the Humanistic Tradition

Individuals should be viewed from a holistic perspective.

The Individual

Individuals live in material, social, cultural, and spiritual dimensions.

Individuals are acutely aware of their existence.

Individuals tend to seek meaning, value, and creativity in their lives.

Individuals are capable of exercising their rational choices.

Second, individuals are aware of their existence. Moreover, they are aware of being aware, which means they are conscious. This statement was a direct challenge to psychoanalysis and its fundamental assumption about the supremacy of the unconscious side of human experience. Although many humanistic psychologists were trained within the psychoanalytic tradition and not all of them had abandoned their belief in the power of unconscious processes to regulate thought and action, their focus was shifting toward consciousness and reason. The focal point of their interest was the knowledgeable, thinking individuals who are aware of their own psychological processes.

The third principle asserts that human beings live in a uniquely human context that is not limited to their immediate surroundings, such as an office, classroom, or dining hall. To fully understand a person's inner world, psychologists have to expand the scientific view of the individual. They have to examine an individual's "cosmic ecology" involving its material, social, cultural, and spiritual dimensions.

Fourth, rational and knowledgeable individuals can exercise their choices. With those choices, however, comes individual responsibility. People make mistakes and learn from them. Humanistic psychologists—contrary to the assumptions of their critics—did not believe in total, unconditional freedom of the individual to do whatever she or he pleases. Choice comes with accountability.

And finally, because human behavior is generally intentional and deliberate, people can control the outcomes of

@
Half a century ago, as well as today, new ideas required promotion, including professional incorporation, publications, and other steps. Learn more about the first steps of humanistic psychology and its later developments on the companion website.

CHECK AND APPLY YOUR KNOWLEDGE

1. What were the "first" and "second" forces in psychology?
2. What is humanistic psychology?
3. Explain humanistic psychology's five points.
4. Imagine that you have founded a new field of research in personality psychology. What would you do today to promote this theory (besides having your own website or blog)?

their behavior. Being aware of their goals, people seek meaning, value, and creativity in their lives, which can become a foundation of happiness.

As you can see, taken as a whole, the main message of humanistic psychology was constructive. People are not necessarily direct "products" of stimuli and circumstances. Neither do they follow the imperatives of the unconscious mind. People are generally rational and logical in setting their goals and choosing the methods to achieve them. Humanistic psychology is also inherently optimistic. Circumstances can affect all of us, but we, as humans, have the power to overcome the challenges.

Yet what if the individual fails to achieve his or her goals despite a sustained effort and good intentions? A person may choose a wrong method or strategy. Sometimes circumstances stand in our way. We fail, and this causes suffering—persistent failures cause persistent suffering. Fortunately, humanistic psychology shows the individual several ways out of this suffering.

Methods and Humanistic Psychology

Humanistic psychologists focus on the actual experience of an individual (Greening, 1971). They generally prefer qualitative research methods to quantitative procedures and stress the importance of in-depth examinations of an individual's concerns, memories, plans, feelings, and actions taken together in unity. Although humanistic psychologists acknowledge several limitations of the experimental method and, above all, the restraints of its formalized, statistics-based view of the individual, they do not reject experiments. In their view, experiments should be conducted but in different combinations with nonexperimental methods such as observations, interviews, content analysis, and so forth. For example, let's assume that some patients have shown improvements in their symptoms after undergoing a certain kind of psychotherapy. Does this finding say anything about what these individuals felt, how they understood their own symptoms, and whether the changes in their behavioral symptoms affected their overall psychological state? The role of humanistic tradition in personality psychology is significant and is better explained if we study it from several angles and see its connections to philosophy, the social sciences, and the humanities (Chapter 2).

Existentialism

Existentialism
An intellectual tradition, existentialism focuses on individual existence, its uniqueness, free will, and responsibility.

The term *existential* refers, above all, to existence and being. **Existentialism**, as an intellectual tradition, focuses on individual existence, its uniqueness, free will, and responsibility. In an existentialist's view, human beings are neither substances with fixed properties, such as bones and brains, nor subjects interacting with a world of objects. A central proposition of existentialism is that human beings, through their conscious efforts, create their own meanings, roles, prescriptions, and values. The problem is that as individuals, we do not necessarily fit well into these meanings and roles.

Existentialism puts forward several candid and controversial assumptions. For convenience, let's put them in sequence:

Human existence is tragic.

Life is painful and absurd.

Life is full of anxiety and depression.

Steps can be taken to address the tragic nature and absurdity of our lives.

Why Is Our Existence Tragic? Existential philosophy celebrates and mourns the heartbreaking uniqueness of each individual's experience. People are free, yet every moment they struggle with the demands of society (Berdyaev, 1931/2009). People are free, yet most individuals have no idea what to do with their freedom. Every moment of our lives, we are breathing, acting, hoping, willing, and . . . getting closer to death. No matter what we do and how hard we try, the final results do not match our expectations. We are left sad and disoriented, according to supporters of existentialism.

Existential crisis
An existential crisis is a period in which an individual questions the very foundations of life and asks whether his or her life has any meaning, purpose, or value.

Why Is Life Absurd? Existentialism holds that there is no true meaning in life, and our attempts to find meaning are fruitless (Sartre, 1943/1969). This futility adds to a sense of confusion, which existentialists call the *existential attitude*. The struggle to comprehend reality often leads to an **existential crisis**, or a period at which an individual questions the very foundations of life and asks whether his or her life has any meaning, purpose, or value. The loss of religious faith and morality in modern life reinforces the existential crisis (Camus, 1951/1992). Finding no answers, people then face anxiety and depression.

Why Is Life Full of Anxiety and Depression? Existentialists say anxiety and depression manifest because people need answers yet do not find them. There is no certainty in life except death. We fear death, and death is a pathway to nonexistence (Sartre, 1943/1969). The individual looks for a distraction from this fear by working harder, making more money, and getting more power. The irony is that these actions make the individual unhappy (Kierkegaard, 1843/1992). Humans try hard to achieve harmony and peace, yet they fail in their attempts at human perfection (Camus, 1951/1992). Uncertainty mounts and anxiety grows. Depression, often called despair, takes over.

Are There Solutions? Existentialists differ in the way they teach about reducing despair. Some advocate action and celebrate the power of human will and power (Nietzsche, 1901/1968). Others encourage people to revolt against their own existence (Camus, 1951/1992). Yet others encourage people to look beyond their prescribed social roles, such as family members, students, or nurses, and stop living lives that fit into the standards defined by professional occupations and roles (Kierkegaard, 1843/1992; Sartre, 1943/1969). Some contemporary philosophers continue to discuss a personal, subjective realm of existence in which an individual lives and extracts pleasure from life only for his or her own sake. We may eventually embrace the shortness of our lives and thus free ourselves from anxiety and despair (Menand, 2009). Other supporters of existential views chose therapy as a means to address the individual's anxieties (Frankl, 1959).

Rollo May and Existential Psychology

Existentialism influenced many disciplines, including psychology. **Existential psychology**, like existential philosophy, embraced a great variety of ideas. Several important themes emerged.

> **Existential psychology**
> An eclectic and diverse field of studies, existential psychology embraces the idea of the exceptionality of human existence, the importance of individual free choice and independent will, and the necessity to consider each person as a unique entity.

First, existential psychology states that the individual's existence and experience are unique, exceptional, and unrepeatable. Each one of us is a universe in itself. When you die, there will never be another "you." This fact is both inspiring and tragic: We simultaneously celebrate our uniqueness and bemoan the shortness of our existence. The second assumption emphasizes the importance of individual free choice and independent will. We make our own choices and take responsibility for them. The third assumption is the necessity to consider every person as a unique entity in the context of his or her circumstances, relationships, conditions, influences, and internal forces (Binswanger, 1963). Although these theoretical principles might appear somewhat eclectic and imprecise, their specific applications are not.

Unlike existential philosophers—most of whom considered the world and individuals in it as disorganized, tragic, and confused—existential psychologists tend to be optimistic. True, the world seems chaotic. But it only seems this way. It happens because many people feel trapped in their daily routines and cannot break some of their habits: We study, work, pay bills, buy property, save for retirement, but forget to be human beings. Our lives are short, but we can discover the path that will lead us to confidence and happiness. This discovery can come naturally through the process of our individual growth. Self-improvement can take place under guidance and deliberate effort.

As you can see, existential psychology intersects—sometimes deliberately and sometimes not—with the Indian philosophical tradition (Chapter 2). One of many applications stemming from this tradition is that self-improvement can be achieved through the changes of self-awareness. A self-improving person overcomes selfish desires and pride. This person keeps away from the material world and practices meditation to reach the state of pure consciousness. Existential psychology suggests that by focusing on awareness of others and self-awareness, a person can pursue pure consciousness and, ultimately, happiness (Rao, Paranjpe, & Dalal, 2008).

Anxiety and Personality According to Rollo May

One of the leading representatives of existential psychology was the American psychologist Rollo May (1909–1994). His personal health problems early in life and his search for inner strength contributed to his relentless and creative insight into personality psychology. As a theorist and practitioner, May considered anxiety one of the most fundamental psychological features of the modern individual. Why did he emphasize anxiety?

He believed that anxiety was provoked by the fundamental technological and social changes taking place in the global world. The individual was caught amid an epic conflict between the old world of tradition and the new world of change. Tradition represented stability and certainty; change was rooted in uncertainty and instability (May, 1950). Another source of anxiety was the emerging threats to the individual's most fundamental family values (May, Angel, & Ellenberger, 1958). So these factors led to anxiety, which led to confusion, which increased the sense of powerlessness. The individual increasingly often feels insignificant, which can lead to anger and even violence (May, 1969).

Certainly, according to May, people seek remedies against anxiety. Some remedies may bring only temporary relief. For example, some people may seek self-isolation. They build psychological shelters of selfishness, disengagement from social life, and apathy: Such individuals disregard other people's interests (Why do I have to care about other people?) or stop pursuing their own goals and dreams (Why do I have to compete and take chances?).

May was not the only thinker who called anxiety the most profound feature of his time. The expression "the age of anxiety" was already popular in the literature (Auden, 1949). However, May was not a pessimist or alarmist. He believed that the modern era was also the "century of psychology." May encouraged people to reduce their anxiety by rediscovering the importance of caring for one another. Only then, he postulated, can people overcome the emerging "bankruptcy of inner values" (May, 1969). Specifically, he taught about the necessity to distinguish between anxiety and fear. Fears usually have an unidentifiable source. Therefore, fears are more manageable than anxiety.

May believed there were two different ways to cope with fear: by avoiding it or confronting it (May, 1969). Yet there is another, third way to manage fear: We can accept it. For example, how do we overcome fear of death? An individual's awareness of death is essential to life, but can we deny death? It is better to accept the existential inevitability of death rather than being afraid of it. As if supporting May's views, Arthur Koestler, a Hungarian British author and journalist who fought with his pen against political oppression, wrote in *Dialogue With Death* (1942) that when he and the other political prisoners knew that they were going to die

FIGURE 9.3 ● Rollo May's Views on Individuals and Anxiety

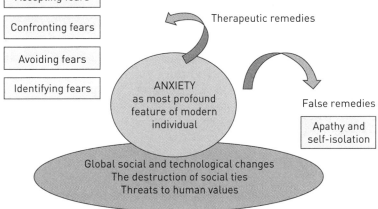

and no longer feared dying, "at such moments we were *free*—men without shadows, dismissed from the ranks of the mortal; it was the most complete experience of freedom" that can be granted a person (see **Figure 9.3**; Menand, 2009).

As we could see, May believed that anxiety could be reduced if we understand it as a certain fear. Another way to overcome anxiety is love. There are different types of love, however. Sexual love is the "lowest" type because it is rooted in predominantly natural impulses. May argued that when a person gives in to the impulses of sexual promiscuity, it does not actually make that person free. Instead, resisting these impulses is about being free. He believed that love can be unselfish and manifested in friendship and dedication to others (May, 1969). May's publications and lectures about anxiety, fear, love, and the possibility for self-improvement drew a significant reading and listening audience.

CHECK AND APPLY YOUR KNOWLEDGE

1. What is existentialism? Explain an existential crisis in an individual.

2. What does the expression "the age of anxiety" mean?

3. How can the individual reduce anxiety, according to Rollo May?

4. How is today's "age of anxiety" different from the period described by May?

Photo 9.2 Maslow described the individual's needs as arranged in a hierarchy in terms of their potency. Can you apply your own life experiences to this hierarchy?

Abraham Maslow and Humanistic Psychology

A significant contribution to personality psychology came from Abraham Maslow (1908–1970), whose name is among the most recognizable in modern psychology and social sciences. Born to a family of poor immigrants from Russia, Maslow developed an early love for learning and chose psychology for his major and career. He did experimental research before turning to a humanistic viewpoint.

Hierarchy of Needs

One of the most notable contributions of Maslow was his theory of motivation and human needs. For Maslow, motivation is a force within an organism that initiates and maintains behavior (Maslow, 1970). How does this motivation work? Maslow argued that when a certain need motivates a living organism, there must be some deficiency within the organism. Hunger, for example, is an indicator of food deficiency. An individual will consume food to reduce or eliminate this deficiency, which will end the subjective experience of hunger. There are other needs, however, that are distinctly human. They are not necessarily related to food, water, or something material. These are needs related to being or becoming. For example, there are needs of becoming a better person, a caring family member, a loving daughter, a decent human being, and more. Maslow described the individual's needs as arranged in a hierarchy in terms of their potency. He grouped these needs into five categorical levels: physiological, safety, love, esteem, and self-actualization (Maslow, 1970).

The concept of hierarchy of needs has an intriguing analogy in the Indian spiritual tradition. To illustrate, Hinduism introduces kama (pleasurable activity), *artha* (activity related to pursuit of a livelihood), and dharma (spiritual duty) as a hierarchy of critical guiding principles of life. However, there is no indication that Maslow knew about these ideas before he published his works on motivation (Collins, 1990).

Not only did Maslow introduce a hierarchy of needs, but he suggested how this hierarchy functioned. In particular, he proposed that once an individual has satisfied the cluster of needs at a particular level, he or she is able to progress to the next hierarchical level (see **Figure 9.4**).

People typically tend not to seek safety and security until they have met their needs for food, water, and shelter (Level 1). After individuals secure their immediate access to basic resources, then they try to meet their safety needs by making sure these recourses remain available in the future (Level 2). For example, if a woman looks for and finds a stable job, this activity is likely to refer to her satisfying the safety needs. Then, on Level 3, individuals are likely to seek social affiliation with other people and groups and pursue affection from others. Then comes Level 4, associated with esteem

FIGURE 9.4 ● Maslow's Hierarchy of Needs	

Level 5:	*Self-Actualization Needs* Completion, sufficiency, morality, etc.
Level 4: ⬆	*Esteem Needs* Achievement, self-esteem, respect by others, etc.
Level 3: ⬆	*Belonging and Love Needs* Friendship, family, intimacy
Level 2: ⬆	*Safety Needs* Security of the body, health, resources, the family, etc.
Level 1: ⬆	*Physiological Needs* Homeostasis, breathing, water, food, sex, etc.

needs: People now pursue approval and appreciation from others. Artists, designers, engineers, and nurses, as well as people of other walks of life and professions, seek respect and recognition. For example, not only is it important for the teacher to teach classes well. Now, on this level, he or she needs feedback—preferably positive—from the students.

Maslow gathered his data more than 50 years ago. Yet contemporary studies show that many of his conclusions are very much applicable to today's word (Konnikova, 2014). A Harvard University project to study digital behavior showed that with a rapid expanding and fragmentation of television, blogs, and social networks, young people tend to find the way to strengthen their identity. They don't want to get lo t in the ocean of information and personal posts. They want to identify self in a special way and find like-minded individuals online (Level 3). Finding like-minded others may be more important than ever before in history (Gardner & Davis, 2013). Studies show that online contacts, in fact (despite many setbacks), can foster a strong sense of identity in a person, stimulate meaningful relationships, and fuel creativity. Esteem and respect (Level 4) received from others can come quickly or it can last—it all depends on how vast and lengthy the impact of the online "self" is.

Maslow's needs on the first four levels are labeled as *deficit needs* or **D-needs** because they are rooted in a scarcity of something, such as food or esteem from others. Maslow noted that as one gradually ascends the hierarchy of needs, this person becomes less animal-like and more human. The highest human function is being achieved on Level 5. If a woman, for example, has been able to satisfy adequately, step by step, the needs on the first four levels, she is in a position to fulfill the highest-order needs—namely, to actualize her unique potential. According to Maslow, once

D-needs
"Deficit needs," or D-needs, are rooted in a scarcity of something, such as food or esteem from others.

Self-actualization
The highest stage
of individual
development,
self-actualization
is governed by the
search for truth,
goodness, beauty,
wholeness, justice,
and meaningfulness.

she enters the top level of the hierarchy, the realm of **self-actualization**, she becomes qualitatively different from those who are still attempting to meet their more basic needs. However, she does not necessarily reach the self-actualization level routinely, simply because she satisfied all other needs. Achieving self-actualization requires time, certain conditions, and, most importantly, significant inner work.

Self-Actualization

Maslow's interest in self-actualizing people began with his great admiration for Max Wertheimer (1880–1943), one of the pioneers of experimental psychology, and Ruth Benedict (1888–1948), the renowned American cultural anthropologist and one of the most ardent critics of the early-20th-century racist theories in social sciences. After learning that these two individuals had many characteristics in common, such as optimism, efficiency, kindness, and generosity, Maslow began to search for other people with similar qualities. The group he finally selected for more a detailed study included European or European American people from different historic periods: American presidents Abraham Lincoln and Thomas Jefferson, physicist Albert Einstein, First Lady Eleanor Roosevelt (wife of President Franklin D. Roosevelt), philosophers Benedict Spinoza and Albert Schweitzer, politician Adlai Stevenson, and educator Martin Buber.

On the basis of his research, Maslow developed a composite, impressionistic profile of an optimally functioning, mature, and healthy human being. Maslow concluded that self-actualizing persons exhibit a number of similar characteristics, including the following:

- Accurate perception of reality
- Continued freshness of appreciation and openness to experience
- Spontaneity and simplicity
- Strong ethical awareness
- Philosophical (rather than hostile) sense of humor
- Need for privacy
- Periodic peak experiences
- Democratic (nonauthoritarian) leadership traits
- Deep interpersonal relations
- Autonomy and independence
- Creativeness
- Problem-centered (rather than self-centered) orientation
- Resistance to enculturation
- Acceptance of self, others, and nature

B-values
Examples of "being-
values," or B-values,
are truthfulness,
goodness, beauty,
wholeness, justice,
and meaningfulness.

The self-actualizing person's life is governed by the search for *being-values*, or **B-values**, such as truth, goodness, beauty, wholeness, justice, and meaningfulness.

Cross-Cultural Applicability

Maslow's research drew criticism. Maslow, like Erikson, focused on a sample of individuals in his research that was not necessarily representative of the global population.

Maslow actually selected people who shared his moral code and his conception of fulfillment and assigned them the honorific status of self-actualizers (Kendler, 1999). Maslow's critics wonder if Maslow simply selected his personal heroes and offered his impressions of them (Smith, 1978).

Maslow's idea of personal independence could be seen as a Western characteristic that was not so dominant in many cultures 50 years ago. The traditional Chinese hierarchy of values, for instance, includes the promotion of interconnectedness, in contrast to the emphasis on self-development in Maslow's version. Nevis (1983) examined Maslow's hierarchy of needs and argued that one of the most basic needs of people in communist China was the need to belong, rather than physiological needs. Moreover, self-actualization could manifest as a devoted service to community. If a person self-actualized by means of contributing to the group, this individual was realizing the value of collectivist self-actualization (Shiraev & Levy, 2013).

Arthur Petrovsky (1978) studied the values and collectivist motivation of people in the Soviet Union in the 1970s. He found that most individuals believed that they achieve their maximum potential not necessarily by self-actualizing but by being part of their society and sharing its values. In both Chinese and Soviet examples, communist ideology and traditions advocated obedience and cooperation but not a kind of self-determination emphasized at that time by many humanistic psychologists in the West (Shiraev & Levy, 2013).

The Autotelic Personality

One of the distinct features of a self-actualizing individual is **peak experiences**—periodic and profound episodes of happiness, optimism, inner harmony, and creativity. These are the most significant, happiest moments of discovery, understanding, accomplishment, or intimacy. Is it possible for a non–self-actualizing person to have peak experiences? It is possible, yet such experiences are likely to be infrequent (Maslow, 1962). Peak experiences can be achieved through meditation. They are common in teachings and practices of Hindu or Buddhist traditions. However, the meditation techniques generally encourage self-focus and detachment from the outside word. Peak experiences require social engagement. These experiences typically involve other people and consistent social engagements.

Years after Maslow descried peak experiences, his ideas found support in the studies of so-called **flow**—a state of complete concentration and joyful immersion in the situation or activity. Flow is a feature associated with the **autotelic personality** (Car, 2011). This is a general term (*auto* in Greek means "self" and *telos* means "goal") to describe a person who tends to be engaged in activities that are naturally rewarding and not necessarily associated with material goals such as money, fame, or high social status. It is also associated with the person's ability to find enjoyment in everyday activities that many people can find tedious (Csikszentmihalyi, 1990). Authentic personality is associated with traits such as curiosity, purposeful behavior, and modesty. Autotelic personalities—compared to others—tend to seek and create situations in which they experience flow states. Compared with other people,

Peak experiences Peak experiences are periodic and profound episodes of happiness, optimism, inner harmony, and creativity.

Flow Flow indicates a state of complete concentration and joyful immersion in the situation or activity.

Autotelic personality Autotelic describes the personality of an individual who tends to be engaged in activities that are naturally rewarding and not necessarily associated with material goals such as money, fame, or high social status (*auto* in Greek means "self" and *telos* means "goal").

autotelic personalities have a greater capacity to initiate, sustain, and enjoy such experiences (Baumann, 2012).

People can be called *autotelic* because they find the right balance between serious activities and play. However, finding this balance is difficult. The individual must learn at least two important things: how to stay focused and how to set realistic goals. This also requires a willingness to learn about one's own limitations. In other words, individuals create their flow experiences because they know that they are achievable. Where nonautotelic individuals see obstacles and problems, the autotelic person believes opportunity is not only fun but also builds skills (Baumann, 2012). This person also has a capacity for disinterested interest, which means the performance may be valued higher than the result of this performance (Csikszentmihalyi, 1997).

Humanistic Tradition and Activism

Should psychologists be impartial observers of facts, or should they bring their values to their research? Should they focus on "what is" in the world, or should they pay attention to "what should be" instead? Should they study individuals, or should they change them? Many humanistic psychologists prefer a more activist position. Maslow's critics maintain that his theory was not necessarily a depiction of a fully functioning person but instead was a reflection of Maslow's own activist value system and beliefs about how people should feel and act. Did Maslow mix ethical considerations with his research logic? Consider, for example, his portrayal of self-actualizing people as open, realistic, spontaneous, possessing democratic leadership traits, resistant to enculturation, and accepting of self, others, and nature. Is this an objective description of human fulfillment? Or is it a prescription of what Maslow wanted people to be?

Maslow (1970) acknowledged that his theorizing and research on self-actualization lacked the rigor of strict, quantitative empirical investigation (Chapter 3). He fervently believed, however, that it was imperative to begin the process of rounding out the field of psychology by attending to "the highest capacities of the healthy and strong man as well as with the defensive maneuvers of crippled spirits" (p. 33). Maslow wanted to inspire others by his research and give them the right knowledge and skills to be liberated and happy. Furthermore, he maintained that science is not value-free because its methods and procedures are developed and used for human purposes.

CHECK AND APPLY YOUR KNOWLEDGE

1. What is self-actualization? Are you a self-actualizer now? If not, do you want to be one? If you do, how soon?

2. What are B-values?

3. Give an example of peak experiences.

4. Explain the autotelic personality.

5. Consider a case: Alex did not like his high school and struggled academically. Maybe he was failing because of his chronic attention problems, or maybe he simply didn't have passion for studying. Few activities interested him, except just two—he loved skateboarding and video games. After finishing high school and changing several jobs, Alex finally found his niche: He now plays video games on an online gaming platform. People from all over the world—for a small subscription fee—log on and watch him play, read his comments, and leave their feedback. Alex has hundreds and sometimes thousands of observers, who are also his paying customers; they are watching Alex's moves, kicks, and other spectacular tricks. Alex is a virtual performer with a salary that is probably less that any minimum-wage job would bring him, so he needs more viewers. This is a challenging task. The viewers can leave as easily as they came to watch. Yet Alex is determined to stay in business, develop his skills, entertain, teach, and inspire others because he loves what he does. Sometimes he works (plays) for 12 hours consecutively or more. He says his performance is not about making money—at least, the material side is not his top priority. By playing video games professionally, he hopes, as he says, to win the battle against his past failures and childhood insecurities. Even though nobody believed he could succeed in anything, he says, he is finally doing something he truly loves and gets attention from others. Some people encourage him to stay in business; one comment said, "I hope this guy makes it." Others suggest getting a "real" tech job, mocking him and his work: "The only thing that is a bigger waste of time than constantly playing video games is watching someone else play" (Kang, 2015).

a) Does Alex, in your view, have features of an autotelic personality?

b) Does Alex's work help him to experience flow?

(Continued)

(Continued)

   c) Do you think he is happy? His work is an emotional roller coaster: He is happy when he has new spectators and miserable when they leave. The work makes him anxious and often sleepless. He lives in a busy world with successes and failures, relationships and strategies. He loves what he does because his activity apparently makes him uniquely human, if you apply Maslow's theory. Yet from your personal standpoint, do you want to experience the same type of happiness that Alex has?

6. Although these days most students suggest that a psychologist should combine the rigor of a researcher and the passion of an activist, they disagree about to what extent. What is your view on this? Choose one statement and explain your choice:

Psychologists should be researchers, not activists.

Psychologists should be researchers first and activists second.

Psychologists should be equally researchers and activists.

Psychologists should be activists first and researchers second.

Psychologists should be activists, not researchers.

Maslow's views were innovative for his time. In contrast to many psychoanalytic theorists preceding him that focused on clinical cases, Maslow created his theory by studying healthy and successful people. His influence in personality psychology was significant. Instead of asking "What does it mean to be mentally ill?" he asked "What does it mean to be mentally healthy?" His approach stimulated the development of numerous studies into personality and the creation of several therapeutic methods. Carl Rogers did both.

Carl Rogers and the Person-Centered Approach

The American psychologist Carl Rogers (1902–1987) was one of the most influential psychologists of the 20th century, and his views remain influential today. He was born near Chicago, obtained his PhD at Columbia University in New York, and worked in several universities, including the University of Chicago and the University of Wisconsin.

Rogers (1947) maintained that all individuals exist in a changing world of their experience. This experience becomes reality for them. The self as a dynamic but stable pattern develops as a result of the individual's interaction with this world of experience. It is true that the organism responds to the outside signals and satisfies its needs, but all this happens within this organism's individual experience. Most of the behaviors we learn are consistent with the subjective concept of self.

Rogers (1947) believed that all living organisms strive to make the very best of their existence—that it is in our nature to do the very best we can. Above other things, people tend to value positive regard, which is love, warmth, attention, and care from others. People also value **positive self-regard**, which refers to high self-esteem and positive emotions toward the self. However, human society sets special conditions for positive regard. We as individuals are raised to understand that only certain behaviors and certain conditions could lead to rewards from others. We need to wash our hands before meals, speak politely to adults, and do our homework. We grow older and, according to Rogers, develop the belief that our personal self-regard also should be conditioned by certain things we do or decisions we make. In other words, we see ourselves in a positive light only when we behave according to certain expectations and accomplishments, not because we realize our potential or simply exist. Because most of us cannot maintain the high standards set for us by our parents, teachers, supervisors, and society in general, we experience incongruity between who we are and who we are supposed to be. This incongruity is the source of our psychological tensions. Here, Rogers echoes assumptions of the German psychologist Karen Horney (Boeree, 2006), whose work we studied in Chapter 5.

> **Positive self-regard**
> A positive self-regard refers to high self-esteem and positive emotions toward the self.

Like Maslow, Rogers saw self-actualization as the highest level of psychological health. Self-actualization, however, does not occur simply because people want it. To achieve self-actualization, they have to make a conscious and sustained effort (Rogers, 1961). Specifically, they must try to be open to new experiences, learn, live each day fully, have trust in their own decisions, enjoy freedom to choose, remain creative without the feeling of conformity, balance their own needs, and participate in the opportunities that life constantly offers. For Rogers, fully functioning people are well adjusted, well balanced, and interested in learning and knowing. Such people tend to be high achievers.

Rogers's critics, however, claim that the profile of fully functioning people is more likely to fit into individualist cultures, which are predominantly Western (see Chapter 2). In other, more collectivist and traditional cultures, individual achievement is valued, yet not as much as the achievement of the group. Furthermore, in traditional cultures, conformity to group norms is valued more than making individual decisions or being open to new experiences. In the age of globalization, as we learned in Chapter 2, we need to reevaluate both Rogers's views and their critical assessments.

As a therapist, Rogers proposed a person-centered (often called client-centered) approach to an individual, and it has become famous and has found many applications in therapeutic practice worldwide. We will discuss this approach a bit later in this chapter.

Positive Psychology

Humanistic psychologists contributed to **positive psychology**, which studies the strengths and virtues that enable individuals and communities to thrive (Compton, 2004). As you remember, Maslow and Rogers encouraged psychologists to study and teach about success and accomplishment, nurture talent, support great initiatives, and

> **Positive psychology**
> Positive psychology studies the strengths and virtues that enable individuals and communities to thrive.

set examples of happiness, thus many psychologists turned to studies of happiness, meaningful life, and achievement. Psychology professionals used methods of positive psychology in the classroom and workplace. The main focus of their work was not problems or weaknesses but mostly growth and improvement. Practical applications of positive psychology included helping individuals find their strength and assisting organizations to identify their potential.

An important contribution of humanistic psychology was the concept of positive mental health. Instead of studying, almost exclusively, psychopathological symptoms and traumatic conditions causing such symptoms, humanistic psychologists turned to the healthy side of an individual, the optimal state of functioning and experience. The concept of self-actualization has become a widely accepted idea in contemporary psychology.

Studying Happiness

Happiness has already become an important measure of social and economic development of a country—the higher the indexes of happiness are, the higher the position of that country on a global scale. Happiness statistics are becoming an important social and economic yardstick. The humanistic tradition, like no other tradition in personality psychology, pays attention to happiness and the ways to reach it. Within this tradition, psychologists are not necessarily interested in an emotion of joy or related emotional states. The focus is on the happy person. How does one become a happy person? How can one be a happy person? By asking these key questions, psychologists will be able to share their knowledge with others and help them to reach their happiness as well.

Critical Assessments of Happiness Approaches

Before offering their own visions of happiness, psychologists working within the humanistic tradition critically examined other views of happiness common in the humanities. These views were also rooted in popular beliefs for centuries.

According to the materialist view, an individual can become happy through the accumulation of material wealth, such as money and products. Happiness is also about possessing power and social status. Things that make an individual's life more comfortable—a cozy home, an impressive savings account, a new car, or a latest version of a smartphone—are important "triggers" of happiness. The higher the social status of an individual, the more power she or he has, and somehow, that status and power translate into happiness. Most of us are aware that although material possessions can make a person happy, this emotional state does not last long. Studies show that happiness and wealth (economic success) are not always strongly correlated (Harari, 2014). In the United Kingdom, for instance, different indicators of happiness haven't changed much for the past 4 decades, even during good and bad economic periods; overall, people in Britain score higher on happiness than people in most countries (Suh et al., 2008).

A slightly different view—the progressive view—adds an important element to the recipe for happiness: social care. Supporters of this view argue that if every individual is guaranteed and given basic social services—including health care, affordable housing, a decent salary, paid vacations, and free tuition (to name a few)—then there will practically be no external factors that contribute to this individual's unnecessary suffering. If the basic needs are secure, the individual ought to be happy. Indeed, people in Denmark or Finland, the Scandinavian countries with the most developed social welfare systems, receive very high scores on the measures of happiness. However, surveys also show that the amount of social welfare does not necessarily affect people's happiness. Iceland, based on studies conducted about a decade ago, spent significantly less on social welfare than Sweden, but people were happier there (Suh et al., 2008). In the past, many psychologists, including Freud and others, were already skeptical about the idea that social reforms alone would make people happy (Menand, 2014).

The situational view maintains that happiness is not necessarily about vast material possessions or generous social services. The entire life situation in which individuals find themselves should determine how happy they are (Lyubomirsky, 2007). The presence or absence of major tragedies in their lives, the quality of the their relationships, especially within the family, the existence of opportunities—all should contribute to happiness. Yet other psychologists argue that even if the conditions are favorable, people still have a tendency to compare themselves to others.

The comparison view suggests that happiness is a state of mind based on appraisals and evaluations of self and others. If we are doing better than others, we tend to feel better about life. Yet what if others do better than we do? Comparisons, unfortunately, often lead to envy: "I wish you did not have it," we may say about others who have more than us (Fiske, 2010). Envy leads to scorn and contributes to unhappiness. Studies also show that in individualistic cultures, people rely on their emotions when they assess their own happiness. In predominantly collectivist cultures, people tend to seek social cues or other people's responses to make a judgment (Suh et al., 2008). In other words, other people may play a role in how we evaluate our happiness.

The expectation view refers to the goals an individual had in the past and the degree to which the individual accomplished those goals. Happiness depends less on material conditions or other people, but rather on what we expect from our lives. If our experiences today match or exceed our expectations yesterday, then we feel happy. However, our expectations do change. When life is getting better, expectations tend to increase, thus increasing our dissatisfaction if our goals aren't met—the better outcomes we expect, the less happy we become if we don't achieve them.

The biological view suggests that people can be happier and less happy primarily because of their genetic and biological makeup. The brain and the body are basically responsible for pleasant sensations, and some people are predisposed to have more of such sensations than others. Evolutionary psychology maintains that happiness is a temporary state that organisms try to achieve. Yet it is quite normal that individuals remain mostly dissatisfied; they always try to survive and always strive to achieve more (Harari, 2014). In sum, with the biological view, unhappiness is biologically predetermined, so some individuals could be happier than others due to their genetic makeup.

The spiritual view stresses the importance of inner factors and emphasizes the search for the higher power within the individual. Philosophers, religious scholars, pundits, and social scientists in many cultures and regions have discussed the ideas about the passing nature of our sensations and emotions. Buddhist and Hindu teachers, philosophers of ancient Greece and Rome, and Central Asian and Chinese philosophers, for example, consistently referred to the possibility for the individual to become and stay happy after turning to inner strengths. Pleasant sensations from the body come and go, a source of happiness tomorrow may disappear today, and people we love may depart, so the path to happiness is in limiting the influence of the world of sensations and cultivating wisdom as well as an introspective mind (Harari, 2014). See these views summarized in **Table 9.1**.

The Humanistic View

Psychologists working within the humanistic perspective embrace other views on happiness but also suggest their own version of how an individual can become and

TABLE 9.1 ● Views of Happiness

View	Brief Description	Practical Steps
Materialist	The individual's happiness is about material possessions, including money and social status, that lead to more possessions and power.	Pursue material values, money, and high social status.
Progressive	Happiness is not about wealth or status. It is about social welfare or guaranteed opportunities and basic necessities, such as health care, jobs, and education.	Make sure that there is a guaranteed level of social support and social services.
Situational	Individuals become happy or unhappy mainly because of favorable and unfavorable circumstances in their lives. Most of these conditions, yet not all, tend to be outside the individual's control.	Life outcomes are basically out of our control, yet we have some power to avoid unfavorable ones.
Comparison	Happiness is based on perceptions. It is relative to the results of comparisons made by the individual between self and other people.	Make sure the comparisons are favorable or avoid comparisons with other people.
Expectation	The individual feels happy or unhappy based on what she or he expected from self.	Make sure your expectations have been met or ignore such expectations.
Biological	Some people are biologically programmed to be either happy or unhappy.	If you believe that you have been "born" unhappy, adjust and work on yourself.
Spiritual	Passing emotions are too shallow to bring happiness. Happiness should be found within yourself.	Happiness is the state of your soul, which should be cultivated through detachment and meditation.
Humanistic	Happiness is a result of many factors. It requires self-growth, hard work on self-improvement, and social engagement.	Think critically, engage socially, practice peace, and provide a positive feedback.

remain happy. There are differences among them, but the most significant similarities can be summarized as follows.

It is quite possible that some individuals are born with a propensity to experience certain emotional states. There are individuals who tend to be happy or sad due to their hormones or the functioning of their brain and the nervous system. It is also possible that material possessions, social protection, and comparisons to other people can bring joy to some individuals. Yet joy is a passing emotion and is not necessarily the *state* of happiness. Happiness is a state of mind, and individuals can be in control of it. So the first point of the humanistic argument is that happiness is achievable and can be learned.

The second point refers to social and interpersonal engagement. Contrary to some religious teachings that encourage self-reflection coupled with detachment and self-isolation, the humanistic perspective encourages interpersonal action, critical thinking, and engagement in social affairs. The humanist view is rooted in the modern philosophical view that scientific knowledge, reasoning, rationality, empiricism, and skepticism have profoundly changed the way individuals perceive morality, justice, and happiness (Lyubomirsky, 2007; Shermer, 2015). Findings indicate, for example, that autotelic individuals are not necessarily happier but more often involved in complex activities, which, in turn, make them feel better about themselves and increase their self-esteem (Csikszentmihalyi, 1997).

The third point is about positive feedback. We need to receive persistent positive feedback about ourselves. Encouragement and praise from others are valuable to us. People often turn to horoscopes for the same reason—to receive validation. As in a fortunate tarot reading, the happier the assessment, the more likely we are to believe it and the more likely we will feel better about ourselves (Konnikova, 2014). Positive assessments encourage optimism in us; optimism stimulates short-term joy; and joy adds to long-term happiness.

Self-growth, described earlier, is one of several applications of the humanistic perspective's approach to personality. Self-growth is difficult to achieve without the practical steps of learning, dedication, and perseverance to the goals one has set. Bottom line: The individual can achieve happiness through self-growth.

CHECK AND APPLY YOUR KNOWLEDGE

1. Explain positive regard.

2. What are the similarities and differences between Rogers's and Maslow's views on self-actualization?

3. Explain positive psychology.

4. Choose and explain at least two of the approaches to happiness presented earlier.

(Continued)

(Continued)

5. The English philosopher and writer Aldous Huxley (1894–1963) in *Brave New World* (1932) imagined a global society of the future in which people live in harmony and are conditioned to work hard and respect their government. They also take a hallucinogenic substance called *soma*. This hangover-free drug makes everyone who takes it happy. Stress and anxiety go away. So do envy and jealousy—after taking soma, people feel content and grateful for what they do and have. They do not experience existential crises. Soma helps everyone experience a high self-esteem. Soma also substitutes for religious feelings and interpersonal attachments; they are no longer needed because the only attachment that people have is to their work and their government. *Brave New World* is a satirical, fictional book full of sarcasm and exaggerations; however, one of Huxley's points is clear: People can be manipulated. Either powerful authorities or scientists can create a reality for them and make them happy while they remain slaves.

(a) Do humanistic psychologists propose another *Brave New World*?

(b) Instead of prescribing a drug like soma, psychologists suggest humanistic methods of self-growth. Do you agree or disagree that they simply teach individuals to change their views of life and ignore the problems that surround them? Explain why or why not.

6. Is bitter truth better and healthier than sweet lies? Explain your choice.

7. Studies show that people who are pessimistic tend to see reality more accurately than optimistic individuals, who tend to see things in rosy colors; however, similar studies show that optimists are happier than pessimists (Konnikova, 2014). What is your position in a difficult alternative: (A) to see the world as it is, with all its pains and tragedies, and be a bit unhappy or (B) to see it from a more optimistic view and remain a bit happy? Explain your choice.

Accomplishments and Limitations of the Humanistic Tradition

Humanistic principles attracted the attention of professionals studying personality and encouraged many dedicated followers around the world. The overall success of this tradition was due to many innovative ideas and practical applications.

Accomplishments

Humanistic psychologists refocused attention back to the individual by redirecting attention to the human factor and the issues that are ultimately unique to an individual's experience. This was quite a reasonable and timely argument. Although most professional psychologists in the end of the 20th century did not switch their research interests dramatically in favor of humanistic principles, many of them turned their attention to the problems that were central for humanistic psychology. In fact, personality psychology today is difficult to imagine without the humanistic principles on which it is based.

The ideas and values of the humanistic tradition became very popular first in Western countries and later around the world. Humanistic psychologists offered an optimistic vision of human beings, their nature, and their experiences. The emphasis on a free, rational, and ever-growing individual was innovative and promising, compared with the widely accepted psychoanalytic assumption about the predetermined trouble hidden in the dungeon of an individual's unconscious mind. The behaviorist assumptions about the value of rewards and conditioning were challenged, too, as the humanistic tradition offered a new set of humanistic values for understanding, teaching, and healing of the individual.

The humanistic tradition offered a hopeful, constructive view of individuals and of their substantial capacity to be self-determining. Ethical values are strong determinants of human behavior. This belief leads to an effort to emphasize human qualities such as choice, imagination, self-improvement, the interaction of the body and mind, and the capacity to become free and happy.

Some existential philosophers claimed that human beings would inevitably become lazy, complacent, and satisfied because of the power of their material possessions (Žižek, 2015). As a challenge to these and other pessimistic assumptions, the humanistic tradition in psychology claimed that the individual path to happiness and care for others should always activate in human beings new individual traits full of passionate intensity.

Shortcomings

One of the obvious shortcomings of humanistic psychology was its relatively poor record of experimental research. You remember that the founders of this tradition were disappointed with the status of what appeared to be mainstream psychology. Psychology as a discipline, they believed, was losing the "tree" of the person in the "forest" of experimental procedures. Unfortunately, humanistic psychology had somewhat distanced itself from empirical studies and statistical interpretations of experimental data. As a result, most empirical facts obtained in this field are based on individual observations, stories, and interviews—all very important, yet imprecise and probably biased. Like the introspection method popular in the 19th century (Remember Wundt?), most research methods of humanistic psychology were very subjective.

Criticisms also came from specialists in theoretical science. They maintained that humanistic psychology and related research orientations in the social sciences were not necessarily scientific. The central argument was that a theory's hypothesis (Chapter 2) should be falsifiable (Popper, 1992). What does that mean? Consider, for example, the following statement: Every person has the right to be happy. It is an unfalsifiable statement because it would be almost impossible to demonstrate its falsehood and prove, for example, that "this person or that individual does not have the right to be happy." A falsifiable statement would be that "this therapeutic method

Photo 9.3 According to client-centered therapy, psychologists show their clients unconditional positive regard. Can you suggest situations when psychologists should criticize and even confront their clients?

© iStockphoto.com/Silvia Jansen

provides successful outcomes 70% of the time" because it is possible to verify empirically. If major statements and findings of humanistic psychology are not falsifiable, the discipline is likely to be just a set of inspirational ideas that exist at the mercy of their creators and supporters. Furthermore, the validity of their assumptions is probably a matter of individual position or social perspective.

Humanistic principles attempted to bring psychologists' attention back to the individual's subjectivity. Cognitive psychology, which we studied in Chapter 8, pursued a relatively similar goal. But despite this common strategic interest, cognitive and humanistic psychologists were very different in how they approached subjectivity. In short, they asked different questions, and this was the crucial difference between the two groups. Psychologist supporters of the humanistic tradition were mostly interested in *why* people do what they do. The cognitive tradition in psychology was studying *how* the individual processes information. Not surprisingly, the first group (humanistic psychologists) turned to moral values and ethical prescriptions. The other group (cognitive psychologists) paid most attention to formal operations, or physiological and mathematical models describing cognitive processes.

Applying the Humanistic Tradition

Humanistic ideas find many applications in clinical practice, education, and other applied fields. One important application is in psychotherapy.

Psychotherapy

Existential Therapy

Most theoretical assumptions of existential psychology find their applications in **existential therapy**. This is the therapeutic and healing method based on the assumption that we, as human beings, make our own choices and should assume full responsibility for the outcomes of our behavior, experiences, and feelings. It is hard to argue that we often feel unhappy because life too often treats us in a very unkind way. Still, every individual possesses the freedom to create his or her own goals. This freedom could generate in every one of us the sense of purpose and meaning. As soon as we have our goals and achieve this sense or purpose, we need to start working on reaching our goals. The responsibility of the psychotherapist is to understand the four basic dimensions of human existence (the physical, the social, the psychological, and the spiritual) and help people set, reset, and eventually achieve their ultimate individual goal, which is happiness (Rogers, 1951).

Any skeptic would quickly comment that this is all easier said than done: Who does not want to be happy? It is a valid critical question. However, existential therapists insist that happiness is not reached overnight or simply because we want to be happy. A fundamental change in our attitudes toward life is needed. We need to stop thinking of what we expect from our lives and think of what our lives expect from us. Life challenges us every moment, and we must respond to these challenges by taking charge of our thoughts and actions and engage in right conduct. Life ultimately means taking responsibility, which is an important condition on the path to happiness (Frankl, 1959).

Client-Centered Therapy

Carl Rogers's theoretical ideas were applied to what he called **client-centered therapy**, which brought him global recognition. According to Rogers, therapists show their clients genuineness, empathy, and unconditional positive regard and create a supportive, nonjudgmental environment in which clients are encouraged to think about their own problems, discuss them, prepare a course of action, and then reach their full potential (Rogers, 1959). A healthy, friendly relationship between the client and the therapist must be achieved, based on openness, trust, and mutual respect. The therapist accepts the client without disapproval or approval; this attitude should facilitate increased self-respect in the clients, which they often lack when they enter therapy. This method has gone through a couple of name changes along the way. Rogers originally called it nondirective therapy because he felt the therapist should not lead the client, but rather be there for the client while the client directs the progress of the therapy. As he became more experienced, he realized that even being "nondirective," he still influenced his client by his very "nondirectiveness." In other words, clients look to therapists for guidance and will find it even when the therapist is trying not to guide (Rogers, 1961).

Existential therapy
A therapeutic and healing method based on the assumption that we make our own choices and should assume full responsibility for their outcomes.

Client-centered therapy
In Rogers's system, client-centered therapy is a therapeutic method in which therapists show their clients genuineness, empathy, and unconditional positive regard and create a supportive, nonjudgmental environment that encourages clients to think about their own problems, discuss them, prepare a course of action, and reach their full potential.

Care With Dignity

Life and Death Decisions

Humanistic ideas have significantly affected contemporary discussions related to end-of-life issues. Does an individual have the right to die if he or she suffers due to incurable illness? Many philosophers and writers of the past, such as Locke in England and Dostoyevsky in Russia, discussed this question and used religion, science, critical thinking, and common sense to offer different opinions. For centuries, countries' laws and religious traditions rendered negative views on the right to die or strictly prohibited an individual's choices in the matters of death. Governments easily put their citizens to death by means of the death penalty yet denied the right to die to citizens. The discussion reemerged in the past decades in the contexts of individual rights and humanistic principles.

In the 20th century, the term *assisted suicide* appeared to identify cases when the suffering person's life is ended with the help of another individual, usually a doctor. Opponents of assisted suicide offer strong legal, religious, moral, and psychological arguments. They suggest, among other things, that further legalization of assisted suicide (some countries as well as some states in the United States have legalized this procedure) would place the most vulnerable and afflicted in an even more susceptible position because someone else makes the decisions for them (Yuill, 2013). Proponents prefer to call the procedure assisted dying (instead of assisted suicide). They also argue that the goal of any treatment is to reduce the individual's suffering and that individuals have the fundamental right to make decisions about their lives (Docker, 2013; Lepore, 2009).

Humanistic principles do not encourage or discourage certain legal or political decisions on the matters of assisted dying. However, these principles simply direct our undivided attention to the individual and his and her right to dignity and a pain-free existence. It is absolutely important that making any end-of-life decisions requires openness, honesty, and complete disclosure of medical information to the patient and the family members. All options should be discussed, and multiple opinions should be sought. The individuals making such decisions must be knowledgeable and free to make the right choice. Still, disagreements persist, and assisted dying remains one of the most controversial issues in medical care today. However, there are other applied areas in which significant progress has been made.

Hospice Care

Hospice care
Hospice care refers to the complex medical and psychological system of help focusing on palliative and other humane principles of medical care.

Humanistic principles in psychology contributed to a global discussion about individual rights, such as the right to live with dignity and the right to be treated humanely. Humanistic psychologists championed the idea that all human beings have the right to be treated with dignity regardless of age, gender, or a social group to which we belong. Moreover, not only do people have the right to live with dignity, but they also have the right to die with dignity (Lepore, 2009). Humanistic principles of the necessity of care and dignity in an individual's existence were crucial in the development of **hospice care**, a complex medical and psychological system of help focusing on palliative and other humane principles of medical care. The major goal of **palliative care** is to prevent and relieve the suffering and distress of individuals affected by a serious illness and to improve their well-being when it is possible (Callanan & Kelley, 1997). Today, hospice care in the United States and many other countries has become a very important part of the health care system.

Holistic Health Movement

Humanistic principles have contributed to the **holistic health movement**, a multidisciplinary applied field focusing on the fundamental assumption that physical, mental, and spiritual factors contributing to an individual's illness are interconnected and equally important in treatment. In fact, the holistic approach in medicine elevates the importance of psychological factors in medical treatment and the prevention of illness (Remen, 1996). Under the influence of humanistic and holistic ideas, during the past 50 or so years, many new centers of holistic treatment appeared, first in North America and Europe, and then across the world. Many trained professionals with medical and psychology degrees began to study spirituality, classic literature, folklore, and traditional methods of healing (in Africa, Asia, and Latin America) to identify and use the effective methods of treatment involving both body and mind. Supporters of holistic treatment used humanistic principles and no longer saw their clients and patients as "sets of symptoms" but rather emphasized the uniqueness of every individual's history of illness and every therapeutic method used in each case.

Basic humanistic principles found another application in **narrative medicine**, a clinical field that helps medical professionals recognize, absorb, interpret, and be moved by the stories of illness (Charon, 1992). Several medical schools and residency programs train physicians and nurses to treat patients and their medical issues not as problems to be solved but to take into account the specific psychological and personal histories of the patients. Narrative medicine helps doctors, nurses, social workers, and therapists improve the effectiveness of care by developing the capacity for attention, reflection, representation, and affiliation with patients and colleagues (Charon, 1993).

Some fields of research turned to empirical studies of specific mechanisms of socialization and development. For example, **narrative psychology** focuses on how published stories and essays shape lives (Murray, 1985). The psychologist James Liu, who was born in Taiwan and now works in New Zealand, showed in his cross-national studies that despite popular assumptions about the existence of profound differences in the way people of different cultures perceive history and major world events, the similarities among individuals are overwhelming (Liu et al., 2005).

Peace Psychology and Public Diplomacy

Principles of humanistic psychology influenced **peace psychology**, a theoretical and applied branch that studies ideological and psychological causes of war and develops educational programs to reduce the threat of violence in international relations and domestic policies of some countries (Greening, 1986). Psychologists working in this field conducted research on a wide range of social issues and topics, including

Palliative care
Palliative care is used to prevent and relieve the suffering and distress of individuals affected by serious illness and to improve their well-being when it is possible.

Holistic health movement
A multidisciplinary applied field, the holistic health movement is focused on the fundamental assumption that physical, mental, and spiritual factors contributing to an individual's illness are interconnected and equally important in treatment.

Narrative medicine
A clinical field that helps medical professionals recognize, absorb, interpret, and be moved by the stories of illness is narrative medicine.

Narrative psychology
Narrative psychology focuses on how published stories and essays shape lives.

Peace psychology
Peace psychology is a theoretical and applied branch of psychology that studies ideological and psychological causes of war and develops educational programs to reduce the threat of violence in international relations and domestic policies of some countries.

forgiveness, social awareness, altruism, and conflict resolution. Specifically, peace psychology teaches that most causes of war and violence are preventable. It takes both political leaders and ordinary people to give up their old images of the enemy and try to find possibilities for dialogue with their adversaries.

Humanistic principles found applications not only in health care but also in other areas. One of them was a global field of **public diplomacy**, which is the organized interaction among citizens of different countries to establish a dialogue intended to find solutions to international disputes or other issues. Public diplomacy is about helping politicians, experts, students, and ordinary people to communicate, understand, and ultimately, reduce international tensions.

Public diplomacy
Public diplomacy refers to the organized interaction among citizens of different countries to establish a dialogue intended to find solutions to international disputes or other issues.

Several pioneers of peace psychology, including Thomas Greening, made an important contribution to the U.S.-Soviet relations during the Cold War, especially in the 1980s (Greening, 1986). Psychologists organized face-to-face meetings between officials, students, teachers, and other professionals in the United States and the Soviet Union to "deconstruct" the old enemy image and promote the new atmosphere of trust. Carl Rogers was also actively engaged in public diplomacy. He conducted multiple seminars and face-to-face meetings between representatives of conflicting groups, including Northern Ireland and South Africa. He traveled to Brazil, Russia, and other countries to conduct seminars of creativity, goodwill, and mutual understanding (Cohen, 2000).

You may ask, "How is it possible to affect international relations by conducting interpersonal group seminars?" Peace psychologists believe that psychological changes should influence policy and global outcomes. Although the direct impact of such interpersonal interactions is difficult to measure, public diplomacy receives high marks from many professionals who acknowledge that a gradual reduction of international tensions is possible to achieve by turning to, among other issues, individual contacts between opinion leaders, including scientists, journalists, and business leaders (Hart, 2013).

Skeptics disagree. They have long maintained that social and political changes cause psychological transformations, not the other way around. To achieve peace, for example, one side has to impose it first, and then people change their attitudes and behavior to adjust to the reality of peace (Kaplan, 2012).

Which side would you support in this argument? If psychologists had enough resources, would they have enough intellectual power to resolve social conflicts?

CHECK AND APPLY YOUR KNOWLEDGE

1. Explain client-centered therapy.
2. Explain narrative medicine and narrative psychology.
3. What is peace psychology?

Visual Review

INTRODUCTION AND CONTEXTS	→	KEY THEORIES AND APPROACHES	→	APPLICATIONS

Humanistic psychologists focus on the individual's care and self-growth	Existential psychology celebrates the uniqueness of human existence, self-growth, and happiness	Psychotherapy
Human beings should be viewed from holistic and optimistic perspectives	Maslow's system • offered a hierarchy of human needs • focused on self-actualization and the autotelic personality	Hospice care
Rational and knowledgeable individuals can exercise choice and take responsibility for their own actions	Rogers's person-centered theoretical ideas were applied in his famous client-centered therapy	Holistic health movement
		Peace psychology

Summary

- In the second half of the 20th century, researchers shared a popular opinion that psychology as a discipline should bring wisdom and compassion in addressing lingering societal problems, especially in the fields of education, mental health, and individual development. Applied to psychology, the humanistic tradition calls for renewed efforts to study the phenomena that distinguish human beings—love, happiness, and self-growth.

- The humanistic tradition is rooted in critical examinations of other traditions. Humanistic psychologists challenged behaviorism and psychoanalysis by emphasizing the importance of individual responsibility, free choice, and intellectual freedom as fundamental human forces guiding a person through life.

- Humanistic psychologists focus on the actual experience of an individual. They generally prefer qualitative research methods to quantitative procedures and stress the importance of in-depth examinations of an individual's concerns, memories, plans, feelings, and actions taken together, in unity.

- Humanistic psychologists based their views, in part, on existentialism in philosophy and on existential psychology. One of the leading representatives of existential psychology was the American psychologist Rollo May, who, like many existential psychologists, believed in self-awareness and self-growth as two important goals that the individual should pursue.

- One of the most notable contributions of Abraham Maslow to personality psychology was his hierarchical theory of motivation and human needs.

- According to Maslow, the highest level of the hierarchy of needs is self-actualization; he concluded that self-actualizing persons exhibit a number of similar behavioral and psychological characteristics.

- One of the distinct features of a self-actualizing individual is peak experiences, which are periodic and profound episodes of happiness, optimism, inner harmony, and creativity. Years after Maslow described peak experiences, his ideas found support in the studies of so-called flow—a state of complete concentration and joyful immersion in the situation or activity. Flow is a feature associated with the autotelic personality.

- Carl Rogers saw self-actualization as the highest level of psychological health. Self-actualization, however, does not occur simply because an individual wants it. To achieve self-actualization, he or she has to make a conscious and sustained effort.

- Humanistic psychology influenced positive psychology, the discipline studying the strengths and virtues that enable the individual and communities to thrive. Positive psychology as well as the humanistic tradition in general pay significant attention to happiness and the ways to reach it.

- Most theoretical assumptions of existential psychology find their applications in existential therapy. Carl Rogers's person-centered theoretical ideas found applications in his famous client-centered therapy.

- Humanistic ideas find significant applications in health care in general, hospice care, the holistic health movement, people's diplomacy, and many other fields.

Key Terms

autotelic personality 277

B-values 276

client-centered therapy 289

D-needs 275

existential crisis 270

existentialism 270

existential psychology 271

existential therapy 289

flow 277

holistic health movement 291

hospice care 290

humanistic psychologists 266

humanistic psychology 267

narrative medicine 291

narrative psychology 291

palliative care 291

peace psychology 291

peak experiences 277

positive psychology 281

positive self-regard 281

public diplomacy 292

self-actualization 276

Evaluating What You Know

Describe the key ideas of the humanistic tradition.

Explain the "five points" related to humanistic psychology.

Explain existentialism and existential psychology.

Explain Rollo May's views on tradition, change, and anxiety.

What is Maslow's hierarchy of needs and self-actualization?

What are peak experiences? Who usually has them?

What is the essence of the person-centered approach?

What are the key views of happiness?

Explain existential therapy.

What is nondirective therapy?

Explain the holistic health movement.

What is narrative psychology?

A Bridge to the Next Chapter

In the previous chapters, we have examined five different traditions of research into personality. Among them were the behavioral-learning, the psychoanalytic, the trait, the cognitive, and the humanistic traditions. It is time now to look into how these major traditions, as well other approaches, explain the individual personality within several major contexts. We will call such contexts domains. They are circumstances or conditions without which major personality traditions cannot be fully understood and assessed. These domains or fields include gender, psychological abnormality, and adjustment. But first, we will turn to the developing person.

WANT A BETTER GRADE?

Get the tools you need to sharpen your study skills. Access practice quizzes, eFlashcards, web exercises, and multimedia at edge.sagepub.com/shiraevpersonality

⑤SAGE edge™

Steve Glass/Getty Images

10

The Developmental Domain

Professor to students: Try, discover, conquer! Before it's too late . . .
Remember a great line from Billy Joel, "Vienna waits for you"?

Student A: Who is Billy Joel?

Student B: Who is Vienna?

> ## Learning Objectives
>
> After reading this chapter, you should be able to:
>
> - Discuss the major milestones in human development and socialization and the influences of nature and nurture
>
> - Explain how biological foundations, cultural influences, and social and political factors affect personality
>
> - Identify ways to apply knowledge about personality psychology in the developmental domain

How different are we from our parents' generation? Do we really share comparable traits with most our peers of the same age, or do these similarities only appear to be true?

A few decades ago, journalists and then social scientists began assigning similar personality traits to entire American generations—the large groups of individuals born and living at about the same time. The baby boomers came first. They were the people born after World War II, approximately between the late 1940s and the early 1960s. Their personalities were described as mostly open-minded, optimistic, family-oriented, resilient, and hardworking.

Then came the hippies. They appeared very much different from the generation before them. They had long hair, wore tie-dyed T-shirts, and spoke a different English (imagine how terrified their parents were). They challenged the old traditions and preferred "peace, love, and rock 'n' roll" to hard work and sacrifice.

The 1980s was the decade of the yuppies. These young professionals challenged the counterculture of the hippie generation. Yuppies were mostly about education and business; they appeared hardworking, rational, and industrious.

After that was generation X with a "softer" view of life. They were active, balanced, happy, tolerant, and family-oriented.

Next came the millennials, whose birth years ranged from the early 1980s to the early 2000s. They seemed community-oriented and supersensitive to injustice. They tended to be more upbeat and happy than their parents. They were mostly detached from official institutions, as well as family-oriented and networked among their friends.

And then came the *app generation*. Most adults older than 30 these days are "app-enabled," and people between 18 and 25 today are mostly "app-dependent." Psychologists say that individuals within the app generation tend to be balancing between two extremes: They vary between a weak and strong sense of identity; they tend to maintain superficial relations with others *and* develop very deep relationships; and they either have little creative imagination or extremely high levels of creativity.

Questions

To which generation do you think you belong?

Do you mostly agree or disagree with those labels assigned to your generation and why?

How would you describe yourself in comparison to your peers? How different are you from them and how similar?

Does our age have anything to do with our personality features?

Sources: Dawson, 2011; Gardner and Davis, 2013.

Human development
The changes in physical, psychological, and social behavior that individuals experience across the life-span, from conception to their last days, are called human development.

Socialization
Socialization is the process by which an individual becomes a member of a society and takes on its ideas and behaviors.

The Essence of the Developmental Domain

This chapter describes personality in the context of development, or a specified state of growth or advancement. Together, we will focus on **human development**—the changes in physical, psychological, and social behavior that individuals experience across the life-span, from conception to their last days. Studying these changes, we will also recognize **socialization**—the process by which an individual becomes a member of a society and takes on its ideas and behaviors.

People accumulate new knowledge and thus develop their beliefs, habits, and individual traits. We dress in particular clothes, avoid specific foods, keep away from certain situations, pursue distinct goals, and avoid discussing some topics because of the way the socialization process works: We tend to behave in the ways that others consider appropriate and normal (Henrich et al., 2010a).

Similar arguments can be applied to the study of the developing personality. Socialization can be a "top-down" process. Social factors shape the behavior of individuals and affect their personality traits. It can also be "bottom-up" process. People change the social world around them according their own perception, ideas, and individual predispositions. As processes, human development and socialization overlap, and neither stops at a particular age. Regardless of how mature you are, you continue to develop and your socialization continues as well. Human development not only involves growth but also decline. Socialization is constant modification and change.

Nature and Nurture Interact

Psychologists have long maintained that the individual's development and socialization depend on the interplay of influences involving nature and nurture. Specifically, a child's development (and the development of his or her personality) is rooted in the child's natural features and direct interaction with other individuals, as well as general societal factors (Whiting & Whiting, 1975). But how does the developing individual learn and acquire individual traits? Two interconnected concepts have emerged.

The first one, which we call "the natural," assumes that children should have certain natural predispositions to think, experience emotions, and act in a particular way. What happens to their personalities in the future is very much dependent on their natural abilities and skills. Social conditions can only modify whatever nature "prescribes" to individuals. Neuroscientists have been able to show that there is an innate predisposition for certain types of learning. Many social scientists and psychologists tend to maintain this point of view.

The other concept, which we will call "the social," assumes that most human beings are born without significant natural "foundations" to have any particular personality traits as adults. This tradition has its roots in the teachings of the English philosopher John Locke (1632–1704), who believed that the child's mind is a "clean board," from the Latin tabula rasa. Experiences can be recorded in the mind in a fashion similar to the way in which teachers use a piece of chalk to write on the board. Although humans may have different natural predispositions, their main features as adults are based on the opportunities they encounter in life. Throughout history, especially in the past several decades, psychologists have maintained that a deliberate, comprehensive, and psychologically sound "intervention" of qualified educators in the child's life could bring significant and positive results. They thought any girl or boy should be capable of developing any features if only this child had opportunities and stimulating conditions (Cravens, 2002). We acquire certain rules of behavior and feeling the same way we obtain food preferences. If what we are given tastes good, we stick with it. If it doesn't, we reject it (Haidt, 2013). Try to recall a few episodes from early in your life in which you think you learned about the importance of being honest, and if you're willing, share these examples with the class.

Quality of Life Is Essential

Development and socialization must be understood in the context of the **quality of life**. This is the general well-being of individuals measured by the availability of resources, physical and financial security, type of living conditions, quality of education and health care, presence or absence of violence, and a number of other factors—all of which significantly affect the individual's development and socialization. Countries vary in overall density of population and number of immediate family members. The child's development and socialization depend on the people with whom the child interacts, the places where they spend time together, and the roles children play (Whiting & Whiting, 1975). Access to resources and educational opportunities

Quality of life   An individual's quality of life refers to her or his general well-being measured by the availability of resources, physical and financial security, type of living conditions, quality of education and health care, presence or absence of violence, and a number of other factors—all of which significantly affect the individual's development and socialization.

Photo 10.1
Contemporary
families have
become significantly
smaller across
the world. Why do
women have fewer
children than 20
years ago? In your
opinion, what does
a smaller family
mean for a child's
development?

© iStockphoto.com/franckreporter

are likely to provide an advantageous environment for the developing child. Poverty
also directly affects relationships within the family. In relatively poor regions, because
of limited access to resources, close cooperation within families becomes a necessity.
In wealthy regions, people tend to be less interdependent (Shiraev & Levy, 2013).

Globalization Affects the Individual

One significant development that affects quality of life is a rapid global decline
in fertility rates during the past 20 years. This trend continues today. General demographic trends in Europe, North and South America, and Asia show fertility rates
of slightly above two children per woman across practically every country except
Africa (Winter & Teitelbaum, 2013). Increasing living standards and educational levels, changing societal norms (especially those concerning women's rights and duties),
plus several other global factors are likely to contribute to the decreasing fertility rates
around the world. What do these changes mean in terms of our study of personality?

Smaller families are likely to mean more material resources available to children
of the new generation. The focus of the family is shifting toward the child; however,
small families could mean the end of the traditional family, in which members of several generations lived under the same roof. Smaller families also mean differences in
socialization patterns in the family. This phenomenon certainly needs more research.

Social scientists have long predicted that globalization would likely threaten many
individuals' identities. In what way? Globalization often promotes somewhat universal
standards for all people and even emphasizes similarities among humans. Thus, many
people living during this period of globalization may feel they are losing their sense of
cultural identity. Will this result in more people turning to the comfort of tradition and

religion? This trend was predicted some time ago—that more individuals would become more conservative in their values, judgments, and decisions (Huntington, 1993).

Other scientists disagree with such assumptions and discuss the weakening of the influence of local cultures on the individual and the development of a new global culture. The ongoing social, economic, technological, and political realities transform traditional cultures (Draguns, 2009; Faiola, 2003). This new global culture with its emphasis on consumption and the Internet is likely to create similar lifestyles and produce somewhat "uniform" personality traits (Ho-Ying Fu & Chiu, 2007). Individual identities thus should become increasingly dynamic, absorbing the commingling backgrounds, interests, ideas, and choices in one individual self.

Global migration also creates a distinctive global culture that is different from anything that existed before (Raghavan, Harkness, & Super, 2010). For example, many immigrants in the United States that came from Latin America are likely to be different from their ancestors in home countries, as well as from the American residents. Specifically, the immigrants are fluent in two languages, support individualistic values in some situations (such as business) and collectivistic values in other contexts (such as community), and identify simultaneously with the United States and with their countries of origin (Chen, Benet-Martinez, & Bond, 2008).

Developmental Stages

Across cultures, personality's development is commonly understood in the context of developmental stages. In the process of development and socialization, individuals go through these **developmental stages**, which are definite periods in the individual's life characterized by certain physical, psychological, behavioral, and social characteristics. Contemporary scholarly books on human development distinguish several common stages within the life-span: prenatal period, infancy, childhood (divided into early and middle childhood), adolescence, and adulthood, which is, in turn, subdivided into three stages: early adulthood, middle adulthood, and late adulthood (see **Figure 10.1**).

Developmental stages In developmental psychology, the definite periods in an individual's life that are characterized by certain physical, psychological, behavioral, and social characteristics are called developmental stages.

Classifications of Stages

Most classifications across cultures include the birth and the death of the individual. Cultural beliefs in immortality and reincarnation promote the understanding of the life-span as an endless cycle. In addition, the views on the beginning of a child's life (i.e., Does it start at conception or at a later stage?) vary cross-culturally and are based on people's educational backgrounds, religion, and their ideological values. There can also be slightly different categorizations of the life-span. For example, according to Hindu tradition, infancy, early childhood, and middle childhood are not necessarily separate stages (Valsiner & Lawrence, 1997). In the Judeo-Christian tradition, life is represented linearly; it begins at conception and its end is death. In Hinduism, life is represented circularly: People live and die many times (Fernandez, Castano, & Singh, 2010). In more than half of the societies in the 20th century studied by Schlegel and Barry (1991), there was no special term for adolescence. Indeed, adolescence is a transitional stage between childhood and adulthood in relatively affluent societies, which can afford the existence of a large segment of the population who may look and feel like adults and yet are not allowed to take on adults' duties, roles, and responsibilities.

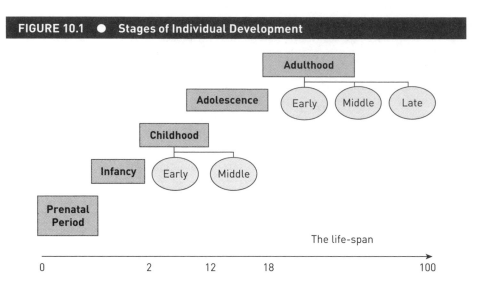

FIGURE 10.1 ● Stages of Individual Development

In some traditional religious teachings, people acquire social status, develop behaviors, and shape personality traits according to a set of prescribed roles. For example, in traditional Hinduism, people have obligations in regard to their positions in society and to their stages of individual development. These classifications and rules refer to traditional beliefs, which most members of today's Hindu community do not practice (Shiraev & Levy, 2013).

Societal positions and the roles attached to them are called castes, and they are hierarchical. The Brahmins (priests) hold the highest position, followed by the nobles or warriors, then the commoners and, finally, the serfs, who are the lowest. The Brahmins teach religion; the nobles practice defense; the commoners plow, tend cattle, and lend money; and the lowest class serves the upper ones. Every person is supposed to come through developmental stages, such as the celibate student, householder, forest dweller, and renouncer. During the first stage, which lasts to approximately the mid-30s, the person learns about religion. After this, the person gets married, starts a family, and becomes a householder. The next stages come after the person retires and returns to the life of self-discipline and ritual. Compassion and giving should dominate this stage. During the last stage, the renouncer gives up daily pleasures and reaches spiritual liberation.

Most classifications of the life-span focus on transition points of the individual's development. Birthdays, initiation rituals, weddings, school graduations, divorces, the birth of children and grandchildren, retirement, and other significant life events mark the most important points of human transition. Legal knowledge matters, too. Reaching the voting age or drinking age, which is 18 and 21 respectively in the United States and 18 in both cases in Russia, for example, could also be interpreted as a sign of legal maturity. It is common to attach developmental labels to other people who reach a transition point in their lives. For example, a person's high school graduation is likely to be considered a sign of maturity. Several biological, behavioral, and physiological changes are also recognized cross-culturally as indicators of reaching particular life stages. Among these natural events are emergence of permanent teeth, first words, first menstruation and menopause in women, growth of facial hair in young men, and so forth. Across cultures, gray hair is commonly viewed as a sign of maturity, despite tremendous individual variation with regard to hair pigmentation. Changes can be gradual, as well as sudden and abrupt: In some cultures it takes just a special ritual or ceremony to "transfer" from a boy into a "man" (McDowell, 1988). In other words, the transition from one state to another is a matter of a social agreement.

In the contemporary world, the amount of education required for young people to enter the workforce is expanding. As these people pursue education for longer periods (to obtain a law degree usually takes at least 7 years of college education in the United States), they also postpone transitions into adult roles. The median ages for these adult transitions are the late 20s in every industrialized society, and it is rising in developing countries (Arnett, 2008; Settersten & Ray, 2010). The fact that transitions into adult roles have become somewhat delayed in many societies has led to the spread of a new period of life, called **emerging adulthood**, that extends from the late teens to the mid-20s (and even later) and is characterized by self-focused exploration of possibilities in work, relationships, interests, and values.

Is There a Midlife Crisis?

You have certainly heard about the midlife crisis. In popular literature, this is a stage or period in people's lives when they realize the pressures of age, question their own accomplishments, experience excessive anxiety about the future, and have doubts about their plans. This period typically occurs between a the 40s to early 60s. In popular novels and movies, this midlife crisis is usually associated with the unusual, unexpected things people do, such as buying flashy cars, digging into some strange projects, falling in love with a seemingly "wrong" person, or giving up a successful career for a more questionable lifestyle, and stories make it appear that every person is expected to go through this crisis.

However, psychological research remains skeptical. Several empirical studies find little evidence about the existence of such a crisis. For example, a study in Canada, one of the most in-depth analyses ever conducted in this area, followed the fortunes of two groups—specifically, 18-year-old Canadian high school students and 23-year-old university seniors—for a period of more than 25 years (Galambos, Fang, Krahn, Johnson, & Lachman, 2015). Participants were regularly asked to report their assessments of happiness, relationship and employment statuses, and how their health fared. Both groups were found to become happier most quickly when they hit their 30s, largely thanks to job and personal relationship upturns, and the 40-year-olds were mostly happy as well. Measures of happiness took a slight downturn by age 43, but this was only in the high school sample. In general, the results of this and most other studies question the myth that there must be a midlife crisis. True, crises take place in our lives, but they are not necessarily confined to any particular age period.

Earlier Stages Affect Later Ones

It is generally assumed that early stages of individual development should influence later ones—that is, whatever happens early in our lives should somehow affect our personality features later on. Ancient philosophers in India, China, and Greece

Emerging adulthood
One of Erikson's developmental stages, emerging adulthood extends from the late teens to the mid-20s (and even later) and is characterized by self-focused exploration of possibilities in work, relationships, interests, and values.

were aware of the impact of a person's early experiences on later developing traits. Aristotle maintained that the habits people acquire when they are growing up are those that determine their lifelong character (Pickard, 2011). Most psychological theories developed in the past 100 years maintain this view. As was discussed in earlier chapters, psychoanalysis and behavioral theories, despite their substantial differences, were essentially in agreement that an individual's early experiences and habits play a significant role in an individual's personality traits and habits during the later stages of life.

Stability and Change: Consistency and Openness Models

Consistency model
The consistency model states that most adults acquire (or learn) behaviors and develop stable traits early in life and tend not to change them later.

Openness model
The openness model states that most people do constantly change their behaviors and adjust their traits to changing life situations.

One of the most important questions developmental psychologists ask is whether individual personality features change during the life-span. The common view is that these features do change. However, how significant are these changes? Two models—**consistency** and **openness**—attempt to explain the process of stability and change in personality features and how they change (Renshon, 1989). According to the first model, consistency, most adults acquire (or learn) behaviors and develop stable traits early in life and tend not to change them later. For example, if a girl grows up in a conservative, religious family in Morocco, she will likely be religious, and she will not tend to seek new experiences—probably no matter where she lives as an adult.

The other model, openness, suggests the opposite: People do constantly change their behaviors and adjust their traits to changing life situations. Early childhood and adolescent experiences do not necessarily determine who you are today as a person. Your traits and habits change throughout your life. Although the consistency approach is somewhat intriguing, most research data suggest that the openness model describes human development somewhat better (Sigel, 1989). Overall, some personality features remain stable during the life-span, while others change. The most important question here is how stable our individual features are.

Development and Stability

Heterotypic stability
A person's heterotypic stability is the psychological consistency of his or her personality features, including behavioral traits, across the life-span.

Homotypic stability
The measure of similarity in the same observable personality feature in a particular period, including the life-span, is referred to as homotypic stability.

Personality psychologists discuss at least two types of stability. **Heterotypic stability** refers to the psychological consistency of an individual's personality features, including behavioral traits across the life-span. Let's think critically. This consistency is not easy to measure and interpret. Overanxious children are more likely to express their fearful reactions openly; however, overanxious adults may not do that. Instead, they might address their anxiety through several obsessive trends, such as perfectionism. Another example is the expectation that an outgoing, gregarious child is likely to be outgoing as an adult. However, this expectation is flawed—there are many influences that can affect this person during the development process. Yet psychologists commonly expect development at the early developmental stages to foreshadow or predict similar personality features later. The patterns of behavior observed in childhood sometimes foreshadow adult personality attributes.

The other type of stability is **homotypic stability**. It refers to the measure of similarity in the same observable personality feature in a particular period, including the life-span. As an illustration, imagine a child who is very organized and has a stable tendency to finish all of her class projects and homework assignments on time. As an adult, she displays the same tendency at her work as a nurse. In sum, heterotypic stability refers to the consistency of the underlying psychological attribute that may have different behavioral manifestations at different ages, but homotypic stability refers to the consistency of the same observable manifestations of a personality attribute (Donnellan, Conger, & Burzette, 2007).

How significant is the trait change? Research suggests two general trends. The first one is that trait changes were more profound in the first half of the transition relative to the second half of the transition from childhood to adulthood. The other is that traits tend to become more stable during the second half of the transition from childhood to adulthood (Hopwood et al., 2011).

Persistence and Change

Personality traits' stability and change should be assessed from different angles. Research shows that most individuals have relatively enduring attributes and that the changes across the life-span are somewhat predictable. Stability of personality features is shaped by a complicated interaction between individuals and their social environments. The stability of traits can be associated with completely different social environments. Consider two examples.

Social and political developments in Afghanistan during the last 40 years have been marked by several devastating developments. Among them were the revolution and dismissal of the king, the Soviet invasion in 1979, the war against the occupation, the emergence of radical religious groups, a new foreign occupation, and then the seemingly endless civil war and instability. Think of an Afghani girl born in 1975. During practically all stages of her life she was exposed to continuous stress, poverty, devastation, and fear for her life and the lives of her loved ones. She had to constantly adjust to the changing conditions and at the same time develop a stable set of personality features necessary to deal with the daily stress of her life (we will learn more about individual coping mechanisms in Chapter 13). The second example sees another girl born in 1975 in a small Norwegian town, likely able to live a life relatively free of cataclysms, significant events, and unexpected turns. Norway is a country that has one of the most developed social welfare systems and one of the highest life expectancy rates in the world. In both cases, individuals are likely to develop relatively stable personality features in response to completely different social and political conditions. In the first case, the stability of traits helps with the changing dangerous circumstances. In the other, the stability of traits can be associated with social stability (Shiraev & Levy, 2013).

The relationship between many personality features and social conditions is a two-way street. Personality attributes seem to shape environmental contexts, and in turn, those contexts often accentuate and reinforce those very personality attributes. Studies show, for instance, that some of our political beliefs—such as being more conservative or more liberal—are associated with our basic personality features. However, some people do not change their beliefs during their life-spans, while others do change their values because of changing social conditions (Caprara & Vecchione, 2009; Sears & Funk, 1999). Personality change or transformation is possible because individuals respond to their environments. Individuals may also want to change certain personality features through their own individual efforts or by turning to counseling or psychotherapy (Donnellan & Robins, 2009).

Of course, certain significant life experiences may change our beliefs, values, and subsequent behaviors as well as personality features and traits. The following case in point, which is borrowed from history, is just one example of a sudden change that takes place in our lives out of a single event or experience.

A Life-Changing Experience

How do we become who we are right now? Contemporary science suggests that changes tend to be gradual and come from different directions. However, we also know from our own experiences and the lives of others that there are some moments in our lives that change our values and expectations. Consider an example. Back in 1893, a young lawyer named Mohandas Gandhi (1869–1948) traveled from England to South Africa on business. While on the train, he was removed from a whites-only carriage on a train because South African law assigned each carriage according to race. Appalled by this act of racial discrimination, Gandhi wanted to return to England immediately. However, the night he spent in a cold waiting room in the train station probably changed his life forever. This humiliation was one of the most inspiring experiences of his life. From that hour, he refused to accept injustice among people. Known to the world today as Mahatma (Sanskrit for "great soul"), Gandhi has become a living symbol for peaceful resistance.

CHECK AND APPLY YOUR KNOWLEDGE

1. Explain human development and socialization.

2. Name the key developmental stages.

3. What is a midlife crisis? Ask a person who is over 40 if he or she has experienced a major crisis; if yes, what caused it?

4. Explain the consistency and oppress models of development.

5. Explain heterotypic and homotypic stability.

6. Have you experienced significant changes in your views of life and other people due to a major event in your life? If yes, what was the event, and what were the changes?

Studying the Developmental Domain

An Individual's Development and Life Sciences

Personality psychologists learn from life sciences about the important biological foundations that affect personality traits and other stable behavioral and emotional characteristics during a life-span.

Hayley Okines was just 17 when she died. This beautiful English girl with blonde hair and blue eyes had a rare premature aging disorder, which gave her the body of a 104-year-old woman at her death. The syndrome, known as *Hutchinson-Gilford progeria syndrome* (HGPS), makes children age about 10 times faster than the normal pace (Harley, 2015). There have been only 70 known cases of this illness on the planet. Hayley was one of them.

We, as human beings, have a naturally determined pace of aging. It is genetically programmed. This means we are supposed to go through physical developmental stages at certain times, but our lifestyles and the events around us can change the pace that nature has set for us. Hayley received a unique genetic program that made her skin look aged, her face small, and her height short. She also suffered from serious and increasing health problems associated with old age, including bone and cardio-vascular issues. Yet even though her body had physically aged, she remained a 17-year-old in her soul. In the book *Old Before My Time* (Okines, 2012), we learn more about Hayley's life, her interests, and her daily routines. Despite the physical aging, she remained a girl just like millions of other girls around her: She was interested in music, games, and was very much involved in thinking about her future—she believed her future would be bright and happy.

Nature has substantial control over the aging process. Age-related physiological mechanisms control the development of our traits, behaviors, stable emotional states, and even the ways we relate to reality and understand it. Nature sets the length of the **prenatal period**, or the time between conception and birth, which is 38 weeks for humans, on average. Yet from conception, the developing embryo in a mother's womb is exposed to either favorable or unfavorable conditions. Across the world, violence, excessive radiation, exposure to chemicals, and air and water pollution, to name a few factors, can cause various complications in pregnancy and serious birth defects. In addition, a lack of professional prenatal care is also a crucial factor affecting children's future development and a variety of their personality traits.

Prenatal period The time between conception and birth, which is 38 weeks for humans on average, is known as the prenatal period.

Age-related changes in the brain affect many personality features. Psychologists examined letters and other documents produced by prominent individuals (such as Napoleon or Freud). The experts compared the letters written long before these individuals' death and ones written just prior to their death. The comparison showed a significant drop in many cognitive functions, such as the degree of integration and differentiation in information processing (Suedfeld & Piedrahita, 1984).

Heredity and harmful environmental conditions affect individuals across their life-spans. The term **degeneration**, a generational regress in physical and psycho-logical traits, was coined in the 1800s (Morel, 1857/1976). For example, a person living in a rough neighborhood who is uneducated, poor, and predisposed to violence and drinking is likely to have children who will remain poor, have few social opportunities, and likely further regress as individuals.

Degeneration Coined in the 1800s, degeneration refers to the generational regress in physical and psychological traits.

Studies show how early physical traumas, illnesses, and other body- and health-related factors affect the development of psychological features in individuals (American Psychiatric Association, 2013). Consider just one example involving studies of children who become addicted to glue at a very early age. Mostly homeless and suffering from hunger and abuse, these children use glue as a narcotic. As it reacts to glue (and may similar toxins), the brain releases endorphins that on the psychological level produce joy, excitement, and, for a brief period, comfort. Unfortunately, children quickly develop glue dependency. As a result of this dependency, not only do they suffer from chronic, long-term kidney problems, but they also have brain seizures, memory loss, and intellectual delays. There are also significant personality changes—they become angry, violent, and irresponsible as brain cells are destroyed by the toxins (Bergmann & Frisén, 2013).

Cross-Cultural Approach

Another approach to studying personality within the developmental domain comes from cross-cultural psychology. Psychologists study how different cultural influences affect the individual's personality. They look for standard, universal personality features as well as cultural differences among personality traits. Social scientists as well as psychologists generally assume that cultures can be described in terms of cultural dichotomies, such as high- versus low-power distance, high- versus low-uncertainty avoidance, and collectivism versus individualism.

Power distance is the extent to which the members of a society accept that power in institutions and organizations is distributed unequally (Hofstede, 1980). People in high-power distance cultures tend to accept inequality between the leaders and the led, the elite and the common, the managers and the subordinates, and breadwinners and other family members. A traditional caste-based Indian society is one of high-power distance. Studies reveal that people in hierarchical, high-power distance cultures tend to assign stricter behavior rules associated with social status (e.g., "A father should always act like a respectable head of the family"). On the other hand, people in egalitarian, low-power distance cultures are less preoccupied with the behavioral rules attached to the status (e.g., "A father should be a friend above all"). In many studies, it has been shown, for instance, that the United States is viewed as a relatively egalitarian, low-power distance culture. Alternatively, Japan and South Korea were commonly viewed as more hierarchical and higher in power distance (Matsumoto, 2007).

Uncertainty orientation refers to common ways used by people to handle uncertainty in their daily situations and lives in general. Uncertainty avoidance is the degree to which the members of a society feel uncomfortable with uncertainty and ambiguity. People in high-uncertainty avoidance cultures tend to support beliefs promising certainty and to maintain institutions protecting conformity. Likewise, people in low-uncertainty avoidance cultures are apt to maintain nonconformist attitudes, unpredictability, creativity, and new forms of thinking and behavior. People who are certainty-oriented tend to defer to rules, customs, or opinions of other people, including authority figures, to resolve uncertainty (Sorrentino et al., 2008). Research shows that people in Eastern and Western cultures tend to differ in how they handle uncertainty. In particular, Eastern cultures such as Japan or China tend to be more "uncertainty avoidant" than Western cultures such as France or Canada (Hofstede, 2010).

Finally, **individualism** is complex behavior based on concern for oneself and one's immediate family or primary group, as opposed to concern for other groups or the society to which one belongs. On the other side of the spectrum is **collectivism**,

Power distance
Power distance is the extent to which the members of a society accept that power in institutions and organizations is distributed unequally.

Uncertainty orientation
A person's uncertainty orientation is the common way he or she handles uncertainty in daily situations and life in general.

Individualism
Complex behavior based on concern for oneself and one's immediate family or primary group (as opposed to concern for other groups or the society to which one belongs) is called individualism.

Collectivism
Collectivism is complex behavior based on concerns for other individuals and care for shared traditions and values.

which is complex behavior based on concerns for other individuals and care for shared traditions and values (Triandis, 1989). While collectivism is high in Asian countries, traditional societies, and the former communist countries, individualism is high in Western countries (Triandis, 1996). North Americans, in comparison to Western Europeans and Asians, show a predominance of independence and individualism, as opposed to the interdependence and collectivism of other groups (Kitayama et al., 2006).

Key processes by which individuals learn cultural norms are socialization and education. School, the family, peers, and social groups provide individuals with knowledge and skills to adjust to the demands of the society (see **Figure 10.2**).

Education is a part of the socialization process. It also plays a major role in influencing personality features of the developing individual (Dahman & Anger, 2014). Highly educated Americans differ from other Americans in many important respects. American undergraduates in particular score higher on some measures of individualism than do their non–college-educated counterparts, particularly for those aspects associated with self-actualization, uniqueness, and locus of control. College-educated Americans were less motivated to conform than were non–college-educated Americans (Stephens, Markus, & Townsend, 2007). American college students respond more favorably toward other groups in society, are more supportive of racial diversity, and are more motivated to mask or explain away negative intergroup attitudes than are Americans who never attended college (Henry, 2009).

According to the **suppression–facilitation model**, behaviors that are discouraged in a culture will be seen infrequently in mental health facilities. For example, if parents punish children for being violent, there should not be many violent mental patients in this country's mental facilities. The suppression–facilitation model

Suppression–facilitation model The suppression–facilitation model states that behaviors that are discouraged in a culture will be seen infrequently in mental health facilities.

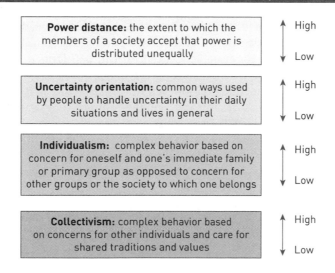

FIGURE 10.2 ● Cultures Described in Terms of Cultural Dichotomies

Power distance: the extent to which the members of a society accept that power is distributed unequally — High / Low

Uncertainty orientation: common ways used by people to handle uncertainty in their daily situations and lives in general — High / Low

Individualism: complex behavior based on concern for oneself and one's immediate family or primary group as opposed to concern for other groups or the society to which one belongs — High / Low

Collectivism: complex behavior based on concerns for other individuals and care for shared traditions and values — High / Low

also assumes that behaviors that are rewarded will be seen excessively. From the standpoint of another model, the adult **distress threshold**, the behaviors that were discouraged in childhood will be seen in clinics more often than "acceptable" behaviors. According to the threshold model, adults in different cultural contexts may have different thresholds for determining which child behaviors are problematic. For example, teachers in Thailand expect that children will not be aggressive and disruptive in school and have low thresholds for tolerating such behavior (Lansford et al., 2010).

Weisz and his colleagues (1987) tested this model in a cross-cultural study that involved Thai and U.S. children. Buddhist traditions in Thailand are generally different from U.S. cultural norms—they emphasize nonaggression, politeness, modesty, and respect for others. Buddhist parents are very intolerant toward impulsive, aggressive, and "undercontrolled" (undisciplined tendencies) behavior in their children. As the suppression–facilitation model predicted, "overcontrolled" problems (aloofness, withdrawal) were reported more frequently for Thai children than they were for U.S. children. Problems such as violence and disorderly behavior were reported more frequently for U.S. children. Thus, the suppression–facilitation model received some empirical support (Weisz, Suwanlert, Chaiyasit, & Walter, 1987).

Social and political factors affect adolescents' cultural identity. A study of Palestinian Arab Christian adolescents in Israel showed that most of them tend to maintain their distinct ethnic and religious identity. However, when compared to Muslim Arabs, they expressed more willingness to adopt elements of the Jewish society. They also feel stronger assimilation pressures from Israeli Jews. Christian Arabs are commonly viewed as a "double minority" because they are Arabs (the majority of Arabs are Muslims) and live in a predominantly Jewish country. The stronger willingness of Palestinian Christian Arabs to engage in social and cultural contact with Israeli Jews may reflect a desire to gain more access to important resources such as education and work. In addition, Palestinian Christian Arabs tend to distinguish themselves historically as a more Westernized cultural group (Horenczyk & Munayer, 2007).

Do parental practices directly affect the child's individual personality features? In other words, if the parents tend to be authoritative and restrictive, do their children grow up as obedient and lacking initiative? Cross-cultural research shows that this is not necessarily the case. For example, Central African Bofi farmers fit the so-called authoritarian parenting style: They demand respect and obedience early and exercise coercive control over their children. However, studies show that Bofi children are not withdrawn, and they do not lack initiative. On the contrary, they display precisely the opposite traits (Baumrind, 1971; Fouts, 2005). We should understand that parenting styles do not affect children in one specific way. There are many different influences that shape our personality profiles and our typical behaviors.

Social and political conditions play a significant role in individual socialization. In a study conducted in Israel, children of North American and Soviet immigrants showed significantly different patterns of behavior in the classroom. Students from North America were peer group-oriented. Students from the Soviet Union were teacher-oriented (Horowits & Kraus, 1984). The Soviet system of education, compared with the U.S. system, had a very strong emphasis on student discipline and obedience. Moving into a new cultural environment, Soviet adolescent immigrants did not change their obedience-oriented behavioral pattern.

CHECK AND APPLY YOUR KNOWLEDGE

1. Explain collectivism, power distance, uncertainty orientation, and individualism.

2. Explain the suppression–facilitation model.

3. Do you personally want to look younger or older? Ask other people in class. Do people want to look older sometimes? Why do so many people want to look younger? What do people do to look younger? Use your personal observations or other sources to discuss in class how people in different families and cultures cope with aging. Which businesses are interested in creating hype about the "younger image"?

The Psychoanalytic Tradition

A study shows that young, middle-aged, and older adults tend to respond to different styles of humor. For example, younger adults tend to prefer the "gaffe" types of jokes and videos, while older adults do not. Young adults endorsed a more aggressive humor style than middle-aged and older adults (Stanley, Lohani, & Isaacowitz, 2014). Why do these differences exist? Of course, there could be various explanations. From the psychoanalytic perspective, however, the differences between the young and the mature are rooted in their individual experiences and the strengths of their ego and superego. The young could have a weaker superego, thus allowing unconscious impulses associated with violence to surface.

Different psychoanalysts had their own classifications for developmental stages and psychological processes that contribute to an individual's personality development. Recall from Chapter 4 and Chapter 5 that the psychoanalytic tradition in psychology emphasizes the importance of early childhood experiences in the future development of the adult. This vision of the individual's development does not seem to be original. Many scientists and psychologists in the past emphasized the importance of the earlier stages of development on the later ones. At least four important points make the psychoanalytic tradition different.

First, the psychoanalytic tradition emphasizes that only the earlier stages are important. They often have a crucial impact on the future personality traits of the individual.

Second, during the process of individual development, a person goes through several distinct stages. Every stage is characterized by a particular conflict, contradiction, or a set of distinct features that the individual acquires. Recall that Freud emphasized human sexuality, while Adler paid attention to human imperfection and inferiority. Erikson believed that at each stage the ego faces a developmental conflict or crisis. If the crisis has been positively resolved, the person's ego strengthens by gaining greater adaptation (Erikson, 1950). But if the crisis has not been resolved, the ego loses strength, which results in poor adaptation.

Third, most likely, the impact of the earlier stages remains outside of the individual's awareness. Only trained psychology professionals are capable of understanding the deep-seated roots of adult behavior and individual traits. Our life is a constant development. If somebody is undergoing psychotherapy, this is, in fact, the act of learning and growing. The individual is developing new virtues that were missing earlier in life (Erikson, 1968). Parents and adults have to play the important role, too. If growing children, for instance, are not allowed to discover their own talents, as adults they will probably lack motivation, have a low self-esteem, and prefer passivity to action.

Fourth, and probably the most important assumption, is that we, as individuals, have the capacity to understand our own problems and weaknesses and then address them to become better people. These views correspond in many ways with Indian, Buddhist, and several religious and philosophical traditions aimed at self-transformation through insight into the nature of self (Paranjpe, 1998). Moreover, Erikson and others wrote about the necessity for developing adults to focus increasingly on others, helping in the community, and society in general. Personal growth is not only about focusing on self but most likely is about the well-being and happiness of others.

A critical assessment of specific psychoanalytic theories of personality appears in Chapter 4 and Chapter 5. The ongoing global demographic changes will show how applicable these theories are to the individuals developing in new conditions, including smaller families, dynamic migration, growth of educational level of parents, and the new forms of communication, such as social networks. Will the impact of family and parents significantly diminish?

Laurence Kohlberg: Personality and Morality

Many psychologists as well as social scientists in the past tried to examine an important question: How do people learn about moral values? A common view prevailed that the child should be "ready" to understand morality before the adults teach it to them. The works of the American psychologist G. Stanley Hall (1844–1924) suggested that the child's development advances through critical periods. Children develop to their full potential if they are not constrained but allowed to go through the stages freely. Before age 6, for example, the child is unable to make sophisticated theoretical judgments and is insensitive to moral values. There is no reason at this age to teach the child sophisticated theories about right and wrong actions. Once the child reaches the next stage at age 8, formal learning should begin. The child is ready to understand moral issues, such as kindness, love, and service to others. It is generally accepted that the child has to go through developmental stages in his or her moral development and that the developing person has to have certain cognitive skills to comprehend moral values. Yet what are the stages?

One of the most prominent theories about moral values and their role in an individual's development came from the American psychologist Lawrence Kohlberg (1981). He described six stages of moral development in which children and adults are able to make several types of moral judgments. In brief, people go from lower stages of reasoning, in which they prefer to avoid punishment for wrongdoing, to the higher stages, where they choose social contract and then universal principles to guide moral actions (see **Table 10.1**).

One of the reasons why this theory was so well received is that empirical studies provided significant support. A comparative study took 45 psychological projects of moral judgment development conducted in 27 countries and showed that the first four stages appear to be practically identical in the subjects of all countries studied (Snarey, 1985). However, some critics expressed skepticism about the cross-cultural validity of this theory. The methodology used in cross-cultural studies on moral development was based on hypothetical stories about moral choices that a person was making. Critics suggested that these stories were more likely to be related to U.S. and other Western subjects (Shweder, Mahapatra, & Miller, 1990).

An interesting cross-cultural examination of Kohlberg's theory was conducted by Ma and Cheung (1996), who compared moral judgments of more than 1,000 Hong Kong Chinese, English, and U.S. college and high school students. The test consisted of four stories, and each story contained a description of a moral problem. The subjects were asked to make judgments about a certain moral dilemma or a similar problem. It was found that Chinese students tended to emphasize the importance of the Stage 3 judgments and considered Stage 4 judgments as more similar to Stage 5 and Stage 6 judgments. The English and U.S. subjects tended to regard Stage 4 judgments as more similar to Stage 2 or Stage 3 judgments.

The authors of the study argued that the differences in choices had cultural roots. Most moral judgments of the Chinese have been reinforced by traditional norms and regulated by conformity to primary groups. Chinese see issues such as concerns for social order, consensus, and abiding by the law from mostly a collectivist perspective. A strong orientation to perform altruistic acts for the sake of close relatives and friends is part of Chinese culture. Chinese are also influenced, as the authors argued, by the Confucian concept of the five cardinal relationships, which emphasizes the harmonious connection between sovereign and subject, father and son, husband and wife, brother and brother, and friend and friend.

TABLE 10.1 ● Kohlberg's (1981) Stages of Moral Development

Stage 1. Preconventional level I: Judgments about what is right and what is wrong are based on fear of punishment.

Stage 2. Preconventional level II: Moral conduct produces pleasure, whereas immoral conduct results in unwanted consequences.

Stage 3. Conventional level I: Any behavior is good if it is approved by significant others.

Stage 4. Conventional level II: The existing laws determine what is moral and immoral.

Stage 5. Postconventional level I: Moral behavior is based on individual rights and underlying social circumstances.

Stage 6. Postconventional level II: Moral conduct is regulated by universal ethical principles that may rise above government and laws.

In contrast, Western people are concerned primarily with individual rights and their interests being protected by the law. In the West, people can easily sue each other because the law often mediates interpersonal relationships. Chinese tend not to resolve their conflicts in legal institutions; they prefer instead to resolve their conflicts by using interpersonal contacts. This practice, however, can become a double-edged sword. On one hand, it may appear that interpersonal orientation is more humane and appealing than the law-based system (indeed, it seems healthier to settle a conflict than seek legal help). On the other hand, an emphasis on an interpersonal system of communications may stimulate nepotism and corruption—two serious problems that Hong Kong officials themselves recognize very well.

Some studies point out that the individual's moral judgments are caused mostly by specific circumstances; the values are not necessarily based on a certain "developmental" level of the person's moral development (Matsumoto, 1994; Vassiliou & Vassiliou, 1973). Other psychologists argue that moral judgments are difficult to examine in a laboratory. Have you heard about the **trolley dilemma**? In the famous exercise, people (imagine yourself in their place) are asked to visualize a runaway trolley, rapidly moving down the railway tracks. You have two options: (1) You do nothing, and the trolley kills the five people in it after an inevitable collision with the wall; or (2) you pull the lever, thus diverting the trolley onto the side track where it will kill just one person, who just happens to be there—however, your act will save the lives of the five. Which will be your choice?

Trolley dilemma
A thought exercise, the trolley dilemma involves rational reasoning and moral choices related to saving a human life by sacrificing another.

Studies show that most people, from 80% to 90%, prefer to save the lives of five people and sacrifice the life of one. However, studies show that we also pay attention to the circumstances and the specific characteristics of the people involved surrounding this hypothetical situation. Significantly more people found it acceptable in general to sacrifice a low-status person than a high-status person. And it was significantly more acceptable to save the lives of "good" people (such as children) by sacrificing a "bad" person (such as a homeless man). Also, they were unwilling to sacrifice the life of a relative or loved one (Fiske, 2010).

The trolley dilemma examines the human capacity for rational justification of moral and immoral decision-making: Is it appropriate to save the lives of five people by sacrificing the life of one? It also shows that people pay attention to the

CHECK AND APPLY YOUR KNOWLEDGE

1. Describe in three sentences the key points of the psychoanalytic approach to an individual's development.

2. Describe the six stages of moral development, according to Kohlberg.

3. Explain the trolley dilemma. How would you personally act in a similar hypothetical situation? Would you sacrifice the life of one person to save the lives of five? Explain your decision.

circumstances surrounding the experimental conditions. Moreover, people's decisions are not attached to their developmental levels. In fact, our moral decisions are caused by a great range of mediating factors.

Developmental psychologists emphasize the interaction of the developing individual with the environment. Jean Piaget from Switzerland and Lev Vygotsky from Russia—two outstanding psychologists of the 20th century—further developed this view. Vygotsky's observations of parent–child interactions led him to a conclusion about an active and adaptive role of the child's adjustment to the changing conditions and demands of life. Piaget's theory emphasized the child's inner developmental mechanisms and their adaptive role. Both theories gained significant international recognition.

Jean Piaget's Developmental Approach

The Swiss psychologist Jean Piaget (1896–1970) believed that the process of development progresses in stages determined by the child's developing brain, skills, and social environment. The movement from one state to another is primarily a natural process. A main lesson we learn from Piaget is that an individual's features are predetermined due to a variety of natural factors that are unfolding within particular interactions and social circumstances. These views had an important impact on personality psychology.

Piaget believed that human development is a process of adapting to the changing contexts of life. Perhaps the most significant contribution made by Piaget was his ideas of **assimilation** and **accommodation**—the two sides of the process of adaptation or learning. Assimilation is adopting operations with new objects into old mind patterns. Accommodation is modifying one's mental structures to fit the new demands of the environment. Assimilation and accommodation are both fundamentally biological processes and work in tandem to help individuals advance their understanding of the world.

Assimilation
In Piaget's system, assimilation is adopting operations with new objects into old mind patterns.

Accommodation
In Piaget's system, accommodation is modifying one's mental structures to fit the new demands of the environment.

Stages of Development

In Stage 1, the *sensorimotor* stage, infants learn about their interaction with their immediate environment through immediate experiences. Around the age of 18 months, children develop the increased ability to hold an image in their minds beyond the immediate experience. During Stage 2, the *preoperational* stage, children acquire language, develop imagination, learn the meaning of symbols, and develop creative play. Children remain generally egocentric, which means they have a diminished capacity to see the world from another person's viewpoint. At this stage, which lasts until approximately age 7, children tend to be animistic in their judgments; for example, they may assign personality features to objects and animals or tend to believe in spiritual beings or actions.

At the third stage of *concrete operations*, children learn the rules of logic and begin to comprehend the laws of physics related to volume, amount, and weight. They become more mechanical in their judgments about nature and things around them. From age 7 to 11, children acquire *operations*, or logical principles to solve most problems. At this stage, the child not only uses symbols to make them represent something but can also logically manipulate those symbols. A child learns to classify and put objects in a series or group according to various rules. The final stage, *formal operations*, which begins at age 11 or 12, indicates the time when adolescents develop the ability to think abstractly. This involves using complex logical operations and hypothetical thinking.

In the process of development, one stage must be accomplished before the next can emerge. The process may resemble construction of a building: Each new level is impossible to build without building the lower ones. As soon as the child has constructed the operations on a new level, he or she learns about more complex objects and performs more complex operations. Thus, children continually renovate the ideas they formed earlier. Transitions between stages are not necessarily gradual—they tend to be rapid and significant.

Do all children develop thinking and move through developmental stages in the way Piaget proposed? Summarizing results from a handful of studies, Dasen (1994) showed that the stage sequence (preoperational, operational, and abstract thinking) appears to be similar across countries. Children tend to move from one stage to another as Piaget predicted. However, more recent research has contradicted Piaget's belief that children go through the animism stage before age 7. Studies of indigenous people (Gardiner, Mutter, & Kosmitzki, 1998) showed that the animistic view of life developed much later and that children up to age 7 were really thinking more like natural scientists (Shweder, 2010).

Piaget's original ideas about the stage-by-stage development of the child have found applications in educational programs in many countries. Critics pointed out that Piaget provoked a temptation to interpret some higher developmental stages as more "valuable" than others. In reality, though, social success, satisfaction, and adaptation strategies, as well as certain activities and professions, do not require that the individual function on the level of formal operations. It is also questionable whether the formal operational stage should be achieved by every child. In both Western and non-Western settings, there are many healthy, happy, and successful individuals who are not that advanced on formal operational tasks (Byrnes, 1988).

Piaget also believed that children made moral judgments based on their own observations of the world. According to Piaget, the child is someone who constructs his own moral worldview, who forms ideas about right and wrong, and fair and unfair, that are not the direct product of adult teaching and that are often maintained in the face of adult wishes to the contrary.

Lev Vygotsky's Developmental Approach

The works of Lev Vygotsky (1896–1934) remained generally unknown to the English-speaking academic world for many years after his death from tuberculosis at age 37. However, his research has had a significant and growing impact on psychology. Many of his ideas related to child development have influenced personality psychology. Like Piaget, he promoted the child-centered approach. His studies directed the attention of parents and teachers toward the child's personality: the child's rational thinking, creativity, individual choices, and nonconforming attitudes.

Vygotsky's research methods were largely observational. His students recalled that he had a habit of coming to the room where preschoolers played and sitting there for hours. After some time, the children in the room would stop paying attention to the man sitting there and begin to act "naturally." This was exactly what Vygotsky wanted to see (Shedrovitsky, 2009). Most of his ideas came from such observations, like the idea about the child's developmental periods. A child's development is not a steady process of a consistent, uninterrupted transformation and change. Periods of gradual change are followed by rapid transitions, sudden transformations, and crises. Vygotsky suggested five stages of such transformation, occurring at birth, at the end of the first year, and then at the ages of 3, 7, and 13. At each stage, new situations and crises occur, and every new situation is a new source of development.

Photo 10.2 According to Vygotsky, a child is typically ready to learn more and understand better than a teacher or parent might assume. Imagine you are in the role of a parent or a teacher and explain this statement in practical terms.

© iStockphoto.com/triloks

Parents and teachers have to understand the entire social situation surrounding the child. The goal of upbringing is not to emphasize a child's inabilities or deficiencies but to pay attention to what this child has already achieved or developed. Finding new potential in a child is a top priority of an educator and parent (Vygotsky, 1933).

Vygotsky also introduced the idea of cultural mediation. Every psychological function, such as thinking, appears twice. First, it is an "outside" social activity or learning. Next, this learning is internalized as thinking. Human consciousness therefore should be understood in the context of interaction of an individual with the outside world. In fact, Vygotsky, in a symbolic way, placed the soul outside the human body. This was a new theoretical way to understand the most difficult question about the nature of consciousness. The essence of human consciousness is in its unity with the cultural environment (Vygotsky, 1934/2005).

Vygotsky introduced and developed the concept of **zone of proximal development**, understood as the difference between a child's learning progress with help or guidance and the child's learning achievement without the guidance of an adult. Children usually have potential, a latent reserve for their intellectual growth. This means that the child is typically ready to learn more and understand better than a teacher or parent assumes. Vygotsky challenged a common belief of the time that the child has to be prepared to understand certain concepts (e.g., a 3-year-old is not ready to study something that a 4-year-old is capable of knowing). In his view, the child can learn more if teachers or adults stimulate the child's intellectual advance within the zone of proximal development (Vygotsky, 1934/2005).

Zone of proximal development The zone of proximal development indicates the difference between a child's learning progress with help or guidance and the child's learning achievement without the guidance of an adult.

Vygotsky thus argued that the task of education is not to offer something that the child is ready to perform. It is greater. Children, as well as adults, have hidden potential that can be developed with some external help. Two tasks should be pursued here.

The first one is to provide detailed information about what specifically each child's "zone" is—some kids may have a greater potential than their peers in some areas but not in others. Second, both psychologists and educational specialists should create tasks, exercises, and even lengthy programs to assist children in developing their knowledge and skills.

Vygotsky originally developed the concept of the zone of proximal development to argue against the use of standardized tests as a means to gauge intelligence. Vygotsky believed that rather than examining what students already know to measure their intelligence, it is better to examine their ability to solve problems independently and with the assistance of an adult. In Vygotsky's view, ideally, teachers and parents should not only follow and accommodate children but also accelerate, improve, and enhance their potential in as many areas as possible.

Vygotsky maintained that creativity and discipline are not mutually exclusive phenomena and that educational programs can promote both imagination and orderliness in the growing individual. Educators should focus on their students as individual personalities, as learners. They add new concepts to prior knowledge and construct, build, and understand themselves—the process that is intrinsically human.

He believed that when we study what a child can do alone at this moment, we actually study his or her development as of yesterday. When we study what this child can do in cooperation, we look at the developments of tomorrow. This was a new, optimistic, and obviously progressive view of human development. Vygotsky believed that human beings could overcome many natural or social limitations to their psychological development. An individual, in his view, is not a mere product of social environment (a popular thesis partially supported by behaviorists). To him, people are independent and active thinkers. He believed that education should involve the process of the child's interaction with teachers and peers and not necessarily memorization and repetition. Vygotsky's ideas resonated well with educational researchers working on advancing teaching techniques to stimulate the child's unknown or underdeveloped potential (Bruner, 1960).

Vygotsky's views also found a reflection in so-called narrative therapy, based on the assumption that an individual's identity reveals itself in certain symbols as short accounts or narratives about his or her life (Charon, 1993). To correct a person's psychological problem is to investigate such narratives and then restructure them to explain new potentials and possibilities for improvement. An externalization of a problem makes it easier to investigate and evaluate it.

Specific Traits

How do individual traits change during the life-span? Do they tend to change in the same way in most individuals? How significant or insignificant are these changes? These questions have intrigued philosophers and scientists for centuries. Early in this chapter, we discussed stability and change of personality traits in the context of consistency and openness models. Even the ancient Greeks debated whether people remain consistent in terms of their traits and other important behavioral features. Consistency of traits in adulthood was seen as a virtue (Donnellan & Robins, 2009).

Similarly, more than 100 years ago American psychologist William James also believed that personality characteristics (they were called "character") are set firmly after the age of 30 and do not change. Psychologist Gordon Allport believed in the biological basis of individual traits—particular personality traits can be traced to certain features of the child's temperament, or a general set of behavioral and emotional responses (Allport, 1937). Behaviorists, however, maintained that personality traits are learned behaviors and thus they can change with circumstances surrounding the individual. As you can see, the views varied significantly.

The Big Five, and other approaches to studying personality, provide some specific answers to the question of trait stability and change (Anusic, Lucas, & Donnellan, 2012; Donnellan et al., 2007). We have already looked at the theory that organizes most personality traits into five categories—extroversion, agreeableness, conscientiousness, neuroticism, and openness to experience (see Chapter 7). Studies show that certain consistent behaviors and responses appear early in life and tend to correlate with some personality features developed later. Extroversion seems to be correlated with the general style of approaching behavior (Is the child interested in exploring a novel object or not?) and the direction of incentive motivation; in other words, to what extent do other people motivate the child to act? Or does the motivation come from within? Research also shows that extroversion is correlated with the balance of the child's inhibited and uninhibited behavior. For instance, children who appear to be inhibited tend to be shy, timid, and fearful of the future, but those who tend to be uninhibited later display bold, sociable, and outgoing behaviors (Kagan & Herschkowitz, 2005). Neuroticism seems to correlate with withdrawal behavior, anxiety, and the ability to recognize threats. Children pay attention to other people and situations that appear to be different from their normal, everyday experiences (Kagan & Snidman, 1991). The child may feel apprehensive and shy because new people and objects appear uncertain and even frightening to a degree. Agreeableness is associated with enjoyment of social attachments and affection toward others. Conscientiousness is associated with the brain's frontal lobes and is correlated with the ability to plan, predict, and anticipate. A few studies agree that openness to experience, as a trait, is likely to be formed a bit later in life and is related to the person's educational and life experiences (Lucas & Donnelan, 2009, 2011).

How stable are these five characteristics within the life-span? **Table 10.2** summarizes a number of studies conducted during the past 10 years. Studies show that average levels of extroversion, especially the attributes associated with self-confidence and independence, tend to increase with age. Agreeableness and conscientiousness appear to increase with age, while neuroticism appears to decrease with the passage of time (Roberts, Walton, & Viechtbauer, 2006). Studies also show that childhood conscientiousness can predict health behaviors of adulthood, which can have an impact on life expectancy. This assumption should make sense: The more careful we are about our bodies and our health, the more likely we are to maintain a healthy lifestyle and seek medical help when necessary.

More conscientious children tend to grow up into more conscientious adolescents and adults. Psychologists tend to see such dynamics in personality traits as positive trends. For example, higher levels of agreeableness and conscientiousness and lower

TABLE 10.2 ● The Big Five Personality Traits and the Life-Span	
Extroversion	• Average levels tend to slightly increase with age, especially attributes linked to self-confidence and independence. • Variations remain less significant with age.
Agreeableness	• Average levels gradually increase across the life-span. • Variations remain less significant with age.
Conscientiousness	• Research is inconclusive. Some studies show that average levels gradually increase across the life-span until midlife or old age when they tend to decline. • Other studies find this relatively stable across the life-span.
Neuroticism	• Level gradually declines across the life-span but has a tendency to increase in old age.
Openness to experience	• Average levels increase during adolescence and then gradually decline by midlife and across the life-span.

Sources: Donnellan and Robins, 2009; Hampson et al., 2015.

levels of neuroticism are associated with stability and quality of relationships, greater success at work, better health, a reduced risk of criminality and mental illness, and even decreased levels of mortality (Hampson, Edmonds, Goldberg, Dubanoski, & Hillier, 2015). This pattern of positive average changes in personality attributes is known as the maturity principle of adult personality development. The basic idea is that attributes associated with positive adaptation and with the successful fulfillment of adult roles tend to increase during adulthood in terms of their average levels. It is also interesting to notice that openness (e.g., openness to new experiences) declines with age, especially after midlife (Roberts et al., 2006). It looks as if most of us develop it for a particular view of life that is increasingly difficult, or even unreasonable, to change during adulthood. Some people develop a stable worldview and feel comfortable with that, but others may feel less comfortable with the way they see the world yet don't find a way to accept new experiences because of their professions, social networks, or their families.

Overall, personality attributes are relatively enduring and become increasingly consistent during adulthood. Personality developments (stability and change) result from the dynamic interplay between individuals and their environment (Donnellan & Robins, 2009). Personality traits are associated with specific responses that promote personality continuity. For example, people who are friendly are likely to evoke more pleasant and supportive responses from other people. This is helpful in other social interactions. Such positive interactions reinforce the disposition to be friendly. In addition, personality traits shape how people construe social situations. A business meeting may have a particular effect on an extrovert and a different effect on an introvert. People with particular personality traits often develop and sustain behaviors relevant to their traits. For example, introverts may feel less comfortable speaking out during business meetings, so they don't make an effort to be active and engaged participants. Finally, individuals play an active role in selecting and manipulating their own social experiences. Many people have a tendency to seek out, modify, and even create certain social environments that are consistent with their individual personality characteristics. For instance, people who are shy and anxious may be less likely to look for careers that require significant social interaction.

CHECK AND APPLY YOUR KNOWLEDGE

1. Describe the stages of development, according to Piaget.

2. What is the zone of proximal development? Which one of your personal features do you think was overlooked when you were a child? What can you do to develop and advance this feature today?

3. What was William James's view of an individual's personality characteristics?

4. Describe how extroversion, agreeableness, openness to experience, neuroticism, and conscientiousness change during the life-span.

Applying the Developmental Domain

Personality psychologists study human development to gain scientific knowledge about the dynamics related to the formation of personality traits. In a simple way, the individual's personality is understood from the standpoint of age and the age-related features that human beings develop in various social contexts. Human beings are seen as developing, changing, and dynamic individuals. This means that every stage of human development has certain features that make this stage somewhat different from all other stages. This also means that our knowledge about human beings should be applied carefully because each person tends to be different. People have different natural backgrounds (such as genetic makeups), but they also go through different developmental stages. The following text will consider several applications of the studies with the developmental domain. We will look at suicide, criminal behavior, and the approaches to educational practices.

Developmental Factors and Suicide

Almost 800,000 people commit suicide globally every year. Approximately every 15 minutes, somebody in the United States takes his or her own life. According to the Centers for Disease Control and Prevention (CDC), 35,000 to 40,000 lives are cut short every year in the United States alone. More than 6,000 of them will be individuals who are over 65. Some countries, such as Estonia and Russia, have higher suicide rates than in America.

Photo 10.3 Suicide is the second-most common cause of death in adolescents. Suicide-prevention centers are always looking for volunteers and qualified professionals.

© David Corby

Others, like Mexico, have lower rates (World Health Organization [WHO], 2016). Around the world, scores of suicide cases go unreported. People tend to maintain a negative view of suicide or prefer not to talk about it at all. In the Western world, males die 3 to 4 times more often by means of suicide than do females, although females *attempt* suicide nearly 4 times as often. Suicide is the second-most common cause of death in adolescents, and in young males, it is second only to accidental death (Värnik, 2012; Yip et al., 2012). Suicide is also the fourth-leading cause of death among young children. While suicide rates among blacks in America remain twice as low as the national average, suicide remains the third-leading cause of death among African Americans ages 15 to 19 (CDC, 2015).

Suicide is a serious problem that requires research and social action. Psychological research shows that individuals who attempt suicide tend to use different reasons to make this fatal decision. There are also risk factors associated with suicide. In this section, we will focus on age-related risk factors and developmental changes in personality associated with age.

Personality Traits

Experts agree that there is no suicidal personality, and there are no personality traits that signal with certainty that the person with them is at risk of taking his or her own life. However, there are indicators that a person is contemplating suicide. Psychologists and medical professionals identify several common warning signs. At least two are the most common globally: depressive illness and substance abuse. Depressive illness remains the most serious contributor to suicide. A combination of depression (a mood disorder) and substance abuse is a lethal blend, leading to a high probability of suicidal behavior (Goldston et al., 2008). Depression almost never leads to suicide by itself. People who attempt or die by suicide can have a variety of problems: relationships breaking down, physical illness, pain and disability, financial or legal difficulties, or alcohol and drug abuse.

Suicidal ideation (such as persistent discussion of death or statements made personally or on social networks) is a factor, too. The presence of a specific plan is considered an additional predictor of suicide. Access to lethal means (such as firearms or sleeping pills) also increases the probability of suicide. It has been found that borderline personality disorder (Chapter 12) is associated with suicidal acts. In addition, suicide is more likely to occur during periods of economic difficulties and family and individual crises (e.g., loss of a significant other, unemployment, or bankruptcy). One of the most important skills psychologists can learn is to identify suicidal risk and to urgently take measures to help at-risk individuals.

Age Factors

There are two critical ages during which most suicides take place in countries where reliable statistics are available. The first critical age period is between late adolescence and young adulthood; younger people are also significantly more likely than those in other age groups to *attempt* suicide and survive. The other period is late adulthood. In the United States, for example, men over 80 years old are especially at risk.

Young People. The most at-risk individuals to attempt suicide among the young are likely to have depressive illness plus substance abuse. Compared to adults, teens and young adults are also likely to have the symptoms of adjustment disorder, which is a serious and distressful inability to cope with life circumstances (Sunesh-Kumar, Anish, & Biju, 2015). We will pay more attention to adjustment disorder in Chapter 13. Studies also have found that impulsivity can be a factor, too—a person focuses on immediate outcomes instead of delayed ones and neglects important information in making decisions. In teens and young adults, several additional risk factors may play a role in suicidal behavior: previous suicide attempts, presence of mental illness, preoccupation with death, family history of mental illness among parents or siblings, and suicidal behavior. Harmful environmental factors also play a role in childhood suicidal behavior (Tishler, Reiss, & Rhodes, 2007).

The Elderly. Unlike the young, older individuals tend to have extensive medical issues that contribute to suicide. A significant number of people in the elderly group have a current diagnosis of depression and might consider themselves a burden to their families (and report such to their psychology professionals). Physical illness and family burden of psychiatric illness are important at-risk predictors in comparison to younger populations (Sunesh-Kumar et al., 2015). The inability to function in daily life, the failure to do what has been done for years with ease, and fear of social disconnection have become significant risk factors that can predict suicide among older age groups (see **Table 10.3**; Span, 2009).

Crime as a Developmental Problem

For centuries, social scientists and psychologists were looking for specific personality features associated with criminal behavior, especially with violent crime. Scientists

TABLE 10.3 ● Risk Factors of Suicide: A Developmental Comparative View		
Risk Factors	**Older Individuals**	**Younger Individuals**
Depressive illness or other mental illness	A significant factor	A significant factor; not common in young children
Substance abuse	A significant factor, especially in combination with depression	A significant factor, especially in combination with depression; not common among young children
Suicidal ideation	A significant factor	A significant factor
Chronic illness	A significant factor	A possible but not common factor
Significant life stressor	A significant factor	A significant factor
Impulsivity, risk propensity	A factor due to the loss of reasoning	A factor due to undeveloped reasoning
Lack of social interaction	A substantial factor	Typically not a factor
Loss of social status, loss of "face"	A substantial factor	A factor, but insignificant among young children
Physical decline	Can be a common factor	Usually not a common factor

identify certain personality traits such as lack of remorse, aggressiveness, low anxiety levels, and antisocial personality disorder as factors predicting crime.

Studying the individual's personality and combining this research with various economic models can produce intriguing results and applications. Some time ago, American economist Gary Becker (1968) suggested that most criminals act as if they were "rational actors"—they, like ordinary citizens, seek to maximize their own well-being, but they use criminal acts instead of legal means. Becker suggested that if society teaches individuals the tough lesson that they will spend some time in prison if they commit a crime, then people should learn to choose better options, such as freedom (in fact, this is an approach that behavioral psychologists would likely suggest). Indeed, it makes sense that being punished for bad behavior with a significant prison term would cause this behavior to change, and after the 1980s in the United States, there were significant increases in sentence length. In Becker's theory, this should have reduced crime, diminished the costs of law enforcement, and resulted in *fewer* people in prison. But in reality, it simply led to more spending on crime control and many more people in prison (Becker, 1968; Tabarrok, 2015). Longer sentences did not reduce crime—why not?

The "Child" Personality?

One of the hypotheses as to why longer sentences didn't reduce crime is rooted in developmental theory. As you should remember from this chapter, Piaget and Vygotsky (and scores of other psychologists) argued the following:

- Individuals have to develop certain psychological skills and functions before they can perform certain operations.
- If we give the child the necessary conditions and encourage the child to act and think, the child is likely to develop better intellectual skills and more adaptive behaviors.

Applied to criminal behavior, the logic can be as follows: What if certain individuals (let's call them "criminal types" for the sake of the argument) have problems forecasting and difficulty regulating their emotions and controlling their impulses? They have these problems not because they're bad people; on the contrary, we label them *bad* because they cannot control their impulses. Why can't they control their impulses? Because their particular personality features are not developed enough to let them judge their behavior and the consequences of their behavior to avoid trouble. In the heat of the moment, the threat of future punishment is just not strong enough to deter their act.

Instead of thinking about criminals as rational individuals, we should think about criminals as resembling children. This means that the punishment for the crime they commit should be quick, swift, and consistent. Inconsistencies in sentencing are detrimental. Studies also show that inconsistencies in the parent's sanctions against the child's misbehavior, in fact, contribute to this misbehavior in the future.

In a brief summary, the developmental reasoning is that when punishment is not quick, children who misbehave have difficulty learning cause and effect—they begin to believe that they can get away with those small bad things that they do. Many adults act the same way, with several types of crime committed on the spur of the moment. We must give people a small opportunity to reflect and consider the consequences of their behavior. They must learn to associate crime with punishment (Scott, Doolan, Beckett, Harry, & Cartwright, 2010).

Education: Discipline Versus Freedom

For decades, philosophers believed that rigorous discipline, drill, and repetition were key factors in the academic success of a child. Many professionals referred to the studies of 19th-century German psychologist Ebbinghaus to emphasize the special importance of repetition and effort (Young, 1985). However, a different viewpoint on education was based on an assumption that children should receive a variety of opportunities and equal choices at school so they can fully develop their intellectual and emotional potential (Vygotsky, 1934/2005). A young child's personality is not fully developed and he or she is still unable to manifest a stable set of traits. Therefore, to help the child achieve his or her personal potential, the teacher and the parent should be given more freedom and creativity in the classroom. In a way, according to Vygotsky, the child should learn according to his or her individual "schedule." The more creative the educational environment is, the more efficient the process of education is. Children need guidance, not drill or punishment. A child's potential skills should be facilitated, not left alone.

This point of view has been challenged by other theories and popular beliefs, which mainly argue that children can be easily trapped in the continual search for gratification of their wishes. To avoid this endless quest for pleasure, children should learn discipline and respect the demands of teachers. The educational system in China, for example, historically emphasized learning and discipline as important tools that help the individual to function properly in society.

There is a third way, however. As the legendary UCLA basketball coach John Wooden said, "Drilling creates a foundation on which individual initiative and imagination can flourish." This means that our individual creativity flourishes only within a certain system of rules; we can improvise with these rules once we understand the systems (Lemov, 2014).

These three views summarize the centuries of intellectual debates about the most appropriate way to raise and educate an individual. Which strategy is the best? Is it mostly about creativity, freedom, and spontaneity? Is it mostly about drill, repetition, and following the rules? Or is it mostly about combining the two approaches?

CHECK AND APPLY YOUR KNOWLEDGE

1. Describe the development factors of suicide. Which age groups are the most susceptible to suicide?

2. Explain why crime can be viewed as a developmental issue.

3. According to your personal view, what is more important in your educational success: drill and memorization or creative discussion?

Visual Review

```
INTRODUCTION          KEY THEORIES AND        APPLICATIONS
AND CONTEXTS     →     APPROACHES         →
```

The individual's development and socialization depend on the interplay of nature and nurture	Nature has substantial control over the development and aging process	Developmental factors in suicide
In the process of development and socialization, individuals go through developmental stages.	Cultural dichotomies explain the impact of culture on the developing personality	Developmental factors in criminality
The consistency and openness models explain the process of stability and change in personality	Developmental stages have been key features in various theories of individual development	Developmental factors in education
	Piaget's stages of development	
	Vygotsky's zone of proximal development	

Steve Glass/Getty Images

Summary

- Human development—the changes in physical, psychological, and social behavior that individuals experience across the life-span, from conception to their last days.

- Socialization—the process by which an individual becomes a member of a society and takes on its ideas and behaviors.

- Psychologists have long maintained—and it has been discussed in previous chapters—that the individual's development and socialization depend on the interplay of influences involving nature and nurture.

- The general well-being of individuals is measured by the availability of resources, physical and financial security, type of living conditions, quality of education and health care, presence or absence of violence, and a number of other factors—all of which significantly affect the individual's development and socialization.

- Global fertility rates and global migration affect the processes of development and socialization.

- In the process of development and socialization, individuals go through developmental stages, which are definite periods in the individual's life characterized by certain physical, psychological, behavioral, and social characteristics. Contemporary scholarly books on human development distinguish several common stages within the life-span.

- It is generally assumed that early stages of individual development should influence the later ones. Two models—the consistency model and the openness model—attempt to explain the process of stability and change in personality features and their changes. According to the consistency model, most adults acquire (or learn) behaviors and develop stable traits early in life and tend not to change them later. The openness model suggests the opposite: People do constantly change their behaviors and adjust their traits to changing life situations.

- Personality psychologists discuss at least two types of stability (among many others): heterotypic and homotypic.

- Nature has substantial control over the aging process. Personality psychologists learn from life sciences about the important biological foundations affecting personality traits and other stable behavioral and emotional characteristics during the individual's life-span.

- Social scientists as well psychologists generally assume that cultures can be described in terms of cultural dichotomies, such as high- versus low-power distance, high- versus low-uncertainty avoidance, and collectivism versus individualism.

- The psychoanalytic tradition in psychology emphasizes the importance of early childhood experiences in the future development of the adult.

- Kohlberg described six stages of moral development in which children and adults are able to make several types of moral judgments. In brief, people go from lower stages of reasoning, when they prefer to avoid punishment for wrongdoing, to the higher stages, when they choose social contract and then universal principles to guide moral actions.

- The Swiss psychologist Jean Piaget believed that the process of development goes in stages determined by the child's developing brain, skills, and social environment.

- According to Vygotsky's view, a child's development is not a steady process of consistent, uninterrupted transformation and change. Instead, periods of gradual change are followed by rapid transitions, sudden transformations, and crises.

- Vygotsky introduced and developed the concept of zone of proximal development, understood as the difference between a child's

learning progress with help or guidance and the child's learning achievement without the guidance of an adult.

- Studies show that average levels of extroversion—especially the attributes associated with self-confidence and independence—tend to increase with age. Agreeableness and conscientiousness also appear to increase with age, while neuroticism appears to decrease with age. Studies also show that childhood conscientiousness can predict health behaviors of adulthood. This can also have an impact on the person's life expectancy.

- Several applications of theories within the developmental domain can be described in the studies of suicide, criminal behavior, and the approaches to educational practices.

Key Terms

accommodation 317

assimilation 317

collectivism 310

consistency model 306

degeneration 309

developmental stages 303

distress threshold 312

emerging adulthood 305

heterotypic stability 306

homotypic stability 306

human development 300

individualism 310

openness model 306

power distance 310

prenatal period 309

quality of life 301

socialization 300

suppression–facilitation model 311

trolley dilemma 316

uncertainty orientation 310

zone of proximal development 319

Evaluating What You Know

What are the key ideas of the developmental domain in personality psychology?

Describe the main developmental stages.

Explain the consistency and openness models.

What do life sciences teach us about individual development?

What is a cross-cultural approach to individual development?

Explain the views of individual development from Piaget, Kohlberg, and Vygotsky.

Describe the application of the developmental domain to studies of education, criminal behavior, and suicide.

A Bridge to the Next Chapter

Developmental factors certainly have a substantial impact on the individual's personality. First, as individuals, we have a number of genetic features that significantly affect our future development. We inherit a certain temperament, life expectancy, the propensity to be tall or short or skinny or overweight, or the predisposition to have certain psychological problems.

As we know, however, biology is not always our destiny. We live and develop in certain cultural conditions. We are influenced by culture and develop patterns of behavior associated with collectivism or individualism, the acceptance or rejection of power distance, the embrace of certainty or uncertainty, and many other cultural factors. Our society, with its customs and norms—through teachers and parents and recently often media and social networks, as well as a wide variety of other influences—shapes our individualities in a certain way. One of the most intriguing factors in this process is gender, to which will turn in the next chapter.

11

The Gender Domain

"You'll never find a rainbow if you're looking down."

—Charlie Chaplin (1889–1977), actor and director

Learning Objectives

After reading this chapter, you should be able to:

- Discuss the role of the gender domain in the study of personality

- Compare traditional and evolving views of the sexes, of gender, and of sexual orientation in the context of personality psychology

- Identify ways to apply knowledge about personality psychology in the gender domain

Kelsy has finally answered the question that most of us do not even have to ask: *Who am I . . . a boy or a girl?* Kelsy already knew that some people are born in female bodies but feel male inside, and some other people have male bodies but feel female. She also knew the meaning of the words *gay, unisex,* and *transgender.* They have become very common in the English language (although, frankly, some people still have only a superficial view of the meaning of these words). Today, more people speak freely about their true identities and overcome the fear of being condemned and discriminated against for their feelings. Yet Kelsey had a more complicated challenge—a feeling that neither *male* nor *female* categories were appropriate for her self-identity: She felt she was neither a girl nor a boy.

Growing up, Kelsy was always puzzled when she needed to cross the box on application forms that referred to male or female identity. Then there were the small but important choices at school: Which sports teams to play on? Which locker room to use? Which doors of gender-specific bathrooms to push? This struggle with self-perception was not about being straight or gay. This was not about being "boyish" or a "manly" girl. This was a matter of Kelsey being honest with herself about who she is.

Finally, Kelsey decided use a pronoun that felt right when describing herself : *they.*

Source: Hesse, 2014.

The Essence of the Gender Domain

Society traditionally divides individuals into large categories. *Women* and *men* are perhaps the most common categories of all. People usually use these words in their descriptions of others. Most of us think of ourselves as either a woman or a man. The "male" and "female" boxes commonly appear on various forms and surveys. In almost every sphere of our lives, we encounter the *gender* category. Gender has been a very important factor affecting our knowledge of personality (Riger, 2002).

What does the gender domain mean to our study of personality? Given the complexity of the topic, it is not surprising to discover a great variety of views and opinions. We will discuss three main facets of the gender factor: sex, gender, and sexual orientation.

The Sexes and the Intersex

Sex Sex refers to the anatomical and physiological characteristics or features of males and females, the two typically assigned sexes.

In the context of personality, the term **sex** refers to anatomical and physiological characteristics or features of males and females, the two typically assigned sexes. These features include at least four commonly recognized clusters, such as external genitalia (the body's reproductive organs), glands, hormones, and chromosomes. For example, females have a uterus and ovaries, and males have a prostate gland and testicles. These anatomical structures are present, by and large, when an individual is born. By looking at a newborn's external genitalia, a designated person (often a doctor) "pronounces" a newborn either a boy (male) or a girl (female). This act of judgment becomes an official assignment of a sex to a newborn individual. The child's parents or caregivers are expected to accept the assigned sex (these days, many parents choose to learn about the sex of their future baby before the child is born). The child is immediately referred to as "he" or "she."

Photo 11.1 From birth, human beings are typically expected to match the behavior and other standards of the assigned sex. Why is it (or isn't it) important to maintain such standards in the 21st century?

As soon as a certain sex is assigned, people start acting toward the child in accordance with the popular norms and expectations. What is expected and in which ways do they act? Consider a simple question: Would you select a blue or a pink baby blanket for a newborn boy? Consider the names parents give their babies—most are sex-specific. Now try to visualize people whose names are John and Joan. Would most people imagine them as men or women? There are exceptions, of course. In every culture, there are certain names that can be assigned to both sexes, but those names are somewhat rare.

Once a particular sex is assigned, boys and girls often begin wearing gender-specific clothes, usually chosen by the parents. As babies get older, the toys tend to be different, too. Many activities, such as play, are often chosen to match what is considered a typical male or female activity. The growing child and then the mature individual is expected to follow the rules, customs, and perceptions that match (or at least are expected to match) the behavioral and other standards of the assigned sex.

However, this common sex dichotomy (either–or) does not accurately represent reality. Some individuals are born with sexual anatomy or reproductive organs, and often chromosome patterns, that do not fit the typical definition of male or female. This evidence may

TABLE 11.1 ● Traditional and Changing Sex Categories		
Traditional Categories	**New Categories**	
Male, female	*Three*	*Five*
	Female, intersex, male	Female, "leaning" female, neither, "leaning" male, male

be apparent at birth or become so later in life (United Nations [UN] for LGBT Equality, 2015). In other words, sex is not strictly dichotomous, but rather a continuous variable. If this is the case, there should be a combination of sex characteristics, such as anatomical structures, that are not exclusively male or female. The **intersex** category is based on the features that are between distinct male and female characteristics. For example, a person can be born with *ambiguous* outer genitalia—those that do not have the typical appearance that allows a child to be assigned immediately to a particular sex. Other people, even if they were born with certain characteristics assigned to a particular sex, choose a different sex at will and accept a surgical and physiological transformation of the body to achieve the physical appearance of their chosen sex.

In a brief review, scientists and medical doctors these days commonly identify a third category in between the two known sex dichotomies. Moreover, some researchers believe that the third category can be further expanded into subcategories so that there could be at least five sexes: the two traditional ones and three in between (see **Table 11.1**; Fausto-Sterling, 2012).

Gender as a Social Construct

Sex as a category is rooted in biological, physiological, and anatomical factors. **Gender** is a complex set of behavioral, cultural, or psychological features associated with an individual's sex. Gender as a concept has a significant social component: It is the state of being male or female and practicing informally prescribed cultural norms (such as customs), following expectations about what a person should do as a member of a particular sex, and adhering to formal legal rules (the law) that mandate or prohibit particular actions. If gender is a social category, it can be viewed from two gender dimensions: the internal and external. The internal, or psychological, dimension refers to the degree of experiencing being male or female. The external, or social, dimension refers to the roles that society assigns to each sex. These dimensions, of course, are interconnected and actively interact with each other.

Let's look at the internal dimension first. **Gender identity** is an individual's self-determination (or a complex self-reflection) as being male, female, intersex (between male and female), or neither. The opening vignette introduced the "neither" identity. Or, for example, consider **androgyny**—a combination, a coexistence, a blend of both male and female behavioral characteristics, features, and reflections. Studies show that for most of us, a gender identity tends to remain stable after we establish it, yet it can change. Therefore, gender identity is a process rather than a "product." Gender identity can strengthen (when an individual feels stronger about this identity than

Intersex
The features that are between distinct male and female characteristics are referred to as intersex.

Gender
The complex set of behavioral, cultural, or psychological features associated with an individual's sex is a person's gender.

Gender identity
An individual's self-determination (or a complex self-reflection) as being male, female, intersex (between male and female), or neither is called gender identity.

Androgyny
A combination and a coexistence of both male and female behavioral characteristics, features, and reflections is known as androgyny.

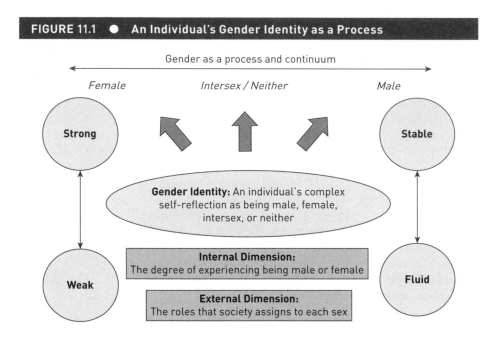

FIGURE 11.1 ● An Individual's Gender Identity as a Process

Gender as a process and continuum

Female   *Intersex / Neither*   *Male*

Strong   **Stable**

Gender Identity: An individual's complex self-reflection as being male, female, intersex, or neither

Internal Dimension: The degree of experiencing being male or female

External Dimension: The roles that society assigns to each sex

Weak   **Fluid**

before), and it may weaken. Although most children refer to self as "I am a boy" or "I am a girl" at a very early age, their understanding or acceptance of the meaning of these words is likely to develop over a significant period. They may never stop evolving; people constantly learn more about gender and gender identity. It may be rediscovered again.

Why does it change or evolve? Many life circumstances influence the ways we identify self: They include physiological factors, our interactions with our parents when we grow up, our experiences with family members, our friendships, or travels—they all matter. Activities such as play or education, exposure to the media, and other life experiences also affect our gender identity in so many ways.

Most individuals develop a specific gender identity that matches their biological sex assigned at birth. However, it is also possible that a person with an assigned sex (a girl, for example) feels differently about the assigned gender identity and roles and develops a different gender (a boy, for example). Some intersex individuals may be raised as a woman or a man but then identify with another gender or none later in life. Also, there can be a strong, core gender identity and a secondary one developing over the core identity (see **Figure 11.1**; UN for LGBT Equality, 2015).

Gender roles
Prescriptions and expectations assigned to genders on the female–male continuum constitute gender roles.

Gender Roles

When an individual learns about or identifies with a particular gender, this process involves understanding, evaluating, and accepting particular patterns of behavior. They are called **gender roles**—prescriptions and expectations assigned to genders on the female–male continuum. These prescriptions and expectations are typically embedded in cultural norms and transmitted from one generation to the next. Ideology, art, and religion play an important role preserving such expectations about gender roles and become embedded into the law. Popular beliefs and everyday customs are also important mediators of the knowledge about gender roles.

Across most cultural groups, two major clusters of gender roles have appeared: masculine (having the qualities attributed to males) and feminine (having the qualities attributed to females). **Masculinity**, traditionally assigned to men, is a general set of features associated with physical strength, decisiveness, and assertiveness. On the other hand, **femininity**, traditionally assigned to women, is a general set of features correlated with beauty, emotionality, and nurture. Notice how imprecise these definitions are. In fact, there is no consensus on how to define these terms. Across cultures and times there was no consistency in what was considered typically masculine and feminine in psychological characteristics, prescribed personality features, or professions. In some cultural settings, gender roles were described as opposing each other, but in others (e.g., Indian philosophies), they were presented and perceived as complementary, adding to each other. Moreover, social prescriptions related to gender roles were changing due to certain political and cultural transformations. The struggle for gender equality has involved gradually eliminating the gaps between gender roles.

Gender roles in history were about the activities the individual should have performed. In traditional cultural settings, women were supposed to be nurturing and caring, while men were supposed to be decisive and physically strong. These prescriptions referred to every area of life, including the family, work, warfare, and education. There were also differences in how social positions and social activities (such as being a warrior or a monk) and occupations (such as being a doctor or a nurse) associated with gender roles. You can easily provide examples from your own experiences.

Contemporary psychology considers gender roles as not exclusively limited to the dichotomous male–female categories. A view that has become increasingly common is that individuals may have many features of masculinity and femininity simultaneously. A person can be physically imposing and dominating (features assigned to masculinity) and at the same time caring and loving (features assigned to femininity). The term **transgender** refers to the roles that do not fit into the traditionally assigned gender dichotomy. Transgender individuals do not identify with distinct, traditional male and female gender roles. About one in every 450 Americans identifies as transgender, according to a 2011 study by the Williams Institute at the UCLA School of Law (Wilson, 2014).

It is critical for psychologists to understand that we all have a choice in how we think of ourselves. This may or may not be based on the type of chromosomes we have or our external genitals or the way we were brought up. Instead, it may be based on how we see and understand the world, other people, and ourselves (Goldberg, 2014).

Sexual Orientation

Being male, female, or transgender, in terms of gender roles, does not necessarily determine our sexuality or sexual orientation. **Sexuality** is the capacity for erotic

Masculinity
Traditionally assigned to men, masculinity is a general set of features associated with physical strength, decisiveness, and assertiveness.

Femininity
Traditionally assigned to women, femininity is a general set of features correlated with beauty, emotionality, and nurture.

Transgender
To be transgender means to feel that one does not fit into the traditionally assigned gender dichotomy, such as male or female.

Sexuality
Sexuality is the capacity for erotic experiences and related behavioral responses.

Sexual orientation
A sexual orientation refers to romantic or sexual attraction to people of a specific sex or gender.

experiences and related behavioral responses. **Sexual orientation** refers to romantic or sexual attraction to people of a specific sex or gender.

Sexual orientation, in most individuals, tends to develop gradually. Although the vast majority of children have a sex assigned to them at birth, and many children have a strong sense of their gender identity, studies show they are not necessarily aware of their sexual orientation. Some children develop this orientation relatively early; some acquire it later in life. Others change it at a certain point in life. For others, sexual orientation is a "work in progress" and remains evolving or undefined throughout their life-spans. Some accept this uncertainty about their sexual orientation. Others struggle with it and may even suffer because of the unsettling challenge of their sexual orientation (Savin-Williams, Joyner, & Rieger, 2012).

Heterosexuality
Heterosexuality is an individual's romantic or sexual attraction to people of opposite sex or gender. In Greek, *heteros* stands for "different" or "other."

Sexual orientation is a continuum. Some people feel asexual. *Asexuality* is the lack of sexual attraction to another person and diminished interest in sexual activity. Asexuality may also be viewed as the person's lack of a sexual orientation. Heterosexuality along with bisexuality and homosexuality are at least three main categories of the continuum of sexual orientation. **Heterosexuality** is an individual's romantic or sexual attraction to people of opposite sex or gender. In Greek, *heteros* means "different" or "other." **Homosexuality** is romantic or sexual attraction between people of the same sex or gender. Bisexuality is romantic or sexual attraction toward both males and females. In Britain, for example, when people were asked to self-identify in terms of their sexual orientation, 72% placed themselves at the completely heterosexual end of the scale, 4% put themselves at the completely homosexual end, and 19% said they are somewhere in between (YouGov, 2015).

Homosexuality
Romantic or sexual attraction between people of the same sex or gender is homosexuality.

In the United States, the term *homosexual* originally carried negative connotations, and it was gradually replaced by *gay* in the 1970s. The terms *gay* and *lesbian* became more common by the end of the 20th century. In more recent years, the term **LGBT** (lesbian/gay/bisexual/transgender) gained popularity; this is an umbrella term for those who are **gender nonconforming**—people whose gender identity or gender expression does not conform to that typically associated with the sex they were assigned at birth. Some who do not identify as either male or female sometimes prefer the term *genderqueer* or *gender-variant* (American Psychological Association [APA], 2015a).

LGBT   LGBT is an acronym for lesbian, gay, bisexual, and transgender.

Gender nonconforming
Individuals whose gender identity or gender expression does not conform to that typically associated with the sex to which they were assigned at birth are referred to as gender nonconforming.

The way we identify ourselves in terms of sex, gender, or sexual orientation influences almost every part of our lives. Society always has paid attention to how individuals acquired sexual identity and expressed their sexual orientation. In a society where gender roles are strictly defined and enforced, people whose behavior differs from such norms have been targeted, isolated, and often prosecuted. These sanctioned sexual orientations were embedded in informal customs, legal rules, and even in politics. There were, of course, societies in which sexual identity and sexual orientation were not strictly defined.

In general, according to the APA (2001), *gender* is cultural and is the term to use when referring to men and women as social groups; *sex* is biological and should be used as a term when the biological distinction is prominent.

CHECK AND APPLY YOUR KNOWLEDGE

1. Define *sex* and *intersex* as categories.

2. What is an individual's gender identity and who (what) determines it?

3. What are gender roles?

4. Explain the term *gender nonconforming* and why you are personally gender-conforming or not. Can it be somewhere in the middle of the spectrum?

Key Approaches to Studying Gender

Traditional Views of the Sexes

A key question for personality psychology is how gender issues influence our knowledge about the individual. Which biological and physiological factors help us in understanding personality features of men, women, and intersex individuals?

For centuries, religion has been a major source of knowledge and prescriptions (authoritative recommendations) about what men and women were supposed to do. Religious prescriptions suggested how men and women were supposed to be treated as members of society. In theory, both sexes were born equal. Judaism, Christianity, and Islam, for example, share the belief that Adam and Eve were the original man and the woman created by God. Eve was created from one of Adam's sides or his ribs so that all people today are descendants from this pair. However, equality wasn't the case in reality.

Science has emphasized for centuries that women and men were born with different natural anatomical features and therefore should be different in their behavior, feelings, outlooks, and personalities. Up until the 20th century, most scientists emphasized the **natural dominance** of men, which was a general assumption about men's physical and biological superiority over women. The natural dominance paradigm focused on men's natural physical strength, firm character, stamina, willpower, intellectual strength, and creativity. As an illustration, the French physician and philosopher La Mettrie wrote that men have solid brains and nerves; therefore, they have stronger personality features and more vigorous minds than women. He wrote that in women, passion is stronger than reason; therefore, women are prone to tenderness, affection, and passing feelings. And, La Mettrie continued, because women generally lack education, men have better opportunities to demonstrate strength of mind and body. Despite men's toughness, they can be very grateful, generous, and constant in friendship. As if attempting to bring some balance to the description of men and women, La Mettrie mentioned women's beauty as their superior feature (La Mettrie, 1748/1994).

Natural dominance
A general assumption about men's physical, biological superiority over women is referred to as the natural dominance of men.

What were the traditional views of the intersex? Descriptions of *intersex* individuals appeared in religious and philosophical traditions dating back many centuries. In ancient Egypt, for example, a male god Hapi represented fertility but had distinct male and female features, including breasts and a large belly, which were both symbols of fertility. In India, the god Ardhanarishvara appeared as half male and half female—like a synergy of two types of spiritual energy. The Navaho people in America believe in Ahsonnutli, a god-creator with male and female features. The ancient Greek philosopher Plato theorized that early in history there were three sexes: male, female, and the third—a union of the two. In ancient myths and Greco-Roman art, Hermaphroditus, the two-sexed child of Aphrodite and Hermes, was portrayed as a female figure with male genitals.

These were, of course, "spiritual" realities. In terms of the realities of human society, intersex individuals are traditionally perceived not only as different but also as odd. But true intersex individuals do live openly in some societies. In India, there is a large category of people known for centuries as the *Hijra*, or the third gender, according to some translations. Some Hijras, born with male sex characteristics, undergo an initiation into the cluster by surgically removing their penis, scrotum, and testicles (Nanda, 1998). In Europe, the 19th-century literary sources contained descriptions of people whom we refer to as intersex today (Kennedy, 1981). However, the social stigma attached to the intersex remains strong. This negative perception is also a source of social discrimination against intersex individuals.

By the early 20th century, an increasing number of doctors and researchers argued that an individual's sex could be determined not only by the external genitalia but also by at least several other biological factors. In some cases, assigning sex to a child became a challenge because some may be born in between the male and female sexes (Dreger, 2000). Another problem was that doctors did not always agree which physical characteristics should be considered as male or female. For example, physicians across countries would agree that *testes* should be considered as male characteristics and *ovaries* as female. In other cases, disagreements were vast: British doctors, for instance, considered facial hair on women as a sign of mental illness (it was assumed that women were not supposed to have masculine features), while in France it was a sign of physical strength (Dreger, 2000).

Early in the 20th century, the developing science, medicine, and experimental psychology fields paid increasing attention to the scientifically proven differences between men and women in terms of their physical characteristics, motor reactions, sensory thresholds, behavioral patterns, and cognitive skills (Dumont, 2010). Scientists in greater numbers were challenging traditional assumptions about the typical men's superior functioning and women's naturally submissive, passive, and nurturing roles.

Evolving Views of the Sexes

Modern studies focus on finding particular physiological, genetic, or evolutionary facts that help to explain sex as a biological category. Contemporary research also supports the view of sex as a continuous variable.

Genetics, Anatomy, and Neurophysiology

Modern genetics (see Chapter 2) has established that females have two of the same kind of sex chromosomes (XX), while males have two distinct sex chromosomes (XY). However, there can be other combinations. Modern science shows that intersex individuals are born with mosaic genetics—some of their cells have XX chromosomes, and some have XY. Genetics research constantly provides new evidence in support of the view that sex is a continuous variable; however, you should remember that in today's society, sex is supposed to be assigned.

Researchers have been identifying particular anatomical brain structures associated with various characteristics of males and females (Kruijver et al., 2000). Studies also identified certain groups of neurons in the hypothalamus that could be related to individuals of the intersex category (Zhou, Hofman, Gooren, & Swaab, 1995). Overall, however, studies show that the human brain can be compared to a dynamic heterogeneous mosaic of different male and female characteristics that should be placed on a continuum. According to research, what is determined as "sex" is influenced by many social and environmental factors unfolding during prenatal and postnatal periods. These "outside" factors influence the brain's structures and specific neuroanatomical types (Joel et al., 2015).

A number of studies over the last couple of decades used various **neuroimaging** methods to demonstrate the differences in responses between men and women. Their analysis is not our goal here, but just to illustrate, some studies showed that women tend to have more neurons relayed to language, hearing, and relational skills compared to men (Brizendine, 2007). Men and women, as groups, showed somewhat different types of responses in the brain related to making moral choices (Jaffee & Hyde, 2000). Females, compared to males, showed increased activity in brain regions associated with caring behavior; males, compared to females, showed increased activity in regions associated with justice-based judgments and behavior (Harenski, Antonenko, Shane, & Kiehl, 2008). Other studies revealed mixed findings, so the discussion of these and other studies continues.

Neuroimaging
Neuroimaging is the use of scanning and other techniques to image (visualize) the structure or function of the nervous system.

As groups, men and women have different physical characteristics. Take height, for example, which is likely to be determined genetically. Overall, globally, men are taller than women. Yet in different parts of the world, the numbers are different. In the United States, for example, the average male is around 5 feet 9 inches, and the average female is 5 feet 4 inches. So women as a group in the United States are shorter than American men but taller than men in Indonesia, whose average height is 5 feet 2 inches. Conversely, women in the Netherlands, whose average height is 5 feet 7 inches, on average, are almost as tall as men in North America.

There are differences between men and women in prevalence of certain illnesses as well. Men have higher rates of autism spectrum disorder (the incidences of autism are 7 times to 10 times greater in boys than in girls), substance abuse, and AIDS. Women have higher rates of breast cancer, Alzheimer's disease, and eating disorders. Although men are stronger than women in throwing velocity and throwing distance, women, globally, on average, live longer than men by about five years.

@

On the companion website, find the links providing additional information about Christine Jorgensen, one of the first individuals to undergo a series of sex-change procedures. Then search the web to find stories about other individuals who underwent a sex change. What kind of problems do these individuals share? Why were they unhappy before the procedure? Were they happy after the surgery? What was the public reaction to their reassignment?

Two comments are important to make here: Some differences are mostly genetic, as in cases of autism spectrum disorder, but physical characteristics and rates for diseases vary significantly across countries and regions. Second, these and other differences are often strongly linked to socioeconomic and social conditions in which people live—chronic poor nutrition, for example, significantly affects body growth and development. Social factors and gender roles often determine what many people do, how they act, take risks, and take care of their bodies and minds.

Evolutionary Theories

Modern evolutionary studies (see Chapter 2) try to identify certain natural mechanisms for explaining the differences between men and women. These studies focus on comparative research and on discussion of natural selection as the main mechanism for determining major sex differences. Several conclusions have been drawn based on this research:

- Evolutionary science does not claim that all behaviors are genetically programmed, but predispositions to acquire them seem to be (Dumont, 2010).
- Evolutionary scientists maintain that sexual selection (the method of selection of a mate) is the strongest factor determining most differences between males and females. Men and women develop certain behavior and "shape" individual features to attract the best possible partners (Geary, 2009; Rusch, Leunissen, & Van Vugt, 2015).
- Children across cultures are raised as boys and girls for a reason, evolutionary scientists claim. The prime reason is survival and preservation of humans as species (Archer, 1996).

How do these conclusions refer to the study and understanding of personality? Evolutionary scientists maintain that women are more likely to be interested in a set of personality traits in men that would secure the future and safety of their children and family. Men tend to be interested in women who display behaviors that are communal, nurturing, and socially oriented. In other words, there must be some evolutionary purpose for men and women to have somewhat different personality features. Men tend to invest more attention to new mates and activities, while women tend give more to parenting. The general difference between men and women is that women naturally tend to act altruistically to show that they can share resources. Alternately, men tend to act heroically or at times greedily to demonstrate that they can protect these resources (Miller, 2000; Rusch et al., 2015).

Societal Practices

Although the differences between males and females can be found on the biological and physiological levels, they are not necessarily significant. Social and environmental factors also shape the behavior of males and females. Human behavior cannot be explained without including psychological mechanisms with cultural and social inputs (Buss, 1996). Social practices continue to influence judgments about an individual's sex.

Globally, with only few exceptions, an intersex person today has to be officially identified as either male or female simply because it is required by tradition and law. In many countries for the last several decades, hormonal treatment and sex change surgery were recommended for those who were born intersex. In Western countries today (as well as in a few other non-Western countries), adults are able to make a decision to change their sex medically, which usually takes several years (Creighton, 2001). To a certain point, gender reassignment is a reversible process, and there are some who change their minds about the procedure (Dreger, 2000; Goldberg, 2014). Yet social norms require and the laws prescribe that a "precise" sex—either male or female—should be given to every individual.

Most studies in psychology so far have focused on similarities and differences among men and women. Research of intersex individuals is still insignificant, but some comparative studies have shown that they do not differ in most characteristics of physical or mental health (Warne et al., 2005).

Traditional Views of Gender

Religion was a major source of human values related to gender. Traditional religions maintained, in general, a contradictory view on gender and gender roles. In theory, men and women were supposed to be equal in the eyes of God, but in reality, they were treated differently. Customs in most countries prescribed women only limited educational choices: elementary education or simple reading-and-writing skills. Women were also expected to play the traditional home-based role of mother and wife. Just a century ago, women were still being strongly cautioned against becoming scientists, engineers, or doctors!

Theoretically, both men and women should practice moderation, self-control, modesty, and chastity. In real life today (and for centuries past), however, women more than men face more serious restrictions and regulations affecting their behavior and individual traits in regard to their clothes, specific behaviors, manners, and even emotional expressions.

In visual arts and literature, **androcentrism**, or placing males or the masculine point of view at the center of a theory or narrative, has always been common. However, written religious traditions contained female images and narratives about women, and there are female saints in Christianity, Islam, and Judaism, as well as female goddesses in Hinduism, even though written religious sources are mostly male (Kinsley, 1986). Science history shows that for centuries scholars believed that prescribed gender roles should exist because they were convenient, customary, and seemingly guaranteed societal stability (Eagly, 1997).

However, during the past 2 to 3 centuries, more philosophers, scientists, and physicians began to understand gender as a social construct. By the 19th century, many believed that although there were some natural differences between men and women, these differences were rooted in societal norms. Furthermore, these norms could

Androcentrism
Androcentrism occurs with placing males or the masculine point of view at the center of a theory or narrative.

change. The popular English philosopher John Stuart Mill (1806–1873) was partic-ularly admired among progressive-minded scholars. Mill's (1869/2010) historic essay *On the Subjection of Women* advocated gender equality, claiming that the differences between men and women were largely the product of social customs and should be overcome.

Ambivalent Prejudice

Many influential scientists, psychologists, and psychiatrists early in the 20th cen-tury accepted the view that women should be equal to men. Seventy and 80 years ago, anthropologists such as Margaret Mead, psychologists such as Lev Vygotsky, and behaviorists such as John Watson all claimed that the socialization practices pre-scribed particular roles to boys and girls to follow were inaccurate. The American psychologist Leta Hollingworth was among the first to find evidence that women's performance on cognitive, perceptual, and motor tasks was consistently similar to that of males (Shiraev, 2015).

Masculine protest
A masculine protest is a psychological reaction of opposing male dominance.

However, women were still viewed as lesser than men. Sigmund Freud, for exam-ple, believed in women's anatomical and psychological inferiority compared to men. Alfred Adler wrote about women's **masculine protest**—a psychological reaction of opposing male dominance. He supported gender equality but was skeptical of the mas-culine protest because it challenged women's natural roles as mothers and caregivers (Dumont, 2010). The Austrian American psychologist and therapist Helene Deutsch believed that women should abandon the traditional roles of mothers and wives, yet she also believed that many women were not ready for this because they would encounter significant psychological difficulties in the process (Deutsch, 1944, 1945).

Gender Discrimination in Psychology

Early in the 20th century and especially in the 1900s, many experimental psychol-ogists in the United States shared the view that only a specially selected and trained group of highly skilled observers could perform the collection and compilation of scientific data in psychological labs—in other words, only trained professionals could conduct scientific observations in strictly controlled conditions of an experiment. Who could argue about the necessity of professional training? The problem was that these trained professionals were expected to be men. What was the logic behind this assumption? Successful researchers were expected to be scrupulous and care-ful observers, and they were not supposed to show any emotion while conducting research. Women were considered unfit as researchers because at that time many thought they were emotionally unstable and overly sentimental (Keller, 1985). Some male experimental psychologists even stated that women should play only secondary, subsidiary roles in psychological research because of their involvement in relation-ships and their commitment to their families and children. A better role for a woman was research assistant, not principal investigator (Noon, 2004). As a result of these beliefs, scores of skilled women were underestimated, overlooked for promotion, or simply ignored.

Functional Inequality

In the first half of the 20th century, many social scientists described gender inequality as **functional inequality**. According to this concept, a person was predisposed to perform a certain function in society. Men were expected to perform mostly instrumental functions, which involved physical work, protection, hunting, and construction. Society assigned expressive functions to women, which involved managing interpersonal conflicts, providing care, educating the young, and so forth. These role differences have created different expectations about what women and men should do. Different expectations placed men and women in different educational and economic sectors and even prescribed behaviors and skills to men and women (Parsons & Bales, 1956).

After the 1950s, more studies focused on gender similarities. They showed the complex interaction between biological and social factors that shape male and female behavior and experience.

Evolving Views of Gender

Gender Studies

Contemporary **gender studies** is a multidisciplinary field dedicated to studying gender and a wide range of gender-related issues. This field has made a significant contribution to personality psychology as a great discussion is taking place about the mechanisms of social construction of gender. Gender is now commonly perceived as a continuum—there is no absolute, invariable "maleness" or masculinity and "femaleness" or femininity in individuals (Rothblatt, 2011a). If gender is a social construct, it is clear that men and women may be different due to different socialization practices and social norms. How significant are such differences? Are there "male" and "female" personalities?

Feminism

One of the most influential sources of gender studies has been feminism, which originated in political and social sciences. **Feminism** is the view that women should have equal rights and opportunities with men, and global changes are needed to achieve social justice (Hirschman, 2010). At least three points are relevant to personality psychology.

First, feminists reject the notion of a "female brain," or significant inborn and physiological changes that distinguish women from men. Second, there are gender differences because, historically, most important positions of power have gone to men, and through them men created customs, laws, and policies that systematically discriminated against women and thus satisfied men's needs to dominate and possess. Indeed, even still today, more than 90% of the world's heads of government are men (outside Western countries, women seldom play a significant role in the positions of power). Third, feminists say, most customs of today's society are rooted in a masculine culture that accepted war and violence rather than consensus and peace (Cohn,

Functional inequality
Functional inequality refers to a concept according to which men and women have to perform a certain function in society. Men were expected to perform mostly instrumental functions, but society assigned expressive functions to women. These role differences have created different expectations about what women and men should do.

Gender studies
Gender studies encompasses the multidisciplinary field dedicated to studying gender and a wide range of gender-related issues.

Feminism
Feminism is the view that women do not have equal rights and opportunities with men, and global changes are needed to achieve social justice.

1987). For centuries, male-dominated societies considered wars essential for conquering, achieving glory, testing patriotism, and dominating the weak. Femininity was little more than "ritualized submission" (Goldberg, 2014), and women's propensity for peace and constructive cooperation were not fully taken into consideration (Ayman & Korabik, 2010).

In modern society, women have gained more power, and 23% of married American women with children now outearn their husbands, up from 4% in 1960. Few women in developed countries now need a man's support to raise a family (Carbone & Cahn, 2013). Feminist scholars continue to argue that women should have the freedom and opportunities to make their own choices in everyday life (Snyder-Hall, 2010).

Comparative Research

In the past 20 years, a significant number of studies examined similarities and differences between men and women and found noteworthy as well as inconsistent or insignificant variations. For example, studies of violent behavior show that violent behavior across the globe is more prevalent in men than it is in women: Young boys are referred to social workers more often than girls (Hyde, 2005); boys are more disruptive at school (Organisation for Economic Co-Operation and Development [OECD], 2011); globally, men are almost 4 times more likely to be murder victims than women. In addition, compared with women, twice as many men commit suicide (United Nations Office on Drugs and Crime [UNODC], 2015; WHO, 2015). Most telling, in America in the 21st century, men have committed approximately 90% of murders and constitute almost 90% of the prison population.

To offer contrast, in terms of higher education women outnumber men as university students in every region except South Asia and sub-Saharan Africa. In the most economically developed countries (such as the United States, Canada, France, or Germany), women earn 58% of college degrees, and this number is on the rise. In the United States, four women graduate from college for every three men (Birger, 2015). At school, boys read somewhat less and do less homework than girls (OECD, 2011). Teenage boys in developed countries are 50% more likely than girls to fail in three basic school subjects, namely, math, reading, and science. Globally among low-achievers in reading, math, and science, boys consistently outnumber girls in poor achievement. More boys than girls are failing at school. In Sweden, for example, among 15-year-olds, 18% of boys were underachievers compared to only 11% of girls; in the United States, the ratio was 15:9 (OECD, 2011). However, considered as groups, girls are somewhat better in verbal reasoning, while boys, as a group, tend to be better in math.

Personality research has systematically found gender differences in two of the three dimensions of the Eysenck model: neuroticism and psychoticism (Escorial, 2007). Studies also consistently show that in the context of the Big Five theory, women tend to produce higher scores than men on extroversion, agreeableness, and neuroticism (Weisberg, DeYoung, & Hirsh, 2011).

Cross-cultural research obtained on samples from more than 25 countries reveals an important finding: The differences between male groups and female groups across

TABLE 11.2 ● A Comparative Summary of Gender Differences in Personality Traits		
Dimensions	**Women Compared to Men**	**Men Compared to Women**
Extroversion	Higher scores	Lower scores
Agreeableness	Higher scores	Lower scores
Neuroticism	Higher scores	Lower scores
Conscientiousness	Lower scores	Higher scores
Openness	No differences	No differences
Neuroticism	Higher scores	Lower scores
Psychoticism	Lower scores	Higher scores

the studied countries were small; however, the variations within both groups were significant and consistent with gender perceptions. Women's scores, compared to men's scores, were somewhat higher in neuroticism, agreeableness, warmth, and openness to feelings, whereas men were higher in assertiveness and openness to ideas (see **Table 11.2**; Costa, Terracciano, & McCrae, 2001).

How can we explain some gender differences obtained in psychological studies? Consider two types of answers discussed by researchers.

The Variability Hypothesis

The *variability hypothesis* is a view that men and women are likely to be similar on many behavioral and psychological measures; nevertheless, men's scores tend to group around the opposite ends of the spectrum. For example, at school there are more boys than girls with extremely high and extremely low grades and test scores (Hyde, 2005). In other words, men are supposed to have a wider range of talents as well as weaknesses and defects than women. Although this hypothesis was tested, the outcomes were inconclusive. To complicate the results, not all gender differences appear equal—some of them are significant and others are not (Hyde & Plant, 1995). In general, again, behavioral and psychological differences within the gender are in most cases far greater than differences between the gender groups.

The Gender Similarities Hypothesis

From the viewpoint of the gender similarities hypothesis, males and females are alike on most—but not all—psychological variables. The early research comes in publications of Eleanor Maccoby and Carol Jacklin (1974). Their most influential work, *The Psychology of Sex Differences*, is based on the review of more than 2,000 studies of gender differences, including memory, aptitudes, personality features, and social behavior. They found that there were differences between men and women on verbal skills, visual spatial ability, math skills, and aggressive behavior. However, the book challenged several common assumptions related to personality, such as girls have lower self-esteem compared to boys; men are less suggestible than women; men do better on difficult cognitive tasks, while women do fine on simple ones; and women have lower achievement motivation than men (Maccoby & Jacklin, 1974). These assumptions were criticized and even dismissed, but the debates about low self-esteem in girls compared to boys has continued for decades later (Hyde, 2005; Pipher, 1994).

Recent research, however, including meta-analysis, gives more support for the gender similarities hypothesis. Men and women as groups may be slightly different in motor skills or aggression. However, other gender differences vary substantially in magnitude at different ages and are based on the context in which measurements occur. For example, there are small gender differences in computational skills (favoring girls) in elementary and middle school, but there are no gender differences in computation in higher grades. Also, there were small gender differences favoring males in solving complex problems, yet this difference surfaces in high school and does not show up in earlier years (Hyde, 2005). Testing conditions matter, too. When they believe that a math test is designed to show gender differences, women underperform (Spencer, Steele, & Quinn, 1999). Many parents as well as teachers expect that boys, compared to girls, should be better at math, thus the adults often overlook many mathematically talented girls. Parents have lower expectations for their daughters' math success than for their sons' (Hyde, 2005).

In the end, men and women are not that different psychologically (Hyde, 2005; Hyde, Lindberg, Linn, Ellis, & Williams, 2008). In part, the beliefs about gender differences were supported by popular stereotypes about female "emotionality," male "assertiveness," and so on. Just remember that stereotypes change with time, and so do social realities. Remember the discussion earlier in the chapter about the difficulties women would have faced 100 years ago as psychology researchers? In 1950, only 15% of all doctoral degrees in psychology were awarded to women. By 1960, the number had risen to just 18%. Yet in the 1970s, the number of women earning doctorates in psychology began to steadily increase, and by the early 1980s, this number had increased dramatically: For the first time in history, the proportion of women doctoral recipients was equal to men. If this trend continues, by 2020 women will receive more than 70% of the doctoral degrees in psychology earned in North America (Stewart, 2009).

Evolving Views on Gender Roles

Views on masculinity and femininity are also changing. Earlier in the chapter, we discussed *masculinity* and *femininity* and how imprecise the definitions of these terms are. Modern developments add more facts and scientific knowledge about the evolving gender roles and the personality and behavioral features associated with these categories. Traditionally, in the past, men were expected to embrace masculinity—that is, to be physically resilient, tough, emotionless, confident, and ambitions. Masculinity was about being heterosexual and also about avoiding femininity at all costs (Levant & Kopecky, 1995). Femininity, on the other hand, was traditionally linked to emotionality, compassion, gentleness, and nurture. It was also about being heterosexual, or attracted to men (Brownmiller, 1985). Although there were some historic and cultural variations, they were few and far between (Shiraev & Levy, 2013).

In which ways are views of masculinity and femininity changing? First, modern global society has become increasingly less demanding about the gender roles that boys and girls and men and women are expected to follow. The perceptions seem to be shifting from labeling human beings who do not follow the prescribed gender roles as *womanly men* or *manly women* to new perceptions that focus less on gender but more on the unique individuality of them.

Studies from some years back showed that many people maintained particular expectations about where men and women were supposed to work, according to the standard gender roles (Eagly, 1997). Today, it appears that women tend to increasingly abandon these stereotypes: They adapt, adjust, and learn new professions better than men do. More women study for and obtain degrees and places in professions that were stereotypically "male." Unfortunately, men have not embraced so-called female professions as eagerly. Women also appear to better embrace new job opportunities. Of the 30 occupations expected to grow fastest in America in the coming years, women dominate 20 of them, including nursing, accounting, child care, and food preparation (Rosin, 2013).

Second, gender roles themselves became more fluid. The term **metrosexual** appeared in the popular literature and then in sociological and psychological research. It means a style of thinking and behavior in men who, contrary to the prescriptions of traditional gender roles, tend to develop and display some feminine features and habits, especially related to appearance, clothes, and grooming (Bais, 2012). Only a few studies have been done; for example, a study in Thailand of urban men who identified themselves as metrosexual showed that they scored higher than average men on traditional femininity and also had high scores for appearance-related variables, such as watching the quality of their body and everyday appearance (Lertwannawit & Gulid, 2010). Metrosexual men can be heterosexual, bisexual, or gay (although most use the term *metrosexual* in reference to heterosexual men). There is a debate in popular sources about whether women can be metrosexual, too, by adopting some traditional masculine features and still paying attention to appearance and romance. In some ways, *metrosexuality* is about avoiding strict standards of gender roles (Simpson & Hagood, 2010).

Third, in the era of global changes, there is an inevitable resistance coming from the supporters of traditional values and gender roles. The rejection of nontraditional roles and bias and discrimination against individuals who do not fit into the traditional standards (under the motto "Men should be men, and women should be women") are likely to continue in some parts of the world and in some cultural groups.

Metrosexual
Metrosexual refers to the style of thinking and behavior in men who, contrary to the prescriptions of traditional gender roles, tend to develop and display some feminine features and habits, especially related to appearance, clothes, and grooming.

CHECK AND APPLY YOUR KNOWLEDGE

1. Explain the natural dominance of the male paradigm.
2. What are the key differences between the traditional and evolving views of the sexes?
3. What is androcentrism?
4. Explain ambivalent prejudice.
5. What are the main assumptions of feminism?
6. Explain the variability hypothesis.
7. Explain the gender similarities hypothesis.

Traditional Views of Sexual Orientation

As in the case of gender, religion throughout the ages has remained a key source of human values (see Chapter 1) about an individual's sexual orientation. Over the past few centuries, most major world religions maintained a strict moral position on what type of sexual orientation individuals should have. With only few exceptions, religion portrayed a heterosexual person as a norm. Any deviation from heterosexuality was considered immoral and thus punishable. Women customarily faced more restrictions related to sexuality and sexual orientation than men. Social customs and laws prosecuted individuals who were accused of homosexual behavior (see **Table 11.3**).

Traditional views on sexual orientation influence scientists. Consider an example. Austro German psychiatrist Richard von Krafft-Ebbing (1840–1902) provided one of the earliest and most detailed scientific analyses of individual sexuality in his famous book *Psychopathia Sexualis* (1886). He maintained a traditional view, according to which heterosexuality was normal, and homosexuality was pathological.

TABLE 11.3 ● Traditional Cultural and Legal Views of Sexual Orientation				
Sexual Orientation	**Legal Status**	**Moral Status**	**Medical Status**	**Social View**
Heterosexual	Legal	Acceptable within marriage	Normal	Normal
Nonheterosexual (homosexual or bisexual)	Illegal, criminal	Unacceptable	Abnormal	Prejudiced, discriminated against

Photo 11.2 Despite significant changes in attitudes, the LGBT community faces significant prejudice around the world. Homosexuality remains criminalized in many countries. What do you think motivates some people to maintain such strict views of gender or sexual orientation?

© iStockphoto.com/Bastiaan Slabbers

In medical research and psychiatric practice, people who had homosexual feelings were assumed to be ill and, therefore, in need of treatment or even punishment (Laqueur, 2004). Most early psychologists until the middle of the 20th century maintained a generally negative view of homosexuality and bisexuality and considered it a form of pathology or even disability. Individuals prone to homosexual and bisexual behavior were expected to receive treatment until they "recovered." In the Soviet Union until the early 1990s, homosexuality was considered a crime punishable by a lengthy prison term. Today, in some countries such as Iran, openly gay and lesbian individuals can be sentenced to death because homosexuality is considered a major offence against religion.

An Evolution of Legal Knowledge

The evolution of views of homosexuality and gays and lesbians is a powerful example of how popular beliefs, science, legal rulings, and ideology have been evolving in the United States over the past 7 decades. Most people's views of gays and lesbians changed along with changing scientific views and legal rulings. Seventy years ago, New York had laws against cross-dressing, onstage depictions of gays, and gatherings of gays in clubs. In the 1930s, the Motion Picture Production Code banned any discussion of or allusion to homosexual behavior. Leading psychiatrists commonly labeled homosexuals as *sexual psychopaths*. President Dwight Eisenhower signed Executive Order 10450, which banned, among other things, "sexual perversion" in government and banned lesbians and gays from working in the federal government. About 50 years ago, homosexual acts were illegal in every state but Illinois. There were no openly gay political candidates or public officials. Even in the liberal press, homosexuality was attacked (Ross, 2012). The popular 1969 bestseller *Everything You Always Wanted to Know About Sex (But Were Afraid to Ask)* said that homosexuality was fixable and curable as long as people asked a psychiatrist to help.

Yet the clinical perceptions and legal ruling were changing. The classification of homosexuality as a mental disorder was scrapped in 1973 from psychiatric manuals in the United States, and by the early 1980s, most states had dropped anti-gay laws. Some public figures, including politicians and celebrities, began openly discussing their sexual identity. Other countries were making changes, too—Russia officially stopped imprisoning gays in the late 1980s. In the 21st century, scores of countries, including the United States, recognized same-sex marriages.

Globally, people do not view homosexuality the same way they treat heterosexual behavior. In a global sample of 40 countries, 59% viewed homosexuality as unacceptable, and only 20% viewed it as acceptable (Pew, 2014). The changes in attitudes are slow. In most African states, homosexuality is still illegal. Russia, for example, recently has adopted a new harsh anti-gay law that limits both printed and online discussion of homosexuality. In some countries, being openly gay and lesbian is punishable by death (Halperin, 2012; Ross, 2012; Warner, 2000).

Evolving Views of Sexual Orientation

Several major developments took place in the 20th century that significantly changed scientific views of sexual orientation. Empirical research was one such development. In the first half of the 20th century, most studies of sexual orientation were conducted within psychiatry and primarily focused on psychopathology. The research samples involved a few individuals, usually patients. The publication of Alfred Kinsey's (1894–1956) *Sexual Behavior in the Human Male* (1948/1998) and later *Sexual Behavior in the Human Female* (1953/1998) were significant developments partly because they were based on large samples. Kinsey, an American physician, and his colleagues believed that humans were not strictly "heterosexual" and "homosexual." Based on the interviews, Kinsey described several types of sexual orientation: those who identified themselves as exclusively heterosexual with no experience with or desire for sexual activity with people of the same sex; those who identified themselves as exclusively homosexual; and those who would identify themselves as bisexual, with varying levels of desire for sexual activity with either sex (Kinsey, 1948/1998). More studies showed that sexual orientation is a continuum with several orientations that may be present in one individual, evolving over time (Sell, 1997). Research also showed that people are not necessarily "stuck" in either of the described groups or categories—although most people do not change their sexual orientation, some evolve during their lives (Savin-Williams et al., 2012). In other words, some individuals are sexually "fluid," and sexual fluidity can be recognized as a kind of sexual orientation (see **Figure 11.2**; Diamond, 2008, 2009).

Debates continue about the most significant factors that influence an individual's sexual orientation. Many studies maintain that sexual orientation, at least to some

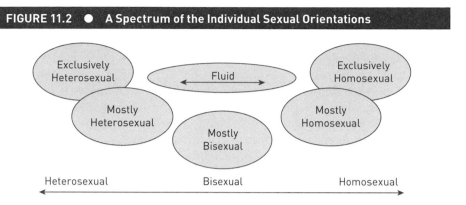

FIGURE 11.2 ●   A Spectrum of the Individual Sexual Orientations

degree, has biological causes, as classical studies of the British-born researcher Simon LeVay showed (1991, 1993). The degree of this connection is further discussed in various studies. Researchers, for example, found that if an identical twin is gay, there is about a 20% chance that the sibling will have the same sexual orientation. That percentage is more than random, but it is lower than expected for two people with the same genetic code (Kremer, 2014). Gay men tend to have more gay brothers, and lesbians tend to have more lesbian sisters than their heterosexual counterparts (Wilson & Rahman, 2008).

Science, however, does not confirm that homosexuality is exclusively or predominantly genetic. Moreover, it is still unclear whether or not the genetic factors and other biological mechanisms for determining male and female sexual orientation are similar (Jeffreys, 2003; Kremer, 2014). Overall, studies have not revealed a clear genetic cause for being gay, lesbian, bisexual, or fluid. Sexuality and sexual behavior are under the control of a complex set of centers in the brain and are certainly shaped by a person's social experiences (LeVay, 2010).

This means that many social and cultural factors play a significant role, too. Homosexual men, for example, tend to be later-born children in respect to their brothers. A similar, yet less strong pattern is found for women (Jones & Blanchard, 1998). Socialization experiences and societal customs play a role, too. Studies show that male participants report more sexual behavior (masturbation, pornography use, and casual sex) and more permissive attitudes (for example, about casual sex) compared to female participants. The gender difference in reported sexual satisfaction is insignificant (Hyde, 2005). Contemporary comparative studies show that, consistent with the gender similarities hypothesis (see earlier in this chapter), most gender differences related to attitudes about sex and sexual behavior are small, and gender differences related to sexuality change over time (Petersen & Hyde, 2010).

Transvestism, Cross-Dressing, or . . . ?

This short case should illustrate the evolution of the individual's sexual orientation and behavior. Magnus Hirschfeld, a German physician, published the first academic study of transvestism in 1910. In the book *Die Transvestiten*, he described the desire and the practice of some individuals (men more often than women) to dress in the clothes of the opposite sex (Hirschfeld, 1910/1991). At the time of the publication, European countries condemned and outlawed cross-dressing. In Germany, for example, people who wanted to cross-dress (mostly men wanting to wear women's clothes) had to apply to the police departments for special permissions (Benjamin, 1966). Doctors considered transvestism as a type of pathological, attention-seeking kind of homosexuality, which was viewed as mental illness. Hirschfeld rejected these views more than 100 years ago. He showed that not only gays and lesbians but also straight individuals could choose transvestism. And it was not a flamboyant act of a capricious individual. For many, cross-dressing was a normal expression of their true personality and individuality. In his publications and lectures, Hirschfeld appeared as an active advocate for equality for gays and lesbians; he fought widespread prejudice and discrimination against them (1910/1991).

More than a century after Hirschfeld's initial publication, prejudice toward cross-dressing still has not disappeared. Some people continue to use the label *cross-dresser* and attach it to individuals as if cross-dressing was a personality type (the same way some people use the labels *criminal* or *mentally ill* to describe someone's entire personality). Cross-dressing has many underlying causes. To some who do it, cross-dressing is an expression of their gender identity. To others, cross-dressing is rooted in their histrionic tendencies (see Chapter 12) and the desire to impress, surprise, and even to shock. Some males cross-dress because they have erotic feelings at the thought of oneself as female, which is called *autogynephilia* (Blanchard, 1989; Goldberg, 2014). Yet to others, the desire to wear particular clothes is not necessarily sexual—they simply admire the opposite sex and want to imitate their behavior. It is important to stress that clinical psychologists and psychiatrists today recognize the term **transvestic fetishism** as a disorder: a condition in which an individual's sexual fantasies, urges, or behaviors that involve cross-dressing also cause clinically significant distress or impairment in social, occupational, or other important areas of functioning.

Transvestic fetishism
A condition in which an individual's sexual fantasies, urges, or behaviors involve cross-dressing, transvestic fetishism also causes clinically significant distress or impairment in social, occupational, or other important areas of function.

CHECK AND APPLY YOUR KNOWLEDGE

1. Behavior considered normal, abnormal, illegal, or acceptable has changed throughout history. This probably means that some of today's definitions of *normal* and *abnormal* in our behavior may no longer be valid a few years from now. Which types of behavior (if any) that we consider abnormal (or pathological) today do you think future generations will consider acceptable or even normal? Explain your view.

2. Consider a woman wearing her brother's T-shirt for a workout and a man wearing his sister's leggings for the same workout. What kind of comments can they both expect behind their backs at the gym? How would you resound to these comments if you heard them?

Applying the Gender Domain

LGBT Psychology

A modern branch of psychology that studies and assists individuals whose orientation is transgender or gender-variant, LGBT psychology is a theoretical and applied field that is gaining support and recognition globally. People who identify with LGBT may have many concerns and challenges for which they seek advice and help.

Many people who identify as transgender have to deal with significant psychological challenges. The San Francisco Unified School District, for example, surveyed middle school children in 2011 and discovered that 50% of transgender kids had attempted suicide (for a wide range of psychological reasons), compared with 6% of straight youth (Wilson, 2014). A 2015 study showed that transsexual youth had a twofold to threefold increased risk of psychological problems, including mood and anxiety disorders, as well as suicide attempts (Reisner et al., 2015).

Another problem that needs recognition and action is the ongoing stigmatization, discrimination, and even open hostility against individuals who are gay, lesbian, transgender, or gender-variant. **Homophobia** is aversion to homosexuality and LGBT individuals. **Biphobia** is aversion toward bisexuality and bisexual people as a social group or as individuals. People of any sexual orientation can experience such feelings of aversion. Biphobia and homophobia are often based on negative stereotypes or irrational fear. In many countries, as we know, homophobia and biphobia are incorporated into the law. People can face significant prison terms for speaking openly on

Homophobia
Homophobia is an aversion to homosexuality and gays, lesbians, bisexual, and gender-variant individuals.

Biphobia
The aversion toward bisexuality and bisexual people as a social group or as individuals is biphobia.

Photo 11.3 Many people still have stereotypical expectations about "male" and "female" professions. Name some of these stereotypes. What can be done to reduce them?

© iStockphoto.com/Robert Carner

behalf of the LGBT community, defending their rights, or just discussing intersex or transgender issues.

True, there are plenty of legal and political issues around the globe related to sex and gender, but public awareness, which can lead to significant social action, is necessary to induce political and social change.

Reducing Gender Stereotypes

Do human names have anything to do with the destructive power of hurricanes? Apparently, they do. The World Meteorological Organization assigns a name to every hurricane: Katrina, Marco, Sandy, Omar, and so on. A study published in the *Proceedings of the National Academy of Sciences* examined 92 most recent hurricanes that made landfall in the United States; it showed that hurricanes with women's names seem to have killed more people than did those with men's names. Why is that? The researchers came to the conclusion that some people do not take hurricanes with women's names as seriously as they take those with men's. As a result of this biased perception, some people tend to act carelessly. They assume that a hurricane named after a woman is not supposed to be that destructive (Jung, Shavitt, Viswanathan, & Hilbe, 2014).

Such biased assumptions are called stereotypes. They are categorical expectations that all members of a given group have particular traits or features. Stereotypes tend to be resistant to change—even when they are fraught with errors. People tend to overlook or reject valid information when it is not consistent with their stereotypes. Propensity to stereotype is one of the most fundamental and pervasive of all human psychological activities. Stereotypes are a form of biased thinking and result in us anticipating what another person will do because we expect this behavior.

In your daily encounters, you can apply the three following strategies to help in overcoming gender stereotypes:

- **Be aware.** Try to monitor the extent to which your gender stereotypes (based on prior beliefs, knowledge, and expectancies) can affect your current experience, impressions, and perceptions. Try to become as aware of your own and other people's stereotypes. Awareness of them will be the first step to increase your ability to modify them.
- **Look for multiple causes.** When you explain gender differences, look for multiple factors that may either explain the differences or show that they are not that significant. Why do girls tend to earn better grades in school than boys? Why are men still far more likely than women to earn degrees in the fields of science, technology, engineering, and mathematics? And why are men on average more likely to be injured in accidents and fights than women (Geary, 2009)?
- **Promote new perceptions.** Reducing gender stereotypes is only a first step in applying your knowledge. The task is to form more accurate perceptions based on facts, including sound psychological research. It is true that in North America more men than women earn doctorate degrees in physics. Does this mean that women are not so great in advanced studies? No. At least half of doctorate degrees in molecular biology and neuroscience are awarded to women. True,

there are more men getting graduate degrees in economics and philosophy, but women get more doctorate degrees in history and psychology (Leslie, Cimpian, Meyer, & Freeland, 2015).

Overcoming Sexism

A vivid case in point of sexism is provided by Dawes (1994), who tells of an incident involving flagrant gender bias in decision-making. The dean of a major medical school, perplexed as to why his institution was unsuccessful in its attempts to recruit female students, asked a colleague of Dawes to investigate the problem. What emerged was striking: One of the interviewers had been rating applicants with respect to their "emotional maturity," "seriousness of interest in medicine," and "neuroticism"; as it turned out, the vast majority of females did not receive positive evaluations on any of his criteria. Specifically, whenever the woman was not married, he judged her to be "immature." When she was married, he concluded that she was "not sufficiently interested in medicine." And when she was divorced? "Neurotic," of course. On the bright side, this example was shared more than 20 years ago, and norms and practices have changed since then. Or have they?

Sexism is prejudice resulting in discrimination based on the views of sex or gender, especially against women and girls. Sexism is often associated with the belief that one sex is superior to or more valuable than another one. Sexism imposes limits on what men and women can and should do. For years, psychologists drew attention to sexism to raise awareness about the oppression of girls and women. Later, sexism as a concept was expanded to include awareness of the discrimination against *any* sex, including men/boys and intersexual/transgender individuals.

Learning about sexism is about gaining professional knowledge and good citizenship skills. Sexism has many forms. It can be open or hostile—think of a person who states that women are incompetent and inferior to men to justify a certain decision, such as hiring or firing a woman. Sexism can also be hidden and disguised (Glick & Fiske, 1997). For example, someone may state that "women are not inferior to men, but they are weak and unprotected; therefore, they need additional help." Sexism incorporates stereotypical statements that explain or prescribe particular behaviors for the entire group.

Sexism
The prejudice and resulting discrimination based on the views of sex or gender, especially against women and girls, is known as sexism.

Visual Review

INTRODUCTION AND CONTEXTS	KEY THEORIES AND APPROACHES	APPLICATIONS
Sex refers to anatomical and physiological characteristics that determine a person's sex category	Traditional views consider a person's sex as a dichotomous category; modern views emphasize its continuity	Counseling and helping the LGBT community with psychological issues
Gender is a complex set of behavioral, cultural, or psychological features associated with an individual's sex	Traditional views on gender tend to be sexist and androgenic; modern views consider a person's gender as a continuum	Reducing gender stereotypes
Gender identity as well as sexual orientation may remain constant or may change, strengthen, or weaken throughout an individual's life	Traditional views consider sexual orientation as strictly attached to each sex and heterosexuality as a norm; modern views see sexual orientation as fluid	Overcoming sexism

D. Sharon Pruitt Pink Sherbet Photography/Moment/Getty Images

Summary

- The term *sex* refers to anatomical and physiological characteristics or features of males and females, the two typically assigned sexes. These features include at least four commonly recognized clusters, such as external genitalia (the body's reproductive organs), glands, hormones, and chromosomes. The intersex category is based on the features that are between distinct male and female characteristics.

- Gender is a complex set of behavioral, cultural, or psychological features associated with an individual's sex. Gender identity is an individual's self-determination (or a complex self-reflection) as being male, female, intersex (between male and female), or neither.

- Gender roles are prescriptions and expectations assigned to genders on the female–male continuum. These prescriptions and expectations are typically embedded in cultural norms and transmitted from one generation to the next. Ideology, art, and religion play an important role in preserving such expectations about gender roles. Masculinity, traditionally assigned to men, is a general set of features associated with physical strength, decisiveness, and assertiveness. Femininity, traditionally assigned to women, is a general set of features correlated with beauty, emotionality, and nurture.

- Sexual orientation, in most individuals, tends to develop gradually. Although the vast majority of children have a sex assigned to them at birth and many children have a strong sense of their gender identity, they are, as studies show, not necessarily always aware of their sexual orientation. Some children develop this orientation relatively early; some acquire it later in life.

- LGBT stands for lesbian, gay, bisexual, and transgender. This is an umbrella term for people who can be called gender nonconforming—that is, those whose gender identity or gender expression does not conform to the one typically associated with the sex to which they were assigned at birth. Some who do not identify as either *male* or *female* sometimes prefer the term *genderqueer* or *gender-variant.*

- For centuries, science emphasized that women and men were born with different natural anatomical features and therefore should be different in their behavior, feelings, outlooks, and personalities. Modern studies focus on finding particular physiological, genetic, or evolutionary facts that help explain sex as a biological category. Contemporary research also supports the view that sex is a continuous variable.

- Human behavior cannot be explained by biological factors alone without including psychological mechanisms with cultural and social inputs. Social practices continue to influence judgments about an individual's sex.

- Religion was a major source of value-based knowledge about gender. Traditional religions maintained, in general, a contradictory view of gender and gender roles. In theory, men and women were supposed to be equal in the eyes of God. In reality, they were treated differently. Traditionally, many influential scientists, psychologists, and psychiatrists early in the 20th century accepted the ambivalent view that (1) women *should* be equal to men; (2) but they are not, and there is a justifiable reason for that.

- Contemporary gender studies is a multidisciplinary field dedicated to the study of gender and a wide range of gender-related issues. Gender studies has many roots and sources. One of the most influential has been feminism, originated in political and social sciences.

- In the past 20 years, a significant number of studies examined similarities and differences between men and women and found both major and insignificant differences, as well as inconsistencies.

- The variability hypothesis and the gender similarities hypothesis attract significant research and discussion.

- Over the past few centuries, most major world religions maintained a strict moral position on what type of sexual orientation individuals should have. With only a few exceptions, religion as well as traditional science portrayed a heterosexual person as a norm. From the beginning of the 20th century, scientific knowledge related to sexual orientation has been changing.

- Gender stereotypes are categorical expectations that all members of a given group have particular traits or features. Sexism is prejudice and results in discrimination based on the views of sex or gender.

- LGBT psychology is a theoretical and applied field that is gaining support and recognition globally.

Key Terms

androcentrism 345

androgyny 337

biphobia 357

femininity 339

feminism 347

functional inequality 347

gender 337

gender identity 337

gender nonconforming 340

gender roles 338

gender studies 347

heterosexuality 340

homophobia 357

homosexuality 340

intersex 337

LGBT 340

masculine protest 346

masculinity 339

metrosexual 351

natural dominance 341

neuroimaging 343

sex 336

sexism 359

sexual orientation 340

sexuality 339

transgender 339

transvestic fetishism 356

Evaluating What You Know

Describe the key points of the gender domain in personality psychology.

Explain the sexes and the intersex.

Define *gender roles* and *sexual orientation*.

What are the traditional views of the sexes?

What are the traditional views of gender?

What are the traditional views of sexual orientation?

Explain the essence of the changing views of the sexes.

Explain the essence of the changing views of gender.

Explain the essence of the changing views of sexual orientation.

Explain LGBT psychology.

Give examples of gender stereotypes and sexism.

A Bridge to the Next Chapter

Sex, gender, and sexual orientation, of course, were not the only topics that underwent significant revision within contrary science during past 50 years or so. Mental illness was another important area, the views of which have significantly evolved after the apparent decline of psychoanalysis. These views continue to change. The clinical domain will be our next area to examine in the following chapter.

WANT A BETTER GRADE?

Get the tools you need to sharpen your study skills. Access practice quizzes, eFlash-cards, web exercises, and multimedia at edge.sagepub.com/shiraevpersonality

$SAGE edge™

12

The Clinical Domain

"Sometimes I think people take reality for granted."

—Francesca Zappia, American author

Learning Objectives

After reading this chapter, you should be able to:

- Discuss the role of the clinical domain in the study of personality
- Describe the methods for diagnosing, classifying, and describing personality disorders
- Describe the personality disorders in the following behavior clusters: odd and eccentric; dramatic, emotional, or erratic; anxious and fearful
- Discuss how philosophy, science, and psychology explain personality disorders
- Explain the concepts of differential diagnosis and comorbidity
- Identify ways to apply knowledge about personality psychology in the clinical domain

Jude Le Grice grew up in a small town in southwest England. Tall and physically imposing, he had a beautiful singing voice and wanted someday to perform in the opera. However, his severe dyslexia was a serious obstacle to a successful music career. After finishing school, he got a job as a laborer and continued taking singing classes. There, he met Rebecca, an aspiring theater student. Jude quickly fell in love with her and asked her to marry him. Rebecca refused, but Jude insisted. Rebecca then told him not to bother her any longer—but Jude continued his pursuit. His affection for Rebecca turned into an obsession. For more than 10 years, his relentless, stubborn pursuit of Rebecca brought him and many people around him emotional pain, anxiety, and fear. Jude became a *stalker*.

Stalkers are engaged in a persistent and unwanted pursuit of another person. A stalker pays excessive attention to a "target," a victim. Stalking is also a form of harassment, which includes repeated following of the victims, spying on them, sending them unsolicited e-mails or texts, posting on their Facebook page, making frequent unwanted calls, loitering near their home or school, leaving unwanted gifts, or destroying or damaging the objects they love. Victims feel confused, intimidated, and profoundly unsafe. They suffer emotionally. Many of them are forced to alter their daily routines, change schools and jobs, or even relocate and hide their identities.

Jude was arrested many times for stalking Rebecca. He went through detentions, court hearings, restraining orders, violations of restraining orders, jail sentences, and probations. Yet he did not give up his obsession. At some point, he was court-ordered to take medication. The doctors believed the medication would change his obsessive thoughts, and eventually, his behavior.

One day, many years after Rebecca and Jude had met in that singing class, Jude learned Rebecca had married. But eyewitnesses said he took this news calmly and promised he would no longer pursue her. What made the difference in his behavior? Did the medication help? Or did he change as a person and finally pick reason over obsession?

We might call Jude a stalker, but the legal system considered him a felon. The mental health system labeled him *mentally ill* and maintained that the illness had caused his obsessive behavior. Today, Jude refuses to believe he was a stalker; instead, he explains that some time ago he simply was passionately in love with another person.

Everybody hopes that this story is over.

Questions

If one has done something wrong, why do you think we attach a negative label to this individual's personality? For example, Jude loved to sing. Why don't we just call him a singer?

Where is the line between falling deeply in love (which is excused) and being a stalker (which is rejected)? Is it wrong to love somebody? Explain.

Clinical domain
In studies of personality, the clinical domain involves approaches to personality from the position of abnormality, illness, and health care.

Was Romeo a stalker? Was Don Quixote a stalker? Why or why not? Are we selectively biased judging individuals? Explain.

What type of care or treatment would you recommend for a stalker: more understanding or more punishment? Explain your answer.

Sources: Knight, 2014; Mohandie, Meloy, McGowan, and Williams, 2006; Mullen, Pathé, and Purcell, 2000; Schwartz-Watts, 2006.

The Essence of the Clinical Domain

The **clinical domain** involves approaches to personality from the position of abnormality, illness, and health care. In the opening case, Jude developed a persistent behavioral pattern labeled *stalking*. This persistent pattern of thought and actions is significantly different from what most people would think and do in compatible circumstances. Jude's behavior also caused significant distress in the lives of many people, including his own. As the experts studying his case maintained, his behavior was associated with an underlying mental illness. The term **illness** (which can be used interchangeably with *disease* and *disorder*) broadly refers to any condition, or functional abnormality or disturbance of the body and mind (although it is debatable how exactly the mind can be "disturbed") that impairs a person's functioning. As you remember from Chapter 1, personality disorders are enduring patterns of behavior and inner experience that deviate markedly from the expectations of the individual's culture. It is not just being different. It is a persistent behavioral pattern that leads to the individual's distress and impairment in one or several important areas of functioning (Akhtar, 2002).

To identify personality disorders (PDs), clinicians study an individual's symptoms that represent a distinct departure from normal appearance, function, desire, or feeling. In this context, **clinicians** are health care practitioners working as primary caregivers to the patient. Health care usually deals with the diagnosis, treatment, and prevention of illness. Clinicians are engaged in the clinical practice and—in most countries these days—are legally qualified to do so.

Psychiatry and Clinical Psychology

For centuries, folk healers, sages, witch doctors, and shamans have been engaged in the process of "correcting" abnormal or undesirable behaviors as well as personality features. Mental illness appeared as a special category in medical journals by the mid-1800s, and psychiatry as a medical discipline dealing with mental illness began taking shape by the end of the 1800s. Doctors working within psychiatry called themselves psychiatrists. Today, this is a mainstream medical profession. Psychiatrists, who are medical schools graduates, use primarily medical methods to diagnose and treat mental illness. Psychiatrists see mental illness mostly as a medical problem, not just an unusual personality feature, deviant behavior, or moral transgression.

Clinical psychologists are not psychiatrists but work closely with them. Clinical psychology, as a field of psychology, traces its roots to university laboratories and clinics emerging approximately early in the 20th century in industrial countries, including the United States. Since the early years of their discipline, clinical psychologists saw an individual's personality as an integrated entity of behavior and experiences that has been disrupted due to certain conditions (Hall & Lindzey, 1957). Clinical psychologists also directed their attention to an individual's experiences. Although they generally disagree on how to explain those experiences, they have accumulated significant knowledge about abnormal symptoms and their associated conditions. Psychiatrists and clinical psychologists also

Illness
An illness refers to any condition, or a functional abnormality or disturbance, of the body and mind (although it is debatable how exactly the mind can be "disturbed") that impairs functioning.

Clinicians Health care practitioners who work as primary caregivers of the patient are clinicians.

Clinical psychologists Professionals educated and trained to provide comprehensive mental and behavioral health care to individuals and families; to consult with agencies and communities; to train, educate, and supervise; and to conduct research.

Photo 12.1 For centuries, folk healers, sages, witch doctors, and shamans have been engaged in the process of "correcting" abnormal or undesirable personality features. What is the difference between such healers and today's professional psychologists?

© iStockphoto.com/chrisfarrugia

CHECK AND APPLY YOUR KNOWLEDGE

An intriguing portrayal of an unusual kind of behavior is depicted in the 1987 movie *Fatal Attraction*. The main female character of the film (Alex Forrest, played by Glenn Close) depicts a wide range of psychological and behavioral flip-flops while she deals with the aftermath of an affair with a married man. Her emotional and behavioral roller coaster storms through ups and downs of seductive tenderness and violent outbursts, fascination and hatred, pitiful vulnerability and rock solid determination, sorrow and loathing, and creativity and idleness.

Questions

What behavioral traits and emotional patterns can you identify in the behavior of Alex Forrest? Does she manifest the symptoms of a particular personality disorder?

believe that personality features under their observation should correspond to specific abnormalities in the brain and nervous system and unfold in particular social circumstances, which must be examined and hopefully corrected or changed with therapeutic procedures based in science (Garfield, 2009).

On "Normal" and "Abnormal" Personality

At least two issues are important to know when we study personality disorders. First, each personality disorder (PD) is characterized by excessive "presence," as compared to the norm of certain traits and behaviors. They are interconnected and can manifest, for instance, as excessive shyness, introversion, anxiety, agitation, suspiciousness, and so on. Consider a young adult who avoids making independent decisions, constantly fears separation from parents, and does not initiate new relationships for fear of rejection. This pattern of stable traits can be labeled *abnormal*. Second, a behavior pattern is called a personality disorder because it appears as significantly different from what is considered a tolerable norm in a given cultural environment. Imagine a person who constantly challenges social norms, has consistent problems with adjustment, and experiences significant distress (Akhtar, 2002). According to this view, personality traits are labels, and each of them stands for a collection of behavioral acts that should be measured against the norm (Bus & Craik, 1984).

Both these views complement each other. Personality disorders can be seen as a kind of disturbing excessiveness of certain personality traits; it also appears that abnormal symptoms taken together are significantly different from what is labeled *normal functioning* in a particular social context. In clinical practice, a majority of symptoms diagnosed as PDs usually represent a pattern of **excessive consistency,** which is different from moderate consistency. To illustrate, moderately present tendencies of being punctual, attentive, and detailed-oriented could be successfully used in business, learning, and other professional areas. However, an extreme or excessive manifestation of these traits, such as a person's adherence to useless ritualistic habits, clinging to orderliness, or

Excessive consistency An individual who exhibits excessive consistency has the condition of feeling and behaving in the same way regardless of changing circumstances and contexts, although a change in such behavior and feelings is generally expected.

constant outbursts of anger at someone who likes to improvise, may result in constant work conflicts and, ultimately, professional failure. As we will see later in the chapter, borderline personality disorder is an exception to the pattern of excessive consistency, as it is characterized by an excessive inconsistency or instability of behaviors and emotional responses and by a lack of continuity and certainty in most aspects of a person's life. The symptoms can manifest as mild, moderate, or severe (Yang, Coid, & Tyrer, 2010).

Most symptoms included in the category *personality disorders* are likely to be present in a person under most life circumstances. This makes the behavior of individuals with personality disorders somewhat predictable.

Clinicians also focus on the significant, abnormal changes that have taken place in an individual's personality. When an illness strikes an individual, it affects this person's functioning, work, sleep, and leisure activities; it shapes daily routines, relationships, and communications; it changes the most significant patterns of thinking and acting. Such illness can have clearly identifiable organic maladies as well as causes that are difficult to establish.

Medicalization of Personality Features

In the 20th century, social scientists began to see many social ills, such as street violence, sex crimes, homelessness, or chronic drug abuse, as mostly medical and not necessarily social problems. Therefore, as these scientists reasoned, these and other social problems required the attention of medical professionals. This was the beginning of **medicalization** of abnormal and deviant behavior. This is the process by which various facets of human behavior are interpreted in medical terms and thus diagnosed and treated by medical methods.

Medicalization Medicalization is the process by which various facets of human behavior are interpreted in medical terms and thus diagnosed and treated by medical methods.

Consider an example. Since the inception of war, military commanders have had to deal with soldiers' fears on the battlefield. Excessive fear was often labeled *cowardice*, and soldiers' complaints about their acute emotional problems were called *malingering*—an intentional falsification of symptoms to avoid certain duties. Malingering was a punishable offense, especially during wartime. Psychology, however, early in the 20th century, brought up the term *shell shock* to describe serious psychological symptoms of traumatic nature. Professionals insisted that some people who exhibited these symptoms needed medical attention, not punishment (Lerner, 2009).

The Stigma of Mental Illness

In general terms, a **stigma** concerns the negative perception and corresponding actions related to a person or group based solely on certain social characteristics they possess or are associated with. The stigma of mental illness affects the manner with which millions of people (including those with personality disorders) are viewed (i.e., prejudged, ignored, or feared) and treated (i.e., mistreated, abused, or discriminated against; Corrigan & Wassel, 2008). Today, people with mental illness are a vulnerable group as a result of the way society treats them. They are subjected to stigma and discrimination on a daily basis, and they experience extremely high rates of physical and sexual victimization (World Health Organization [WHO], 2014).

Stigma A stigma is the negative perception and corresponding actions related to a person or group based solely on certain social characteristics they possess or are associated with.

For centuries, popular beliefs held that the label *mental illness* explained personal features and behavior that was difficult to describe by other, more understandable causes,

Is There a "Criminal Personality"?
Social scientists and psychologists have repeatedly attempted to make the psychological profile of a typical criminal. Visit the companion site to learn about some of such studies. There you also can see how clinicians associated certain types of mental illness (such as madness, neurasthenia, or hysteria) with important personality features.

such as an external incentive, fear, or greed. If a person was "mentally ill," then he or she must have been profoundly different from "normal" people. This individual was expected to act and think in predictable yet disturbing ways. In fact, these individuals were placed into a special category. For example, in the 19th century, clinicians applied the label *insane* to people with behavioral patterns ranging from alcoholism to fire setting to compulsive theft and to senility (Quen, 1983). The terms *idiocy* or *degeneration* were attached to individuals with a wide range of developmental problems (Krafft-Ebbing, 1886).

Religion was also a very powerful source of deep-seated beliefs about mental illness and its impact on personality. Across times and cultures, religion taught that psychological abnormalities must have been caused by the devil or other forms of curse. It was also seen as God's payback for an individual's inappropriate violence, shameful desires, dishonesty, or perversity. Even today, many people believe that mental illness is the result of an individual's deviation from God, tradition, and family (Shiraev & Levy, 2013). Religious prescriptions today continue to identify "appropriate" personality characteristics and "abnormal" ones.

A significant sociocultural shift in attitudes toward mental illness took place during the second half of the 20th century. A person with symptoms of mental illness was no longer labeled as an *alcoholic*, a *schizoid*, an *addict*, or an *obsessive-compulsive*, but rather as an individual who has been affected by a range of symptoms. Instead of labeling people with mental illness with catchy words or phrases or stigmatizing them, psychologists began to see them as needing professional treatment and care (Shorter, 1997).

CHECK AND APPLY YOUR KNOWLEDGE

1. What is excessive consistency? Give examples.

2. Explain medicalization of behavior. Give examples.

3. Define and explain *stigma*.

4. Does it really matter how we label people with psychological problems? Do you see the difference between calling a woman "a drug addict" compared to calling her "a person affected by a drug addiction"? Explain.

5. If you have serious avoidant tendencies in interpersonal relationships, would you prefer to be called "one with avoidant tendencies" or "an avoidant person"? Explain.

Diagnosing Personality Disorders

Diagnosing personality disorders is difficult. Although many symptoms of PDs should have an underlying biological basis (Livesley & Jang, 2008), clinicians do not yet have reliable genetic, biochemical, or electrophysiological methods to detect them. Behavioral observations tend to have only limited reliability and validity due to substantial variability of symptoms within each type of PD. Other disorders may be masked under the same symptoms. This is another complicating issue, which we shall examine later.

Self-report questionnaires and inventories are commonly used in clinical practice, despite their diagnostic limitations. Many personality assessment inventories are available today. They provide psychologists with important information about the magnitude of personality traits such as extroversion, anxiety, agreeableness, openness, conscientiousness, independence, aggression, focus on physical symptoms, denial, and some others. After a psychologist examines various traits and their combinations, he or she can establish a clinical diagnosis of a certain type of PD. However, the **interrater reliability** of these diagnostic methods remains low. This usually means that if several professionals separately diagnose one individual, they would often come to different diagnostic conclusions (Tyrer et al., 2007).

Interrater reliability The interrater reliability is the degree of agreement among several professionals when they separately diagnose an individual.

Because people with personality disorders tend to exhibit abnormal behavioral traits in a consistent way across time and situations, clinicians often use *behavioral functional analysis* (BFA) for their assessments. This method requires a systematic observation of the immediate causes of behavior, the contextual characteristics of the behavior itself, and the consequences of this behavior. Accordingly, the analysis of a PD in an individual focuses on (1) self-reported personality characteristics and (2) the duration, intensity, and frequencies of observable behaviors consistent across time and situations. This work takes significant time.

Among common issues related to personality questionnaires are **test-taking attitudes**. Some people tend to either give positive (socially desirable) evaluations of self ("I am always honest" or "I never lose my temper"), or they exaggerate negative symptoms ("I feel completely empty" or "I cannot focus on anything"). They may do this to draw attention to themselves, claim serious illness, receive special health benefits, or influence legal action involving them. In addition, even though many people want to give sincere answers, their insights into their psychological problems may be shallow and misleading (Krueger et al., 1996; Reich et al., 1986; Trull & Sher, 1994).

Test-taking attitudes An individual's view about taking a particular test or taking tests in general is referred to as a test-taking attitude.

Although clinicians frequently use personality questionnaires for assessment, only a few of them have specific scales that help professionals identify psychological distortions that stem from the test-taking attitudes. Such scales have been long used by the authors of the Minnesota Multiphasic Personality

H.S. Photos/Alamy Stock Photo

Photo 12.2 In the United States, *The Diagnostic and Statistical Manual of Mental Disorders* (5th ed.; *DSM–5*) is the main diagnostic source for personality disorders. Different countries have their own traditions in defining personality disorders.

Inventory (MMPI–2) and its later versions (Brief History of the MMPI Instruments, 2016). Look, for example, at just three **validity scales, L, F, K**):

L: The lie scale measures social desirability, or the extent to which a person wants to present self in a best positive light, in accordance with cultural norms.

F: The frequency scale measures the degree to which a person has a feeling that he or she is different from others.

K: The correction scale is aimed at measuring the defensiveness of a person, or self-protection from criticism and exposure of own shortcomings.

These scales help clinicians assess an individual better and make a more informed judgment about other answers in this personality inventory.

Factors Contributing to Diagnosis

Psychologists pay serious attention to a variety of factors that could contribute to diagnostic practices. For instance, the use of mental health services is significantly lower among people of lower socioeconomic status (SES). Individuals with affordable health insurance are more likely to see a psychologist than individuals who must pay high premiums for a visit. If we compare people with personality disorders that receive psychological help, we are likely to find that individuals of higher SES have less pronounced symptoms of personality disorders than do individuals of lower SES (WHO, 2014).

Although there are international diagnostic and classification systems of mental health that are often used, such as *The ICD–10 Classification of Mental and Behavioural Disorders* (WHO, 1993), as well as a classification system used in the United States called *The Diagnostic and Statistic Manual of Mental Disorders* (5th ed.; *DSM–5*; American Psychiatric Association [APA], 2013), countries have different traditions in defining personality disorders.

Classification and Description of Personality Disorders

Clinical practice and psychological research provided important observations of many distinct abnormal features in the individual's behavior and experience. French doctor Philippe Pinel (1745–1826) described cases of impulsive rage combined with relatively normal reasoning ability and called these symptoms *manie sans delire* (mania without delirium). Chronic aggressive behavior was labeled *moral insanity, egopathy, sociopathy,* and *psychopathy.* These individuals were described as manipulative, impulsive, self-centered, lying, and joy-seeking; they were also lacking in features such as remorse, empathy, or guilt (Cleckley, 1976;

Hare, 1998). Jean-Étienne Esquirol (1772–1840), another French physician, studied *erotomania* as an excessive, irrational obsession with another person. Esquirol saw it as a grossly exaggerated affection. The difference between love, which is socially acceptable, and erotomania was not in type but in degree: People with erotomania pursue unreasonable goals, develop unrealistic fantasies, and have inaccurate views of themselves. What we call *stalking* today may well fit into this pattern of behavior and thought. Early in the 1900s, clinicians discussed cases involving individuals who were extremely arrogant and preoccupied with self-importance. Some doctors thought this phenomenon was a sexual deviation; others postulated pathological self-love; yet others talked of an extreme form of introversion (Campbell, 1999).

For years, psychoanalysts (see Chapter 4 and Chapter 5) held a monopoly on clinical understanding of PDs. Psychoanalysts used the term **neurotic character**— one basic trait or a set of traits developed in early childhood that lead to the overt manifestation of neurosis. Traditional psychoanalytic classifications of personality-related dysfunctions included the following types: schizoid, paranoid, inadequate (avoidant), cyclothymic (narcissistic or borderline), emotionally unstable (histrionic), passive-aggressive (dependent), compulsive, and sociopathic (English & English, 1958). With the decline of psychoanalysis, the usage of the term *neurotic* became less frequent. Other psychoanalytic terms were disappearing from the professional vocabulary, and at the same time, the term *personality disorders* was gaining popularity. It obtained support from many clinicians several decades ago and signified a separation of modern psychology from the conceptual "storage" of psychoanalysis.

Neurotic character In psychoanalysis, a neurotic character is a basic trait or a set of traits developed in early childhood that lead to the overt manifestation of neurosis.

The Diagnostic and Statistical Manual of Mental Disorders (3rd ed.; *DSM–3*), which was released in 1980, included the category *Personality Disorders* and emphasized that attention should be given to personality traits, which are inflexible and maladaptive and cause either significant impairment in social or occupational functioning or subjective distress (APA, 1980). The *DSM–3-R*, released by the APA 7 years later, provided 11 officially recognized diagnoses for personality disorders (four new descriptions were added: narcissistic, borderline, schizotypal, and avoidant), and two more were included in the appendix (sadistic and self-defeating), although the latter two were deleted entirely from the *DSM–4* (APA, 1994). Instead, passive-aggressive and depressive personality disorders were added to the appendix in *DSM–4*, but they were removed from the *DSM–5*.

Our understanding and clinical classifications of PDs continue to evolve and are likely to change in the future. Even though the *DSM–5* was published in 2013, there are still some controversies over the classifications, given the imprecise boundaries between "normal" and "pathological" features. Many diagnostic criteria for one disorder overlap with the diagnostic criteria for another, and several of the symptoms are related to other emotional and cognitive abnormalities. Contemporary scientific classifications of personality disorders are still "works in progress." For review, see **Table 12.1.**

TABLE 12.1 ● Summarizing the *DSM–5* (APA, 2013): Classifications and Descriptions of Personality Disorders

Cluster: Odd and Eccentric Behavior	Brief Description of Symptoms	Cautionary Statement
Paranoid personality disorder	A prevalent distrust and suspiciousness of others and their motives	Should not be confused with reasonable cautious behavior and doubts about loyalty
Schizoid personality disorder	A pervasive pattern of detachment from social relationships and a restricted range of emotions in interpersonal settings	Should not be confused with someone's shyness, reasonable lack of interest, or social inhibitions
Schizotypal personality disorder	A persistent pattern of social and interpersonal deficits marked by cognitive or perceptual distortions and eccentricities of behavior	Should not be confused with attention-seeking behavior or other culturally appropriate responses
Cluster: Dramatic, Emotional, or Erratic Behavior	**Brief Description of Symptoms**	**Cautionary Statement**
Histrionic personality disorder	A pervasive pattern of excessive emotionality and attention seeking	Should not be confused with socially adaptive responses
Narcissistic personality disorder	A persistent pattern of grandiosity in fantasy or behavior, need for admiration, and lack of empathy	Should not be confused with certain patterns of leadership behavior and responses in extreme situations
Borderline personality disorder	A prevalent pattern of instability and unpredictability of thought, emotion, and behavior	Should not be confused with responses caused by frequently changing, highly unpredictable, and confusing situations
Antisocial personality disorder	A long-standing pattern of disregard for other people's rights, often crossing the line and violating those rights	Should not be confused with adaptive responses to extraordinary, dangerous, and threatening situations
Cluster: Anxious and Fearful Behavior	**Brief Description of Symptoms**	**Cautionary Statement**
Avoidant personality disorder	A long-standing pattern of feelings of inadequacy and social inhibition	Should not be confused with the lack of social skills and reasonable self-isolation
Dependent personality disorder	A pervasive pattern of dependency and fear of abandonment	Should not be confused with temporary lack of social skills
Obsessive-Compulsive personality disorder	A pervasive pattern of preoccupation with orderliness, perfectionism, and mental and interpersonal control, done at the expense of flexibility, openness, and efficiency	Should not be confused with adaptive skills of discipline and perfection that may lead to eventual success

Cluster: Odd and Eccentric Behavior

Clinicians use the characteristics of this cluster to diagnose individuals who demonstrate a stable pattern of remarkably unusual behavior. In the United States, we recognize three forms of such odd and eccentric behavior: paranoid, schizoid, and schizotypal.

Paranoid Personality Disorder

The development of paranoid personality disorder symptoms goes hand to hand with an elevated interpersonal sensitivity—individuals feel that they are capable of seeing and knowing more about potentially dangerous or dreadful developments than other people do. Because this eminent sensitivity typically manifests in suspiciousness, a central feature of this syndrome is pervasive mistrust. High self-esteem and beliefs in one's own exclusivity contribute to suspiciousness. The individual displays emotional coldness, detachment from others, and unforgiving behavior. The world seems extremely hostile. Unjustified doubts about the loyalty or trustworthiness of associates, friends, and family members prevail. "I have done so much for them, and what did I get in return?" is a common pattern of thinking. Interpersonal sensitivity also manifests in a great susceptibility to criticism from others. Such criticisms appear to the individual as another sign of other people's ill intentions. Individuals with these symptoms seldom seek clinical help (Harper, 2010).

Schizoid Personality Disorder

Exaggerated introversion may be considered a prime feature of schizoid personality disorder. Introverted individuals tend to display a constant pattern of reserved and withdrawn behavior, but they do not draw clinical attention just because of this trait. Individuals with schizoid PD display a pervasive pattern of withdrawn behavior. They tend to choose solitary activities and do not have warm, emotional, and close relationships (Millon, Millon, Meagher, Grossman, & Ramnath, 2004). They rarely display their feelings to others. Not only do they have limited relationships with others but they also seem to have almost no desire for such relationships. They often seem self-absorbed and oblivious to what is going on around them and demonstrate few social skills. Most of them do not seek marriage. The person with schizoid PD can have fantasies and creative ideas. Consider Steve, a 52-year-old man living in a small studio apartment in Westwood Village (Los Angeles) for the past 20 years. The only two people with whom he communicates regularly are his landlord and a doctor. Steve reads several books a month, usually modern philosophy, and often rereads them to understand the authors' "inner worlds." He loves modern science fiction and mocking contemporary pop culture. He has no friends, except his dog, a brown spaniel. He dresses up in clean but clearly outdated clothes. Steve occasionally communicates with clerks at a neighborhood grocery store, where he works part time. Steve had a girlfriend, but they broke up several years ago.

Schizoid PD should be diagnosed with caution and related to particular circumstances. Persistent and seemingly unreasonable avoidance of social contacts and the lack of desire to develop meaningful relationships can appear in many cases as abnormal and maladaptive features. However, being quiet, reticent, and more observing than participating can also be indicative of a person's conscientiousness. In addition, temporary social withdrawal can be a useful means to achieve a professional or educational goal, such as when studying for exams. Sometimes individuals reduce their social contact for a reason that is not obvious to an impatient observer.

Schizotypal Personality Disorder

To be diagnosed with schizotypal personality disorder, an individual should display profound peculiarities of perceiving, thinking, acting, and communicating. The ability to express thoughts is diminished, and speech contains odd and unusual words and awkward phrases. Standard words may be said in peculiar ways. One of the features of this disorder is the belief in extraordinary, even magical personal powers. Although emotions tend to be shallow, social anxiety is persistent and elevated. Most affected individuals lack social skills, seek seclusion, and avoid friendships. Clinicians try not to confuse these symptoms with those of schizoid and paranoid personality disorders (note the common symptoms). Some consider this disorder as a midpoint type between healthy individuals and those with symptoms of schizophrenia (McGlashan, 1986).

It seems appropriate to consider an individual's bizarre beliefs, concerns, and communication patterns that interfere with the person's professional or educational activities as abnormal symptoms. Some of them can disrupt the clinician's efforts to treat medical or other psychological problems (such as substance addition or depression)

CHECK AND APPLY YOUR KNOWLEDGE

1. Explain test-taking attitudes such as social desirability and malingering.

2. On the companion website, see the list of personality disorders identified in the *DSM–5* and in the *ICD–10*. Which similarities and differences did you find between the two?

3. What does the label *neurotic character* mean?

4. Name three disorders within the odd and eccentric behavior cluster.

5. Exaggerated introversion may be considered a prime feature of which PD?

6. Which occupations do you think will be the least suitable for individuals with PDs from the odd and eccentric behavior cluster?

7. Clinicians have to be cautions when diagnosing paranoid PD. Persistent, unfounded, and obviously irrational suspiciousness should probably require clinical attention. The same can be said about a person's unrelenting and inflexible accusations of other people's maliciousness. However, questioning someone's loyalty can be appropriate in certain circumstances. There are also professions that require constant vigilance. What are some?

that the person with schizotypal PD may have. Nevertheless, in some cultural groups, beliefs in extraordinary and magical powers seem appropriate and even welcome. Unusual thinking and odd ideas may also be indicators of a person's creativity in certain social contexts.

Cluster: Dramatic, Emotional, or Erratic Behavior

Disorders in the dramatic, emotional, or erratic behavior cluster share problems with the individual's impulse control and emotional regulation and include histrionic, narcissistic, borderline, and antisocial personality disorders.

Histrionic Personality Disorder

Lilia underwent a psychological evaluation as an alleged victim of sexual abuse. She told the psychologist that she became a prostitute 7 years earlier, when she was 13, after her stepfather had sexually molested her. She provided a very detailed and disturbing account of the continuous abuse that she encountered. The psychologist who examined her turned to her medical records. According to the most recent medical examination, Lilia was a virgin (she had never had sexual intercourse). Next, the psychologist learned that she never had a stepfather and had made up her entire story about being a prostitute. Why did she lie? What was her incentive?

Individuals diagnosed with histrionic PD constantly look for attention. Their personality features resemble an extreme, exaggerated form of extroversion. Lilia, as well as other people diagnosed with this disorder, tend to grossly exaggerate their experiences. Anything—weather, traffic, friends, world economy, fashion—may be described as wonderful or horrible, stunningly beautiful or unbelievably ugly. Being egocentric, those affected wish to remain the center of attention, which is their major motivation and thrill (such individuals are often labeled *sensitizers*). Anything is used to turn people's heads, including wearing provocative or revealing clothes or lying to a therapist. They make dramatic moves just to get people's attention.

As always, do not confuse clinical symptoms and conventional behaviors. Frequent, dramatic, and mostly unwarranted emotional outbursts or other peculiar actions that affect the person's relationships or academic or professional careers and overall well-being should draw clinical attention. These symptoms easily interfere with the treatment of other disorders (panic disorder or learning disabilities) in an individual. However, histrionic traits can be appropriate in certain activities and professions, including entertainment, the arts, politics, and some areas of teaching (Millon et al., 2004). Performing arts or politics may create conditions that attract individuals with certain personality traits because of possible and significant public exposure associated with these occupations.

Narcissistic Personality Disorder

The term *narcissistic* comes from the classical Greek myth about Narcissus, the young man who fell in love with his own reflection in the water. Refusing the love of others and being unable to fall in love, he suddenly discovered that only his own reflection was worth his affection. Like Narcissus, people diagnosed with narcissistic personality disorder are typically preoccupied with self-appearance. They feel self-important and expect special favors from others. They need constant approval and admiration. They also tend to think that everything they do is exceptional and that other people do not appreciate them enough. They also have a fragile self-esteem (Campbell, 1999). To compensate for the perceived lack of admiration from others, they tend to develop a grandiose but unrealistic self-image, including fantasies of unlimited success, love, and power (John & Robbins, 1994). They pursue exploitative, even "parasitic" relationships because they feel they have the right to control others. *A profound feeling of entitlement* summarizes their attitudes toward others and self.

Diagnosing narcissistic PD requires caution and patience. Clinical symptoms often overlap with conventional behaviors. A person's pattern of self-absorption, egotism, and envy that bring harmful consequences to this person's life should certainly draw clinical attention. These individuals tend to have poor recognition of their psychological problems and need help. Yet an individual's self-confidence, self-appreciation, pride for personal accomplishments, or attention to appearance should be seen as appropriate in particular circumstances.

SELF-REFLECTION

The Drama of the Gifted Child by Alice Miller (1994) put forward a controversial hypothesis: Many professional psychotherapists are likely to be narcissistic. They do not become narcissistic after they become professionals—quite the contrary, she writes. Many individuals seek degrees in psychology because of childhood experiences that make them narcissistic.

Imagine, she argues, a mother who is emotionally insecure, weak, or desperate, yet who always tries to appear confident, independent, and strong. This mother has a child who is sensitive and smart and who is capable of understanding her or his mother's struggles. The child wants to help and thus develops sensitivity to the needs of the mother and other people. The child earns a good reputation for helping others. Unlike business, such amateur "psychological practices" generate no money; however, they bring approval from others. The child, a teenager now, becomes a home-grown "therapist" and feels important. He or she now seeks people's praise. That is why many of these children later choose psychology as a profession. To them, Alice Miller argues, psychological practice is about much more than money. Helping other people with their emotional issues feeds the psychologists' childhood narcissism—the desire to maintain a good image of self and feel special.

Questions

As a high school student, were you ever asked to help other people with their emotional problems? Did you enjoy helping or guiding others? What is the difference between (1) enjoying every opportunity to help another person and (2) having narcissistic features?

Borderline Personality Disorder

The symptoms of borderline personality disorder (BPD) point to a profound inconsistency of personality traits. In contrast to other PDs, such inconsistency represents a pervasive pattern of instability in behavior, emotions, and thinking. One of the most basic features of this disorder is the feeling of emptiness, which is often associated with extreme instability and shallowness in self-perception, habits, and opinions. Relationships are highly unbalanced—a person's kindness and compassion are followed by anger and physical aggression a few hours later. A strong need for a relationship leads persons with borderline symptoms to fear abandonment and feel anger about a possible separation. They usually demand dedication and exclusiveness from others but do not show dedication themselves. Impulsivity, or behavior with little or no forethought, is common and includes sexual promiscuity, spending sprees, or excessive drinking or eating. People with this disorder are highly manipulative. They make threats, including suicidal ones, and frequent swings in emotions are typical (Kreger, 2008).

If an individual displays behavioral and emotional instability, impulsivity, anger, and self-destructive tendencies, these symptoms should certainly receive clinical attention. It is important, however, not to perceive occasional instability and impulsivity in someone's behavior as symptoms of this disorder. We routinely change our plans, depending on the circumstances. We sometimes make abrupt decisions. Many outside factors affect an occasional emotional swing. It is always important to pay attention to the duration and severity of these and other symptoms and determine how they affect an individual's functioning in a variety of circumstances.

Antisocial Personality Disorder

Individuals with symptoms of antisocial personality disorder have difficulty controlling their own impulses and have little or no regret for the harmful things they do. The diagnosis is usually given to people over the age of 18, yet some key symptoms of this disorder tend to occur a few years earlier. Some individuals diagnosed with this disorder say in self-reports that they regard life as a "big game" in which they use every opportunity to manipulate others. Excitement about risks and winning seems to be especially important. People with symptoms of antisocial PD have a callous lack of concern for the rights and feelings of others. They also have little insight into their own behavior and blame others for "provoking" them into deviant acts. Some individuals turn to violence and recklessness, while others can appear charming and caring. They frequently lie and do not keep their promises and commitments. Symptoms of this disorder make other psychological problems more difficult to treat. Moreover, some of those affected use therapy to learn manipulation techniques: how to lie, hide emotions, and exploit other people's vulnerabilities.

Diagnosing antisocial PD should be done with caution. Persistent manipulative or violent behavior, uncontrollable anger, and lying could result in self-destruction or endangerment of other people—these are serious clinical symptoms. Under specific social conditions, however, some features of this disorder become somewhat useful coping strategies that help the individual survive in extreme conditions. Try to name such conditions.

Cluster: Anxious and Fearful Behavior

Personality disorders included in the anxious and fearful behavior cluster represent a range of symptoms for abnormal manifestations of apprehensive, timid, or frightened behavior. Such symptoms become significant and distressful in an individual's life and have a significant impact on daily activities. The disorders include avoidant, dependent, and obsessive-compulsive PDs.

Avoidant Personality Disorder

Y. M. is a 27-year-old graduate of the prestigious law school at Waseda University in Tokyo, Japan. A hardworking man, he spent significant time after graduation to prepare for the bar exam. Only a handful of law school graduates in Japan pass this extremely difficult exam that allows them practice law. Y. M. passed the exam with a high score, which meant he was eligible to apply for a job in a prominent firm. However, he did not apply. He feared accepting responsibility for thousands of people at his new job as a lawyer. Such avoidant tendencies started when Y. M. was a boy: He felt uncomfortable discussing things publicly; he was extremely embarrassed for being clumsy or messy at a party. He also developed an irrational fear about his body's odor (he believed that people knew about his odor problem but were too polite to tell him). His avoidant tendencies grew. His lengthy preparation for the bar exam had shielded him from other people for some time, but when the time came to apply for a job, his symptoms returned.

One of the major psychological features associated with avoidant personality disorder (in Japan, this phenomenon is known as *Taijin confusho*) is elevated social anxiety. Low self-esteem, fear of criticism, and concerns about negative evaluation are distinct characteristics. Those affected have constant doubts about their own appearance, abilities, and competence, have only a few friends, and tend to evade intimacy. Individuals with these symptoms are not likely to enter into a relationship unless they become sure another person likes and appreciates them. They tend to be extremely vigilant about their ongoing relationships, while constantly anticipating the potential pain of rejection and disenchantment. They are sensitive to negative evaluation, deception, mocking, or other negative reactions from others. They exaggerate concerns about looking foolish or incompetent in social situations.

Clinicians should pay attention to serious and persistent avoidant tendencies that thwart a person's ability to function in everyday situations such applying for a job, establishing a personal contact, asking for directions, registering a car at the DMV office, or making a doctor's appointment. On the other hand, shyness and some other mild avoidant tendencies can be adaptive or culturally appropriate. Some avoidant tendencies, for example, may "protect" a person from making unrealistic promises or engaging in risky enterprises.

Dependent Personality Disorder

The movie *What About Bob?* (1991) is a Hollywood comedy in which the panicky, helpless, and annoying patient called Bob, played by Bill Murray, follows his therapist everywhere he goes and keeps asking for extra therapy sessions. In exchange for therapy, Bob promises his friendship and devotion. Bob's dependent behavior is depicted as a series of irritating and intrusive acts: He does unpleasant things just to be close to the therapist, constantly craves support and assurances from others, and feels extremely uncomfortable being alone.

Symptoms of dependent personality disorder include two basic subtypes: an individual's persistent delegation of important decisions to other people, and subordination of his or her own needs to the wishes of others. Individuals with symptoms of this disorder appear overly submissive and clingy. Their elevated anxiety is related to possible abandonment by a relative or friend. Many of these individuals believe they are irrelevant, incompetent, unattractive, or ugly. They assume that there is no reason for another person to stay in a relationship with them, which further increases their anxiety and dependent tendencies. They often make themselves available or pleasing to others, expecting that this behavior will keep them close to each other (Loranger, 1996).

Contrasting clinical symptoms with conventional behaviors is an important critical-thinking method in the diagnosis of dependent PD. Certain dependent tendencies require clinical attention if they seriously thwart a person's ability to have meaningful relationships; develop a career; or decide about education, employment, housing, or medical treatment. Yet a person's commitment to a relationship or selfless tendencies should be judged with caution. Only evident frequency, degree, or intensity of such selfless manifestations in particular social and cultural contexts can explain whether an individual should be diagnosed with this personality disorder.

Obsessive-Compulsive Personality Disorder

Individuals diagnosed with obsessive-compulsive disorder (OCD) display ritualized thought patterns and behavior. They seem to be extremely self-controlling and exceptionally organized. They prefer routines and standard procedures and reject improvisation. They appear serious, moralistic, grumpy, and demanding. They do not appreciate jokes and prefer not to make jokes themselves. As extraordinary perfectionists, they tend to focus on small details. These individuals feel disturbed when rules are not followed or when things are not where they are supposed to be at home or

SELF-REFLECTION

Imagine that you have become a licensed psychologist who treats personality disorders (in fact, you may only be a few years away from it). Which one of the disorders discussed in this chapter appears most interesting and intriguing to you? Why?

CHECK AND APPLY YOUR KNOWLEDGE

1. Name four disorders within the dramatic, emotional, or erratic behavior cluster.

2. The symptoms of which disorder point at a profound inconsistency of personality traits?

3. Which occupations do you think will be least suitable for individuals with PDs from this cluster?

4. Under specific social conditions, some features of antisocial PD become somewhat useful strategies that help individuals survive in extreme conditions. Name some of these conditions.

5. Name three disorders within the anxious and fearful behavior cluster.

6. Low self-esteem, fear of criticism, and concerns about negative evaluation are distinct characteristics of which PD?

7. Which occupations or professions do you think will be least suitable for individuals with PDs from the anxious and fearful behavior cluster?

in the office. Although anxiety is often reported as a significant underlying feature, individuals with OCD are unlikely to engage in irrational compulsive acts.

Clinical attention is likely required when significant preoccupation with rules and routines prevent an individual from successfully coping with changing life conditions. When a person loses flexibility and abandons common sense, clinicians should help. However, there are many healthy and efficient people among us who are extremely organized and who dislike improvisation. In fact, some professions require us to be rigid and extremely organized.

Etiology of Personality Disorders

Which factors cause and contribute to the symptoms of personality disorders? How do philosophy, science, and psychology explain personality disorders?

The Biomedical Perspective

For centuries, scientists assumed that bodily humors were foundations of four classical types of personality: the sanguine, the phlegmatic, the choleric, and the melancholic. A misbalance in bodily humors caused the person to be either persistently and unreasonably elated or constantly withdrawn and grumpy or stubbornly belligerent and unpredictable or consistently sad or easily disturbed. Although science no longer uses the concept of body humors, it is accepted that PDs have underlying biological and physiological causes, including genetic predispositions.

Twin studies show a genetic contribution to borderline PD (Lehman, 2003). First-degree relatives of patients with schizophrenia are more likely than people in the general population to develop schizotypal PD (Battaglia & Torgensen, 1996). Presence of mood disorders in the family also increases probability of schizotypal symptoms in close relatives (Erlenmeyer-Kimlig et al., 1995). Persistent and unreasonable suspiciousness, a key symptom of paranoid PD, runs in the family as well (Costello, 1995). Studies also show the impact of hereditary factors on "antisocial" traits (Lykken, 1995). For example, impulsive physical violence and aggression—often associated with antisocial PD—have long been linked to very low levels of neurotransmitter serotonin and one of its metabolites in the spinal cord (Virkkunen, 1983). Having a biological parent with antisocial features increases the child's chances of developing antisocial PD as well (Langbehn & Cadoret, 2001). Physiological factors also affect an individual's heightened or lowered anxiety levels. Low anxiety, for example, is a common condition for antisocial tendencies that include persistent reckless behavior and impulsivity and are associated with an individual's failing to predict the consequences of personal actions (Hare, 1983; Patrick, 1994). Slow alpha waves in the brain and several features of antisocial behavior are also correlated (Volavka et al., 1990), which again may suggest that people with antisocial symptoms have a low measure of arousal level (in normal individuals slower alpha waves indicate nonanxiety states).

Hereditary and environmental factors both contribute to the symptoms of PDs. To illustrate, Cadoret et al. (1995) studied people who were separated at birth from biological parents who both had antisocial PD. The children who grew up in unfavorable, difficult, and stressful environments had more antisocial symptoms than their counterparts raised in more favorable social environments. Can genetics or social factors explain these differences? One example might point to high testosterone levels (which may be caused by genetic factors) as a cause of aggressive behavior; however, testosterone levels can also increase due to the impact of constantly stressful situations, such as difficult social or living environments. In contrast, there are many individuals with high testosterone scores who choose prosocial forms of behavior and exercise moderation and self-control. Instead, it is likely that people have certain genetic **overarching liabilities**. They affect behavior and traits under particular, unfavorable conditions; for example, internalizing liabilities are linked to emotional problems, while externalizing liabilities refer to behavioral conduct such as lack of inhibition or aggressiveness (see **Table 12.2**; Krueger & Markon, 2006).

Overarching liabilities
An individual with overarching liabilities has a genetic predisposition that affects his or her behavior and traits under particular, unfavorable, conditions.

The Psychoanalytic Tradition

Traditional psychoanalytic models focus on unconscious psychological mechanisms usually rooted in early childhood and heavily influenced by early experiences (English & English, 1958). A child's oversensitivity or resistance, selfishness or alienation from reality, instability or playfulness, maliciousness or clinging behavior—all may contribute to this child's behavioral and psychological problems later in life.

Psychoanalysts generally believe that personality disorders refer to a person's social maladjustments. See several examples of psychoanalytic interpretations in **Table 12.3**. Although they may appear intriguing, they do not find significant empirical support in contemporary research. Psychoanalytic theories deserve credit, nevertheless, for directing attention to family-related psychological problems and early childhood experiences and their impact on personality disorders.

TABLE 12.2 ● The Biomedical Perspective: A Summary	
Personality Disorder Clusters	**Descriptions**
Odd and eccentric behavior	Genetic and other biological factors determine some people's hypersensitivity, which can lead to paranoid tendencies; natural inclinations for reclusive behavior and solitary activities are commonly labeled as *schizoid* characteristics.
Dramatic, emotional, or erratic behavior	Genetic and other biological factors contribute to excessive anxiety, instability in coping mechanisms, impulsivity, and other psychological responses—which manifest in various forms described as antisocial, histrionic, borderline, or narcissistic behaviors.
Anxious and fearful behavior	All of these disorders involve behavioral traits that may be related to a heightened susceptibility (liability) to anxiety and a common category of behavioral and psychological efforts to ward off anxiety.

TABLE 12.3 ● Selected Psychoanalytic Interpretations of Personality Disorders	
Personality Disorder	**Interpretations of Causes**
Narcissistic	A redirection of a person's love inward takes place because a child does not get enough love from his or her parents. The child also has to suppress anger for the perceived abandonment. Shame formed in early childhood can also be a powerful cause of narcissistic symptoms.
Antisocial	The individual lacks the authoritative power of the superego as a moral guide or censor. A lack of trust toward parents in early childhood may also weaken the desire to respect any authority in the future.
Borderline	Aggressive impulses toward parents are directed inward. The weak ego allows infantile impulses pushing for the immediate satisfaction of desires.
Paranoid	Angry, threatening, and demanding parents launch the child's unconscious defenses, which later results in deep suspiciousness toward other people.
Dependent	Overprotective parents stimulate defense mechanisms that later contribute to dependent tendencies.

Sources: Broucek, 1991; Freud, 1914/1957; Gabbard, 1990; Kernberg, 1992; Kohut, 1977; Loranger, 1996; Morrison, 1989.

The Behavioral Learning Tradition

Personality disorders are also formed in individual daily interactions and learning. People learn by means of reinforcement or example. Facing challenging life situations, some individuals learns successful strategies, but others learn poor strategies, which, if they become persistent, can appear as symptoms of PDs.

For example, a boy learns that friendship and intimacy bring no benefits, and at the same time, his parents constantly tell him that he is better than everybody else. The boy learns to diminish others to benefit himself. Such behavioral patterns could lead to narcissistic PD (Watson, Grisham, Trotter, & Biderman, 1984). Some people learn how to excel in life through hard work and perseverance, while others learn about drawing unwarranted attention to self and being manipulative in romantic relationships to build narcissistic features (Campbell, 1999).

Studies gave psychologists supportive evidence about the impact of interpersonal relationships on PDs. For instance, overly demanding and constantly angry parents tend to contribute to a child's paranoid symptoms (Manschreck, 1996). Parental abuse, neglect, separation, and excessive violence during childhood or adolescence contribute to the symptoms of borderline PD (Gunderson & Lyoo, 1997). Schizoid personality features are rooted in the child's profound dissatisfaction with interpersonal relationships: Lacking positive reinforcement in the family, the person learns that human relationships bring nothing but trouble. Therefore, avoiding interpersonal contacts and focusing on solitary activities becomes rewarding (Horner, 1991).

It is still unclear why, under similar circumstances, some people develop distinct symptoms of a PD while others do not. Troubled learning experiences can contribute to specific personality features. Nevertheless, in many cases such personality traits do not develop into a personality disorder.

The Cognitive Tradition

The cognitive tradition focuses primarily on how people process information related to self and how they use this information in relation to their experience and behavior. Psychologists have long established a connection between self-focused cognitions and emotional responses and actions. An example helps illustrate this point:

Imagine a person develops the belief that she is unattractive, and therefore, nobody is paying attention to her. She further concludes that she is unlovable, assuming that attention from somebody is a path to love. However, she wants to be lovable, so she looks for a way to get attention from others. One way is to appear extremely provocative, exaggerate emotions, and behave in unpredictable ways. If this pattern persists for years, it may be associated with histrionic PD. The cognitive tradition suggests that relatively stable cognitive constructs, such as expectations of outcomes, regulate our behavior in a wide range of social situations (Gramzow & Tangney, 1992).

Various cognitive variables have been linked with narcissistic PD (Emmons, 1987). These variables include exaggerated self-focus in conversations, such as the pervasive use of the pronoun *I* in spontaneous speech (Raskin & Shaw, 1988). Another variable is the exaggerated belief in personal uniqueness (Emmons, 1984), exceptional importance (Raskin, Novacek, & Hogan, 1991), or the belief in superior personal features compared with other people (Gabriel, Critelli, & Ee, 1994).

Individuals diagnosed with antisocial PD have cognitive difficulty recognizing nonconfrontational or nonviolent solutions to most problems they face (Kosson & Newman, 1986). They may lack self-reflection of their own anxiety (Schalling, 1978), yet they also show a heightened responsiveness to threat (Hodgins, De Brit, Chhabra, & Côté, 2010). The individual's cognitive features and abnormal symptoms are interconnected. A belief that one looks ugly may contribute to this person's avoidance, and avoidance further enhances this irrational belief.

The Trait Tradition

From the trait tradition perspective, personality disorders represent "anomalous" configurations of basic, "normal" dimensions of personality. If we understand these basic dimensions well enough, then we better understand PDs. Basic research into personality, therefore, is central in the study of abnormal symptoms. One of the most popular models of personality—but not the only one—is the five-factor model (FFM) of personality (see Chapter 7). Recall that this model was originally derived from the words in the English language that describe personality traits (Lynam & Widiger, 2001). There are five broad domains of personality: extroversion (positive affectivity), neuroticism (negative affectivity), agreeableness, conscientiousness, and openness to experience. Each of these domains can be further differentiated.

If we place known PDs into the left column and arrange the five personality traits horizontally, the intersections between the rows that represent disorders and the columns representing traits become the "diagnostic cells" in reference to which specific observations and measurements can be made (see **Table 12.4**). For example, an individual can be assessed along the personality dimensions first, and then an attempt

Personality Disorders	Personality Traits				
	Neuroticism	Extroversion	Openness	Agreeableness	Conscientiousness
Paranoid	High	Low	Low	Low	Low
Schizoid	Mixed	Low	Low	Mixed	High
Schizotypal	High	Low	High	Low	Low
Borderline	High	High	High	Low	Low
Narcissistic	High	High	Low	Low	High
Histrionic	High	High	High	High	Low
Antisocial	High	Mixed	Mixed	Low	Low
Dependent	High	High	High	High	Low
Avoidant	High	Low	Low	Low	High
Obsessive-Compulsive	Mixed	Low	Low	Low	High

TABLE 12.4 ● Understanding Personality Disorders From the Trait Tradition

can be made to associate these assessments with specific personality symptoms. Some features have been established empirically, such as a negative correlation of narcissism with agreeableness (Rhodewalt & Morf, 1995). Others are results of assumptions about how things "should be." Feel free to make your own judgments about such assumptions.

Many uncertainties require further studies. For example, psychologists often agree on how to describe a specific individual along the personality dimensions, but they tend to disagree about which combinations of traits represent a specific PD. One of the arguments is that any diagnostic method in psychology should take into consideration the cultural conditions in which the individual grows up and functions. Not only do we as individuals think, feel, and act according to cultural norms, but we also judge other people based on such norms.

The Cross-Cultural Approach

Some cross-cultural psychologists suggest that if human beings think, act, and feel according to particular cultural prescriptions, then people who are brought up in diverse cultural settings should understand what is "normal" and "abnormal" differently. This view is called the **relativist perspective of abnormal behavior** because it puts this behavior in a relative, comparative perspective (Shiraev & Levy, 2013). What is considered pathological in one culture could be regarded as simply different in another—for example, pinching somebody in one cultural environment can be seen as a friendly sign, whereas in another environment it is recognized as an inappropriate, violent act.

Other cross-cultural psychologists believe that despite cultural differences, people share a great number of features, including common social norms, values, and behavioral responses (Beardsley & Pedersen, 1997). Therefore, the overall understanding of normal and abnormal individual features ought to be universal. This view is called the **universalist perspective of abnormal behavior** because it suggests the existence of some universal psychological and behavioral features shared in individuals. Deviant and abnormal phenomena across countries and cultures tend to be universal in terms of their origin and expression. Almost everywhere, people disapprove of unprovoked hostility, reject excessive suspiciousness, or condemn persistent lying (Penny, Newton, & Larkin, 2009). In a unique comparative study sponsored by the WHO, 58 psychiatrists interviewed 716 patients in 11 countries in North America, Europe, Africa, and Asia and found that personality disorders have relatively similar features (Loranger et al., 1994). They can be assessed with a reasonably high degree of reliability across different nations, languages, and cultures. Additional studies support this point of view (Fountoulakis et al., 2002).

Which view—universalist or relativist—better describes personality disorders? We can accept both (1) the relative cultural uniqueness and (2) the universal nature of psychological symptoms. Each PD, therefore, can manifest as follows:

- A set of central symptoms that are abnormal, maladaptive, and distressful that can be observed in practically all world populations
- A set of peripheral symptoms that are culturally specific

Relativist perspective of abnormal behavior Using a relativist perspective of abnormal behavior puts it in a relative, comparative perspective. What is considered pathological in one culture could be regarded as simply different in another.

Universalist perspective of abnormal behavior The universalist perspective on abnormal behavior suggests the existence of some universal psychological and behavioral features shared in individuals. Deviant and abnormal phenomena across countries and cultures tend to be universal in terms of their origin and expression.

For example, central symptoms for a case of a histrionic PD can be an individual's profound desire to be in the center of attention, a propensity for dramatic acts, and emotional exaggerations. Peripheral symptoms can include the preferred style of clothes (every region has its own requirements) or seductiveness in behavior (judged differently in separate cultures). In other words, our judgments about "appropriate" and "excessive" behaviors and traits vary across cultures. Psychologists should decide whether the diagnosis is applicable to the individual given the cultural context in which this person lives. Someone's flashy and provocative clothes may cause negative comments from people in one culture but not in another. What is labeled *provocative* or *promiscuous* behavior in rural Iran may easily be tolerated in North America or Europe. The term *tolerance threshold*, again, is applicable here (Chapter 1). Low thresholds indicate relative societal intolerance against specific behaviors and underlying personality traits, while high thresholds designate relative tolerance. If a society accepts the diversity of behaviors, then tolerance thresholds should be relatively high.

Specific social and cultural circumstances serve as "filters" for evaluations of personality traits and disorders. Some traits can be seen as common and standard from a particular national or cultural standpoint, while they can be seen as excessive and even abnormal (if they fit specific criteria) from another cultural point of view. For instance, if a woman from a traditional culture stays away from public places, prefers solitary activities at home, does not have close relationships with anyone outside her family, and appears "cold" or unemotional in conversations with strangers (such as a Western psychologist who interviews her), these characteristics should not be considered indicative of schizoid PD. Her behavior should be judged from a broader cultural context that contains specific gender scripts, or rules of behavior for men and women.

Now take, for example, discussions about obsessive-compulsive personality traits in Japan. As one Japanese educator put it, in Japanese society many people were brought up to model themselves faithfully on "role models" or general behavioral standards. This environment creates conditions that stimulate people's preoccupation with discipline, formal rules, and procedures (Esaki, 2001). If these behavioral traits are taken out of cultural context, there could be a temptation to view them as symptoms of OCD. However, within the Japanese context, to a degree, these personality traits are considered normal.

Certain personality traits may "flourish" in particular circumstances and be "blocked" in others. Some personality types can contribute to successful coping in a set of cultural conditions—take, for example, avoidant traits. In China, traditionally, interpersonal relationships have been largely based on a deep cultural tradition of exchange of favors, or, in Western language, reciprocal relationships guided by moral norms. If people believe that under specific circumstances they are not capable of exchanging favor with others, this could be an embarrassing blow to their reputations. Therefore, to save face, it is generally appropriate for such individuals to develop avoidant tendencies because avoidance is perceived as less embarrassing than the inability to exercise appropriate social acts. Foreign observers may be inclined to perceive these persistent behaviors as symptoms of avoidant PD. Similarly, one study shows it is common for young adults from Greece to seek support (both emotional

CHECK AND APPLY YOUR KNOWLEDGE

1. What is the essence of the biomedical perspective of PDs?

2. What is the key difference between the behavioral learning and cognitive perspectives of PDs?

3. Compare the universalist and relativist perspectives of abnormal behavior.

4. *Hikikomori* is a complex form of withdrawal behavior common in Japan. It has been the topic of numerous television documentaries and newspaper and magazine articles (Rees, 2002; Saitō, 2012). Hikikimori is found mostly in men who shut themselves in the homes of their parents and have very limited face-to-face contact with other people (according to estimates, there are over 1 million of them). They spend their days browsing the web or chatting online and only occasionally see their parents, who help them financially. These young individuals claim they lost the incentive for hard work and abandoned their ambitions, but their lives are comfortable, and the web gives them a chance to interact with others without face-to-face contact. They do not have a prevalence of any psychological disorder, compared to the general population, and studies in other countries suggest that this is not exclusively a Japanese phenomenon (Sax, 2007).

   (a) Do you see Hikikomori as a kind of schizoid personality disorder? Why or why not?

   (b) Do you think these individuals are suffering psychologically? Have they failed as society members?

   (c) How will the society in which you live change if most people in it chose Hikikomori as their lifestyle? Explain your opinions.

and financial) from their parents until the age of 30. However, a foreign observer may construe this as a form of dependent behavior (Fountoulakis et al., 2002).

To summarize, some symptoms of PDs in the *DSM–5* could be valued as nonexcessive, nonpathological, and even normal in certain cultural settings. Cultural knowledge is essential when attempting to apply *DSM*-based diagnoses to individuals from different cultural environments.

Differential Diagnosis and Comorbidity

Comorbidity is the presence of one or several additional disorders in an individual. These disorders can be independent or related to one another. Comorbidity makes diagnostic procedures more difficult. A **differential diagnosis** is a method to identify and separate one disorder from others. This method also allows possible alternatives to an initial diagnosis.

Comorbidity
The simultaneous presence of more than one disorder in an individual.

Differential diagnosis
A differential diagnosis is a method to identify and separate one disorder from others This method also might identify possible alternatives to an initial diagnosis.

Comorbidity of personality disorders is the norm rather than the exception. Despite the diagnostic guidelines that prescribe that only one PD diagnosis should be given, people who meet diagnostic criteria for one PD will likely meet the criteria for another or several other PDs (Lenzenweger, Lane, Loranger, & Kessler, 2007; Widiger & Spitzer, 1991). For example, many symptoms of antisocial PD, including manipulativeness, grandiosity, and a lack empathy, are found in individuals with symptoms of narcissistic PD (Hare, 1991). Personality disorders are comorbid with other psychological problems—there is evidence of connections between pathological gambling and antisocial PD (Slutske et al., 2001). In addition, avoidant PD and a range of mood and anxiety disorders, such as social phobia, tend to be comorbid (Brieger, Ehrt, & Marneros, 2003).

A person diagnosed with a PD should have a history of inflexible, maladaptive, and distressful behavioral patterns. However, it is usually a challenge for clinicians to establish such a history. The person under evaluation is likely to regard these behavioral patterns as normal; he or she seems not to realize or refuses to acknowledge the problem. Another potential diagnostic problem relates to the degree of the problem, or the scope of the observable behaviors—for instance, an individual may exhibit only one trait that requires clinical attention (such as excessive punctuality) or a couple of traits of different PDs, such as excessive fascination with one's own self-appearance put together with an inability to delegate tasks to others. And although many symptoms of PDs tend to appear early in life, this is not true in every case. Late onset of PDs can take place under specific circumstances, such as the occurrence of other major psychological or physical disorders like Alzheimer's disease or substance-related disorders.

Personality disorders are especially difficult to differentiate from anxiety-related disorders. It is expected that individuals who develop symptoms of an anxiety disorder typically regard their anxiety and subsequent behavior as unusual and different from their "normal" behavior (Jansen, Arntz, Merckelbach, & Mersch, 1994). In contrast, individuals who exhibit several symptoms of a PD tend to explain their behavior as generally normal. A person with OCD may have difficulty accepting the fact that many people are late for their appointments, disregard written rules, or do not live according to a rigid schedule.

Now consider key distinctions between several pairs of PDs. Using the examples in **Table 12.5**, try to establish differences for the following pairs of disorders: avoidant and schizoid; narcissistic and histrionic; and paranoid and obsessive-compulsive.

A cautionary statement is necessary here. Studying personality from the position of illness is a work in progress. Looking for a clear-cut set of symptoms that describe an "abnormal" personality to distinguish it from a "normal" one is often unproductive. The methods used by clinicians, psychiatrists, psychologists, and social workers are not necessarily precise or reliable. We psychologists still know little about the impact of cultural factors on key symptoms of PDs. Experiments in this area are often difficult to conduct, and many research hypotheses remain untestable. To summarize, there is not a quick blood test or an express questionnaire to recognize a personality disorder. Not yet.

TABLE 12.5 ● Key Distinctions Between Several Pairs of Personality Disorders

Overlapping and Common Symptoms	Some Differences
Dependent and Borderline: Individuals demonstrate "clinging" behavior, suffer from separation anxiety, and report fear of abandonment.	In borderline cases, individuals are likely to be angry and move from being caring to being demanding and manipulative; in dependent cases, they tend to be agreeable, trusting, and submissive.
Avoidant and Schizoid: Introversion is a common underlying personality trait; self-isolation is a significant behavioral symptom.	Avoidant symptoms are accompanied by anxiety-related symptoms—individuals are afraid to make a mistake; individuals with schizoid symptoms tend to display low neuroticism and a lack of social motivation.
Schizotypal and Borderline: Common features include bizarre behavioral manifestations, inappropriate emotional displays, and general unpredictability.	Borderline symptoms are likely to be associated with impulsivity, aggression, and reckless behavior, all of which are almost uncommon in schizotypal symptoms.
Histrionic and Antisocial: Common features include seemingly flamboyant, shocking, provocative, and inappropriate behavior.	Histrionic behavior is likely to take place within the established social norms and may be judged as eccentric; symptoms are attention-seeking behaviors. Antisocial behavior is a more blatant challenge to norms, and symptoms are related to pragmatic or egotistic motives.
Paranoid and Narcissistic: Both have common features associated with lack of trust in other people, anger, inadequate self-esteem, and beliefs in self-exclusivity.	Paranoid symptoms are likely to be connected to withdrawal tendencies and elevated anxiety, as well as low self-esteem. Narcissistic tendencies are likely to be connected with attention-seeking behavior, envy, and the feeling of entitlement.
Complete the columns by comparing the following disorders. For discussion, visit the companion website.	
Avoidant and Dependent	
Narcissistic and Histrionic	
Paranoid and Obsessive-Compulsive	

CHECK AND APPLY YOUR KNOWLEDGE

1. Explain comorbidity in psychology.
2. Explain differential diagnosis in the context of PDs.

Applying Knowledge to the Clinical Domain

Treatment of Personality Disorders

There is no "magic pill" to treat personality disorders. While understanding the complexity of this type of illness and the inability of common individuals to recognize their problems, clinicians need to find the most effective, often "tailor-made" therapeutic approach to each patient. Some individuals need lengthy therapy, while others need it for just a short period. Some individuals thrive on strong support from their families, yet others do not. As we have learned, PDs usually appear in conjunction with other illnesses. Some clinicians advance the traditional psychoanalytic methods of treatment, whereas others turn to new forms of treatment such as *schema therapy*, which is a creative combination of several therapeutic techniques (Young, Klosko, & Weishaar, 2006). Despite the fact that PDs are very difficult to treat, there is evidence that many people diagnosed with them can improve over time (Zanarini, Frankenburg, Hennen, Reich, & Silk, 2005).

Personality disorders are likely to have a significant impact on other psychological disorders and the outcomes of their treatment (Lenzenweger et al., 2007). Patients with bipolar disorder who are also diagnosed with PDs have poorer treatment outcomes than those diagnosed as only bipolar. Clinical trials show that a key to successful treatment can be an emphasis on educating patients about their behavior and emotions (Colom et al., 2004).

Suicide Prevention

Some personality disorders, especially borderline and histrionic, are risk factors that contribute to suicide and self-destructive behavior (Lineham et al., 2000). Early recognition of symptoms and clinical attention to such individuals can save lives. Some assume that individuals with PDs make suicidal threats simply because they need attention and that they aren't serious about taking their own lives. This assumption should be dismissed. Suicide may take place even though it might have initially been planned as a theatrical gesture. Any suicidal threats, talk about death, or comments about "ending it all" should be taken with extreme seriousness. Some individuals with PDs will respond to the arguments of clinicians and friends who persuade them to avoid any harm to themselves or others. Such arguments can be designed according to the specific patient's situation and can be used in preventive therapies (McGirr, Paris, Lesage, Renaud, & Turecki, 2007).

© iStockphoto.com/Murika

Photo 12.3 Some personality disorders, especially borderline and histrionic, are risk factors that contribute to self-destructive behavior. Discuss the ways that we can attempt to help such individuals without violating their privacy.

Criminal Justice

By studying personality disorders and associating them with behavior, specialists in criminal justice (with the help from clinicians) gather information to identify, recognize, and deal with antisocial, deviant, and criminal behavior. Let's return to the chapter's opening example to illustrate: Reports suggest that 2 million to 3 million people in the United States may be stalked every year (Knight, 2014). Many different factors and circumstances cause stalking, so which cases should be addressed by the criminal justice system alone, and which cases also require clinical intervention?

First, experts draw a "profile" of the stalker. On average, stalkers are single males. About half of the victims are in a relationship with the stalker, about 15% are just acquaintances, and only 10% of cases involve people who have never met. Basic indicators, such as the stalker's age (under 30), the number of threats made, the presence of substance abuse, and the tendency to produce high levels of fear in the victim, are accurate predictors of violence in stalking cases and assist the law enforcement and criminal justice systems in creating a profile.

What about the psychological factors affecting a stalker's behavior and mind? There are at least five types of key stalking types or mind-sets. The *rejected* cannot accept their rejection or loss and try to achieve their goals by receiving acceptance. *Intimacy chasers* tend to ache from unrequited love and try to reduce their suffering. *Incompetent suitors* typically lack many important social and communication skills. The *resentful* believe they have been mistreated and hope to restore "justice." Finally, the *predatory* tend to behave as seekers and hunters (Mohandie et al., 2006). Which personality disorders, in your view, could be connected to the five types described here?

Those who stalk strangers and acquaintances are often mentally ill, and psychopathology is associated with more persistent and recurrent stalking behavior.

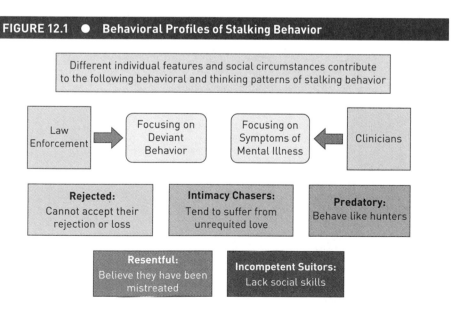

FIGURE 12.1 ● Behavioral Profiles of Stalking Behavior

Different individual features and social circumstances contribute to the following behavioral and thinking patterns of stalking behavior

Law Enforcement → Focusing on Deviant Behavior

Focusing on Symptoms of Mental Illness ← Clinicians

Rejected: Cannot accept their rejection or loss

Intimacy Chasers: Tend to suffer from unrequited love

Predatory: Behave like hunters

Resentful: Believe they have been mistreated

Incompetent Suitors: Lack social skills

These findings strongly support the argument for routine mental health assessment of stranger and acquaintance stalkers who become involved with the criminal justice system (McEwan & Strand, 2013).

Perhaps there are certain personality traits that contribute to stalkers' behavior, such as narcissistic tendencies, high or low self-esteem, compulsive habits, or impulsivity (see **Figure 12.1**). Some stalkers realize that their behavior is wrong and soon enough stop pursuing their victims, but others do not stop and carefully calculate their next step. Unfortunately, almost every third stalking case results in physical or sexual assault.

Visual Review

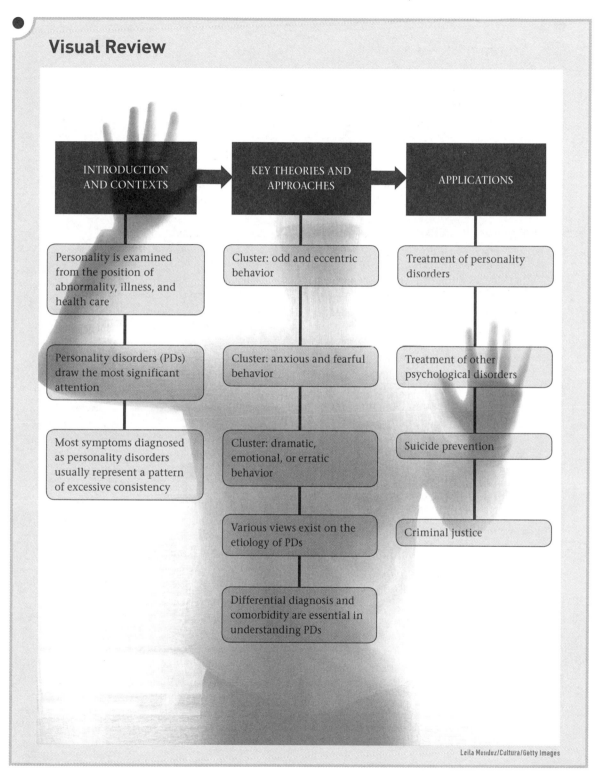

INTRODUCTION AND CONTEXTS → KEY THEORIES AND APPROACHES → APPLICATIONS

INTRODUCTION AND CONTEXTS

- Personality is examined from the position of abnormality, illness, and health care
- Personality disorders (PDs) draw the most significant attention
- Most symptoms diagnosed as personality disorders usually represent a pattern of excessive consistency

KEY THEORIES AND APPROACHES

- Cluster: odd and eccentric behavior
- Cluster: anxious and fearful behavior
- Cluster: dramatic, emotional, or erratic behavior
- Various views exist on the etiology of PDs
- Differential diagnosis and comorbidity are essential in understanding PDs

APPLICATIONS

- Treatment of personality disorders
- Treatment of other psychological disorders
- Suicide prevention
- Criminal justice

Summary

- The clinical domain involves approaches to personality from the position of abnormality, illness, and health care. The term *illness* can be used interchangeably with the terms *disease* and *disorder* and broadly refers to any *condition*, or a functional abnormality or disturbance of the body and mind. Psychiatry and clinical psychology, together with other disciplines, contributed to this approach.

- Personality disorders are enduring patterns of behavior and inner experience that deviate markedly from the expectations of the individual's culture. In clinical practice, a majority of symptoms diagnosed as PDs usually represent a pattern of excessive consistency.

- Medicalization is the process by which various aspects of human behavior are interpreted in medical terms and thus diagnosed and treated by medical methods. Stigma is marked by the negative perception and corresponding actions related to a person or group based solely on certain social characteristics they possess or are associated with.

- Psychologists use various methods to diagnose PDs. Clinicians are aware of the many unresolved issues with these methods and constantly improve them.

- Clinicians use the classification of PDs based on *The Diagnostic and Statistical Manual* (*DSM–5*). There are three clusters.

- The first cluster is odd and eccentric behavior. Disorders of this cluster deal with stable patterns of remarkably unusual behavior. Clinicians in the United States recognize three PDs related to this cluster: paranoid, schizoid, and schizotypal.

- The second cluster is dramatic, emotional, and erratic behavior. Disorders in this cluster share problems with the individual's impulse control and emotional regulation. Named disorders include histrionic, narcissistic, borderline, and antisocial PDs.

- The third cluster is anxious and fearful behavior. Personality disorders here represent a range of symptoms for abnormal manifestations of apprehensive, timid, or frightened behavior. The disorders include avoidant, dependent, and obsessive-compulsive PDs.

- Different philosophical, sociological, and other models explained the etiology of PDs. Traditional psychoanalytic models focus on unconscious psychological mechanisms usually rooted in early childhood and heavily influenced by early experiences. According to the biomedical perspective, PDs should have underlying biological causes such as genetic or other natural predispositions that impact specific individual functions and subsequent thought, behavior, and emotion. The learning perspective states there should be social factors and corresponding learning experiences that impact PDs. The cognitive perspective focuses primarily on how people process information related to self and how they use this information to regulate their emotions and behavior. From the trait perspective, PDs represent abnormal configurations of basic, "normal" dimensions of personality. The cross-cultural approach investigates PDs from the standpoint of common, universal, and culture-specific factors.

- To better understand personality disorders, we should apply two key perspectives: the relativist perspective on abnormal behavior that puts psychological phenomena in a relative, cultural perspective; and the universalist perspective on abnormal behavior, which suggests the existence of some universal psychological and behavioral features within individuals. Judgments about appropriate and inappropriate traits vary across cultures. In the context of culture, tolerance threshold indicates a measure of tolerance or intolerance toward specific personality traits in a cultural environment.

- Personality disorders are comorbid and require differential diagnoses. Comorbidity is the presence of one or several additional disorders in an individual. These disorders can be independent or related to one another. A differential diagnosis is a method to identify and separate one disorder from others that appear with similar symptoms.

- Scientific knowledge about PDs is used—among other areas—in treatment of mental illness, in suicide prevention, and in the criminal justice system.

Key Terms

clinical domain 366

clinical psychologists 367

clinicians 367

comorbidity 389

differential diagnosis 389

excessive consistency 368

illness 367

interrater reliability 371

L, F, and K validity scales 372

medicalization 369

neurotic character 373

overarching liabilities 383

relativist perspective of abnormal behavior 387

stigma 369

test-taking attitudes 371

universalist perspective of abnormal behavior 387

Evaluating What You Know

Explain the essence of the clinical domain.

Explain the features of the "normal" and "abnormal" personality.

Explain excessive consistency referring to personality.

Describe key features of the following personality disorders: paranoid, schizoid, schizotypal, histrionic, narcissistic, borderline, antisocial, avoidant, dependent, and obsessive-compulsive.

Explain the relationship between differential diagnosis and comorbidity.

Explain the relativist and universalist perspectives on abnormal behavior.

How do we apply the clinical domain in personality psychology? Explain the use of knowledge in treatment of personality disorders, suicide prevention, and in criminal justice.

A Bridge to the Next Chapter

The majority of symptoms that appear together and are diagnosed as personality disorders usually represent a pattern of excessive consistency. We now better understand what it means: The individual experiences serious and constant problems with either a constantly changing environment or particular social norms that require from this individual corrections and adjustments. When a new challenge occurs, we take the valuable lessons from our experience and adjust to these new demands. Our ability or inability to adjust to new conditions plays a significant role in how we live our lives, how we feel, and who we become. This is the subject of the next chapter.

13

The Adjustment Domain

"None will improve your lot if you yourself do not."

—**Berthold Brecht (1898–1956),** German playwright

Learning Objectives

After reading this chapter, you should be able to:

- Identify areas of change that require adjustment and coping in individuals
- Describe the various types of adjustment and coping and their outcomes
- Compare "helpful" personality traits with traits that are unhelpful in the coping process
- Compare adaptive and maladaptive coping strategies
- Identify ways to apply knowledge about personality psychology in the adjustment domain

Her life was full of hardship. Yet through all of her tragedies and challenges, Christina persevered, learned, and found renewed will and strength. She was the oldest of 15 siblings, five of whom died very young because of illness and poverty. She took care of her surviving brothers and sisters, and her first full-time job was when she was just 11 years old. She quit school so she could work. While still a young girl, she witnessed a bloody revolution and civil war in her country. She lived through many years of adversity and political repression. She survived World War II and dealt with the loss of her brothers and a husband who died on the battlefield. As a widow with two small children, she migrated from one war-torn town to another, looking for any opportunity that would help her cope and survive. She found a job. She sent both her children to college. She continued working. She maintained an active lifestyle until well into her 90s when Alzheimer's finally took away her memories and her relentless energy.

Today, some people facing just a smidgeon of Christina's problems would give up and fall apart. She did not.

She adjusted to every challenge and resolved the problems she faced.

She was resilient. She never gave up, and she remained hardy and tough on every difficult curve of her life and in every tragic situation.

She was proactive. She disliked procrastination, and she chose preventive actions instead of late reactions.

She was optimistic. She always saw a positive side of life, and she believed that tomorrow definitely would be better than today. She always had a reason to look forward to every day.

She was my grandmother.

Questions

Who in your family has or had the great ability to overcome difficulties and challenges better than others? What specific traits does this person have?

The Essence of Adjustment and Coping

Life is about change. Everything evolves. Some changes are slow, and we prepare for them. Other changes strike like lightening. Some changes are exciting and enjoyable. Others are unpleasant and painful. How do we deal with significant challenges and changes? Most probably, we try to adjust to them.

In general terms, adjustment is an alteration to achieve a desired result or condition. Such alteration takes place to reduce a discrepancy between (a) what is expected or desired and (b) the reality of it. Adjustments can be small, such as a slight modification or fine-tuning—for example, we sometimes alter our clothes. As with food or music preferences, we develop our own "styles" of adjustment. Imagine you are driving and suddenly see a traffic jam ahead of you. What do you usually do in such cases? Do you immediately seek a detour? Or do you prefer moving slowly through the traffic?

Many of our adjustments seem almost automatic. For example, every day when we communicate with others, we tend to automatically match other people's language style. Research shows that almost immediately after we establish contact with another person, verbal and nonverbal behaviors become—to some degree—more synchronized than they were prior to the contact (Ireland & Pennebaker, 2010). Other adjustments can be significant. For instance, to many people, a transition from high school to college requires a major effort—they have to adjust to a new place away from home, to new friends, and to the new anxieties of college life. In the context of personality, this type of adjustment should probably interest us the most.

In personality psychology, **adjustment** refers to relatively significant changes in an individual's behavior and experiences in response to external and internal challenges. Adjustment is somewhat similar to **coping**, which is a deliberate and conscious effort to adjust to challenges, changing situations, and new conditions (adjustment is not necessarily conscious and deliberate).

Adjustment
Relatively significant changes in an individual's behavior and experiences in response to external and internal challenges are known as the process of adjustment.

Coping The process of coping includes deliberate and conscious efforts to adjust to challenges, changing situations, and new conditions.

Why Individuals Cope

Why do species adjust? They do it because adjustment is essential for their survival. For example, some birds

TABLE 13.1 ● Types of Challenges That Require Adjustment and Coping	
Type	Range
Occurrence	Sudden, unexpected to expected, planned
Duration	Fast emerging, quick to slowly developing, prolonged
Origin	Avoidable to inevitable
Significance	Major, significant to minor, insignificant

fly to warmer places in the fall and some mammals, like bears, hibernate during winters to avoid the harmful impact of cold temperatures. Humans also tend to avoid dangerous environments, physical threats, and anything that causes or may cause physical harm, pain, or discomfort. We tend to perceive and recognize the discrepancy between (a) how things are now and (b) how they should be. This discrepancy is based on a subjective experience and is influenced by many underlying physical and psychological conditions and contexts. Subjectively, this discrepancy is unpleasant and occurs in many forms, such as a mild psychological discomfort or distress or significant suffering. Challenges that disturb the individual's physical or mental equilibrium are called stressors. The reaction to a condition that disturbs an individual's physical or mental balance is called **stress**. Almost one third of adults in the United States report that stress has a strong impact on their physical and mental health (see **Table 13.1**; American Psychological Association [APA], 2015b).

Photo 13.1
Hibernation is a state of inactivity and metabolic depression as a response to cold temperatures or when sufficient food is unavailable. Do some humans have a somewhat similar response of inactivity to harsh conditions? Suggest examples.

© iStockphoto.com/Dieter Meyrl

Stress
Stress is the reaction to a condition that disturbs an individual's physical or mental balance.

Areas of Change Requiring Coping and Adjustment

To study the process of coping, you have to identify the stressors the individual has to face. A stressor can be a single event in one area of life; it also can be a continuous development, involving many areas of an individual's activities. In the United States, the top three stressors are problems with money, problems with work, and family responsibilities (APA, 2015b). Stress—especially continuous stress—significantly contributes to individual problems that might include various disorders, including mental illness (see Chapter 12). Many areas of life and its activities produce stressors, and they require us to cope with them. Let's mention just a few of such areas and activities. Feel free to suggest other areas not mentioned here.

Aging

Regardless of how old you are now, remember how much you enjoyed getting older when you were a child? Conversely, once we become adults, aging is sometimes unpleasant, stressful, and even traumatic. Simply ask around and listen to what people say about how they feel about getting older. Every age has some unpleasant realizations that are fairly typical but can still be stressful. A few significant physical and psychological changes are associated with aging that require coping (Lazarus & Lazarus, 2006). One feature of aging is that many people never feel their age—they feel younger. In a 2009 survey, people over 50 in the United States claimed to feel at least 10 years younger than their chronological age; those over 65 said they felt up to 20 years younger (Segal, 2013). Why is this disconnection between actual age and perceived age stressful? Because physical decline and other changes associated with aging do not match people's perception of their age.

Physical Illness

Some health maladies, such as heart attacks, strokes, and accidents, are sudden and devastating. Such serious life-threatening events immediately alter the lives of the victim and their loved ones. To recover from an acute illness and get back to day-to-day life requires considerable effort. It is about making adjustments and coping in several areas of life. The uncertainty that is associated with the illness (some injuries may remain life-threatening for a long time) adds to the stress.

Other illnesses develop slowly and remain chronic. In fact, two thirds of adults in the United States report having at least one chronic illness (APA, 2015b). Suffering from these illnesses also demands from the individual significant behavioral and psychological adjustments. Serious illnesses are frequently connected with **disabilities**, which involve impairments (significant problem with a physical or psychological functioning), activity limitations (inability to perform certain tasks), and participation restrictions (problems with particular social activities). Of course, not every illness becomes a disability (see **Table 13.2**).

Disabilities
Disabilities take the form of impairments (significant problems with physical or psychological functioning), activity limitations (inability to perform certain tasks), and participation restrictions (problems with particular social activities).

Changes in the Family

Significant changes in family life may become major stressors and require adjustment and coping. Not all of these changes, whether sudden or continuing, are catastrophic; many major life events are supposed to be easy to deal with—take marriage as an example. It can be stress-free, but it can also be a significant stressor, sometimes requiring big adjustments in habits and even personality traits. Now, think of divorce. Not only does a person have to cope with moral and psychological problems associated with the divorce but also with many interpersonal, financial, and legal challenges. There are other major changes associated with the family as well. Some parents (after they have sent their grown sons and daughters off to college) experience a stressful "empty-nest syndrome"—a persistent state of sadness and loneliness. Some parents cope with this new situation somewhat quickly; others do not.

TABLE 13.2 ● Areas of Change That May Require Adjustment and Coping	
Area of Change	**Types of Challenges**
Aging	Physical decline, cognitive decline, stigma of aging
Physical illness	Physical decline, uncertainty of the outcome
Disability	Physical decline, stigma of disability
Family changes	Marriage, divorce, moving in or out, new or lost members
Professional changes	Getting a new job or promotion, losing a job, retirement
Relationships	Breakup, loss of an attachment figure, chronic or acute conflicts
Social changes	War and violence, hardship, migration and immigration
Other	What other challenges not mentioned here could an individual face?

Professional Changes

The process of getting a new job is as exciting as it is stressful. A new job sometimes requires adjusting to a different geographic area, a tough work schedule, additional or unfamiliar job requirements, daily commuting, and so on—all may require personal changes and significant adjustment. Individuals who are not ready to face these challenges may develop serious psychological problems, including burnout. Losing a job is also often very stressful. This event can cause significant, long-term psychological consequences in an individual. The loss of income is certainly an issue, but being out of work is also about loss of dignity, respect, and meaningful social interactions. Research suggests that an individual's unemployment is associated with social withdrawal, tension in the family, and many other stressful symptoms (Brand, 2015).

There is also noteworthy psychological research about the stressors associated with retirement. It is true that some people look forward to their retirement; yet for others, retirement can be a period they dread. Some people delay the decision to retire or never make it. They may worry about financial security, fear boredom and isolation, and fret about no longer being able to do something meaningful or make a difference in other people's lives (Knoll, 2011).

Changes in Personal Relationships

Friendship and love are supposed to be fulfilling and rewarding, and for many people, they are. However, relationships often involve conflict. Studies show that many individuals experience significant challenges and stress during a crisis in their relationships with a significant other (Borelli & Sbarra, 2011). Such a crisis may involve separation, infidelity, dishonesty, or emotional and physical abuse, which can have a profound impact on an individual and often requires serious psychological coping.

A large cross-cultural study in 96 countries (Morris, Reiber, & Roman, 2015) showed that people experience an average of three significant breakups in their relationships by age 30, and at least one of those breakups affects them strongly enough that it substantially decreases their quality of life for weeks or even months.

Immigration

Acculturation
The individual's process of coping with the new cultural conditions is acculturation.

Immigration (the movement of people into a country) is another source of significant stress, as it often requires individuals to cope and adjust to new social and cultural conditions. The process of coping with new cultural conditions is called **acculturation**. Each generation of newcomers faces the unavoidable challenge of adapting to their new country and its culture, and the process of adjustment is an extremely stressful period of their lives. They have left something significant back in their home countries: They have to learn a new language, adapt to a different value system, make friends, find new reinforcements, seek social support networks, and get used to a different climate, food, and the little nuances that constitute culture. Individuals who fail to cope with the acculturation stressors are more likely to develop psychopathological symptoms. We will return to this subject again later in this chapter.

Significant Social Changes

There are different types of social changes. Most people—especially those who grew up in economically developed countries such as the United States, Canada, or Japan—are shielded against devastating social cataclysms. They do not have to encounter famine, violent revolutions, or a protracted civil war. Unfortunately, this is not the case for people living in underdeveloped places. Today, hundreds of millions of people remain vulnerable to serious abuse and violations of their safety and most basic rights. Additionally, rampant poverty is a major and constant challenge in their lives.

Other social changes are of a different nature. Recall from Chapter 10 the American psychologist Rollo May's belief that individuals are caught between an epic conflict of the old world of tradition and the new world of change. The old world represented stability and certainly; the new world is about uncertainty and instability. As a result, individuals lose their ability to learn and adjust to the rapidly changing surroundings (May, 1950), and their poor adjustment causes anxiety—also caused by consistent threats to their most fundamental values (May, Angel, & Ellenberger, 1958). Anxiety brings more confusion, which in turn increases the sense of powerlessness. People no longer know how to influence their lives or other people. This leads to anger, which can lead to violence (May, 1969).

Although May and his colleagues wrote about these problems more than 50 years ago, their analysis tends to reflect very well the challenges that we experience these days in the globalizing world. For example, the spread of fundamentalist ideas and the resulting violence are seen by some scholars as a psychological byproduct of the ongoing globalization (Huntington, 1996, 2004).

CHECK AND APPLY YOUR KNOWLEDGE

1. Describe the similarities and differences between adjustment and coping.

2. Name three features of disability.

3. How many significant breakups does an average person expect to have by age 30?

4. What is acculturation? Why does it require coping?

Types of Coping and Adjustment

Assisting people with adjustment requires a very diverse knowledge of their personalities. The **psychology of adjustment** studies problems and conditions that cause people's need for adjustment, the psychological mechanisms of adjustment, and the ways to help them in their coping process. Some people avoid dealing with challenges, while others tend to confront them. Some individuals cope by transforming their personal features, including their habits and traits, yet others remain stubborn and unchanged. Based on age, experience, and education, people choose different coping strategies (Folkman, Lazarus, Pimley, & Novacek, 1987; Powell, 2015), and many small variables and ever-changing circumstances affect the way they adjust and cope.

What do we do when we face stressors or significant challenges in our lives? Consider several general strategies. Two of them refer to the individual, and the other two have to do with the social environment.

Psychology of adjustment
The psychology of adjustment is the study of problems and conditions that cause the individual's need for adjustment, the psychological mechanisms of adjustment, and the ways to help individuals in their coping process.

The Individual

Facing a stressor, we can choose—if we think logically—between two alternatives: to change something internally (such as our own thinking, emotional responses, and behavior) or not to change anything. The choice between these two strategies ("To change or not to change?") depends on our personality features as well as on specific circumstances and contexts. In the first case, coping will require some personal transformation and correction. New assessments of the stressors and innovative responses should be sought and found. A change of habits and even personality features may also be required.

There are some individuals who are more flexible and, thus, have a greater propensity for constant adjustments to changing environment and stressors. **Flexibility** can be viewed as a trait measured by the degree (scope and depth) or the extent to which a person can cope in novel ways. There is evidence that flexibility can form early in life and is based on parenting style. For instance, authoritarian parents are likely to diminish psychological flexibility in their children by constantly restricting the ways their children cope with stressors in life (Williams, Ciarrochi, & Heaven, 2012). The power of psychological flexibility in the workplace is correlated with better mental

Flexibility
Flexibility is a trait measured by the degree (scope and depth) or the extent to which a person can cope in novel ways.

health and job performance. Allowing workers more job control would likely increase work productivity as well as job satisfaction (Bond & Flaxman, 2006). Studies also show that psychological flexibility is a factor that affects long-term coping—people who are better "managers" of their emotional responses are less likely to be stressed over time (Bonanno, Papa, Lalande, Westphal, & Coifman, 2004).

Individuals who choose the second alternative—not changing anything—keep most of their evaluations, responses, habits, and personality features unchanged when faced with a stressor. We may use the adjective *stubborn* to describe this pattern. Stubbornness may result in successful coping, or it may be harmful and cause significant psychological suffering.

The Stressor

Which challenges—or stressors—do we accept, and which do we contest? The discussion has been ongoing in social sciences and the humanities for centuries. Some philosophers in the past called for the individual's active engagement in life events in attempts to transform them. Others called for more wisdom and acceptance of one's own fate (Yakunin, 2001). Both sides offered reasonable arguments in defense of their positions: On the one hand, we should be able to overcome life's challenges by standing tall against them; on the other, there are many challenges that we are incapable of overcoming, and, thus, we should not falsely believe that we can resolve every problem and negotiate every obstacle (you may recall similar arguments in Chapter 9).

Coping and adjustment can be active or passive, with many variations in between the "active" and "passive" alternatives of the imaginary spectrum. On one end of it is **approaching**, which is a type of coping that refers to deliberate attempts at changing self as well as the sources of stress. A person who is approaching is also is seeking internal (self) and external (others) resources to deal with a stressor or a problem (Zeidner & Endler, 1995). Approaching involves cognitive operations, such as thinking, as well as actions. Approaching can be proactive when an individual is aware of a problem or anticipates a stressor to emerge and thus has one or more strategies to deal with them. For instance, a couple expecting a baby is proactive about understanding the challenges that new families face, such as night feeding, changing diapers, and having much less free time for a while, and they prepare for these challenges in advance. Approaching can also be reactive, as a response to the changes. Approaching might be mostly behavioral (involving actions) or mostly cognitive (involving thinking) or both.

Approaching Some patients use approaching, a type of coping that refers to deliberate attempts at changing self as well as the sources of stress.

Coping may also take a form of **avoiding**, which is keeping oneself away from addressing a challenge or a stressor. There are several types of avoidant behavior. Avoidant behavior can be rational, which means that we consciously try to discount or ignore an apparent problem for some time, even though we are aware of it. Many of us, from time to time, avoid certain unpleasant challenges because we have a realistic understanding that we have little time or opportunity to address known stressors that confront us. On the other hand, avoiding can be a way of ignoring or hiding from a problem. This often leads to a more serious problem that arises because the original stressor is not addressed. Avoiding can be behavioral (not doing anything to address the problem), cognitive (not thinking about the problem), or both. Avoiding can take

Avoiding Keeping oneself away from addressing a challenge or a stressor is called avoiding.

a form of compensatory behavior, which may distract the individual from addressing the stressor. Such behavior is often associated with certain unhealthy activities. For example, approximately two in five adults in America report overeating or eating unhealthy foods in the past month due to stress (APA, 2015b). Avoiding can also be a result of our lack of knowledge and understanding, our deliberate ignorance ("I don't even want to know"), our inability to correctly assess the problem and its significance, or our specific individual psychological features, including mental illness. Recall the discussion of avoidant personality disorder in Chapter 12. It is important for psychologists to study and recognize the differences between an individual's use of avoiding as a healthy, successful way to cope and avoiding that is an unhealthy, harmful behavioral style (see **Figure 13.1**).

In terms of the dynamics, or speed, of coping, some people tend to adjust quickly. As soon as the stressor appears or as soon as they realize an adjustment is necessary, they think about what to do and then act. Others display a persistent pattern of behavior and thought called **procrastination**—putting off impending tasks to a later time. We procrastinate for various reasons and tend to be aware of the consequences of our procrastination. How often do you hear the phrase "I wish I had done this earlier"? It is true that for many people occasional procrastination is not a serious problem, but it may become significant when it becomes a consistent pattern. Chronic procrastinators have a deficiency in their self-regulation: There is a gap between their intentions and actions, as studies show (Pychyl, Lee, Thibodeau, & Blunt, 2000). Procrastinators often fail to correct their behavior and face the same problem in new situations and create a false excuse that turning to their problem later is a better choice (Pychyl et al., 2000). Research finds that procrastinators tend to carry accompanying feelings of guilt, shame, or anxiety associated with their constant choice to delay (Jaffe, 2013; Sirois & Pychyl, 2013). Some procrastinators act more efficiently when they work under time pressure; however, many of them use this argument, as studies show, to justify their

Procrastination
Putting off impending tasks to a later time is called procrastination.

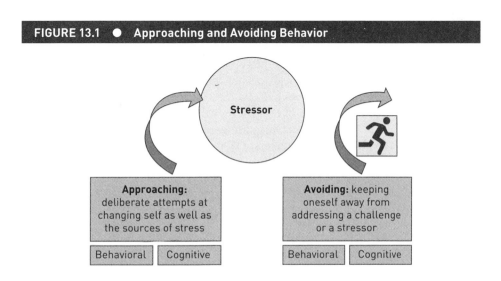

FIGURE 13.1 ● Approaching and Avoiding Behavior

Stressor

Approaching: deliberate attempts at changing self as well as the sources of stress

Behavioral | Cognitive

Avoiding: keeping oneself away from addressing a challenge or a stressor

Behavioral | Cognitive

Passive adjustment
Putting off
impending tasks to
a later time is called
procrastination.

chronic inaction now and in the future (Sirois & Pychyl, 2013).

Passive adjustment, or passive coping, is a general pattern of relying on others to address or resolve stressful events or life situations. This pattern of dependency is rooted in an individual's feeling of helplessness and the inability to deal with the stressor (recall dependent personality disorder from Chapter 12). Those who engage in passive coping tend to relinquish control of the stressful situation to others. These individuals often want others to help them find the best way of coping (Carroll, 2013).

Although there are several ways we can classify different kinds of adjustment and coping, our behavior doesn't always fall into the same category from stressor to stressor. While some individuals tend to maintain a particular adjustment style, others do not. Sometimes we may use an approaching style, other times we may use an avoiding style, or we may use a combination of the two, depending on the situation.

Outcomes of Coping and Adjustment

Coping has a continuum of outcomes, ranging from successful to unsuccessful. On one end of the spectrum, successful coping responses allow an individual to maintain a happy and productive life, score high on the measures of subjective well-being (see Chapter 9), and be free of distressful symptoms. In a famous study, the psychologist Shelly Taylor (1983) was looking for successful coping strategies in women treated for breast cancer. She wanted to identify the inner resources that help women return to their previous, "normal" level of functioning after going through traumatic experiences associated with their illness. The interviews conducted with the women revealed that rather than simply "getting back" to what their healthy lives used to be, most of the women reported that their lives had changed for the better in many ways. Some noted that they had a new sense of themselves as being strong and resilient; others talked about their ability to stop procrastinating, reestablish priorities, and make time for the activities that were most important (Taylor et al., 2004).

Adjustment disorder
Someone unable to
cope with a major life
stressor experiences
a cluster of symptoms
associated with
significant distress
and is diagnosed with
adjustment disorder.

On the other end of the outcomes scale is unsuccessful adjustment and coping associated with the inability to adjust to a stressor and continuous emotional distress. One of the most severe forms of such distress is adjustment disorder (see **Figure 13.2**).

Adjustment disorder refers to a cluster of symptoms associated with significant distress that occurs in someone who is unable to cope with a major life stressor. This stressor is associated with an individual's immediate social network (e.g., separation from a significant other) or broader network (e.g., becoming a refugee and moving to

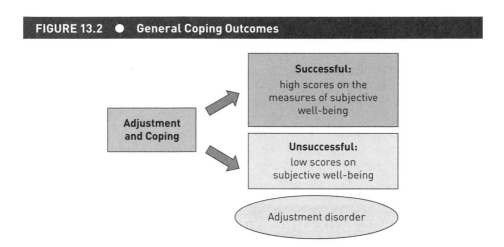

FIGURE 13.2 ● General Coping Outcomes

a foreign country), or it is caused by a life transition or crisis (e.g., becoming a parent or being diagnosed with a serious illness). The manifestations include persistent depressed mood, anxiety, irritability, sleep problems, and feelings of helplessness. Individual personality features and circumstances may worsen the manifestation of the symptoms. Once the individual is able to cope with the stressor, the harmful symptoms diminish and can disappear. The challenge is in finding the right path to an individual's coping strategies (Powell, 2015).

One of the negative outcomes of coping is **burnout**—a state of a significant exhaustion and disappointment brought about by devotion to an activity (often work related) that failed to produce the expected result or reward. Burnout is a problem usually born out of the individual's attempts to achieve unrealistic goals or take on undeliverable promises. Those who experience burnout feel extremely fatigued, distrustful, pessimistic, and tend to be increasingly inefficient despite their efforts (Maslach, Jackson, & Leiter, 1996). They also tend to maintain a negative attitude toward work and are at risk of developing serious health problems (Bakker, Demerouti, & Sanz-Vergel, 2014). One who once was enthusiastic and full of energy becomes irritable, frustrated, and bitter. Burnout may resemble some symptoms of depression, but one of the differences is that depression is likely to impact an individual's whole life, while burnout relates mostly to the job context (Plieger, Melchers, Montag, Meermann, & Reuter, 2015).

Although earlier research showed that differences in how genders handle general coping were relatively small (Billings & Moos, 1981), psychologists were often looking at specific stressors and situations. Some earlier studies suggested that women tend to have a harder time coping with a breakup (Davis, Matthews, & Twamley, 1999). However, more recent cross-cultural research shows that this is not the case. Researchers measured the subjective rate of the emotional and physical pain in the immediate aftermath of the breakup on a sample of more than 5,700 people in 96 countries. While breakups affect women the hardest emotionally and physically, this is true only immediately after the breakup. Men tend to have more emotional issues in the long

Burnout
Often a work-related term, burnout is a state of a significant exhaustion and disappointment brought about by a devotion to an activity that failed to produce the expected result or reward.

term. In other words, women tend to recover more fully and come out emotionally stronger after a breakup than men (Morris et al., 2015).

There are different explanations for this phenomenon. Evolutionary psychologists suggest that women cope better in the long term because they have better skills in finding "substitutions" (in other words, a new partner) for the lost relationship (Morris et al., 2015). Men also tend to reevaluate their losses, and once they have a new partner, they realize their new partner may be not as great as the one they lost. Other research suggests that men tend to cope by either confronting the stressor or avoiding it; women, on the other hand, when a relationship becomes a source of stress, tend to be better "negotiators" than men (Wang et al., 2007).

CHECK AND APPLY YOUR KNOWLEDGE

1. Define and explain *flexibility*.

2. Explain proactive approaching.

3. Ferrari (2010), in *Still Procrastinating? The No Regrets Guide to Getting It Done*, would like to see a general cultural shift from punishing procrastination to rewarding the "early bird." The author proposed, among other things, that the federal government and other agencies give financial incentives to those who do things (such as paying taxes) early, long before the deadlines. Discuss whether this strategy could reduce procrastination or would just reward the people who are too anxious and do everything very early.

4. In one of the most famous plays by Shakespeare, the main character Hamlet posed probably the most frequently quoted question: "To be or not to be?" In the monologue that followed, he complained about life's pains and unfairness yet was also afraid that the alternative, which is suicide, might be worse. What kind of coping was Hamlet choosing from?

5. Define *adjustment disorder*.

6. Explain burnout.

7. Have you ever experienced burnout? How did you cope with it?

Identifying "Helpful" Personality Traits

Stress tolerance
Stress tolerance is a stable pattern of behavior and experience that appears helpful in the process of coping with significant stressors.

Psychologists have identified a stable pattern of behavior and experience that appears helpful in the process of coping with significant stressors (Block & Block, 2012). This pattern has different names, but we can call it **stress tolerance**. At least three specific traits have been identified as contributing to stress tolerance: openness to experience, hardiness, and individual impulse control (Weiten, Dunn, & Hummer, 2011). We studied openness to experience and impulse control in earlier chapters (remember, for instance, instant gratification in Chapter 2). Psychological research also provides interesting data about **hardiness**—the individual's general ability to withstand difficult conditions. Hardiness may resemble stubbornness, which was described earlier in this chapter. Hardiness and stubbornness share some common psychological features, yet stubbornness is usually a pattern of resistance to change by all costs. Hardiness has three specific characteristics (Kobasa, 1979). It involves these actions:

- Changes in strategies and behavior, as well as a commitment or sustained effort to achieve a goal
- Control, or the belief in and ability to rely on your own efforts, to solve a problem
- A challenge, or a commitment to test self and confront difficulties

These features help the individual to launch effective coping and actively seek solutions, seek and receive social support, and engage in effective self-care (Maddi, 2006). Hardiness is a continuous variable. Research shows that it is likely to be correlated with internal locus of control and self-efficacy (Bandura, 1997), which we studied in Chapter 6.

Another feature that tends to be helpful in successful coping is **optimism**—the general belief in positive or successful outcomes. Optimism involves an act of cognitive assessment of the present and the future. We call people *optimists* if they tend to believe things that belong to them and around them (a) are better than they seem or (b) will be better in the future. These beliefs refer to material things and developments (such as the stock market or weather) as well as social and psychological phenomena (such as personal health and professional career). When facing challenges, optimists tend to think they will overcome the difficulties, or the challenges will just go away. Leonel Tiger, in *Optimism: The Biology of Hope* (1979), argued that optimism is an evolutionary useful feature, mostly because of its role in coping: It allows human beings to counteract their fears, manage their anxiety, and cope with significant problems and crises. Optimism is also associated with exploratory behavior, such as finding alternative solutions and experiences. For example, a person's exploratory activities affect building more new neurons in the hippocampus (a process called neurogenesis), which is the brain's center for learning and memory (Bergmann & Frisén, 2013). Optimistic views of self are connected to the person's views of others: Individuals who scored high on self-coherence also perceive life as comprehensible, cognitively meaningful, and manageable (Antonovsky, 1987).

Optimism can be a situational, short-lived phenomenon or a stable personality feature or trait. Scheier and Carver (1992) were among the first to study **dispositional optimism**—a general and stable belief that good things and positive outcomes will happen. People who possess this trait tend to expect that in most life situations, the balance between good and bad things will be in favor of good things. "In uncertain times, I usually expect the best," says an optimist. Dispositional optimism is likely to affect behavior since optimists tend to sustain their efforts to pursue their goals, while pessimists tend to give up (Peterson, 2000). Optimism has also been tied to active and preventive coping efforts, which enable people to guard against undesirable

Hardiness
An individual's general ability to withstand difficult conditions is called hardiness.

Optimism
The general belief in positive or successful outcomes is referred to as optimism.

Dispositional optimism
An individual's general and stable belief that good things and positive outcomes will happen is displayed as dispositional optimism.

life changes caused by significant stressors (Aspinwall & Taylor, 1997). Because optimism is associated with effective social relationships and interpersonal coping strategies, optimists develop a stronger sense of personal control and tend to have greater social support during times of stress.

Pessimism is the general belief in negative or unsuccessful outcomes. A pessimistic person tends to believe in the likelihood of bad outcomes and anticipates that difficulties will continue and troubles will prevail. As a famous saying goes, optimists see a glass "half full," while pessimists see the same glass "half empty."

Traits That Negatively Affect the Coping Process

Even in ancient times, philosophers in India, China, and Greece stated that many individuals had a distorted way of looking at things, and they could not effectively cope with difficulties (Isaeva, 1999). Modern research provides supporting evidence for those philosophical assertions. As in the case of "helpful" traits, there are also features that negatively affect coping.

Consider again procrastination, which we discussed earlier in this chapter. Research shows that constant procrastination becomes particularly maladaptive in an individual's coping strategies. It becomes especially harmful if a person is measured high on impulsivity and low on self-discipline (Jaffe, 2013). People who procrastinate persistently create false excuses that turning to their problem later is a better choice (Pychyl et al., 2000).

Consistent cognitive distortions (we discussed them in Chapter 8 and Chapter 9) also can negatively affect the coping process. These are thoughts and assumptions that cause individuals to perceive reality inaccurately. They are rooted in negative emotions (Burns, 1989). An individual, for example, is angry that the college courses are too difficult for her and therefore she is failing academically. Instead of changing her learning habits, she is preoccupied with her anger and other negative emotions. Consider, for example, consistent **catastrophic thinking**—the stable tendency to overestimate the probability of very negative outcomes. People who are prone to this type of thinking tend to focus on their negative emotions—a process that is called rumination. These individuals see threats when there are few or none of them. They tend to exaggerate minor threats. They also tend to be **dispositional pessimists**—people who have the general and stable belief that bad things and negative outcomes will happen. Studies show that people who have a tendency for catastrophic thinking have problems coping with pain (Wideman & Sullivan, 2011).

Catastrophic thinking as a thought pattern has been linked to certain personality characteristics. Psychologists, for example, identify the **Type D personality** (*D* stands for *distressed* in cognitive and behavioral terms). The Type D personality is linked to the persistent tendency toward negative affectivity (being constantly irritable, anxious, and expecting failure) and social inhibition (which involves both self-restraint and a lack of self-assurance). This type is also associated with the development of burnout (Geuens, Braspenning, Van Bogaert, & Franck, 2015).

Contemporary studies also show the existence of so-called **latent vulnerability traits**, which are specific behavioral and psychological features that individuals

Catastrophic thinking The stable tendency to overestimate the probability of very negative outcomes is catastrophic thinking.

Dispositional pessimists People who have the general and stable belief that bad things and negative outcomes will happen.

Type D personality A Type D personality has the persistent tendency toward (a) negative affectivity (being constantly irritable, anxious, and expecting failure) and (b) social inhibition (involving both self-restraint and a lack of self-assurance).

Latent vulnerability traits Specific behavioral and psychological features that individuals may develop at any period in life that are harmful in the process of coping are latent vulnerability traits.

may develop at any period in life (e.g., bad eating habits, substance use or abuse, or propensity for hostile behavior). These features may later develop into stable traits that are harmful in the process of coping (Beauchaine & Marsh, 2006). American psychologist Karen Matthews demonstrates in her research how certain habits, such as smoking and physical immobility, contribute to physical changes in the cardiovascular system and make individuals more vulnerable in coping with their health problems (Matthews, 2005; Matthews & Gallo, 2011). John Curtin and colleagues showed that an alcohol or drug habit can also become a latent vulnerability trait for some people when a difficult life situation arises, and they turn to substances to cope rather than address the problem (Curtin, McCarthy, Piper, & Baker, 2005).

Identifying Adaptive Coping Strategies

Successful adaptive coping strategies improve the individual's functioning in everyday situations and reduce the impact of life-changing stressors. These strategies should have significant, long-term impact. There are at least three types of such strategies that are interconnected: problem-focused, appraisal-focused, and emotion-focused (see **Table 13.3**; Bond & Bince, 2000).

Problem-focused strategies center on changing or eliminating the source of an individual's problems. Here, the individuals act independently or seek advantageous social support, including practical advice and guidance from another person or people. For instance, a person diagnosed with a serious illness immediately studies several available treatment options and chooses one. If the problem persists, the individual seeks other options. Success of these strategies is not necessarily about the speed of the decision. These strategies can be effective in part because they are informed (an individual's knowledge is based on a range of facts) and efficient (an individual critically analyzes and chooses the best option).

Quite often, we cannot tackle our problems head on. **Appraisal-focused strategies** center on the way we see the problem (or a particular life development), its causes, its impact on us, and the expected outcome of our coping behavior. The goal here is to gain knowledge about the stressor to help better understand and discuss the

Problem-focused strategies Problem-focused strategies are methods that center on changing or eliminating the source of an individual's problems.

Appraisal-focused strategies Appraisal-focused strategies are methods that center on the way we see the problem (or a particular life development), its causes, its impact on us, and the expected outcome of our coping behavior.

TABLE 13.3 ● Adaptive and Maladaptive Coping Strategies: A Comparison	
Adaptive Strategies	**Maladaptive Strategies**
• Problem-focused strategies center on eliminating the stressor.	• Denial is a belief that something is untrue. It may appear as ignoring a problem.
• Appraisal-focused strategies usually refer to internal, stable, and global causes of the individual's problems.	• Ruminative strategies refer to behaviors and thoughts that focus on the individual's negative experiences, failing strategies, and distressful psychological symptoms.
• Emotion-focused strategies center on the emotional meaning of the stressor and on reducing anxiety.	• Learned helplessness is the belief that there is no connection between actions and their outcomes.

anticipated outcomes. Optimistic strategies, for example, help to deal with unfortunate events in these ways:

- Explaining a misfortune or a difficult period in a circumscribed way: "This may be difficult, but it will not ruin my life. I will deal with my problems, one day at a time."
- Identifying external, unstable, and limited causes of the problem: "I am just unlucky; bad things happen. I will be better tomorrow; things change for the better."

Emotion-focused strategies
Methods that center on the emotional meaning of the stressor, on distraction, and on relaxation are called emotion-focused strategies.

Distraction
Distraction is an avoidant coping strategy that diverts attention away from a stressor and toward other thoughts or behaviors that are unrelated to the stressor.

People can turn to **emotion-focused strategies** that center on the emotional meaning of the stressor, on distraction from it, and on relaxation. These strategies include actively reevaluating the psychological impact of the existing problem, gaining emotional strength, switching attention to something else, or seeking emotional support from other people and new sources (learning about spirituality, for instance). Of course, we do not choose just one strategy and reject others. We use a mixture of coping strategies and skills, which develop and change over time.

Consider distraction, for example. **Distraction** refers to avoidant coping strategies that are employed to divert attention away from a stressor and toward other thoughts or behaviors that are unrelated to the stressor. Simple distraction, such as focusing on an external object like a painting on the wall or imagining a peaceful place like a mountain lake, may ease pain and discomfort during or after serious medical procedures. Other examples of distraction include deliberate daydreaming or engaging in substitute activities to keep one's mind from several stressors related to a chronic illness (Traeger, 2013). These are called calming behaviors that can grow into a habit of engaging in a pleasant activity to reduce anxiety. Successful distraction often involves daily activities, such as working out, playing sports, or getting busy as a volunteer.

Empirical research has long suggested that quality of social support is linked to coping and improvement in well-being (Stanley, Beck, & Zebb, 1998; Weissman, Markowitz, & Klerman, 2007). Interpersonal psychotherapy (IPT) aims at improving the quality of relationships and usually addresses unresolved grief, social isolation, or the significant lack of social skills. We will turn to other strategies—in the context of therapies—in the section on applications.

Psychologists do not encourage people to forget about their troubles or ignore them or see all adversities in a positive light. Instead, they teach that to cope with changing circumstances, we should learn from mistakes and find a way to recover and win. The death of a friend, an illness in the family, personal setbacks—no matter how unpleasant and devastating their impacts can be on our lives, they should make us reexamine what happened (to see everything from a new perspective), reevaluate our strategies (to seek a way out), and mobilize our resources (and if there are none left, then seek help from others). The state of helplessness causes inaction.

We all know that, unfortunately, life is full of unpleasant "surprises." We all eventually will die, and illness strikes practically everyone. How do people cope with the inevitable threat of an illness? Weinstein (1989) examined people's perception of personal risk for illnesses and various mishaps. When people were asked to provide a percentage estimate of the likelihood that they will someday experience a particular illness or injury, most respondents underestimated their risks. The average individual sees himself or herself as far below average at risk for a variety of maladies and misfortunes. These results spark a critical argument: What if some individuals who do not foresee many dangers in life are not necessarily optimistic? What if they are somewhat careless or ignorant about illnesses? It is known, for example, that if some people were more vigilant about their health, many illnesses could have been diagnosed at earlier stages and many lives could have been saved. However, if people are not vigilant enough about their health, this does not mean they are pessimistic. On the other hand, educating people to be aware of possible health dangers is not necessarily a process that evokes people's pessimism.

Identifying Maladaptive Strategies

While adaptive coping strategies improve functioning, maladaptive coping strategies do not. Sure, some maladaptive techniques may be effective in the short term, but they tend to be harmful for the long-term coping process. Maladaptive coping strategies often lead to increased anxiety, other emotional problems, and even substance abuse.

Denial

Denial, in a psychological context, is the belief that something is untrue and often presents itself as ignoring an issue or a fact. Though denial has been sometimes called an adaptive strategy, there has been little evidence that it is actually helpful for long-term coping or reduces a person's stress-related anxiety.

Denial involves several interconnected strategies. Fantasy involves persistently using creative imagination in attempts to avoid facing the problem, and it becomes a substitution for the real coping strategy. **Anxious avoidance** involves a person who dodges thinking about the stressor and refuses dealing with it in all situations and by all means. Anxious avoidance often presents in alcohol and substance abuse, both common maladaptive strategies. Giving up is a form of passive coping and results when the individual stops paying attention to the problem, most likely when the bad consequences of inaction increase. In contrast to distractive strategies (focusing on pleasant activities), giving up is mostly about withdrawal and depressive thinking. This strategy is sometimes called dismissive.

Ruminative Strategies

In contrast to denial, **ruminative strategies** refer to behaviors and thoughts that focus on the individual's negative experiences, failed strategies, and distressful psychological symptoms associated with the inability to cope with a stressor. Examples of ruminative responses include expressing how unhappy one feels, wondering why one feels unhappy, and thinking about how difficult it will be tomorrow. Individuals who use ruminative strategies are highly involved in their attachment experiences and focus on the possible negative outcomes that might affect their attachment.

Denial
In a psychological context, denial is the belief that something is untrue.

Anxious avoidance
A person exhibits anxious avoidance if he or she dodges thinking about a stressor and refuses to deal with it in all situations and by all means.

Ruminative strategies
Ruminative strategies are behaviors and thoughts that focus on the individual's negative experiences, failing strategies, and distressful psychological symptoms associated with the inability to cope with a stressor.

TABLE 13.4 ● Examples of Learned Hopelessness Statements and Consecutive Plans	
Statement	**Pattern of Inaction**
"I have tried two times, and still my LSAT (or MCAT or GRE) score is too low."	"There is no reason to study for the tests; I will never improve."
"I have tried several medications, but my illness does not go away."	"There is no reason to continue treatment; I am hopeless."
"I have tried to ask for help many times; nobody helped me."	"People are just selfish; the whole world is unhelpful."

Learned Helplessness

Learned helplessness
When they experience uncontrollable, aversive events or a crisis, some people exhibit learned helplessness—they become passive and unresponsive—presumably because they have learned during the crisis that there is nothing they can do to help themselves.

Experiencing uncontrollable aversive events or a crisis, some people become helpless—passive and unresponsive—presumably because they have learned during the crisis that there is nothing they can do to help themselves. This phenomenon has been called **learned helplessness** (Abramson, Metalsky, & Alloy, 1989; Abramson, Seligman, & Teasdale, 1978). People believe there is no connection between their actions and the outcomes of these actions—no matter what they do, it will be irrelevant. Therefore, during a crisis the chances of resolving it will be next to zero. This expectation becomes prevailing, affects individual activities, and interferes with subsequent learning from self and others. Individuals then become passive and withdrawn. Learned helplessness may be a result of a certain parenting style, unsafe social environment, accidents, and a variety of other contributing circumstances and conditions (see **Table 13.4**).

CHECK AND APPLY YOUR KNOWLEDGE

1. Describe the Type D personality.
2. What are latent vulnerability traits?
3. Some say, "Optimism is costly if it is unrealistic." Give examples of unrealistic and realistic optimism.
4. Describe and give an example of a problem-focused strategy.
5. Describe and give an example of an emotion-focused strategy.
6. Denial involves several interconnected strategies. Describe them.
7. Explain ruminative strategies and give an example. Do you use these strategies and how often?
8. Have you experienced learned helplessness? How did it affect your life? What is your advice on how to overcome learned helplessness?

© iStockphoto.com/FangXiaNuo

Photo 13.3
Sensitization is a
protective coping
effort to prevent
negative emotions
and despair. Have
you ever used
sensitization to help
yourself and others?

Applying the Adjustment Domain

Coping With Serious Illness

When the Australian scientist Denis Wright was diagnosed in 2009 with an aggressive brain cancer, his doctors said the illness was incurable. While his health was slowly deteriorating, he started a blog called *My Unwelcome Stranger* (the title referred to his illness) in which he shared his daily experiences. He gave his most sincere advice about how we can live fulfilling and happy lives even with a terminal illness (Wright, 2013). His blog shares a very optimistic, caring, and powerful story of coping.

The coping strategy Wright used is called **sensitization**. This is a strategy to learn about, rehearse, and anticipate fearful events in a protective coping effort to prevent negative emotions and despair. Recall from Chapter 9 that psychologist Rollo May believed people can be happy only if they confront the difficult circumstances of their lives, especially those that are manageable (May, 1967). Yet how can we manage the fear of an outcome as frightening as our own death? One strategy is to focus on acceptance—we cannot deny death. It is better to accept the existential inevitability of death rather than be afraid of it (Fernandez, Castano, & Singh, 2010). Recall from Chapter 9 that the humanistic tradition in personality psychology considers the issue of acceptance as important in an individual's life.

From their research, Shelly Taylor and her colleagues (1983) formulated and applied the **cognitive adaptation theory**, which was described earlier in this chapter. Their

Sensitization
Sensitization is a
strategy to learn
about, rehearse, and
anticipate fearful
events in a protective
coping effort to
prevent negative
emotions and despair.

**Cognitive adaptation
theory**
The cognitive
adaptation theory
is rooted in a set of
ideas suggesting that
adjustment depends
on personal ability to
sustain and modify
positive illusions.

research evolved from a psychological study of breast cancer patients. Psychologists showed that human perception tends to be marked by three *positive illusions*, which are mild and positive distortions of reality: self-enhancement, unrealistic optimism, and an exaggerated perception of personal control (Taylor, 2000). They are called illusions because they may contradict, to some degree, the facts. Self-enhancement is a tendency to think better of yourself. Unrealistic optimism is a tendency to believe mostly in positive outcomes (even when the facts do not suggest the same). And finally, personal control is the belief that the individual can exercise control over many events in his or her life.

Studies show that positive illusions tend to promote healthy behaviors. People who develop (1) a positive sense of self-worth, (2) beliefs in their own control, and (3) optimism are more likely to practice conscientious health habits, including healthy dieting and exercising. Positive illusions appear to have protective psychological effects and become especially important in the context of predicaments and threatening events. Positive beliefs, such as those that form the core of positive illusions, might influence the course of various illnesses, including depression (Taylor, 1989).

Fighting Alcoholism

One of the most harmful coping strategies is substance abuse. Some people use substances as a distraction. They turn to alcohol to relax and "forget" about their problems or stressors. A short-term effect of substance use may actually seem positive since alcohol, as a depressant, may temporarily reduce an individual's painful anxiety and physical tension. However, drinking (and other substance use) does not address the stressor itself, and it does not produce adaptive coping strategies. On the contrary, many individuals end up turning to substances again and again, which can lead to dependency and addiction. Psychologists have a professional responsibility to spread awareness about the harmful effects of drinking, especially as a coping strategy. This "strategy" quickly becomes a habit, the consumption of alcohol increases, and the dependency grows.

Many interventions related to alcoholism require face-to-face interaction between a professional therapist and a person who seeks help. Support groups gained popularity as well. During the past 2 decades, research has provided evidence about the effectiveness of online groups in providing help to find social support, distributing new facts about coping strategies with alcoholism, and encouraging members to share personal experiences and success stories with others (Das & Rae, 1999; Griffiths et al., 2012). Studies suggest that online support groups for people with alcohol-related problems could strengthen a person's "circle of support" in almost the same way as face-to-face groups (National Council on Alcoholism and Drug Dependence, 2016).

Relaxation Techniques

Close your eyes, and relax . . .

Relaxation training
Relaxation training is a technique or method to cope with stress.

Millions of people over the years have heard this phrase in the beginning of their sessions of relaxation therapies. **Relaxation training** is a technique or method to cope with stress. This method has been used in developing effective skills of self-control—the skills that can be an asset in coping with serious life problems (Davis, Eshelman, & McKay, 2008). In the 1920s, German physician Johannes Shultz suggested the method of **autogenic training (AT)**, which is a self-administered technique for physical and emotional relaxation. For many years, it has been used as a stress management procedure to build and improve self-control skills (Sadigh, 2012). The main technique is autosuggestion. In a relaxed sitting position, the person who learns AT concentrates on heaviness in the arms and legs, warmth in the body, respiratory and cardiac regularity, abdominal warmth and comfort, coolness of the forehead, and overall feelings of harmony and peace. Each of these experiences is learned and practiced with a professional and then alone at home for several weeks until the intended effects are achieved (Krampen, 1999). Once learned, autogenic exercises may provide relief for psychological and somatic symptoms associated with stressors. Individuals reduce their anxiety and improve their memories and cognitive skills as well as report greater levels of self-control (Stetter & Kupper, 2002).

With a measure of imagination, we can find many similarities between AT and several techniques in Chinese and Japanese holistic treatments, which emphasize the balanced interaction of the body and the mind (Sutton, 1998). These techniques have been very popular among millions of people around the world. For example, according to academic research, the methods of tai chi, which originated in China, have been found to be beneficial for individual physical and emotional health (Lee & Ernst, 2011). More recently, contemporary health psychology has accumulated evidence that regular relaxation can be more beneficial if it is combined with proper diet and physical exercises (Lewis, 2001; McCarthy, 2013). A combination of physical and talk therapy is welcome if it helps the client overcome persistent anxiety or chronic pain (Clay, 2002). Physical therapy can reduce a client's constant anxiety, thus easing a therapeutic dialogue with a psychologist.

To achieve deep relaxation or concentration, therapists can teach their clients various forms of meditation. In fact, during the 1960s, various relaxation methods rooted in Eastern philosophies and religious traditions, including Hinduism and Buddhism, gained significant popularity (Aanstoos, Serlin, & Greening, 2000). These methods remain very popular today, gaining popularity because they place self-awareness, forgiveness, and growth-seeking experiences at the center of therapeutic treatment. Interest in mindfulness (internal and external experiences occurring in the present moment) and the practice of meditation is growing (Kabat-Zinn, 2012). Richard Davidson at the University of Wisconsin, who founded the Center for Investigating Healthy Minds, has developed a serious research base to support and further develop many traditional methods of therapy (Davidson & Begley, 2012).

Along the way, the implementation of key principles of the humanistic tradition (see Chapter 9) inadvertently invited psychologists and their clients to discover the incredible world of Indian and Asian philosophy and mythology.

Overcoming Acculturative Stress

Acculturative stress (sometimes called culture shock) is a distressful psychological reaction to an unfamiliar cultural environment. The symptoms include significant psychological changes in individuals who undergo major cultural transitions usually

Autogenic training (AT)
Autogenic training, or AT, is a self-administered technique for physical and emotional relaxation.

Acculturative stress
Also known as culture shock, acculturative stress is a distressful psychological reaction to an unfamiliar cultural environment.

associated with immigration and might manifest as persistent anxiety, sadness, pessimistic thoughts, and low self-esteem (see **Table 13.5**).

Acculturative stress can be short-term and continuous (Tsytsarev & Krichmar, 2000). Significant language barriers, lack of knowledge about local norms, detachment from familiar environments, and the challenges of a new country can be very stressful (Shiraev & Levy, 2013). Individuals who cope with the negative consequences of their lives as immigrants often need the acquisition and development of the skills and habits required in the new cultural settings. Several steps are necessary to help individuals cope with acculturative stress:

1. *Gaining knowledge.* The person should be aware of the symptoms of acculturative stress.

2. *Overcoming stigma.* Many individuals do not want to accept that they have developed a psychological disorder. The phrase *mental illness* terrifies them. The less educated a person is, the stronger the stigma (or negative perception) of mental illness in this person's mind (Wood & Wahl, 2006). It takes a significant effort to explain that suffering from the symptoms of acculturative stress should not be embarrassing, and it is not a sign of personal failure—it is a treatable problem that social workers or psychologists can help with.

3. *Commitment.* Several forms of cognitive and behavioral intervention can be used to reduce the harmful impact of acculturative stress. However, the key to the successful coping with this problem is the person's commitment and perseverance where treatment is concerned.

TABLE 13.5 ● Symptoms of Acculturative Stress (Culture Shock)

Symptoms	Description
Nostalgic feelings	Longing for relatives, friends, familiar scenes, foods, and other precious experiences
Disorientation and loss of control	Inability to solve simple problems, lack of power, anxiety, and depressive symptoms
Dissatisfaction over communication barriers	Lack of spoken and written language skills create frustration and affective symptoms
Loss of habits and lifestyle	Inability to do many previously enjoyed activities, which causes negative affective symptoms
Dissatisfaction over perceived differences	Differences between the new and "old" cultures are exaggerated and seem difficult to accept
Dissatisfaction over perceived value gap	Differences in values typically exaggerated, new values seem difficult to accept

Source: Shiraev and Boyd, 2008.

Visual Review

INTRODUCTION AND CONTEXTS	KEY THEORIES AND APPROACHES	APPLICATIONS

INTRODUCTION AND CONTEXTS

Adjustment is a change in an individual's behavior and experiences in response to challenges

Changes differ in occurrence, duration, origin, and significance

Adjustment is needed for:
- Aging
- Physical illness
- Disability
- Family changes
- Relationships
- Professional and social changes

KEY THEORIES AND APPROACHES

Approaching is a deliberate attempt at changing self as well as the sources of stress

Avoiding is keeping oneself away from addressing a challenge or a stressor

The inability to cope with a major life stressor can lead to adjustment disorder

There are stable patterns of behavior and experience that appear helpful in the process of coping with significant stressors

APPLICATIONS

Coping with illness

Fighting alcoholism

Relaxation techniques

Overcoming acculturative stress

Thomas Darwick/Iconica/Getty Images

Summary

- Adjustment refers to relatively significant changes in an individual's behavior and experiences in response to external and internal challenges. Adjustment is somewhat similar to coping, which is a deliberate and conscious effort to adjust to challenges, changing situations, and new conditions.

- Many areas of life and activities produce stressors and thus require adjustment. Among them are aging, illness, changes in the family, professional changes, migration, and many others.

- Psychology of adjustment studies problems and conditions that cause the individual's need for adjustment, the psychological mechanisms of adjustment, and the ways to help individuals in their coping process.

- Different types of adjustment exist. They can relate to the individual or to the stressor.

- Coping and adjustment can be active or passive, with many variations in between the "active" and "passive" alternatives. One style is approaching, which is a type of coping that refers to deliberate attempts at changing self as well as the sources of stress. Another is avoiding; contrary to approaching, it is keeping self away from addressing a challenge or a stressor.

- In terms of the dynamics, or speed of coping, some people tend to adjust quickly. As soon as the stressor appears or as soon as they realize that an adjustment is necessary, they think about what to do and then act. Others display

a persistent pattern of behavior and thought called procrastination—putting off impending tasks to a later time.

- Successful coping responses that allow the individual to maintain a happy and productive life score high on the measures of subjective well-being. Unsuccessful coping is associated with the inability to adjust to a stressor or continuous problem and includes emotional distress—the most severe version of which is adjustment disorder.

- Another feature that tends to be helpful in successful coping is optimism—the general belief in positive or successful outcomes. Optimism involves an act of cognitive assessment of the present and future.

- As in the case of "helpful" traits, there should be individual features that negatively affect coping.

- Adaptive, successful coping strategies improve the individual's functioning in everyday situations and reduce the impact of life-changing stressors. These strategies should have significant, long-term impact. On the other hand, maladaptive coping strategies often lead to increased anxiety, other emotional problems, and even substance abuse.

- Scientific knowledge of adaptive strategies can be applied to a wide variety of problems that people face in their daily lives. These problems range from coping with illness to alcoholism to stress-reduction techniques.

Key Terms

acculturation 406

acculturative stress 421

adjustment 402

adjustment disorder 410

anxious avoidance 417

appraisal-focused strategies 415

approaching 408

autogenic training (AT) 421

avoiding 408

burnout 411

catastrophic thinking 414

cognitive adaptation theory 419

coping 402

denial 417

disabilities 404

dispositional optimism 413

dispositional pessimists 414

distraction 416

emotion-focused
     strategies 416

flexibility 407

hardiness 413

latent vulnerability traits 414

learned helplessness 418

optimism 413

passive adjustment 410

problem-focused
     strategies 415

procrastination 409

psychology of adjustment 407

relaxation training 420

ruminative strategies 417

sensitization 419

stress 403

stress tolerance 412

Type D personality 414

Evaluating What You Know

What is the focus of the adjustment domain?

What are the areas of changes requiring adjustment?

Describe the types of coping and adjustment.

What are key outcomes of coping and adjustment?

Describe traits that affect coping and adjustment.

Provide an example for each of the areas of application: coping with serious illness, fighting alcoholism, relaxation techniques, and overcoming acculturative stress.

A Bridge to the Next Chapter

The next, final chapter of this book should be studied at the very end of the semester or quarter. A pessimist would say that the odds are very high that (1) many unforeseen circumstances have arisen during these past weeks to make this class schedule extremely packed and that (2) your time will be absolutely, indisputably scarce to study this chapter. An optimist would certainly disagree.

Whether this chapter is included in your final exam or not, please read it. It is not structured the same way that the other chapters are (What do we study? How do we study? How do we apply?). It does not contain Check Your Knowledge boxes. It has no questions to practice. It is all about the new research of personality that does not necessarily "fit" into traditional approaches or domains. It may appear to you down-to-earth, contentious, obvious, daring, useful, and useless—all at the same time. It is up to you now what to make out of it. The journey continues.

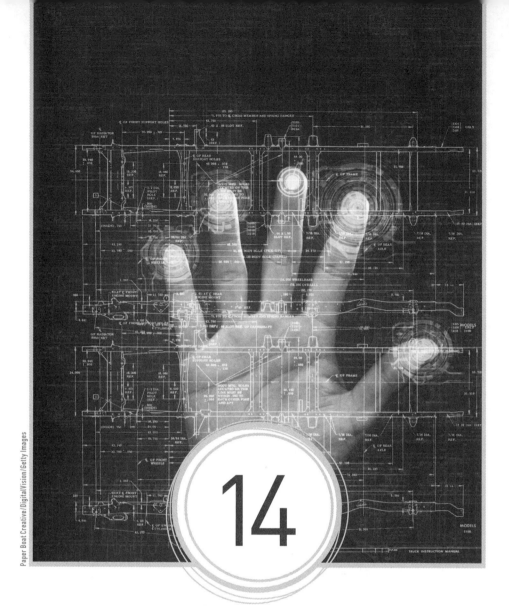

14

Personality Theories in the 21st Century

"Real generosity towards the future lies in giving all to the present."

—Albert Camus (1913–1960), French philosopher and author

n 10 years, some of you will be conducting your own research into personality. Some of you will be reading and critically reviewing this research. Yet others will be applying it to various practical fields, including education, health care, counseling, business, conflict resolution, and many more. How will personality psychology evolve in the coming 10 years? On what type of research will personality psychologists focus? What will they discover, and how will they apply their findings? In the past, social scientists have not been very accurate in predicting social trends. Forecasting what humans will do in the future and what their society will look like is difficult for at least three reasons. First, there are too many variables that require researchers' attention. Second, these variables tend to be too complex and interconnected in unpredictable ways. Third, there are even more variables that remain unknown to the researcher. Scientists can predict the movement of comets and space objects, and yet do you know what we are going to be doing exactly 2 years from now? For these and other reasons, it is particularly difficult to predict the specific developments of psychology and personality psychology. However, we can probably suggest something about the general direction of this research. At least three trends should emerge.

First, personality psychologists will receive significant feedback from neuroscience. Studies of the brain and its functioning should be making almost revolutionary changes in the ways we understand individual behavior, experience, and personality. Second, personality psychology will also receive a significant boost from cognitive psychology and computer science. And third, psychologists will make significant progress effectively applying their research to practice.

Let's suggest some examples of these research trends. On these next pages, you will find several hypothetical scenarios involving research of personality. There are several cases based on studies conducted in the recent past. Each case is then followed by a hypothetical research scenario about specific follow-up research that might be conducted about 10 years from now. As you read about the possible future scenarios, consider whether you agree or disagree and answer the questions that follow.

Case 1: "Hacking" Living Cells for a Good Cause

Scientists at MIT have conducted successful experiments that allow them to "hack" living cells and give them special programs and new tasks. In other words, cells are now able to directly receive new information and act accordingly. Scientists have put together a new programming language for various cells, including bacteria (Nielsen et al., 2015). This is a text-based language, similar to what computer scientists use to develop a software or program for a computer. Cells, like students, learn in several steps, and each step involves the performance of a more complex task. First, they learn to act differently in various environmental conditions, such as in changing levels of oxygen. Then cells learn new tasks about carrying and delivering information. One of the goals of this research is to teach human cells to transport and then release cancer drugs upon encountering a tumor in the body or teach cells in plants to discharge natural insecticide to fight insects. In the future, researchers hope that they will be able to find significant breakthroughs in the treatment of most diseases by creating special informational programs for the living cells. These programs are likely to replace many medications or be significantly more effective than most of them.

Possible Research in 2027: "Hacking" Living Cells to Change Personality Traits

Based on the series of studies initiated by MIT researchers, a team of behavioral psychologists and neuroscientists who work in several universities in the United States, India, and China will find a way to install special "educational codes" into the living cells of the human body, including the brain cells. First, the educational "cell software" will be created. After several educational "sessions," the cells will learn to create specific physiological conditions and change the function of several brain structures, such as the amygdala and the prefrontal cortex, so that the individual begins to respond differently to various environmental conditions. Cells continue to learn, and the changes in an individual's behavior and emotions become more or less permanent.

To test their technique, the researchers will conduct a series of preliminary experiments on anger management. The subjects who volunteer for these experiments will have had significant anger-related behavioral troubles in the past; some of them will have had problems with the law as the result of their anger and violence. After several learning sessions involving their "hacked" brain cells, more than 70% of the subjects will significantly reduce the number of angry reactions during 1 year of postexperimental, drone-monitored observations. Many of these individuals' personality traits will be affected as well. For example, about 90% of the subjects who display high scores on the measure of neuroticism will show significantly lower scores on this measure 1 year later. Some years later, researchers will claim that within a 22-month period they will be able to create special cell programs to reduce the number of angry responses in an individual by more than 75% and replace them with joyful responses. Will this be the end of anger as we know it?

Questions

- Do you think that this type of a study with this type of results is (a) very likely, (b) somewhat likely, or (c) very much unlikely to take place in 2027?
- Assume that this research has taken place. What ethical limitations do you see in these research applications?
- Would you personally support the idea that human beings be able to change their personality features and even traits at will via computerized methods of cell modification? What is wrong with the idea that under the influence of the "hacked cells" most of us, if not all, would feel happier, less angry, and more optimistic then we felt yesterday?

Case 2: Understanding Multimorbidity

Do you want to live a long time? Is our life expectancy genetically programmed?

If this is not completely determined by our genes, then do you want to know what you have to do to live as long as possible?

For many years, scientists studied individual cases of healthy men and women, especially those who remained healthy through old age. There were also several studies using significantly larger samples. Scientists in the United Kingdom turned to a massive research database involving 1,200,000 people who were tracked and studied for years (Danesh, 2015). The researchers were interested in multimorbidity, which is the co-occurrence of two or more chronic medical conditions in one person (Glynn, 2009). They found a relatively simple formula for the unhealthiest lifestyle—specifically, it involves little exercise, poor diet, and smoking. The forecast is staggering: An individual who maintains this lifestyle is likely to cut his or her life-span by 23 years. It is estimated that around 80% of premature deaths could be prevented by keeping weight under control, exercising more, eating a healthy diet, and not smoking. Researchers did not suggest that medications could or should be abandoned. The main conclusion of this massive study was that people should learn about, agree on, and sustain a healthier lifestyle (Danesh, 2015). However, to change one's lifestyle may take a serious personality change.

Possible Research in 2027: Understanding Psychological Multimorbidity

Inspired by the multimorbidity study conducted by British doctors back in 2015, an international group of researchers from 11 universities will collect data from 57 countries from most world regions over 10 years. The key idea of the research will be to establish the most significant personality factors involved in multimorbidity. The researchers will offer a hypothesis: If there is a particular lifestyle (described in the 2015 study) that negatively affects the individual's longevity, then there should be a particular trait or a combination of traits or other individual features that negatively affect the person's life expectancy. Earlier studies described healthy traits affecting longevity, such as conscientiousness, optimism, and social connectedness (Kern & Friedman, 2008). Yet this research focused on the traits that increased, rather than decreased, an individual's longevity. These studies were also conducted on relatively small samples.

The 2027 study will be different: It will involve 300,000 individuals across many cultures and 35 countries. Online surveys will be combined with face-to-face and Skype interviews. Using factor analysis, researchers will establish several personality features as multimorbid. Among them, three will turn out to be most significant: (1) high-level neuroticism, (2) high frequency of lying, and (3) low measures of sense of humor (in particular, understanding sarcasm and irony). People who score high on neuroticism and lying and very low on sense of humor tend to reduce their life expectancy up to 10 years. One of the study's applications will be discussed with educational ministries of several countries. A proposal will circulate about the establishment of a mandatory training program for schoolchildren on how to manage stress and anxiety, how to be honest and avoid lying in most circumstances, and how to better understand irony and sarcasm in interpersonal communications.

Questions

- Do you think that this type of study with this type of results is (a) very likely, (b) somewhat likely, or (c) very much unlikely to take place in 2027? Research online to see if similar studies have been conducted. What were their results?
- Suppose this research on multimorbidity of personality traits has taken place. What moral or legal limitations do you see in this research's applications? Would you personally support the idea that schoolchildren should undergo special training to develop certain personality traits that could increase their longevity? What is wrong with that idea that some of us (maybe even most of us), if we act and feel in a certain way as a result of special training, would live longer?

Case 3: Height, Mind, and Self-Esteem

In 2014, researchers at Oxford University in the United Kingdom used virtual reality technology to "reduce" the perceived height of female volunteers traveling on a computer-simulated subway train by 10 inches (25 cm). In a series of experiments, scientists found out that when people feel smaller than they really are, they are more frustrated, scared, and less trustful of others. Feeling shorter than normal makes people think others are staring or talking about them. Reducing a person's perceived height also results in more negative views of the self (Freeman et al., 2014).

At about the same time, researchers at the Federal Centers for Disease Control in Atlanta, Georgia, studied "male discrepancy stress"—an unpleasant feeling of falling short of traditional masculine gender norms that emphasize physical strength and decisiveness (Reidy, Berke, Gentile, & Zeichner, 2015). The men who considered themselves less masculine than average and who experienced male discrepancy stress were nearly 3 times more likely to have committed violent assaults than those who didn't worry about such "male discrepancy." Both studies indicate a discrepancy between how we want to appear and the way we actually are (as seen by ourselves or others) can cause significant emotional and behavioral challenges and problems.

Possible Research in 2027: Matching Self-Esteem and Social Perception

Following years of research on self perception and self-esteem, psychologists in Japan, with the cooperation of their colleagues in Russia and the United States, will create a battery of tests that allow researchers to instantly measure not only major personality traits of individuals but also their secret expectations about which traits and characteristics they would love to have in themselves. Such tests will involve online self-assessment questionnaires, as well as assessments based on brain imaging and several scanning techniques, allowing the detection of unconscious impulses, thoughts, and desires. This research will provide some explanations regarding the function of defense mechanisms introduced by psychoanalysts in the 20th century. The results of these tests will also allow researchers to create a new model for an individual's personality, which would take into consideration the discrepancy between a person's ideal self and real self. A 1-hour online interview with simultaneous brain scanning and instantaneous data analysis will produce a detailed description of participants' individual traits, as well as their level of aspirations, propensity for envy and forgiveness, ability to love and be loved, and their "actual" sexual orientation and preferred gender role (with varying degrees of masculinity and femininity).

Eventually, this method will be available commercially. Not only will people who pay for the services be able to examine their individual profiles, but they also will be able to obtain a list of individuals (upon their agreement) with similar psychological profiles for matchmaking. This method will be free for parents who want to test their children for potential personality conflicts and discrepancies.

Questions

- Do you think that this type of a study with this type of results is (a) very likely, (b) somewhat likely, or (c) very much unlikely to take place in 2027? Research online to see if similar studies have been conducted. What were their results?
- Would you personally want to study your own relational and unconscious discrepancies?
- What are the advantages and disadvantages of knowing about such discrepancies?

Case 4: A Personality Profile of the Internet Troll

An "Internet troll" is someone who enters an online discussion and posts comments almost exclusively to upset the discussants or disrupt the conversation. Although some trolls are hired by companies or politicians to either promote a certain idea or product or disrupt and harm the opponents or competitors, that is not the kind of troll this research viewed.

Trolls commonly exaggerate, lie, mislead, sometimes praise, yet mostly offend. A few studies have shown similar personality characteristics among typical Internet trolls (Buckels, Trapnell, & Paulhus, 2014). They are most likely to be sadistic, angry, antisocial (with low-remorse levels), and narcissistic. They tend have a high expectation of themselves and enjoy what they consider "power" (which, in this case, is their ability to disrupt conversations and cause harm to others with their words). Trolls also dislike successful people but are not brave or bold people themselves. They vent their negative emotions and antisocial impulses on strangers because they can remain anonymous and unpunished.

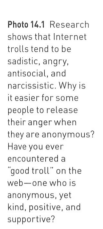

Photo 14.1 Research shows that Internet trolls tend to be sadistic, angry, antisocial, and narcissistic. Why is it easier for some people to release their anger when they are anonymous? Have you ever encountered a "good troll" on the web—one who is anonymous, yet kind, positive, and supportive?

© iStockphoto.com/DragonImages

Possible Research in 2027: Researching, Understanding, and Punishing Trolls

Let's punish trolls! Researchers from Stanford University—in cooperation with Facebook, Twitter, and several other social networks—will conduct a 5-year study that examines posting patterns and personality profiles of 100 million people around the globe. Inspired by studies of trolling conducted a decade earlier, psychologists and computer scientists will be able to identify trolls' most significant and stable personality traits by looking at their postings, comments, "likes," and pictures over the course of 1 week. Researchers will also examine billions of private messages (assuring that people's privacy will be protected) and incorporate their findings into the main study's results. To accomplish this seemingly daunting task, the research team will use a specially designed web engine by Google. As a result of this project, all users of Facebook and Twitter will be able to install an app called PersonApp that will instantly reveal the personality profiles of every person who is communicating with them via these social networks. Users will have their most salient personality traits appear as multicolored emojis next to their online profiles.

Critics openly say that PersonApp will be a significant violation of personal privacy. Imagine that you are posting a message and your personality features (e.g., kind, disorganized, open to experience, overanxious, or masculine) are immediately revealed to other users. Proponents, however, insist that the presence of PersonApp will encourage millions of people to communicate in a more responsible, kind, and considerate way.

According to one of the principal investigators of this hypothetical study, "This feature will essentially reduce and even eliminate trolling on the web. Who wants to appear online as a mean and angry person?"

Another researcher added, "In real life, most of us smile and say hello to each other. Why this should be different online?"

Questions

- Do you think this type of study with this type of results is (a) very likely, (b) somewhat likely, or (c) very much unlikely to take place in 2027? Conduct research online to see if similar studies have been already been done. What were their results?
- Would you support the idea that users of social networks should have several emojis attached to their profiles based on the scientific analysis of these users' postings?
- If you are using these emojis, will it somehow change your online behavior? Will it make you at least "kinder"?
- In real life, you normally don't want to talk to people who are visibly angry or agitated. Why would you do this online?

A Conclusion: Understanding an Individual's Personality

In the classic 1989 movie *Dead Poets Society,* the late actor Robin Williams played an eccentric teacher, Mr. Keating, at an elite, private high school. At one point in the movie, Mr. Keating angrily declared, "No one can measure poetry!" He lashed out at a textbook's author, whose method quantified the creative verses of the poet's mind. Mr. Keating touched upon a centuries-old scientific debate about whether it is proper to use gadgets, numbers, and formulas to measure the complexity of human experience and behavior. Of course, scientists do not use yardsticks and barometers to study personality, but to better understand human beings, we need to have some reliable ways to understand, assess, and then critically evaluate individual personalities.

Today, the argument is not *if* we can scientifically examine and measure personality features—we know that we *can* do it better than yesterday. A more intriguing question is whether we can correctly explain the results of these research procedures. Can we interpret scientific knowledge in the most unbiased way? Can we as psychologists then use this knowledge to effectively help people develop particular personality traits, feel happier, or avoid a potentially harmful relationship? Will we be able to, for example, design a questionnaire and a corresponding brain to imagine a technique to predict a person's successful professional career or a happy marriage? Or are we on the wrong path? Should understanding individual personalities involve something dramatically different than is known to us today through research procedures and their critical evaluations? The psychological jury is still out on this.

• Glossary •

16PF The Sixteen Personality Factor Questionnaire was developed by Raymond Cattell.

Absentmindedness In behavioral terms, absentmindedness can be called a lack of practical skills, common sense, or attention.

Academic traditions These traditions bring together scholars that share similar views on a particular scientific approach, subject, or method.

Accommodation In Piaget's system, accommodation is modifying one's mental structures to fit the new demands of the environment.

Acculturation The individual's process of coping with the new cultural conditions is acculturation.

Acculturative stress Also known as culture shock, acculturative stress is a distressful psychological reaction to an unfamiliar cultural environment.

Adjustment Relatively significant changes in an individual's behavior and experiences in response to external and internal challenges are known as the process of adjustment.

Adjustment disorder Someone unable to cope with a major life stressor experiences a cluster of symptoms associated with significant distress and is diagnosed with adjustment disorder.

Agility of the nervous system The quickness of the activation of excitement or the quickness of change between inhibition and excitement is known as the agility of the nervous system.

Aircrib Designed by Skinner to form good habits in children, an Aircrib is a thermostatically controlled crib with a safety-glass front and a stretched-canvas floor.

Alpha males Alpha males are the strongest and most aggressive males and are able to reproduce better than other, weaker males.

Amygdala The amygdala is the almond-shaped part of the brain crucial for processing emotions.

Analysand An analysand, also known as a psychoanalyst's patient or client, is a person undergoing psychoanalysis.

Analysis Analysis occurs with the breaking of something complex into smaller parts to understand their essential features and relations.

Analytical psychology Jung called his views analytical psychology to distinguish them from Freud's.

Androcentrism Androcentrism occurs with placing males or the masculine point of view at the center of a theory or narrative.

Androgyny A combination and a coexistence of both male and female behavioral characteristics, features, and reflections is known as androgyny.

Anthropomorphism Anthropomorphism is portraying animal behavior in human terms.

Anxious avoidance A person exhibits anxious avoidance if he or she dodges thinking about a stressor and refuses to deal with it in all situations and by all means.

Appraisal-focused strategies Appraisal-focused strategies are methods that center on the way we see the problem (or a particular life development), its causes, its impact on us, and the expected outcome of our coping behavior.

Approaching Some patients use approaching, a type of coping that refers to deliberate attempts at changing self as well as the sources of stress.

Archetypes According to Jung, archetypes are the content of the collective unconscious that consist of images of the primordial (elemental, ancient) character. These archetypes manifest in three universal ways: dreams, fantasies, and delusions.

Art Art is the expression of human imagination through creativity.

Artificial intelligence (AI) Artificial intelligence, or AI, is the study and design of intelligent machines.

Assimilation In Piaget's system, assimilation is adopting operations with new objects into old mind patterns.

Atavism Atavism is the reversion of behavior to some earlier developmental stages.

Attitudes The cognitive representations and evaluations of various features of the social and physical world are present in attitudes.

Attribution An attribution is the explanation individuals use to explain the causes of behavior and events.

Authoritarian personality An authoritarian personality is exhibited in a complex pattern of behavior and thought based on the individual's faithful acceptance of the power of authority, order, and subordination.

Autogenic training (AT) Autogenic training, or AT, is a self-administered technique for physical and emotional relaxation.

Autotelic personality Autotelic describes the personality of an individual who tends to be engaged in activities that are naturally rewarding and not necessarily associated with material goals such as money, fame, or high social status (*auto* in Greek means "self" and *telos* means "goal").

Avoiding Keeping oneself away from addressing a challenge or a stressor is called avoiding.

Bad-me In Sullivan's system, the bad-me is an early awareness of self as disapproved by the adults.

Balance of the nervous system The equilibrium between excitement and inhibition within the nervous system is known as the balance of the nervous system.

Basic anxiety In Karen Horney's system, basic anxiety is exhibited in feelings of loneliness, hopelessness, and counter-hostility (emotional responses to hostile situations).

Behavioral economics The study of the effects of individual factors on personal economic decisions is behavioral economics.

Behaviorism The rich and diverse interdisciplinary tradition that focuses on observable behavior is called behaviorism.

Big Five The Big Five personality theory states that individual traits are likely to fall into these five categories: openness to experience, conscientiousness, extroversion, agreeableness, and neuroticism.

Biphobia The aversion toward bisexuality and bisexual people as a social group or as individuals is biphobia.

Burnout Often a work-related term, burnout is a state of a significant exhaustion and disappointment brought about by a devotion to an activity that failed to produce the expected result or reward.

B-values Examples of "being-values," or B-values, are truthfulness, goodness, beauty, wholeness, justice, and meaningfulness.

Catastrophic thinking The stable tendency to overestimate the probability of very negative outcomes is catastrophic thinking.

Categorization The process of categorization entails a variety of mental shortcuts, or heuristics, that tend to reduce complex and time-consuming tasks of describing and analyzing to seemingly more simple, manageable, practical, and efficient labeling strategies.

Censorship Censorship is practicing the dissemination or restriction of what is deemed "appropriate" or "inappropriate" knowledge.

Central Central personality features tend to be somewhat wide-ranging and present—to various degrees—in most people, most of the time.

Class consciousness Members of social classes possess a set of core beliefs and perceptions about their life and the world around them based on their position in society.

Client-centered therapy In Rogers's system, client-centered therapy is a therapeutic method in which therapists show their clients genuineness, empathy, and unconditional positive regard and create a supportive, nonjudgmental environment that encourages clients to think about their own problems, discuss them, prepare a course of action, and reach their full potential.

Clinical domain In studies of personality, the clinical domain involves approaches to personality from the position of abnormality, illness, and health care.

Clinical–pathological method Using the clinical–pathological method, clinical observations of a patient's abnormal symptoms are compared with reliable data of brain pathology, most likely obtained during an autopsy.

Clinical psychologists Professionals educated and trained to provide comprehensive mental and behavioral health care to individuals and families; to consult with agencies and communities; to train, educate, and supervise; and to conduct research.

Clinicians Health care practitioners who work as primary caregivers of the patient are clinicians.

Cognitive adaptation theory The cognitive adaptation theory is rooted in a set of ideas suggesting that adjustment depends on personal ability to sustain and modify positive illusions.

Cognitive dissonance Individuals experience the unpleasant psychological state known as cognitive dissonance when they perform an action that is contradictory to their beliefs and ideas or when they are confronted by new information that conflicts with their beliefs or ideas.

Cognitive map In Tolman's system, a cognitive map results from the internal processing by which individuals code, store, recall, and decode information about particular elements of their experience.

Cognitive neuroscience The study of cognitive neuroscience examines the brain mechanisms that support the individual's mental functions and subsequent behaviors.

Cognitive revolution The cognitive revolution refers to the gradual yet significant shift of focus within university psychology from being primarily behavioral (studying actions) to being increasingly cognitive (studying the work of the mind).

Cognitive science The field of cognitive science includes cognitive neuroscience, computer science, philosophy, and linguistics, among others.

Collaborative empiricism When a therapist and a client engage in collaborative empiricism, they form a therapeutic alliance in which they become coinvestigators and together examine the evidence to accept, support, reevaluate, or reject the client's thoughts, assumptions, intentions, and beliefs.

Collective unconscious In Jung's theory, the collective unconscious is an impersonal layer in the human psyche that is different from the individual unconscious, as well as inherited and shared with other members of the species.

Collectivism Collectivism is complex behavior based on concerns for other individuals and care for shared traditions and values.

Comorbidity The simultaneous presence of more than one disorder in an individual.

Compensation In Adler's vocabulary, compensation refers to attempts to overcome the discomfort and negative experiences caused by a person's feelings of inferiority.

Conditioned reflexes In Pavlov's theory, conditioned reflexes appear only under certain conditions.

Confident arrogance The behavior and thinking to support people's belief that their ability to do something outweighs their actual ability to do it is called confident arrogance.

Consistency model The consistency model states that most adults acquire (or learn) behaviors and develop stable traits early in life and tend not to change them later.

Constructs In Kelly's system, constructs are stable assumptions that the individual develops about other people, the self, and the world in general.

Continuous variables Continuous variables consist of a theoretically infinite number of points lying between two polar opposites.

Coping The process of coping includes deliberate and conscious efforts to adjust to challenges, changing situations, and new conditions.

Correlation A correlation is a statement about the relationship or association between two (or more) variables.

Critical thinking The process of critical thinking is an active and systematic strategy for understanding knowledge on the basis of sound reasoning and evidence.

Cross-cultural psychology The critical and comparative study of cultural effects on human psychology is cross-cultural psychology.

Culture A large group of people share a culture, or a set of beliefs, behaviors, and symbols that is usually communicated from one generation to the next.

Cynicism The persistent distrust of other people's motives is shown in cynicism.

Death wish Often called a death instinct or death drive, a death wish is the repressed instinctual tendency that leads toward destruction.

Defense mechanisms The specific unconscious structures that enable individuals to avoid awareness of unpleasant, anxiety-arousing issues are called defense mechanisms.

Degeneration Coined in the 1800s, degeneration refers to the generational regress in physical and psychological traits.

Deindividuation After joining a group, an individual may go through deindividuation, or the weakening of the awareness of self.

Denial In a psychological context, denial is the belief that something is untrue.

Dependent variable(s) The aspect of human activity that is studied and expected to change under the influence of the independent variable is the dependent variable.

Determinism Determinism is the view that psychological phenomena are causally determined by preceding events or some identifiable factors.

Developmental stages In developmental psychology, the definite periods in an individual's life that are characterized by certain physical, psychological, behavioral, and social characteristics are called developmental stages.

Developmental stages (Erikson's) In Erikson's view, developmental stages are the periods of a life-span in which the ego faces age-related developmental challenges, usually resulting in a conflict.

Dichotomous variables Dichotomous variables are phenomena that may be divided into two mutually exclusive or contradictory categories.

Differential diagnosis A differential diagnosis is a method to identify and separate one disorder from others. This method also might identify possible alternatives to an initial diagnosis.

Disabilities Disabilities take the form of impairments (significant problems with physical or psychological functioning), activity limitations (inability to perform certain tasks), and participation restrictions (problems with particular social activities).

Dispositional optimism An individual's general and stable belief that good things and positive outcomes will happen is displayed as dispositional optimism.

Dispositional pessimists People who have the general and stable belief that bad things and negative outcomes will happen.

Distraction Distraction is an avoidant coping strategy that diverts attention away from a stressor and toward other thoughts or behaviors that are unrelated to the stressor.

Distress threshold Behaviors that were generally discouraged in childhood will be seen in clinics more often than generally acceptable behaviors—the resulting proportion is the distress threshold.

D-needs "Deficit needs," or D-needs, are rooted in a scarcity of something, such as food or esteem from others.

Dual-evaluation attitudes Dual-evaluation attitudes contain an ambivalent emotional component.

Ego In psychoanalysis, the ego is the component of the psyche that is guided by the reality principle and makes compromises between the id and the environment.

Ego psychology Ego psychology focuses on how the ego interacts with its social environment.

Emerging adulthood One of Erikson's developmental stages, emerging adulthood extends from the late teens to the mid-20s (and even later) and is characterized by self-focused exploration of possibilities in work, relationships, interests, and values.

Emotion-focused strategies Methods that center on the emotional meaning of the stressor, on distraction, and on relaxation are called emotion-focused strategies.

Enlightenment Enlightenment is the view of validating knowledge and education based on science and reason rather than on religious dogmas.

Eros In psychoanalysis, Eros refers to all the tendencies that strive toward the integration of a living substance.

Ethnic disidentification Detaching an individual's self from the ethnic group with which he or she has been previously associated or is currently associated.

Ethnocentrism Ethnocentrism is the view that supports judgment about other ethnic, national, and cultural groups and events from the observer's own ethnic, national, or cultural group's outlook.

Evolutionary psychology The study of evolutionary psychology combines the knowledge of evolutionary science and psychology and explores the ways in which complex evolutionary factors affect human behavior, experience, and personality features.

Evolutionary science The study of evolutionary science explains how large populations of organisms—plants, animals, and human beings—evolve over time.

Excessive consistency An individual who exhibits excessive consistency has the condition of feeling and behaving in the same way regardless of changing circumstances and contexts, although a change in such behavior and feelings is generally expected.

Existential crisis An existential crisis is a period in which an individual questions the very foundations of life and asks whether his or her life has any meaning, purpose, or value.

Existentialism An intellectual tradition, existentialism focuses on individual existence, its uniqueness, free will, and responsibility.

Existential psychology An eclectic and diverse field of studies, existential psychology embraces the idea of the exceptionality of human existence, the importance of individual free choice and independent will, and the necessity to consider each person as a unique entity.

Existential therapy A therapeutic and healing method based on the assumption that we make our own choices and should assume full responsibility for their outcomes.

Experimental introspection Experimental introspection is the method according to which the researcher has to carefully observe his or her own experience as a response to a physical stimulus delivered in laboratory surroundings.

External locus of control An external locus of control is an individual tendency to explain events as influenced by uncontrollable external factors, such as powerful others, luck, the great complexity of the "outside" forces, and so on.

Extinction The process of extinction is the act of abandoning a bad habit or decreasing a fearful reaction.

Extroversion In Jung's view, extroversion is the attachment by a person of his or her psychological energy to other people.

Extroversion (E) In Eysenck's system, extroversion (E) is characterized by talkativeness, positive emotions, and the need to seek external sources of stimulation.

Eysenck's E and N Hans Eysenck studied two personality dimensions, extroversion (E) and neuroticism (N).

Factor analysis Factor analysis is a method to deal with large numbers of observed variables that are thought to reflect a smaller number of underlying variables.

Fatalism The view that humans are not in control of their lives because something or somebody else predetermines or "programs" them is called fatalism.

Femininity Traditionally assigned to women, femininity is a general set of features correlated with beauty, emotionality, and nurture.

Feminism Feminism is the view that women do not have equal rights and opportunities with men, and global changes are needed to achieve social justice.

Field theory Lewin's approach to combining the main principles of Gestalt psychology and topology is called field theory. According to this approach, the acting and thinking individual is part of a dynamic field of interdependent forces.

Fixed-role therapy In Kelly's system, fixed-role therapy is a method to change the individual's perception of self during a relatively short period.

Flexibility Flexibility is a trait measured by the degree (scope and depth) or the extent to which a person can cope in novel ways.

Flow Flow indicates a state of complete concentration and joyful immersion in the situation or activity.

Four Noble Truths The four basic statements reflecting the key positions of Buddhism are known as the Four Noble Truths.

Functional inequality Functional inequality refers to a concept according to which men and women have to perform a certain function in society. Men were expected to perform mostly instrumental functions, but society assigned expressive functions to women. These role differences have created different expectations about what women and men should do.

Gender The complex set of behavioral, cultural, or psychological features associated with an individual's sex is a person's gender.

Gender identity An individual's self-determination (or a complex self-reflection) as being male, female, intersex (between male and female), or neither is called gender identity.

Gender nonconforming Individuals whose gender identity or gender expression does not conform to that typically associated with the sex to which they were assigned at birth are referred to as gender nonconforming.

Gender roles Prescriptions and expectations assigned to genders on the female–male continuum constitute gender roles.

Gender studies Gender studies encompasses the multidisciplinary field dedicated to studying gender and a wide range of gender-related issues.

Gene A gene is a segment or portion of the DNA (a complex molecule) that contains codes or "instructions" as biological information about how to build new protein structures.

Genetics Genetics is the study of heredity through genetic transmission and genetic variations.

Genius In Adler's vocabulary, a genius is the type of individual who overcomes the old inferiority problems and achieves success and happiness.

Genotypes In Allport's theory, genotypes are individual forces that relate to how we keep information and use it to interact with the social and physical world around us.

Gestalt therapy The Gestalt therapy uses ideas about the holistic nature of human experience, the disruption of its structure, and the emphasis on the actuality of the moment.

Good-me In Sullivan's system, the good-me is an early awareness of an aspect of self that brings rewards from the parents or other adults.

Habit disturbance In Watson's system, the habit disturbance is the cause of mental illness.

Habit formation The process by which new behaviors become automatic is habit formation.

Hardiness An individual's general ability to withstand difficult conditions is called hardiness.

Heterosexuality Heterosexuality is an individual's romantic or sexual attraction to people of opposite sex or gender In Greek, *heteros* stands for "different" or "other."

Heterotypic stability A person's heterotypic stability is the psychological consistency of his or her personality features, including behavioral traits, across the life-span.

Holistic Holistic refers to the study of systems with multiple interconnected elements.

Holistic health movement A multidisciplinary applied field, the holistic health movement is focused on the fundamental assumption that physical, mental, and spiritual factors contributing to an individual's illness are interconnected and equally important in treatment.

Homophobia Homophobia is an aversion to homosexuality and gays, lesbians, bisexual, and gender-variant individuals.

Homosexuality Romantic or sexual attraction between people of the same sex or gender is homosexuality.

Homotypic stability The measure of similarity in the same observable personality feature in a particular period, including the life-span, is referred to as homotypic stability.

Hospice care Hospice care refers to the complex medical and psychological system of help focusing on palliative and other humane principles of medical care.

Human development The changes in physical, psychological, and social behavior that individuals experience across the life-span, from conception to their last days, are called human development.

Humanist tradition Also called humanism, the humanist tradition in science emphasizes the subjective side of the individual—the sense of freedom, beauty, creativity, and moral responsibility.

Humanistic psychologists Humanistic psychologists encourage efforts to study the phenomena that distinguish human beings—love, happiness, and self-growth.

Humanistic psychology Humanistic psychology refers to a tradition or a value orientation in psychology that holds a hopeful and constructive view of people and of their substantial capacity to be self-determining.

Humanities In general terms, the field of humanities studies human culture.

Hypotheses Expectations or proposed explanations for something that you study are called hypotheses.

Id In psychoanalysis, the id is the component of the psyche that contains inborn biological drives (the death wish and the life instinct); the id seeks immediate gratification of its impulses.

Identity crisis An identity crisis is an inner state of tension due to a person's inability to see and accept self with confidence and certainty.

Idiographic The idiographic approach is person-centered and focuses on many characteristics integrated in a unique person. It refers to specific features within an individual and uses various assessments and measurements.

Illness An illness refers to any condition, or a functional abnormality or disturbance, of the body and mind (although it is debatable how exactly the mind can be "disturbed") that impairs functioning.

Independent variable In an experiment, an independent variable is a condition that is controlled—that is, it can be changed by the experimenter.

Individualism Complex behavior based on concern for oneself and one's immediate family or primary group (as opposed to concern for other groups or the society to which one belongs) is called individualism.

Individuation In Jung's view, individuation is the process of fulfilling an individual's potential by integrating opposites into a harmonious whole and by getting away from the aimlessness of life (a condition most of his patients were suffering from).

Inheritance Inheritance refers to how certain traits in living organisms were handed down from parents to offspring.

Inkblot test An inkblock personality test involves the evaluation of a subject's response to ambiguous inkblots.

Instinct A person's instinct is an inherent pattern or a complex behavior.

Interrater reliability The interrater reliability is the degree of agreement among several professionals when they separately diagnose an individual.

Internal locus of control A person's internal locus of control is the individual tendency to explain events as influenced by somewhat controllable, internal, relatively permanent characteristics such as skill, preparedness, will, and the like.

Intersex The features that are between distinct male and female characteristics are referred to as intersex.

Introversion In Jung's view, introversion happens when a person attaches his or her psychological energy back to self.

Knowledge Information that has a purpose or use is also called knowledge.

Lack of control The intention of doing something important but getting engaged in some other unimportant activity instead.

Latent vulnerability traits Specific behavioral and psychological features that individuals may develop at any period in life that are harmful in the process of coping are latent vulnerability traits.

Laws of learning In Thorndike's system, the laws of learning are the most essential principles on which learning is based.

Learned helplessness When they experience uncontrollable, aversive events or a crisis, some people exhibit learned helplessness—they become passive and unresponsive—presumably because they have learned during the crisis that there is nothing they can do to help themselves.

Learning curve In Thorndike's theory, the learning curve is a concept that describes the dynamic of learning a habit; it also indicates the connection between learning and the time it takes to learn.

Least-effort principle The least-effort principle is the tendency to minimize the number of cognitive operations to reach a goal.

Legal knowledge Legal knowledge emerges in official, legal prescriptions by authorities (ranging from tribal leaders to countries' governments).

Level of aspiration The degree of difficulty of the goal toward which a person is striving is the level of aspiration.

L, F, and K validity scales The three validity scales that help professionals identify psychological distortions that stem from the test-taking attitudes are called the L, F, and K scales.

LGBT LGBT is an acronym for lesbian, gay, bisexual, and transgender.

Libido In psychoanalysis, libido is the energy of the sexual drive or an erotic desire common in women and men.

Marshmallow experiments The psychologist Walter Mischel, a Stanford University professor, conducted the marshmallow experiments, a series of studies of delayed gratification in children.

Masculine protest A masculine protest is a psychological reaction of opposing male dominance.

Masculinity Traditionally assigned to men, masculinity is a general set of features associated with physical strength, decisiveness, and assertiveness.

Medicalization Medicalization is the process by which various facets of human behavior are interpreted in medical terms and thus diagnosed and treated by medical methods.

Meta-analysis Meta-analysis is the analysis of analyses (usually called combined tests) of a large collection of individual results in an attempt to make sense of a diverse selection of data.

Metrosexual Metrosexual refers to the style of thinking and behavior in men who, contrary to the prescriptions of traditional gender roles, tend to develop and display some feminine features and habits, especially related to appearance, clothes, and grooming.

Mindclones Mindclones are digital versions of human individuals that live forever.

Molar responses In Holt's system, a molar response is the reaction that has something to do with the meaning of the situation—that is, the way an animal or human interprets the situation.

Naïve scientists Naïve scientists are individuals who seek rational and reasonable answers yet lack scientific knowledge and critical judgment.

Narrative medicine A clinical field that helps medical professionals recognize, absorb, interpret, and be moved by the stories of illness is narrative medicine.

Narrative psychology Narrative psychology focuses on how published stories and essays shape lives.

Natural dominance A general assumption about men's physical, biological superiority over women is referred to as the natural dominance of men.

Natural science Natural science is concerned with the description, prediction, and understanding of natural phenomena.

Nature–nurture debate The general discussion about biological and social factors that affect human development, behavior, and experience is known as the nature–nurture debate.

Neuroimaging Neuroimaging is the use of scanning and other techniques to image (visualize) the structure or function of the nervous system.

Neuropsychoanalysis Neuropsychoanalysis is a discipline that provides a link between psychoanalysis and the neurosciences.

Neuroscience The scientific study of the nervous system is called neuroscience.

Neurotic character In psychoanalysis, a neurotic character is a basic trait or a set of traits developed in early childhood that lead to the overt manifestation of neurosis.

Neuroticism (N) In Eysenck's system, neuroticism (N) refers to an individual's level of emotionality. People who measure high in neuroticism have the tendency to see danger in many people, events, and developments around them.

Neurotransmitters Neurotransmitters are endogenous chemicals that enable neurotransmission between two cells. They are associated with a variety of behavioral and psychological functions, including propensity to depression, anxiety, and even social delinquency.

Nomothetic A nomothetic strategy, or approach, uses the same method to compare many people or subjects to a certain average, standard, or norm. This approach focuses on comparisons and generalizations.

Not-me In Sullivan's system, not-me refers to the early awareness of certain individual features that the child does not want to consider as part of his or her experience.

Observation Observation is the acquisition of information about identifiable variables from a primary source.

Observer ratings Observer ratings are structured observations of behaviors or features that require assessment of these actions and features.

Openness model The openness model states that most people do constantly change their behaviors and adjust their traits to changing life situations.

Operant conditioning In Skinner's system, operant conditioning is based on using activities to produce effects.

Optimism The general belief in positive or successful outcomes is referred to as optimism.

Organ inferiority In Adler's view, organ inferiority refers to a wide range of physical problems that become psychological impediments.

Overarching liabilities An individual with overarching liabilities has a genetic predisposition that affects his or her behavior and traits under particular, unfavorable, conditions.

Palliative care Palliative care is used to prevent and relieve the suffering and distress of individuals affected by serious illness and to improve their well-being when it is possible.

Parsimony Parsimony is the scientific principle that refers to the necessity to seek the simplest explanations available to explain complex phenomena.

Passive adjustment Passive adjustment is a general pattern of relying on others to address or resolve stressful events or life situations.

Peace psychology Peace psychology is a theoretical and applied branch of psychology that studies ideological and psychological causes of war and develops educational programs to reduce the threat of violence in international relations and domestic policies of some countries.

Peak experiences Peak experiences are periodic and profound episodes of happiness, optimism, inner harmony, and creativity.

Peripheral Peripheral personality features tend to be more specific and also tend to appear in specific individual or cultural circumstances, such as being polite and cooperative in some contexts but not in others.

Personality A personality is a stable set of behavioral and experiential characteristics of an individual.

Personality disorders Personality disorders are enduring patterns of behavior and inner experience that deviate markedly from the expectations of the individual's culture.

Personality psychology Personality psychology is a branch of psychology that studies personality.

Pessimism Pessimism refers to a persistent, broad-spectrum belief in and anticipation of undesirable, negative, or damaging outcomes.

Phenotypes In Allport's theory, phenotypes are internal and external forces that reflect the way individuals accept their environments and how others influence their behavior.

Philosophy Philosophy is the study of the most general and basic problems of nature, human existence, mind, and society.

Plasticity Plasticity is the capacity for new habit formation or change of old habits.

Pleasure principle The pleasure principle is a demand that an instinctual need be immediately gratified.

Political psychology Political psychology is the field of study that examines psychological factors in politics as well as an individual's political behavior.

Pop psychology Pop psychology is a type of knowledge related to personality and designed for mass consumption; it reaches people primarily through the media—television, radio, popular books, magazines, and the Internet.

Popular (or folk) beliefs Observations and assumptions that represent a form of "everyday psychology" created by the people and for the people are referred to as popular (or folk) beliefs (*folk* is an old Germanic word meaning "people").

Positive psychology Positive psychology studies the strengths and virtues that enable individuals and communities to thrive.

Positive psychotherapy Positive psychotherapy is a therapeutic procedure based on the scientific premise that the human mind is capable of changing itself through behavior.

Positive self-regard A positive self-regard refers to high self-esteem and positive emotions toward the self.

Post hoc error With post hoc error, there is mistaken logic that because Event B follows Event A, then B must have been caused by A. This error is also known as parataxic reasoning.

Power distance Power distance is the extent to which the members of a society accept that power in institutions and organizations is distributed unequally.

Prenatal period The time between conception and birth, which is 38 weeks for humans on average, is known as the prenatal period.

Problem-focused strategies Problem-focused strategies are methods that center on changing or eliminating the source of an individual's problems.

Procrastination Putting off impending tasks to a later time is called procrastination.

Progressivism Progressivism is a general way of thinking and a social movement based on the deep belief that human beings and their society can be improved through social reform, education, and opportunity available to all people.

Projective methods In personality psychology, projective methods require the respondent to ask

questions or perform particular tasks—the results of which are expected to reveal certain meanings that are typically concealed from a direct observation.

Psychoanalysis Psychoanalysis is a broad term that encompasses the psychological views and the psychotherapeutic methods attributed to Sigmund Freud and his followers.

Psychobiography Psychobiography is the genre of historical biography based on psychoanalysis.

Psychodrama Psychodrama is the method that requires participants to explore their own internal conflicts through acting out their emotions in front of one another, not through a private discussion with a therapist.

Psychology of adjustment The psychology of adjustment is the study of problems and conditions that cause the individual's need for adjustment, the psychological mechanisms of adjustment, and the ways to help individuals in their coping process.

Psychoticism Psychoticism is a personality pattern that manifests as persistent aggressiveness and hostility toward others.

Public diplomacy Public diplomacy refers to the organized interaction among citizens of different countries to establish a dialogue intended to find solutions to international disputes or other issues.

Purposive or operational behaviorism In Tolman's system, purposive or operational behaviorism involves the idea of purpose or a goal.

Qualitative research Qualitative research does not involve measurement or statistical procedures.

Quality of life An individual's quality of life refers to her or his general well-being measured by the availability of resources, physical and financial security, type of living conditions, quality of education and health care, presence or absence of violence, and a number of other factors—all of which significantly affect the individual's development and socialization.

Quantitative research Quantitative research uses systematic investigation of behavioral or psychological phenomena by means of statistical or mathematical data and various computational techniques.

Reality principle The reality principle involves the realization of the demands of the environment (which is, mostly, the social world) and the adjustment of behavior to these demands.

Reciprocal determinism Reciprocal determinism offers the suggestion that individuals influence their environment and vice versa.

Reflexology In Bekhterev's system, reflexology is a unifying science to study reflexes.

Relativist perspective of abnormal behavior Using a relativist perspective of abnormal behavior puts it in a relative, comparative perspective. What is considered pathological in one culture could be regarded as simply different in another.

Relaxation training Relaxation training is a technique or method to cope with stress.

Reliability The extent to which a particular method gives consistent results is its reliability.

Religion The beliefs, practices, and prescriptions relevant to the supernatural and the relationships between the individual and the supernatural make up religion.

Representative sample A representative sample's characteristics should accurately reflect the characteristics of the population.

Retention In behaviorism, retention is the ability of individuals to keep their habits ready to be used in a new situation.

Ruminative strategies Ruminative strategies are behaviors and thoughts that focus on the individual's negative experiences, failing strategies, and distressful psychological symptoms associated with the inability to cope with a stressor.

Sample By studying a sample, or a part of a larger group, the researcher can generalize the results to that larger group.

Sampling error A sampling error indicates the extent to which the sample is different from the population it represents.

Scarcity mindset A scarcity mindset is a reaction to a shortage of resources.

Schedules of reinforcement In Skinner's system, schedules of reinforcement are conditions involving different rates and times of reinforcement.

Scientific knowledge Scientific knowledge is based on science, or systematic empirical observation, measurement, and evaluation of facts.

Scientific method The scientific method uses careful research procedures designed to provide reliable and verifiable evidence.

Self The self is the representation of one's identity or the subject of experience.

Self-actualization The highest stage of individual development, self-actualization is governed by the search for truth, goodness, beauty, wholeness, justice, and meaningfulness.

Self-awareness Self-awareness is a reflection of a state of awareness of our own existence; it allows us to perceive our existence with a sense of consistency.

Self-control therapy A behavioral method in dealing with emotional problems, self-control therapy contains three phases: self-monitoring, self-evaluation, and self-reinforcement.

Self-determination Self-determination is the view that we, as individuals, generally are in control of our plans, actions, responses, minds, and personality features.

Self-efficacy Self-efficacy is our belief in our own ability to manage our lives and to exercise control over events that affect our lives.

Self-enhancement The tendency to deem our self as superior to peers is self-enhancement; in other words, we tend to believe that we are somewhat better, smarter, and more reasonable than others.

Self-esteem Self-esteem is a person's general subjective evaluation, both emotional and rational, of his or her own worth.

Self-fulfilling prophecy A perceiver's assumptions about another person that may lead that person to adopt those expected attributes is known as self-fulfilling prophecy.

Self-serving bias The tendency to assess our own features as better or more advanced than those of the "average" person is known as self-serving bias.

Sensation seeking Sensation seeking is the constant tendency to search for new experiences and feelings.

Sensitization Sensitization is a strategy to learn about, rehearse, and anticipate fearful events in a protective coping effort to prevent negative emotions and despair.

Sex Sex refers to the anatomical and physiological characteristics or features of males and females, the two typically assigned sexes.

Sexism The prejudice and resulting discrimination based on the views of sex or gender, especially against women and girls, is known as sexism.

Sexual orientation A sexual orientation refers to romantic or sexual attraction to people of a specific sex or gender.

Sexuality Sexuality is the capacity for erotic experiences and related behavioral responses.

Significant other The most intimate and important person in a person's life—a partner, a fiancé(e), or a spouse—is known as a significant other.

Single-evaluation attitudes Single-evaluation attitudes have a single composition of the affective component, such as either liking or disliking.

Social desirability bias The tendency of respondents to give answers that are supposed to be received favorably by others is the social desirability bias.

Social identity People's perceived membership in one or several social groups is their social identity.

Social interest In Adler's view, social interest is the desire to be connected with other people and to adapt positively to the perceived social environment.

Socialization Socialization is the process by which an individual becomes a member of a society and takes on its ideas and behaviors.

Social learning theory Generally, social learning theory states, among other things, that learning does not necessarily need reinforcement and conditioning.

Social science The study of social science is concerned with society and the relationships among individuals within it.

Social status A social status is a position within the society and can be a measure of an individual's access to resources and power.

Sociology Sociology is the study of society and the social action of humans.

Stereotyping Stereotyping is a generalization of others' behaviors and traits based on their social status or membership in a particular gender, age, ethnic, or professional group.

Stigma A stigma is the negative perception and corresponding actions related to a person or group based solely on certain social characteristics they possess or are associated with.

Strength of the nervous system The strength of the nervous system is a reflection of the functional ability of the neurons to maintain the state of activation or excitement without developing self-protecting inhibition.

Stress Stress is the reaction to a condition that disturbs an individual's physical or mental balance.

Stress tolerance Stress tolerance is a stable pattern of behavior and experience that appears helpful in the process of coping with significant stressors.

Striving toward superiority In Adler's view, striving toward superiority is an individual's vigorous exertion or effort to achieve security, improvement, control, and conquest.

Style of life In Adler's view, the style of life is a technique for dealing with one's inadequacies and inferiorities and for gaining social status.

Superego In psychoanalysis, the superego is the moral guide that passes on imperatives regarding appropriate or inappropriate actions and thoughts.

Suppression–facilitation model The suppression–facilitation model states that behaviors that are discouraged in a culture will be seen infrequently in mental health facilities.

Taxonomies Taxonomies are descriptive models or classifications based on similarity, function, structure, size, origin, and the like.

Test-taking attitudes An individual's view about taking a particular test or taking tests in general is referred to as a test-taking attitude.

Thanatos According to Freud, thanatos ("death" in ancient Greek) means striving for destruction, humiliation, pain, and death.

Themas In Murray's system, themas are stories or interpretations that project fantasy imagery onto an objective stimulus.

Theory Applied to personality, theory is a type of comprehensive, scientific explanation about what personality is, how it develops, and how it functions.

Tolerance threshold An individual's tolerance threshold is a measure of tolerance or intolerance toward specific personality traits in a society or within a cultural group.

Traits Traits are distinguishable and stable patterns of behavior and experience.

Transcendental Transcendental refers to the spiritual, nonphysical side of human experience.

Transgender To be transgender means to feel that one does not fit into the traditionally assigned gender dichotomy, such as male or female.

Transpersonal psychology Transpersonal psychology is a theoretical and applied field that focuses on spiritual and transcendent states of consciousness.

Transvestic fetishism A condition in which an individual's sexual fantasies, urges, or behaviors involve cross-dressing, transvestic fetishism also causes clinically significant distress or impairment in social, occupational, or other important areas of function.

Trolley dilemma A thought exercise, the trolley dilemma involves rational reasoning and moral choices related to saving a human life by sacrificing another.

Type D personality A Type D personality has the persistent tendency toward (a) negative affectivity (being constantly irritable, anxious, and expecting failure) and (b) social inhibition (involving both self-restraint and a lack of self-assurance).

Type A type refers to a kind or category of elements or features sharing similar characteristics or qualities.

Uncertainty orientation A person's uncertainty orientation is the common way he or she handles uncertainty in daily situations and life in general.

Unconscious The unconscious refers to the psychological activities not open to direct rational scrutiny but that influence individual experience and behavior.

Universalist perspective on abnormal behavior The universalist perspective on abnormal behavior suggests the existence of some universal psychological and behavioral features shared in individuals. Deviant and abnormal phenomena across countries and cultures tend to be universal in terms of their origin and expression.

Validity The degree to which an assessment measures what it is supposed to measure and not other variables is its validity.

Values Stable perceptions about the individual's place and his or her role in the world are represented by values.

Witchcraft Witchcraft is the alleged practice or art of witches.

Yoga Yoga is a system of beliefs and practices to facilitate the transformation of body and consciousness.

Zone of proximal development The zone of proximal development indicates the difference between a child's learning progress with help or guidance and the child's learning achievement without the guidance of an adult.

• References •

Aanstoos, C., Serlin, I., & Greening, T. (2000). History of division 32 (humanistic psychology) of the American Psychological Association. In D. Dewsbury (Ed.), *Unification through division: Histories of the divisions of the American Psychological Association* (Vol. 5, pp. 85–112). Washington, DC: American Psychological Association. Retrieved from **http://www.apa.org/pubs/books/431640A.aspx**

Abramson, L., Metalsky, G., & Alloy, L. (1989). Hopelessness depression: A theory-based subtype of depression. *Psychological Review, 96*, 358–372.

Abramson, L. Y., Seligman, M. E. P., & Teasdale, J. D. (1978). Learned helplessness in humans: Critique and reformulation. *Journal of Abnormal Psychology, 87*, 49–74.

Aczel, B., Palfi, B., & Kekecs, Z. (2015). What is stupid? People's conception of unintelligent behavior. *Intelligence, 53*, 51–58.

Adler, A. (1930). *Problems of neurosis.* New York, NY: Cosmopolitan.

Adorno, T. W., Frenkel-Brunswik, E., Levinson, D. J., & Sanford, R. N. (1950). *The authoritarian personality.* New York, NY: Harper & Row.

Akerlund, D., Gronqvist, H., & Lindhal, L. (2014, May). Time preferences in criminal behavior. *IZA Discussion Paper Series.* N. 8168. Retrieved from **http://ftp.iza.org/dp8168.pdf**

Akhtar, S. (2002). *Broken structures: Severe personality disorders and their treatment.* Northvale, NJ: Aronson.

Alexander, M. G., & Fisher, T. D. (2003). Truth and consequences: Using the bogus pipeline to examine sex differences in self-reported sexuality. *Journal of Sex Research, 40*, 27–35.

Alloy, L., Abramson, L., Walshaw, P., Cogswell, A., Grandin L., Hughes, M., . . . Hogan, M. (2008). Behavioral approach system and behavioral inhibition system sensitivities and bipolar spectrum disorders: Prospective prediction of bipolar mood episodes. *Bipolar Disorders, 10*(2), 310–322.

Allport, F. (1924). *Social psychology.* New York, NY: Houghton-Mifflin.

Allport, G. (1937). *Personality: A psychological interpretation.* New York, NY: Henry Holt.

Allport, G. W. (1935). Attitudes. In C. Murchinson (Ed.), *A handbook of social psychology* (pp. 798–844). Worcester, MA: Clark University Press.

Allport, G. W., & Odbert, H. S. (1936). *Trait-names: A psycho-lexical study.* Albany, NY: Psychological Review.

Ambedkar, B. R. (2012). *Castes in India.* Ulan Press. (Original work published 1917)

American Psychiatric Association. (1980). *The diagnostic and statistical manual of mental disorders* (3rd ed.). Washington, DC: Author.

American Psychiatric Association. (1994). *The diagnostic and statistical manual of mental disorders* (4th ed.; text revision). Washington, DC: Author.

American Psychiatric Association. (2013). *The diagnostic and statistical manual of mental disorders* (5th ed.). Washington, DC: Author.

American Psychological Association. (2001). *Publication manual of the American Psychological Association* (5th ed., p. 63). Washington, DC: Author.

American Psychological Association. (2014). Psychology topics: Personality. Retrieved February 19, 2015, from **http://www.apa.org/topics/personality/**

American Psychological Association. (2015a). Psychology topics: Lesbian, gay, bisexual, transgender. Retrieved from **http://www.apa.org/topics/lgbt/index.aspx**

American Psychological Association. (2015b). Stress in America. Retrieved from **http://www.apa.org/news/press/releases/stress/index.aspx?tab=1**

American Veterinary Medical Association. (2016). U.S. pet ownership statistics. Retrieved from **https://www.avma.org/KB/Resources/Statistics/Pages/Market-research-statistics-US-pet-ownership.aspx**

Amidon, S. (2006, August 12). I didn't like sex at all. *Salon.com.* Retrieved from **http://www.salon.com/2006/08/12/gellhorn/**

Anderson, C. (1987). Temperature and aggression: Effects on quarterly, yearly, and city rates of violent and nonviolent crime. *Journal of Personality and Social Psychology, 52*, 1161–1173.

Andreason, N. J. C., & Canter, A. (1974). The creative writer: Psychiatric symptoms and family history. *Comprehensive Psychiatry, 15*(2), 123–131.

Andreason, N. J. C., & Powers, P. S. (1975). Creativity and psychosis: An examination of conceptual style. *Archives of General Psychiatry, 32*, 70–73.

Antonovsky, A. (1987). *Unraveling the mystery of health: How people manage stress and stay well.* San Francisco, CA: Jossey-Bass.

Anusic, I., Lucas, R. E., & Donnellan, M. B. (2012). Cross-sectional age differences in personality: Evidence from nationally representative samples from Switzerland and the United States. *Journal of Research in Personality, 46*, 116–120.

Archer, J. (1996). Sex differences in social behavior. Are the social role and evolutionary explanations compatible? *American Psychologist, 51*(9), 909–917.

Armstrong, K. (2014). *Fields of blood: Religion and the history of violence.* New York, NY: Knopf.

Arnett, J. J. (2002). The psychology of globalization. *American Psychologist, 57*(10), 774–783.

Arnett, J. J. (2008). The neglected 95%: Why American psychology needs to become less American. *American Psychologist, 63*, 602–614.

Aspinwall, L. G., & Taylor, S. E. (1997). A stitch in time: Self-regulation and proactive coping. *Psychological Bulletin, 121*(3), 417–436.

Association for Humanistic Psychology. (2014). *Humanistic psychology overview.* Retrieved from **https://www.ahpweb.org/about/ what-is-humanistic-psychology.html**

Astuli, R., & Bloch, M. (2010). Why a theory of human nature cannot be based on the distinction between universality and variability: Lessons from anthropology. *Behavioral and Brain Sciences, 33*(2/3), 23–24.

Auden, W. H. (1949). *The age of anxiety.* London, England: Faber & Faber.

Ayman, R., & Korabik, K. (2010). Why gender and culture matter. *American Psychologist, 65*(3), 157–170.

Bacon, F. (1970). *The essays or counsels, civil and coral, of Francis Ld. Verulam, Viscount St. Albans.* Peter Pauper Press. (Original work published 1625)

Bais, A. (2012). Relevance of metrosexuality in the post modern society. *Research Journal of Humanities and Social Sciences, 3*(1), 154–157.

Bakker, A. B., Demerouti, E., & Sanz-Vergel, A. I. (2014). Burnout and work engagement: The JD–R approach. *Annual Review of Organizational Psychology and Organizational Behavior, 1*, 389–411.

Bandura, A. (1963). *Social learning and personality development.* New York, NY: Holt, Rinehart, & Winston.

Bandura, A. (1977). *Social learning theory.* Oxford, England: Prentice-Hall.

Bandura, A. (1986). *Social foundations of thought and action: A social cognitive theory.* Englewood Cliffs, NJ: Prentice-Hall.

Bandura, A. (1997). *Self-efficacy: The exercise of control.* New York, NY: Freeman.

Bandura, A. (2001). Social cognitive theory: An agentic perspective. *Annual Review of Psychology, 52*, 1–26.

Bandura, A., Ross, D., & Ross, S. A. (1961). Transmission of aggression through the imitation of aggressive models. *Journal of Abnormal and Social Psychology, 63*(3), 575–582.

Bandura, A., Ross, D., & Ross, S. A. (1963). Imitation of film-mediated aggressive models. *Journal of Abnormal and Social Psychology, 66*(1), 3–11.

Banerjee, A., & Duflo, E. (2011). *Poor economics: A radical rethinking of the way to fight global poverty.* New York., NY: Public Affairs.

Banks, D., & Rose, D. (2010). Diversity in representations, uniformity in learning. *Behavioral and Brain Sciences, 33*(2/3), 30–31.

Barrett, P., & Eysenck, S. B. G. (1984). The assessment of personality factors across 25 countries. *Personality and Individual Differences, 5*, 615–632.

Battaglia, M., & Torgensen, S. (1996). Schizotypal disorder: At crossroads of genetics and nosology. *Acta Psychiatrica Scandinavica, 94*, 303–310.

Baumann, N. (2012). Autotelic personality. In S. Engeser (Ed.), *Advances in flow research* (pp.165–186). Heidelberg, Germany: Springer.

Baumeister, R. (2010). *Is there anything good about men?: How cultures flourish by exploiting men.* New York, NY: Oxford University Press.

Baumeister, R., & Tierney, J. (2012). *Willpower.* New York, NY: Penguin Books.

Baumrind, D. (1971). Current patterns of parental authority. *Developmental Psychology Monographs, 4*(1–2), 1–10.

Bayanova, L. (2013). Vygotsky's Hamlet: The dialectic method and personality psychology. *Psychology in Russia: State of the Art, 6*(1), 35–42.

Beard, M. (2014). *Laughter in ancient Rome: On joking, tickling, and cracking up.* Berkeley: University of California Press.

Beardsley, L., & Pedersen, P. (1997). Health and culture-centered intervention. In J. Berry & C. Kagitcibasi (Eds.), *Handbook of cross-cultural psychology: Social behavior and applications* (Vol. 3, pp. 413–448). Boston, MA: Allyn & Bacon.

Beauchaine, T. P., & Marsh, P. (2006). Taxometric methods: Enhancing early detection and prevention of psychopathology by identifying latent vulnerability traits. In D. Cicchetti & D. Cohen (Eds.), *Developmental psychopathology* (2nd ed., pp. 931–967). Hoboken, NJ: Wiley.

Beck, A. T. (1964). Thinking and depression: II. Theory and therapy. *Archives of General Psychiatry, 10*, 561–571.

Beck, A. T. (1991). Cognitive therapy: A 30-year retrospective. *American Psychologist, 46*(4), 368–375.

Beck, A. T., & Weishaar, M., (2013). Cognitive therapy. In D. Wedding & R. J. Corsini (Eds.), *Current pyschotherapies* (10th ed., pp. 231–264). Belmont, CA: Brooks/Cole, Cengage Learning.

Becker, G. (1968). Crime and punishment: An economic approach. *Journal of Political Economy, 76*, 169–217.

Bekhterev, V. (1907, September). *Personality and the conditions of its development and health.* In proceedings of the second symposium of Russian Psychiatrists, Kiev. Retrieved from **http://testmetod.ru/index.php/stati/73statibehterev**

Bekhterev, V. (1922). Personality and work. [Lichnost I Trud] In V., Bekhterev, H. Munsterberg (Eds.), *Reader of applied psychology.* Moscow: Gostehizdat.

Bekhterev, V. M. (1904). *Psikhicheskaia deiatelnost i Zhizn* [Psychological activity and life]. St. Petersburg, Russia: Military Medical Academy.

Bekhterev, V. M. (1933). *General principles of human reflexology: An introduction to the objective study of personality* (Translation of the 4th Russian ed.). London, England: Jarrolds. (Original work published 1918)

Bekhterev, V. M. (2001). *Collective reflexology: The complete edition* (E. Lockwood & A. Lockwood, Trans.). New Brunswick, NJ: Transaction. (Original work published 1921)

Bekhterev, V. M. (2001). Immortality from a scientific point of view. *Journal of Russian and East European Psychology, 39*(5), 34–70. (Original work published 1916)

Bélanger, J. J., Caouette, J., Sharvit, K., & Dugas, M. (2014). The psychology of martyrdom: Making the ultimate sacrifice in the name of a cause. *Journal of Personality and Social Psychology, 107*(3), 494–515.

Bellows, A. (2013, November 22). Three thrown over the cuckoo's nest [Web log post]. Retrieved from **http://www.damninteresting.com**

Bemak, F., & Chung, R. C.-Y. (2004). Culturally oriented psychotherapy with refugees. In U. Gielen, J. Fish, & J. Draguns (Eds.), *Culture, therapy and healing* (pp. 121–132). Mahwah, NJ: Lawrence Erlbaum.

Bemak, F., Chung, R. C.-Y., & Pedersen, P. B. (2003). *Counseling refugees: A psychosocial approach to innovative multicultural interventions.* Westport, CT: Greenwood Press.

Benedict, R. (1946). *The chrysanthemum and the sword: Patterns of Japanese culture.* Boston, MA: Houghton Mifflin.

Bengson, J., Kelley, T., Zhang, X., Wang, J.-L., & Mangun, G. (2014). Spontaneous neural fluctuations predict decisions to attend. *Journal*

of Cognitive Neuroscience, 26(11), 2578–2584.

Benight, C. C., & Bandura, A. (2004). Social cognitive theory of post-traumatic recovery: The role of perceived self-efficacy. *Behaviour Research and Therapy, 42*(10), 1129–1148.

Benjamin, H. (1966). *The transsexual phenomenon.* New York, NY: Julian Press.

Bennis, W., & Medin, D. (2010). Weirdness is in the eye of the beholder. *Behavioral and Brain Sciences, 33*(2/3), 25–26.

Berdyaev, N. (2009). *The destiny of man.* Semantron Press. (Original work published 1931)

Berger, K. (1994). *The developing person through the life span* (3rd ed.). New York: Worth Publishers.

Bergmann, O., & Frisén, J. (2013). Why adults need new brain cells. *Science, 340*(6133), 695–696.

Berman, P. (2004). *Terror and liberalism.* New York, NY: Norton.

Bérubé, A. (1990). *Coming out under fire: The history of gay men and women in World War II.* New York, NY: Penguin.

Bharati, A. (1970). The Hindu renaissance and its apologetic patterns. *Journal of Asian Studies, 29*(2), 267–287.

Bhikkhu, T. (2002). *The karma of questions.* Valley Center, CA: Metta Forest Monastery.

Bilger, B. (2004, April 5). The height gap. *The New Yorker.* Retrieved from **http://www.newyorker.com/magazine/2004/04/05/the-height-gap**

Billings, A. G., & Moos, R. H. (1981). The role of coping responses and social resources in attenuating the stress of life events. *Journal of Behavioral Medicine, 4*(2), 139–157.

Binswanger, L. (1963). *Being-in-the-world: Selected papers of Ludwig Binswanger* (J. Needleman, Trans.). New York, NY: Basic Books.

Birger, J. (2015). *Date-onomics: How dating became a lopsided numbers game*. New York, NY: Workman.

Birmingham, K. (2014). *The most dangerous book: The battle for James Joyce*. London, England: Penguin Press.

Biswas, U. N., & Pandey, J. (1996). Mobility and perception of socioeconomic status among tribal and caste group. *Journal of Cross-Cultural Psychology, 27*(2), 200–215.

Bjerre, P. (1916). *The history and practice of psychoanalysis*. Boston, MA: Richard Badger.

Blanchard, R. (1989). The concept of autogynephilia and the typology of male gender dysphoria. *Journal of Nervous and Mental Disease, 177*(10), 616–623.

Block, J. (2001). Millennial contrarianism: The five-factor approach to personality description 5 years later. *Journal of Research in Personality, 35*, 98–107.

Block, S., & Block, C. (2012*). Mind-body workbook for stress: Effective tools for lifelong stress reduction and crisis management*. Oakland, CA: New Harbinger.

Boeree, C. G. (2006). *Carl Rogers*. Retrieved from **http://webspace .ship.edu/cgboer/rogers.html**

Bonanno, G. A., Papa, A., Lalande, K., Westphal, M., & Coifman, K. (2004). The importance of being flexible: The ability to both enhance and suppress

emotional expression predicts long-term adjustment. *Psychological Science, 15*(7), 482–487.

Bond, F. W., & Bince, D. (2000). Mediators of change in emotion-focused and problem-focused Woodside Stress Management Interventions. *Journal of Occupational Health Psychology, 5*(1), 156–163.

Bond, F. W., & Flaxman, P. E. (2006). The ability of psychological flexibility and job control to predict learning, job performance, and mental health. *Journal of Organizational Behavior Management, 26*(1–2), 113–130.

Bond, M., & Tak-Sing, C. (1983). College students' spontaneous self concept: The effects of culture among respondents in Hong-Kong, Japan, and the United States. *Journal of Cross-Cultural Psychology, 14*, 153–171.

Bond, R., & Smith, P. B. (1996). Culture and conformity: A meta-analysis of studies using Asch's line judgment task. *Psychological Bulletin, 119*(1), 111–137.

Boninger, G. F., Boninger, D. S., Strathman, A., Armor, D., Hetts, J., & Ahn, M. (1995). With an eye toward the future: The impact of counterfactual thinking on affect, attitudes, and behavior. In N. Roese & J. Olson (Eds.), *What might have been: The social psychology of counterfactual thinking* (pp. 283–304). Hillsdale, NJ: Lawrence Erlbaum.

Borelli, J. L., & Sbarra, D. A. (2011). Trauma history and linguistic self-focus moderate the course of psychological adjustment to divorce. *Journal of Social and Clinical Psychology, 30*, 667–698.

Boring, E. G. (1950). *A history of experimental psychology* (2nd ed.). New York, NY: Century. (Original work published 1929)

Bornstein, R. F. (2001). The impending death of psychoanalysis. *Psychoanalytic Psychology, 18*, 3–20.

Boster, J. (1985). Selection for perceptual distinctiveness: Evidence from Aguaruna Cultivars of Manihot Esculenta. *Economic Botany, 39*(3), 310–325.

Bouchard, T., Lykken, D., McGue, M., Segal, N. L., & Tellegen, A. (1990). Sources of human psychological differences: The Minnesota study of twins reared apart. *Science, 250*, 223–228.

Bouchard, T. J., & McGue, M. (2003). Genetic and environmental influences on human psychological differences. *Journal of Neurobiology, 54*(1), 4–45.

Boucher, H. C., Peng, K., Shi, J., & Wang, L. (2009). Culture and implicit self-esteem: Chinese are "good" and "bad" at the same time. *Journal of Cross-Cultural Psychology, 40*(1), 24–45.

Boyle, G., & Helmes, E. (2009). Methods of personality assessment. In P. Corr & G. Matthews (Eds.), *The Cambridge handbook of personality psychology* (pp. 110–126). Cambridge, United Kingdom: Cambridge University Press.

Brand, J. (2015). The far-reaching impact of job loss and unemployment. *Annual Review of Sociology, 41*, 359–375.

Bray, J. (2010). The future of psychology practice and science. *American Psychologist, 65*(5), 355–369.

Brewer, M. B. (1991). The social self: On being the same and different at the same time. *Personality and Social Psychology Bulletin, 17*, 475–482.

Brewer, M. B., & Pierce, K. P. (2005). Social identity complexity and outgroup tolerance. *Personality and Social Psychology Bulletin, 31*, 428–437.

A Brief History of the MMPI Instruments. (2016). University of Minnesota Press. Retrieved from **https://www.upress.umn.edu/test-division/bibliography/mmpi-history**

Brieger, P., Ehrt, U., & Marneros, A. (2003). Frequency of comorbid personality disorders in bipolar and unipolar affective disorders. *Comprehensive Psychiatry, 44*(1), 28–34.

Brizendine, L. (2007). *The female brain.* New York, NY: Harmony.

Broad, W. (2012). *The science of yoga: The risks and the rewards.* New York, NY: Simon & Schuster.

Bronfenbrenner, Y. (1979). *The ecology of human development: Experiments by nature and design.* Cambridge, MA: Harvard University Press.

Broucek, F. (1991). *Shame and the self.* New York, NY: Guilford.

Browder, L. (2000). *Slippery characters: Ethnic impersonators and American identities.* Durham: University of North Carolina Press.

Brown, J. D., & Cai, H. (2010). Self-esteem and trait importance moderate cultural differences in self-evaluations. *Journal of Cross-Cultural Psychology, 41*(1), 116–123.

Brownmiller, S. (1985). *Femininity.* New York, NY: Ballantine Books.

Bruehl, E. (1990). *Anna Freud: A biography.* New York, NY: Pocket Books.

Bruner, J. (1990). *Acts of meaning.* Cambridge, MA: Harvard University Press.

Bruner, J., & Goodman, C. (1947). Value and need as organizing factors in perception. *Journal of Abnormal and Social Psychology, 42*, 33–44.

Bryan, A., Aiken, L. S., & West, S. G. (2004). HIV/STD risk among incarcerated adolescents: Optimism about the future and self-esteem as predictors of condom use self efficacy. *Journal of Applied Social Psychology, 34*, 912–936.

Buckels, E. E., Trapnell, P. D., & Paulhus, D. L. (2014). Trolls just want to have fun. *Personality and Individual Differences, 68*, 97–102.

Bugental, J. (1964). The third force in psychology. *Journal of Humanistic Psychology, 4*(1), 19–25.

Burgess, R., & Akers, R. (1966). Differential association-reinforcement theory of criminal behavior. *Social Problems, 14*(2), 128–147.

Burns, D. D. (1989). *The feeling good handbook: Using the new mood therapy in everyday life.* New York, NY: W. Morrow.

Bus, D., & Craik, K. (1986). Acts, dispositions, and clinical assessment: The psychopathology of everyday conduct. *Clinical Psychology Review, 6*, 387–406.

Buss, A., & Plomin, R. (1984). *Temperament: Early developing personality traits.* Hillsdale, NJ: Erlbaum.

Buss, D. (1996). Paternity uncertainty and the complex repertoire of human mating strategies. *American Psychologist, 51*(2), 161–162.

Buss, D. M., & Duntley, J. D. (2008). Adaptations for exploitation. *Group Dynamics, 12*, 53–62.

Byrnes, J. P. (1988). Formal operations: A systematic reformulation. *Developmental Review, 8*, 66–87.

Cadoret, R., Yates, W., Troughton, E., Woodworth, G., & Stewart, M. (1995). Genetic-environmental interaction in the genes of aggressivity and conduct disorders. *Archives of General Psychiatry, 52*(11), 916–924.

Calkins, M. W. (1906). A reconciliation between structural and functional psychology (Calkins' APA presidential address). *Psychological Review, 8*, 61–81.

Callanan, K., & Kelley, P. (1997). *Final gifts: Understanding the special awareness, needs, and communications of the dying.* New York City, NY : Bantam Books.

Campbell, D. (2006). *Inner strength defies the skeptic: A psychological and spiritual guide from fear to freedom.* Los Angeles, CA: Immediex.

Campbell, W. K. (1999). Narcissism and romantic attraction. *Journal of Personality and Social Psychology, 77*(6), 1254–1270.

Camus, A. (1992). *The rebel.* New York, NY: Vintage. (Original work published 1951)

Caplan, E. (1998). Popularizing American psychotherapy: The Emmanuel movement, 1906–1910. *History of Psychology, 1*, 289–314.

Caprara, G., Barbaranelli, C., &. Zimbardo, P. (1997, February). Politicians' uniquely simple personalities. *Nature, 385*, 493.

Caprara, G., & Vecchione, M. (2009). Personality and politics. In P. Corr & G. Matthews (Eds.), *The Cambridge handbook of personality psychology* (pp. 589–607). Cambridge, United Kingdom: Cambridge University Press.

Car, A. (2011). *Positive psychology. The science of happiness and human strengths.* New York, NY: Routledge.

Carbone, J., & Cahn, N. (2013). *The end of men or the rebirth of class?* Boston University Law Review 871. Retrieved June 15, 2015, from **http://scholarship.law.umn.edu/facultyarticles/125**

Carey, B. (2011, November 2). Fraud case seen as a red flag for psychology research. *The New York Times*. Retrieved from **http://www.nytimes.com/2011/11/03/health/research/noteddutchpsychologiststapelaccusedofresearchfraud.html**

Carroll, L. (2013). Passive coping strategies. In M. Gellman & J. R. Turner (Eds.), *Encyclopedia of Behavioral Medicine* (p. 1442). New York, NY: Springer.

Carver, C. S., & Harmon-Jones, E. (2009). Anger is an approach-related affect: Evidence and implications. *Psychological Bulletin, 135*, 183–204.

Carver, C. S., & White, T. L. (1994). Behavioral inhibition, behavioral activation, and affective responses to impending reward and punishment: The BIS/BAS scales. *Journal of Personality and Social Psychology, 67*, 319–333.

Casey, B., Somerville, L., Gotlib, I., Ayduk, N., Franklin, M., Askren, J., . . . Shoda, Y. (2011). Behavioral and neural correlates of delay of gratification 40 years later. *Proceedings of the National Academy of Sciences, 108*(36), 14998–15003.

Cashdan, M., & Steele, E. (2013). Pathogen prevalence, group bias, and collectivism in the standard cross-cultural sample. *Human Nature, 24*(1), 59–75.

Cattell, R. B. (1946). *The description and measurement of personality.* New York, NY: Harcourt, Brace, & World.

Cattell, R. B. (1957). *Personality and motivation structure and measurement.* New York, NY: World Book.

Cattell, R. B. (1965). *The scientific analysis of personality.* Baltimore, MD: Penguin.

Cattell, R. B. (1978). *The scientific use of factor analysis in behavioral and life sciences.* New York, NY: Plenum.

Cattell, R. B. (1983). *Structured personality-learning theory: A holistic multivariate research approach* (pp. 419–457). New York, NY: Praeger.

Cattell, H. E. P., & Mead, A. D. (2008). *The sixteen personality factor questionnaire (16PF).* In G. J. Boyle, G. Matthews, & D. H. Saklofske. (Eds.), *The SAGE handbook of personality theory and assessment: Vol. 2– Personality measurement and testing.* Los Angeles, CA: Sage.

Centers for Disease Control (CDC). (2015). Deaths and mortality. Retrieved from **http://www.cdc.gov/nchs/fastats/deaths.htm**

Chajes, J. (2011). *Between worlds: Dybbuks, exorcists, and early modern Judaism.* Philadelphia: University of Pennsylvania Press.

Charon, R. (1992). To build a case: Medical histories as traditions in conflict. *Literature and Medicine, 11*(1), 93–105.

Charon, R. (1993). The narrative road to empathy. In H. Spiro (Ed.), *Empathy and the medical profession: Beyond pills and the scalpel* (pp. 147–159). New Haven, CT: Yale University Press.

Chaudhary, N. (2010). [Review of the book *Handbook of Indian psychology,* by K. R. Rao, A. C. Paranjpe, & A. K. Dala (Eds.)]. New Delhi, India: Cambridge University Press.

Chen, S. X., Benet-Martinez, V., & Bond, M. H. (2008). Bicultural identity, bilingualism, and psychological adjustment in multicultural societies: Immigration-based and globalization-based acculturation. *Journal of Personality, 76*, 803–838.

Chiao, J., & Cheon, B. (2010). The weirdest brains in the world. *Behavioral and Brain Sciences, 33*(2/3), 28–30.

Chiraag, M., & Griskevicius, V. (2014). Sense of control under uncertainty depends on people's childhood environment: A life history theory approach. *Journal of Personality and Social Psychology, 107*(4), 621–663.

Clay, R. A. (2002). A renaissance for humanistic psychology: The field explores new niches while building on its past. *American Psychological Association Monitor, 33*(8), 42.

Cleckley, H. (1976). *The mask of sanity* (5th ed.). St. Louis, MO: CV Mosby.

Cloninger. C. R., Dragan, M. S., & Thomas R. P. (1993). A psychobiological model of temperament and character. *Archives of General Psychiatry 50*, 975–990.

Cochran, G., & Harpending, H. (2010). *The 10,000-year explosion: How civilization accelerated human evolution.* New York, NY: Basic Books.

Cohen, D. (2000). *Carl Rogers: A critical biography.* London, England: Constable.

Cohn, C. (1987). Sex and death in the rational world of defense intellectuals. *Signs, 12*(4), 687–718.

Colamonico, J., Formella, A., & Bradley, W. (2012). Pseudobulbar affect: Burden of illness in the USA. *Advances in Therapy, 29*(9), 775–798.

Collins, F. S. (2010). *The language of life: DNA and the revolution in personalized medicine.* New York, NY: HarperCollins.

Collins, S. (1990). *Selfless persons: Imagery and thought in Theravada Buddhism.* New York, NY: Cambridge University Press.

Colom, F., Vieta, E., Sánchez-Moreno, J., Torrent, C., Reinares, M., Goikoela, J. M., . . . Comes, M. (2004). Psychoeducation in bipolar patients with comorbid personality disorders. *Bipolar Disorders, 6*(4), 294–298.

Compton, W. C. (2004). *An introduction to positive psychology.* Belmont, CA: Wadsworth.

Confer, J., & Cloud, M. (2010). Sex differences in response to imagining a partner's heterosexual or homosexual affair. *Personality and Individual Differences, 50*(7), 11–55.

Confer, J., Easton, J., Fleischman, D., Goetz, C., Lewis, D., Perilloux, C., & Buss, D. (2010). Evolutionary psychology: Controversies, questions, prospects, and limitations. *American Psychologist, 65*(2), 110–126.

Connelly, B., & Ones, D. (2010). Another perspective on personality: Meta-analytic integration of observers' accuracy and predictive validity. *Psychological Bulletin, 136*(6), 1092–1122.

Converse, P. E. (1964). The nature of belief systems in mass publics. In D. E. Apter (Ed.), *Ideology and discontent* (pp. 206–261). New York, NY: Free Press.

Coonan, C. (2012, August 27). Wanted: 'Innocent' brides for China's ultra-rich. *The Independent.* Retrieved from **http://www.independent .co.uk/news/world/asia/wanted-innocent-brides-for-chinas-ultrarich-8082065.html**

Cooper, D. (2003). *World philosophies.* Malden, MA: Blackwell.

Corr, P., & Matthews, G. (Eds.). (2009). *The Cambridge handbook of personality psychology* (pp. 110–126). Cambridge,

United Kingdom Cambridge University Press.

Corrigan, P. W., & Wassel, A. (2008). Understanding and influencing the stigma of mental illness. *Journal of Psychosocial Nursing and Mental Health Services, 46*(1), 42–48.

Costa, P. T., Terracciano, A., & McCrae, R. R. (2001). Gender differences in personality traits across cultures: Robust and surprising findings. *Journal of Personality and Social Psychology, 81*(2), 322–331.

Costa, P. T., Jr., & McCrae, R. R. (1985). *The NEO Personality Inventory manual.* Odessa, FL: Psychological Assessment Resources.

Costa, P. T., Jr., & McCrae, R. R. (1988). Personality in adulthood: A six-year longitudinal study of self-reports and spouse ratings on the NEO Personality Inventory. *Journal of Personality and Social Psychology, 54,* 853–863.

Costa, P. T., Jr., & McCrae, R. R. (1992). *NEO PIR professional manual.* Odessa, FL: Psychological Assessment Resources.

Costello, C. G. (Ed.). (1995). *Personality characteristics of the personality disordered.* New York, NY: John Wiley & Sons.

Craighead, W. E., Miklowitz, D. J., & Craighead, L. W. (Eds.). (2013). *Psychopathology: History, diagnosis, and empirical foundation* (2nd ed.). New York, NY: John Wiley & Sons.

Cramer, P. (1991). *The development of defense mechanisms: Theory, research, and assessment.* New York, NY: Springer-Verlag.

Cravens, H. (2002). *Before Head Start: The Iowa station and America's children.* Chapel Hill: University of North Carolina Press.

Creighton, S. (2001). Surgery for intersex. *Journal of the Royal Society of Medicine, 94,* 218–220.

Csikszentmihalyi, M. (1990). *Flow: The psychology of optimal experience.* New York, NY: Harper & Row.

Csikszentmihalyi, M. (1997). *Finding flow: The psychology of engagement with everyday life.* New York, NY: Basic Books.

Cuddihy, J. M. (1974). *The ordeal of civility: Freud, Marx, Levi-Strauss, and the Jewish struggle with modernity.* New York, NY: Basic Books.

Curtin, J. J., McCarthy, D. E., Piper, M. E., & Baker, T. B. (2005). Implicit and explicit drug motivational processes: A model of boundary conditions. In R. Reinout & A. Stacy (Eds.), *Handbook on implicit cognition and addiction* (pp. 233–250). Thousand Oaks, CA: Sage.

Da Conceição, C. G., & De Lyra Chebabi, W. (1987). Psychoanalysis and the role of black life and culture in Brazil. *International Review of Psycho-Analysis, 14,* 185–202.

Dahlsgaard, K., Peterson, C., & Seligman, M. (2005). Shared virtue: The convergence of valued human strengths across culture and history. *Review of General Psychology, 9,* 203–213.

Dahman, S., & Anger, S. (2014). The impact of education on personality: Evidence from a German high school reform. *Institute for Study of Labor.* Retrieved from **http://ftp.iza.org/dp8139.pdf**

Damasio, A. (2012). *Self comes to mind: Connecting the conscious brain.* New York, NY: Vintage Books.

Danesh, J. (2015). Association of cardiometabolic multimorbidity with mortality. *Journal of the American Medical Association, 314*(1), 52–60.

Das, G., & Rae, A. (1999). *The new face of self-help: Online support for anxiety disorders. Dissertation Abstracts International: Section B. Sciences and Engineering, 59*(7B), 36–91.

Dasen, P. R. (1994). Culture and cognitive development from a Piagetian perspective. In W. J. Lonner & R. Malpass (Eds.), *Psychology and culture* (pp. 145–149). Boston, MA: Allyn & Bacon.

David, E. J. R. (2013). *Brown skin, white minds: Filipino American postcolonial psychology.* Information Age.

Davidson, A. R., & Thompson, E. (1980). Cross-cultural studies of attitudes and beliefs. In H. C. Triandis & W. J. Lonner (Eds.), *Handbook of cross-cultural psychology: Vol. 5. Basic Processes* (pp. 25–35). Boston, MA: Allyn & Bacon.

Davidson, R., & Begley, S. (2012). *The emotional life of your brain.* New York, NY: Plume.

Davies, J. (2014). *Life unfolding: How the human body creates itself.* New York, NY: Oxford University Press.

Davis, M., Eshelman, E. R., & McKay, M. (2008). *The relaxation and stress reduction workbook.* Oakland, CA: New Harbinger.

Davis, M. C., Matthews, K. A., & Twamley, E. W. (1999). Is life more difficult on Mars or Venus? A meta-analytic review of sex differences in major and minor life events. *Annals of Behavioral Medicine, 21*(1), 83–97.

Davis, M. L., Morina, N., Powers, M. B., Smits, J. A. J., & Emmelkamp, P. M. G. (2015). A meta-analysis of the efficacy of acceptance and commitment therapy for clinically relevant mental and physical health problems. *Psychotherapy and Psychosomatics, 84*(1), 30–36.

Dawes, R. M. (1994). *House of cards: Psychology and psychotherapy built on myth.* New York, NY: Free Press.

Dawson, A. (2011, October 26). Study says generation X is balanced and happy. *CNN.* Retrieved from **http://www.cnn.com/2011/10/26/living/gen-x-satisfied/**

Dawson, J. (1975). Socioeconomic differences in size judgments of discs and coins by Chinese primary VI children in Hong Kong. *Perceptual and Motor Skills, 41,* 107–110.

Deshpande, S., Nagendra, H., & Nagarathna, R. (2009). A randomized control trial of the effect of yoga on *gunas* (personality) and self esteem in normal healthy volunteers. *International Journal of Yoga, 2*(1), 13–21.

Deutsch, H. (1944). *The psychology of women: A psychoanalytic interpretation: Vol. 1. Girlhood.* New York, NY: Grune & Stratton.

Deutsch, H. (1945). *The psychology of women: A psychoanalytic interpretation: Vol. 2. Motherhood.* New York, NY: Grune & Stratton.

Devereux, G. (1953). Cultural factors in psychoanalytic therapy. *Journal of the American Psychoanalytic Association, 1,* 629–655.

Dewey, J. (1884). The new psychology. *Andover Review, 2,* 278–289.

Diamond, L. (2009). *Sexual fluidity: Understanding women's love and desire.* Cambridge, MA: Harvard University Press.

Diamond, L. M. (2008). Female bisexuality from adolescence to adulthood: Results from a 10-year longitudinal study. *Developmental Psychology, 44*(1), 5–14.

DiClemente, D., & Hantula, D. (2000). *John Broadus Watson, IO*

psychologist. Retrieved from **http://www.siop.org/tip/backissues/TipApril00/7Diclemente.aspx**

Dijksterhuis, A. (2004). Think different: The merits of unconscious thought in preference development and decision making. *Journal of Personality and Social Psychology, 87,* 586–598.

Dijksterhuis, A., Bos, M. W., Nordgren, L. F., & van Baaren, R. B. (2006). On making the right choice: The deliberation without attention effect. *Science, 311,* 1005–1007.

Dilthey, W. (2002). The formation of the historical world in the human sciences. New York, NY: Princeton University Press. (Original work published 1910)

Djikic, M., Oatley, K., & Carland, M. (2012). Genre or artistic merit? The effect of literature on personality. *Scientific Study of Literature, 2*(1), 25–36.

Dobreva-Martinova, T., & Strickland, L. H. (Eds.). (2001, September/October). The many sides of Bekhterev [Special issue]. *Journal of Russian and East European Psychology, 39,* 5.

Docker, C. (2013). *Five last acts—The exit path: The arts and science of rational suicide in the face of unbearable, unbelievable suffering.* CreateSpace.

Dolan, M. (2014, January 28). Disgraced journalist Stephen Glass unlikely to ever be lawyer. *The Los Angeles Times.* Retrieved from **http://www.latimes.com/local/lanow/la-me-ln-stephen-glass-lawyer-ruling-20140128-story.html#axzz2rixUCEx0**

Dollard, N., & Miller, J. (1964). *Social learning and imitation.* New Haven, CT: Yale University Press.

Dombrowski, A. Y., Szanto, K., Clark, L., Reynolds, C. F., & Siegle, G. J. (2013). Reward signals, attempted suicide, and impulsivity in late-life depression. *Journal of the American Medical Association—Psychiatry, 70*(10), 1020–1030.

Donnellan, M. B., Conger, R. D., & Burzette, R. G. (2007). Personality development from late adolescence to young adulthood: Differential stability, normative maturity, and evidence for the maturity-stability hypothesis. *Journal of Personality, 75,* 237–267.

Donnellan, M. B., & Robins, R. (2009). The development of personality across the lifespan. In P. Corr & G. Matthews (Eds.), *The Cambridge handbook of personality psychology* (pp. 191–204). Cambridge, United Kingdom Cambridge University Press.

Draguns, J. (2009). Personality in cross-cultural perspective. In P. Corr & G. Matthews (Eds.), *The Cambridge handbook of personality psychology* (pp. 556–576*).* Cambridge, United Kingdom: Cambridge University Press.

Drake, B. (2013). Americans see growing gap between rich and poor. Pew Research Center. Retrieved from **http://www.pewresearch .org/facttank/2013/12/05/ americansseegrowing gapbetweenrichandpoor/**

Dreger, A. (2000). *Hermaphrodites and the medical invention of sex.* Cambridge, MA: Harvard University Press.

Drob, S. L. (1999). Jung and the kabbalah. *History of Psychology, 2*(2), 102–118.

Dubal, D. B., Yokoyama, J. S., Zhu, L., Broestl, L., Worden, K., Wang, D., . . . Mucke, L. (2014). Life extension factor

KLOTHO enhances cognition. *Cell, 7,* 4. Retrieved from **http://www.ncbi .nlm.nih.gov/pubmed/24813892**

Dufresne, T. (2003). *Killing Freud.* London, England: Continuum International.

Dumont, F. (2010). *A history of personality psychology.* New York, NY: Cambridge University Press.

Dunlap, K. (1920). *Mysticism, Freudianism, and scientific psychology.* St. Louis, MO: Mosby.

Dunning, D., & Kruger, J. (1999). Unskilled and unaware of it: How difficulties in recognizing one's own incompetence lead to inflated self-assessments. *Journal of Personality and Social Psychology, 77*(6), 1121–1134.

Eagly, A. H. (1997). Sex differences in social behavior: Comparing social role theory and evolutionary psychology. *American Psychologist, 52*(12), 1380–1383.

Economist. (2013a, August 24). Defense lawyer of the bad: Jacques Vergès, 82. Retrieved from **http:// www.economist.com/news**

Economist. (2013b, July 6). Filial impropriety. Retrieved from **http://www.economist.com/news/ china/21580492childrenmustvisit theirparentsfilialimpropriety**

Edin, K., & Kefalas, M. (2011). *Promises I can keep: Why poor women put motherhood before marriage.* Los Angeles: University of California Press.

Einstein, A. (1905). On the electrodynamics of moving bodies. *Annalen der Physik, 17,* 891–921.

Eisold, K. (2002). Jung, Jungians, and psychoanalysis. *Psychoanalytic Psychology, 19,* 501–524.

Elia, I. E. (2013). A foxy view of human beauty: Implications of the farm fox experiment for understanding the origins of structural and experiential aspects of facial attractiveness. *Quarterly Review of Biology, 88,* 3. Retrieved from **http://www.jstor .org/stable/10.1086/671486**

Ellens, J. H. (Ed.). (2011). *Explaining evil.* Westport, CT: Praeger.

Ellis, H. H., & Symonds, J. A. (2006). *Sexual inversion.* Charleston, SC: Bibliobazaar. (Original work published 1897)

Erne, R. (2008). Male life-course persistent antisocial behavior: A review of neurodevelopmental factors. *Aggression and Violent Behavior, 14,* 348–358.

Emmons, R. A. (1984). Factor analysis and construct validity of the narcissistic personality inventory. *Journal of Personality Assessment, 48,* 291–300.

Emmons, R. A. (1987). Narcissism: Theory and measurement. *Journal of Personality and Social Psychology, 52,* 11–17.

Emmons, R. A., & McCullough, M. E. (2003). Counting blessings versus burdens: Experimental studies of gratitude and subjective well-being in daily life. *Journal of Personality and Social Psychology, 84,* 377–389.

English, H., & English, A. C. (1958). *A comprehensive dictionary of psychological and psychoanalytical terms.* New York, NY: Longmans, Green.

Epel, E. (2009). Psychological and metabolic stress: A recipe for accelerated cellular aging? *Hormones (Athens), 8,* 7–22.

Epel, E. (2012). How reversible is telomeric aging? *Cancer Prevention Research, 5*(10), 1163–1168.

Erikson, E. (1950). *Childhood and society.* New York, NY: Norton.

Erikson, E. (1962). *Yong man Luther.* New York, NY: Peter Smith.

Erikson, E. (1968). *Identity: Youth and crisis.* New York, NY: Norton.

Erikson, E. (1969). *Gandhi's truth: On the origins of militant nonviolence.* New York, NY: W. W. Norton.

Erlenmeyer-Kimlig, L., Squires-Wheeler, E., Adamo, U., Bassett, A., Cornblatt, B., Kestenbausm, C., . . . Gottesman, I. (1995). The New York high-risk project—Psychoses and cluster: A personality disorders in offspring of schizophrenic patients at 23 years of follow-up. *Archives of General Psychiatry, 52,* 857–865.

Esaki, L. (2001, April 1). Connecting to the 21st century educational reform in Japan and reflections on global culture. *The Daily Yomiuri,* p. 6.

Escorial, S. (2007). Analysis of the gender variable in the Eysenck personality questionnaire–Revised scales using differential item functioning techniques. *Educational and Psychological Measurement, 67*(6), 990–1001.

Esterson, A. (2002). The myth of Freud's ostracism by the medical community in 1896–1905: Jeffrey Masson's assault on truth. *History of Psychology, 5*(2), 115–134.

Etkind, L. (1993). *Eros nevozmozhnogo: Istoriya psychoanalyza v Rossii* [Eros of impossible: A history of psychoanalysis in Russia]. Moscow, Russia: Meduza.

Evans, D. (2005). From Lacan to Darwin. In J. Gottschall & D. S. Wilson (Eds.), *The literary animal: Evolution and the nature of narrative.* Evanston, IL: Northwestern University Press.

Eysenk, H. (1948). *Dimensions of personality.* New York, NY: Routledge & Kegan.

Eysenck, H. J. (1956). *Sense and nonsense in psychology.* London, England: Penguin Books.

Eysenck, H. J. (1993). Creativity and personality: Suggestions for a theory. *Psychological Inquiry, 4*(3), 147–178.

Eysenck, H. J. (1997). Personality and the biosocial model of antisocial and criminal behavior. In A. Raine, P. A. Brennan, D. P. Farrington, & S. A. Mednick (Eds.), *Biosocial bases of violence.* New York, NY: Plenum.

Eysenck, H. J., & Eysenck, S. B. G. (1975). *Manual of the Eysenck personality questionnaire.* London, England: Hodder & Stoughton.

Eysenck, H. J., & Eysenck, S. B. G. (1976). *Psychoticism as a dimension of personality.* London, England: Hodder & Stoughton.

Fairbairn, W. R. D. (1963). Synopsis of an object-relations theory of the personality. *International Journal of Psycho-Analysis, 44,* 224–225.

Faiola, A. (2003, December 27). Japan's empire of cool: Country's culture becomes its biggest export. *Washington Post,* p. A01.

Fairhall, J. (2012). Nature, existential shame, and transcendence: An ecocritical approach to Ulysses. *Joyce Studies Annual,* 66–95.

Faja, S., & Dawson, G. (2013). Reduced delay of gratification and effortful control among young children with autism spectrum disorders. *Autism.* Retrieved from **http://aut.sagepub.com/content/ early/2013/12/09/ 1362361313512424.long**

Farmer, R., & Chapman, A. (2007). *Behavioral interventions in cognitive*

behavior therapy: Practical guidance for putting theory into action. Washington, DC: American Psychological Association.

Farrington, D. P. (2002). Families and crime. In J. Q. Wilson & J. Petersilia (Eds.), *Crime: Public policies for crime control* (2nd ed., pp. 129–148). Oakland, CA: Institute for Contemporary Studies Press.

Fausto-Sterling, A. (2012). *Sex/gender: Biology in a social world.* New York, NY: Routledge.

Fazio, R. (1989). On the power and functionality of attitudes: The role of attitude accessibility. In A. R. Pratkanis et al. (eds.), *Attitude structure and function* (pp. 153–179). Hillsdale, NJ: Lawrence Erbaum Associates.

Fazio, R., Williams, C., & Powell, M. (2000). Measuring associative strength: category-item associations and their activation from memory. *Political Psychology, 2*(1), 7–27.

Feldman, R., Forrest, L., & Happ, B. (2002). Self-presentation and verbal deception: Do self-presenters lie more? *Journal of Basic and Applied Social Psychology, 24*(2), 163–170.

Fernald, A. (2010). Getting beyond the "convenience" sample in research on early cognitive development. *Behavioral and Brain Sciences, 33*(2/3), 31–32.

Fernandez, S., Castano, E., & Singh, I. (2010). Managing death in the burning grounds of Varanasi, India: A terror management investigation. *Journal of Cross-Cultural Psychology, 41,* 182–194.

Ferrari, J. R. (2010). *Still procrastinating? The no regrets guide to getting it done.* Hoboken, NJ: Wiley.

Festinger, L. (1957). *A theory of cognitive dissonance.* Stanford, CA: Stanford University Press.

Festinger, L., Riecken, H. W., & Schachter, S. (1956). *When prophecy fails: A social and psychological study of a modern group that predicted the destruction of the world.* Minneapolis: University of Minnesota Press.

Fincher, C. L., Thornhill, R., Murray, D., & Schaller, M. (2008). Pathogen prevalence predicts human cross-cultural variability in individualism-collectivism. *Proceedings of the Royal Society B: Biological Science, 275,* 1279–1285.

Finkel, E. J., Eastwick, P., Karney, B., Reis, H., & Specher, S. (2012, January). Online dating: A critical analysis from the perspective of psychological science. *Psychological Science in the Public Interest 13,* 3–66.

Finlayson, C. (2014). *The improbable primate: How water shaped human evolution.* New York, NY: Oxford University Press.

Fischer, R., & Smith, P. (2003). Reward allocation and culture: A meta-analysis. *Journal of Cross-Cultural Psychology, 34*(3), 251–268.

Fisher, H. (2004). *Why we love: The nature and chemistry of romantic love.* New York, NY: Henry Holt.

Fisher, R. (1971). *The design of experiments.* New York, NY: Macmillan. (Original work published 1935)

Fiske, S. (2010). Envy up, scorn down: How comparison divides us. *American Psychologist, 65*(8), 688–706.

Fiske, S. T., Gilbert, D. T., & Lindzey, G. (2009). *Handbook of social psychology.* Hoboken, NJ: Wiley.

Flood, G. (2012). *An introduction to Hinduism.* New York, NY: Cambridge University Press.

Folkman, S., & Lazarus, R. S. (1988). Coping as a mediator of emotion.

Journal of Personality and Social Psychology, 54(3), 466–475.

Folkman, S., Lazarus, R. S., Pimley, S., Novacek, J. (1987). Age differences in stress and coping processes. *Psychology and Aging, 2*(2), 171–184.

Fountoulakis, K. N., Iacovides, A., Ioannidou, C., Bascialla, F., Nimatoudis, I., Kaprinis, G., et al. (2002). Reliability and cultural applicability of the Greek version of the international personality disorders examination. *BMC Psychiatry, 2*(1), 6.

Fouts, H. N. (2005). Families in Central Africa: A comparison of Bofi farmer and forager families. In J. L. Roopnarine (Ed.), *Families in global perspective* (pp. 347–363). Boston, MA: Pearson.

Fowers, B. J., & Richardson, F. C. (1996). Why is multiculturalism good? *American Psychologist, 51,* 609–621.

Fraher, A. (2004). Systems psychodynamics: The formative years of an interdisciplinary field at the Tavistock. *History of Psychology, 7*(1), 65–84.

Frank, H., Lueger, M., & Korunka, C. (2007). The significance of personality in business start-up intentions, start-up realization and business success. *Entrepreneurship & Regional Development: An International Journal, 19*(3), 227–251.

Frankl, V. (1959). *Man's search for meaning.* New York, NY: Pocket.

Freeman, D., Evans, N., Lister, R., Antley, A., Dunn, G., & Slater, M. (2014). Height, social comparison, and paranoia: An immersive virtual reality experimental study. *Psychiatry Research, 218*(3), 348–352.

Freud, A. (1966). *The ego and the mechanisms of defense.* Madison, CT: International Universities Press. (Original work published 1936)

Freud, S. (1957). On the history of the psychoanalytic movement. In J. Strachey (Ed. & Trans.), *The standard edition of the complete psychological works of Sigmund Freud* (Vol. 14, pp. 3–66). London, England: Hogarth. (Original work published 1914)

Freud, S. (1990). *Beyond the pleasure principle.* New York, NY: Norton. (Original work published 1920)

Freud, S. (1990). *Civilization and its discontents.* New York, NY: Norton. (Original work published 1930)

Freud, S. (1990). *The future of an illusion.* New York, NY: Norton. (Original work published 1927)

Freud, S. (2000). *Three essays on the theory of sexuality.* New York, NY: Basic Books. (Original work published 1905)

Freud, S. (2009). *The psychopathology of everyday life.* New York, NY: General Books LLC. (Original work published 1901)

Freud, S., & Bullitt, W. (1966). *Thomas Woodrow Wilson: A psychological study.* Boston, MA: Houghton Mifflin.

Friedman, M., & Ulmer, D. (1984). *Treating type A behavior and your heart.* New York, NY: Knopf.

Fromm, E. (1947). *Man for himself: An inquiry into the psychology of ethics.* New York, NY: Rinehart.

Fromm, E. (1994). *Escape from freedom.* New York, NY: Holt. (Original work published 1941)

Frosh, S. (2009). *Hate and the "Jewish science": Anti-Semitism, Nazism and psychoanalysis.* New York, NY: Palgrave.

Frost, E. P. (1912). Can biology and physiology dispense with consciousness? *Psychological Review, 19,* 246–252.

Fung, Y.-L. (1948). *A short history of Chinese philosophy.* New York, NY: Free Press.

Funkhouser, C. T. (2012). *New directions in digital poetry.* New York, NY: Continuum.

Furnham, A., & Baguma, P. (1999). A cross-cultural study from three countries of self-estimates of intelligence. *North American Journal of Psychology, 1,* 69–77.

Furnham, A., Rakow, T., Sarmany-Schuller, I., & Fruyt, F. (1999). European differences in self-perceived multiple intelligences. *European Psychologist, 4*(3), 131–138.

Gabbard, G. (1990). *Psychodynamic psychiatry in clinical practice.* Washington DC: American Psychiatric Press.

Gabriel, M. T., Critelli, J. W., & Ee, J. S. (1994). Narcissistic illusions in self-evaluations of intelligence and attractiveness. *Journal of Personality, 62*(1), 143–155.

Gachter, S., Renner, E., & Sefton, M. (2008). The long-run benefits of punishment. *Science, 322*(5907), 1510.

Gaertner, L., Sedikides, C., Cai, H., & Brown, J. (2010). It's not weird, it's wrong: When researchers overlook underlying genotypes, they will not detect universal processes. *Behavioral and Brain Sciences, 33*(2/3), 33–34.

Galambos, N. L., Fang, S., Krahn, H. J., Johnson, M. D., & Lachman, M. E. (2015). Up, not down: The age curve in happiness from early adulthood to midlife in two longitudinal studies. *Developmental Psychology, 51*(11), 1664–1671.

Gangestad, S. W., Haselton, M. G., & Buss, D. M. (2006). Evolutionary foundations of cultural variation: Evoked culture and mate preferences. *Psychological Inquiry, 17,* 75–95.

Gardiner, H., Mutter, J., & Kosmitzki, C. (1998). *Lives across cultures: Cross-cultural human development.* Boston, MA: Allyn & Bacon.

Gardner, H., & Davis, K. (2013). *The app generation: How today's youth navigate identity, intimacy, and imagination in a digital world.* New Haven, CT: Yale University Press.

Garfield, S. (2009). The clinical method in personality assessment. In J. Wepman & R. Heine (Eds.), *Concepts of personality* (pp. 474–501). New Brunswick, NJ: Transaction.

Gay, P. (1998). *Freud: A life for our time.* New York, NY: Norton.

Geary, D. (2009). *Male, female: The evolution of human sex differences.* Washington, DC: American Psychological Association.

Gensler, H. (2013). *Ethics and the golden rule.* New York, NY: Routledge.

Gerber, A., Huber, G., Doherty, D., Dowling, C., & Ha, S. (2010). Personality and political attitudes: Relationships across issue domains and political contexts. *American Political Science Review, 104*(1), 111–133.

Gerber, A., Kocsis, J., Milrod, B., Roose, S., Barber, J., Thase, M., Perkins, P., & Leon, A. (2011). A quality-based review of randomized controlled trials of psychodynamic psychotherapy. *American Journal of Psychiatry, 168*(1), 19–28.

Gergen, K. (2001). Psychological science in a postmodern context. *American Psychologist, 56,* 803–813.

Gethin, R. (1998). *Foundations of Buddhism.* New York, NY: Oxford University Press.

Geuens, N., Braspenning, M., Van Bogaert, P., & Franck, E. (2015). Individual vulnerability to burnout in nurses: The role of type D personality within different nursing specialty areas. *Burnout Research, 2*(2/3), 80–86.

Gibson, C. (2013, May 2). Connie Picciotto has kept vigil near the White House for 32 years. Why, and at what cost? *The Washington Post.* Retrieved from **http://www.washingtonpost.com/sf/feature/wp/2013/05/02/conniepicciottohaskeptvigilnearthewhitehousefor32yearswhyandatwhatcost/**

Gibson, M. (2002). *Born to crime: Cesare Lombroso and the origins of biological criminology.* Westport, CT: Praeger.

Gilligan, C. (1982). *In a different voice: Psychological theory and women's development.* Cambridge, MA: Harvard University Press.

Glass, S. (2003). *The fabulist.* New York, NY: Simon & Schuster.

Glick, P., & Fiske, S. T. (1997). Hostile and benevolent sexism. *Psychology of Women Quarterly, 21,* 119–135.

Glynn, L. G. (2009). Multimorbidity: Another key issue for cardiovascular medicine. *Lancet, 374*(9699), 1421–1422.

Goldberg, L. R. (1982). From ace to zombie: Some explorations in the language of personality. In C. D. Spielberger & J. N. Butcher (Eds.), *Advances in personality assessment, Vol. 1.* Hillsdale, NJ: Erlbaum.

Goldberg, L. R. (1993). The structure of phenotypic personality traits. *American Psychologist, 48,* 26–34.

Goldberg, M. (2014, August 4). What is a woman? *The New Yorker,* pp. 24–28.

Goldston, D., Molock, S., Whitbeck, L., Murakami, J., Zayas, L., & Hall, G. C. N. (2008). Cultural considerations in adolescent suicide prevention and psychosocial treatment. *American Psychologist, 63*(1), 14–31.

Gollob, H., & Levine, J. (1967). Distraction as a factor in the enjoyment of aggressive humor. *Journal of Personality and Social Psychology, 5*(3), 368–372.

Gordon, D. (2012). A flood of emotions: Treating the uncontrollable crying and laughing of pseudobulbar affect. *Neurology Now, 8*(1), 26–29.

Gottfredson, M. R. (2007). Self-control theory and criminal violence. In D. J. Flannery, A. T. Vazsonyi, & I. D. Waldman (Eds.), *The Cambridge handbook of violent behavior and aggression* (pp. 533–544). New York, NY: Cambridge University Press.

Graham, J., & Haidt, J. (2010). Beyond beliefs: Religions bind individual into moral communities. *Personality and Social Psychology Review, 14,* 140–150.

Gramzow, R., & Tangney, J. P. (1992). Proneness to shame and the narcissistic personality. *Personality and Social Psychology Bulletin, 18,* 369–376.

Gray, J. A. (1987). *The neuropsychology of anxiety.* New York, NY: Oxford University Press.

Greenberg, J., Pyszczynski, T., & Solomon, S. (1986). The causes and consequences of the need for self-esteem: A terror management theory. In R. F. Baumeister (Ed.), *Public self and private self* (pp. 189–212). New York, NY: Springer-Verlag.

Greening, T. (1971). *Existential humanistic psychology.* Belmont, CA: Brooks/Cole.

Greening, T. (1986). Passion bearers and peace psychology. *Journal of Humanistic Psychology, 26*(4), 98–105.

Griffiths, K., Mackinnon, A., Crisp, D., Christensen, H., Bennett, K., &

Farrer, L. (2012). The effectiveness of an online support group for members of the community with depression: A randomized controlled trial. *PLOS Online.* Retrieved from **http://dx.doi .org/10.1371/journal.pone.0053244**

Gunderson, J., & Lyoo, K. (1997). Family problems and relationships for adults with borderline personality disorder. *Harvard Review of Psychiatry, 4,* 272–278.

Hafiz, Y. (2014, May 13). Exorcism conference at Vatican addresses the need for more demon-fighting priests. *Huffington Post.* Retrieved from **http://www.huffingtonpost .com/2014/05/13/exorcism-conference-rome-priestsn 5316749.html**

Haidt, J. (2013). *The righteous mind: Why good people are divided by politics and religion.* New York, NY: Vintage.

Hall, C., & Lindzey, G. (1957). *Theories of personality.* New York, NY: Wiley.

Hall, G. S. (1904). *Adolescence: Its psychology and its relations to physiology, anthropology, sociology, sex, crime, religion, and education* (2 vols.). New York, NY: Appleton.

Halperin, D. (2012). *How to be gay.* Cambridge, MA: Belknap Press.

Hampson, S. E., Edmonds, G. W., Goldberg, L. R., Dubanoski, J. P., & Hillier, T. A. (2015). A life-span behavioral mechanism relating childhood conscientiousness to adult clinical health. *Health Psychology, 34*(9), 887–895.

Harari, Y. N. (2014, September 5). Were we happier in the stone age? *The Guardian.*

Hare, R. D. (1983). Diagnosis of antisocial personality disorder in two prison populations. *American Journal of Psychiatry, 140,* 887–890.

Hare, R. D. (1991). *The Hare psychopathy checklist—revised.* Toronto, ON: Multi-Health Systems.

Hare, R. D. (1998). The PCL-R assessment of psychopathy: Some issues and concerns. *Legal and Criminological Psychology, 3,* 101–122.

Harenski, C., Antonenko, O., Shane, M., & Kiehl, K. (2008). Gender differences in neural mechanisms underlying moral sensitivity. *Social Cognitive and Affective Neuroscience, 3*(4), 313–321.

Harkness, S. (1992). Human development in psychological anthropology. In T. Schwartz, G. M. White, & C. A. Lutz (Eds.), *New directions in psychological anthropology* (pp. 102–121). New York, NY: Cambridge University Press.

Harley, N. (2015, April 3). Progeria sufferer Hayley Okines dies, aged 17. *The Telegraph.* April 3. Retrieved from **http://www.telegraph.co.uk/news/ health/children/11513990/ Hayley-Okines-who-had-the-body-of-a-104-year-old-has-died-aged-17.html**

Harper, R. (2010). Paranoid personality disorder. *Corsini Encyclopedia of Psychology.* Retrieved from **http://onlinelibrary.wiley .com/doi/10.1002/9780470479216 .corpsy0637/full**

Harrington, A. (1996). *Reenchanted science: Holism in German culture from Wilhelm II to Hitler.* Princeton, NJ: Princeton University Press.

Hart, J. (2013). *Empire of ideas: The origins of public diplomacy and the transformation of US foreign policy.* New York, NY: Oxford University Press.

Hart, J., Nailling, E., Bizer, G. Y., & Collins, C. K. (2015). Attachment theory as a framework for explaining engagement with Facebook.

Personality and Individual Differences, 77, 33–40.

Hartmann, H. (1958). *Ego psychology and the problem of adaptation.* New York, NY: International Universities Press.

Haun, D. B. M., Call, J., Janzen, G., & Levinson, S. (2006). Evolutionary psychology of special representations in the Hominade. *Current Biology, 16*(17), 1736–1740.

Hawley, J. (Ed.). (1987). *Saints and virtues.* Berkeley: University of California Press.

Hayward, R. D., & Kemmelmeier, M. (2011). Weber revisited: A cross-national analysis of religiosity, religious culture, and economic attitudes. *Journal of Cross-Cultural Psychology, 42*, 1406–1420.

Heider, F. (1944). Social perception and phenomenal causality. *Psychological Review, 51*, 358–374.

Heider, F. (1958). *The psychology of interpersonal relations.* New York, NY: Wiley.

Heiman, G. (1996). *Basic statistics for the behavioral sciences.* Boston, MA: Houghton Mifflin.

Heine, S., Lehman, D., Markus, H., & Kitayama, S. (1999). Is there a universal need for positive self-regard? *Psychological Review, 106*(4), 766–794.

Heine, S., Lehman, D., Peng, K., & Greenholtz, J. (2002). What's wrong with cross-cultural comparisons of subjective Likert scales? The reference group effect. *Journal of Personality and Social Psychology, 82*(6), 903–918.

Heine, S. J. (2008). *Cultural psychology.* New York, NY: W. W. Norton.

Henrich, J., Boyd, R., Bowles, S., Camerer, C. F., Fehr, E., Gintis, H.,

. . . Tracer, D. (2005). "Economic man" in cross-cultural perspective: Behavioral experiments in 15 small-scale societies. *Behavioral and Brain Sciences, 28*(6), 795–815.

Henrich, J., Boyd, R., Bowles, S., Camerer, C., Gintis, H., McElreath, R., & Fehr, E. (2001). In search of Homo economicus: Experiments in 15 small-scale societies. *American Economic Review, 91*(2), 73–79.

Henrich, J., Heine, S., & Norenzayan, A. (2010a). The weirdest people in the world? *Behavioral and Brain Sciences, 33*(2/3), 123.

Henrich, J., Heine, S. J., & Norenzayan, A. (2010b). Most people are not WEIRD. *Nature, 466*, 29.

Henry, P. J. (2009). College sophomores in the laboratory redux: Influences of a narrow database on social psychology's view of the nature of prejudice. *Psychological Inquiry, 19*, 49–71.

Herdt, G. (1993). *Ritualized homosexuality in Melanesia.* Berkeley: University of California Press.

Hesse, M. (2014, September 20). When no gender fits: A quest to be seen as just a person. *The Washington Post*, pp. A1, 14–15.

Hilsenroth, M. J. (2007). A programmatic study of short-term psychodynamic psychotherapy: Assessment, process, outcome, and training. *Psychotherapy Research, 17*(1), 31–45.

Hirschfeld, M. (1991). *The transvestites: The erotic drive to cross-dress.* Buffalo, NY: Prometheus Books. (Original work published in German 1910)

Hirschman, N. (2010). Choosing betrayal. *Perspectives on Politics, 8*(1), 271–278.

Ho, D. (1998). Indigenous psychologies: Asian perspectives.

Journal of Cross-Cultural Psychology, 29(1), 88–103.

Hock, R. (2013). Personality. In C. Campanella, J. Mosher, S. Frail, & M. Schricker (Eds.), *Forty studies that changed psychology* (pp. 190–197). Upper Saddle River, NJ: Pearson Education.

Hodges, A. (1983). *Alan Turing: The enigma.* London, England: Burnett.

Hodgins, S., De Brit, S., Chhabra, P., & Côté, G. (2010) Anxiety disorders among offenders with antisocial personality disorders: A distinct subtype? *Canadian Journal of Psychiatry, 55*(12), 784–791.

Hofstede, G. (1980). *Culture's consequences: International differences in work-related values.* Beverly Hills, CA: Sage.

Hofstede, G. (2010). The GLOBE debate: Back to relevance. *Journal of International Business Studies, 41*(8), 1339–1346.

Hogan, R., & Bond, H. (2009). Culture and personality. In P. Corr & G. Matthews (Eds.), *The Cambridge handbook of personality psychology* (pp. 577–588). Cambridge, United Kingdom: Cambridge University Press.

Hogan, R., Hogan, J., & Roberts, B. W. (1996). Personality measurement and employment decisions: Questions and answers. *American Psychologist, 51*, 469–477.

Hollingworth, L. S. (1928). *The psychology of the adolescent.* New York, NY: Appleton.

Hooker, R. (1982). *The complete works of Richard Hooker.* Cambridge, MA: Harvard University Press.

Hopwood, C., Donnellan, B., Blonigen, D., Krueger, R., McGue, M., Iacono, W. G., & Burt, A. (2011). Genetic and environmental influences on personality trait stability and growth during the transition to adulthood: A three-wave longitudinal study. *Journal of Personality and Social Psychology, 100*(3), 545–556.

Horenczyk, G., & Munayer, S. J. (2007). Acculturation orientations toward two majority groups: The case of Palestinian Arab Christian adolescents in Israel. *Journal of Cross-Cultural Psychology, 38,* 76–86.

Horner, A. J. (1991). *Psychoanalytic object relations therapy.* Northvale, NJ: Jason Aronson.

Horney, K. (1950). *The collected works of Karen Horney* (2 vols.). New York, NY: Norton.

Hornstein, G. (1992). The return of the repressed: Psychology's problematic relations with psychoanalysis, 1909–1960. *American Psychologist, 47,* 254–263.

Horowits, R., & Kraus, V. (1984). Patterns of cultural transition. *Journal of Cross-Cultural Psychology, 15*(4), 399–416.

Ho-Ying Fu, J., & Chiu, C-Y. (2007). Local culture's responses to globalization: Exemplary persons and their attendant values. *Journal of Cross-Cultural Psychology, 38*(5), 636–653.

Hsu, F.-H. (2002). *Behind deep blue: Building the computer that defeated the world chess champion.* New York, NY: Princeton University Press.

Hufeland, C. M. (2009). *Art of prolonging life.* Bibliolife. (English translation of 1794)

Huizinga, J. (2013). *The waning of the middle ages.* New York, NY: Dover. (Original work published 1924)

Hume, D. (1987). *Essays: Moral, political, and literary.* Indianapolis,

IN: Liberty Classics. (Original work published 1777)

Huntington, S. (1993). Clash of civilizations. *Foreign Affairs, 72,* 22–49.

Huntington, S. (1996). *The clash of civilizations and the remaking of world order.* New York: Simon and Schuster.

Huntington, S (2004). *Who are we? The challenges to America's national identity.* New York: Simon and Schuster.

Huntington, S. (2006). *The clash of civilizations and the remaking of the world order.* New York, NY: Simon & Shuster.

Hyde, J. (2005). The gender similarities hypothesis. *American Psychologist, 60*(6), 581–592.

Hyde, J., & Plant, E. (1995). Magnitude of psychological gender differences: Another side to the story. *American Psychologist, 50,* 159–161.

Hyde, J. S., Lindberg, S. M., Linn, M. C., Ellis, A., & Williams, C. (2008). Gender similarities characterize math performance. *Science, 321,* 494–495.

Ireland, M., & Pennebaker, J. (2010). Language style matching in writing: Synchrony in essays, correspondence, and poetry. *Journal of Personality and Social Psychology, 99*(3), 549–571.

Isaeva, N. (1999). *From early Vedanta to Kashmir Shaivism.* Albany: State University of New York Press.

Iusitini, L., Gao, W., Sundborn, G., & Paterson, J. (2011). Parenting practices among fathers of a cohort of Pacific infants in New Zealand. *Journal of Cross-Cultural Psychology, 42*(1), 39–55.

Iwato, S., & Triandis, H. (1993). Validity of auto- and heterostereotypes

among Japanese and American students. *Journal of Cross-Cultural Psychology, 24*(4), 428–444.

Iyengar, S., Wells, R., & Schwartz, B. (2006). Doing better but feeling worse: Looking for the "best" job undermines satisfaction. *Psychological Science, 17,* 143–150.

Jabr, F. (2015). Life's big leaps: Critical moments in evolution. *Quanta Magazine.* Retrieved from **https://www.quantamagazine.org/20151110-evolution-of-big-brains/**

Jacobs, H. (2013, April 25). Woman accused of using ambulances for free rides. *wistv.com.* Retrieved on December 31, 2013, from **http://bit.ly/1ililNi**

Jaffe, E. (2013). Why wait? The science behind procrastination. *The Observer.* Retrieved from **http://www.psychologicalscience.org/index.php/publications/observer/2013/april-13/why-wait-the-science-behind-procrastination.html**

Jaffee, S., & Hyde, J. S. (2000). Gender differences in moral orientation: A meta-analysis. *Psychological Bulletin, 126,* 703–726.

Jamison, K. R. (1993). *Touched with fire: Manic-depressive illness and the artistic temperament.* New York, NY: Free Press.

Jang, K., Livesley, W. J., & Vernon, P. A. (1996). Heritability of the Big Five personality dimensions and their facets: A twin study. *Journal of Personality, 64*(3), 577–591.

Jansen, M., Arntz, A., Merckelbach, H., & Mersch, P. P. (1994). Personality disorders and features in social phobia and panic disorder. *Journal of Abnormal Psychology, 103*(2), 391–395.

Jefferson, T., Herbst, J. H., & McCrae, R. R. (1998). Associations between birth order and personality traits: Evidence from self-reports and observer ratings. *Journal of Research in Personality, 32*(4), 498–509.

Jeffreys, S. (2003). *Unpacking queer politics.* Cambridge, United Kingdom: Polity.

Jenkins, A. (1995). *Psychology and African Americans* (2nd ed.). Boston, MA: Allyn & Bacon.

Jensen-Campbell, L., & Knack, J. (2009). Personality and social relations. In P. Corr & G. Matthews (Eds.), *The Cambridge handbook of personality psychology* (pp. 506–523). Cambridge, United Kingdom: Cambridge University Press.

Jeronimus, B. F., Riese, H., Sanderman, R., & Ormel, J. (2014). Mutual reinforcement between neuroticism and life experiences: A five-wave, 16-year study to test reciprocal causation. *Journal of Personality and Social Psychology, 107*(4), 751–764.

Jessup, J. (1948, June 28). The newest utopia. *Life,* 38.

Joel, D., Berman, Z., Tavor, I., Wexler, N., Gaber, O., Stein, Y., Shefi, N., Pool, J., Urchs, S., Margulies, D., Liem, F., Hänggi, J., Jäncke, L., & Assaf, Y. (2015). Sex beyond the genitalia: The human brain mosaic. *Proceedings of the National Academy of Sciences USA, 112*(50), 15468–15473.

John, O., & Srivastava, S. (2001). The big-five trait taxonomy: History, measurement, and theoretical perspectives. In L. Pervin & O. John (Eds.), *Handbook of personality: Theory and research* (2nd ed.). New York, NY: Guilford Press.

John, O. P., & Robbins, R. W. (1994). Accuracy and bias in self-perception: Individual differences in self-enhancement and the role of

narcissism. *Journal of Personality and Social Psychology, 66*(1), 206–219.

Johnson, J. (2001). Personality psychology: Methods. In N. Smelser & P. Baltes (Eds.), *International encyclopedia of the social and behavioral sciences.* Oxford, England: Pergamon.

Johnson, K., White, A. E., Boyd, B. M., & Cohen, A. B. (2011). Matzah, meat, milk, and manna: Psychological influences on religio-cultural food practices. *Journal of Cross-Cultural Psychology, 42,* 1421–1436.

Johnson, W., & Krueger, R. F. (2005). Higher perceived life control decreases genetic variance in physical health: Evidence from a national twin study. *Journal of Personality and Social Psychology, 88,* 165–173.

Johnston, A. (2014). Jacques Lacan. In E. N. Zalta (Ed.), *The Stanford encyclopedia of philosophy* (Summer 2014 Ed.). Retrieved from **http://plato.stanford.edu/archives/sum2014/entries/lacan**

Johnston, T. D. (2002). An early manuscript in the history of American comparative psychology Lewis Henry Morgan's "Animal Psychology" (1857). *History of Psychology, 5,* 323–355.

Jones, H. E. (2008). Scientific evidence and practical experience with methadone-assisted withdrawal of heroin-dependent pregnant patients. *Heroin Addiction and Related Clinical Problems, 10,* 33–38.

Jones, M. B., & Blanchard, R. (1998). Birth order and male homosexuality: Extension of Slater's index. *Human Biology, 70,* 775–787.

Jost, J. (2006). The end of the end of ideology. *American Psychologist, 61*(7), 651–670.

Jung, C. G. (1924). *Psychological types or the psychology of individuation.* New York, NY: Random House.

Jung, C. G. (1961). *Memories, dreams, reflections* (Recorded and edited by A. Jaffe). New York, NY: Random House.

Jung, C. G. (1964). *Man and his symbols.* New York, NY: Dell.

Jung, C. G. (1967). *C. G. Jung collected works: Alchemical studies.* Princeton, NJ: Princeton University Press. (Original work published 1929)

Jung, C. G., & Hinkle, B. M. (1912). *Psychology of the unconscious: A study of the transformations and symbolisms of the libido, a contribution to the history of the evolution of thought.* London, England: Kegan Paul, Trench, Trubner.

Jung, K., Shavitt, S., Viswanathan, M., & Hilbe, J. (2014). Female hurricanes are deadlier than male hurricanes. *Proceedings of the National Academy of Sciences, 111*(24), 8782–8787.

Kabat-Zinn, Jon. (2012). *Mindfulness for beginners: Reclaiming the present moment—And Your Life.* Louisville, CO: Sounds True.

Kagan, J., & Herschkowitz, N. (2005). *Young mind in a growing brain.* New York, NY: Psychology Press.

Kagan, J., & Snidman, N. (1991). Temperamental factors in human development. *American Psychologist, 46,* 856–862.

Kahan, D. (2012). Ideology, motivated reasoning, and cognitive reflection: An experimental study. *Judgment and Decision Making, 8,* 407–424.

Kahneman, D., & Tversky, A. (1979). Prospect theory: An analysis of decisions under risk. *Econometrica, 47,* 313–327.

Kakar, S. (1989). The maternal-feminine in Indian psychoanalysis. *International Review of Psycho-Analysis, 16,* 355–362.

Kakar, S. (1995). Clinical work and cultural imagination. *Psychoanalytic Quarterly, 64*, 265–281.

Kallgren, C. A., & Wood, W. (1986). Access to attitude-relevant information in memory as determinant of attitude-behavior consistency. *Journal of Experimental Social Psychology, 22*, 328–338.

Kandel, E. (2012). *The age of insight.* New York, NY: Random House.

Kang, C. (2015, January 4). The "halo" effect. *The Washington Post Magazine*, pp. 12–17.

Kaniel, R., Massey, C., & Robinson, D. (2010, September). The importance of being an optimist: Evidence from labor markets. *NBER Working Paper* No. 16328.

Kant, I. (1956). *Groundwork for a metaphysics of morals.* New York, NY: Harper & Row. (Original work published 1785)

Kaplan, R. (2012). *The revenge of geography: What the map tells us about coming conflicts and the battle against fate.* New York, NY: Random House.

Kaplan, R. M., & Saccuzzo, D. P. (2013). *Psychological testing: Principles, applications, and issues* (8th ed.). Belmont, CA: Wadsworth.

Kaplan-Solms, K., & Solms, M. (2000). Clinical studies in neuro-psychoanalysis: Introduction to a depth neuropsychology. London, England: Karnac.

Karlsson, G. (2010). *Psychoanalysis in a new light.* New York, NY: Cambridge University Press.

Karon, B. P., & Widener, A. J. (2001). Repressed memories: Avoiding the obvious. *Psychoanalytic Psychology, 18*, 161–164.

Kasule, O. (2000). *Personality development in Islam.* Paper presented at the Leadership Training Programme, Islamic College of South Africa 1922 June. Retrieved from **http://omarkasule02.tripod.com/id611.html**

Keller, E. F. (1985). *Reflections on gender and science.* New Haven, CT: Yale University Press.

Kelley, H. H. (1967). Attribution theory in social psychology. In D. Levine (Ed.), *Nebraska Symposium of Motivation* (Vol. 15, pp. 192–240). Lincoln: University of Nebraska Press.

Kelley, H. H. (1979). *Personal relationships: Their structures and processes.* Hillsdale, NJ: Erlbaum.

Kelley, T. L. (1927). *Interpretation of educational measurements.* New York, NY: Macmillan.

Kelly, G. A. (1955). *The psychology of personal constructs: Vol. 1–2.* New York, NY: W. W. Norton.

Kelly, G. A. (1963). *A theory of personality: The psychology of personal constructs.* New York, NY: W. W. Norton.

Keltner, D., & Haidt, J. (2003). Approaching awe: A moral, spiritual, and aesthetic emotion. *Cognition and Emotion, 17*, 297–314.

Kendler, H. H. (1999). The role of value in the world of psychology. *American Psychologist, 54*, 828–835.

Kennedy, H. (1981). The "third sex" theory of Karl Heinrich Ulrichs. *Journal of Homosexuality, 6*(1–2), 103–111.

Kenny, D. (2015). Stairway to hell: Life and death in the pop music industry. *The Conversation.* Retrieved from **https://theconversation.com/stairway-to-hell-life-and-death-in-the-pop-music-industry-32735**

Kenrick D., & Funder, D. (1988). Profiting from controversy: Lessons from the person-situation debate. *American Psychologist, 43*, 23–34.

Kenrick, D. T., Li, N. P., & Butner, J. (2003). Dynamical evolutionary psychology: Individual decision rules and emergent social norms. *Psychological Review, 110*, 3–28.

Kern, M. L., & Friedman, H. S. (2008). Do conscientious individuals live longer? A quantitative review. *Health Psychology, 27*(5), 505–512.

Kernberg, O. (1992). *Aggression in personality disorders and perversions.* New Haven, CT: Yale University Press.

Kierkegaard, S. (1992). *Either/or: A fragment of life.* New York, NY: Penguin. (Original work published 1843)

Kim, E., Zeppenfeld, V., & Cohen, D. (2013). Sublimation, culture, and creativity. *Journal of Personality and Social Psychology, 105*(4), 639–666.

Kimmelman, M. (2014, June 19). The art Hitler hated. *The New York review of books.* Retrieved from **http://www.nybooks.com/articles/archives/2014/jun/19/arthitlerhated/**

Kinsey, A. (1998). *Sexual behavior in the human male.* Bloomington: Indiana University Press. (Original work published 1948)

Kinsey, A. (1998). *Sexual behavior in the human female.* Bloomington: Indiana University Press. (Original work published 1953)

Kinsley, D. (1986). Hindu goddesses: Visions of the feminine in the Hindu religious tradition. Berkeley: University of California Press.

Kitayama, S., Ishii, K., Imada, T., Takemura, K., & Ramaswamy, J. (2006). Voluntary settlement and the spirit of independence: Evidence from Japan's "northern frontier." *Journal of Personality and Social Psychology, 91*, 369–384.

Klages, L. (1929). *The science of character*. London, England: George Allen & Unwin.

Kleinman, A., & Kleinman, J. (1991). Suffering and its professional transformation: Toward an ethnography of interpersonal experience. *Culture, Medicine, and Psychiatry, 15,* 275–301.

Knight, S. (2014, February). A God more powerful than I. *Harper's*, 53–62.

Knoll, M. (2011). Behavioral and psychological aspects of the retirement decision. *Social Security Bulletin, 71*(4), 15–32. Retrieved from **http://www.ssa.gov/policy/docs/ssb/v71n4/v71n4p15.html**

Kobasa, S. C. (1979). Stressful life events, personality, and health—Inquiry into hardiness. *Journal of Personality and Social Psychology, 37*(1), 1–11.

Koenigsberg, R. (2007). *The nation: A study in ideology and fantasy*. New York, NY: Information Age.

Koenigsberg, R. (2014). *The delusion of rationality*. Retrieved from **http://blog.libraryofsocialscience.com/the-delusion-of-rationality/**

Köhler, W. (1959). Gestalt psychology today. *American Psychologist, 14*, 727–734.

Kohut, H. (1977). *The restoration of the self*. Madison, CT: International Universities Press.

Kohut, H. (2009). *The analysis of the self: A systematic approach to the psychoanalytic treatment of narcissistic personality disorders*. Chicago, IL: University of Chicago Press. (Original work published 1971)

Kohlberg, L. (1981). *The philosophy of moral development: Moral states and the idea of justice*. San Francisco, CA: Harper & Row.

Konnikova, M. (2014, April 30). I want you to know that I'm Tyrion Lannister. *The New Yorker*. Retrieved from **http://www.newyorker.com/science/maria-konnikova/i-want-you-to-know-that-im-tyrion-lannister**

Kosson, D. S., & Newman, J. P. (1986). Psychopathy and allocation of attentional capacity in a divided-attention situation. *Journal of Abnormal Psychology, 95*(3), 257–263.

Kozaryn, M. (1998). *Martha Gellhorn: War reporter, D-Day stowaway*. DoD News. Retrieved from **http://www.au.af.mil/au/awc/awcgate/dod/n03061998_9803063.htm**

Krafft-Ebbing, R. (1886). *Psychopathia sexualis*. Stuttgart, Germany: Verlag von Ferdinand Enke.

Krampen, G. (1999). Long-term evaluation of the effectiveness of additional autogenic training in the psychotherapy of depressive disorders. *European Psychologist, 4*(1), 11–18.

Krantz, D. L., & Wiggins, L. (1973). Personal and impersonal channels of recruitment in the growth of theory. *Human Development, 16*(3), 133–156.

Kreger, R. (2008). *The essential family guide to borderline personality disorder: New tools and techniques to stop walking on eggshells*. Center City, MN: Hazeldenc.

Kremer, W. (2014). The evolutionary puzzle of homosexuality. *BBC News Magazine*. Retrieved from **http://www.bbc.com/news/magazine-26089486**

Kreml, W. P. (1977). *The anti-authoritarian personality*. New York, NY: Pergamon Press.

Krueger, R., Caspi, A., Moffitt, T., & Silva, P. (1996). Personality traits are differentially linked to mental disorders: A multitrait–multidiagnosis study of an adolescent birth cohort. *Journal of Abnormal Psychology, 105*(3), 299–312.

Krueger, R. F., & Markon, K. E. (2006). Reinterpreting comorbidity: A model-based approach to understanding and classifying psychopathology. *Annual Review of Clinical Psychology, 2,* 111–133.

Kruijver, F. P., Zhou, J. N., Pool, C. W., Hofman, M. A., Gooren, L. J., & Swaab, D. F. (2000). Male-to-female transsexuals have female neuron numbers in a limbic nucleus. *Journal of Clinical Endocrinology and Metabolism, 85*, 2034–2041.

Kumpulainen, K., & Wray, D. (2002). *Classroom interaction and social learning: From theory to practice*. New York, NY: Routledge Falmer.

Kurth, F., Cherbuin, N., & Luders, E. (2015). Reduced age-related degeneration of the hippocampal subiculum in long-term mediators. *Psychiatry Research, 232*(3), 214–218.

Kurtz, S. N. (1992). *All the mothers are one: Hindu India and the cultural reshaping of psychoanalysis*. New York, NY: Columbia University Press.

Kurzweil, R. (2005). *The singularity is near*. New York, NY: Viking.

Kurzweil, R. (2013). *How to create a mind*. New York, NY: Penguin Books.

Kusch, M. (1999). *Psychological knowledge: A social history and philosophy*. New York, NY: Routledge.

Lacan, J. (1988). *The seminar of Jacques Lacan*. Cambridge, United Kingdom: Cambridge University Press.

Lacan, J. (2007). *Ecrits*. London, England: Routledge.

La Mettrie, J. O. (1994). *Man a machine, man a plant* (R. A. Watson & M. Rybalka, Trans.). Indianapolis, IN: Hackett. (Original work published 1748)

Lammers, J., & Galinsky, A. (2010). Power increases hypocrisy: Moralizing in reasoning, immunity and behavior. *Psychological Science, 21*, 737–744.

Laney, M. O. (2002). *The introvert advantage.* Markham, Ontario: Thomas Allen & Son.

Lang, F., Weiss, D., Gerstrof, D., & Wagner, G. (2013). Forecasting life satisfaction across adulthood: Benefits of seeing a dark future? *Psychology and Aging, 28*(1), 249–261.

Langbehn, D. R., & Cadoret, R. J. (2001). The adult antisocial syndrome with and without antecedent conduct disorder: Comparisons from an adoption study. *Comprehensive Psychiatry, 42*(4), 272–282.

Lansford, J., Malone, P., Dodge, K., Chang, L., Chaudhary, N. T. S., Oburu, P., & Deater-Deckard, K. (2010). Children's perceptions of maternal hostility as a mediator of the link between discipline and children's adjustment in four countries. *International Journal of Behavioral Development, 34*(5), 452–461.

Laqueur, T. (2004). *Solitary sex: A cultural history of masturbation.* Cambridge, MA: Zone Books.

Lavine, H., Bordiga, E., & Sullivan, J. (2000). On the relationship between attitude involvement and attitude accessibility: Toward a cognitive-motivational model of political information-processing. *Political Psychology, 21*(1), 81–107.

Lazarus, R., & Lazarus, B. (2006). *Coping with aging.* New York, NY: Oxford University Press.

Le Bon, G. (1896). *The crowd: A study of the popular mind.* London, England: Ernest Benn.

Lea, M., & Spears, R. (1991). Computer-mediated communication, de-individuation and group decision-making. *International Journal of Man-Machine Studies, 34*, 283–301.

Lee, M. S., & Ernst, E. (2011). Systematic reviews of tai chi: An overview. *British Journal of Sports Medicine, 46*(10), 713–718.

Leenen, I., Givaudan, M., Pick, S., Venguer, T., Vera, J., & Poortinga, Y. H. (2008). Effectiveness of a Mexican health education program in a poverty-stricken rural area of Guatemala. *Journal of Cross-Cultural Psychology, 39*(1), 198–214.

Lehman, C. (2003). Genes may play key role in impulsive aggression in BPD. *Psychiatric News, 38*(2), 20.

Lehrer, J. (2012, January 30). Groupthink: The brainstorming myth. *The New Yorker,* pp. 22–27.

Leibin, V. M. (1994). *Zigmund Freid, psychoanalys, I russkaya mysl* [Sigmund Freud, psychoanalysis, and the Russian thought]. Moscow, Russia: Respublika.

Leibovitz, L. (2014). *The broken halleluiah.* Dingwall, Scotland: Sandstone Press.

Leichsenring, F., Biskup, J., Kreische, R., & Staats, H. (2005). The Gottingen study of psychoanalytic therapy: First results. *International Journal of Psychoanalysis, 86*, 433–455.

Lemov, D. (2014). *Teach like a champion 2.0: 62 techniques that put students on the path to college.* Hoboken, NJ: Jossey-Bass.

Lenzenweger, M., Lane, M., Loranger, A., & Kessler, R. (2007). *DSM-IV* personality disorders in the national

comorbidity survey replication. *Biological Psychiatry, 62*(6), 553–564.

Lepore, J. (2009, November 30). The politics of death. *The New Yorker,* pp. 60–67.

Lerner, P. (2009). *Hysterical men: War, psychiatry, and the politics of trauma in Germany, 1890–1930.* Ithaca, NY: Cornell University Press.

Lertwannawit, A., & Gulid, N. (2010). Metrosexual identification: Gender identity and beauty-related behaviors. *International Business & Economics Research Journal, 9*(11), 85.

Leslie, S. J., Cimpian, A., Meyer, M., & Freeland, E. (2015). Expectations of brilliance underlie gender distributions across academic disciplines. *Science, 347*, 262–265.

Levant, R. F., & Kopecky, G. (1995). *Masculinity reconstructed: Changing the rules of manhood—At work, in relationships, and in family life.* New York, NY: Dutton.

LeVay, S. (1991). A difference in hypothalamic structure between homosexual and heterosexual men. *Science, 253*, 1034–1037.

LeVay, S. (1993). *The sexual brain.* Cambridge, MA: MIT Press.

LeVay, S. (2010). *Gay, straight, and the reason why: The science of sexual orientation.* New York, NY: Oxford University Press.

Levine, M., Taylor, P. J., & Best, R. (2011). Third parties, violence, and conflict resolution: The role of group size and collective action in the microregulation of violence. *Psychological Science, 22*(3), 406–412.

Levitt, S., & Dubner, S. (2005). *Freakonomics: A rogue economist explores the hidden side of everything.* New York, NY: Harper.

Levy, D. (1997). *Tools of critical thinking*. Needham Height, MA: Allyn & Bacon.

Levy, D. (2009). *Tools of critical thinking: Meta thoughts for psychology* (2nd ed.). Long Grove, IL: Waveland Press.

Lewin, K. (1942). *Field theory in social science*. Chicago, IL: University of Chicago Press.

Lewin, K. (1943). Defining the "field at a given time." *Psychological Review, 50*, 292–310. (Republished in *Resolving Social Conflicts & Field Theory in Social Science*. Washington, DC: American Psychological Association, 1997.)

Lewin, K. (1944). Constructs in psychology and psychological ecology. *University of Iowa Studies in Child Welfare, 20*, 1–29. (Republished in *Resolving Social Conflicts and Field Theory in Social Science*. Washington, DC: American Psychological Association, 1997.)

Lewinsohn, P. M., Rohde, P., Seeley, J. R., Klein, D. N., & Gotlib, I. H. (2003). Psychosocial functioning of young adults who have experienced and recovered from major depressive disorder during adolescence. *Journal of Abnormal Psychology, 112*, 353–363.

Lewis, M. (2001). *Multicultural health psychology: Special topics acknowledging diversity*. Boston, MA: Pearson.

Li, J. (2003). The core of Confucian learning. *American Psychologist, 58*(2), 146–147.

Linehan, M., L., Rizvi, S., Welch, S. S., & Page, B. (2000). Psychiatric aspects of suicidal behaviour: Personality disorders. In K. Hawton & K. van Heeringen (Eds.), *The international handbook of suicide and attempted suicide*. West Sussex, England: John Wiley & Sons.

Liu, J. H., Goldstein-Hawes, R., Hilton, D. J., Huang, L. L., Gastardo-Conaco, C., Dresler-Hawke, E., & Hidaka, Y. (2005). Social representations of events and people in world history across twelve cultures. *Journal of Cross-Cultural Psychology, 36*, 171–191.

Livesley, W., & Jang, K. (2008). The behavioral genetics of personality disorder. *Annual Review of Clinical Psychology, 4*, 4247–4274.

Lock, A. (1981). Ingenious psychology and human nature: A psychological perspective. In P. Heelas & A. Lock (Eds.), *Indigenous psychologies* (pp. 183–204). London, England: Academic Press.

Loehlin, J., & Nichols, R. (1976). *Heredity, environment, & personality: A study of 850 sets of twins*. Austin: University of Texas Press.

Lombroso, C., & Ferrero, G. (1959). *The female offender*. New York, NY: Appleton. (Original work published 1895)

Long, A. A. (1968). The stoic concept of evil. *The Philosophical Quarterly, 18*(7), 329–343.

Loranger, A. (1996). Dependent personality disorder: Age, sex, and axis I comorbidity. *Journal of Nervous and Mental Disease, 184*(1), 17–21.

Loranger, A. W., Sartorius, N., Andreoli, A., Berger, P., Buchheim, P., Channabasavanna, S. M., et al. (1994). The international personality disorder examination. *Archives of General Psychiatry, 51*(3), 215–224.

Lovelock, J. (2009). *The vanishing face of Gaia: A final warning—Enjoy it while you can*. London, England: Allen Lane.

Lucas, R. E., & Donnellan, M. B. (2009). Age differences in personality: Evidence from a nationally representative sample of Australians. *Developmental Psychology, 45*, 1353–1363.

Lucas, R. E., & Donnellan, M. B. (2011). Personality development across the lifespan: Longitudinal analyses with a national sample from Germany. *Journal of Personality and Social Psychology, 101*, 847–861.

Luders, E., Cherbuin, N., & Kurth, F. (2010). Forever young(er): Potential age-defying effects of long-term meditation on gray matter atrophy. *Frontiers in Psychology, 5*, 1551.

Luper, S. (2000). *Existing*. Houston, TX: Mayfield.

Lykken, D. (1995) *The antisocial personalities*. Mahwah, NJ: Lawrence Erlbaum.

Lynam, D., & Widiger, T. (2001). Using the five-factor model to represent the *DSM—IV* personality disorders: An expert consensus approach. *Journal of Abnormal Psychology, 110*(3), 401–412.

Lyubomirsky, S. (2007). *The how of happiness: A scientific approach to getting the life you want*. New York, NY: Penguin Press.

Ma, H. K., & Cheung, C. K. (1996). A cross-cultural study of moral stage structure in Hong Kong Chinese, English, and Americans. *Journal of Cross-Cultural Psychology, 27*(6), 700–713.

Maass, A., Karasawa, M., Politi, F., & Suga, S. (2006). Do verbs and adjectives play different roles in different cultures? A cross-linguistic analysis of person representation. *Journal of Personality and Social Psychology, 90*, 734–750.

Maccoby, E., & Jacklin, C. (1974). *The psychology of sex differences*. Stanford, CA: Stanford University Press.

Macur, J. (2015, June 28). The line between male and female athletes remains blurred. *The New York Times*. Retrieved from

http://www.nytimes.com/2015/07/29/
sports/win-for-dutee-chand-but-
line-between-male-and-female-
athletes-remains-blurred.html?hp
&action=click&pgtype=Homepage
&module=mini-moth&region=top-
stories-below&WT.nav=top-stories-
below&r=0

Maddi, S. R. (2006). Hardiness: The
courage to grow from stresses.
Journal of Positive Psychology, 1(3),
160–168.

Mahbubani, K. (1999). *Can Asians
think?* Singapore: Times Books
International.

Maier, B. N. (2004). The role of
James McCosh in God's exile from
psychology. *History of Psychology, 7*,
323–339.

Malouf, E., Stuewing, J., & Tangney, J.
(2012). Self-control and jail inmates'
substance misuse post-release:
Mediation by friends' substance use
and moderation by age. *Addictive
Behaviors, 37*(11), 1198–1204.

Maltby, J., Day, L., & Macaskill,
A. (2013). *Personality, individual
differences and intelligence*. Essex,
England: Pearson Education Limited.

Mandler, G. (2007). *A history of
modern experimental psychology: From
James and Wundt to cognitive science*.
Cambridge: MIT Press.

Manschreck, T. C. (1996). Delusional
disorder: The recognition and
management of paranoia. *Journal of
Clinical Psychiatry, 57*(3), 32–38.

Markus, H. R., & Kitayama, S. (1991).
Culture and the self: Implications for
cognition, emotion, and motivation.
Psychological Review, 98, 224–253.

Maslach, C., Jackson, S. E, & Leiter,
M. P. (1996). *MBI: The Maslach burnout
inventory—Manual*. Palo Alto, CA:
Consulting Psychologists Press.

Maslow, A. (1962). *Toward a psychology
of being*. Princeton, NJ: Van Nostrand.

Maslow, A. (1970). *Motivation and
personality* (2nd ed.). New York, NY:
Harper & Row.

Mathers, D., Miller, M., & Ando,
O. (Eds.). (2009). Self and no-self:
Continuing the dialogue between
Buddhism and psychotherapy. New
York, NY, Routledge.

Matsumoto, D. (1992). American-
Japanese cultural differences in the
recognition of universal expressions.
*Journal of Cross-Cultural Psychology,
23*(1), 72–85.

Matsumoto, D. (1994*). People:
Psychology from a cultural perspective*.
Pacific Grove, CA: Brooks/Cole.

Matsumoto, D. (2007). Individual
and cultural differences on
status differentiation: The status
differentiation scale. *Journal of Cross-
Cultural Psychology, 38*(4), 413–431.

Matthews, K. (2005). Psychological
perspectives on the development of
coronary heart disease. *American
Psychologist, 60*, 783–796.

Matthews K., & Gallo, L. (2011).
Psychological perspectives on
pathways linking socioeconomic
status and physical health. *Annual
Review of Psychology, 62*, 501–530.

May, R. (1950). *The meaning of anxiety*.
New York, NY: Ronald Press.

May, R. (1969). *Love and will*. New York,
NY: Norton.

May, R. (1994). *The courage to create*.
New York, NY: W. W. Norton.

May, R., Angel, E., & Ellenberger, H. F.
(Eds.). (1958). *Existence*. New York, NY:
Basic Books.

McCarthy, J. (2013). *The
psychology of spas and wellbeing*.

CreateSpace. Retrieved from **http://
psychologyofwellbeing.com/
psychology-of-spa**

McCrae, R., & Costa, P. (1990).
Personality in adulthood. New York, NY:
Guilford Press.

McCrae, R., & Costa, P. (1999). A
five-factor theory of personality.
In L. A. Pervin & O. P. John (Eds.),
Handbook of personality (pp. 139–153).
New York, NY: Guilford.

McCrae, R. R., & Costa, P. T. (1987).
Validation of the five-factor model of
personality across instruments and
observers. *Journal of Personality and
Social Psychology, 52*(1), 81–90.

McCrae, R. R., & Costa, P. T., Jr.
(1997). Personality trait structure
as a human universal. *American
Psychologist, 52*, 509–516.

McDougall, W. (1908). *An introduction
to social psychology*. London, England:
Methuen.

McDowell, N. (1988). A note on cargo
cults and cultural construction of
change. *Pacific Studies, 11*(2), 121–134.

McEwan, T., & Strand, S. (2013). The
role of psychopathology in stalking by
adult strangers and acquaintances.
*Australian and New Zealand Journal of
Psychiatry, 47*(6), 546–555.

McFadden, R. (2013, August 16).
Jacques Vergès, defender of
terrorists and war criminals, is
dead at 88. *The New York Times*.
Retrieved from **http://www.nytimes.
com/2013/08/17/world/europe/
jacques-verges-88-defender-of-
war-criminals-and-terrorists.
html?pagewanted=all&r=1&**

McGirr, A., Paris, J., Lesage, A.,
Renaud, J., & Turecki, G. (2007).
Risk factors for suicide completion
in borderline personality disorder:
A case-control study of cluster
B comorbidity and impulsive

aggression. *Journal of Clinical Psychiatry, 68*, 721–729.

McGlashan, T. (1986). Schizotypal personality disorder. *Archives of General Psychiatry, 43*, 329–334.

Mehrabian, A., & Bloom, J. (1997). Physical appearance, attractiveness, and the mediating role of emotions. *Current Psychology, 16*(1), 20–42.

Meinert, D. (2015). What do personality tests really reveal? *SHRM Online*. Retrieved from **https://www .shrm.org/publications/hrmagazine/ editorialcontent/2015/0615/ pages/0615-personality-tests.aspx**

Meissner, S. J. W. W. (2006). Prospects for psychoanalysis in the 21st century. *Psychoanalytic Psychology, 23*, 239–256.

Menand, L. (2009, December). Road warrior: Arthur Koestler and his century. *The New Yorker*. Retrieved from **http://www.newyorker.com/ arts/critics/atlarge/2009/12/21/ 091221cratatlargemenand? printable=true#ixzz27jCrWmP7**

Menand, L. (2010, January 11). Top of the pops: Did Andy Warhol change everything? *The New Yorker*, pp. 57–65.

Menand, L. (2014, January 27). The prisoner of stress. *The New Yorker*, pp. 64–68.

Metzl, J. (2005). *Prozac on the couch.* Durham, NC: Duke University Press.

Mill, J. S. (2010). *On the subjection of women.* Berlin, Germany: Nabu Press. (Original work published 1869)

Miller, A. G. (Ed.). (2004). *The social psychology of good and evil.* New York, NY: Guilford Press.

Miller, G. (2000). *The mating mind: How sexual choice shaped the evolution of human nature.* London, England: Heineman.

Miller, G., Galanter, E., & Pribram, K. (1960). *Plans and the structure of behavior.* New York, NY: Holt.

Miller, J. D., & Lynam, D. (2001). Structural models of personality and their relation to antisocial behavior: A meta-analytic review. *Criminology, 39*, 765–798.

Millon, T., Millon, C., Meagher, S., Grossman, S., & Ramnath, R. (2004). *Personality disorders in modern life.* New York, NY: Wiley.

Mills, E., & Singh, S. (2007). Health, human rights, and the conduct of clinical research within oppressed populations. *Globalization and Health, 3*(10). Retrieved from **http://www .globalizationandhealth.com/ content/pdf/ 1744-8603-3-10.pdf**

Mills, J. (2001). Reexamining the psychoanalytic corpse from scientific psychology to philosophy. *Psychoanalytic Psychology, 19*, 552–558.

Mirandola, G. (1996). *Oration on the dignity of man.* Washington, DC: Gateway Editions. (Original work published 1486)

Mischel, W. (1993). Behavioral conceptions. In W. Mischel (Ed.), *Introduction to personality* (pp. 295–316). New York, NY: Harcourt Brace.

Mischel, W. (2014). *The marshmallow test: Mastering self-control.* New York, NY: Little, Brown.

Mischel, W., Ebbesen, E., & Raskoff, Z. (1972). Cognitive and attentional mechanisms in delay of gratification. *Journal of Personality and Social Psychology, 21*(2), 204–218.

MMPI History. (2016). Retrieved from **https://www.upress.umn.edu/test-division/bibliography/mmpi-history**

Moffitt, T. E. (1990). The neuropsychology of juvenile delinquency: A critical review. In M.

Tonry & N. Morris (Eds.), *Crime and Justice* (Vol. 12, pp. 99–169). Chicago, IL: University of Chicago Press.

Mohandie, K., Meloy, J. R., McGowan, M. G., & Williams, J. (2006). The RECON typology of stalking: Reliability and validity based upon a large sample of North American stalkers. *Journal of Forensic Science, 51*(1), 147–155.

Mondak, J., Hibbing, M., Canache, D., Seligson, M., & Anderson, M. (2010). Personality and civic engagement: An integrative framework for the study of trait effects on political behavior. *American Political Science Review, 104*(1), 85–110.

Moorehead, C. (2003). *Gellhorn: A twentieth-century life.* New York, NY: Holt.

Morel, B. A. (1976). *Traite des degenerescence physique, et intellectuelles et morales de l'espece humaine* [Degenerative physical, intellectual and moral traits in human beings]. New York, NY: Arno. (Original work published 1857)

Moreno, J. (1977). *Who shall survive? Foundations of sociometry, group psychotherapy, and sociodrama.* New York, NY: Beacon House. (Original work published 1934)

Morris, C. E., Reiber, C., & Roman, E. (2015). Quantitative sex differences in response to the dissolution of a romantic relationship. *Evolutionary Behavioral Sciences.* Advance online publication. **http://dx.doi. org/10.1037/ebs0000054**

Morrison, A. P. (1989). *Shame: The underside of narcissism.* Hillsdale, NJ: Analytic Press.

Mosing, M., Madiason, G., Pedersen, N., Kuja-HAlkola, R., & Illen, F. (2014, July 30). Practice does not make perfect: No causal effect of music practice on music ability. *Psychological Science.* doi:10.1177/0956797614541990

Mullainathan, S., & Shafir, E. (2013). *Scarcity: Why having too little means so much.* New York, NY: Times Books.

Mullen, P. E., Pathé, M., & Purcell, R. (2000). *Stalkers and their victims.* Cambridge, United Kingdom: Cambridge University Press.

Münsterberg, H. (1915). *Psychology: General and applied.* New York, NY: Appleton.

Murray, H. (1943, October). *Analysis of the personality of Adolf Hitler.* Retrieved from **http://library.lawschool .cornell.edu/WhatWeHave/ SpecialCollections/Donovan/Hitler/**

Murray, H. A. (1938). *Explorations in personality.* New York, NY: Oxford University Press.

Murray, K. (1985). Life as fiction. *Journal for the Theory of Social Behaviour, 15*(2), 173–188.

Mursalieva, S. (2003, July 18). Sudba psychoanalyze v Rossii [Psychoanalysis' fate in Russia]. *Novaya Gazeta.* Retrieved from **http://www.novayagazeta.ru/ data/2002/51/21.html**

Myers, D. (2008). *A friendly letter to skeptics and atheists: Musings on why god is good and faith isn't evil.* New York, NY: Jossey-Bass/Wiley.

Myers, K. M., & Davis, M. (2002). Behavioral and neural analysis of extinction: A review. *Neuron, 36,* 567–584.

Nagasawa, M., Kawai, E., Mogi, K, & Kikusui, T. (2013). Dogs show left facial lateralization upon reunion with their owners. *Behavioural Processes, 98,* 112–116.

Naito, T., & Gielen, U. (1992). Tatemae and Honne: A study of moral

relativism in Japanese culture. In U. Gielen, L. Adler, & N. Milgram (Eds.), *Psychology in international perspective.* Amsterdam, the Netherlands: Swets & Zeitlinger.

Nakamura, T., Kiyono, K., Yoshiuchi, K., Nakahara, R., Struzik, Z. R., & Yamamoto, Y. (2007). Universal scaling law in human behavioral organization. *Physical Review Letters, 99*(13), 138103.

Nanda, S. (1998). *Neither man nor woman: The Hijras in India.* New York, NY: Wadsworth.

Nanda, S., & Warms, R. (2010). *Culture counts.* Boston, MA: Cengage.

Nardone, I. B., Ward, R., Fotopoulou, A., & Turnbull, O. H. (2007). Attention and emotion in anosognosia: Evidence of implicit awareness and repression? *Neurocase, 13*(5), 438–445.

National Council on Alcoholism and Drug Dependence. (2016). Self-support groups. Retrieved from **https://www.ncadd.org/people-in-recovery/hope-help-and-healing/ self-help-recovery-support-groups**

Nave, C. S., Sherman, R. A., Funder, D. C., Hampson, S. E., & Goldberg, L. R. (2010). On the contextual independence of personality: Teachers' assessments predict directly observed behavior after four decades. *Social Psychological and Personality Science, 1*(4), 327–334.

Neurath, O. (1931). Physicalism: The philosophy of the Vienna circle. In R. S. Cohen & M. Neurath (Eds.), *Philosophical papers 1913–1946* (pp. 48–51). Dordrecht: D. Reidel.

Nevis, E. C. (1983). Cultural assumptions and productivity: The United States and China. *Sloan Management Review, 24,* 17–29.

Nevo, O., & Nevo, B. (1983). What do you do when asked to answer

humorously? *Journal of Personality and Social Psychology, 44*(1), 188–194.

Nicholson, I. A. M. (1998). Gordon Allport, character, and "culture of personality," 1897–1937. *History of Psychology, 1,* 52–68.

Nicholson, I. A. M. (2000). "A coherent datum of perception": Gordon Allport, Floyd Allport, and the politics of "personality." *Journal of the History of Behavioral Sciences, 36,* 463–470.

Nielsen, A., Der, B. S., Shin, J., Vaidyanathan, P., Paralanov, V., Strychalski, E. A., . . . Voigt, C. A. (2015). Programming circuitry for synthetic biology. *Science, 352,* 7341.

Nietzsche, F. (1968). *The will to power.* New York, NY: Vintage Books. (Original work published 1901)

Nolen-Hoeksema, S. (1991). Responses to depression and their effects on the duration of the depressive episode. *Journal of Abnormal Psychology, 100,* 569–582.

Noon, D. H. (2004). Situating gender and professional identity in American child study, 1880–1910. *History of Psychology, 7,* 107–129.

Norenzayan, A., & Gervais, W. M. (2013). The origins of religious disbelief. *Trends in Cognitive Sciences, 17,* 20–25.

Nugent, W. (2009). *Progressivism: A very short introduction.* New York, NY: Oxford University Press.

Ochse, R., & Plug, C. (1986). Cross-cultural investigation of the validity of Erikson's theory of personality development. *Journal of Personality and Social Psychology, 50*(6), 1240–1252.

Odajnyk, W. (2012). *Archetype and character: Power, eros, spirit, and matter personality types.* New York, NY: Palgrave Macmillan.

Offermann, L., & Hellmann, P. (1997). Culture's consequences for leadership behavior: National values in action. *Journal of Cross-Cultural Psychology, 28*(3), 342–351.

Oishi, S. (2010). The psychology of residential mobility: Implications for the self, social relationships, and wellbeing. *Perspectives on Psychological Science, 5*, 521.

Okines, H. (2012) *Old before my time.* Abercynon, UK: Accent Press.

Onnela, L. P., Waber, B., Pentland, A., Schnorf, S., & Lazer, D. (2014). Using sociometers to quantify social interaction patterns. *Scientific Reports, 4*, 5604.

Oppenheimer, S. (2003). *The real Eve: Modern man's journey out of Africa.* New York, NY: Carroll & Graf.

Orbuch, T. (2015). *Five simple steps to take your marriage from good to great.* Austin, TX: River Grove Books.

Organisation for Economic Co-Operation and Development. (2011). *Against the odds: Disadvantaged students who succeed in school.* OECD. Retrieved from **http://bit.ly/1MTXJxF**

Panksepp, J. (1998). *Affective neuroscience: The foundations of human and animal emotions.* New York, NY: Oxford University Press.

Paranjpe, A. (1998). *Self and identity in modern psychology and Indian thought.* New York, NY: Plenum Press.

Paris, B. (1994). *Karen Horney: A psychoanalyst's search for self-understanding.* New Haven, CT: Yale University Press.

Park, C. L. (2005). Religion and meaning. In R. F. Paloutzian & C. L. Park (Eds.), *Handbook of the psychology of religion and spirituality* (pp. 295–314). New York, NY: Guilford Press

Park, N., & Peterson, C. (2010). Does it matter where we live? The urban psychology of character strengths. *American Psychologist, 65*(6), 535–547.

Parsons, T., & Bales, R. (1956). *Family, socialization and interaction process.* Milton Park, England: Routledge.

Parvizi, J., & Damasio, A. (2001). Consciousness and the brainstem. *Cognition, 79*(12), 135–160.

Patrick, C. J. (1994). Emotion and psychopathy: Startling new insights. *Psychophysiology, 31*, 319–330.

Paul, M. (2014, Winter). First blood test to diagnose depression in adults. *Northwestern Medicine Magazine, 2*(1). Retrieved from **http://magazine .nm.org/winter-2014/research-briefs/blood-test-adult-depression/**

Peltzman, S. (2011). Offsetting behavior, medical breakthroughs, and breakdowns. *Journal of Human Capital, 5*(3), 302–341.

Penny, E., Newton, E., & Larkin, M. (2009). Whispering on the water: British Pakistani families' experiences of support from an early intervention service for first-episode psychosis. *Journal of Cross-Cultural Psychology, 40*(6), 969–987.

Perelli-Harris, B. (2014). How similar are cohabiting and married parents? Second conception risks by union type in the United States and across Europe. *European Journal of Population, 30*(4), 437–464.

Perez-Arce, F. (2011, March). The effects of education on time preferences. *Rand Corporation Working Papers.* WR-844. Retrieved from **http://www.rand.org/pubs/ workingpapers/WR844.html**

Perls, F. (1968). *Gestalt therapy verbatim.* Moab, UT: Real People Press.

Perls, F., Hefferline, R., & Goodman, P. (1951). *Gestalt therapy: Excitement and growth in the human personality.* New York, NY: Julian.

Perry, K. (2014, June 4). Hidden in her bedroom, a young cancer victim's secret message of hope. *Telegraph.* Retrieved from **http://bit.ly/TgA986**

Persinger, M. (1987). *Neuropsychological bases of God beliefs.* Westport, CT: Praeger.

Petersen, J. L., & Hyde, J. S. (2010). A meta-analytic review of research on gender differences in sexuality, 1993–2007. *Psychological Bulletin, 136*(1), 21–38.

Peterson, B., Smirles, K., & Wentworth, P. (1997). Generativity and authoritarianism: Implications for personality, political involvement, and parenting. *Journal of Personality and Social Psychology, 72*(5), 1202–1216.

Peterson, C. (2000). The future of optimism. *American Psychologist, 55*(1), 44–55.

Petrovsky, A. (1978). *Psichologicheskaya teorija kollektiva* [The psychological theory of the collective]. Moscow, Russia: Academy of Sciences.

Pew. (2014). *Global views of morality.* Retrieved from **http://www. pewglobal.org/2014/04/15/global-morality/**

Pew. (2016). *Five facts about online dating.* Retrieved from **http:// www.pewresearch.org/fact-tank/2016/02/29/5-facts-about-online-dating/**

Phillips, H. (2015, July 28). Four women bond over the beauty in their baldness. *The New York Times.* Retrieved from **http://nyti .ms/1N27bC6**

Pickard, H. (2011, May 4). What Aristotle can teach us about personality disorder. *National Personality Disorder Website*. Available from author by request at **http://www.philosophy.ox.ac.uk/members/researchstaff/hannapickard**

Piekkola, B. (2011). Traits across cultures: A neo-Allportian perspective. *Journal of Theoretical and Philosophical Psychology, 31*, 2–24.

Pinsky, D., & Young, S. M. (2006). Narcissism and celebrity. *Journal of Research in Personality, 40*(5), 463–471.

Pinsky, D., & Young, S. M. (2009). *The mirror effect: How celebrity narcissism is seducing America*. New York, NY: HarperCollins.

Pipher, M. (1994). *Reviving Ophelia: Saving the selves of adolescent girls*. New York, NY: Ballantine Books.

Plieger, T., Melchers, M., Montag, C., Meermann, R., & Reuter, M. (2015). Life stress as potential risk factor for depression and burnout. *Burnout Research, 2*(1), 19–24.

Plomin, R., Caspi, A., Corley, R., Fulker, D. W., & DeFries, J. (1998). Adoption results for self-reported personality: Evidence for nonaddictive genetic effects? *Journal of Personality and Social Psychology, 75*, 211–218.

Pluck, G. (2013). Cognitive abilities of "street children": A systematic review. *Chuo Journal of Policy Sciences and Cultural Studies, 21*, 121–133.

Pluck, G. (2015). The street children of Latin America. *The Psychologist*. Retrieved from **https://thepsychologist.bps.org.uk/volume-28/january-2015/street-children-latin-america**

Popper, K. (1992). *The logic of scientific discovery*. New York, NY: Routledge. (Original work published 1950)

Post, J., & George, A. (2004). *Leaders and their followers in a dangerous world: The psychology of political behavior*. Ithaca, NY: Cornell University Press.

Powell, A. D. (2015). Grief, bereavement, and adjustment disorders. In T. A. Stern, M. Fava, T. E. Wilens et al. (Eds.), *Massachusetts general hospital comprehensive clinical psychiatry* (2nd ed., pp. 428–432). Philadelphia, PA: Elsevier.

Powell, L. H., Shahabi, L., & Thoresen, C. E. (2003). Religion and spirituality: Linkages to physical health. *American Psychologist, 58*, 36–52.

Power, R., Verweij, K., Zuhair, M., Montgomery, G., Henders, A., Heath, A., . . . Martin, N. (2014). Genetic predisposition to schizophrenia associated with increased use of cannabis. *Molecular Psychiatry, 19*, 1201–1204.

Pratkanis, A. (1988). The attitude heuristic and selective fact identification. *British Journal of Social Psychology, 27*, 257–263.

Pychyl, T. A., Lee, J. M., Thibodeau, R., & Blunt, A. (2000). Five days of emotion: An experience sampling study of undergraduate student procrastination. *Journal of Social Behavior and Personality, 15*, 239–254.

Quas, J. A., Malloy, L., Goodman, G. S., Melinder, A., Schaaf, J., & D'Mello, M. (2007). Developmental differences in the effects of repeated interviews and interviewer bias on young children's false reports. *Developmental Psychology, 43*, 823–837.

Quen, J. (1983). Psychiatry and the law: Historical relevance to today. In L. Freedman (Ed.), *By reason of insanity: Essays on the psychiatry and the law* (pp. 153–166). Wilmington, DE: Scholarly Resources.

Radhakrishnan, S. (2007). *Eastern religions and Western thought*. New York, NY: Oxford University Press.

Raghavan, C., Harkness, S., & Super, C. (2010). Parental ethnotheories in the context of immigration: Asian Indian immigrants and Euro-American mothers and daughters in an American town. *Journal of Cross-Cultural Psychology, 41*(4), 617–632.

Rai, T., & Fiske, A. (2010). ODD (observation and description deprived) psychological research. *Behavioral and Brain Sciences, 33*(2/3), 46–47.

Raine, A. (2014). *The anatomy of violence: The biological roots of crime*. New York, NY: Vintage.

Ramanujan, A. K. (1989). Is there an Indian way of thinking? *Contributions to Indian Sociology, 23*(1), 41–58.

Rang, H. P. (2003). *Pharmacology*. London, England: Churchill Livingstone.

Rao, K. R., Paranjpe, A. C., & Dalal, A. K. (Eds.). (2008). *Handbook of Indian psychology*. New Delhi, India: Cambridge University Press.

Raskin, R. N., Novacek, J., & Hogan, R. (1991). Narcissism, self-esteem, and defensive self-enhancement. *Journal of Personality, 59*(1), 19–38.

Raskin, R. N., & Shaw, R. (1988). Narcissism and the use of personal pronouns. *Journal of Personality, 56*, 393–404.

Ray, O. (2004). How the mind hurts and heals the body. *American Psychologist, 59*, 29–40.

Rees, P. (2002, October 20). Japan: The missing million. *BBC News, World Edition*. Retrieved from **http://news.bbc.co.uk/2/hi/programmes/correspondent/2334893.stm**

Reich, J., Noyes, R., Coryell, W., & O'Gorman, T. W. (1986). The effect of state anxiety on personality measurement. *American Journal of Psychiatry, 143*(6), 760—763.

Reid, J. (2011). Crime and personality: Personality theory and criminality examined. *Student Pulse, 3*(1), 1–26. Retrieved from **http://www.studentpulse. com/articles/377/crime-and-personality-personality-theory-and-criminality-examined**

Reidy, D., Berke, D., Gentile, B. C., & Zeichner, A. (2015, August). Discrepancy stress, substance use, assault, and injury in a survey of U.S. men. *Injury Prevention.* Retrieved from **http://bit.ly/1Ua4ltG**

Reisner, S., Vetters, R., Leclerc, M., Zaslow, S., Wolfru, S., Shumer, D., & Mimiaga, M. (2015, January). Mental health of transgender youth in care at an adolescent urban community health center: A matched retrospective cohort study. *Journal of the Adolescent Health, 56*(3), 274–279.

Remen, R. N. (1996). *Kitchen table wisdom: Stories that heal.* New York, NY: Riverhead Books.

Renshon, S. (1989). Psychological perspectives on theories of adult development and the political socialization of leaders. In R. Sigel (Ed.), *Political learning in adulthood: A sourcebook of theory and research* (pp. 203–264). Chicago, IL: University of Chicago Press.

Rhodewalt, F., & Morf, C. C. (1995). Self and interpersonal correlates of the narcissistic personality inventory. *Journal of Research in Personality, 29,* 1–23.

Rich, N. (2013, November). The man who saves you from yourself: Going undercover with a cult infiltrator. *Harper's,* pp. 35–44.

Riger, S. (2002). Epistemological debates, feminist voices: Science, social values, and the study of women. In W. Pickren & D. Dewsbury (Eds.), *Evolving perspectives on the history of psychology* (pp. 21–44). Washington, DC: American Psychological Association.

Rioch, D. (1985). Recollections of Harry Stack Sullivan and of the development of his interpersonal psychiatry. *Psychiatry, 48*(2), 141–158.

Ritvo, L. R. (1990). *Darwin's influence on Freud: A tale of two sciences.* New Haven, CT: Yale University Press.

Robbie, N. (2014). Thirteen Christian personality types. Retrieved from **http://transforminggrace .wordpress.com/2008/06/04/ 13christianpersonalitytypes/**

Roberti, J. W. (2004). A review of behavioral and biological correlates of sensation seeking. *Journal of Research in Personality, 38*(3), 256.

Roberts, B. W., & Friend-DelVecchio, W. (2000). Consistency of personality traits from childhood to old age: A quantitative review of longitudinal studies. *Psychological Bulletin, 126,* 3–25.

Roberts, B. W., Walton, K., & Viechtbauer, W. (2006). Patterns of mean-level change in personality traits across the life course: A meta-analysis of longitudinal studies. *Psychological Bulletin, 132,* 1–25.

Roer-Strier, D., & Kurman, J. (2009). Combining qualitative and quantitative methods to study perceptions of immigrant youth. *Journal of Cross-Cultural Psychology, 40*(6), 988–995.

Roese, N. J., & Olson, J. M. (1994). Self-esteem and counterfactual thinking. *Journal of Personality and Social Psychology, 65,* 199–206.

Rogers, C. (1947). Some observations on the organization of personality. Address of the retiring president of the American Psychological Association. The 1947 Annual Meeting. *American Psychologist, 2,* 358–368.

Rogers, C. (1951). *Client-centered therapy: Its current practice, implications and theory.* London, England: Constable.

Rogers, C. (1959). The essence of psychotherapy: A client-centered view. *Annals of Psychotherapy, 1,* 51–57.

Rogers, C. (1961). *On becoming a person: A therapist's view of psychotherapy.* New York, NY: Houghton Mifflin.

Rokeach, M. (1964). *The three Christs of Ypsilanti.* New York, NY: Vintage.

Roland, A. (2006). Across civilizations: Psychoanalytic therapy with Asians and Asian Americans. *Psychotherapy: Theory, Research, Practice, Training, 43,* 454–463.

Romanes, G. J. (1882). *Animal intelligence.* Whitefish, MT: Kessinger.

Roscoe, W., & Murray, S. (2001). *Boywives and female husbands: Studies in African homosexualities.* New York, NY: Palgrave Macmillan.

Rosenthal, R., & Jacobson, L. (1968). *Pygmalion in the classroom: Teacher expectation and pupils' intellectual development.* New York: Holt, Rinehart, & Winston.

Rosin, H. (2013). *The end of men.* New York, NY: Riverhead Books.

Rosin, H. (2014, November 10). Hello, my name is Stephen Glass, and I'm sorry. *New Republic.* Retrieved from **http://bit.ly/1oE5hMZ**

Roskies, A. (2010). How does neuroscience affect our understanding of volition? *Annual Review of Neuroscience, 33,* 109–130.

Ross, A. (2012, November 12). Love on the march: Reflections on the gay community's political progress—and its future. *The New Yorker*, pp. 45–53.

Rothblatt, M. (2009, May 4). What are mindclones? *Mindflies, Mindware, and Mindclones* [Web log post]. Retrieved from **http://ieet.org/index.php/IEET/more/rothblatt20090502**

Rothblatt, M. (2011a). *From transgender to transhuman: A manifesto on the freedom of form.* Publisher: Rothblatt.

Rothblatt, M. (2011b, January 27). How can a mindclone be an exact copy of a person's mind? *Mindflies, mindware, and mindclones* [Web log post]. Retrieved from **http://ieet.org/index.php/IEET/more/rothblatt20110127**

Rotter, J. (1958). *Social learning and clinical psychology.* Englewood Cliffs, NJ: Prentice Hall.

Rotter, J. (1966). Generalized expectations for internal versus external control of reinforcement. *Psychological Monographs, 80*, 1–28.

Rotter, J. (1990). Internal versus external control of reinforcement: A case history of a variable. *American Psychologist, 45*(4), 489–493.

Rozin, P. (2010). The weirdest people in the world are a harbinger of the future of the world. *Behavioral and Brain Sciences, 33*(2/3), 48–49.

Rusch, H., Leunissen, J., & Van Vugt, M. (2015). Historical and experimental evidence of sexual selection for war heroism. *Evolution and Human Behavior.* Retrieved from **http://www.ehbonline.org/article/S1090-5138%2815%2900023-9/fulltext**

Sabatier, C., Mayer, B., Friedlmeier, M., Lubiewska, K., & Trommsdorff, G. (2011). Religiosity, family orientation, and life satisfaction of adolescents in four countries. *Journal of Cross-Cultural Psychology, 42*, 1375–1393.

Sackett, P. R, & Walmsley, P. T. (2014). Which personality attributes are most important in the workplace? *Perspectives on Psychological Science, 9*(5), 538–551.

Sadigh, M. (2012). *Autogenic training: A mind-body approach to the treatment of chronic pain syndrome and stress-related disorders.* Jefferson, NC: McFarland.

Saitō, T. (2012). *Social withdrawal: Adolescence without end.* Minneapolis: University of Minnesota Press.

Salzberg, S. (2002). *Loving kindness: The revolutionary art of happiness.* Boston, MA: Shambhala.

Sandler, J. (1985). *The analysis of defense: The ego and the mechanisms of defense revisited.* New York, NY: International Universities Press.

Saroglou, V. (2011). Believing, bonding, behaving, and belonging: The big four religious dimensions and cultural variation. *Journal of Cross-Cultural Psychology, 42*, 1320–1340.

Saroglou, V. (2014). *Religion, personality, and social behavior.* New York, NY: Psychology Press.

Sartre, J. P. (1969). *Being and nothingness.* New York, NY: Washington Square Press. (Original work published 1943)

Sasaki, J. Y., Kim, S. H., & Xu, J. (2011). Religion and well-being: The moderating role of culture and the oxytocin receptor (OXTR) gene. *Journal of Cross-Cultural Psychology, 42*, 1394–1405.

Savin-Williams, R. C., Joyner, K., & Rieger, G. (2012). Prevalence and stability of self-reported sexual orientation identity during young adulthood. *Archives of Sexual Behaviour, 41*(1), 103–110.

Sax, L. (2007). *Boys adrift: The five factors driving the growing epidemic of unmotivated boys and underachieving young men.* New York, NY: Basic Books.

Scarr, S., Webber, P. L., Weinberg, R. A., & Wittig, M. A. (1981). Personality resemblance among adolescents and their parents in biologically related and adoptive families. *Journal of Personality and Social Psychology, 40*(5), 885–898.

Schalling, D. (1978). Psychopathology-related personality variables and the psychophysiology of socialization. In R. Hare & D. Schalling (Eds.), *Psychopathic behavior: Approaches to research.* Chichester, Great Britain: Wiley.

Scheier, M. F., & Carver, C. S. (1992). Effects of optimism on psychological and physical well-being: Theoretical overview and empirical update. *Cognitive Therapy and Research, 16*, 201–228.

Schlegel, A., & Barry, H. (1991). *Adolescence: An anthropological inquiry.* New York, NY: Free Press.

Schmitt, D., Allik, J., McCrae, R., & BenetMartínez, V. (2007). The geographic distribution of big-five personality traits: Patterns and profiles of human self-description across 56 nations. *Journal of Cross-Cultural Psychology, 38*(2), 173–212.

Schmitt, D., Realo, A., Voracek, M., & Alik, J. (2008). Why can't a man be more like a woman? *Journal of Personality and Social Psychology, 94*, 168–182.

Schneider, K., Pierson, J. F., & Bugental, J. (Eds.). (2014). *The handbook of humanistic psychology: Theory, research, and practice* (2nd ed.). Thousand Oaks, CA: Sage.

Schoepflin, R. (2002). *Christian science on trial: Religious healing in America.*

Baltimore, MD: Johns Hopkins University Press.

Schwartz-Watts, D. M. (2006). Commentary: Stalking risk profile. *Journal of the American Academy of Psychiatry the Law, 34*(4), 455–457.

Scott, S., Doolan, M., Beckett, C., Harry, S., & Cartwright, S. (2010). How is parenting style related to child antisocial behaviour? Preliminary findings from the Helping Children Achieve Study. UK Department of Education. Retrieved from **http://learning.gov.wales/docs/learningwales/publications/121127parentingstylechildbehaviouren.pdf**

Scott, W. D. (1908). And interpretation of the psychoanalytic method in psychotherapy with a report on a case so treated. *Journal of Abnormal Psychology, 3,* 371–379.

Searle, J. (1992). *The rediscovery of the mind.* Cambridge, MA: MIT Press.

Searle, J. (1998). *The mystery of consciousness.* London, England: Granta.

Sears, D., & Funk, C. (1999). Evidence of long-term persistence of adults' political predispositions. *Journal of Politics, 61,* 128.

Segal, L. (2013). *Out of time: The pleasures and the perils of ageing.* New York, NY: Verso.

Segal, N. (2012). *Born together reared apart: The landmark Minnesota twin study.* Cambridge, MA: Harvard University Press.

Segall, M. H., Dasen, P. R., Berry, J. W., & Poortinga, Y. H. (1990). *Human behavior in global perspective: An introduction to cross-cultural psychology.* New York, NY: Pergamon.

Seligman, M. (2006). *Learned optimism: How to change your mind and your life.* New York, NY: Vintage.

Seligman, M. E. P., Rashid, T., & Parks, A. C. (2006). Positive psychotherapy. *American Psychologist, 61,* 774–788.

Sell, R. L. (1997). Defining and measuring sexual orientation: A review. *Archives of Sexual Behavior, 26*(6), 643–658.

Settersten, R., & Ray, B. (2010). What's going on with young people today? The long and twisting path to adulthood. *The Future of Children, 20*(1). Retrieved from bit.ly/1V7PG77

Shalvi, S., & De Dreu, C. (2014). Oxytocin promotes group-serving dishonesty. *Proceeedings of the National Academy of Science of the USA, 111*(15), 5503–5507.

Sharpe, M. (2008). In the name of the Father: God in Lacan, Judaic or Christian? *Psychoanalytische perspectieven, 26*(3/4), 267–285.

Shedrovitsky, P. (2009). Lev ygotsky I sovremennaja pedagogicheskaya antropologiya [Lev Vygotsky and modern pedagogical anthropology]. *Russian Archipelago.* Retrieved from **http://www.archipelag.ru/authors/shedrovickypetr/?library=1308**

Shermer, M. (2015). *The moral arc: How science and reason lead humanity toward truth, justice, and freedom.* New York, NY: Holt.

Shiner, R., & Caspi, A. (2003). Personality differences in childhood and adolescence: Measurement, development, and consequences. *Journal of Child Psychology and Psychiatry, 44*(1), 2–32.

Shiraev, E. (2013). *A history of psychology: A global perspective.* Thousand Oaks, CA: Sage.

Shiraev, E. (2015). *A history of psychology* (2nd ed.). Thousand Oaks, CA: Sage.

Shiraev, E., & Boyd, G. (2008). *The accent of success.* Ann Arbor, MI: University of Michigan Press.

Shiraev, E., & Fillipov, A. (1990). Cross-cultural social perception. *St. Petersburg University Quarterly, 13,* 53–60.

Shiraev, E., & Levy, D. (2013). *Cross-cultural psychology* (5th ed.). Needham Heights, MA: Pearson.

Shiraev, E., & Zi, Y. (2014). In M. Icks & E. Shiraev (Eds.), *Character assassination throughout ages.* New York, NY: Palgrave.

Shiraev, E. B., & Levy, D. A. (2013). *Cross-cultural psychology: Critical thinking and contemporary applications* (5th ed.). New York, NY: Pearson.

Shorter, E. (1997). *A history of psychiatry.* New York, NY: Wiley.

Shweder, R. (2010). Donald Campbell's doubt: Cultural difference or failure of communication? *Behavioral and Brain Sciences, 33*(2/3), 49–50.

Shweder, R., Mahapatra, M., & Miller, J. (1990). Culture and moral development. In J. Stigler, R. Shweder, & G. Herdt (Eds.), *Cultural psychology* (pp. 130–204). New York: Cambridge University Press.

Sigel, R. (1989). Introduction: Persistence and change. In R. Sigel (Ed.), *Political learning in adulthood: A sourcebook of theory and research.* Chicago, IL: University of Chicago Press.

Silva, P., & Stanton, W. (Eds.). (1996). *From child to adult: The Dunedin multidisciplinary health and development study* (pp. 1–10). New York, NY: Oxford University Press.

Simpson, M., & Hagood, C. (2010, June 13). On wo-metrosexuality and the city. *Huffington Post.* Retrieved from **http://www.huffingtonpost .com/caroline-hagood/ metrosexuality-and-the- cib535333.html**

Singer, M. (2003). *Cults in our midst: The continuing fight against their menace.* Jossey-Bass.

Sinha, J., & Verma, J. (1983). Perceptual structuring of dyadic interactions. *Journal of Cross-Cultural Psychology, 14,* 187–199.

Sirois, F. M., & Pychyl, T. A. (2013). Procrastination and the priority of short-term mood regulation: Consequences for future self. *Social and Personality Psychology Compass, 7,* 115–127.

Skinner, B. F. (1938). *The behavior of organisms.* New York, NY: Appleton-Century-Crofts.

Skinner, B. F. (1960). Pigeons in a pelican. *American Psychologist, 15,* 28–57.

Skinner, B. F. (1971). *Beyond freedom and dignity.* New York, NY: Bantam Vintage Books.

Skinner, B. F. (2005). *Walden two.* Indianapolis, IN: Hackett. (Original work published 1948)

Skya, W. (2009). *Japan's Holy War: The ideology of radical Shinto ultranationalism.* Durham, NC: Duke University Press.

Slater, D. (2013). *Love in the time of algorithms: What technology does to meeting and mating.* New York, NY: Current Hardcover.

Slater, M., Rovira, A., Southern, R., Swapp, D., Zhang, J. J., Campbell, C., & Levine, M. (2013). Bystander responses to a violent incident in an immersive virtual environment. *Plos One, 8*(1). Retrieved from h**ttp:// www.plosone.org/**

Slife, B. (1993). *Time and psychological explanation.* New York, NY: State University of New York Press.

Slutske, W., Eisen, S., Xian, H., True, W., Lyons, M., Goldberg, J., & Tsuang, M. (2001). A twin study of the association between pathological gambling and antisocial personality disorder. *Journal of Abnormal Psychology, 110*(2), 297–308.

Small, D. J. (2005). *Power interest and psychology.* Ross-on-Wye, England: PCCS Books.

Smith, J. (1982). *Imagining religion, from Babylon to Jonestown.* Chicago, IL: University of Chicago Press.

Smith, K. (2011). Neuroscience vs. philosophy: Taking aim at free will. *Nature, 477*(7362), 23–25.

Smith, M. B. (1978). Psychology and values. *Journal of Social Issues, 34,* 181–199.

Snarey, J. (1985). Cross-cultural universality of social-moral development: A critical review of Kohlbergian research. *Psychological Bulletin, 97,* 202–232.

Snyder, M., & Swann, W. B., Jr. (1978). Behavioral confirmation in social interaction: From social perception to social reality. *Journal of Experimental Social Psychology, 14,* 148–162.

Snyder-Hall, R. C. (2010). Third-wave feminism and the defense of "choice." *Perspectives on Politics, 8*(1), 255–261.

Solms, M., & Turnbull, O. (2011). What is neuropsychoanalysis? *Neuropsychoanalysis, 13*(2), 133–145.

Sorrentino, R. M., Nezlek, J. B., Yasunaga, S., Kouhara, S., Otsubo, Y., & Shuper, P. (2008). Uncertainty orientation and affective experiences: Individual differences within and across cultures. *Journal of Cross-Cultural Psychology, 39*(2), 129–146.

Span, L. (2009). *When the time comes: Families with aging parents share their struggles and solutions.* New York, NY: Grand Central Life & Style.

Spencer, S. J., Steele, C. M., & Quinn, D. M. (1999). Stereotype threat and women's math performance. *Journal of Experimental Social Psychology, 35,* 4–28.

Sperry, R. (1961). Cerebral organization and behavior. *Science, 133,* 1749–1757.

Spillett, R. (2014, June 6). Maybe it's not about the happy ending, maybe it's about the story. *Daily Mail.* Retrieved from **http://dailym. ai/1EBXYNg**

Staddon, J. (2001). *The new behaviorism: Mind, mechanism, and society.* London, England: Taylor & Francis.

Stanley, J., Lohani, M., & Isaacowitz, D. (2014). Age-related differences in judgments of inappropriate behavior are related to humor style preferences, *Psychology and Aging, 29*(3), 528–541.

Stanley, M., Beck, J., & Zebb, B. (1998). Psychometric properties of the MSPSS in older adults. *Aging and Mental Health, 2*(3), 186–193.

Starcevic, V. (1999). Neurosthenia: Cross-cultural and conceptual issues pertaining to chronic fatigue syndrome. *General Hospital Psychiatry, 21*(4), 249–255.

Stephens, N. M., Markus, H. R., & Townsend, S. S. M. (2007). Choice as an act of meaning: The case of social class. *Journal of Personality and Social Psychology, 93*(8), 14–30.

Stern, J. (2010). Mind over martyr: How to deradicalize Islamist extremists. *Foreign Affairs, 89*(1), 95–108.

Sternberg, R. (1997). The concept of intelligence and its role in lifelong learning and success. *American Psychologist, 52*(10), 1030–1037.

Stetter, F., & Kupper, S. (2002). Autogenic training: A meta-analysis of clinical outcome studies. *Applied Psychophysiology and Biofeedback, 27*(1), 45–98.

Stevens, S. (1946). On the theory of scales of measurement. *Science, 103*(2684), 677–680.

Stewart, C. (2009). *APA membership: Past, present, and possible futures.* Paper presented at the annual meeting of the American Psychological Association, Toronto, Ontario, Canada.

Steyer, R., Mayer, A., Geiser, C., & Cole, D. (2015). A theory of states and traits—Revised. *Annual Review of Clinical Psychology, 11*, 71–98.

Stossel, S. (2014). *My age of anxiety.* New York, NY: Knopf.

Streeter, C., Whitfield, T., Owen L., Rein, T., Karri, S., Yakhkind, A., . . . Jensen, J. (2010). Effects of yoga versus walking on mood, anxiety, and brain GABA levels: A randomized controlled MRS study. *Journal of Alternative and Complementary Medicine, 16*(11), 1145–1115.

Strickland, L. H. (1997). Who? V. M. Bekhterev? A field theorist? *SAFT Newsletter, 13*(1), 2–3.

Strickland, L. H. (2001). Introduction. In *L. Bekhterev's collective reflexology: The complete edition* (E. Lockwood & A. Lockwood, Trans., pp. 15–19). New Brunswick, NJ: Transaction.

Suedfeld, P., & Piedrahita, L. E. (1984). Intimations of mortality: Integrative simplification as a precursor of death. *Journal of Personality and Social Psychology, 47*(4), 848–852.

Suh, E. M., Diener, E. D., & Updegraff, J. A. (2008). From culture to priming conditions: Self-construal influences on life satisfaction judgments. *Journal of Cross-Cultural Psychology, 39*(1), 3–15.

Sullivan, E., & Greene, R. (2015, February 24). States predict inmates' future crimes with secretive surveys. Associated Press. Retrieved from **http://hosted2.ap.org/PASCR/ a5050f4ad4f44dafab85bb41a 15281cf/Article2015–02–24–US– Risky%20Justice/id-6720085e6d 184f07839a6b2126a39b94**

Sullivan, H. (1953). *The interpersonal theory of psychiatry.* New York, NY: W. W. Norton.

Sulloway, F. (1996). *Born to rebel: Birth order, family dynamics, and creative lines.* New York, NY: Pantheon.

Sulloway, F. (1997). *Born to rebel.* New York, NY: Vintage.

Sunesh-Kumar, P. N. S., Anish, P. K., & Biju, G. (2015). Risk factors for suicide in elderly in comparison to younger age groups. *Indian Journal of Psychiatry, 57*(3), 249–254.

Sutherland, S. (2014). How yoga changes body and mind. *Scientific American, 25*(2). Retrieved from **http://www.scientificamerican.com/ article/how-yoga-changes-the- brain/**

Sutton, J. (1998). *Philosophy and memory traces: Descartes to connectionism.* New York, NY: Cambridge University Press.

Szasz, T. S. (1960). The myth of mental illness. *American Psychologist, 15*, 113–118.

Tabarrok, A. (2015, September 16). What was Gary Becker's biggest mistake? *Marginal Revolution.* Retrieved from

http://marginalrevolution.com/ marginalrevolution/2015/09/ what-was-gary-beckers-biggest- mistake.html

Tafarodi, R., Shaughnessy, S. C., Yamaguchi, S., & Murakoshi, A. (2011). e reporting of self-esteem in Japan and Canada. *Journal of Cross-Cultural Psychology, 42*(1), 155–164.

Tafarodi, R., & Swann, W. (1996). Individualism-collectivism and global self-esteem: Evidence for a cultural trade-off. *Journal of Cross-Cultural Psychology, 27*, 651–672.

Talhelm, T., Zhang, X., Oishi, S., Shimin, C., Duan, D., Lan, X., & Kitayama, S. (2014). Large-scale psychological differences within China explained by rice versus wheat agriculture. *Science, 344*(6184), 603–608.

Tarde, G. (1903). *The laws of imitation.* New York, NY: Holl.

Taylor, F. W. (1911). *The principles of scientific management.* New York, NY: Harper.

Taylor, S. E. (1983). Adjustment to threatening events: A theory of cognitive adaptation. *American Psychologist, 38*(11), 1161–1173.

Taylor, S. E. (1989). *Positive illusions: Creative self-deception and the healthy mind.* New York, NY: Basic Books.

Taylor, S. E. (2000). Psychological resources, positive illusions, and health. *American Psychologist, 55*(1), 99–109.

Taylor, S. E., Sherman, D., Kim, H. S., Jarcho, J., Takagi, K., & Dunagan, M. (2004). Culture and social support: Who seeks it and why? *Journal of Personality and Social Psychology, 87*(3), 354–362.

Terracciano, A., AbdelKhalek, A. M., Adam, N., Adamovova, L., Ahn, C. K., & Ahn, H. N. et al. (2005). National character does not reflect mean personality trait levels in 49 cultures. *Science, 310,* 96–100.

Thorndike, E. L. (1911). *Animal intelligence: Experimental studies.* New York, NY: Macmillan.

Thorne, A., & Nam, V. (2009). The storied construction of personality. In P. Corr & G. Matthews (Eds.), *The Cambridge handbook of personality psychology* (pp. 491–505*).* Cambridge, United Kingdom: Cambridge University Press.

Tishler, C. L., Reiss, N., & Rhodes, A. (2007). Suicidal behavior in children younger than twelve: A diagnostic challenge for emergency department personnel. *Academic Emergency Medicine, 14*(9), 810–818.

Tolman, E. C. (1932). *Purposive behavior in animals and men.* New York, NY: Century.

Tolman, E. C. (1948). Cognitive maps in rats and men. *Psychological Review, 55,* 189–208.

Tomkins, S. S. (1963). Left and right: A basic dimension of ideology and personality. In R. W. White (Ed.), *The study of lives* (pp. 388–411). Chicago, IL: Atherton.

Toner, K., Leary, M., Asher, M., & Jongman-Sereno, K. (2013). Feeling superior is a bipartisan issue: Extremity (not direction) of political views predicts perceived belief superiority. *Psychological Science.* Retrieved from **http:// pss.sagepub.com/content/ early/2013/10/04/ 0956797613494848.full**

Tori, C. D., & Bilmes, M. (2002). Multiculturalism and psychoanalytic psychology: The validation of a defense mechanisms measure in an Asian population. *Psychoanalytic Psychology, 19,* 701–721.

Traeger, L. (2013). Distraction. In M. Gellman & J. R. Turner (Eds.), *Encyclopedia of behavioral medicine* (pp. 610–611). New York, NY: Springer.

Triandis, H. (1989). The self and social behavior in different social contexts. *Psychological Review, 96,* 506–520.

Triandis, H. (1994). *Culture and social behavior.* New York, NY: McGraw-Hill.

Triandis, H. C. (1996). The psychological measurement of cultural syndromes. *American Psychologist, 51*(4), 407–415.

Trull, T. J., & Sher, K. J. (1994). Relationship between the five-factor model of personality and axis I disorders in a nonclinical sample. *Journal of Abnormal Psychology, 103*(2), 350–360.

Tsytsarev, S. V., & Krichmar, L. (2000). Relationship of perceived culture shock, length of stay in the US, depression and self-esteem in elderly Russian-speaking immigrants. *Journal of Social Distress and the Homeless, 9*(1), 35–49.

Tucker W. H. (2009). *The Cattell controversy: Race, science, and ideology.* Chicago: University of Illinois Press.

Turing, A. (1950). Computing machinery and intelligence. *Mind, 50,* 433–460.

Turner, J. F. (1920). *The frontier in American history.* New York, NY: Henry Holt.

Tutty, L., Rothery, M., & Grinnell, R. (1996). *Qualitative research for social work.* Boston, MA: Allyn & Bacon.

Tversky, A., & Kahneman, D. (1973). Availability: A heuristic for judging frequency and probability. *Cognitive Psychology, 5,* 207–232.

Tversky, A., & Kahneman, D. (1974). Judgment under uncertainty:

Heuristics and biases. *Science, 185,* 1124–1131.

Tversky, A., & Kahneman, D. (1982). Judgments of and by representativeness. In D. Kahneman, P. Slovic, & A. Tversky (Eds.), *Judgment under uncertainty: Heuristics and biases* (pp. 153–160). New York, NY: Cambridge University Press.

Tyler, A. (1944). *Freedom's ferment.* Minneapolis: University of Minnesota Press.

Tyrer, P., Coombs, N., Ibrahimi, F., Mathilakath, A., Bajaj, P., Ranger, M., . . . Din, R. (2007). Critical developments in the assessment of personality disorder. *British Journal of Psychiatry, 190,* 51–59.

Tyrer, P., & Johnson, T. (1996). Establishing the severity of personality disorder. *American Journal of Psychiatry, 153*(12), 1593–1597.

United Nations for LGBT Equality. (2015). LGBT rights: Frequently asked questions. Retrieved May 22, 2015, from **http://bit.ly/1RwMHAZ**

United Nations Office on Drugs and Crime. (2015). Statistics. Retrieved June 22, 2015, from **https://www .unodc.org/ accessed**

U.S. Department of Labor. (2016). Statistics. Retrieved from **http:// www.dol.gov/general/topic/ statistics**

Uzzi, B. (2008). A social network's changing statistical properties and the quality of human innovation. *Journal of Physics A: Mathematical and Theoretical, 41*(22).

Vaihinger, H. (1952). *The philosophy of "as if."* London, England: Routledge. (Original work published 1924)

Valsiner, J., & Lawrence, J. (1997). Human development in culture across the life span. In J. W. Berry, P. R. Dasen, & T. S. Saraswathi (Eds.), *Handbook of cross-cultural psychology: Basic processes and human development* (Vol. 2, pp. 69–106). Boston, MA: Allyn & Bacon.

Van de Vliert, E. (2006). Autocratic leadership around the globe: Do climate and wealth drive leadership culture? *Journal of Cross-Cultural Psychology, 37,* 42–59.

Vandewater, E., Ostrove, J., & Stewart, A. (1997). Predicting women's well-being in midlife: The importance of personality development and social role involvements. *Journal of Personality and Social Psychology, 72*(5), 1147–1160.

Värnik, P. (2012). Suicide in the world. *International Journal of Environmental Research and Public Health, 9*(3), 760–771.

Vassiliou, V., & Vassiliou, G. (1973). The implicative meaning of the Greek concept of philomoto. *Journal of Cross-Cultural Psychology, 4*(3), 326–341.

Veenhoven, R. (2008). Sociological theories of subjective well-being. In M. Eid & R. Larsen (Eds.), *The science of subjective well-being: A tribute to Ed Diener* (pp. 44–61). New York, NY: Guilford Press.

Verhulst, B., Eaves, L., & Hatemi, P. (2012). Correlation not causation: The relationship between personality traits and political ideologies. *American Journal of Political Science, 56*(1), 34–51.

Verhulst, B., Hatemi, P. K., & Martin, N. G. (2010). Personality and political attitudes. *Personality and Individual Differences, 49*(4), 306–316.

Vernon, P. (1969). *Intelligence and cultural environment.* London: Methuen.

Vich, M. A. (1988). Some historical sources of the term "transpersonal." *Journal of Transpersonal Psychology, 20,* 107–110.

Virkkunen, M. (1983). Insulin secretion during the glucose tolerance-test in anti-social personality. *British Journal of Psychiatry, 142,* 598–604.

Volavka, J., Crowner, M., Brizer, D., Convit, A., Van Praag, H., & Suckow, R. (1990). Tryptophan treatment of aggressive psychiatric patients. *Biological Psychiatry, 28,* 728–732.

von Mayrhauser, R. (2002). The mental testing community and validity: A prehistory. *American Psychologist, 47,* 244–253.

Vygotsky, L. (1933, April 20). *Kriticheskie vozrasta* [Critical periods]. Leningrad, Russia: Leningrad Pedagogical Institute's Archive.

Vygotsky, L. (2005). Myshlenie i rech [Thought and language]. In *Psychology of the individual's development.* Moscow, Russia: Smysl. (Original work published 1934)

Wade, N. (2015) *A troublesome inheritance: Genes, race, and human history.* New York, NY: Penguin Books.

Wairaven, G. (2013). *Health and poverty: Global health problems and solutions.* New York, NY: Routledge.

Wallace, A., & Shapiro, S. (2006). Mental balance and well-being. *American Psychologist, 61*(7), 690–701.

Wallace, B. A. (2004). The four immeasurables: Cultivating a boundless heart (Rev. ed.). Ithaca, NY: Snow Lion.

Wallis, L. (2013, April 24). Living a conjoined life. *BBC News.* Retrieved from **http://www.bbc.com/news/magazine-22181528**

Wang, J., Korczykowski, M., Rao, H., Fan, Y., Pluta, J., Gur, R. C., . . . Detre, J. A. (2007). Gender difference in neural response to psychological stress. *Social Cognitive and Affective Neuroscience, 2*(3), 227–239.

Warburton, N. (2012). *Philosophy: The Classics* (2nd ed.). New York, NY: Routledge.

Warne, G., Grover, S., Hutson, J., Sinclair, A., Metcalfe, S., Northam, E., & Freeman, J. (2005). A long-term outcome study of intersex conditions. *Journal of Pediatric Endocrinology and Metabolism, 18*(6), 555–568.

Warner, M. (2000). *The trouble with normal.* Cambridge, MA: Harvard University Press.

Watson, J. B. (1919). *Psychology from a standpoint of a behaviorist.* Philadelphia, PA: Lippincott.

Watson, J. B. (1924). The unverbalized in human behavior. *Psychological Review, 4,* 273–280.

Watson, J. B. (1927). Can psychology help in the selection of personnel? *J. Walter Thompson News Bulletin, 129,* 113.

Watson, J. B., & Rayner, R. (1920). Conditioned emotional responses. *Journal of Experimental Psychology, 3,* 1–14.

Watson, J. M. (2012). Educating the disagreeable extravert: Narcissism, the big five personality traits, and achievement goal orientation. *International Journal of Teaching and Learning in Higher Education, 24*(1), 76–88.

Watson, P. J., Grisham, S. O., Trotter, M. V., & Biderman, M. D. (1984). Narcissism and empathy: Validity evidence for the narcissistic personality inventory. *Journal of Personality Assessment, 45*, 159–162.

Weber, E. (1998). What folklore tells us about risk and risk taking: Cross-Cultural comparisons of American, German, and Chinese proverbs. *Organizational Behavior and Human Decision Processes. 75*(2), 170–186.

Weber, M. (2003). *The Protestant ethic and the spirit of capitalism.* Mineola, NY: Dover. (Original work published 1904)

Wegner, B. (2000). *The Waffen-SS: Organization, ideology and function.* Hoboken, NJ: Wiley-Blackwell.

Weiner, I. (2003). *Principles of Rorschach interpretation.* Mahwah, NJ: Lawrence Erlbaum.

Weinstein, L. B. (1989). Transcultural relocation: Adaptation of older Americans to Israel. *Activities, Adaptation & Aging, 13*, 33–42.

Weisberg, Y., DeYoung, C., & Hirsh, J. (2011). Gender differences in personality across the ten aspects of the big five. *Frontiers in Psychology.* Online Publication. Retrieved from **http://www.ncbi.nlm.nih.gov/pmc/articles/PMC3149680/**

Weiss, A., Bates, T., & Luciano, M. (2008). Happiness is a personal(ity) thing: The genetics of personality and well-being in a representative sample. *Psychological Science, 19*, 205–210.

Weissman, M. M., Markowitz, J. C., & Klerman, G. L. (2007). *Clinician's quick guide to interpersonal psychotherapy.* New York, NY: Oxford University Press.

Weisz, J., Suwanlert, S., Chaiyasit, W., & Walter, B. (1987). Over and undercontrolled referral problems among children and adolescents from Thailand and the United States. *Journal of Counseling and Clinical Psychology, 55*, 719–726.

Weiten, W., Dunn, D., & Hummer, E. (2011). *Psychology applied to modern life: Adjustment in the 21st Century.* Boston, MA: Cengage.

Weizenbaum, J. (1976). *Computer power and human reason.* London, England: W. H. Freeman.

Wertz, A., & Wynn, K. (2014). Selective social learning of plant edibility in 6- and 18-month-old infants. *Psychological Science, 25*(4), 874–882.

Whiting, B. B., & Whiting, J. W. M. (1975). *The children of six cultures: A psycho-cultural analysis.* Cambridge, MA: Harvard University Press.

Wideman, T., & Sullivan, M. (2011). Reducing catastrophic thinking associated with pain. *Pain Management, 1*(3), 249–256.

Widiger, T. A., & Spitzer, R. L. (1991). Sex bias in the diagnosis of personality disorders: Conceptual and methodological issues. *Clinical Psychology Review, 11*, 1–22.

Williams, K. E., Ciarrochi, J., & Heaven, P. C. (2012). Inflexible parents, inflexible kids: A 6-year longitudinal study of parenting style and the development of psychological flexibility in adolescents. *Journal of Youth Adolescence, 41*(8), 1053–1066.

Wilson, G., & Rahman, Q. (2008). *Born gay: The psychobiology of sex orientation.* London, UK: Peter Owen Publishers.

Wilson, E. O. (2000). *Sociobiology: The new synthesis.* Cambridge, MA: Harvard University Press.

Wilson, K. (2014, August 6). Transgender at 10. *Willamette Week.* Retrieved July 3, 2015, at **http://www.wweek.com/portland/article-22897-transgenderat10.html**

Win-Gallup International. (2012). *Global index of religion and atheism.* Retrieved from **http://bit.ly/P2OIr3**

Winter, J., & Teitelbaum, M. (2013). *The global spread of fertility decline: Population, fear, and uncertainty.* New Haven, CT: Yale University Press.

Wolfe, R. (1993). A commonsense approach to personality measurement. In K. Craik, R. Hogan, & R. Wolfe (Eds.), *Fifty years of personality psychology* (pp. 269–290). New York, NY: Plenum Press.

Wood, A. L., & Wahl, O. W. (2006). Evaluating the effectiveness of a consumer-provided mental health recovery education presentation. *Psychiatric Rehabilitation Journal, 30*, 46–52.

World Health Organization. (1993). *The ICD–10 international classification of diseases.* Retrieved from **http://www.who.int/classifications/icd/en/**

World Health Organization. (2014). *Mental health, poverty and development.* Retrieved June 12, 2015, from **http://bit.ly/1j7j4az**

World Health Organization. (2015). *Preventing suicide: A global imperative.* Retrieved June 23, 2015, from **http://www.who.int/mentalhealth/suicide-prevention/worldreport2014/en/**

World Health Organization. (2016). *Suicide data.* Retrieved from **http://www.who.int/mental_health/**

prevention/suicide/suicide
prevent/en/

Wozniak, R. (1993). *The roots
of behaviorism*. New York, NY:
Routledge.

Wright, D. (2013, December 7). My
unwelcome stranger [Web log post].
Retrieved from **http://deniswright
.blogspot.com.au/**

Wundt, W. (1916). *Elements of folk
psychology: Outlines of a psychological
history of the development of mankind*
(E. L. Schaub, Trans.). New York, NY:
Macmillan.

Xu, J., & Harvey, N. (2014). Carry
on winning: The gamblers' fallacy
creates hot hand effects in online
gambling. *Cognition, 131*(2), 173–180.

Yakunin, V. (2001). *Istoriya Psikhilogii*
[A history of psychology]. St.
Petersburg, Russia: Mikhailov.

Yamagata, S., Suzuki, A., Ando, J.,
Ono, Y., Kijima, N., Yoshimura, K., .
. . Jang, K. L. (2006). Is the genetic
structure of human personality
universal? A cross-cultural twin
study from North America, Europe,
and Asia. *Journal of Personality and
Social Psychology, 90*, 987–998.

Yang, M., Coid, J., & Tyrer, P. (2010).
Personality pathology recorded by
severity: National survey. *The British
Journal of Psychiatry, 197*(3), 193–199.

Yeager, D. S., Henderson, M. D.,
Paunesku, D., Walton, G. M., D'Mello,
S., Spitzer, B. J., & Duckworth, A. L.
(2014). Boring but important: A self-
transcendent purpose for learning
fosters academic self-regulation.
*Journal of Personality and Social
Psychology, 107*(4), 559–558.

Yip, P. S., Caine, E., Yousuf, S.,
Chang, S. S., Wu, K. C., & Chen,
Y. Y. (2012). Means restriction for
suicide prevention. *Lancet, 379*(9834),
2393–2399.

YouGov. (2015). YouGov survey
results. Retrieved from **https://
yougov.co.uk/news/2015/08/16/
half-young-not-heterosexual/**

Young, J., Klosko, J., & Weishaar,
E. (2006). *Schema therapy: A
practitioner's guide*. New York, NY:
Guilford Press.

Young, R. K. (1985). Ebbinghaus:
Some consequences. *Journal of
Experimental Psychology: Learning,
Memory, and Cognition, 11*, 491–495.

Yuill, K. (2013). *Assisted suicide:
The liberal, humanist case against
legalization*. New York, NY: Palgrave.

Zanarini, M. C., Frankenburg, F. R.,
Hennen, J., Reich, D. B., & Silk, K. R.
(2005). The McLean study of adult
development (MSAD): Overview and
implications of the first six years of
prospective follow-up. *Journal of
Personality Disorders, 19*(5),505–523.

Zeidner, M., & Endler, N. (Eds.). (1995).
*Handbook of coping: Theory, research,
applications*. New York, NY: Wiley.

Zelinsky, W. (1992). *The cultural
geography of the United States*.
Englewood Cliffs, NJ: Prentice Hall.

Zhou, J. N., Hofman, M. A., Gooren,
L. J., & Swaab, D. F. (1995). A sex
difference in the human brain and its
relation to transsexuality. *Nature, 378*,
68–70.

Žižek, S. (2015, January 10). Slavoj
Žižek on the Charlie Hebdo massacre:
Are the worst really full of passionate
intensity? *New Statesman*. Retrieved
from **http://www.newstatesman
.com/world-affairs/2015/01/slavoj-
i-ek-charlie-hebdo-massacre-
are-worst-really-full-passionate-
intensity**

Zuckerman, M. (1979). *Sensation
seeking: Beyond the optimal level of
arousal*. Hillsdale, NJ: Lawrence
Erlbaum.

Zuckerman, M. (1990, December).
Some dubious premises in research
and theory on racial differences
in scientific, social, and ethical
issues. *American Psychologist, 45*(2),
1297–1303.

Zuckerman, M. (2007a). *Sensation
seeking and risky behavior*.
Washington, DC: American
Psychological Association.

Zuckerman, M. (2007b). The
sensation seeking scale V (SSS–V):
Still reliable and valid. *Personality
and Individual Differences, 43*(5),
1303–1305.

• Index •